Professional Style Sheets for HTML and XML

Frank Boumphrey

Wrox Press Ltd. ®

Professional Style Sheets for HTML and XML

Published by Wrox Press Ltd. 30 Lincoln Road, Olton, Birmingham, B27 6PA
Printed in Canada
1 2 3 4 5 TRI 00 99 98

ISBN 1-861001-65-7

Trademark Acknowledgements

Credits

Authors
Frank Boumphrey

Development Editor
Anthea Elston

Editors
Sonia Mullineux
Jon Duckett

Index
Simon Gilks

Cover
Andrew Guillaume

Technical Reviewers
David Bostock
Michael Corning
Andy Enfield
Alex Fedorov
Rick Kingslan
Craig McQueen
Benoit Marchal

Design/Layout
Frances Olesch

Cover photo supplied by The Image Bank

About the Author

Frank Boumphrey currently works for Cormorant Consulting, a firm that specializes in medical and legal documentation.

He started programming in the dark ages of punch cards and machine language. One of his first projects was to help write a program that differentiated between an incoming Soviet ICBM and a flock of geese. The fact that we are reading this is evidence that it probably worked!

Burnt out by thinking in hexadecimals, he left programming and became a medical doctor, ending up as a Professor and the chief of spine surgery at a large American Midwest institution. Along the way he was involved with the introduction of the MRI to the medical world.

Semi-retirement returned him to his first interest of computing and now he tries to get medical institutions to organize their medical records in a semi-rational fashion, and on the side lectures to medical personal and healthcare executives on documentation issues. Interestingly he is most in demand by legal firms that want to rationalize their medical databases!

His main objective at the present is to help XML to become the language of choice in web documents.

Author Acknowledgments

To Rona

Thanks etc.

My thanks to the many people who made this book possible, in particular to the editorial staff led by Anthea Elston, who put up with my foibles and kept me on the straight and narrow. They made me aware that deadlines were approaching without once breathing a single threat!

A special word of thanks also goes to the technical reviewers who made great suggestions, most of which I have incorporated in the text. Even if I did exercise the author's privilege to disagree with them from time to time, I want them to know that I read every one of their criticisms and pondered each one deeply. That there are so few inaccuracies in the book is chiefly due to them. Any errors that remain are, of course, entirely my responsibility. I feel that if more publishers followed the Wrox example of multiple technical reviewers the standard of computer books would escalate.

I owe a special debt to my long-suffering family, who have had to put up with my absorption in this project. They have done so without complaint, and have even encouraged me!

Lastly I need to apologize to my cat Hergie, who has made it quite clear that she is not getting the attention that she feels is her due. Her chief tactic has been to sit on my computer keyboard and growl at me–Hergie, I promise, I will make it up to you!

Table of Contents

An Introduction to Styling and Style Sheets

This book is about style sheets; the exciting new development that is going to put a great deal more spice into the web. Up until now authors wishing to present their page in anything other than a bland and uninteresting manner have had to resort to all kinds of guru tricks and hacks. Any desire for compelling presentation has been required to make heavy use of graphics to ensure satisfactory results. This has resulted in a number of deleterious effects including:

Page Bloat

All the extra tags and attributes necessary to format pages double the size of the document.

Excessive Use of Graphics

To ensure that a heading looks the way you want it a graphic is used. The temptation is always there to make something look just that bit more impressive. Look at any quality magazine. They, for the most part, use stylish headings in pure text. Why shouldn't we do the same on the Web?

Lack of Legibility

All the extra markup for styling has made it almost impossible to read the document content. This has led to problems in the field of page maintenance.

Excessive Coding

Most commercial pages, other than the very basic, either write their code using a script or make heavy use of script for presentation. This also adds to maintenance difficulty and page bloat.

Maintenance Difficulty

The cluttered up pages make it very difficult to maintain a site and to revise pages.

Style sheets change all of this. Now authors can put all styling information in one place, halving the size of their files, reducing by a factor of 3 or 4 their need for images, and easing all their maintenance problems.

Furthermore, the exciting new development XML–which allows authors to custom design their documents–requires authors to use style sheets and this book also covers the styling of XML documents.

Who Should Read this Book?

First this book assumes a basic understanding of HTML. If you don't know any HTML you will have difficulty following many of the arguments. Why not pick up a copy of *Instant HTML Programmer's Reference ISBN 1861001568 (Wrox 1997)* to read alongside it.

This book assumes no knowledge of XML, we will teach you enough to get you writing and publishing web documents. If of course you need to do some heavy-duty enterprise document publishing, this book will act as a great introduction, but you should probably also read a book such as *Professional XML Applications ISBN 1861001525* which is coming very soon from Wrox Press.

You should read this book if:

- You want to add excitement and spice to your web pages.
- You are interested in learning about styling and the basics of XML.
- You are fed up spending hours updating your old web pages.
- You want to impress your boss by showing him how to save money.
- You are the boss and you want to save money
- You actually want to learn all about style sheets in HTML and XML.

How Should you Read this Book

This book covers a very wide range of subjects, in an effort to be as comprehensive as possible about styling and style sheets. To aid comprehension and for ease of use, we've divided it up into three parts. Part One gives a basic introduction to style sheets, Cascading Style Sheets, XML and XSL. Part Two gives an advanced and detailed breakdown of all the available CSS properties that you can use to style your web pages, plus much more detail on Cascading Style Sheets. This is the real meat of the book. Part Three looks to the future. It gives you more detail about XSL, looks at styling with script, possible future languages for styling XML, and the properties provided by CSS2 for styling canvases other than the computer screen. The book ends with a chapter of examples of the different styling effects that can be achieved for your web pages!

What You Need to Use this Book

You will definitely need a CSS compatible browser i.e. Netscape Navigator/Communicator 4 or IE4. If you have room you are advised to download both of them. An older non-compatible browser is also helpful for checking the look of your pages if the style sheet is not called up. You can, however, also check this by just commenting out your style sheet.

To try out the examples with XSL you will need either the ActiveX control (if you have IE4) or the command line converter. This can be obtained from:

```
http://www.microsoft.com/workshop/author/xml/xmldata-f.htm
```

Look under XSL. While you are about it download their example files. The converter only works on Windows95.

Some simple XML and XSL teaching tools written by the author are also available from the Wrox web site at:

`http://rapid.wrox.co.uk/books/1657`

These tools also only work on Windows 3 and 95. (It hasn't been tested on NT but it is unlikely to work.) If you have a different platform you will still be able to do 95% of the examples and exercises in this book.

The most valuable tool for testing the examples will be a friendly text editor, such as Notepad. If you can't try the examples for yourself as you go along, you can download them or run them from our web site at:

`http://rapid.wrox.co.uk/books/1657`

So now we've given an overview of what the book is about and explained what previous knowledge and current tools you need to get the most of it, let's spend the rest of the introduction defining our terms, beginning with that most fundamental question–what are style sheets?

What are Style Sheets?

Style sheets are as old as printing

In the days of manual type-setting style sheets were nothing more than a set of written instructions from the publisher to the printer telling the printer what kind of style to use when printing up the publisher's manuscript. Traditionally, the editor used to deliver a "marked up" manuscript full of terse notations like dele and stet–beloved of crossword fans everywhere. The printer would then consult the style sheet of that particular publishing house for a range of specifications. These specifications would encompass such details as what size the pages were to be, what size and family of font to use for chapter titles, sub-headings, body text and so on. Plus, how much leading to put between the lines, what margins to leave and whether, and by how much, to indent the paragraphs.

> *Printers used to set the distance between the lines by putting in pieces of lead, hence the term leading. It is pronounced like the metal, rather than as in the term "leading the way".*

In these days of electronic type setting the style sheet is much more likely to be in binary form, but it is still there.

However, before more detailed forays into the subject of style sheets, and before an examination of the relationship between style sheets and computers it would be extremely helpful to highlight both technical necessities and frequently used terminology.

Some Basic Terminology

Here are some basic explanations of terms which will be used frequently in this book.

SGML

If it wasn't for HTML hardly anyone would have heard of SGML (Standardized General Mark up Language), although it has been an international standard since 1986. It is really a document that lays down rules on how to describe a set of markup tags. HTML is its best-known product. However, it has been used with great success to manipulate very large documents, and relies on the fact that a document marked up according to the rules of SGML can be widely understood on a variety of platforms.

Its great strength is that it allows the use of semantic tagging, which can accurately describe a document's content.

Its chief draw back is its complexity, which makes it difficult for the occasional user and an unattractive prospect in terms of SGML compatible software.

DSSSL

Document Style Semantics and Specification Language. If you thought SGML was difficult just wait till you see this language. This is the official styling language for SGML and as such is extremely powerful. It is really a full programming language in its own right, and extremely complicated. As we will see later, one of the problems with having a complicated language is that few people speak it, and so anyone making software to support the language can expect few sales. This and the fact that the complexity of the language makes the software difficult to write, resulting in expensive software, fewer sales and, therefore, a general lack of language adoption. In effect a vicious circle.

HTML

HTML (Hypertext Markup Language) will need no introduction to readers of this book. However, it is worth saying a little about its origins. It was originally devised by Tim Berners-Lee as a way to submit documents over the Internet and still maintain their form. As originally conceived, it was a mixture of semantic and stylistic markup. The language itself was based on SGML (this relationship is explained in more detail later) although it wasn't until HTML version 2 came out that it formally became an SGML dialect. It probably owes its explosive growth to its hypertext features. These features allow readers to "surf" the Internet. It has, however, now outgrown its humble origins.

XML

XML (eXtensible Markup Language) is a recent language that is 100% compatible with SGML. It has been designed by the W3C as a version of SGML suitable for use over the Internet. It is still very much in the development stage, although the Specification has reached the point of being made a W3C recommendation (see the W3C entry for the importance of this label). There is still much work to be done on the form of linking called XLL and the related style sheets to use with it. Originally a simplified version of DSSSL called DSSSL-0 or XS (extensible styling) was to be used, but both of these are horribly complicated. Currently it appears that CSS will be used for every day declarative styling and XSL (as we will see later in the book) will be used when more powerful document manipulation is required. These are covered elsewhere.

Most people who have been exposed to this language are wildly enthusiastic and very optimistic about XML's future. It has nearly all the power of SGML without any of the difficulty.

DTD

A DTD is a Document Type Definition. This is a term used mainly with XML and SGML (and HTML which, as we will see, is a form of SGML) and is related to the fact that these languages allow the use of a user generated set of tags. How these tags relate to each other, what attributes they can take, and what rules they have to follow are all laid out in the document type definition. HTML has a DTD. Its URL is given in the References section at the end of this chapter.

CSS

This is short for Cascading Style Sheets and the main subject of this book. When several style sheets are present they will form a cascade with properties being taken from all the sheets, and where conflict occurs they are resolved according to a set of rules. Don't worry if you don't understand what this means for now it will become clear as we progress.

XSL

This is the eXtensible Style Language Based on both XML and XS, this has been proposed as the prime style sheet language for XML. It is still in the form of a "note" and undoubtedly its merits are being widely debated in the Ivory towers of the W3C right at this very minute. It does, however, have impressive credentials. XSL was introduced by both Sun and Microsoft, and in fact seems an extremely well thought out and put together language. As well as drawing on DSSSL it also uses CSS syntax. It is difficult to believe that XSL will not be the final choice for an XML styling language. This author believes that although possible major changes to XSL may be in the offing, these changes will only affect the form of the reserved keywords and not the syntax of the language.

XLL

This is the eXtensible Linking Language and is the work in progress on the way XML will link with other documents. It is discussed in some detail in Chapter 6.

XS

Also known as DSSSL-0, this was the first attempt at writing a simplified form of DSSSL for use with XML. Most people, apart from the DSSSL gurus, however, found that it was way too complicated and that it would not fly with the Internet crowd. We will look very briefly at XS at the end of the book.

User Agent

User agent describes anything which is acting on behalf of a user. You are a user agent working for your boss, your computer is a user agent working for you, your browser is a user agent working for your computer, and so it goes on. It is not the best term in the world, but a very useful one nevertheless, so like it or not it's probably going to stick around.

Canvas

The artist paints on his canvas, so why shouldn't you and your user agent paint on yours. This canvas could be your monitor screen, your printer, a projection screen, a sound system, or even a Braille reader.

Flow Objects

Text flows and as it flows it creates flow objects. A chapter is a flow object, a paragraph is a flow object, an element is a flow object even a sentence, a word or an individual character is a flow object. Although these latter few are probably smaller than we care to deal with.

When we are creating text and then styling it, we are continuously creating flow objects and if we want to manipulate them we can. For example, all the heading flow objects in this chapter could be taken out and used to generate a table of contents. (We will do this as an exercise later.)

ASCII

The numerical representation of the Latin character set, plus some special notations including the numbers 0 to 32. For example, 0 represents null, 9 represents a tab, 10 a line feed and 13 a carriage feed. The numbers you will come across most often are:

- **32**–a space.
- **60**–the < character.
- **62**–the > character.
- **36**–the ampersand.

As you probably know, in HTML an ASCII character can be represented by its decimal notation, its hexadecimal notation or its entity name.

The decimal syntax is `&` `[`*decimal number*`];` so by typing `<` we see `<` on the screen

ISO10646

Also known as ISO/IEC-10646 Universal Multiple-Octet Coded Character Set. This contains the numeric equivalent of most of the entire world's characters. Although mention will be made of this character set from time to time, this book confines it self to the ASCII character set, mainly because its the only character set the author can read apart from some Greek symbols used in math.

The point is–if I wanted this book translated into Arabic then I would use the Arabic Unicode symbols.

XML, however, supports Unicode, so XML and XSL can be used to style any language you like (provided you can read it).

Unicode

Unicode is not quite the same thing as ISO10646 although their character set is identical. For a full (and readable) discussion on the subject see:

`http://plan9.bell-labs.com/plan9/doc/utf.html`

The Unicode Consortium's Home Page is at:

`http://www.unicode.org`

Also helpful is Marc Andreessen's column entitled *The World Wide Web* which can be found at:

`http://home.netscape.com/comprod/columns/techvision/international.html`

For further information my advice would be to run a search on Yahoo for Unicode.

Some Basic Definitions

At this point it would also be helpful to examine some other definitions in slightly more detail.

Tags and Elements

Strangely, the terms 'tag' and 'element' are the ones that most people familiar with HTML have difficulty with.

A tag is special piece of text that indicates that an action should take place. In SGML (of which HTML is an example) and XML, a tag is the text between the angled brackets e.g.**<BODY>.**

Some examples of tags used in HTML are the following:

> **<P>** is a tag that marks the beginning of a new paragraph.
> **<B>** is a tag indicating that the following text should be rendered in bold type.
> **</B>** is a tag indicating that this is the end of the text to be rendered in bold .

In general terms tags are a label that tells a user-agent to do something to whatever is encased in the tags.

Elements on the other hand are the tags plus their content. The following is an element:

```
<B> This is bold text</B>
```

Tags don’t have to be HTML or XML or any other *ML. This is because tags can mean exactly what we want them to mean. "~~" "`~" are a pair of tags often used to indicate that the enclosed text, "flow object", in the sentence "A ~~flow object`~ is..." should be included as a word in the index of a book. A special program could then run through a piece of text and generate an index. Us oldies remember the days when we had to bribe our children to make the indexes. Aren't computers wonderful!

In XML you can use (almost) anything you want as a tag provided it is enclosed in a pair of angled brackets. **<helena>** is an example of an opening tag, **</helena>** would be an example of a closing tag.

In HTML (and XML) tags can be either open or empty. An open tag implies a closing tag, whereas an empty tag has no closing tag. **<IMG>** is an example of an empty tag in HTML. Note that **<P>** is not an empty tag because **</P>** is implied by the structure of the document.

In XML empty tags must take a special form for reasons that we will go into later. **<IMG/>** is the correct rendering of the **<IMG>** tag in XML.

An element consists of an opening tag, the text it contains, and the closing tag. Text is not the only thing that can be included between tags to form an element, but we're going for the simple definition here and will move on to more complex stuff later.

- **<H1>Professional Style Sheets</H1>** is an element.
- **<hamlet>To be or not to be...</hamlet>** is an element.

To be absolutely clear: An element is a pair of tags together with its enclosed text. An element is not a tag.

The following diagram illustrates the parts of an element.

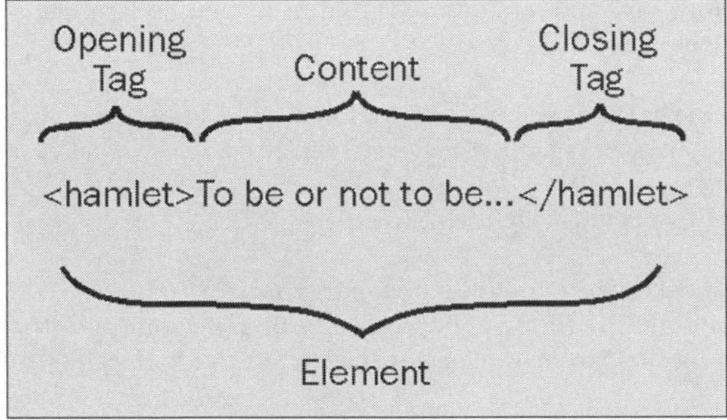

Attributes

Any tag can have an attribute as long as it is defined in the DTD. You are probably most used to the attributes of the **<IMG>** tag which can have many attributes including **ALT**, **HREF**, **VSPACE**, etc.

```
<IMG HREF="smiley.gif" ALT= "Smiley face" VSPACE=30>.
```

In XML the last attribute would be illegal. This is because all values must be in quotes.

```
<IMG HREF="smiley.gif" ALT= "Smiley face" VSPACE= "30"/>
```

The above would be the equivalent tag in XML. Note the penultimate forward slash.

Although we are getting a little ahead of ourselves here an explanation is necessary. In XML the closing forward slash is absolutely essential because the user-agent, namely the parser, has no intrinsic knowledge of the meaning of the tags, and so has to be told up front which is an empty and which is an open tag.

Markup Languages

A markup language is the set of rules, the grammar and the syntax that specifies how a language that marks up documents should be "spoken". SGML is a markup language, and HTML is the vocabulary of a particular dialect of that language, albeit a very widely spoken dialect. Correctly authored HTML follows the rules of SGML.

XML is also a mark up language with a grammar that is based on, but is substantially simpler than, SGML.

Markup is the symbolic tag sets that are used to indicate that something needs to be done to the text. The **<B></B>** pair is markup in HTML. In XML and SGML markup corresponds to the tags. Markup can take one of three forms, semantic, stylistic, or structural.

Semantic markup gives information about the text that the markup is marking. In the XML element:

```
<hamlet> To be or not to be...</hamlet>
```

the tag **<hamlet>** logically tells us that the words are being spoken by Hamlet. In the following HTML element:

```
<CODE>For i= 0 to ubound(chapterArray)</CODE>
```

<CODE> tells us that the enclosed text should be rendered as code.

Stylistic markup tells us about the style that should be used to display a document item.

In HTML the element:

```
<I>This is italic text</I>
```

indicates that the style of the document should change to italic.

Structural markup tells us something about the structure of a document. Again in HTML 4.0

```
<P>
```

infers that the text that occurs until one comes across another similar tag is a paragraph and should be treated as such.

The XML equivalent of this could be:

```
<para> The text that occurs......</para>
```

and is structural markup.

The old editor's notations of dele and stet are structural mark up.

Style Sheets and Computers

Style sheets are widely used by word processing programs. For example here is what WordPerfect, the word processor that I happen to use, has to say about styles in the help file:

"Styles provide an easy way to format similar types of text, such as headings and lists. Use a style repeatedly to save time and ensure that your document has a consistent format."

It is possible in almost any modern word processor to create your own style sheet. This sheet, however, is usually stored in binary form and is, therefore, not readable to the human eye. When the document is stored all the information about styling is kept with the document in binary form. Try opening up a word processor document in a text editor such as Notepad. The screenshot below shows what this chapter looks like. It is just possible to make out the text among the binary information, although it is clearly not a particularly user friendly format.

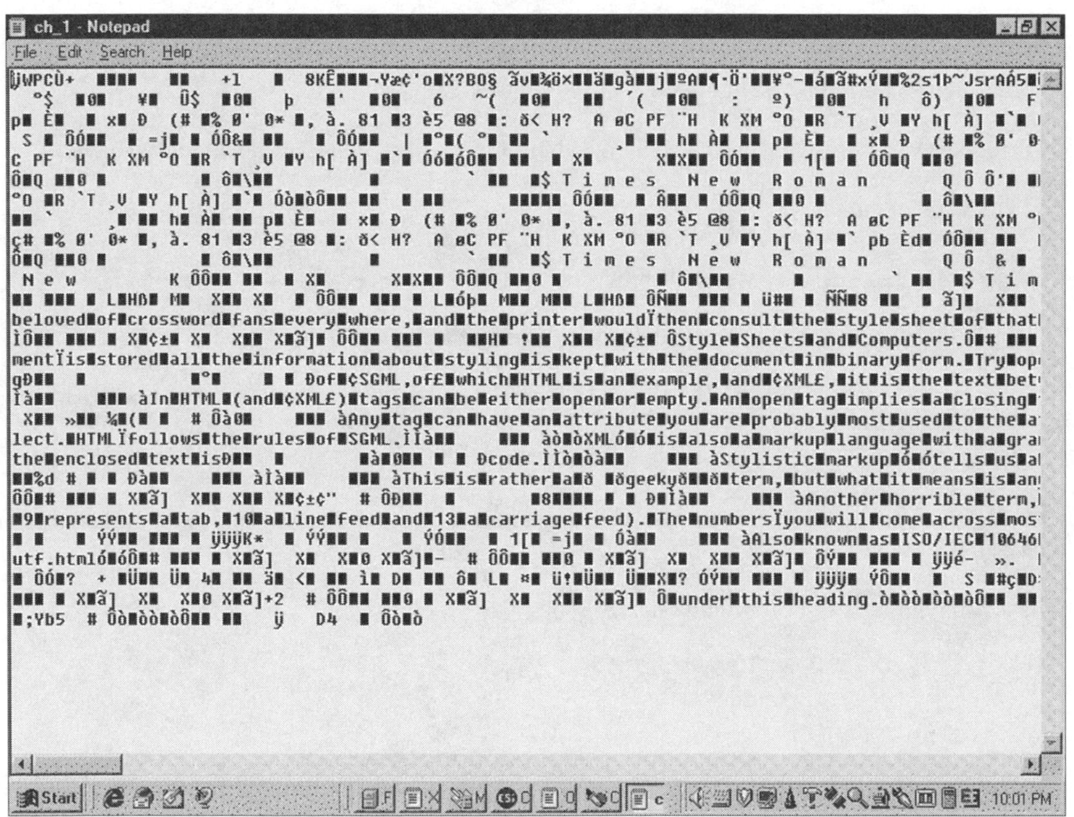

The problem arises when we want to exchange files across different platforms and different formats. Anyone who has tried to do this is only too aware of the problems that can arise when converting one binary form to another. About the only standard that all platforms and processors have in common is the text itself, in other words the ASCII format. Part of the success of HTML is that it used ASCII format to allow publication of documents on differing platforms. One solution that word processors have come up with is RTF (Rich text format) which codes the text style in an

ASCII format. We will examine this in more detail later. Although RTF is successful, it is designed to be read by computers not humans. Wrox Press requires all chapters to be submitted in Word format, so I convert this Word Perfect file to RTF then import it into WordPad and convert the RTF to Word format. Because both WordPerfect and Word understand plain text (ASCII), there is very little scrambling in the conversion process.

WordPerfect gives me the option of converting their format directly into the Word format, however, if I try the binary to binary conversion the results are unpredictable to say the least.

Clients and Servers

On the Web, when a client–for example your computer–wants a document, it makes a request to the server via HTTP using a URL. The server will then look up the document requested in its document store. If the server finds said document, then it will be returned. First, however, the server sends a message ahead using a MIME type and sub-type (text/css or image/jpeg) in the HTTP header. The client sometimes also sends a message ahead, as when the XML link is used e.g. `<?XML-stylesheet type="text/css" href="shaksper.css"?>` , but usually the type of document is just implied in its suffix. For example, `document.htm` tells the processor to expect an HTML document, `document.txt` a text document, and `document.xml` an XML document.

Once a client has a document it will cache it and keep it for a period of time. So whenever a document is requested, the client will look in its cache first to see if the requested document is held there. This illustrates one of the great advantages of style sheets. If you are looking at a whole series of documents over the Internet which share one style sheet, the style sheet only has to be down loaded once. This not only speeds up viewing but also saves bandwidth.

Another example of saving bandwidth that we will meet in XML is when a request is made for a DTD preceded by the keyword `PUBLIC`.

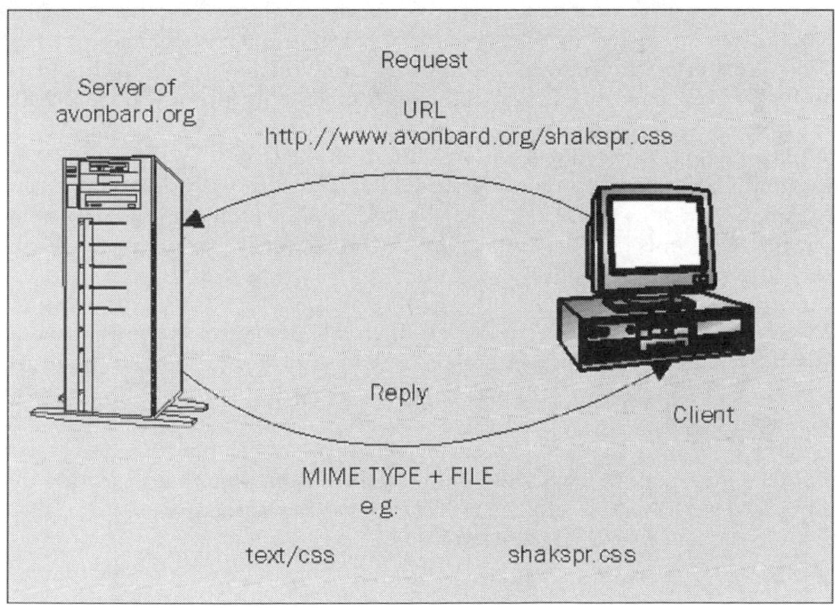

The above diagram shows a simplified depiction of the client/server relationship.

The World Wide Web Consortium

The World Wide Web Consortium (W3C) is the nearest thing there is on the Web to an official standards body. It is supported by various grants and the fees paid by its members. Company membership costs megabucks, but Microsoft can probably afford it! Individual membership last time I looked was about $10,000 a year. There are about 300 members, but they compromise an enormous pool of wealth and, more importantly, expertise.

A new standard is first of all introduced as a note or a proposal. The note for XSL was introduced in August 1977. See it at the following address:

`http://www.w3.org/TR/NOTE-XSL.html`.

This note becomes a draft that is then mulled over and altered by the members, usually on closed mailing lists of members and invited experts. This draft is usually made public, and public discussion takes place on the Public mailing lists. Anyone can join these. Some of the lists are owned by W3C and others such as the DSSSL list (hosted by ArborText) are outside. There is every indication that the members listen to the public's views.

Finally the members come up with a proposed recommendation which the members vote on over a 6 week period. Depending on the result of the vote it either becomes an official standard, or it goes back to the draft stage.

Microsoft, Netscape, and the W3C

When it boils down to it, it doesn't really matter what we write in this book, what protocols are issued by bodies such as the W3C, what international standards we promulgate, if they are ignored by the majority of the world. And realistically 95% of the world uses Netscape or Microsoft browsers. Recent figures suggest that it's about a 60/40 split (but this changes in accordance with the day and the pollster) with Microsoft gaining fast. So if the major players don't support style sheets what then? This section briefly views the level of support for the CSS and XSL protocols.

Firstly, both players have pledged to give full support to the CSS proposals, although most have not fully implemented CSS1 as of yet. As of today IE4 has 97% implementation for Windows, but only 68% for the Mac. Netscape is worse. This issue is discussed at some length later in the book. As far as the XSL protocol is concerned five out of the eleven authors came out of the Microsoft camp, so they are likely to give it major support.

Netscape, of course, is the company that started the implementation of proprietary tags, but they are a little distracted at the moment and both companies have fallen behind the proposed W3C standard for CSS. Netscape give no support to XSL at present, but then XSL has not yet reached the proposal stage.

As far as XML is concerned, the evolution of the Web is something that is needed by industry, and as such will be driven by the marketplace rather than by the marketing efforts of the major players. You can take it as a given that XML is here to stay.

My bet is that the next generation of browsers will provide much greater support for XML with CSS type style sheets. IE (Internet Explorer) will use ActiveX to support XSL and the final implementation will support both XSL and CSS. Certainly IE will support both these standards. Netscape beat off the VBScript challenge and JavaScript is now the defacto scripting language of the Internet. It is, however, unlikely they will be able to beat off XSL, so they might as well join them.

CSS1, CSS2, XML and XSL Specifications

The specifications of these languages are freely available and the URLs are given in the References section at the end of this chapter. You are urged to download them before starting the relevant chapters. In short they lay out all the rules pertaining to the language in question. The XSL notation is still at a basic note form at the time of writing.

Conventions

We have used a number of different styles of text and layout in the book to help differentiate between the different kinds of information. Here are examples of the styles we use and an explanation of what they mean:

Advice, hints, or background information comes in this type of font.

Important pieces of information come in boxes like this

Quotes from sources such as official specifications come in boxes like this

- **Important Words** are in a bold type font
- Words that appear on the screen in menus like the File or Window are in a similar font to the one that you see on screen
- Keys that you press on the keyboard, like *Ctrl* and *Enter*, are in italics
- Code has several fonts. If it's a word that we're talking about in the text, for example, when discussing the **For...Next** loop, it's in a bold font. If it's a block of code that you can type in as a program and run, then it's also in a gray box:

```
<STYLE>
... Some VBScript ...
</STYLE>
```

- Sometimes you'll see code in a mixture of styles, like this:

```
<HTML>
<HEAD>
<TITLE>Cascading Style Sheet Example</TITLE>
<STYLE>
```

```
style1 {color: red;
     font-size: 25}
```

```
</STYLE>
</HEAD>
```

- The code with a white background is code we've already looked at and that we don't wish to examine further.

These formats are designed to make sure that you know what it is you're looking at. I hope they make life easier.

Tell Us What You Think

We've worked hard on this book to make it enjoyable and useful. Our best reward would be to hear from you that you liked it and that it was worth your money. We've done our best to try to understand and match your expectations.

Please let us know what you think about it. Tell us what you have liked best and what aspects have made you regret spending your hard-earned money. If you think this is just a marketing gimmick, then test us out–drop us a line!

We'll answer, and we'll take whatever you say on board for future editions. The easiest way is to use email:

`feedback@wrox.com`

You can also find more details about Wrox Press on our Web site. There, you'll find the code from out latest books, sneak previews of forthcoming titles, and information about the authors and the editors. You can order Wrox titles directly from the site, or find out where your nearest local bookstore with Wrox titles is located. The address of our site is:

`http://www.wrox.com`

Customer Support

If you find a mistake, please have a look at the errata page for this book on our web site first. Appendix H outlines how can you can submit an errata in much greater detail, if you are unsure. The full URL for the errata page is:

`http://www.wrox.com/Scripts/Errata.idc?Code=1657`

If you can't find an answer there, tell us about the problem and we'll do everything we can to answer promptly!

Just send us an email to **`support@wrox.com`**.

Note

Some of the code-foreground listing blocks within the book have reproduced with faint white horizontal lines. These lines are the result of unforseen pre-production circumstances, and have no bearing or effect on the content of the code.

Summary

In the introduction you have learnt what a style sheet is, and have looked at some definitions that we will be using time and time again.

In the next chapter we will look at various forms of styling that are available today, and in particular we will see how present day HTML can be used to style a web page.

References

The URL of the W3C organization:

`http://www.w3.org`

Unicode references:

`http://plan9.bell-labs.com/plan9/doc/utf.html`

A very readable general introduction to the subject is featured on The Unicode Consortium's Home Page at:

`http://www.unicode.org`

Read Marc Andreessen's column on Unicode and the Web:

`http://home.netscape.com/comprod/columns/techvision/international.html`

Microsoft's XML pages:

`http://www.microsoft.com/xml`

The DTD for HTML 4:

`http://www.w3.org/TR/REC-html40/loose.dtd`

Exercises

This chapter is available as a text file. Mark it up in HTML. Hint use a search program to look for and alter all **<** and **>** symbols to **<** and **>** respectively.

If you want to, mark it up using semantic tags of your own devising. The rules that need to be followed are:

- Put tags in angle brackets
- Use lowercase only
- Make sure every opening tag has a closing tag of the form **</tag>**
- Make sure the tags nest.

You are going to spend some time wandering around the W3C web site. Contact it and look up the XML, the XSL, and the CSS specs. Download them if you wish.

Part 1

The first of the three sections of this book takes you through chapters one to five. These easily accessible slices of information lay down the foundations of what is to be investigated in more detail later.

Chapter 1 is an introduction to styling and style sheets. It is, very basically, a comparison between styling in HTML with style sheets and without. This comparison serves to highlight the fundamental advantages of style sheets in general by showing how you can save time and money by producing faster more easily maintained Web pages.

By the time you have read **Chapter 2**, you will be producing external style sheets that link to your HTML documents, and you will have seen how to put in-line styling in HTML documents. On the way, you will learn about the anatomy of style sheets, the positioning and syntax of rules, and the differences between simple, compound and contextual selectors.

Chapters 3 and **4** introduce the exciting new innovation that is XML. Before you can use XSL–the style sheet wing–it is important to have an understanding of the language itself. Chapter 3 helps you develop well-formed XML documents, write a simple DTD and enables you to display XML documents on the Internet. Whereas Chapter 4 will show you how to output the contents of your document using an XML processor and a back end processor and give a brief introduction to style sheets and XML.

Having learnt about XML, your mind will be buzzing with ideas about its possibilities. Before you have time to catch your breath, **Chapter 5** will stride ahead into the realms of XSL–the styling language currently under development for use with XML. By the end of this chapter you should be satisfied that what you have learnt about CSS (and what you will continue to learn about CSS) will be invaluable in the future when XML and XSL get a stronger hold on the Web. But don't worry, CSS is not about to be replaced by XSL, rather it will be just another thing we'll all have to learn about in greater detail sometime in the future...

1

Styling and Style Sheets in General

From the beginning, HTML has been a mixture of semantic, stylistic and structural markup. Structural markup was predominant in the early versions of HTML. However, HTML has now developed to the point where appearance can be seen as the more dominant force.

A style sheet is nothing more than a written set of rules laying out the style of a document, and is usually quite separate from the document to be marked up, or at the least is contained in a separate section of the document.

Styling markup on the other hand is markup on the document itself indicating how certain parts of the document are to be styled, and in HTML consists of certain tags and their attributes.

As such, styling markup is quite different from semantic and structural mark up. Structural markup defines the structure of a document, "put a paragraph here, put a heading there", and semantic markup gives information about the content of the document part. It states that "this part of a document is the title, this part is an address" etc.

In this chapter, as a prelude to getting down to a serious examination of style sheets, we will examine the following:

- Styling in HTML, and the complications this can introduce into your coding
- Styling using style sheets, and how this can simplify your coding
- Summarize the advantages of style sheets.

We will do this by looking at how a typical simple page is styled in HTML, and hopefully in the process the problems associated with HTML styling will become obvious. Just in case they don't we will review them, and then we will look at the potential for style sheets to untangle the mess. We will also take a quick historical look at the reasons behind this mess.

We won't actually look at any of the details of style sheets in this chapter we will leave that to later. First the emphasis will be upon the potential of style sheets to untangle the mess that exists now.

Styling in HTML

Styling in HTML is carried out using a combination of techniques. We will only cover their use very briefly here as books on HTML, such as *Instant HTML Programmer's Reference, ISBN 18610001568 from Wrox Press*, give more than adequate coverage. We will then run through a quick tutorial. If you don't know much about styling using HTML this should be enough for you to get a basic grasp of the subject and, more importantly, make you realize that there must/should be a better way.

First let's look at the various tags and attributes used to style HTML documents.

Styling Tags

These can be divided into tags concerned with paragraph and document layout, and those involved with text and font styles. Also to be considered are attributes of the tags that alter the elements display in some way.

Document Layout

The following table shows the tags most commonly used for document layout.

HTML Tag	Definition
** **	Causes a line break to be inserted into the text. It is also useful for creating horizontal white space in HTML.
<CENTER>	Anything contained between the **<CENTER>** tags will be centered on the page. This tag has no good substitution in style sheets, because the browsers do not implement correctly the properties that are designed to center the elements centering. This means that until the browsers improve the **<CENTER>** tag still has a place in a style-sheet driven document.
<H1><H2> <H3><H4> <H5><H6>	The various headings, display text with a font size that is dependent on the browser, and have a variable amount of white space before or after them.
<HR>	According to many design gurus this should be given a ceremonial burial. Always consider using white space to divide up your page rather than the using horizontal rule.
<P>	The paragraph is the 'work-horse' of HTML. It creates a block of text, usually with a line of white space before and after it.

Text and Font Styling

There are numerous tags that can be used for styling, many of them redundant and seldom used. For a full list see Appendix B of *Instant HTML Programmer's Reference ISBN 1861000156 8 from Wrox Press* or check out the Ultimate HTML Reference Database at the Reference section of **`http://rapid.wrox.co.uk`**. Here, however, are some of the more commonly used ones. All these tags really act as switches to switch a particular type of styling on or off. Switching on and off style, however, is not a good thought process when we are thinking about styling a page. Instead we need to think of blocks of content with a certain style applied to them. A later paragraph entitled *Switches and Style Blocks* deals with this issue.

HTML Tag	Definition
`<B>`	Turns on **bold** text
`<I>`	Turns on *italic* text
`<U>`	Turns on underlined text
`<S>`	Turns on ~~strikethrough~~ text
`<EM>`	Designed to emphasize text. The text is usually rendered in *italic.*
`<PRE>`	Maintains all the original formatting. Type is usually monospaced.
`<FONT>`	Sets font face, size and color. This is the most powerful of all the HTML tags and as such deserves a subheading of its own.

The FONT Element

The font element is used to switch font characteristics on and off. Among its attributes it has:

Size

This takes the form **`size=n`**, where n can be any number from 1 to 7. **`SIZE=3`** corresponds to a font size used in the main text and **`7`** to an H1 font size. The font can also be made larger by using, for example, **`SIZE=+2`** which would make the font size two sizes bigger, or **`SIZE=-1`** which would make it one size smaller.

Face

This specifies the font family you want to use. It takes the form:

```
FACE= "fontname1, fontname2, fontname3 etc."
```

The browser will check the user's system for the requested font in the order specified.

Color

Specifies the font color as an RGB hexadecimal number, for example,

```
COLOR=#FF0000
```

This would produce a red colored text.

Styling Attributes

Elements can also take attributes that style and format the document. The following table is a partial list of styling and formatting attributes.

HTML Attribute	Definition
BGCOLOR	Can be used on the **<BODY>** tag or any of the table tags to provide a background color.
BACKGROUND	Takes a URL as its value. Can be used on any of the table or body tags to provide a tiled image.
LINK, VLINK, ALINK	Sets the color of a link using an RGB hexadecimal.
TEXT	Used on the **<BODY>** tag. Sets the text color for the page.
LEFTMARGIN, RIGHTMARGIN and TOPMARGIN	The syntax is **LEFTMARGIN=*n***, where ***n*** is the size of the margin expressed in pixels. Only works on IE.
CLEAR	An attribute that can be used with the ** ** or **<BODY>** tags, it takes the values **CLEAR=LEFT | RIGHT | ALL | NONE**. If, for example, the tag **<BR CLEAR=LEFT>** is employed, the browser will wait until there is a clear margin on the left before rendering the text. The pipestem symbol "|" indicates alternatives.
ALIGN	Applies to numerous elements and is used to align the element. The syntax is **ALIGN=LEFT | RIGHT | CENTER**

Whereas the following table refers to styling attributes associated with tables:

HTML Attribute	Definition
BORDER	Sets the border width in pixels.
BORDERCOLOR	Sets the border color.
CELLPADDING	**CELLPADDING** is the amount of space between the cell content and the border.

HTML Attribute	Definition
CELLSPACING	**CELLSPACING** is the amount of space between individual cells.
HEIGHT	Specifies the height either as a percentage or in pixels.
WIDTH	Specifies the width either as a percentage or in pixels.

Positioning

This was a perennial headache for the web author, until the advent of style sheets. Let's take a look at a few of the tricks and workarounds they came up with in the interim.

Using Tables

Because authors felt the need to control the placement of their content on the screen they took to using tables to do this. This worked fairly well but at the expense of complicating document design and making the source document difficult to read.

The following code would produce a nice margin down the left side of any written material.

```
<TABLE WIDTH=80%>
<TR>
<TD WIDTH=15%>
<BR>
</TD WIDTH=80%>
<TD>All the text goes here. We have made this text long enough to wrap to
illustrate the margin.
</TD>
</TR>
</TABLE>
```

The following screenshot shows the above in Communicator.

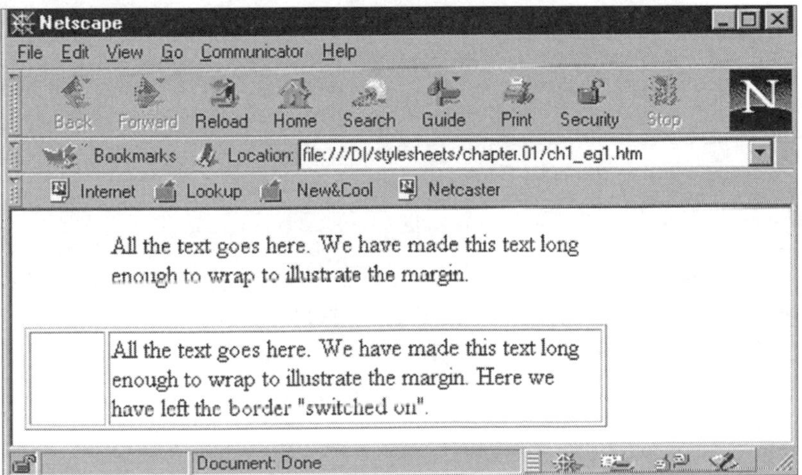

We have also repeated the code with the border switched on by setting:

```
<TABLE WIDTH=80% BORDER=1>
```

Note, we have added content in the form of a **
** to the empty table cell, otherwise some browsers will not render the cell.

So in order to position text accurately on the page, the web page author would have to create multiple tables and then ensure they were invisible to the viewer. Not terribly intuitive. Before the arrival of style sheets, the only alternative to this was to use the single pixel trick, which we cover next.

Using the Single Pixel Trick

Although tables give quite a bit of control over positioning, to precisely position content without using style sheets, we must resort to the single pixel trick.

The trick here is to make a **.gif** image consisting of a single pixel, then make that pixel transparent. We then use the **VSPACE** and **HSPACE** attributes to provide a border round the single pixel.

We can use this trick for precise positioning of objects and text, and also to make sure that our tables are the precise dimensions we want them.

```
<HTML>
<BODY BGCOLOR=WHITE>
   <IMG SRC="dot_clear.gif " HSPACE=25 VSPACE=25 ALIGN=RIGHT><BR>
   <BR CLEAR=RIGHT>
   <IMG SRC="dot_clear.gif" HSPACE=25 VSPACE=25 ALIGN=LEFT>
   Here is some text which should have a border of 50 pixels above it and a
margin of 50       pixels to the left of it
   <IMG SRC="dot_red.gif" HEIGHT=50 WIDTH=50 ALIGN=RIGHT><BR>
   <BR CLEAR=RIGHT>
   <IMG SRC="dot_red.gif" HEIGHT=50 WIDTH=50 ALIGN=LEFT>
   Here is some text which should have a border of 50 pixels above it and a
margin of 50       pixels to the left of it.
   <BR CLEAR=LEFT>
   <BR>
   <IMG SRC="dot_red.gif" HEIGHT=2 WIDTH=10 ALIGN=LEFT>
   This line of text is indented 10 pixels. We have used the solid color
here, but this of      course should be converted to a clear pixel in our
final document.
</BODY>
</HTML>
```

The above code shows how to accomplish this using the single pixel trick. In the second paragraph of text we have used a red colored single pixel with height and width properties so that you can visualize the process.

In fact you are encouraged to do this while you are laying out your documents, just remember to halve the width and height when you substitute the **VSPACE** and **HSPACE** attributes, because these are added to both sides of the single pixel image.

The following screenshot shows what this looks like in practice.

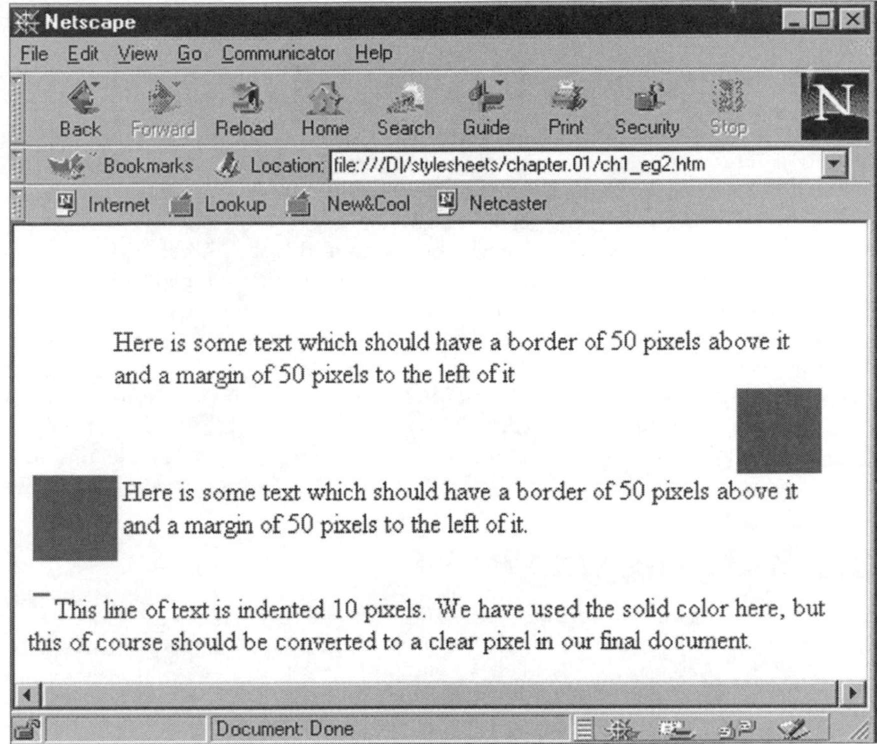

Using a combination of tables and the single pixel trick it is really possible to lay out a page any way we want. The problem with this approach is that the HTML source rapidly becomes cluttered up with styling tags. To be effective each page really has to be hand crafted.

To change the look and feel of a series of pages would be a huge task. In fact the effort would be almost as great as designing the pages in first place, without the excitement that goes with creativity.

The single pixel trick is a hack, a useful hack but a hack none the less. Thank goodness style sheets will obviate the need for it.

Using Images

The final way to make sure that the page is presented just as we want it is to convert the content to an image. However, this is a very wasteful use of resources. For example, the very simple page above is 450 bytes when sent as HTML and 15,000 bytes when sent as a 16-color **`.gif`**.

Again images can be expensive (good artists don't come cheap), they take time to download plus, you can't search on them, you can't copy the text, you can't change the size of the image there are major maintenance problems and so on and so on.

Image elements are best reserved for headings with special fonts and for visual clipart, **`.gif`**, and **`.jpg`** images.

Switches and Style Blocks

It is customary to think of a tag as a switch that switches various styles on and off. This may be a valid way of thinking of style if one is writing a simple text document, but it is a poor thought process to use when we are styling anything more sophisticated.

Whether we are designing a page for a magazine, a newspaper, or the Web, we are moving blocks of text and images around our page. It is, therefore, better to think of styling in terms of styling blocks of content.

All the styling languages make use of this concept, so we should force ourselves to think in these terms straight off. Cascading Style Sheet language (CSS) uses the box concept, eXtensible Style Language (XSL) and Document Style Semantics and Specification Language (DSSSL) use the flow-object concept, but they mean the same thing–blocks of material to which we can apply styling.

Experience from teaching style languages tells me that, although this is an easy concept for beginners to grasp, it can be a difficult concept for experienced HTML buffs to adapt to. So if you fall into the latter category, it would be helpful to start thinking in terms of blocks of content rather than switches.

An Example of Styling with HTML

In order to understand what kind of styling is possible with old HTML let's look at an example. A good and fairly simple example would be a page from a Wrox Instant book. We have chosen page 82 from *Instant HTML Programmer's Reference.* Read the text on this page as well, it is applicable. The code for this page is listed as **`Ch1_1.htm`**.

First let's set the page background. The following line provides a soothing mint green.

```
<BODY BGCOLOR="#EEFFEE"><!--A pleasant mint green-->
```

Now we need to set the outline of the page. The best way to do this is via a table with a border. The width of the page should be about 6 inches. As we can only depict the width in pixels, in HTML we need a ruler and experimentation to carry this out. As a rule of thumb there are about 80 pixels to a logical inch, but the actual pixel size will depend on your monitor.

> *The "logical inch" is what your monitor thinks an inch should be. When I ask the browser to draw a box 6in. wide on my monitor the actual measured width is 8.5in, which makes the "logical inch" about 1.4 actual inches on my monitor. The measurement in the y direction may even be different. Most programming languages have a function that allows you to get this information, in VB it is* `Screen.TwipsPerPixelX` *and* `TwipsPerPixelY`. *It is likely that XSL will have a similar function built into it, but it is unlikely that we will be able to have such precise control in CSS.*

What we come up with is the following:

```
<!--The page itself-->
<TABLE BORDER="1" BGCOLOR="white">
```

```
<TR>
<TD WIDTH="500">
<BR>
<IMG SRC="dot_clear.gif" VSPACE="418" ALIGN="left">
```

The page color of course is white, the border of the table we have depicted as one pixel thick. Because we wanted to make sure of the height of the page as nine inches, we used the Single Pixel Trick, which we demonstrated earlier in this chapter.

Now we want to set the various elements in the page, and to get these set in exactly the right position we will nest in our main table some more tables and use the single pixel trick over and over again.

First we will put in the page heading. A good trick is to leave the border switched on until we have got the material exactly where we want it, then switch it off to display the completed page.

```
<TABLE BORDER="0" BGCOLOR="white">
<!--page heading type-->
<TR>
   <TD>
      <IMG SRC="dot_clear.gif" HSPACE="8" ALIGN="left">
      <FONT SIZE="2" FACE="arial">
      <B>Chapter 4 - Images and Inclusions</B>
   </TD>
</TR>
</TABLE>
```

The first lot of text is a regular paragraph. If we take care with our table construct we can use it as a template for all our other paragraphs.

```
<TABLE WIDTH=480 CELLPADDING="10" BORDER="0" BGCOLOR="white">
<!--para type-->
<TR>
   <TD>
      <FONT SIZE="2" FACE="times new roman">
      <IMG SRC="dot_clear.gif" VSPACE="8" HSPACE="5" ALIGN="left">
      In fact this page uses a table to seperate the page......etc
   </TD>
</TR>
</TABLE>
```

The **VSPACE** attribute will have to be set for each individual paragraph. Note how we have used the **CELLPADDING** attribute to provide space above and below the paragraph. We could also have used the single pixel trick, but this way is neater.

As an exercise for you, we have not made **VSPACE** high enough and so the third line does not line up with the others. Try adjusting it so that every thing looks just right.

Now to format the block of code shown on the page.

```
<!--Set the gray box in from the edge of the page.-->
<IMG SRC="dot_clear.gif"VSPACE="12" HSPACE="14" ALIGN="left">
```

```
<TABLE WIDTH=430  BORDER="0" BGCOLOR="#CCCCCC">
<TR>
   <TD>
<!--code type-->
      <FONT SIZE="1" FACE="courier new">
      <IMG SRC="dot_clear.gif"VSPACE="12" HSPACE="12" ALIGN="left">
      &lt;IMG SRC="world.gif" ALIGN="LEFT" WIDTH=75 HEIGHT=75&gt;<BR>
      &lt;B&gt;The internet is the most cost effective way to <BR>
      advertise &lt;I>your&lt;/I&gt; business today ... etc
   </TD>
</TR>
</TABLE>
```

Note the use of the escape entities for **<** and **>**. There are no new tricks here just a lot of fiddling about. The same with the heading

```
<TABLE BORDER="0" BGCOLOR="white">
<TR>
   <TD>
      <IMG SRC="dot_clear.gif" HSPACE="8" ALIGN="left">
      <FONT SIZE="3" FACE="arial">
<!--Sub Heading 2 type-->
      <I><B>Using the HTML 4.0 'float' Style Property</B></I>
   </TD>
</TR>
</TABLE>
```

One of the problems we run into is that in HTML we can't set the font size exactly, we have to use a scale of 1-7, where 3 corresponds to what the default value for the browser usually is.

Again we have to fiddle around and experiment to make things look right.

The rest of the page doesn't introduce any thing new. Here's the complete code for the page.

```
<HTML>
<TITLE> Chapter1 Tutorial1. A Wrox Page in HTML.</TITLE>
<BODY BGCOLOR="#EEFFEE"><!--A pleasant mint green-->

<!--set our page in about 1" from the left of the screen-->
<IMG SRC="dot_clear.gif" HSPACE="30" ALIGN="left">

<!--The page itself-->
<TABLE BORDER="1" BGCOLOR="white">
<TR>
<TD WIDTH="500">
<BR>
<IMG SRC="dot_clear.gif" VSPACE="418" ALIGN="left">

<TABLE BORDER="0" BGCOLOR="white">
<!--page heading type-->
<TR>
<TD>
<IMG SRC="dot_clear.gif" HSPACE="8" ALIGN="left">
<FONT SIZE="2" FACE="arial">
```

```
<B>Chapter 4 - Images and Inclusions</B>
</TD>
</TR>
</TABLE>

<TABLE WIDTH=480 CELLPADDING="10" BORDER="0" BGCOLOR="white">
<!--para type-->
<TR>
<TD>
<FONT SIZE="2" FACE="times new roman">
<IMG SRC="dot_clear.gif"VSPACE="8" HSPACE="5" ALIGN="left">
In fact this page uses a table to seperate the page into two sections.
We'll look at how tables work in chapter 6. In the meantime the important
line is the one that inserts the left-hand image:
</TD>
</TR>
</TABLE>

<!--Set the gray box in from the edge of the page.-->
<IMG SRC="dot_clear.gif"VSPACE="12" HSPACE="14" ALIGN="left">
<TABLE WIDTH=430  BORDER="0" BGCOLOR="#CCCCCC">
<TR>
<TD>
<!--code type-->
<FONT SIZE="1" FACE="courier new">
<IMG SRC="dot_clear.gif"VSPACE="12" HSPACE="12" ALIGN="left">
&lt;IMG SRC="world.gif" ALIGN="LEFT" WIDTH=75 HEIGHT=75&gt;<BR>&lt;B&gt;The
internet is the most cost effective way to <BR>advertise
&lt;I>your&lt;/I&gt; business today ... etc
</TD>
</TR>
</TABLE>

<TABLE WIDTH=480 CELLPADDING="10" BORDER="0" BGCOLOR="white">
<!--para type-->
<TR>
<TD>

<FONT SIZE="2" FACE="times new roman">
<IMG SRC="dot_clear.gif"VSPACE="40" HSPACE="8" ALIGN="left">
You can see that we've used the value <B> "LEFT" </B> for the <B>ALIGN</B>
attribute (the quotaton marks are in fact optional, because the value is a
single word with no spaces). This causes the image to be aligned with the
left margin, and the text wraps to the right of it. If it appears to be too
close, we could use the <B>HSPACE</B> and the <B>VSPACE</B> attributes to
give it more room, although in our case we wanted it to wrap as closely as
possible.
</TD>
</TR>
</TABLE>

<TABLE BORDER="0" BGCOLOR="white">
<TR>
<TD>
<IMG SRC="dot_clear.gif" HSPACE="8" ALIGN="left">
<FONT SIZE="3" FACE="arial">
<!--Sub Heading 2 type-->
```

```
<I><B>Using the HTML 4.0 'float' Style Property</B></I>
</TD>
</TR>
</TABLE>

<TABLE WIDTH=480 CELLPADDING="10" BORDER="0" BGCOLOR="white">
<TR>
<TD>
<!--para type-->
<FONT SIZE="2" FACE="times new roman">
<IMG SRC="dot_clear.gif"VSPACE="16" HSPACE="8" ALIGN="left">
Of course, we should be using the new HTML 4.0 style sheet standards to
place our image, instead of the attributes of the <B>&lt;IMG&gt;</B>
element directly:
</TD>
</TR>
</TABLE>

<!--Set the gray box in from the edge of the page.-->
<IMG SRC="dot_clear.gif"VSPACE="12" HSPACE="14" ALIGN="left">
<TABLE WIDTH=430  BORDER="0" BGCOLOR="#CCCCCC">
<TR>
<TD>
<!--code type-->
<FONT SIZE="1" FACE="courier new">
<IMG SRC="dot_clear.gif"VSPACE="12" HSPACE="12" ALIGN="left">
&lt;IMG SRC="world.gif" <BR>
<!--indent STYLE>-->
<IMG SRC="dot_clear.gif" HSPACE="12" ALIGN="left">
STYLE="float:left;width:75, height:73; &gt;"
</TD>
</TR>
</TABLE>

<TABLE WIDTH=460 CELLPADDING="10" BORDER="0" BGCOLOR="white">
<TR>
<TD>
<!--para type-->
<FONT SIZE="2" FACE="times new roman">
<IMG SRC="dot_clear.gif"VSPACE="30" HSPACE="8" ALIGN="left">
Here, the CSS1 <B>float</B> property is used to move the element to the
left margin of the page and wrap the text round it. This will only work in
browsers that support the CSS1 standard, but you could always take the
'belt and braces' approach and include both the direct attributes and the
style attribute with the matching properties:
</TD>
</TR>
</TABLE>

<!--Set the gray box in from the edge of the page.-->
<IMG SRC="dot_clear.gif"VSPACE="12" HSPACE="14" ALIGN="left">
<TABLE WIDTH=430  BORDER="0" BGCOLOR="#CCCCCC">
<TR>
<TD>
<!--code type-->
<FONT SIZE="1" FACE="courier new">
<IMG SRC="dot_clear.gif"VSPACE="12" HSPACE="12" ALIGN="left">
```

```
&lt;IMG SRC="world.gif" ALIGN="LEFT" WIDTH=75 HEIGHT=73 <BR>
<!--indent STYLE>-->
<IMG SRC="dot_clear.gif" HSPACE="12" ALIGN="left">
STYLE="float:left;width:75, height:73; &gt;
</TD>
</TR>
</TABLE>

<TABLE WIDTH=480 CELLPADDING="10" BORDER="0" BGCOLOR="white">
<TR>
<TD>
<!--para type-->
<FONT SIZE="2" FACE="times new roman">
<IMG SRC="dot_clear.gif"VSPACE="16" HSPACE="8" ALIGN="left">
 The only problem now is that behavior may be erratic in browsers that
partly support CSS1. If they don't handle it properly, and it takes
precedence over the direct properties (as it should), the results could be
less than appealing.
</TD>
</TR>
</TABLE>

<TABLE BORDER="0" BGCOLOR="white">
<TR>
<TD>
<!--Sub Heading 1 type-->
<IMG SRC="dot_clear.gif" HSPACE="8" ALIGN="left">
<FONT SIZE="4" FACE="arial">
<B>The Single Pixel GIF Trick</B>
</TD>
</TR>
</TABLE>

<TABLE WIDTH=480 CELLPADDING="10" BORDER="0" BGCOLOR="white">
<TR>
<TD>
<!--para type-->
<FONT SIZE="2" FACE="times new roman">
<IMG SRC="dot_clear.gif"VSPACE="30" HSPACE="8" ALIGN="left">
 This is a useful trick that many web authors use to achieve precise
control over layout and formatting. It's a little out of date now, because
you should be using style sheets (see the previous chapter) to control the
placement and alignment of all the elements in your pages. However, until
more browsers fully support the style sheet proposals, it can be useful.
</TD>
</TR>
</TABLE>

<TABLE WIDTH=480 CELLPADDING="10" BORDER="0" BGCOLOR="white">
<TR>
<TD>
<!--para type-->
<FONT SIZE="2" FACE="times new roman">
<IMG SRC="dot_clear.gif"VSPACE="38" HSPACE="8" ALIGN="left">
 It basically works like this. You have an image, in this case
<B><CODE>dot_clear.gif</CODE></B> which consists of one pixel. The
pixelcolor is defined as being the invisible, a trick that GIF version 89a
```

```
files can achieve. When you want to add a precise amount of space across or
down, you insert the image and use the <B>HSPACE</B> and/or the
<B>VSPACE</B> attributes to move the following elements around as required.
The code is something like this:
</TD>
</TR>
</TABLE>

<!--Set the gray box in from the edge of the page.-->
<IMG SRC="dot_clear.gif"VSPACE="1" HSPACE="14" ALIGN="left">
<TABLE WIDTH=430  BORDER="0" BGCOLOR="#CCCCCC">
<TR>
<TD>
<!--code type-->
<FONT SIZE="1" FACE="courier new">
<IMG SRC="dot_clear.gif"VSPACE="12" HSPACE="12" ALIGN="left">
&lt;IMG SRC="dot_clear.gif" HSPACE=x VSPACE=y &gt;
</TD>
</TR>
</TABLE>

<!--PAGENUMBER.-->
<IMG SRC="dot_clear.gif"VSPACE="32" HSPACE="2" ALIGN="left">
<TABLE WIDTH=50  BORDER="0" BGCOLOR="white" >
<TR>
<TD VALIGN=center>

<FONT SIZE="4" FACE="arial">
<IMG SRC="dot_clear.gif"VSPACE="18"  >
82<BR>
</TD>
</TR>
</TABLE>
</TD>
</TR>
</TABLE>
</BODY>
</HTML>
```

The following screenshot shows how it displays on IE4.

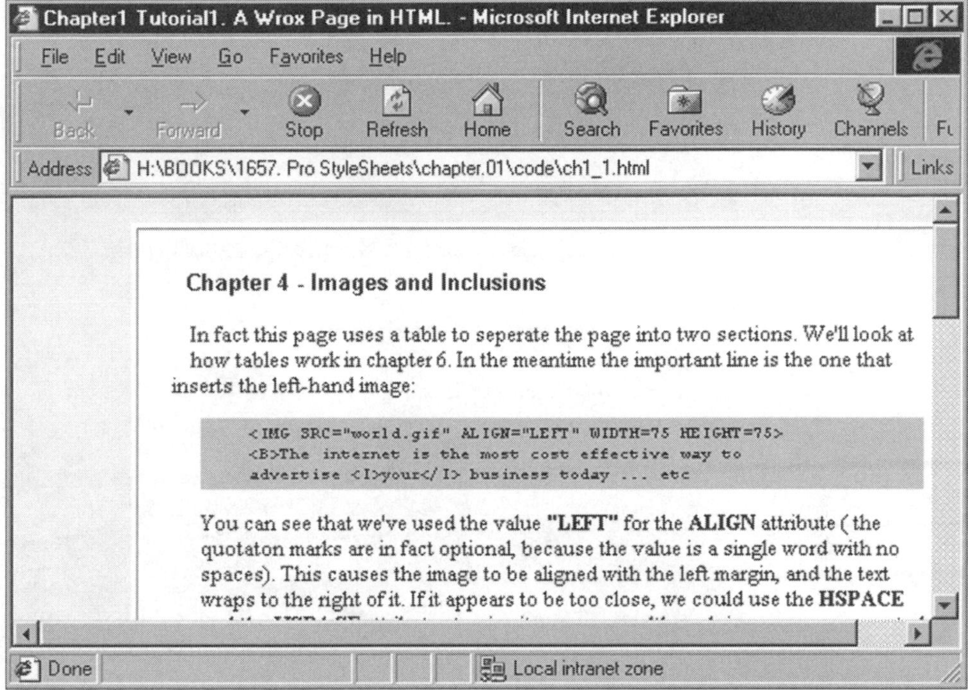

It looks the same on Communicator. On my monitor it is 6 inches wide, it may be more or less on your monitor.

So, styling with HTML is complex, messy and time consuming. To see a summary of problems facing the web designer before the advent of style sheets, check out an article called *"Severe Tire Damage on the Information Superhighway"* by David Siegel, which you'll find at: **`http://www.dsiegel.com/damage/index.html`**.

OK, we've seen the problems, now let's see the solution.

Styling with Style Sheets

Style sheets changed all this. They made styling much quicker, easier and cleaner. We aren't going to cover them in detail in this chapter, we'll leave that until Chapter 2. We are just going to show you how great they are by repeating the same tutorial using a style sheet instead of HTML.

An Example of Styling with Style Sheets

The picture below shows how our page that has been styled using HTML and a style sheet looks.

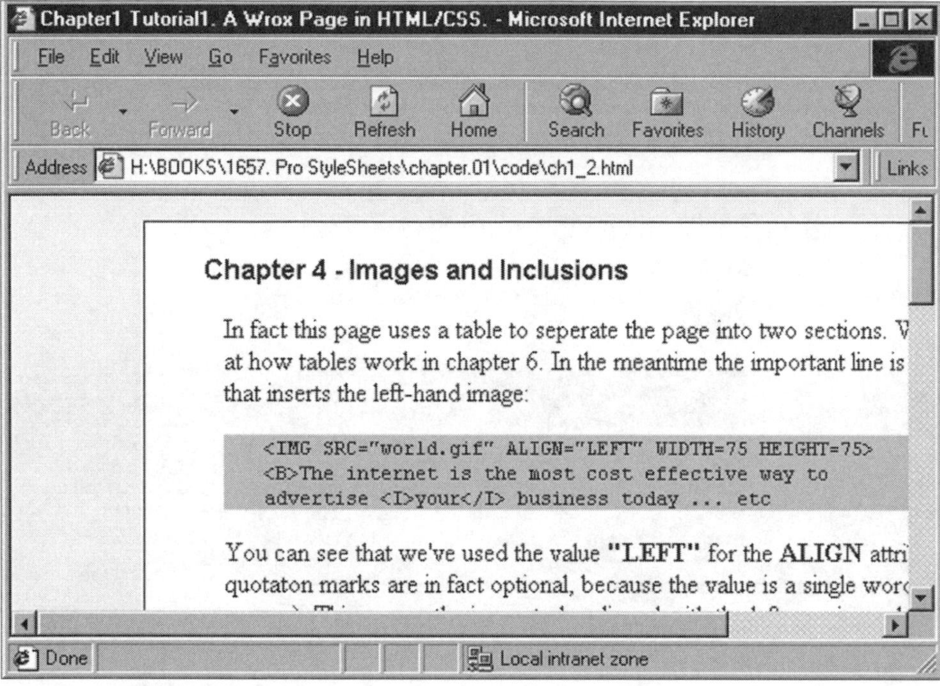

The next figure shows the HTML.

```
<HTML>
<HEAD>
<TITLE> Chapter1 Tutorial1. A Wrox Page in HTML/CSS.</TITLE>
<LINK REL="stylesheet" TYPE="text/css" HREF="ch1_2.css">
</HEAD>
<BODY>
<DIV CLASS="page">

<DIV CLASS="phead">
Chapter 4 - Images and Inclusions
</DIV>

<DIV CLASS="para">
In fact this page uses a table to seperate the page into two sections.
We'll look at how tables work in chapter 6. In the meantime the important
line is the one that inserts the left-hand image:
</DIV>

<DIV CLASS="code">
&lt;IMG SRC="world.gif" ALIGN="LEFT" WIDTH=75 HEIGHT=75&gt;<BR>
&lt;B&gt;The internet is the most cost effective way to <BR>
advertise &lt;I>your&lt;/I&gt; business today ... etc
```

```
</DIV>

<DIV CLASS="para">
You can see that we've used the value <B> "LEFT" </B> for the <B>ALIGN</B>
attribute (the quotation marks are in fact optional, because the value is a
single word with no spaces). This causes the image to be aligned with the
left margin, and the text wraps to the right of it. If it appears to be too
close, we could use the <B>HSPACE</B> and the <B>VSPACE</B> attributes to
give it more room, although in our case we wanted it to wrap as closely as
possible.
</DIV>

<DIV CLASS="head2">
Using the HTML 4.0 'float' Style Property
</DIV>

<DIV CLASS="para">
Of course, we should be using the new HTML 4.0 style sheet standards to
place our image, instead of the attributes of the <B>&lt;IMG&gt;</B>
element directly:
</DIV>

<DIV CLASS="code">
&lt;IMG SRC="world.gif" <BR>
<!--indent STYLE>-->
<SPAN CLASS="indent">
STYLE="float:left;width:75, height:73; &gt;</SPAN>
</DIV>

<DIV CLASS="para">
Here, the CSS1 <B>float</B> property is used to move the element to the
left margin of the page and wrap the text round it. This will only work in
browsers that support the CSS1 standard, but you could always take the
'belt and braces' approach and include both the direct attributes and the
style attribute with the matching properties:
</DIV>

<DIV CLASS="code">
&lt;IMG SRC="world.gif" ALIGN="LEFT" WIDTH=75 HEIGHT=73 <BR>
<!--indent STYLE>-->
<SPAN CLASS="indent">
STYLE="float:left;width:75, height:73; &gt;</SPAN>
</DIV>

<DIV CLASS="para">
The only problem now is that behavior may be erratic in browsers that
partly support CSS1. If they don't handle it properly, and it takes
precedence over the direct properties (as it should), the results could be
less than appealing.
</DIV>

<DIV CLASS="head1">
<B>The Single Pixel GIF Trick</B>
</DIV>

<DIV CLASS="para">
```

```
This is a useful trick that many web authors use to achieve precise control
over layout and formatting. It's a little out of date now, because you
should be using style sheets (see the previous chapter) to control the
placement and alignment of all the elements in your pages. However, until
more browsers fully support the style sheet proposals, it can be useful.
</DIV>

<DIV CLASS="para">
It basically works like this. You have an image, in this case
<B>dot_clear.gif</B> which consists of one pixel. The pixelcolor is defined
as being the invisible, a trick that GIF version 89a files can achieve.
When you want to add a precise amount of space across or down, you insert
the image and use the <B>HSPACE</B> and/or the <B>VSPACE</B> attributes to
move the following elements around as required. The code is something like
this:
</DIV>

<DIV CLASS="code">
&lt;IMG SRC="dot_clear.gif" HSPACE=x VSPACE=y &gt;
</DIV>

<DIV CLASS="pnum">
82
</DIV>
<BR>
<!--end of div class=page-->
</DIV>
</BODY>
</HTML>
```

Finally there is the style sheet.

```
/* style sheet for ch1_2.htm*/


BODY{

background-color:#EEFFEE;
}

DIV.page{


background-color:white;
margin-left:0.75in;
border:solid 1px;
width:6in;
}

DIV.phead{
font:bold 12pt arial,sans-serif;
margin-top:0.2in;
margin-left:0.375in;

background-color:white;
}
```

```
DIV.para{
font:normal 12pt 'times new roman',serif;
margin-left:0.5in;
margin-top:1em;
margin-bottom:1em;
margin-right:0.5in;
background-color:white;
}

DIV.code{
font:normal 9pt 'courier new',monospaced;
margin-left:0.5in;
padding-left: 0.25in;
margin-right:0.5in;
border:none 1px;
background-color:#CCCCCC;
}

DIV.head1{
font:bold 16pt arial,sans-serif;
margin-left:0.375in;
background-color:white;
}

DIV.head2{
font:bold italic 12pt arial,sans-serif;
margin-left:0.375in;
background-color:white;
}

DIV.pnum{
font:bold 16pt arial,sans-serif;
margin-top:0.25in;
padding-bottom:0.25in;
margin-left:0.25in;

}

SPAN.indent{
margin-left:0.4in;
}
```

The output pages are virtually identical. The page using a style sheet looks better because it is 6 virtual inches across (8.5 real inches on my computer screen) as opposed to 6 actual inches in the page styled with HTML tags.

Look at the HTML page and compare it with the tagged page. This page is actually readable without much effort.

Now look at the Style Sheet page and, although you may not know any CSS, at this stage you can tell at a glance that the styling language is logical, understandable and precise. We'll go into detail on how to create and apply style sheets in the next chapter.

HTML Styling versus Style Sheet Styling

First, let's examine the problems that come out of our HTML styling example.

Time is Money

In the first example above we tackled a reasonably straight forward job of formatting a file using some tried and trusty HTML guru work-arounds and tricks, and the result is just as we wanted it.

The problem is connected to how long the entire exercise took. I started off by just typing in the text, (I'm a slow typist, so I didn't want that to flavor this experiment) and then timed how long it took to get every thing right. It took almost two hours. I then tried another page using the templates that I had already created, and it took me almost an hour. Calculate that for the book. 400 pages times 3/4 hour (assume I get better as I go along), times $25 an hour (and that's cheap). The end result is $7500 to put up a web site containing these pages in this format.

Actually most commercial pages, are generated on-the-fly using script, or are generated using proprietary software.

Also look and see how difficult it is to read the actual content in all that formatting, consider that intranets are putting up hundreds of pages of information a day, and you realize that we have a major problem with HTML type styling. The answer of course is style sheets. Later on we will consider the advantages of CSS type style sheets, but before doing this lets look at some of the other problems associated with the current HTML type of styling.

Download Speeds

Most pages use a lot of images to compensate for the difficulty of styling with HTML tags, and this takes time to download. As an experiment try going to a graphics heavy site, and navigate between their pages. For example:

`http://www.microsoft.com`

On my 56 kbps modem it takes between 30 and 40 seconds for each page of this site, which makes heavy use of headers in the form of graphics, to download.

Now go to a site that uses style sheets.

`http://www.hypermedic.com/style`

After emptying my cache, it took less than a second for each page to download, making for very fast navigation.

Admittedly some sites need to be graphics heavy, but users certainly appreciate the speed that style sheets bring.

Even if we don't use graphics, but use HTML type styling, the pages themselves are larger. The Wrox page in the example above is 7K. This is twice the size of the page using style sheets and those extra bytes all come from the styling tags.

Admittedly the style sheet file that is necessary to display non HTML styled pages weighs in at 1K, but this same sheet could be used for all 400 pages of the book. This represents an overall saving of about 1.5 megabytes for a single simple documentation project.

Maintenance

It is great fun to design and build pages, but unfortunately in the real world they have to be maintained, and maintaining pages with a lot of HTML styling can be a nightmare. The following list charts the various parts of said nightmare.

- First the content of the pages can be difficult to read because of all the styling elements and tags.
- Secondly if we change the content, the balance of the page is often upset, and we have to alter our tags and attributes and get things right by trial and error.
- Thirdly there is no easy way to alter the overall style of a set of pages without altering every tag individually, usually by hand.
- In fact it is often easier to write a one-off program to handle the problem with code or script.

Style sheets have none of these disadvantages, and have the additional advantages set out below.

The single style sheet we developed above can be applied to as many documents as you want with a single line of code in the HTML document—**`<LINK REL="stylesheet" TYPE="text/css" HREF="ch1_2.css">`**.

- If you wish to change any of the styling in a family of documents, you just have to alter one document, the style sheet, not thousands of HTML sources.
- The size of your HTML document is almost half of the document written up in tagged HTML.
- It makes it possible to separate authoring, and styling. Your copywriters can concentrate on the copy, and your artists/typographers can concentrate on the styling.
- You will save both time and money.
- If you really want extra kudos, suggest to your boss what styling all your pages in XML/XSL will do for productivity, profitability, and his stock options. But I am afraid you will have to read further before you can pitch this line to him/her.

Why did Styling get so Complicated in HTML?

To answer this question we have to go back to the origins and original purposes of HTML.

HTML was originally designed for the transfer of referenced (with links) scientific documents across numerous different platforms and the Internet. It is difficult to realize now that in the very recent past Windows was not so dominant a platform.

The original HTML was very good at what it was designed to do, namely transfer document content. However, somewhere along the line it crossed a divide from being a mere content provider for scientists to being a means of communication for the average consumer. Most are agreed this process started with the first Mosaic browser which allowed transfer of images, and accelerated with the release of Netscape 1.1.

The "Old Guard" fought an unsuccessful rearguard action to maintain the so-called "purity" of the Web, but as soon as commercial forces became involved, they were doomed to failure. They were done in by self-proclaimed "web-terrorists" such as David Siegel who were intent on making the Web a stylish and consumer oriented place. The web-terrorists were provided with tools by "gun-runners" such as Marc Andreessen intent on making the Netscape browser the dominant browser. His chief tool to accomplish this was to create proprietary tags to make the Web a more stylish and attractive place.

Once Microsoft realized that they had almost missed the boat, they threw their massive resources into the struggle, again using proprietary styling and Multimedia tags as their chief weapon. The purist's battle to keep the Web content driven was doomed–and styling tag followed styling tag. Individuals such as David Siegel invented new tricks like the single pixel gif, new uses were found for tables, layout and styling improved, but all at the expense of document clarity.

While David Siegel took to boasting "the Web is ruined and I ruined it", the W3 consortium lagged behind the browsers to such an extent that the HTML 3 proposals were never finished, becoming out of date before they ever became a recommendation! And so the web and HTML became a disordered mishmash of styling tags and guru hacks. The next chapter shows how this dilemma was resolved using Cascading Style Sheets.

Summary

In this chapter we looked at various forms of web page styling.

- We saw how styling markup differs from semantic and structural mark up, and how using mark up to style is different from using a style sheet.
- We looked briefly at some of the more common styling tags and tricks used in HTML, and then used them to style a relatively simple document.
- We looked at some of the problems that style sheets should be asked to solve, and looked at how CSS in particular offers a solution.
- We enumerated the advantages of using style sheets over styling markup.

In the next chapter we will jump right into basic CSS style sheets, and then in the rest of the first part of this book we will have a look at basic XML and how CSS can be used with it. We will also take a first look at XSL, a style language that is very much in the formative stages, but will probably be used to add powerful styling capabilities to XML.

Exercises

1. Take any 'commercial' page on the Web, and remove all the images and formatting tags. See what you are left with.
2. Try and make the page interesting again, just using text.
3. Take a series of pages on a site, and time the average download time on your site.
4. Now time the average amount of time you spend reading the pages. (Research suggests that we spend 70% of our time waiting for pages to download, 30% of our time reading.)

2

Basic Cascading Style Sheets

The scene we described at the end of the last chapter was the one that confronted Hakon Lie and Bert Bos. Almost single handedly they pioneered style sheets and thereby put some order back into the Web. In December 1996 they created a standard called **Cascading Style Sheet Level 1 Recommendation (CSS1)** which you can read at **`http://www.w3.org/TR/REC-CSS1`**. It can be a bit daunting when you first look it up, so we've included an appendix which explains how it is set out and gives tips on the best way to read it.

CSS1 enabled web designers to attach styles, in the form of fonts, colors, spacing and so on, to web pages. The cascading part of the recommendation referred to the fact that more than one style sheet may apply to the same HTML document. The author may specify a style sheet, so may the reader, particularly if they need to apply certain styles to documents to overcome a visual impairment. Both Communicator 4 and IE4 support CSS1. Certain properties are not implemented in one or the other, but we highlight this on our way through the book, and in the appendices covering CSS1 and CSS2 properties at the back of this book.

Not satisfied with revolutionizing design on the Web once, Lie and Bos, together with Chris Lillie and Ian Jacobs, produced a second specification, **Cascading Style Sheets Level 2 (CSS2)**, adopted as a recommendation by W3C in May 1998. You can find this at **`http://www.w3.org/TR/REC-CSS2`**.

CSS2 introduces media-specific style sheets which allow the web author to make their work suitable for visual browsers, aural devices, printers, braille devices, handheld devices, and so on. It also brings support for content positioning, downloadable fonts, table layout, features for internationalization, automatic counters and numbering, and some properties related to user interface. It is not yet supported to any extent by either Microsoft or Netscape, but both will surely seek to implement its recommendations in the next versions of their browsers.

By now, hopefully you are convinced of the need for style sheets, and understand what we mean when we refer to CSS1 and CSS2, which we will do constantly throughout this book. Let's get down to some practical programming! In this chapter we'll:

- Introduce you to a simple style sheet example to get you going,
- Then take you through style sheet rules in some detail,
- And finally introduce some of the other features of style sheets which we will cover in depth later in the book.

Let's begin with a reiteration of the definition of a style sheet.

What is a Style Sheet?

You learnt in the introduction that a style sheet is just a set of rules informing the compositor how to set up his page for printing. A Cascading Style Sheet is a similar set of rules for a computer user agent. The agent is usually browser software loaded on to a computer.

In this chapter you will learn the basic syntax of a Cascading Style Sheet and how to use some of the various properties. This will all be expanded on later in this book, but at the end of this chapter you should know enough to start writing your own style sheets.

Probably the best way to get acquainted with Cascading Style Sheets is to start with a simple example, like the one displayed below.

A Simple Style Sheet Example

This is the first of many examples we'll take you through in this book. The best way to use them is to type the code from the book into your text editor and run it yourself, following the instructions. You might want to set up a directory to hold your examples. Alternatively, if you're short of time you can just run the example code straight from our web site at **`http://rapid.wrox.co.uk/books/1657`** or copy and paste the source from the web site.

Type or paste the following code into your text editor:

```
<HTML>
<HEAD>
<TITLE> Chapter 2 First example</TITLE>
<STYLE TYPE="text/css">
BODY{
color:red;
}
</STYLE>
</HEAD>
<BODY>
Hello World- in red!

</BODY>
</HTML>
```

Then save it in your example folder or directory as **ch2_1.htm** and open it in your browser.

If you have Communicator go to File—Open Page (*Ctrl+O*) then click Choose File. If you have IE4 go to File—Open (*Ctrl+O*) then click Browse

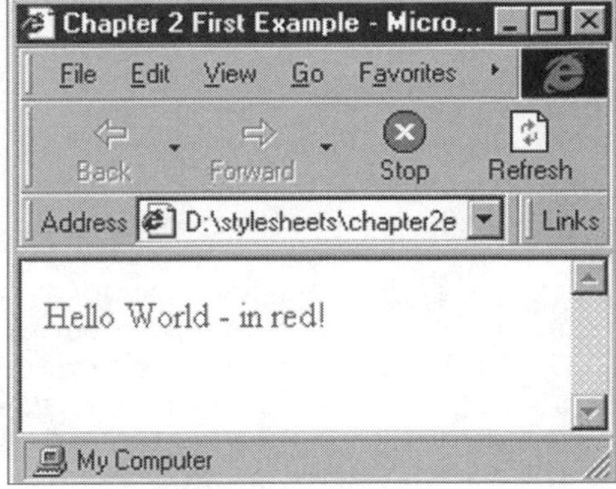

Nothing very fancy here, just a line of red text. If your browser displays black text then I'm afraid that you have a browser that either doesn't support style sheets, or one in which the style sheets are disabled. See the instructions in the Introduction on how to get one, or how to enable style sheets.

The only way this differs from a regular HTML 2 file is that in the **<HEAD>** there is a new HTML element **<STYLE></STYLE>**. Inside it is a statement or **rule**.

```
BODY{
color:red;
}
```

Quite simply, from the browser's point of view, this tells it to print everything in the document in red unless told otherwise. The following box explains this in more detail if you aren't quite sure what's happening.

> **Every browser has a list of default values, which are consulted whenever it comes across a markup tag. This tells the browser what action it has to take. The default color for text in a document body is usually black, but here the style sheet is telling the browser to override the default color and print everything in red instead. The browser will carry on doing this until told to do otherwise.**

Anatomy of a Cascading Style Sheet Rule

Let's examine this rule in a bit more detail.

First of all it could have been written:

```
BODY{color:red;}
```

Or:

```
BODY{color:red}
```

For the most part **white-space** is ignored by the browser. Formatting is only important from the point of view of clarity. For considerations of space the single line version will be used quite often in this book, but I urge you to always expand your code for maximum clarity. The following information box explains the importance of clarity in a computer context.

> **Anyone who has done any programming will tell you that clarity is probably the most important thing in writing code. What seems abundantly clear to you today will seem a complete mystery when you review it in the weeks ahead. Also remember that someone else is likely to be reviewing your efforts and they will have no insight into your thinking. The important thing is to develop you own clear style and stick to it. If you have any doubts at all as to the clarity of what you have done, or if the reason for doing it is not abundantly clear, comment it (see later). It will save endless headaches.**

The semi-colon, which is used to separate multiple properties, is optional if you have just one value. However, it's best to always put it in as experience tells us that we are going to be adding to and subtracting from the properties, and the absence of a single semi-colon can cause your whole page not to display. When it comes to style sheets browsers are **very** finicky about the correct syntax. The most commonly over looked errors are getting a colon or semi-colon wrong, or leaving out a unit designation such as pt in **`font-size:12pt`**. The browser is just meant to ignore the incorrect property, but often it skips over the whole rule, sometimes the whole sheet and occasionally the whole page.

Let's examine this statement in more detail.

```
BODY{color:red;}
```

It is made up of two parts–what is present before the curly brackets–the **selector,** which in this example is the HTML tag **`<BODY>`** and that which is contained within–the **declaration**.

The declaration is made up of another two parts–the **property name** and the property's **value**. A colon (**`:`**) separates the property name and the value. In this case the declaration is **`{color:red;}`** The whole thing i.e. the selector (in this case **`<BODY>`**) plus its declaration (enclosed in curly brackets) is known as a rule.

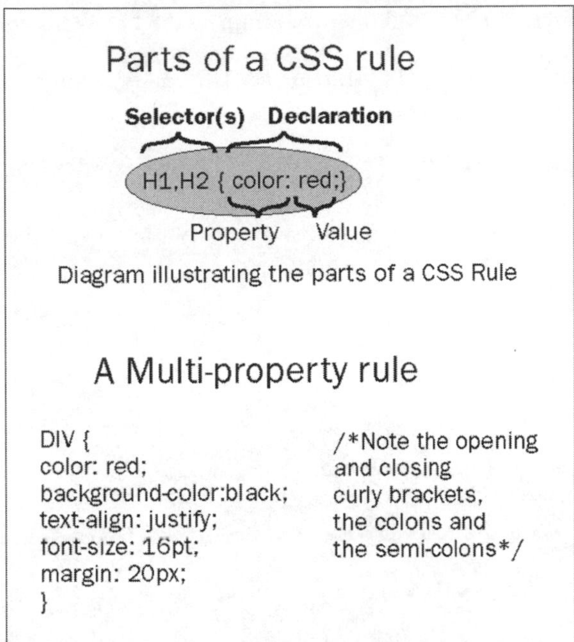

Parts of a CSS rule
Selector(s) Declaration
H1,H2 { color: red;}
Property Value
Diagram illustrating the parts of a CSS Rule
A Multi-property rule
DIV {
color: red;
background-color:black;
text-align: justify;
font-size: 16pt;
margin: 20px;
}
/*Note the opening
and closing
curly brackets,
the colons and
the semi-colons*/

What then is a Cascading Style Sheet? A style sheet is no more than a collection of **rules** written with the correct syntax. Whereas a **cascade** is when compliant browsers allow multiple style sheets to have control over the same document at the same time, it's as simple as that!

A style sheet can either be contained in the **.htm** file itself, usually in the **<HEAD>** element between a pair of **<STYLE>[***style rules and css type comments here***]</STYLE>** tags, or in a separate file with the format **.css**.

Much of the rest of this book is nothing more than an explanation and expansion of the syntax that applies to selectors, properties and values, i.e. an exposition on the above paragraph.

Commenting

Before going any further we should just touch on the very important subject of commenting.

What is commenting? It is textual notes meant for the programmer's eyes only and ignored by the computer when displaying the page.

In a style sheet everything placed between **/*** and ***/** will be ignored by the browser. Although CSS rules are fairly straightforward and self-explanatory, it is still very important to comment.

```
/*This is a css style comment*/
```

Why is commenting important? Well unless you are very different from the rest of us mortal humans, code that seems lucid and self-documenting today can appear as a mysterious tangle of spaghetti-code when re-read 2-3 months down the road. My advice is that if anything is not in the least bit clear it is probably best to comment it.

It is true to say that the more experienced the programmer, the better his commenting.

As you probably know commenting in HTML (and XML/XSL) is accomplished by using the following notation:

```
<!--This is a comment-->.
```

Because a browser that is not CSS compliant will show everything inside the **<STYLE>** tags you should always comment out the rules–as shown below.

```
<HTML>
<HEAD>
<TITLE> Chapter 2 First example</TITLE>
<STYLE TYPE="text/css">
<!–(This was not meant to be rendered as written. Leave out the etc.etc.
and it will be fine, although Communicator presents the code correctly and
IE4 incorrectly. The etc.etc. should just be ignored.)
/*Style rules are included within html style type comments to hide them
from older browsers*/
/*Style rules go here*/

BODY{
color:red;
[etc. etc.]
}
/*End of rules*/
-->
</STYLE>
</HEAD>
<BODY>
Hello World- in red!

</BODY>
</HTML>
```

The next screen shot shows what a similar "Hello World in Red" example, looks like on Netscape 3 with the HTML style comments omitted. This is probably not what was intended.

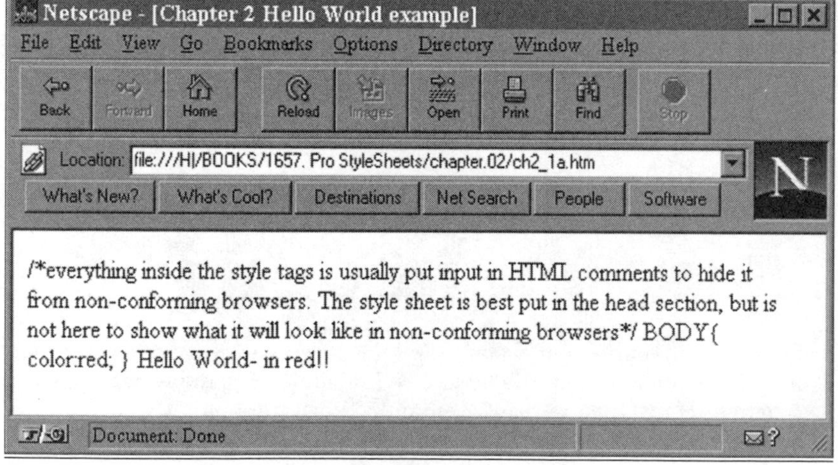
Netscape - [Chapter 2 Hello World example]
File Edit View Go Bookmarks Options Directory Window Help
Back Forward Home Reload Images Open Print Find Stop
Location: file:///H|/BOOKS/1657. Pro StyleSheets/chapter.02/ch2_1a.htm
What's New? What's Cool? Destinations Net Search People Software
/*everything inside the style tags is usually put input in HTML comments to hide it from non-conforming browsers. The style sheet is best put in the head section, but is not here to show what it will look like in non-conforming browsers*/ BODY{ color:red; } Hello World- in red!!
Document: Done

In the book, comments have been left out for the sake of clarity of display as well as space considerations, but you should never omit them or you will end up with what is shown above.

The original code for the example that produced this screenshot is on the web site and can be found at:

`http://rapid.wrox.co.uk/books/1657/`

Testing for Non-Compliant Browsers Example

There is one other time when it is essential to use comments. The only browsers that support CSS are IE4 and Communicator 4, and both of these have major errors of implementation. Therefore, it is essential to either view your document in a non-compliant browser, such as Netscape 3, or comment out the whole of the style sheet when testing your pages. This will enable you to make sure that your page is still readable, albeit a trifle dull, for all those people using non-compliant browsers. Note that you must remove the comments **inside** the style sheet otherwise you have nesting comments, which are a no-no. The code below shows an example of commenting out the style sheet.

```
<!--
Start of HTML style comment.

Comment out the whole style sheet to make sure that your page is
understandable to a non-conforming browser. Note that the HTML style
comments inside the style sheet have been removed as you can't have nesting
comments.
<STYLE TYPE="text/css">

/*Style rules are included within html style comments to hide them from
older browsers*/
/*Style rules go here*/

BODY{
color:red;
}
/*End of rules*/

</STYLE>
End of HTML style comments.
-->
```

Forms of Cascading Style Sheet Rules

There are four basic forms a CSS rule can take, but they all follow the same structure of **`selector{property:value;}`**. Here is a table that shows the four types, their syntax and examples of each one:

Type	Syntax	Example
Simple Selector, single declaration	SELECTOR1{property1:value1;}	**BODY{color:red;}**
Multiple or grouped Selectors, multiple declarations	SELECTOR2,SELECTOR3{property1:value1;property2:value1;}	**H1,H2{font-size:32pt;color:#FF0000;text-align:center;}**
Property with multiple values	SELECTOR4{property1:value1 value2 value3;}	**P{font: italic bold 12pt Arial, sans-serif;}**
Contextual selector	SELECTOR5 SELECTOR6{property1:value1;}	**DIV EM{font-style:italic;}**

The rest of this book concerns the ins and outs of writing rules, although as you might have guessed sometimes the rules can get a little complex. For now let's look at the syntax above and run through some examples.

We've already covered the first type, **Simple Selector, single declaration**. They are just like our first example. It is as basic as it gets, so let's look at examples of the other types. After working through the following three examples you should have enough basic understanding to actually start writing your own style sheets.

Multiple or Grouped Selectors

The following example demonstrates the use of this type of selector in style sheets.

```
<HTML>
<HEAD>
<TITLE>Chapter2 Second Example</TITLE>
<STYLE TYPE="text/css">
/*An example of multiple selectors and multiple properties */

H1,H2{

font-size:32pt;

color:#FF0000;
text-align:center;

}

</STYLE>

</HEAD>

<BODY>

Here is some dumb old text, it should be in the browsers default color
(probably black) and font size (probably 12 points)
```

```
<H1>Heading one</H1>

This heading should be red and 32 points and centered.

<H2>Heading two</H2>

This heading should be centered, red and 32 points i.e. exactly the same

<H3>Heading three</H3>
This heading should be in the default values. Left aligned, black and
probably 16 points

</BODY>

</HTML>
```

The following screen shot shows how the above code is rendered on IE4.

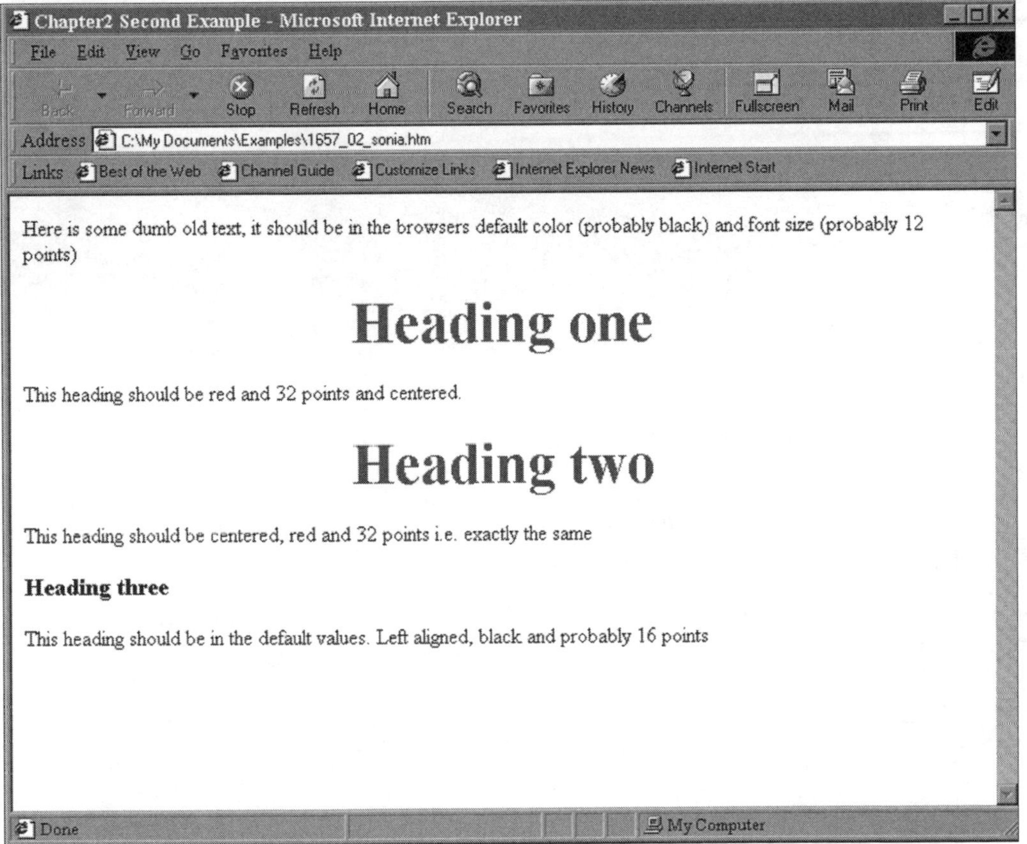

Note the form of the style sheet selector:

```
H1,H2{...
```

What we have is two HTML tags separated by a comma. This tells the browser that the properties between the curly brackets apply to **both** the tags. The **<H3>** tag just appears in the browser's default style. There is no limit to the number of tags you can group in this way as long as each one is separated by a comma.

That concludes our look at multiple or grouped selectors, let's move on to the third form of CSS rule–properties with multiple values.

Properties with Multiple Values

Several of the CSS properties (see Appendix B) can take multiple values, and we will go into this later in the book. For now, let's take a look at one of them–the font property.

We could write a rule applying to fonts like the following:

```
P{
font-style: italic;
font-weight: bold;
font-size:12pt;
line-height:14pt;
font-family: Arial, sans-serif;
}
```

CSS, however, allows us to combine them into one property like this:

```
P{
font: italic bold 12pt/14pt Arial, sans-serif;
}
```

Don't worry what line-height is for now. This is covered in more detail in Chapter 6 Font and Text Properties.

The above two rules are identical; it's just that one is compressed.

There are several properties that take multiple values and we will be looking at them through the course of the book. For now note that, in general, they don't have to take all the properties, and the order the properties appear in is usually important.

Consider the following code, and if you can, type or paste it into a text editor, save it as **ch2_ex3.htm** and display it in your browser:

```
<HTML>

<HEAD>

<TITLE> Chapter 2 third example</TITLE>

<STYLE TYPE="text/css">

/*An example of a property with multiple values*/
```

```
P{

font: italic bold 16pt/18pt Arial,sans-serif;

}

</STYLE>

</HEAD>

<BODY>

Here is some dumb old text , it should be in the browsers default color
(probably black) and font size (probably 12 points)

<P>

We are now in the P section, the text should be, 16 points bold, italic and
in the arial or a sans-serif font.

</P>

Here is some more dumb old text , again it should be in the browsers
default color (probably black) and font size (probably 12 points)

</BODY>

</HTML>
```

Your screen should look like the one below, which shows the code rendered on IE4.

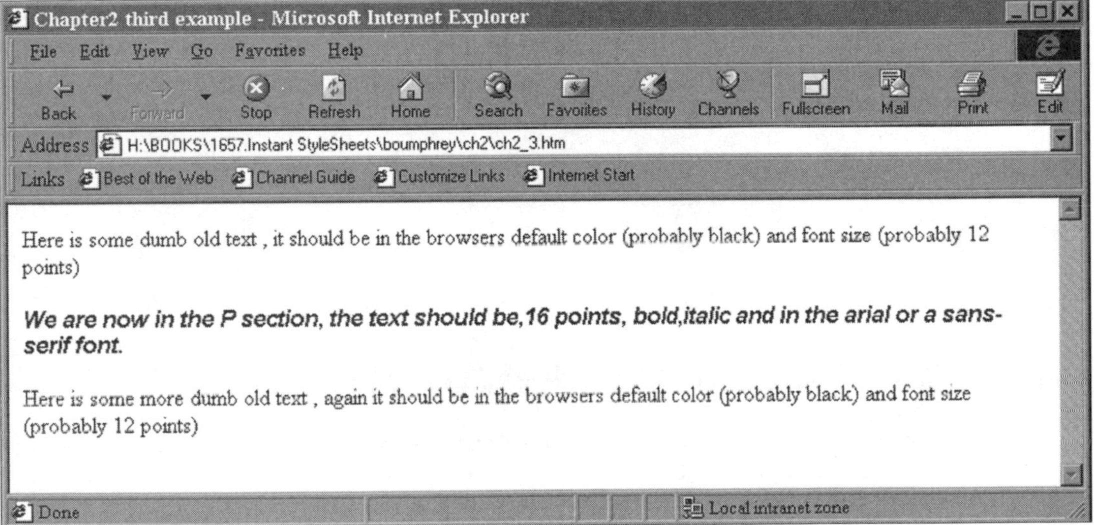

We don't want to make a big deal of this right now as we will be covering it in some detail later. In brief, the paragraph inherits the properties of the body. It takes its color and all other relevant properties from the body, unless we specify different ones–as shown above. The paragraph is said to be a **child** of the body and the body is said to be an **ancestor** of the paragraph.

Exercise 1

First fire up your favorite text editor and remove the closing **`</P>`** from the last example. Save it as **`ch2_3a.htm`** and reload your browser. Of course the browser now interprets everything after the **`<P>`** as applying to **`<P>`** and puts it all in 16pt Arial including the paragraph that once followed the now deleted **`</P>`**. The screen shot below shows how this is indeed the case.

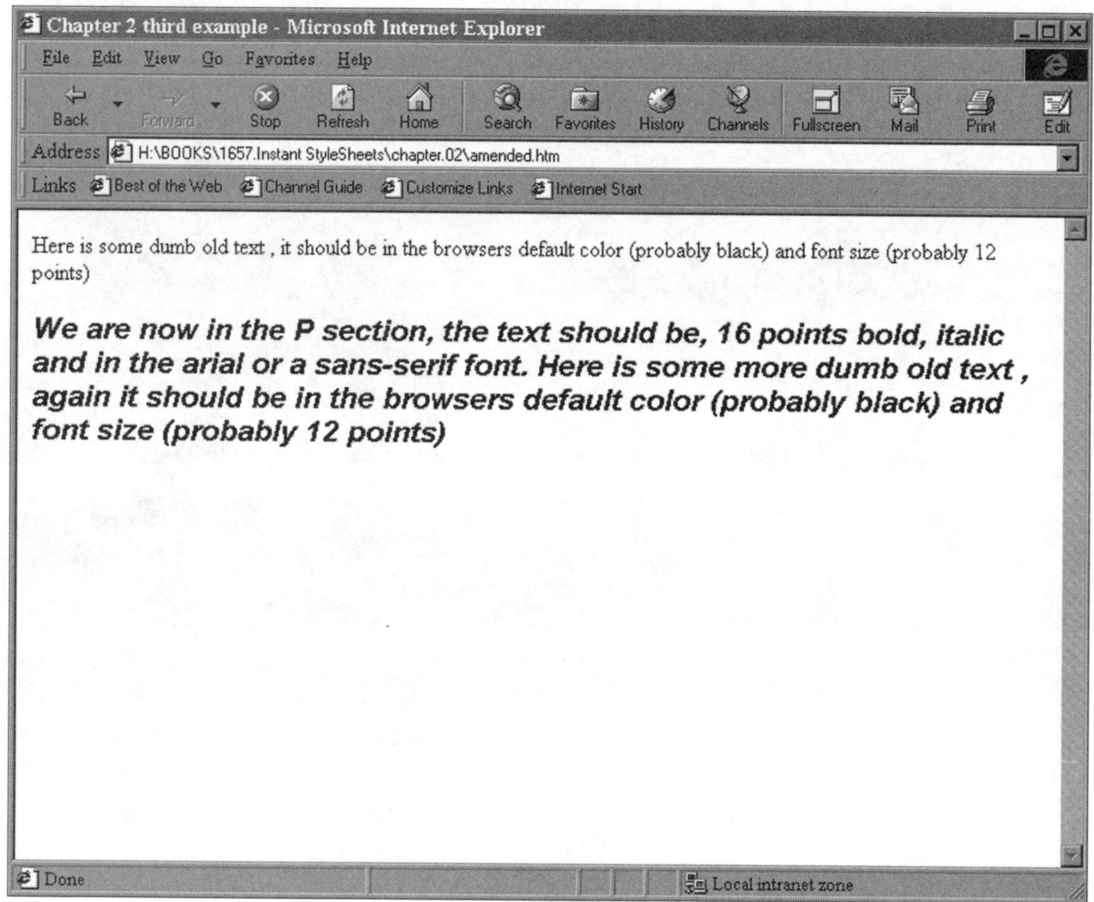

The font property can compress the properties for **`font-variant`**, **`font-style`**, **`font-weight`**, **`font-size`**, **`line-height`**, and **`font-family`**. As noted above, the order they appear in **is** important. **`Font-variant`**, **`font-style`** and **`font-weight`** can appear in any order, but they must appear before **`font-size`** and **`line-height`**. These must, in turn, appear before **`font-family`**. Added to this is the fact that **`font-size`** and **`line-height`** must be separated by a forward slash.

Don't worry about the details for now they will be covered in more detail later. **`Line-height`** was used in this example, but it's not used in the on-line example. This property will be discussed later on.

See the Language Reference at Appendix A for other properties that can take multiple values.

Exercise 2

First fire up **`ch2_ex3.htm`**. Then place **`underline`** somewhere in the value for font.

> *This value is not taken by the property font. It is in fact a value of the text property* **`text-decoration`**.

Then save and reload. What happens? Probably nothing even though you now have an illegal statement. Actually, this is what is meant to happen–the browser ignores values it doesn't understand.

Secondly remove **`underline`** and replace it with **`#FF0000`**. This is, as I'm sure you are well aware, a color value which is not taken by the **`font`** property. Again save and re-load. Now the browser will probably ignore the whole thing. If it doesn't try sticking **`#FF0000`** at the beginning. If you use "**`red`**" instead of the Hex number nothing will happen. The text won't be red, if it is you may have a problem, you may be inadvertently sharing a room with the son of Hal.

> *You probably know this already but computers are incredibly dumb. They do exactly what they are told. They are quite unlike HAL; the rogue computer in 2001. I like to think that HAL had a dumb Brother-in-Law called Marvin. My computer is Marvin, and being a control freak, I want to keep it that way, the faster the better, and the dumber the better.*

Finally, cut out **`bold`** and **`italic`** and put them before the font names. It may still work, but it probably won't. The browser either does nothing or presumes that it is the name of a font. I repeat–in properties that take multiple values the order in which the values appear **is** important.

The other moral of the story is that you should test everything.

Now return **`ch2_ex3.htm`** to its original form. So, on to the final form of CSS rule, contextual selectors.

Contextual Selectors

As we explained in the Introduction, an opening tag, a closing tag and the contents of the tags, i.e. anything that comes in between, is called an **element**, and elements can be nested. For example:

```
<DIV>
Here is some <I> italicized</I> text. The &lt;I&gt; is nested in the
&lt;P&gt;
<P>
This &lt;DIV&gt; is nested in the &lt;P&gt; tags
Here is some <I> italicized</I> text. The &lt;I&gt; is nested in the
&lt;DIV &gt; which is in turn nested in the &lt;P&gt;
</P>
```

```
</DIV>
<P>
Here is some <I> italicized</I> text which is just nested in a &lt;DIV &gt
and NOT in a &lt;P&gt;.
</P>
```

Here italic elements are nested at various levels. The first is in the **<DIV>** element alone. It is, therefore, a child of **<DIV>**. The second is in the **<DIV>** element and the **<P>** element. It is, therefore, a child of the **<P>** element and a grandchild of the **<DIV>** element. The third is just in the **<P>** element. It is a child of the **<P>** element.

We can make a different rule for each of these **<I>** elements by using a contextual selector. In other words by identifying the context in which we find them.

```
DIV I{.....
```

would refer to the first.

```
DIV P I{...
```

would refer to the second.

```
P I{...
```

would refer to the third.

For that matter

```
DIV P{...
```

would refer to the contents of the first **<P>** element and not the second.

With this in mind, it is helpful to consider the following example concerning contextual selectors in style sheets. If you can, type or copy and paste this into your text editor, save it as **ch2_ex4.htm** and display it in your browser.

```
<HTML>
<HEAD>
<TITLE>Chapter 2 Fourth Example</TITLE>
<STYLE TYPE ="text/css">
P{
font: 14pt 'Times New Roman',serif;
color:black;
}

DIV{
font: italic bold 12pt Arial,sans-serif;
color:red;
}
EM{
color:red;
```

```
}
/*note the tokeniser is a space (ascii32)*/
DIV EM{
color:green;
font-style:normal;
}

</STYLE>
</HEAD>
<BODY>
This <EM>emphasised</EM> text is just in the body.
<P>
This <EM>emphasised</EM> text is in a &lt;P&gt;.
</P>
<DIV>
This <EM>emphasised</EM> text is in a &lt;DIV&gt;.
</DIV>
</BODY>
</HTML>
```

What we have here is a difference between the ways that emphasized text is displayed, depending on the context of the **<EM>** tag. The screenshot below shows how these variations appear on IE4.

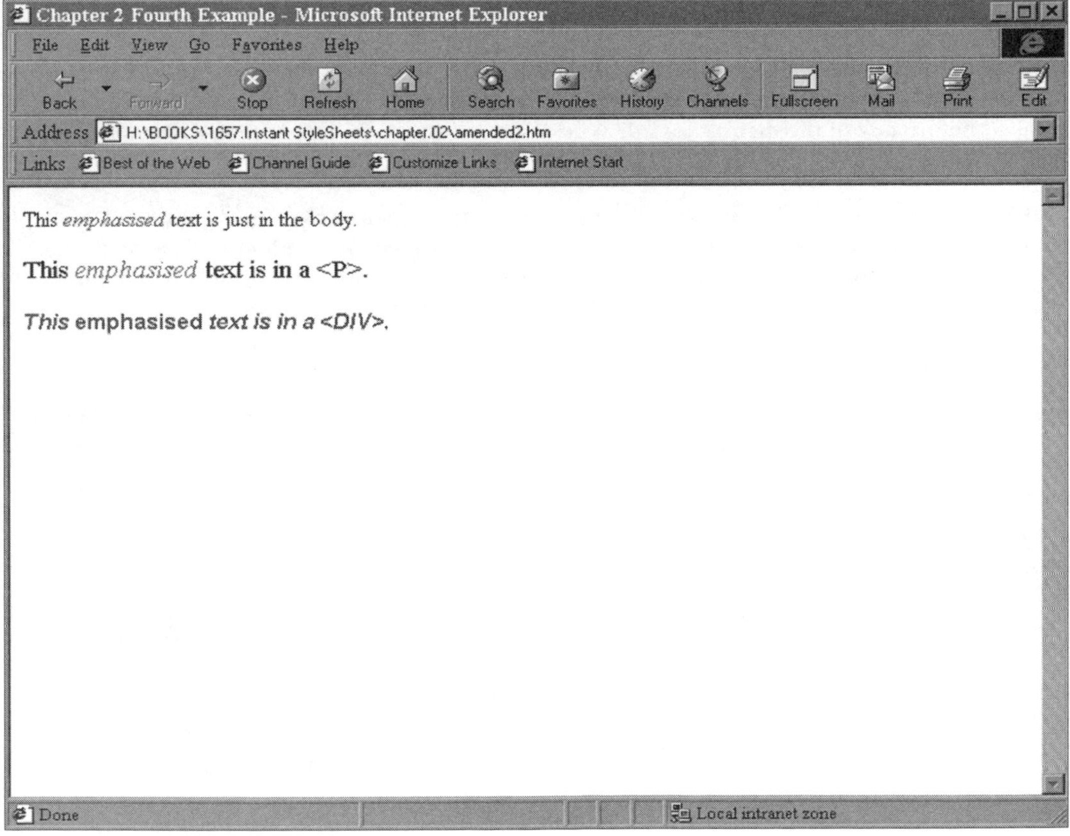

When the **<EM>** tag is used outside a **<DIV>** it has a red color because that's how we asked for it to be displayed in the style sheet. It is in italic because that is the way browsers usually display emphasized text and, of course, it inherits the font size of the container it is in. (See below)

When the **<EM>** tag is in the **<DIV>** container. For example, when it is the child of a **<DIV>** or, to put it another way, when it has a **<DIV>** parent–it is in green and non-italicized.

Notice how a space is used as a tokenizer to separate the two tags in the selector.

An interesting alteration that can be made is by reversing the order of **DIV** and **EM** and see what happens. It is important to place the **DIV** tag back at the beginning of the line when you have finished however .

We've now covered the format of the four types of style sheet rule, now let's look where in your code the style rules should be located.

Location of Style Rules

Style rules can be located inside or outside the document they are styling. We'll go through the options available to you.

Internal Style Sheets

The style rules we've seen so far in this chapter have all been included in the HTML document they are styling. The browser reads the document from top to bottom, so the style rules must be placed before any of the display text. The best place to put them is just before the **</HEAD>** or **<BODY>** tag.

With HTML 4 you don't even have to put in a **<BODY>** or a **<HEAD>** tag, it is implied. The only place you really need to put the style rules is before your content. In older browsers, if put after **<HEAD>**, they may show up, as in the example we saw in the *Comments* section. They must, however, be placed within the document i.e. after the **<HTML>** tag.

External Style Sheets

We can also write our rules in a separate document and then import it into our style sheet. For now, we will just look at one way to do this and will discuss the other ways in the Language Reference in Appendix A.

We create an external style sheet by putting all the rules into a separate file with a **.css** extension e.g.

```
"my_style.css"
```

We import it into our HTML document using the **<LINK>** element thus:

```
<LINK REL="stylesheet" TYPE="text/css" HREF="my_style.css">
```

This is placed in the **<HEAD>** of the HTML document.

A CSS style sheet should contain **nothing** but CSS comments, CSS rules and white space. This of course has several advantages, including the fact that it enables us to write just one style sheet for several documents–very useful if we want to maintain a house style for our pages. We will see how we can modify this sheet in our own pages when we examine cascading in more detail in Chapter 7.

Inline Style Rules

All HTML elements that are capable of display can take the **`STYLE`** attribute. Although extensive use of this undermines one of the advantages of CSS, namely its universality, it can occasionally be useful.

> *It should be noted that the Microsoft XML/XSL command line processor converts all XML tags into HTML tags with a* **`STYLE`** *attribute. So you are going to see a lot of this in those chapters!*

Here are a couple of examples:

```
<DIV STYLE ="background-color:blue; color:red">.....</DIV>
```

```
<SPAN STYLE="font-size:22pt">.....</SPAN>
```

Note that the syntax is just the declaration with the curly brackets removed.

Cascading Style Rules

We have just seen that it is possible to have style rules outside the **`<HEAD>`** of our HTML document. It is also possible for the user to have a style sheet. The browser also has its own built in set of style rules. We will discuss this in more detail in Chapter 7. What happens when we have the same property with two or three different values? For example, in the external style sheet:

```
P{color:red;}
```

in the internal style sheet:

```
P{color:black;}
```

and in line:

```
<P STYLE="color: green;">
```

In this case, the cascade rule comes into effect. This will be studied in much greater depth later, but for now you should keep these two golden rules in mind:

- Server style sheets take precedence over client style sheets. i.e. those sheets that the HTML designer writes will take precedence over those requested by the viewer.
- The last style sheet read takes precedence over the previous ones.

It is possible to override the precedence by using the !important parameter.

> *Actually the above is correct in CSS1 compliant browsers, but in CSS2 compliant browsers, the User preference will take preference over the Author when the !Important parameter is used.*

Let's look briefly at this **`!important`** parameter.

The !important Parameter

This parameter is applied to a property as follows:

```
P{font-weight:bold !important;}
```

This ensures that the value **`bold`** will be used with the **`font-weight`** property in place of any other **`font-weight`** values in almost all circumstances.

When conflicting rules apply to a flow object, a cascade is set up to produce a result. In this case, the last rule applies.

The following figure shows a cascade in action.

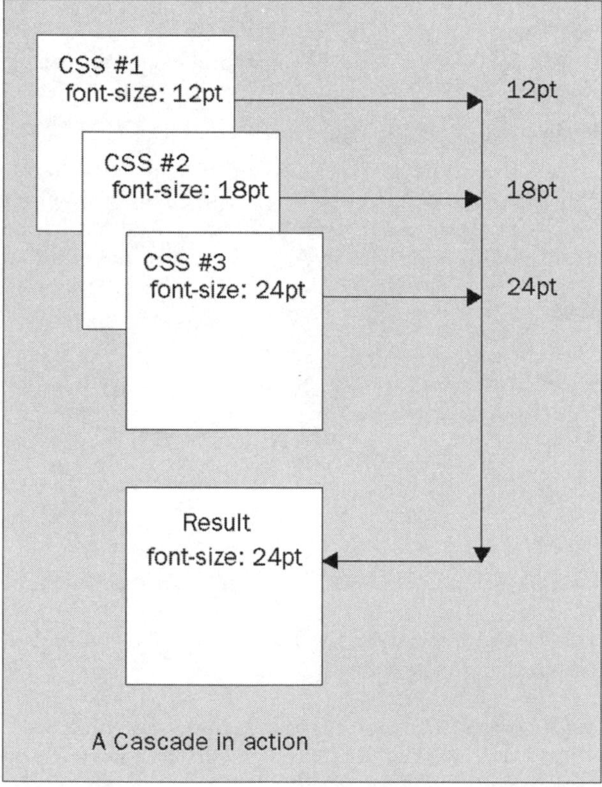

A Cascade in action

It might be very tempting for a designer to sprinkle his style sheets with **!important**, but this is bad practice. Many people, such as the visually impaired, have special requirements and this may make the pages unusable for them.

> *You should note that browsers, and in particular Communicator 4, are **very, very** picky about the syntax. One **small mistake** can cause the whole of your cascade to collapse (see below). It is very important to test run your efforts. The author had to test run the following simple tutorial 3 times before he got it right. A simple tip is to make use of comments to comment out sections of your code, to narrow down the offending syntax.*

A Simple Example Cascade

Download or type out the following two code samples. Save the first file as **ch2_7.css** and the second file as **ch2_7.htm**. Make sure that they are in the same directory or else give a path. Then run them in your browser. Unfortunately this demonstration will not run correctly in Communicator as it does not under stand the CSS **!important** parameter.

```
/* chapter two sample css file. Save this file as ch2_ex7.css*/

DIV{
font-size:24pt;
color: red;
}
```

```
<HTML>
<!--save this file as ch2_ex7.htm-->
<HEAD>
<TITLE>Cascading example.</TITLE>

<STYLE TYPE="text/css">
DIV{
color:green !important;
font-size:44pt;
}
</STYLE>
<LINK REL="stylesheet" TYPE="text/css" HREF="ch2_ex7.css">

</HEAD>

<BODY>

<DIV>Hello Cascade!</DIV>

<DIV STYLE="color:blue; font-size:32pt;"> A second cascade!</DIV>
</BODY>
</HTML>
```

Under IE4 you will see two statements, the first is in the font size that we specified in our **.css** file, namely 24 pts, because this comes **after** the style rule that we typed into our document. The inline style rule overrides the **.css** file. However both of the statements are in green because we assigned the color property an **!important** parameter. Here's the screenshot which illustrates this, but again, you don't get the benefit of color unless you run it yourself.

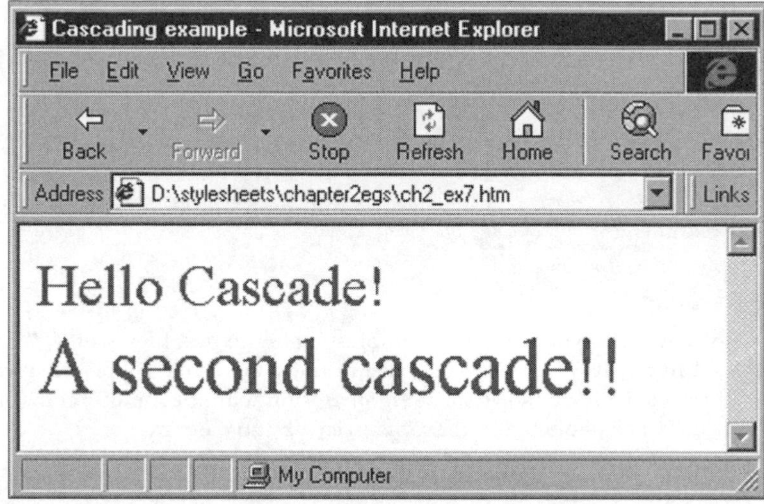

Because Communicator doesn't understand the **!important** parameter the colors will appear as declared in the dominant style sheet.

Cut out the !**important** parameter, save the file as **ch2_ex7a.htm** and run again, to prove to yourself that it really is controlling the colors used in this example.

Now cut the **<LINK>** element out, paste it above the **<STYLE>** element and run the browser again and see what happens. You should see the first line of text shown at 44 pt font, because the inline style rule now comes after the reference to the **.css** file and so overrides it.

That concludes the section on CSS rules. We're now going to introduce you to some other terms and concepts which are important in CSS, which we'll cover in greater depth later in the book. Let's start with a quick look at inheritance.

Inheritance

We really don't want to get into much detail here but it is necessary to introduce you to the idea of inheritance.

A pair of tags can be thought of as containing material. For example, a **<DIV> </DIV>** pair of tags can contain text as can a **<P> </P>** pair, even though the closing **</P>** is often inferred. The closing **</P>** was not required, just optional in early specifications of HTML. However, with the advent of XML get used to putting closing tags in all your documents.

As a shorthand way of speaking we call this pair of tags a **container**. A container can also contain another container. For example, another **<DIV></DIV>** pair or an **<EM></EM>** pair.

When one container contains a second container then the second container will inherit the properties of the first. So, if we have the font size of a **<P>** set to 16 then a pair of **<EM></EM>** contained in the **<P>** container will also be font-size 16 and **not** the default font size.

The diagram here illustrates this process. Although the colors change, the size of the text remains a constant inherited factor.

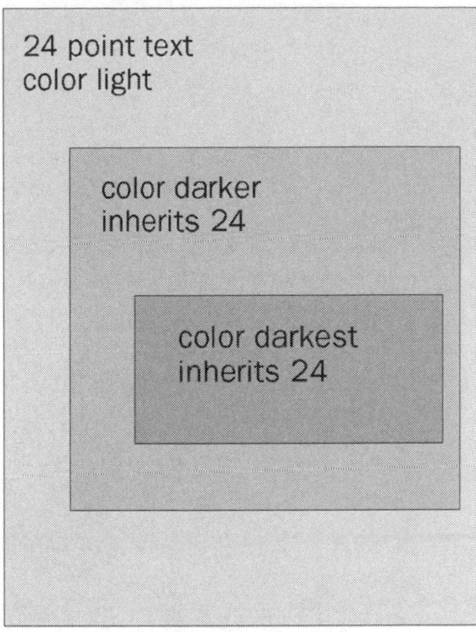

Inheritance in action

Inheritance in Action

In the last example, **ch2_ex4.htm,** the **<EM>** pair would be called a child of **<P>** and **<P>** would be referred to as the parent of **<EM>**.

Ancestor and parent are different, a parent is an ancestor but not necessarily vice versa.

The next example is especially useful, as the text in the markup is self-explanatory. After finishing it, you should have a basic understanding of what is meant by inheritance and how it works, and you should understand why the ubiquitous **<P>** tag should not be over used in the near future. We recommend that a **<DIV>** tag (which requires a closing tag) should be used instead. However, because much legacy HTML markup code contains the **<P>** tag it is important to understand how to work around the current browser limitations.

Type this code into your text editor, save it as **ch2_ex5.htm** and display it in your browser. Alternatively, run or copy the file from the web site at **http://rapid.wrox.co.uk/books/1657**.

```
<HTML>
<HEAD>
<TITLE>Chapter2 fifth example</TITLE>
<STYLE TYPE="text/css">
/*A simple example of inheritance*/

BODY{
```

```
fontsize: 12pt;
}
P{
fontsize: 16pt;
}

DIV{
color:red;
}

</STYLE>
</HEAD>
<BODY>
Here is some dumb old text, it should be in the browsers default color
(probably black) and font size of 12 points.<EM> Emphasized text</EM> is
also black and 12 points.
<P>
Here is some text in a &lt; P&gt; tag all by itself. Font size should be 16
points. <EM> Emphasized text</EM> is also black and 16 points
</P>
<DIV>
Here is some text in a &lt; DIV&gt; tag all by itself. Font size should be
12 points and its color should be red, as should be the <EM> Emphasized
text.</EM>
</DIV>

<DIV>
We are in the DIV section but outside the P this should be a red 12 point
font. <EM> Emphasized text.</EM>
<P>
This P is in the DIV section so it inherits the red color because the P is
now a child of the DIV and has its own 16 Pts.<EM> Emphasized text.</EM>
</P>
Back in DIV only, red 12pt's.<EM> Emphasized text.</EM>
</DIV>
<P>
We are now in the P section, the text should be black 16 points.<EM>
Emphasized text.</EM>
<DIV>
We are in the DIV section nested in a &lt;P&gt;. We intended that this
should be a red, 16 point font, 16 point because it should have inherited
the fontsize property from P, but it probably isn't because the dumb
browser (?wrongly) inferred a &lt;/P&gt; when it met the &lt;DIV&gt;, so it
is just interpreted as a plain div with red 12 pt text.<EM> Emphasized
text.</EM> But is it wrong? See the next section!
</DIV>
Back in the P only section, we intended this should be black and 16 points,
but it probably isn't because the browser (not wrongly) inferred a
&lt;/P&gt; when it met the &lt;DIV&gt;, so it's just interpreted as a plain
body text (black 12pts). <EM> Emphasized text.</EM> Why do I say "not
wrongly"? Because the element declaration in the HTML DTD is &lt;!ELEMENT P
O (%text)*&gt; which in SGMLspeak says that only text and various low level
elements are allowed inside the &lt;/P&gt;. Quite honestly I have not read
the whole DTD to find out whether a &lt;DIV&gt; is considered high or low
level, (nor do I intend to!), but common sense would suggest it is a high
level element. Luckily things are much more explicit and understandable in
XML!
```

```
</P>
Here is some more dumb old text, again it should be in the browsers default
color (probably black) and font size 12 points.<EM> Ephasised text.</EM>
<BR>Note how throughout this document the emphasised text inherits all the
characteristics (except the italics) of its ancestors.

</BODY>
</HTML>
```

Here is a screenshot displaying the beginning of the page, but it's far too large to show here in its entirety, you really need to run it for yourself.

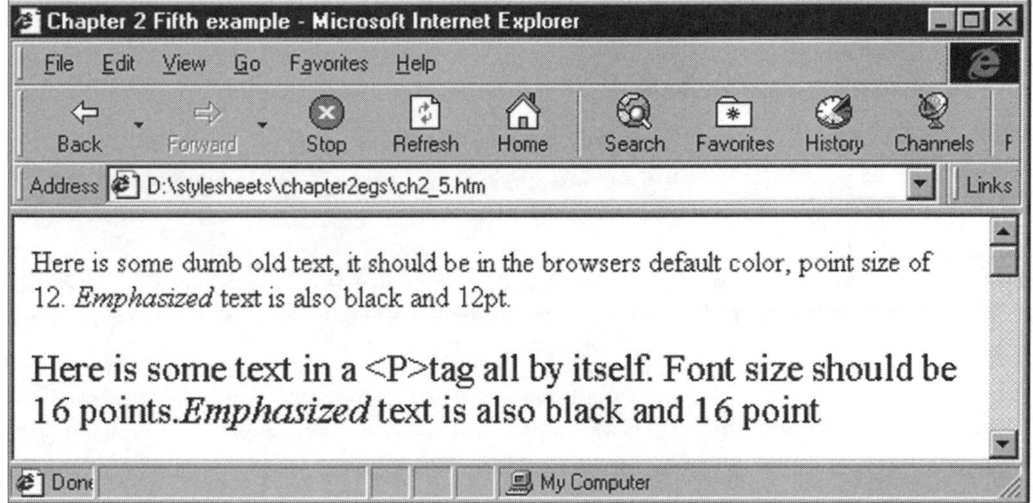

We have several containers of text here and several containers within containers.

- First we have the **<BODY>** tag pair
- Next we have a **<P>** within a **<BODY>**
- Then a **<DIV>** within a **<BODY>**
- Then a **<P>** within a **<DIV>** within a **<BODY>**. Both the **<P>** and the **<DIV>** have an **<EM>** as a child.
- Then a **<DIV>** within a **<P>** within a **<BODY>**. Both the **<P>** and the **<DIV>** have an **<EM>** as a child.

Note how the contained inherits the characteristics of the container, and also note how **<P>** does not work as a container.

The problem we encounter with the second set of contained tags i.e. when we are trying to use **<P>** as a container for the **<DIV>**, is a hang over from the old HTML specification where a closing **</P>** tag was inferred when a new tag floating tag was encountered.

For us to produce what was intended, we must put in separate **<P>** tags. However, it is probably just easier to use separate classes of **<DIV>** tags. Classes will be explained in the next section.

This browser bug will probably be fixed sometime but not in the near future. For this reason it is probably better to use the `<P>` tag sparingly from now on and use the `<DIV>` tag instead. This will allow code to be easily updated.

The moral in all this is of course to try and obey the rules even if you can't see the significance of them at the time, because you may get burnt later.

The <P> Problem

This is a typical problem of legacy code. When the first HTML specification was written, cool web sites were not even in the mind of Mr. Berners-Lee.

When the first browsers were written the programmers thought, quite reasonably, why bother insisting on a closing `</P>`, when all we are going to do is put in another `<P>`. Therefore, they wrote their code that way, and in the DTD of HTML they did not insist on a closing tag.

> *Actually SGML, of which HTML is an example, allows this. XML does not. You should start closing your* `<P>` *tags for two reasons, so that the style mechanism is not confused–as we saw above– and to bring it into conformance with XML.*

New browsers came and incorporated the code of the old and now here comes CSS insisting they go back to using a closing `</P>`. The browser companies thought they would have to ferret through all their code, and heavens only knows what problems that would cause.

The problem is that to change this in the browsers–which were built on the backs of previous browsers–may cause other bugs. Plus a change could also break thousands of web pages already out there and that would make the users really mad at the companies.

That concludes our introduction to inheritance. It's an important concept which we'll look at in detail in Chapter 7 of this book.

Selector Classes

One of the great things about CSS is that it allows you to define your own classes of selectors. This can be quite a complex subject but the basics are simple enough, and we will just look at enough here to allow you to start using them.

Take this dialog from **A Midsummer Night's Dream**:

Hermia. I frown upon him, yet he loves me
Helena. O that your frowns would teach my smiles such skill!
Hermia. I give him curses, yet he gives me love.
Helena. O that my prayers could such affection move!
Hermia. The more I hate, the more he follows me.
Helena. The more I love the more he hateth me.
Hermia. His folly, Helena, is no fault of mine.
Helena. None, but your beauty: would that fault were mine!

If you wanted to distinguish between the two in your HTML document you could assign both Hermia and Helena a class and make their dialog different in your HTML document.

```
DIV.hermia{font-style:italic; color:blue;}
```

```
DIV.helena{font-style:normal; color:black;}
```

Note how this was done–simply a period followed by a name. The name must contain alpha-numeric content. Hyphens (-) are also allowed, but the name cannot begin with a number or a hyphen.

Now when we write our HTML we can use the **CLASS** attribute:

```
<HTML>
<HEAD>
<TITLE> Chapter 2 Play example </TITLE>
<STYLE>
DIV.hermia{font-style:italic; color:blue;}
DIV.helena{font-style:normal; color:black}
</STYLE>
</HEAD>
<BODY>
<DIV CLASS="hermia">Hermia. I frown upon him, yet he loves me still </DIV>
<DIV CLASS="helena">Helena.O that your frowns would teach my smiles such
skill!</DIV>
</BODY>
</HTML>
```

Look at the sample **ch2_play.htm** to see what it looks like in practice. Here's a screenshot. You can't see the color, but you can see the italic effect.

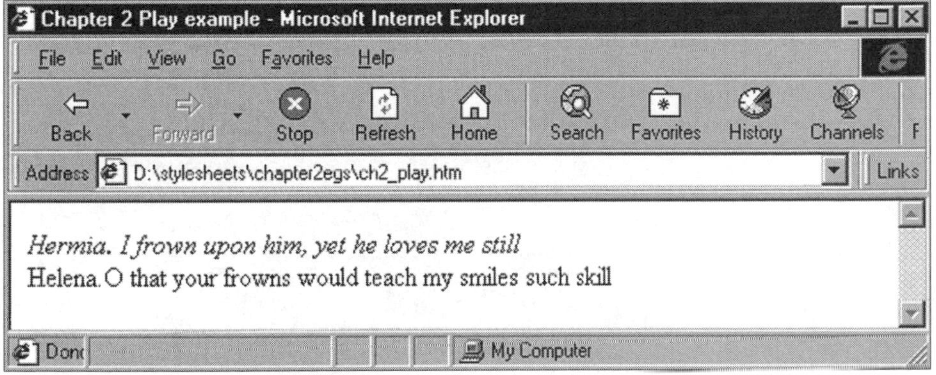

Note that the class name was semantically marked up i.e. the class didn't just give us a description of the style, which would be a stylistic markup, but rather gave us a description of the content viz. Hermia's words, Helena's words. Although this is not necessary, it is good practice because you can now use your **CLASS** attribute to do meaningful searches on your HTML document. For example, return all of Hermia's lines by looking for **CLASS="hermia"**.

Thus you can give HTML some of the semantic advantages of XML.

One other thing, HTML is case insensitive, but XML is case sensitive, so start getting into the habit of putting all your HTML tags in upper case, and all your XML tags in lower case. This is a suggested convention in XSL and XML.

So, enough of selector classes for the moment. We'll cover them in depth in Chapter 7 of this book. Let's move on to the next section–boxes.

Boxes

We referred to 'containers' above implying that they were containers for text and elements. They are, but in CSS they go by the much more plebeian name of boxes, as I am sure you are not surprised to learn, boxes have numerous properties. They will be covered in some detail in Chapter 8 later in the book but we will just have a brief look at them here.

Any block of text can be contained in a box, and this box is then placed on the "canvas" i.e. your browser desktop. The three basic properties that apply to the box are **`margins`**, **`border`**, and **`padding`**.

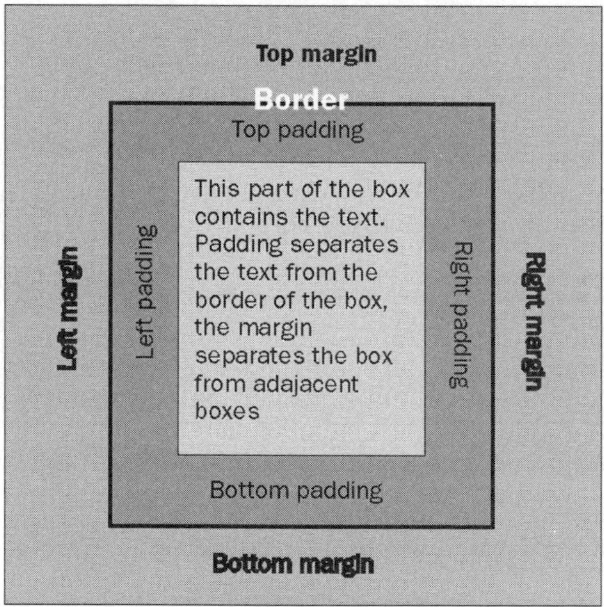

First, every box has a border–even if it is not visible–which separates it from the edge of the canvas, or from adjacent boxes. The distance between the border and the outer edge of the adjacent box, or between the border and its containing box is called its margin. The distance between the contents of the box and its border, e.g. text, images, etc., is called its padding.

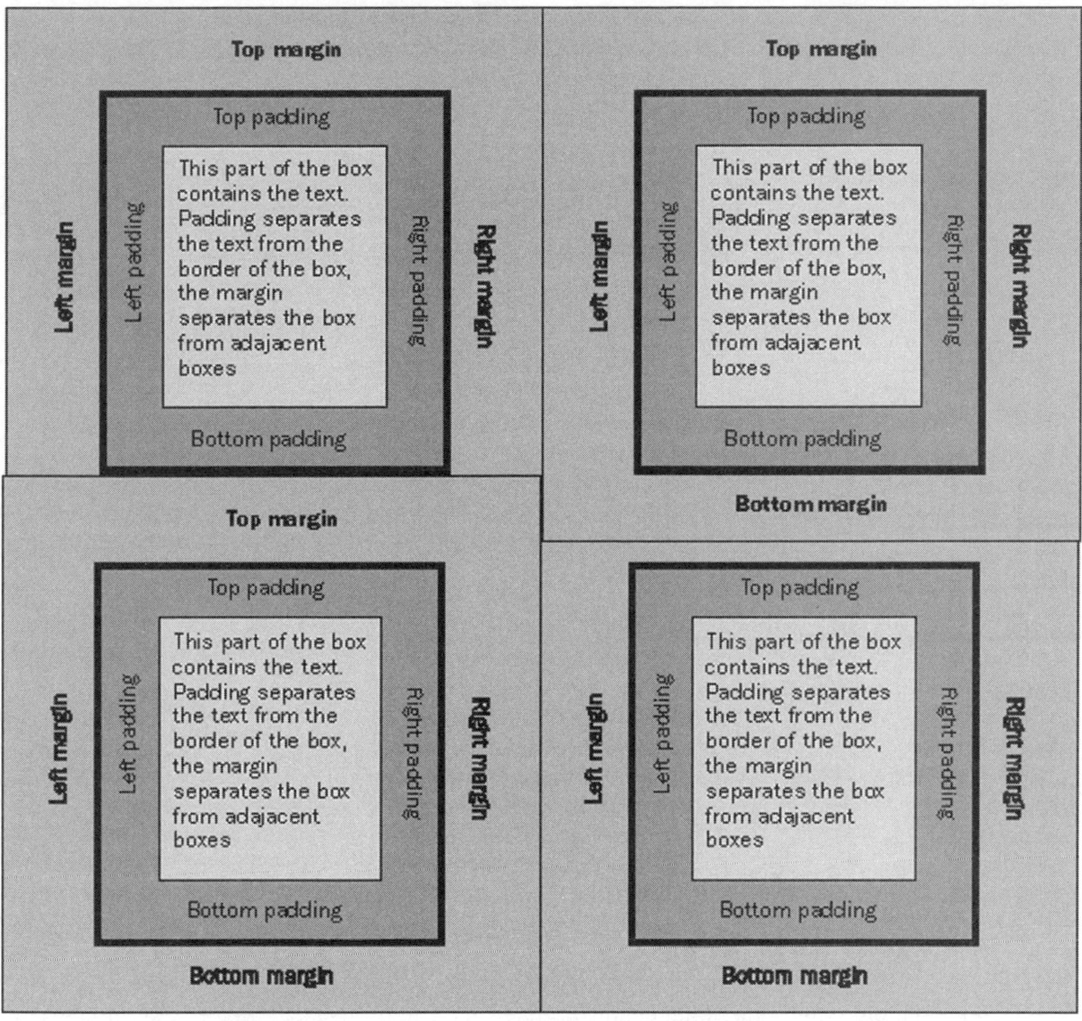

Note that in the vertical axis the margins are collapsed, so that only the larger margin is displayed, but in the horizontal axis, both margins are maintained.

What follows is a simple example of boxes. Either type it into your text editor, save it and run it in your browser, or run it off the web site as **boxes.htm**. However, there are differences in implementation between the two browsers–read on to find out what these are.

```
<HTML>
<HEAD>
<TITLE>Boxes</TITLE>
<STYLE TYPE="text/css">
P{
font: 14pt 'Times New Roman',serif;
color:black;
```

```
margin:0.75in;
padding:0.5in;
border:solid blue;
}

DIV{
font: italic bold 12pt Arial,sans-serif;
color:red;
margin:0.5in;
padding:0.5in;
border:solid green;
}

EM{
color:red;
}

DIV EM{
color:green;
font-style:normal;
}
</STYLE>
</HEAD>
<BODY>
This text is just in the body.
<P>
This text is in a &lt;P&gt;.
</P>
<DIV>
This text is in a &lt;DIV&gt;.
</DIV>
Here's a line of text, in the body.
<DIV>
This text is again in a &lt;DIV&gt;.
</DIV>
</BODY>
</HTML>
```

Here we have highlighted one of the major problems with style sheets at the present moment in time. The fact that Netscape and IE4 give very different interpretations of the above.

The correct presentation is that of IE4 as shown next:

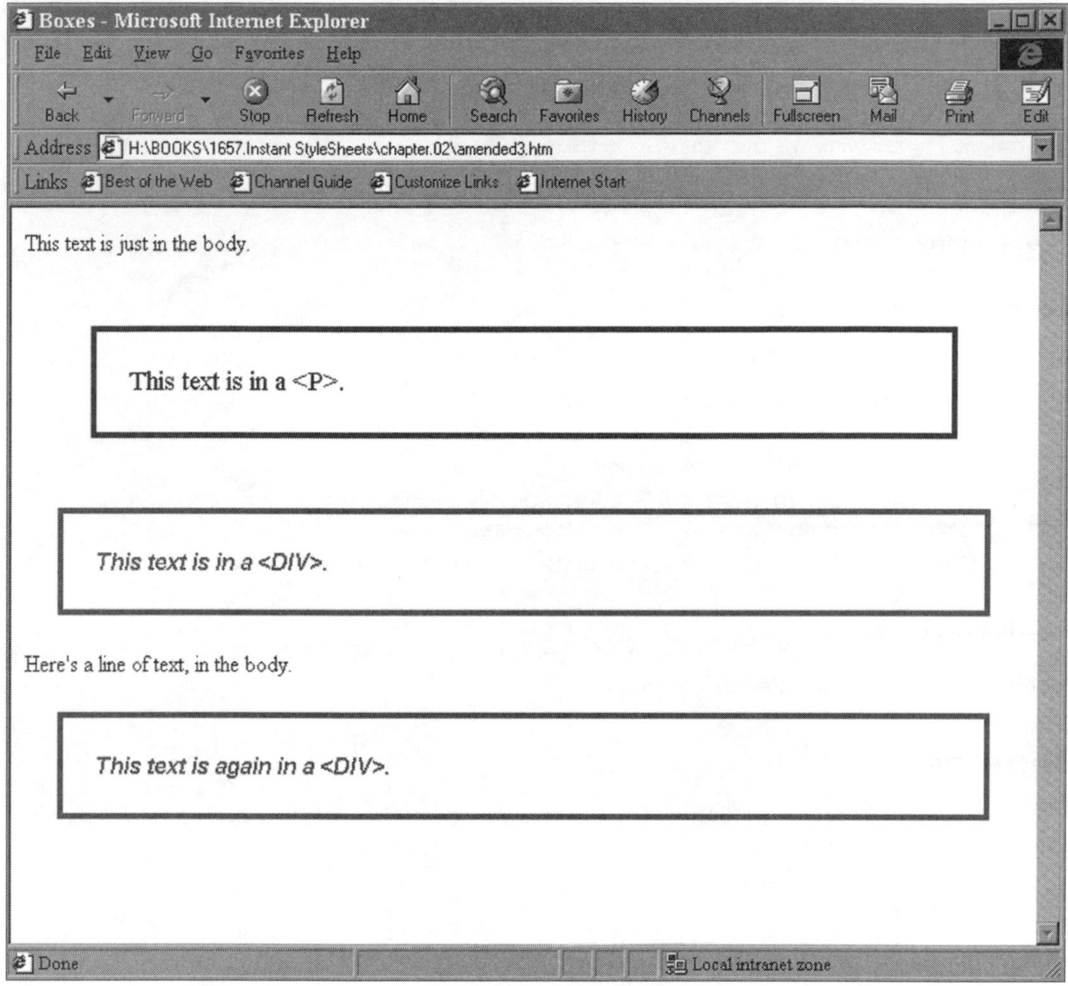

As you can see, neat boxes are made around the specified text. There is a logical half inch padding between the text and the border, and there is a half inch margin all round.

> *A very small word of warning: If you paste text from a word processor to a text editor, the text editor will sometimes put in a different opening and closing quotation, i.e. other than ASCII 34. When this happens, your code will not work so if you have done this look very carefully at the nature of your single and double quotes.*

Where boxes abut from top to bottom (in a vertical orientation), the margins are collapsed on each other so that the space between the **<P>** and the **<DIV>** is .75 inches not .75 + .5 inches.

Netscape just doesn't do anything to the **<P>** at all, and how it calculates the space between the two **<DIV>** elements is completely beyond my reasoning.

Perhaps by the time you read this they will have got their act together. Who knows?

Properties

In this chapter you have you have been introduced to a few of the 130 odd properties that are available in CSS2. If you want to start writing style sheets now you can, and you can use the rest of the book as a reference. All the other properties will be covered in the succeeding chapters.

Summary

In this chapter you have:

- Learnt what a CSS rule is.
- You have learnt the basic syntax of the rules.
- Learnt what the differences between simple, compound and contextual selectors are. (You will learn more about selectors in Chapter 7).
- Learnt about external style sheets, inline style rules, the **!important** parameter and what is meant by cascading.
- Been introduced to the concept of inheritance, selector classes, boxes and properties.

You should now be able to write a simple style sheet. In the next two chapters, we are going to have a look at XML before going on to XSL. After that, we are going to look at the CSS properties in detail which can be applied to XSL as well.

References

Web sites change. The given URLs were current at the time of writing. We will try and keep the URL's updated on the web site:

`http://www.wrox.com`

If you find a broken one please let us know and we will try to fix it.

A good place to start is the following URL which has an excellent summary of the CSS1 properties.

`http://htmlhelp.com/reference/css/all-properties.html`

The W3C's home page on style sheets. From here, you can go anywhere in the style world!

`http://www.w3.org/Style/`

Exercises

1. Write a style sheet to mimic the left hand page of this book.

Hint–there are three kinds of headings in a sans-serif font, and the text is in a serifed font. Some text is italicized. You may want to use the **`margin-left`**, the **`margin-top`**, the **`margin-right`** and the **`margin-bottom`** properties, as well as **`border-right`**, **`border-left`**, **`padding-right`**, **`padding-left`**. Don't forget the heading and the page number.

2. Use your favorite programming language to write a simple program that prints out all of Hermia's lines in the sample.

Hint–search the string for **`CLASS ="hermia"`**.

3

Basic XML

The object of this and the next chapter is to take you to the level where:

- You can write a well-formed XML document.
- You can write a simple Document Type Definition (DTD).
- You can display the document on the Internet.

If you are already conversant with XML you can skip the next two chapters, but because XML is a relatively recent innovation this will probably not apply to most readers. As XSL (the style sheet for XML) is built with XML, clearly you must understand XML before you can create XSL style sheets.

It is important to be able to create a well-formed XML document. This chapter and the next provide most of the information you need to reach this standard, and the examples included in these next two chapters will demonstrate your understanding of this important topic. These two chapters cover most of XML between them, and if you read them and work through the examples you should have enough knowledge to start writing useful XML documents. Some topics are only mentioned briefly, others are covered in some depth. The following topics are not covered at all– Conditional Sections, User Switches, Groves, but don't worry these are not important to the general topic of XSL. To review these or other XML related topics, look out for *Professional XML Applications, ISBN 1861001525* from Wrox Press.

The first part of this chapter deals with the history of markup and sets XML in the context of SGML and HTML. If you want to get straight to the practicalities of XML, skip to page 83 and the section entitled– *Writing an XML Document*.

A Brief History of Markup Languages

So, let's get straight down to business by dealing with the most fundamental question–what is a markup language?

What is a Markup Language?

Markup is anything we care to put on a document that has a special meaning, (a coffee stain is **not** markup, unless you spill it everywhere and, even then, not in our desired sense), and as such we use it all the time. Highlighted text is markup. A series of check marks on your bank statement are markup.

If we want others to understand what our markup means we need a set of rules encompassing the following points:

- To declare what constitutes markup
- To declare exactly what our markup means

A markup language is just such a set of rules. For example in Standardized Generalized Markup Language (SGML) anything in angle brackets is considered markup. **`<This-is-mark-up>`**.

Markup can be divided into the following three categories.

Stylistic Markup

This indicates how the document is to be styled. The **`<I>`**, **`<B>`**, and **`<U>`** tags are all stylistic markup in HTML.

Structural Markup

This informs us of how the document is to be structured. The **`<H>`**, **`<P>`** and the **`<DIV>`** tags are examples of structural markup.

Semantic Markup

This tells us something about the content of the data. **`<TITLE>`** and **`<CODE>`** are examples of semantic markup in HTML.

HTML has proven very adept at preparing documents for display over the Web. However, a document marked up in HTML tells us very little about the content of the document, and it so happens that for most documents to be useful in a business situation there is a need to know about the document's content.

As an example, if a patient's medical records were marked up in HTML and I, as a doctor, wanted to find out about the patient's allergies I would, at present, have to download the whole record (several thousand bytes), and then do a manual search through that document.

If, however, the patients records were marked up in XML and one of the tags was **`<allergies>`**, I could just send a request to the server for that part of the document, and receive a few bytes of information instead of hundreds of thousands of bytes.

Using the same example of patient's records, what if we wanted someone to have access to some part of the records, but not others? For example, the accounts department would not need access to a patient's clinical records. You could instruct the server to withhold certain parts of the document. For example, in the above illustration anything marked up **`<psych.-note>`** or **`<confidential>.`**

Thus the ability for individuals, groups of individuals, and institutions to write their own markup language will expedite information transfer and provide other benefits such as confidentiality.

The Importance of Markup Languages

The great thing about a language is that it can be understood by all who understand it. I know that is an idiotic, redundant statement, but I need to make a point. What if no one else understands the language you speak? Sure you can get by somehow, but there is ample scope for confusion, ambiguity and wasted time.

This is where Standard Generalized Markup Languages (**SGML**) come in. If you have a document marked up in a language that is standardized, several agents–human or computer–can understand it. This means that it is easy to carry out operations on that document, whatever the form of the agent (Human, PC, Mac, UNIX, etc.).

As more and more businesses use the Web to transmit their information, there is a clear need to be able to transmit marked up documents. Sure I can convert all my documents to HTML, but if I do this the original markup is lost, together with all the advantages that correct markup confers. I can use various work-rounds, but then we are back to the same situation we discussed in Chapter 1, namely the accumulation of quick fixes until the tail starts wagging the dog.

As we also saw in Chapter 1 the Web is becoming fragmented because of individuals attempts to display information in different ways, and because of the proprietary formats that have been developed to meet those needs. Now, if an author could just make up a tag and assign it attributes whenever he wanted to, and transmit the information on how to display that tag with his page.....well wouldn't that be just wonderful.....

In fact there is indeed such a way!

SGML

Standard Generalized Markup Language has been around for a long time in computer years–the international standard was published in 1986–long before the Web was ever thought of. It has been used by large institutions and Government departments to mark up their documents for exactly those reasons that we mentioned above. SGML was one of several such competing languages, although it was its offspring, HTML, which gave it prominence over the others.

Let's take a quick look at the composition of a document marked up in SGML.

Which comes first the Horse or the cart?

Which comes first the markup or the content?

We are proceeding on the assumption that we have a document that we wish to markup in XML. We, therefore, write the document, and apply all our tags in the appropriate places. Correct?

Actually this is not the way things are usually done in the real SGML/XML world, especially when dealing with technical documents. In practice the text is usually poured into the XML container in accordance with the DTD.

Obviously there is the marked up text itself containing a whole series of elements. But how do you read these tags? How do you know what they mean? From your knowledge of HTML you (probably) know that a tag can have attributes. For example the **`<P>`** tag can have the **attribute `"align"`**, which indicates whether the text is to be centered on the page, aligned to the left margin or aligned to the right margin. Most attributes also have a default value, which in the case of the **`<P>`** tag is **`align="left"`**.

If you are making up your own tags, how is the browser going to know what the tag means? How will it know whether the tag has any attributes, and if the tag does have attributes how does the browser know what to do with them? The answer is that you send two separate sets of instructions with your document. One set, the **Document Type Definition,** (or **DTD**), tells the **user agent** what the tags mean. The second set of instructions, the **Style Sheet,** tells the browser what to do with the tags.

We will look at a DTD in some detail in the second part of this chapter, but essentially it is a set of rules. These rules can be either part of the marked up document, or a separate document that the user-agent refers to in order to understand how to interpret the contents of the document. Style Sheets, or how to display the document, are of course the topic of this book!

If SGML has been around for so long and is so useful, why hasn't it been used before on the Web? Well the truth is SGML is rather complicated, and the style sheet system it uses (**DSSSL**) is even more complex. In fact, it's probably true to say that the number of programmers who truly understand DSSSL could be put into a single (largish) room! (The DSSSL mailing list in fact has about 300 members, but many may be like myself, we don't really understand it we just have to try and use it!) If you wanted to use SGML, you either had to learn this rather complicated language yourself, or you had to find someone who already knew it and they were few and far between. This complexity is the very reason that HTML was invented, the idea being that reasonably intelligent scientists could use the language to mark up a document with little extra knowledge or work. In the case of HTML both the DTD and the style sheet were wired into the browser, so all the author had to worry about was the markup.

HTML of course has a DTD. If you want to see it, point your browser at:

`http://www.w3.org/TR/REC-html40/sgml/dtd.html`

SGML and HTML

HTML is often called (incorrectly) a subset of SGML, but this is not true. All SGML is, is a set of rules that tell us how to create a markup language. Every time we create a new tag, we are creating a new markup language, and if we create that tag according to the rules of SGML the markup language becomes an SGML conforming language, and so can be understood by all agents, human or machine who understand the SGML rules.

In other words HTML is the language, and SGML is the grammar and Syntax of that language. Technically HTML is known as an application of SGML.

Just as you can speak a language without understanding a single rule of grammar, there are hundreds of thousands of people out there merrily speaking HTML knowing only the most basic rules. It is a language understood by numerous varieties of browsers as well as humans.

HTML has tags that mark up text and indicate how it should be presented. Tim Berners-Lee (now the head of the W3C) first created HTML as a means of transferring scientific documents. As such it was very successful. Probably no one at that time foresaw that it marked the dawn of a new era in communication, something that future historians might well define as the "Age of Information" .

All that was being aimed at was a set of tags to mark up a document so that it could be intelligible at the other end. What follows are a few handy examples:

- **<H1>** This is a primary heading**</H1>**
- **<PRE>** This is text where formatting is important**</PRE>**
- **<P>** The text between these two tags is a paragraph **</P>**

As long as the document came over with the same meaning it really wasn't important how it looked. Headings could be anywhere from 20-32 points, and be underlined or not!

Information is transferred over the Internet using various **protocols**, and the protocol that HTML uses is HTTP (Hypertext Transfer Protocol). Several other protocols were widely used, and before HTML came along the most popular was **FTP** (File Transfer Protocol), which of course is still widely used today.

What really separated HTTP from the other protocols was the ease of connecting to another document and, in retrospect, it was a foregone conclusion that as soon as the non-scientific crowd got hold of it, its use would explode. And of course the non-scientific crowd using HTML for non-scientific purposes started being worried about the appearance of their pages, and the browser companies were only to happy to fuel their desires for style.

SGML and XML

It has been said that the lords of SGML were somewhat jealous of the success of their offspring, and that they really had very little to do with the Web, carrying on with their serious business of designing document specifications. Whether that was true or not I don't know. I do know, however, that there was little software available that was affordable or simple enough to be useable by the average web citizen.

By 1996 it was also becoming obvious that the Web needed fixing for the reasons already mentioned in Chapter 1. It also appeared to those running the Web that using some kind of SGML was the way to go, but it was clear that the current version of SGML was way too complicated. Somehow the two sides got together and a group of about 80 SGML specialists and some members of the World Wide Web Consortium (W3C) formed a task-force under the chairmanship of Jon Bosak to develop a markup language suitable for the Web. This resulted in eXtensible Markup Language (XML). The group's objectives were (and this is pasted directly from the specification at **`http://www.w3.org/TR/PR-xml-971208`**) as follows:

> "The design goals for XML are:
>
> XML shall be straightforwardly usable over the Internet.
> XML shall support a wide variety of applications.
> XML shall be compatible with SGML.
> It shall be easy to write programs which process XML documents.
> The number of optional features in XML is to be kept to the absolute minimum, ideally zero.
> XML documents should be human-legible and reasonably clear.
> The XML design should be prepared quickly.
> The design of XML shall be formal and concise.
> XML documents shall be easy to create.
> Terseness in XML markup is of minimal importance."

It is worth looking at some of these goals in a little more detail.

"..It shall be easy to write programs which process XML documents."

One of the major drawbacks of SGML was the complexity of the language, and this in turn made it very difficult to write programs that dealt with the language. There were so many side rules and each one had to be programmed for. Taking one simple example–the complexity of comments allowed in SGML meant that to cope with all the permutations using Visual Basic, I had to write over two hundred lines of code, and even then I was not sure I had covered every eventuality. To take the comments out of an XML document takes about 10 lines!

```
Function remove_comments (xmldoc As String) As String

'removes xml comments and returns a string without comments.

    Dim ltxt$
    Dim rtxt$
a$ = xmldoc

    Do Until InStr(a$, "<!--") = 0

        b% = InStr(a$, "<!--")
        c% = InStr(a$, "-->")
        ltxt$ = Left$(a$, b% - 1)
        rtxt$ = Mid$(a$, c% + 3)
        a$ = ltxt$ & rtxt$
    Loop

  remove_comments = a$
End Function
```

This means that software can be written quickly and cheaply.

I've written a basic XML parser, which we'll use in later chapters, and it took me less than two days to write. It would have taken me a minimum of two days just to design the format for a similar SGML parser. I know this fact because I've done it!

"..The design of XML shall be formal and concise"

HTML has got to the point where you can write sloppy markup and get away with it, and the browser vendors have been conniving at this. I am told that over half the code in one of the popular browsers is to enable sloppy code to be displayed without error. By insisting on formality from the beginning it becomes easier and cheaper to write software. Certain modifications have been made to the SGML specification that makes this easier, for example closing tags, optional in SGML, are compulsory in XML.

"...XML documents shall be easy to create"

The specification as published for approval in Dec 1997 is a mere 40 pages (the SGML specification is about 270 pages last time I looked) Anyone familiar with HTML can write an XML document in a really short time.

I'm not sure who first used the phrase, but XML is bandied as the "80/20" solution, i.e. SGML with 80% of its functionality, and 20% of its complexity. This was probably an SGML guru, because to a non-guru such as myself the ratio appears to be closer to 90/10!

Anyway XML is here and became a W3C recommendation on the 10th of February 1998. At the time of writing the formal process of adopting a style-sheet language is just getting under way.

XML and HTML

Is XML going to replace HTML? Although anyone who tries to predict in this game is usually doomed to failure, I would have to say "ABSOLUTELY NOT!"

HTML (with style sheets) will almost certainly be used for the majority of informative or declarative pages.

I predict that XML will be used in the following circumstances:

- Where the content of the document is more important that its presentation, e.g. in the transfer of technical and medical records.
- Where the document needs to be searched on a semantic basis.
- In long documents that need to be split up into various sections.
- Where it is advantageous to be able to present the same information in different formats, e.g. financial dealings.
- When security is necessary.
- Where the powerful formatting abilities of XSL are advantageous (as opposed to the more declarative style of CSS).

Having said that there will be a generation of programmers who grow up finding it *easier* to use XML. After all you won't have to memorise a whole lot of tags, and when that happens HTML will, like an old soldier, slowly fade away.

XSL as presently envisioned (and it is only at the note stage) relies heavily on HTML and CSS for its functionality, so whatever happens this knowledge of HTML and CSS will not be wasted.

This book is about style sheets but to understand XSL it is necessary to go into the fundamentals of XML a little bit more deeply. Whereas HTML has been around for some time, XML is the new kid on the block. We must spend a little time getting to know him, but with some knowledge of HTML this should be fairly easy, although as an HTML web developer some things will seem rather strange.

What is XML?

XML is a simplified version of SGML designed for use on the Web, which immediately brings us to the question of what SGML is.

To recap:

SGML is an international standard that contains the rules of how to write a markup language. You are almost certainly familiar with what a markup language is because HTML is a markup language and is written according to the rules of SGML.

If you think of SGML as a primer containing the rules of grammar and syntax of HTML, and of HTML as the vocabulary of a language you will not be far wrong. There are several other languages written according to SGML rules, HTML just happens to be the most widespread and well known. This way you can think of HTML as the dialect of a group of SGML languages.

This concept should present little difficulty. English is a dialect of a group of languages called Old German. Hundreds of millions of people speak English. Tens of millions speak German. Millions speak Dutch. How many speak Friesian?

It so happens that the rules of SGML are very complicated, so if you wanted to design your own markup language using SGML you would have to do a lot of ground work. Because there is a clear need for new languages (see next section) there was clearly a need for a simplified grammar. XML is that simplified grammar.

Who needs XML?

Everyone who needs to send data that needs to be manipulated in various ways over the Internet needs XML. (You can still make your cool display pages using HTML!)

XML allows us to markup a document with a set of tags of our own devising.

Is XML difficult?

No! XML was designed to be easy. The official specification is a mere 40 pages. You can download it from **http://www.w3.org/TR/PR-xml-971208** and is written in (almost) readable language. They use Extended Backus-Naur Form (EBNF) notation to describe the keywords.

Unless you are familiar with EBNF read section 6, the last section, of this document first.

Anyone with a basic under standing of HTML can be writing XML documents in no time at all.

So, we've covered the history and development of XML, and its relationship with SGML and HTML. Now let's move on to look at the practicalities of the language.

Writing an XML Document

In this part of the chapter, we cover the basics you need to understand in order to be able to write an XML document. We cover the concepts of tags, elements and attributes, which you will already be familiar with from HTML, and highlight how they are different in XML. Then we go on to cover two vital concepts in XML; the **well-formed document** and the **valid document**. As part of our coverage of the valid document, we cover the **Document Type Definition** in detail. By the time you get to the end of this chapter, you will know all you need to know about the rules and structure of an XML document to enable you to write one of your own.

Required Software

All you need to write an XML document is a text editor. Various HTML authoring packages help you to author XML documents. However, at the time of writing, in order to display an XML document in a browser, you need to convert it into HTML first. There are tools already available which will do this for you automatically, and we will cover these in the next chapter. It is also likely that, in the very near future, browsers will provide direct support for XML.

Tags and Elements

These two words are **not** inter-changeable. In XML a tag is what is written between angled brackets e.g. **<atag>**. This is an example of an opening tag. In XML all opening tags must have closing tags of the form **</atag>**. The way the **<P>** tag is used in HTML is illegal in XML. In XML an opening **<P>** tag requires a closing tag **</P>**.

An element, as we explained in the Introduction, is an opening and a closing tag and what comes inbetween. For instance:

```
<greeting>Hello XML! </greeting >
```

is an element.

Empty tags must be in a special format, namely **<emptytag/>**, (note where the forward slash is), or else you are allowed to write **<emptytag></emptytag>**. The **<IMG>** tag is illegal in XML. However, try using the legal form, **<IMG/>**, on your HTML browser. If it's like mine it probably won't accept it!

By convention put HTML tags in uppercase, XML tags in lower case.

XML is case sensitive. So, **<Atag>**, **<atag>**, and **<ATAG>** are three different kinds of tags.

A tag name must start with a letter (a-z, A-Z) or an underscore (_) and can contain letters, digits 0-9, the period (.), the underscore (_) or the hyphen (-). Neither white space nor other markup are allowed.

> *A tag name can also contain other unicode characters, but this is somewhat advanced in nature and beyond the scope of this book.*

The colon (:) is reserved for experimental use, and although it is legal at present it might well acquire special meaning in the future, so it is probably best to avoid using it if you can.

No name can begin with the sequence **xml...** This sequence is reserved for use by the XML Working Group.

Your tags should have semantic meaning otherwise why bother using XML?

With these few simple rules and conventions in mind you are safe to surge forward and make tags that describe your document.

Attributes

Tags can contain attributes.

You are almost certainly familiar with what an attribute is from your knowledge of HTML. The following example shows some of the attributes used by the image tags. An attribute(a quality ascribed to something) gives **added meaning** to the tag.

The example you are probably most familiar with is the HTML **<IMG>** tag. For example;

```
<IMG ALT="smileyface" URL="smiley.gif" VSPACE=75>
```

In XML an attribute takes the form of an equals sign and a value, keeping in mind that the value must be quoted. So, for example, the **VSPACE** attribute above would have to be **VSPACE="75"** to be legal in XML. Also, in HTML, some tags can take an attribute without a value such as **<UL COMPACT>**. This too would be illegal in XML. You must give an attribute a quoted value such as **<UL COMPACT="anything">**, even **<UL COMPACT= "">** would do.

Attributes should obey the following rules:

They can only take a restricted range of characters. This range is the same as the range allowed in tag names, although of course the < and > which open and close the tag, are not allowed

- All values must be quoted.
- Attributes can only appear in start tags and empty element tags.
- No attribute may appear more than once in the same start tag.
- All attributes must be declared in the DTD, and the attribute's value must be of the correct type (see below under attributes).
- An attribute cannot contain a reference to an external entity (See under the later heading: *Defining Entities*).

The Well-formed Document in XML

XML introduces the concept of a well-formed document. For a document to be well-formed it must obey the following simple rules:

- (a) It must contain at least one element .
- (b) It must contain a unique opening and closing tag that contains the whole document, forming what is called the ROOT element .
- (c) All the other tags must be nested, i.e. there must be an opening and a closing tag and the tags can't overlap.

Nesting

Nesting is a concept that is not always that easy to grasp, so the following is added by way of explanation. By all means skip it if you know what nesting means in the above context.

The Oxford English Dictionary describes once sense of the verb "to nest" *as follows:*

> ".... packed one inside another"

And this is exactly what we mean here.

Let's look at three tag pairs `<a></a>` `<b></b>` `<c></c>`

As written above, none of them are nested, they are all separate.

In the following example the `<b>` tags are nested in the `<a>` tags. The `<c>` tags are separate.

```
<a> <b> </b> <a> <c> </c>
```

In the following example the `<b>` tags are nested in the `<a>` tags and the `<c>` tags are nested in the `<b>` tags

```
<a> <b> <c> </c> </b> <a>
```

In the following example the **<b>** tags are **not** nested in the **<a>** tags, they overlap. The **<c>** tags are separate.

```
<a> <b> <a> </b> <c> </c>
```

Now after that short interlude it is back to the central XML issue of well-formedness.

Well-Formedness in XML

This **is** a well-formed XML document, because it conforms to rule (a) and contains a complete element;

```
<greeting> Hello XML!</greeting>
```

This XML document is **not** well-formed because it violates rule (a) by failing to contain any elements;

```
"Hello World!"
```

The following XML document is **not** well-formed. It violates rule (b) because there is no unique opening and closing tag containing the whole document.

```
<greeting> Hello World!</greeting>
<greeting> Hello XML!</greeting>
```

This XML document is now well-formed. It no longer violates rule (b) because there is now a unique set of **ROOT** tags, **<document>** and **</document>**.

```
<document>
<greeting> Hello World!</greeting>
<greeting> Hello XML!</greeting>
</document>
```

This XML document is **not** well-formed. It violates rule (c). It has an incorrect closing bracket for the second tag.

```
<document>
<greeting> Hello World!</greeting]
<greeting> Hello XML!</greeting>
</document>
```

This XML document is **not** well-formed. It violates rule (c). The closing bracket has been fixed, but the tags do not nest. The **<greeting>** and **<emphasis>** elements overlap.

```
<document>
<greeting> Hello World!</greeting>
<emphasis> <greeting> Hello XML!</emphasis> </greeting>
</document>
```

This XML document is well-formed, as it violates none of our defined rules. The end **</emphasis>** and **</greeting>** tags have changed places so that the elements no longer overlap.

```
<document>
<greeting> Hello World!</greeting>
<emphasis> <greeting> Hello XML! </greeting></emphasis>
</document>
```

This is also a well-formed XML document. Again the tags are nested properly, with no overlapping.

```
<document>
<greeting> Hello World!</greeting>
<greeting><emphasis> Hello XML! </emphasis></greeting>
</document>
```

The Valid Document in XML

XML also uses the SGML concept of a valid document. None of the above well-formed documents are valid documents. What do we mean by this?

Remember we said markup languages should have a set of rules declaring what the markup means and how to use it? In SGML this is called the DTD, or Document Type Definition.

All SGML documents must have a DTD and this is indeed a set of rules describing the tags of a document. Well, it is advisable but not obligatory for an XML document to have a DTD. However, if a well-formed XML document has a DTD and abides by its rules then it is also a valid document.

Why is a DTD necessary in SGML and not in XML? Well XML rules of construction are much stricter (simpler, but stricter) than SGML, and because of this an XML processor can infer what rules apply from a well-formed document. It does this by constructing a tree of all the nested elements, and establishing the relationships of the various parts. As we will see when we get to styling, the relationships of XML document elements are very important. SGML does not require that elements have closing tags, so it would be impossible for an SGML processor to construct such a tree without a DTD.

Another way of looking at this is to ask why a DTD may **not** be necessary in XML. XML is designed to be used over the web; i.e. to display documents. Downloading a DTD is just extra baggage. As long as the document can be meaningfully displayed (and it can be if it is well-formed) the browser, both human and machine are happy, and don't really care whether the document is valid or not as long as it conforms to its DTD.

In the last of the well-formed document examples shown above, the processor can infer that there is a root element called "**document**" that contains two other elements, a "**greeting**" element and an "**emphasis**" element, and that **emphasis** is a child of **greeting**.

In SGML, the SGML processor would have to look at the DTD to obtain this information.

It is still advisable for an XML to have a DTD because if several people are authoring documents, the DTD will set out the ground rules that they can all work by. More importantly they can use a special piece of software called a validity checker to make sure that they are not violating those rules. More work for the computer means less work for the authors, and isn't that what computers are about?

In XML document authoring the DTD is most useful in ensuring that the author (and there may be several authors working on several documents using the same DTD) sticks to a plan, and that everything is included where it should be included. This will ensure that all the documents using a certain DTD will have a certain structure and feel to them. For example the SGML DTD used to write Military Technical manuals enforces numerous headings and sub-headings, so that the user; often a technician in a "mission critical" situation, can easily hone in on the part they need.

The XML DTD can either be in the prolog of the document, or it can be in a separate file that is referenced in the prolog. The diagram below illustrates an XML document, consisting of a prolog containing a version declaration, a DTD and the body of the document with at least one pair of tags.

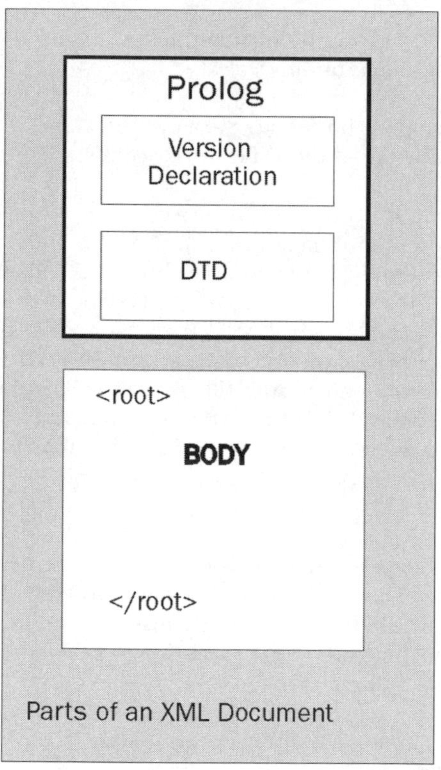

Parts of an XML Document

The rest of the chapter explains in detail what a prolog is and what a DTD is and how you can construct your own!

The Prolog

Actually according to the official specification, every well-formed XML document must contain a prolog, but the prolog can consist of nothing at all. Therefore, in the well-formed examples above imagine a prolog consisting of nothing but white space.

The prolog abides by the following simple rules:

- It must come before the first element in the document i.e. before the opening root tag.
- It can contain a **version declaration**, a **document type declaration, comments** and **processing instructions**, but it needn't contain all or for that matter any of them!

Let's look at each of these in turn.

Version declaration

All XML documents should contain a simple version declaration, which tells the processor what version of XML the document conforms to. Here is the form that it takes.

```
<?xml version="1.0"?>
```

Here is the body of the document that the above version declaration applies to.

```
<greeting> Hello XML!</greeting>
```

The version declaration can also contain other information, such as an encoding declaration that informs the processor what kind of code the document uses. For example, UTF 8 (which, up to number 255, is the same character set as ASCII) and a standalone declaration that tells the processor whether the document can be read as a standalone document, or whether it needs to look outside the document for other rules. This is rather advanced stuff and you are directed to the specification or books such as *Professional XML Applications, ISBN 1861001525* from Wrox Press for more information. Here is an example, however:

```
<?xml version="1.0"-encoding="UTF-8" standalone="yes"  ?>
<--the document body follows-->
<greeting> Hello XML!</greeting>
```

Note that if you do include the encoding and the standalone declaration they must appear in this order.

Document Type Declaration

The document type declaration takes the following form **<!DOCTYPE......>** and can contain the following;

- The document's name
- A reference to an external DTD (document type definition **not** declaration!)
- A markup declaration
- Parameter entity references

Declaraton v's Definition

> **Whoever decided to define document type DEFINITION and make it so similar to document type DECLARATION obviously had a perverse sense of humor. Even old SGML hands are constantly tripping up on the two, especially as they are described by the same acronym. However we are stuck with it! Just remember the declaration refers to an external definition, or else contains one in the form of markup declaration.**

The document's name by convention is the name of the opening tag of the document. Here is a document type declaration with a system identifier.

```
<?xml version="1.0" encoding="UTF-8" ?>
<!DOCTYPE greeting SYSTEM "hello.dtd">

<greeting> Hello XML!</greeting>
```

Here is the same document with a local definition.

```
<?xml version="1.0"? encoding="UTF-8">
<!DOCTYPE greeting [
<!ELEMENT greeting (#PCDATA)>
]>

<greeting> Hello XML!</greeting>
```

This will be explained more fully below, but note for now that "**`hello.dtd`**" would contain nothing but comments and:

```
<!ELEMENT greeting (#PCDATA)>
```

Don't worry for now what this actually means. If, however, you can't bear the suspense then jump ahead to the section entitled *Defining Elements: Element Declarations.*

XML Comments

These are the same as HTML comments. **`<!--this is a comment-->`**. See the remarks at the start of Chapter 2 on the importance of comments, they definitely apply when designing a DTD.

The XML processor is not required to pass this information on to the user agent.

- A comment can contain anything except -->
- A comment cannot nest

XML CDATA

Sometimes an XML document needs to contain code. CDATA gives a simple means in XML of passing tags and entities through the user agent without the tags being interpreted.

For example I might be writing a book on HTML which contains the sentence:

> "The **<P>** tag should always have a closing **</P>** tag if using strict HTML 4."

To put this in my XML (or HTML) document I would need to mark it up as follows:

```
<DIV> The &lt;P&gt; tag should always a closing &lt;/P&gt;  tag if using
strict HTML4.</DIV>
```

Similarly the sentence:

> "The less-than symbol "**<**" cannot appear inside markup but must always be escaped using the entity **<**."

would need to be rendered as follows:

```
<DIV> The less-than symbol "&lt;" cannot appear inside markup but must
always be escaped using the entity &amp;lt;. </DIV>
```

XML gives us a method to treat markup as text (or CDATA) in our documents, so there is no necessity to escape every **&** and **<** or **>**. Simply enclose the text with markup that we want displayed (as opposed to interpreted) in a CDATA element.

```
<![CDATA [The <P> tag should always have a closing </P> tag if using strict
HTML 4. ]]>
```

will be displayed as:

The **<P>** tag should always have a closing **</P>** tag if using strict HTML 4.

and

```
<![CDATA [The less-than symbol "<" cannot appear inside markup but must
always be escaped using the entity &lt;.]]>
```

will be displayed as:

The less than symbol "**<**" cannot appear inside markup but must always be escaped using the entity **<**.

Unfortunately CDATA does not work in HTML documents.

Processing Instructions

Processing instructions take the following form:

```
<?this is a processing instruction?>
```

Processing instructions cannot start with any form of the string **xml** this is reserved for the xml declaration processing instruction that we've seen already namely:

```
<?xml version="1.0"? encoding="UTF-8">
```

They can occur anywhere on the form and contain information that the processor must pass on to the user agent. The version declaration is an example of a processing instruction. That concludes our look at the prolog, now let's examine the DTD in detail.

The XML DTD

The Document Type Definition is the place where all the rules about your elements and their attributes are declared. It is a good thing because it makes sure that the layout of your document follows certain rules and we can use a piece of software called a validator or validating parser to tell us whether we have a valid document.

The validator will use our DTD to check the document. Again, less work for the human and more for the computer which can't be bad.

You can really make these rules as loose or as restrictive as you want to. We will work backwards and use an example of a well-formed document to build a DTD. We will make a contact card such as a sales-person might use for his clients.

We might want the card to contain the following information:

- The name of the client, first, middle, last, nicknames
- Company name
- Phone number
- History of all contacts, particularly the first and the last
- Level of Interest in our products–hot, warm or cool
- Personal information
- A photo

Here's an XML document with some appropriate tags. We are doing this backwards as we would probably write the DTD before we filled out any data, but it is easier to visualize the concept this way.

```
<client>
   <name id="CPQ142">
      <honorific> Dr.</honorific>
      <first> Pierre</first>
      <middle> R. </middle>
      <last> LeBlanc </last>
```

```
        <nickname> Butch</nickname>
    </name>
    <phone> 440-123-4567</phone>
    <company lang="french"></company>
    <contact type="first" >
        <date> Jan 1992</date>
    </contact>
    <contact type="last">
        <date> Dec 19 1997</date>
    </contact>
    <attitude interest="warm"/>
    <personal> Baby Girl b.
        <date> Nov 1997</date>
    golf mad!, handicap 7, likes Mexican food, completely bi-lingual French
and English
    </personal>
</client>
```

Let's now see how we would go about writing a DTD.

Writing a Document Type Definition

Writing a DTD involves specifying the DOC type, and defining the elements, attributes and entities which your XML document will use. We'll examine each of these in turn.

Defining the DOCTYPE

First of all we set down the **DOCTYPE**. Remember that, by convention, the name is the same as the root element.

```
<!DOCTYPE client  [
(element, attribute, and entity definitions go in here.)
]>
```

The **<!DOCTYPE>** tag of course contains the DTD, and the name of this **DOCTYPE** , **client**, is used to distinguish it from other **DOCTYPES**.

Defining Elements: Element Declarations

Now let's go through each of our elements and define them. The definition will tell us what is allowed in each element, whether it be text or other elements.

An element declaration takes the following general form:

```
<!ELEMENT [element_name] ([names of allowed elements])>
```

First the root element, obviously this must contain the other elements so:

```
<!ELEMENT client (name, phone, company, contact, attitude, personal)>
```

Writing the rule with commas separating the element names, as shown above, means that each of the elements **must** occur once, only once, and in the exact order they are declared in. We might find this a little restrictive, so for now note that we can also use the pipe-stem (|) as a tokenizer, which is the equivalent of and/or and allows the contained elements to appear in any sequence.

Note also that honorific, first, middle, last and nickname have not been included. This is because they will be included in the name element.

Getting back to our list, we would certainly want the client's name, and this should obviously be the first thing in our document.

We would also like to keep a record of the client's phone number, but we may not yet have it. Alternatively the client may have several phone numbers, so we would like the option of having none or several phone numbers.

We indicate this by putting an asterisk (*****) after the element name thus

```
phone*
```

This tells the validator that there don't have to be any **`phone`** tags, but on the other hand there might be several.

We may not have his company name but we only want to include one company name, not several. We indicate this by putting a question mark after the element name (**?**) thus

```
company?
```

This tells the validator that there may not be a **`company`** tag, but, if there is, there can only be one. In other words the tag is optional.

We certainly want to include at least one contact, and we hope there will be several more so we follow this element with a plus (**+**) thus:

```
contact+
```

This tells the validator that there must be at least one **`contact`** element, but there can be several.

By a similar reasoning we might mark the **`personal`** element:

```
personal*
```

the date element:

```
date*
```

and the attitude element:

```
attitude+
```

In summary, markup notation tells us the following about the element they are applied to:

- **+** occurs once or more
- ***** occurs zero or more
- **?** occurs zero or once

We now have the following:

```
<!ELEMENT client(name, phone*, company?, contact+, attitude+, personal*)>
```

We may find the ordering too restrictive, but we can change this by writing

```
<!ELEMENT client(name| phone| company| contact| attitude| personal)>
```

By using the pipestem (|) as a tokenizer, instead of the comma, the code now says that the elements can occur in **any** order.

Indeed to be completely unrestrictive we could write:

```
<!ELEMENT client(name| phone| company|contact| attitude| personal)*>
```

Which means that the elements can occur either not at all or as many times as you wish and in any order.

```
<!ELEMENT client ANY>
```

Means that any declared element can be contained (for example last) in any order.

To compromise we will settle for the following

```
<!ELEMENT client(name, phone*, company?, (contact| attitude| personal)*)>
```

Which means that the first three elements must occur in the given order, but the last three elements can occur in any order and are optional.

We now work down the list of elements

```
<!ELEMENT name (first, middle?, last, nickname*)>
<!ELEMENT phone (#PCDATA)>
```

`#PCDATA` is short for Parsed Character Data and means any text or other characters that is neither markup nor **`"`**, **`&`** or **`]]`**. In short–it means plain old writing.

```
<!ELEMENT contact (#PCDATA| date)*>
```

can contain text or the date element.

The last two examples are called mixed content declarations. Note that to mix content and elements the form **must** be as in the second example, the asterix (*) is compulsory as is the pipestem (|).The other definitions would look like this:

```
<!ELEMENT first (#PCDATA)>
<!ELEMENT middle (#PCDATA)>
<!ELEMENT last (#PCDATA)>
<!ELEMENT nickname (#PCDATA)>
<!ELEMENT company (#PCDATA)>
<!ELEMENT date (#PCDATA)>
<!ELEMENT personal (#PCDATA| date)*>

<!ELEMENT attitude EMPTY>
```

This last line of code is self explanatory, an empty element can't contain either text or another element, but it must be declared.

Summary of Element Definitions

Let's summarize what we've learnt about element definitions.

- The general form is **<!*ELEMENT NAME content_specification*>**
- The content specification can be elements, mixed content , EMPTY or ANY
- Mixed content and multiple element content is contained in parentheses i.e. (p, br, etc)
- Mixed content MUST take the form **(#PCDATA|A|B|...)***
- Mixed content need not contain elements **(#PCDATA)**
- The comma (**,**) is used as a tokenizer in a sequential series of elements
- The pipestem (|) is used as a tokenizer in an alternative series of elements
- The question mark (**?**) indicates that an element can occur 0 or once
- The asterix (*) indicates an element can occur 0 or several times
- The plus mark (+) indicates an element can occur once or several times.
- Parentheses can be used to nest e.g. **(title, chapter, (text|heading|code)*)**

So, that concludes our look at elements in the DTD, let's move on to look at how we define and declare attributes.

Defining Attributes: Attribute Declarations

The general form of an attribute declaration is:

```
<!ATTLIST element_name
attribute_name attribute_type defaultvalue>
```

Now, let's look at what forms of attribute there are.

Types of Attribute

We'll cover the three main types of attribute here and show examples of their use. There are several other types which we shall not cover here. Consult a specialized text or the specification for details of them.

The CDATA Attribute

This is the most common type. It means any text. (Do not confuse this with the **CDATA** used as a comment, even though they have the same name).

An example of an attribute where the value can be any text-string would be:

```
role CDATA #IMPLIED
<!ATTLIST actor
role CDATA #IMPLIED>
```

For example:

```
<actor role="hamlet">
```

The default value **#IMPLIED** tells the validator that no value is specified, and it's OK if the attribute does not occur, so the following element:

```
<actor> To be or not to be..</actor>
```

would not flag an error.

The ID Attribute

An ID must be unique within the document. There must be no other ID of the same name. Here's an example of an attribute that defines a unique value, an ID.

```
id ID #REQUIRED

<!ATTLIST name
id ID #REQUIRED>
```

For example:

```
<name id="OH615">
```

The default value **#REQUIRED** tells the validator that the ID must be present and a value **must** be specified.

```
<name>Frank</name>
```

would flag an error.

An Enumerated Attribute

This is one of a specific list of declared values.

An example of an attribute that provides a value choice and specifies a default:

```
interest (hot|warm|cool|unknown) "unknown"
<!ATTLIST attitude
interest (hot|warm|cool|unknown) "unknown">
```

For example:

```
<attitude interest="warm"/>
```

Note the default, like the value in the document, must be quoted. If the document just contained

```
<interest/>
```

then the attribute "**unknown**" would be presumed by the validating software.

An example of an attribute where only one value is allowed, that must be included:

```
method CDATA #FIXED "POST"

<!ATTLIST form
method CDATA #FIXED "POST">
```

For example:

```
<form method ="POST">

<form>
```

Here the attribute is fixed and its value is passed through to the user-agent, whether it is written in the document or not. Both the above have the same effect. Note that

```
<form method ="GET">
```

would flag an error with this DTD.

Here are the other attribute declarations we would use in our contacts DTD example.

```
<!ATTLIST company
lang (english|french) "english">

<!ATTLIST contact
type (first|last|other) "other">
```

White Space Handling

The XML processor is required to pass all white space on to the user agent. How it is dealt with is up to the agent. If white space is important, (as it is in poetry, math, and code) XML provides the following built in attribute that instructs the agent to preserve all white space. Note that, even though it is described as built in, it must be declared in the DTD, like this;

```
xml:space(default|preserve) #IMPLIED
```

So that you can use it like this:

```
<!ATTLIST poem
xml:space(default|preserve) "preserve">
```

As stated in the XML spec:

> "This declared intent is considered to apply to all elements within the content of the element where it is specified, unless overridden with another instance of the `"xml: space"` attribute"

In other words child elements inherit the attribute, so, if you declared it in the root element, white space would be preserved throughout the whole document.

Note that xml:space is one of the few attributes that XML reserves for itself.

So, we've looked at defining elements and element declarations, and defining attributes and attribute declarations. Let's look at the final part of writing a DTD–entities.

Defining Entities: Entity Declarations

An entity is a storage unit for data, either character data or binary data. Every entity has a name and content, and the idea is that by quoting the entity name in your document you get the content of your entity storage unit.

An entity quotation takes the general form:

```
&[entity_name];
```

If you know HTML you are familiar with entities. > is an entity. When the user agent comes across it, it substitutes >.

In XML, an entity has to be declared before it can be used and, of course, the place it is declared is in the DTD.

Declaring an Entity

An entity declaration takes the general form:

```
<!ENTITY [entity_name] [entity_content]>
```

Before we go any further it would be handy to consider the following example.

```
<?xml version="1.0"?>
<!DOCTYPE greeting [
<!ELEMENT greeting (#PCDATA)>
<!ENTITY XML "Extensible Markup Language">
]>

<greeting> Hello &XML;!</greeting>
```

This would be rendered by the XML browser as:

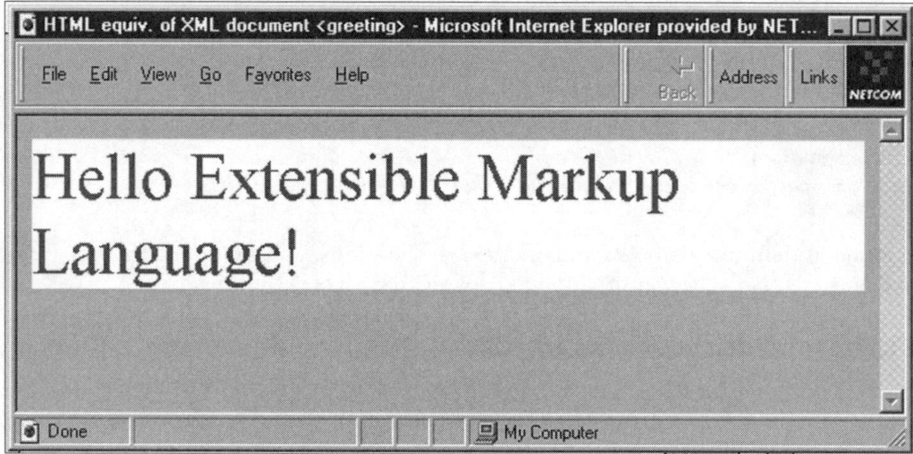

This is an internal entity. Entities can also be external.

`<!ENTITY tutorial SYSTEM "xmltut.txt">` could refer to the text file that contains this tutorial so that:

```
<?xml version="1.0"?>
<!DOCTYPE tutorial [
<!ELEMENT tutorial (#PCDATA)>
<!ENTITY tutorialtxt SYSTEM "xmltut.txt">
]>

<tutorial> &tutorialtxt;</tutorial>
```

Would be a valid, well-formed XML document containing this tutorial.

Supposing we saved this resulting document as **`xmltut.xml`**;

```
<?xml version="1.0"?>
<!DOCTYPE tutorial [
<!ELEMENT tutorial (#PCDATA)>
<!ENTITY tutorialxm SYSTEM "xmltut.xml">
]>

<tutorial> &tutorialxm;</tutorial>
```

This would **not** be a valid well-formed document.

> *To find out why expand out the document and look at rule (b) under XML is a Well-formed Document.*

In short we would have the following:

```
<tutorial><tutorial> ..The tutorial text is here.. </tutorial></tutorial>
```

In other words there is no longer a single all encompassing root element.

Note how the identifier keyword **`SYSTEM`** is used to refer to an external entity.

The other identifier for external entities is **`PUBLIC`**. This can be used when the entity is so common that the user-agent may have the resource cached locally. For example

```
<!ENTITY HTML.Version PUBLIC "-//W3C//DTD HTML 4.0//EN"
"http://www.w3.org/TR/REC-html40/loose.dtd" >
```

brings up the HTML4 DTD and if it is not available locally provides a URL.

In an internal entity the document gets the substitution directly from the DTD, as illustrated here.

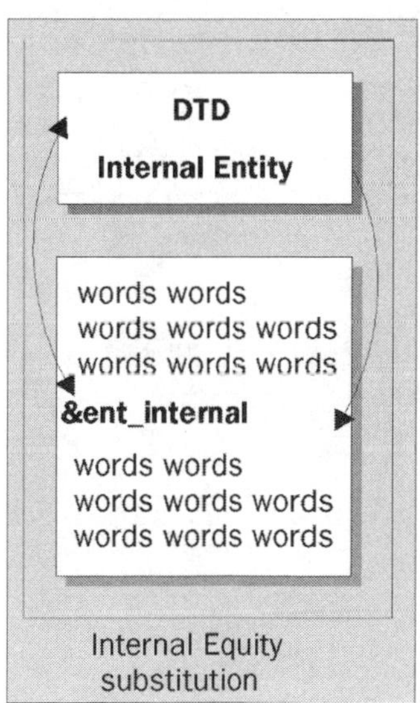

Internal Equity substitution

In an external entity the document gets the address of the document from the DTD, and the outside source is directly substituted in the document.

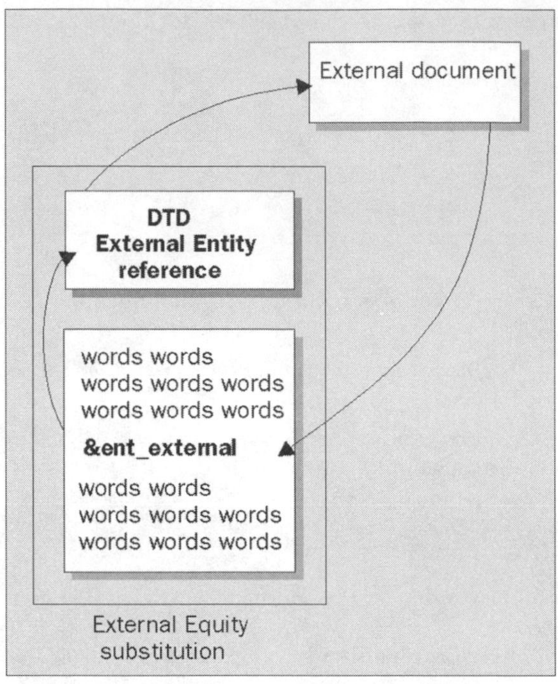

Other Types of Entity

So far we have looked at text entities both internal and external. Let's look at the other forms of entities.

Character References

Any Unicode character can be referenced as follows:

```
&#[unicodeDecimalNumber];
```

Although XML specifically uses UNICODE rather than ASCII, the first 256 Unicode characters correspond with the ASCII character set, so in practice entities that work in HTML (which uses ASCII) also work in XML. However, in XML you are allowed to use a hexadecimal reference as well as a decimal reference.

The copyright symbol is **©**. It can also be written in the hexadecimal form as **&x#A9;** in XML. Note that this later hexadecimal form doesn't work in HTML

Binary Entities

A binary entity is anything that is not an XML document. (In this sense a text file is a binary entity, but they are usually declared just like an XML document!). They have to be declared in a special way, like this;

```
<!ENTITY smileyface SYSTEM "Smiley.gif" NDATA GIF>
```

This tells the XML processor that it is dealing with a **GIF** file. How does the processor handle that? Well, it doesn't have to, but, if it wants to, it uses a helper agent. This helper agent must be declared in a notation declaration, which we will deal with next.

Notation Declaration

Notation declarations take this form

```
<!NOTATION [name] SYSTEM (or PUBLIC) "url">
```

For example:

```
<!NOTATION GIF SYSTEM "gws.exe">
```

Would signal to the processor to open any **GIF** files in the popular shareware program–*Graphics Workshop*

Pre-defined Entities

The following entities are built into XML and all processors that check for well-formedness must recognize them:

- **<** = <
- **>** = >
- **&** = &
- **'** = '
- **"** = "

However, if a DTD is provided they must be declared in the DTD for the document to be valid. Here is the form their declaration takes–note that the **<** and **&** characters in the declarations of **lt** and **amp** are doubly escaped to meet the requirement that entity replacement be well-formed.

```
<!ENTITY lt     "&#38;#60;">
<!ENTITY gt     "&#62;">
<!ENTITY amp    "&#38;#38;">
<!ENTITY apos   "&#39;">
<!ENTITY quot   "&#34;">
```

Parameter Entities

Parameter entities are entities that can be used in the DTD and are useful for organizing the DTD. They take the general form:

```
<!ENTITY % [name] "[names]">
```

The topic is a little advanced, but here is a general idea of what they do.

In the HTML DTD the following combination of tags are being referenced as a group all the time:

- **UL|OL|DIR|MENU**

as are:

- **H1|H2|H3|H4|H5|H6**

They can be declared as an entity thus:

```
<!ENTITY % list " UL | OL | DIR |MENU ">

<!ENTITY % headings " H1|H2|H3|H4|H5|H6 ">
```

Now, instead of writing

```
<!ELEMENT BODY (H1|H2|H3|H4|H5|H6|P|UL|OL|DIR|MENU|PRE|HR|IMG)*>
```

we can write:

```
<!ELEMENT BODY (%headings | P | %list | PRE | HR | IMG)*>
```

Note that the entity has to be declared **before** it is used.

Summary of DTD

All you have to do to write a DTD is:

- 1.Declare and define your elements
- 2.Declare and define their attributes.
- 3.Declare and define any entities and notations, both external and internal.

Here is the DTD for our contact example:

```
<!-- DTD for a client document-->

<!DOCTYPE client  [

<!--beginning of element declarations-->
<!--the root tag of client-->
<!ELEMENT client(name, phone*, company?, (contact| attitude|
personal|image)*)>

<!ELEMENT name (first, middle?, last, nickname*)>

<!ELEMENT phone (#PCDATA)>
<!ELEMENT company (#PCDATA)>
<!ELEMENT contact (#PCDATA| date)*>
<!ELEMENT first (#PCDATA)>
<!ELEMENT middle (#PCDATA)>
<!ELEMENT last (#PCDATA)>
<!ELEMENT nickname (#PCDATA)>

<!ELEMENT date (#PCDATA)>
<!ELEMENT personal (#PCDATA| date)*>
```

```
<!ELEMENT attitude EMPTY>
<!--We may want to have a picture in our document-->

<!ELEMENT image EMPTY>

<!--end of element declarations-->

<!--beginning of attribute declarations-->

<!-- we are commenting out this requirement for now
<!ATTLIST name
id ID #REQUIRED>
-->

<!ATTLIST attitude
interest (hot|warm|cool|unknown) "unknown">
<!--the in house language of communication-->
<!ATTLIST company
lang (english|french|spanish) "english">

<!ATTLIST contact
type (first|last|other) "other">

<!ATTLIST image
type (bmp|gif|jpg|other) "gif">

<!--include for white space handling in name-->
<!ATTLIST name
xml:space(default|preserve) #IMPLIED>

<!ATTLIST

<!--end of attribute declarations-->

<!-- beginning of entity declarations-->
<!--declare pre-defined entities to be a validating document-->

     <!ENTITY lt      "&#38;#60;">
     <!ENTITY gt      "&#62;">
     <!ENTITY amp     "&#38;#38;">
     <!ENTITY apos    "&#39;">
     <!ENTITY quot    "&#34;">
<!--declare eacute, egrave, and atilde for spelling of french and spanish
names-->
<!ENTITY eacute  "&#233"  >
<!ENTITY egrave  "&#232"  >
<!ENTITY atilde  "&#227"  >

<!--declare boiler plate, our %&@* lawyers want this-->
<!ENTITY boilerplate  "Any opinions expressed in this contact note are the
opinions of the individual sales person and do not necessarily represent
the opinions of megacorp"  >

<!NOTATION gif SYSTEM  "gwswin/gws.exe">
<!NOTATION bmp SYSTEM  "gwswin/gws.exe">
<!NOTATION jpg SYSTEM  "gwswin/gws.exe">
```

```
<!NOTATION other SYSTEM  "gwswin/gws.exe">

<!--end of entity declarations-->
]>
<!--end of DTD-->
```

We can either paste this into the beginning of each document or preferably we save it as **client.dtd**, **BUT REMEMBER TO REMOVE "<!DOCTYPE client [" at the beginning and "]>"** at the end! To declare it we put

```
<?xml version="1.0"? encoding="UTF-8">
<!DOCTYPE client SYSTEM "client.dtd">
<client>.....
</client>
```

The screenshot below shows how this DTD appears when you open it up in Notepad.

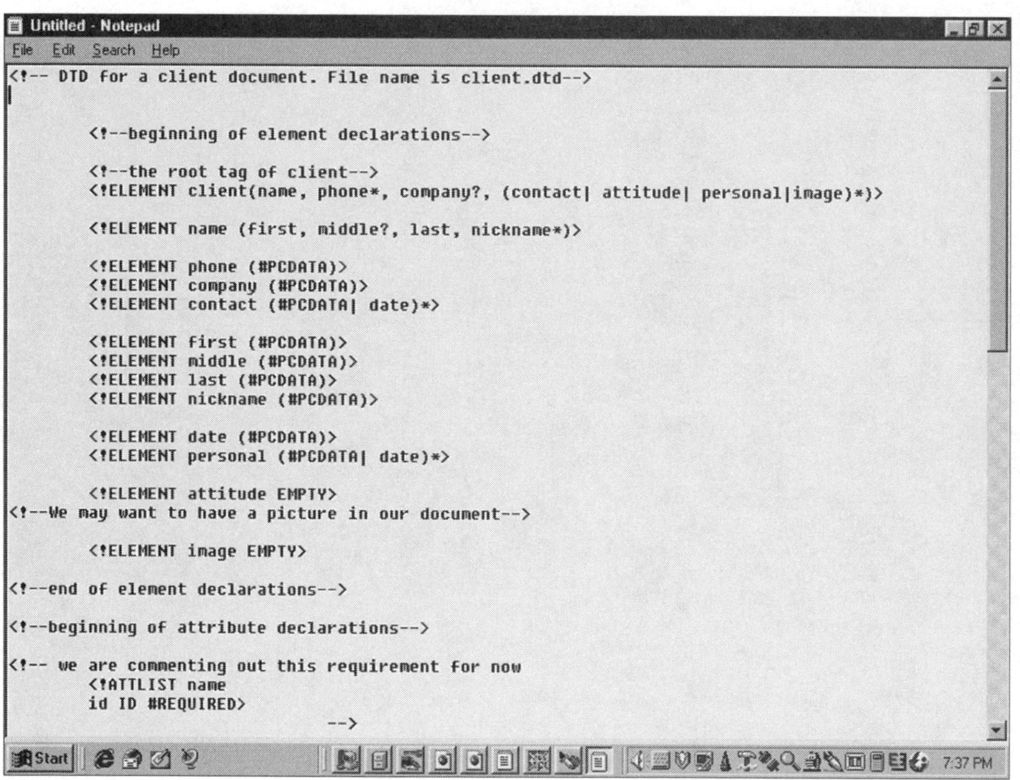

```
<!-- DTD for a client document. File name is client.dtd-->


        <!--beginning of element declarations-->

        <!--the root tag of client-->
        <!ELEMENT client(name, phone*, company?, (contact| attitude| personal|image)*)>

        <!ELEMENT name (first, middle?, last, nickname*)>

        <!ELEMENT phone (#PCDATA)>
        <!ELEMENT company (#PCDATA)>
        <!ELEMENT contact (#PCDATA| date)*>

        <!ELEMENT first (#PCDATA)>
        <!ELEMENT middle (#PCDATA)>
        <!ELEMENT last (#PCDATA)>
        <!ELEMENT nickname (#PCDATA)>

        <!ELEMENT date (#PCDATA)>
        <!ELEMENT personal (#PCDATA| date)*>

        <!ELEMENT attitude EMPTY>
<!--We may want to have a picture in our document-->

        <!ELEMENT image EMPTY>

<!--end of element declarations-->

<!--beginning of attribute declarations-->

<!-- we are commenting out this requirement for now
        <!ATTLIST name
        id ID #REQUIRED>
                                   -->
```

As you can see it is quite a bit of work just to make a simple declaration like this. It, however, only has to be made once, and then it can be used over and over again.

You probably won't have to write your own DTD's, I'm sure that in the near future there will be a number of DTD's in the public domain that you can just pick up for the asking. However, you must know how to read them to see if they meet your needs, and there is no better way of understanding how they work than by building your own at least once.

Summary

We covered a huge amount in this chapter! After briefly reviewing markup we:

- Covered the history of XML
- Learnt what a well-formed XML document is and how to write one
- Looked into the contents of a prolog
- Saw what a document declaration is and what it can contain
- Discovered what a DTD contains, and learnt about element declarations, attribute declarations and entity declarations
- Wrote a DTD for a simple client contact sheet

In the next chapter we will learn the difference between physical and logical structure, and how to string a whole series of documents together.

We will also have a look at linking to other documents and styling our documents, and we will see how we can use the power of XML on the Web today.

References

The official specification for XML. You may want to check out EBNF in the appendix before reading this document.

`http://www.w3.org/TR/PR-xml-971208`

The XML page with links to just about every thing that is going on in the XML world.

`http://www.w3.org/xml`

Microsoft's XML page:

`http://www.microsoft.com/xml`

The provisional DTD for HTML 4 can be found at:

`http://www.w3.org/TR/REC-html40/loose.dtd`

Exercises

1. Write a DTD for a home nursing agency that wants to keep track of their patients in a single file. The document should include the patient's name, address, referring doctor's name, allergies and diagnoses. (We will add to this document in the next chapter.)
2. Add an address tag to the Contacts DTD we've examined in this chapter. Use either attributes or separate elements to delineate state, city ZIP code etc. The clients can be in Canada, the US or Mexico.

4

More XML

If the general press is to be believed HTML is on the way out and XML is already here! Well neither of these statements is true, or even likely to become true. XML, however, is clearly going to become a major player on the Web.

This chapter aims to give you just enough XML to get you started on the Web. We will look at:

- How to make complex documents out of a series of simple documents by using external entities.
- How we can output the contents of our document using an XML processor, and a back-end processor.
- How we can sort the document to extract the information we need.
- How we can modify documents.
- XML links (only very briefly, as they are not really a part of style sheets.)
- Some new and developing XML topics.

So, let's start by looking at how you take a series of simple documents and combine them into a single complex document using entities.

Creating an XML Document using Entities

In this section we're going to look at how you combine the contents of a series of XML documents into a single XML document using external entities. First, we'll examine the theory of an entity by looking at the contrast between the logical and physical structure of the XML document. Then we'll move on to see what this theory means in practical terms by using a tool developed for this book to actually expand a series of external entities to create a single document. Later in the chapter we'll demonstrate how to display the XML document we've created in your browser using style sheets, but we're getting a bit ahead of ourselves here, so let's get back to looking at entities, beginning with a look at logical and physical structure.

Any XML document has both a logical and a physical structure. What is meant by these terms?

Logical Structure

Consider the following well-formed and valid (assuming it conforms to the external DTD **doc.dtd**) XML document.

```
<?XML version="1.0"?>
   <!DOCTYPE doc SYSTEM "doc.dtd" [
   <!ENTITY contact1 SYSTEM "\stylesheets\chapter.04\ch3xml1.xml">
   <!ENTITY contact2 SYSTEM "\stylesheets\chapter.04\ch3xml2.xml">
   <!ENTITY contact3 SYSTEM "\stylesheets\cha.04\ch3xml3.xml">
   <!ENTITY contact4 SYSTEM "\stylesheets\chapter.04\ch3xml4.xml">

   <!ENTITY XML  "eXtensible Markup Language">
]>
<doc>
   <para>Expanding entities in XML (&XML;)</para>
   <para>&contact1;</para>
   <para>&contact2;</para>
   <para>&contact3;</para>
   <para>&contact4;</para>
</doc>
```

This document has a logical structure in that all its elements are nested, and that it conforms to a DTD. Its content, however, consists merely of entity references. In fact the first paragraph does have some text in it, but we will not know what the physical structure of the document is until we have expanded those entities.

The diagram below illustrates a similar document.

```
<?XML version "1.0"?>
<!DOCTYPE doc SYSTEM "doc.dtd" [
<!ENTITY contact1 SYSTEM "cont1.xml">
<!ENTITY contact2 SYSTEM "cont2.xml">
<!ENTITY contact3 SYSTEM "cont.3xml">
<!ENTITY contact4 SYSTEM "cont.4xml">
]>

<doc>
<body>
&contact1;
&contact2;
&contact3;
&contact4;
</body>
</doc>
```

A logical document structure with 4 external entities and their declarations

Physical structure

The physical structure of the above document consists of the actual document with all the entities expanded out. The following diagram shows this actually being done.

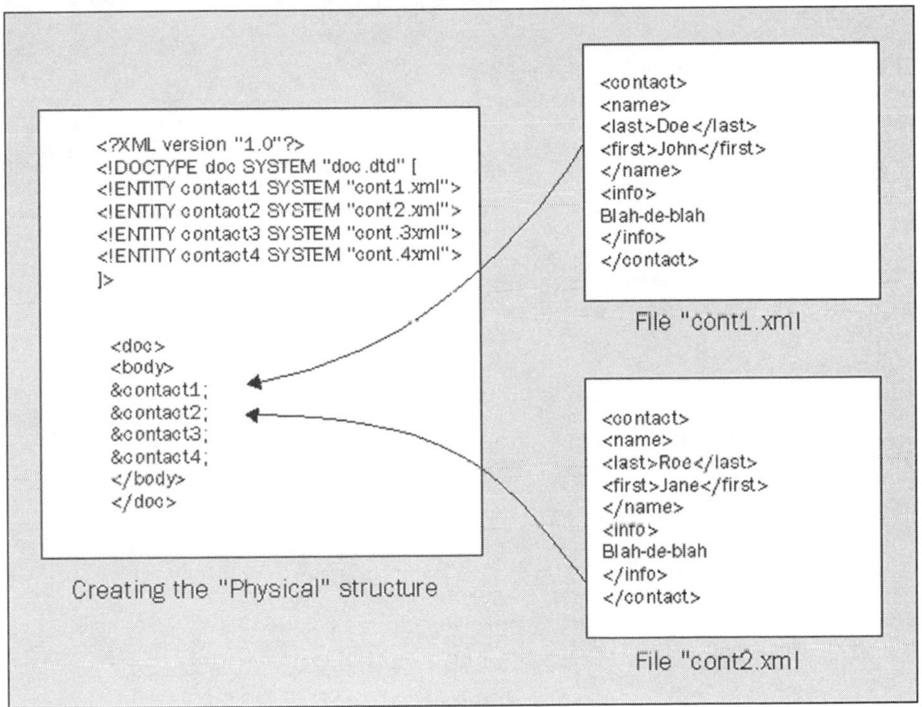

Creating the "Physical" structure

The XML processor goes through the following processes:

- On encountering an entity (`&[entity name];`) it decides whether it is an entity that it needs help with, i.e. is it other than a pre-defined entity? (See the section on *Pre-defined Entities* in the previous chapter if you are unsure about this term). If it does need help it will consult the DTD.

> **A reminder: Even though the user agent should be able to expand pre-defined entities (`<="<",>=">",&="&",'="'","="" "`.) without help from the DTD they should still be declared in the DTD for the document to be valid.**

- On consulting the DTD, if it is an internal entity (e.g. `&XML;` in the first paragraph in the example above) it will substitute the relevant text right away.
- If, on consulting the DTD it finds it is an external entity, it must discover what type the file is (binary or text) by looking for an **NDATA** attribute. If no **NDATA** attribute exists the processor assumes that it is another text, or rather XML, file.
- If the file is a pure text file, i.e. a file with no markup, this is, in theory, a binary entity and should be declared as follows: `<!ENTITY atxtfile SYSTEM "txtfile.txt" NDATA TXT>`. However, in practice, the **NDATA TXT** is left out, and the text file is treated as a text file.
- If the file is a binary file, the processor looks for a notation declaration to see how it is to handle the file. The example we gave in the last chapter `<!NOTATION GIF SYSTEM "gwswin/gws.exe">` would instruct the processor to open `gws.exe` to display a `.gif` file.
- If the file is another XML file the processor expands it.

The diagram here shows what the file looks like when the text entities have been expanded.

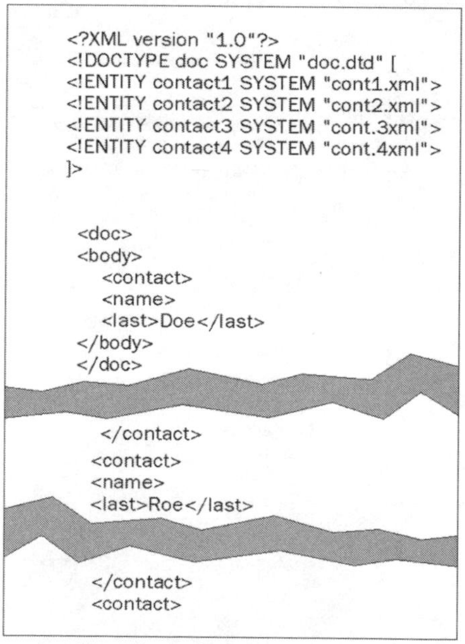

```
<?XML version "1.0"?>
<!DOCTYPE doc SYSTEM "doc.dtd" [
<!ENTITY contact1 SYSTEM "cont1.xml">
<!ENTITY contact2 SYSTEM "cont2.xml">
<!ENTITY contact3 SYSTEM "cont.3xml">
<!ENTITY contact4 SYSTEM "cont.4xml">
]>

 <doc>
 <body>
    <contact>
    <name>
    <last>Doe</last>
 </body>
 </doc>

    </contact>
  <contact>
  <name>
  <last>Roe</last>

  </contact>
  <contact>
```

The "Physical" document with entities expanded (P1)

Some Notes on Valid Text Entities

Text entities are something of a misnomer because, as we have just seen, they don't refer to files containing unmarked up text, but to marked up XML files. In practice, however, a text file will behave like a marked up XML file when imported into the physical document.

There are several things to be observed about importing another XML file.

Firstly, the file itself should be a well-formed file with all its elements nested.

Actually to be well-formed the file has to have a unique opening and closing tag, and this is really not necessary for entities, so the file merely has to have its tags nested. In practice though, in case we ever want to display the entity by itself, it is better that the file should be able to stand alone as an XML file, so we should indeed put in a pair of unique opening and closing tags.

This well-formed file is a valid text entity

```
<contact>
   <name> Frank Boumphrey</name>
</contact>
```

as is this one

```
   <name> Frank Boumphrey</name>
```

This will also be treated as a valid entity even though in (XML) theory it is a binary file (of course it's not!):

```
Frank Boumphrey
```

as will this:

```
Frank <nickname>Boomer </nickname>Boumphrey
```

whereas this entity is not a valid entity:

```
<contact>
   <name> Frank Boumphrey</name>
```

because it is not well-formed. It lacks a closing tag.

The other thing to note is that XML files that are called in cannot have DTDs. All DTDs have to be in the prolog position, i.e. before the root element, and obviously, this would not apply if the entity contained a DTD that was also imported!

To summarize:

- The logical structure of a document consists of well-formed document elements with or without a DTD.
- The physical structure of a document consists of a well-formed or valid document with its entities expanded.
- Entities can consist of:

  Another well-formed document without its DTD.
  A text string or text file.
  A binary file.
- All entities have to be declared in the DTD (even predefined ones if a DTD is present).

Storage Units for Entities

In the example above our entity is defined as a local disc file.

```
<!ENTITY contact1 SYSTEM "\stylesheets\chapter.04\ch3xml1.xml">
```

The processor will open that file and place its contents in the correct part of our document. However, there is no need for the entity to be a file, the entity can be stored in any manner it is possible to conceive of provided the actual content meets the above rules. For example, the contents could be just part of a file, or stored in a database, or even generated through code.

So, that's the theory behind external entities, now let's see them in action with a concrete example of entity expansion.

An Example of Expanding Entities

In order to further illustrate entities we are now going to do some practical entity expansion. This will be done using a simple tool developed by the author. This tool, unfortunately, only runs under Windows.

`Entity.exe` is a very simple teaching tool that simply expands entities that are stored as files, or referenced as internal entities. What it does, in essence, is read the XML file, and when it comes across an entity reference, it expands it and puts it in the correct place in the text.

This is only a "toy", do not try and do any heavy duty work with it!

Download it from the Wrox web site at:

`http://rapid.wrox.co.uk/books/1657`

or from:

`http://www.hypermedic.com/style/tools/index.htm`.

When you run the **.exe** file this is what you should see:

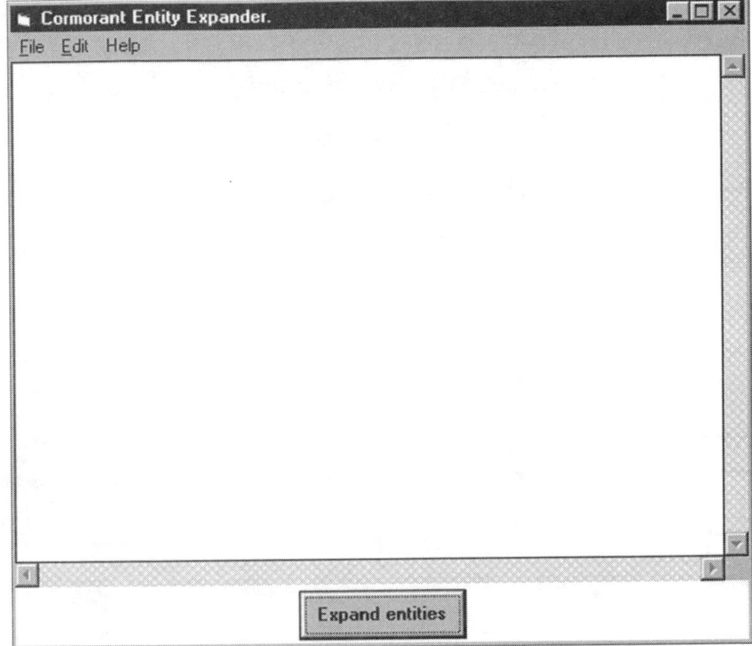

Now let's see how we can use it in an example.

Here is a well-formed and valid XML file **entit.xml**, with four external and one internal entity declaration. We will open this file in **entity.exe**.

To reproduce this example yourself, you need to download the files **entit.xml**, **ch3xml1.xml**, **ch3xml2.xml**, **ch3xml3.xml** and **ch3xml4.xml**, as well as downloading **entity.exe** from our web site. Place them all in the same directory, and make sure the path to the **.xml** files in **entit.xml** points to where you have placed them. i.e. **\stylesheets\chapter.04** is the path in my computer, it may not be the same in yours.

```
<?XML version="1.0"?>
   <!DOCTYPE doc SYSTEM "doc.dtd" [
   <!ENTITY contact1 SYSTEM "\stylesheets\chapter.04\ch3xml1.xml">
   <!ENTITY contact2 SYSTEM "\stylesheets\chapter.04\ch3xml2.xml">
   <!ENTITY contact3 SYSTEM "\stylesheets\cha.04\ch3xml3.xml">
   <!ENTITY contact4 SYSTEM "\stylesheets\chapter.04\ch3xml4.xml">

   <!ENTITY XML  "eXtensible Markup Language">
]>
<doc>
   <para>Expanding entities in XML (&XML;)</para>
   <para>&contact1;</para>
   <para>&contact2;</para>
   <para>&contact3;</para>
   <para>&contact4;</para>
</doc>
```

To open the file, use the File-Open option from the File dropdown menu. The screenshot below shows what the file **entit.xml** looks like opened in **entity.exe**.

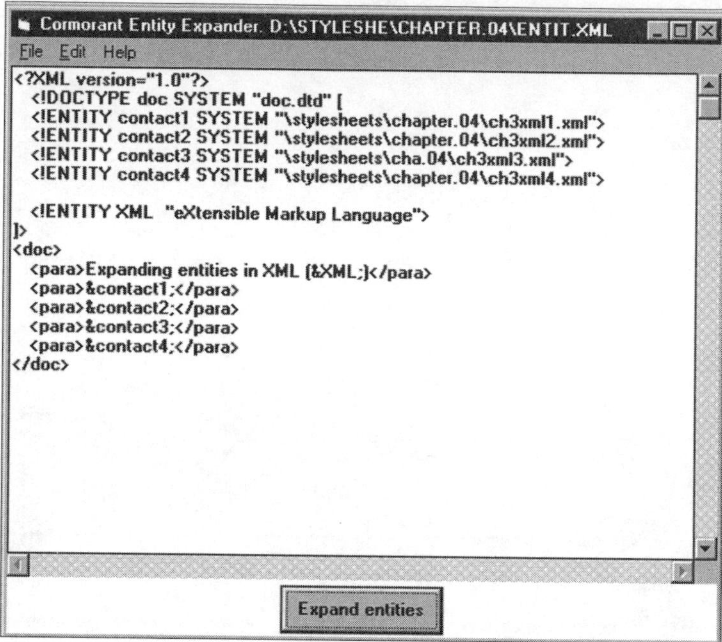

To expand the file we click on the Expand entities button. The next screenshot shows what happens.

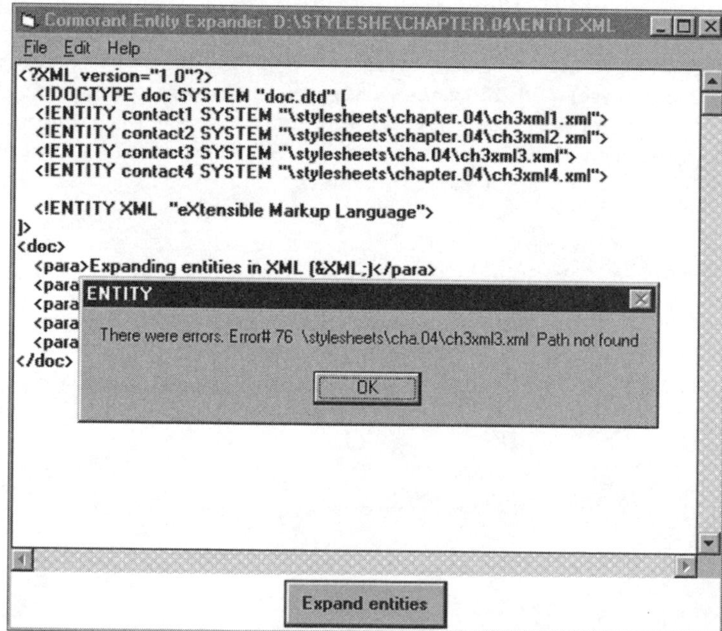

As you can see, we have an error on the line;

```
<!ENTITY contact3 SYSTEM "\stylesheets\cha.04\ch3xml3.xml">
```

`\cha.04` is an obvious typo. The message box informs us of this.

`Entity.exe` will carry on and expand all the entities that it can find a valid path for, but obviously not the entity that it cannot expand. We fix the typo, reload the file and expand it again successfully. The screenshot below shows what **`entit.xml`** looks like with all the entities expanded.

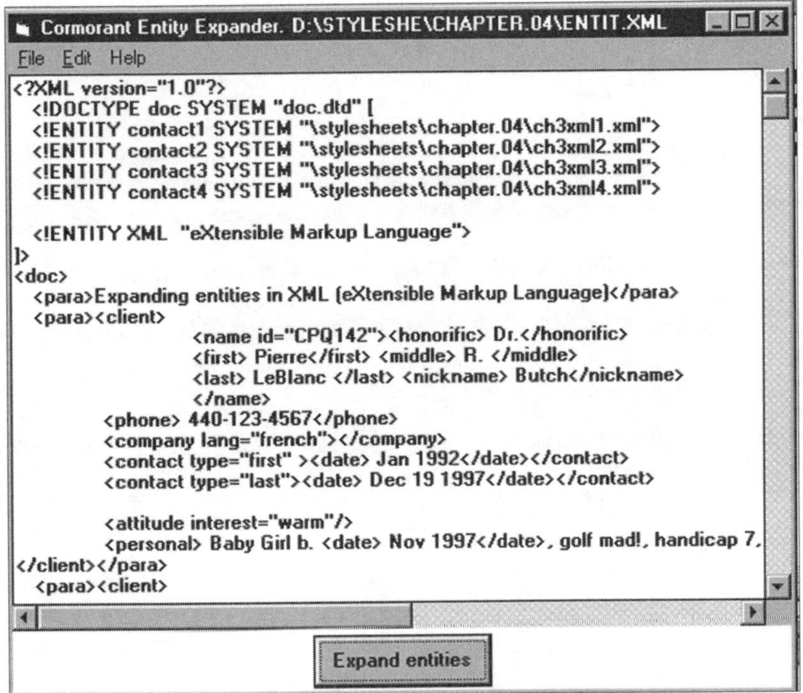

Warning this is only a toy and will not handle full-blown DTDs, but it should give you a good idea of how the physical structure of a document is created.

Let's examine what's happened here. In the last chapter, we used the example of creating a summary of contact information in order to illustrate the concept of the DTD, and we got you to do some more work on it in one of the exercises at the end of the chapter. This example imagines that you created a number of XML documents, each giving the contact details for one client. Then you decide that you want to incorporate them all into a single new XML document. You have just performed this task by defining them as entities, giving the entity expander the correct path to find them and clicking the Expand entities button.

So, now that you've created your master XML document, what if you want to output it to a browser or some other file type or user agent? We'll cover that next.

Outputting XML

This section has the same structure as the previous one. First, we will cover the theory of outputting XML by examining how we currently output HTML, then look at how we will output XML in the future. Then we look at the current practical method of displaying XML–applying CSS style rules to it and converting it to HTML. We'll finish this section with a practical example which uses another utility devised for this book to take one of the files we used in the example above, convert it into styled HTML and display it.

So, let's begin with a look at the theory of outputting documents. Before we look at outputting XML, let's look at outputting a document with which you are doubtless familiar, an HTML document.

Outputting HTML

If you have a browser, outputting HTML is simplicity itself, you type the URL or file reference into the appropriate place, press enter, and hey presto! There's your document neatly displayed and styled on the screen. It is so commonplace that we tend to forget the processes that the browser must go through.

- After fetching the document via HTTP or the file system it must take the raw document and strip it of its tags, and make an array of the elements content.
- Next it must figure out what each tag means, and look for any styling associated with the tag. The browser has a knowledge of the HTML tags built into it.
- Then it must display the content on the screen.

This is a very simplistic description. A more sophisticated one is given in the chapter on flow objects and selectors: Chapter 7.

The diagram below illustrates this process.

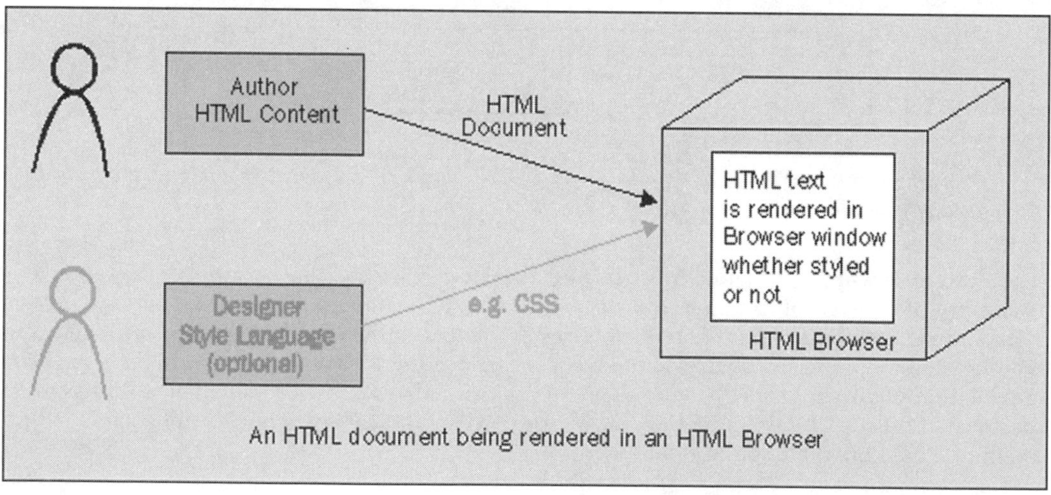

An HTML document being rendered in an HTML Browser

Because the HTML browser has a built-in ability to display HTML the styling process is optional.

The XML Browser

Firstly at the time of writing there are no XML browsers on the market, but if one did exist, it would have to go through a similar process.

- The first step would be the same, the browser would have to take the raw document and strip it of its tags, and make an array of the elements content.
- The second step, however, would be different. Because there are no set tags in XML, the XML browser has no intrinsic knowledge of the tag's meaning. It would have to look for information on how to display the element. This information is displayed in a style sheet, so every XML document would need a style sheet in order to be displayed.
- The next step would be the same, it would have to display the document on the screen, but again the XML browser would do this a little differently. The HTML browser has its own built-in display window, but the XML browser might choose to convert the document into a different format and display the document in a helper application. For example, it might convert the XML document into **`.rtf`**, and display it in a word processor, or it might convert the XML into HTML and display the document on an HTML browser. In fact it might give the user the option on how they would like the document displayed.

The diagram below illustrates this process.

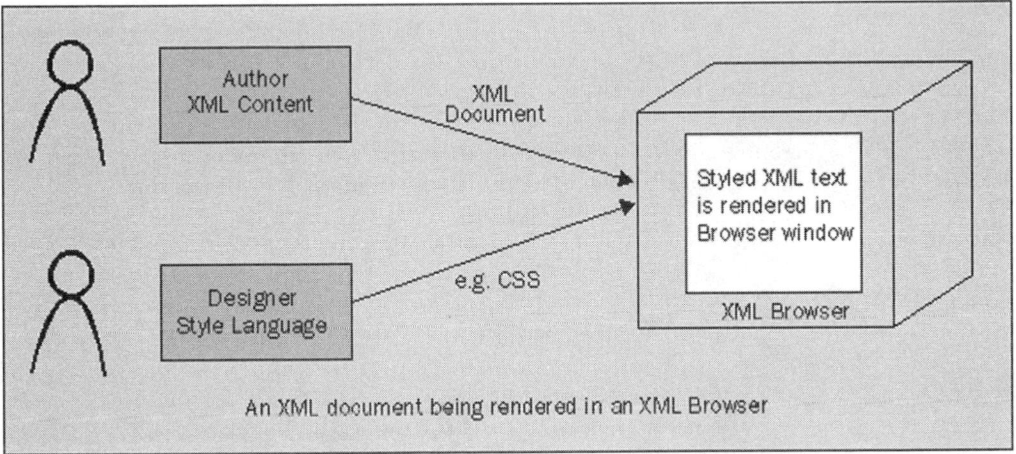

An XML document being rendered in an XML Browser

Because an XML browser couldn't have any built-in knowledge of how the XML elements should be displayed, the styling process is essential. Of course, you are not limited to outputting XML only to a browser. We'll look at non-browser XML output in a moment, but first we need to give you a brief introduction to flow objects.

An Introduction to Flow Objects

We will have a look at flow objects in some detail in Chapter 7. For now let's just look at a couple of simple concepts to help us understand how an XML processor operates.

Essentially a flow object is a piece of content that is created by the processor from the source document.

Take the following simple well-formed XML document.

```
<doc>
   <para>
   There is no emphasized text in this paragraph.
   </para>
   <para>
   However there is <emph>emphasized text</emph> in this paragraph.
   </para>
</doc>
```

For practical purposes the processor will create three flow objects from this document–two paragraphs and a line of emphasized text. Because the processor has no intrinsic knowledge of how to render the tags it must look around for a style sheet, and this is what it finds, a CSS type style sheet.

```
para{display:block}
emph{display:inline; font-style:italic}
```

The processor will therefore create two **block** flow objects and an **inline** flow object. Quite simply a block flow object has a line break before and after it, and an inline flow object doesn't.

So the processor will send this message to the rendering agent (in binary or coded form of course).

```
[put a line break here]
[print the following in your default type] "there is no emphasized text in
this paragraph."
[put a line break here]
[put a line break here]
[print the following in your default type] "However there is"[print the
following in italic] "emphasized text"[print the following in your default
type] "in this paragraph"
[put a line break here]
```

This is a very simplistic description of what a flow object is. In theory every piece of content down to the last ASCII character is a flow object, but it is usually not productive to think in terms of flow objects this small.

The block flow object can be moved about the display canvas using positioning code, but the inline flow object must keep its place in the line, unless of course it is positioned elsewhere by code. But that's a story for later! Finally, in this theory section, let's examine how you output XML other than to a browser.

Non-Browser XML Output

We have got used to thinking of an all-inclusive browser, which downloads a document, processes it and then displays it. But this does not have to be the case, in fact in SGML it is more usual to have the SGML processor take the marked up document, and output it in a different format.

This is so with XML at the present. The XML processor that is used in this chapter takes an XML document, marries it with a CSS type style sheet, and outputs the result as an HTML document. The diagram below illustrates this process.

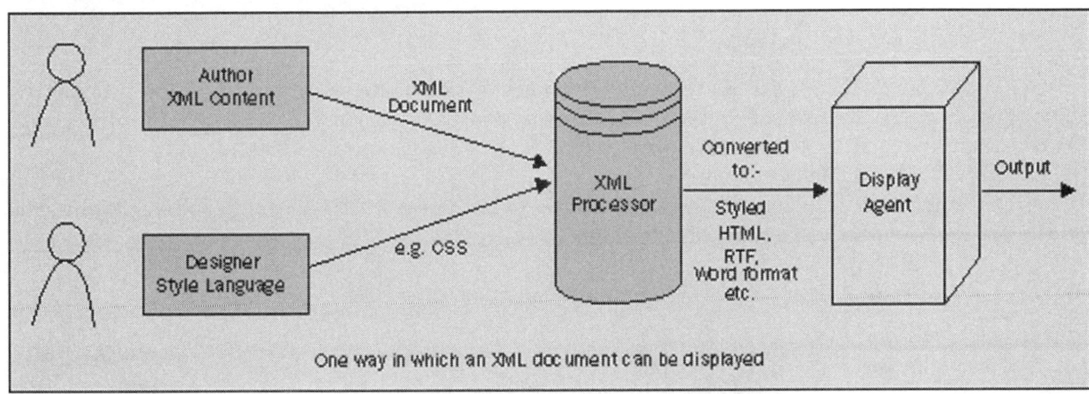

One way in which an XML document can be displayed

The processor converts the XML to another format that is then fed to an agent for display.

At the present time, where XML is being used it is usually being converted to HTML "on the fly", by a script located on the server and then sent out over the Internet. The diagram below illustrates this process.

Displaying an XML document on the Internet

In the next chapter we will look at Microsoft's XSL processor which marries an XML document to an XSL style sheet and outputs it as a single HTML file with inline styling.

Jade, which you are encouraged to download if you get serious about XML, uses a command line format and can output our XML document in RTF or HTML. The mechanisms of using it are not covered in this book, but there is documentation accompanying the software. The url to download it from is: **`http://www.mulberrytech.com/dsssl/dssslist/archive/1019.html`**.

That concludes our examination of the theory of outputting XML, now let's look at what is practically possible today. In this chapter we'll limit ourselves to looking at what you can achieve with CSS styling; in the next chapter we'll look at XML's own form of styling, XSL. So, let's begin with a simple example.

Style Sheets in XML

As we pointed out above, the XML document markup carries no styling information it is purely semantic. If we do not provide any styling information, most processors usually strip off the tags and present every item as an inline display (the XML equivalent of a **`<SPAN>`** tag).

The most important information for a style sheet to convey in XML is whether the element should be treated as an inline or a block display item.

Here is a simple well-formed XML document.

```
<doc>
   <heading> MRI of the Lumbar Spine</heading>
   <author> Frank Boumphrey</author>
   <para> Magnetic Resonance Imaging,<acronym> MRI </acronym>, has given us
a powerful new way to look at the soft tissue of the spine...</para>
</doc>
```

We will want our heading, our author and our paragraph to be block elements. **`<acronym>`** should obviously be an inline element, so we start our style sheet:

```
doc, heading, author, para {display: block}
acronym {display: inline}
```

The display property is covered in Chapter 8, Boxes and Layers.

We will want the heading to be in larger type so we add:

```
heading {font-size: 18pt}
```

and we may also add:

```
author {font-size: 16pt; font-style: italic}
acronym {font-weight: bold}
```

This should result in output as follows:

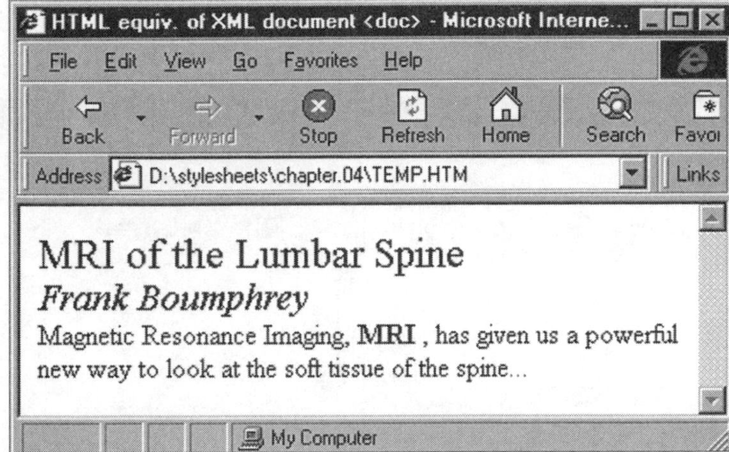

This output was produced using an XML parser, **XMLparse.exe**, developed for this book, which we will cover in detail shortly.

There are many actual and proposed style languages for XML, but the important thing to realize is that one of them must be used to get anything other than the most basic output. (If you open an XML document in IE4 it will strip off the tags and treat every element as an inline flow object.)

Linking XML Documents to Style Sheets

One proposal for linking to a style sheet is to use a processing instruction.

```
<?XML:stylesheet type="text/css" href="mri.css"?>
```

It should be possible to set up a cascade of style sheets (see Chapter 7) using similar processing instructions, and each style sheet can use an **@import** property to import further style sheets.

There is no provision in the XML spec for using a **<STYLE>** tag, and the attribute **CLASS** is not reserved in XML for applying class styling to a tag.

At time of writing the W3C is just beginning to address this issue. A note can be found at:

http://www.w3.org/TR/1998/NOTE-xml-stylesheet-19980405

An Example of Applying CSS to XML

XMLparse.exe is a simple tool developed by the author for teaching purposes. It allows you to open up an XML document, check that its structure is valid, style it and then convert it to HTML to display it. To run it, download it from the Wrox web site at **http://rapid.wrox.co.uk/books/1657** and place it in the same directory as the XML files you want to use it with. It comes complete with a **Readme.txt** file which gives more details on installation.

It should be made quite clear up front that this is just a simple teaching tool, and not suitable for any heavy manipulation of XML documents.

The utility looks like this:

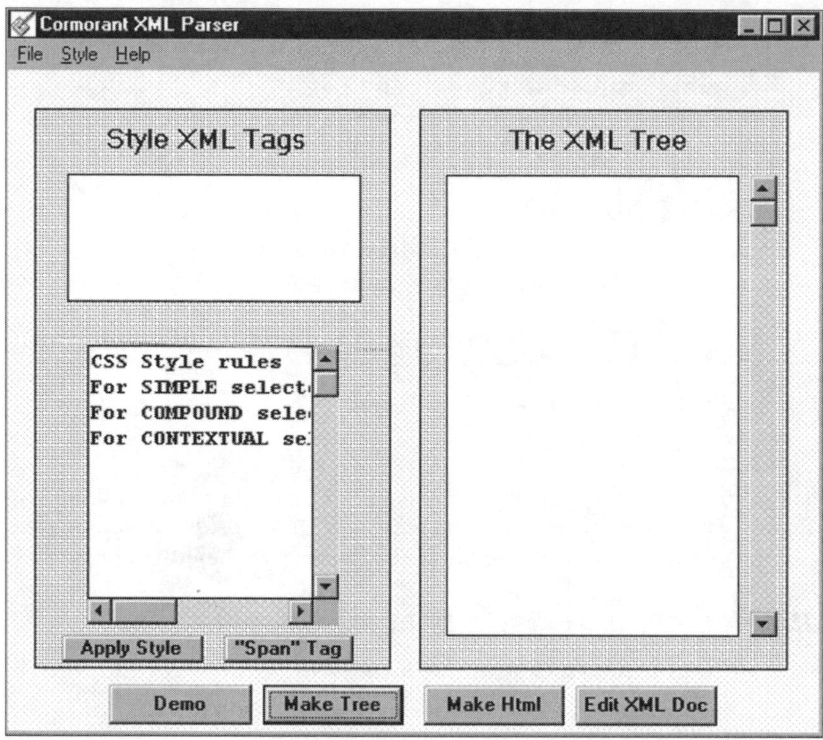

As a file to work with we will use one of the contacts which we developed a DTD for in the previous chapter. All the files used in this example can be downloaded for the Wrox site at:

`http://rapid.wrox.co.uk/books/1657`.

Here is the XML file **`ch4_ex2.xml`**.

```
<client>
   <name id="CPQ142">
      <honorific> Dr.</honorific>
      <first> Pierre</first>
      <middle> R. </middle>
      <last> LeBlanc </last>
      <nickname> Butch</nickname>
   </name>
   <phone> 440-123-4567</phone>
   <company lang="french"></company>
   <contact type="first" ><date> Jan 1992</date></contact>
   <contact type="last"><date> Dec 19 1997</date></contact>
```

```
    <attitude interest="warm"/>
    <personal> Baby Girl b. <date> Nov 1997</date>, golf mad!, handicap 7,
likes Mexican food, completely bi-lingual French and English</personal>
</client>
```

First of all we open the document in the parser, using the Open command off the File dropdown menu:

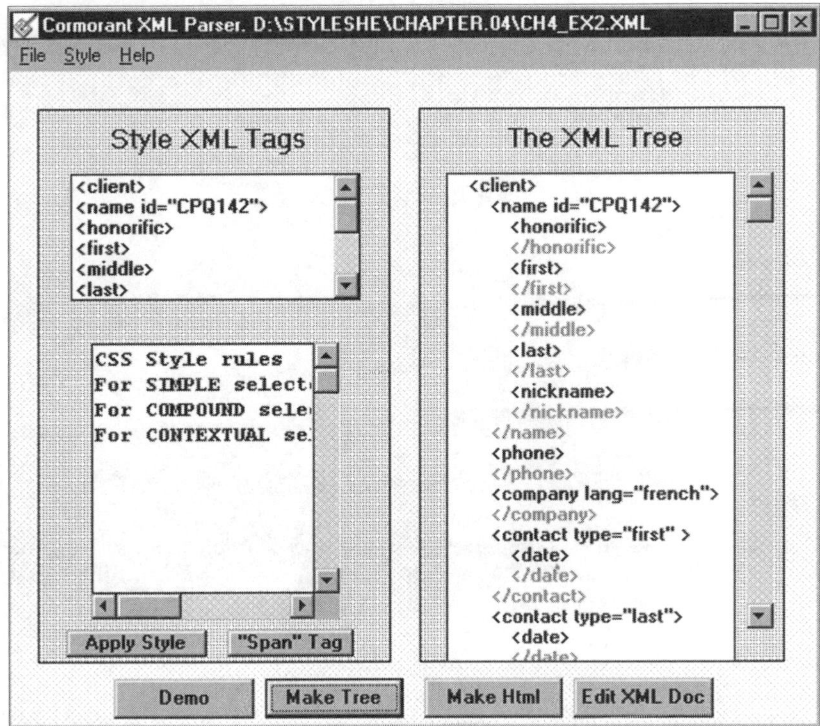

As you can see, the document is automatically parsed and a tree of the document is presented in the right hand XML Tree window.

In the upper left window a list of all the tags appear, plus simple instructions on how to make compound or contextual selectors.

Right-clicking anywhere on an opening tag in the tree will open the XML file in a window with the relevant tag highlighted.

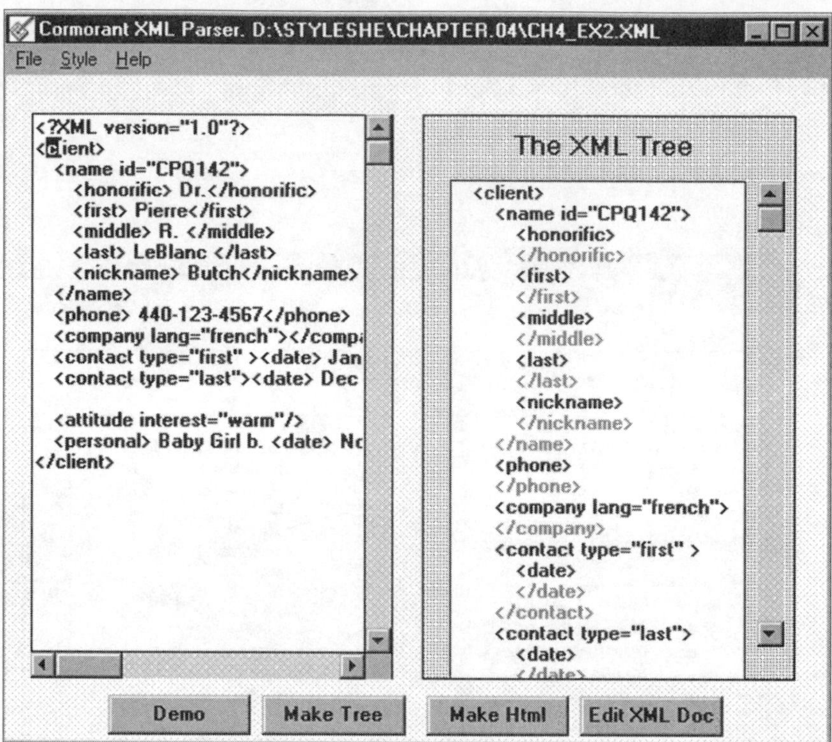

To style the document we first of all decide which of the elements should be inline elements. To make an element inline, we simply click on the name in the list box and then click on the "Span" Tag button. Note that the default is to make the element a block element.

We might decide that all the name tags and the date tag should be inline.

To apply styling to a tag we left click on the appropriate element in the Style XML Tags list box and a selector with an empty declaration will appear in the window below the box. The next screenshot shows **`personal`** being assigned a declaration of

```
{font-size:16pt;color:navy}
```

Once the rule has been entered in the empty declaration, you must click the Apply Style button to apply it. This should mean that when we convert the XML document to HTML anything contained within the **`<personal>`** tags will be displayed in 16point navy blue font.

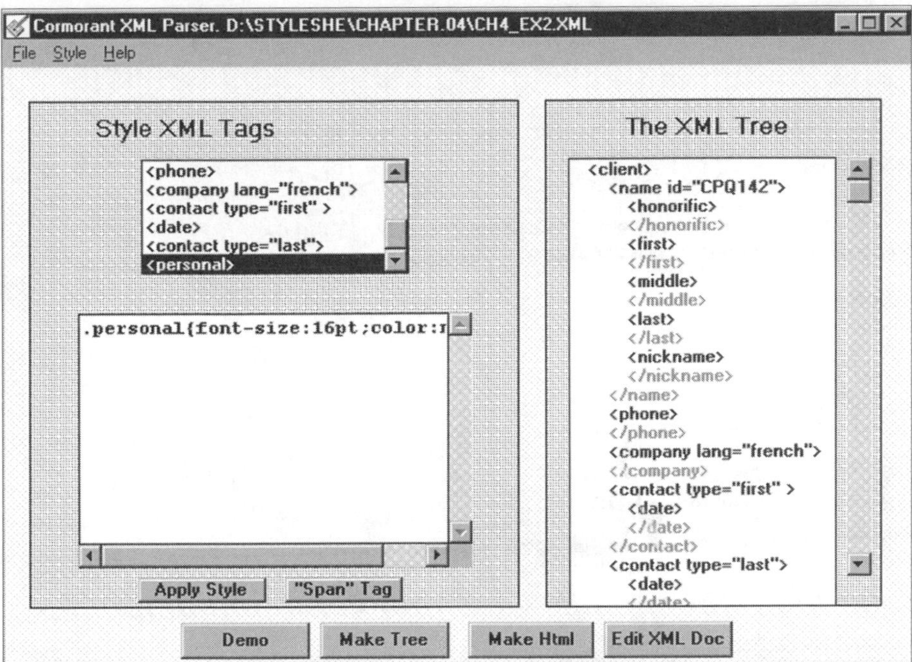

We repeat the process outlined above to apply the following styles:

- Make the last name display in bold type,
- Make the nickname display in red,
- Make the phone number and personal display in 16pt type,
- Make a contextual selector out of the **`<date>`** in **`<personal>`**, highlighting that date in red.

To convert our XML document into HTML we simply click the Make HTML button. The parser creates a **`temp.htm`** file containing the HTML code. A Notepad window will open up with our code in it. We can tweak our code any way we want, and then we use the Save As from the Notepad File menu to save it as an HTML file. We'll save this file as **`ch4_ex2.htm`**.

The parser assumes that **`Notepad.exe`** is in the same drive and at **`\windows\notepad.exe`**. If its not, as may be the case if you are running on a network, then place a copy of it there.

```
Temp.htm - Notepad
File  Edit  Search  Help

<!-- special formatting for the XML tag "<date>" -->
.personal .date{color:red;}

<!-- special formatting for the XML tag "<date>" -->
.personal{font-size:16pt;color:navy}

</STYLE>
</HEAD>
<BODY>
<DIV>
<DIV CLASS="client">
   <DIV CLASS="name">
      <SPAN CLASS="honorific"> Dr.</SPAN>
      <SPAN CLASS="first"> Pierre</SPAN>
      <SPAN CLASS="middle"> R. </SPAN>
      <SPAN CLASS="last"> LeBlanc </SPAN>
      <SPAN CLASS="nickname"> Butch</SPAN>
   </DIV>
   <DIV CLASS="phone"> 440-123-4567</DIV>
```

The screenshot above shows some of the style sheet, and how the XML tags have been converted into HTML **<DIV>** and **<SPAN>** tags with appropriate **CLASS** attributes. The screenshot below shows what the converted XML file looks like opened in Communicator.

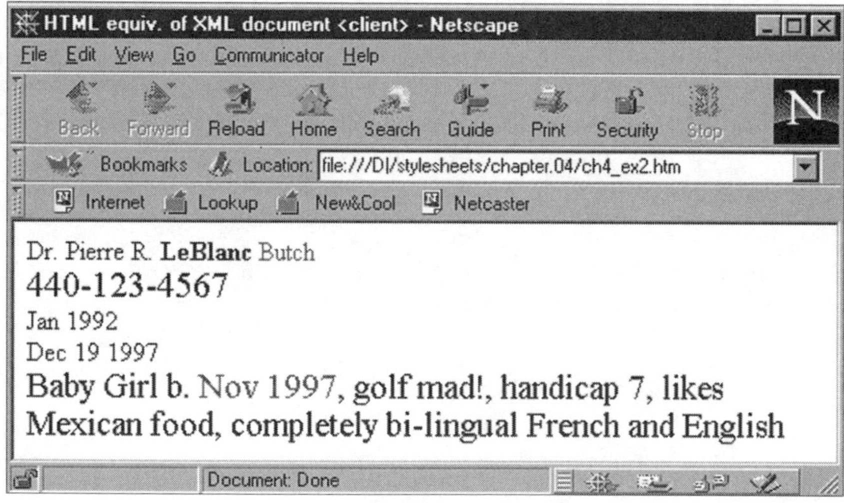

For just a little bit more, try opening up the expanded document **entit.xml** in **entit.exe**, expand it, save the expanded document as say **compxml.xml**, then open that document in **XMLParse.exe** and style it.

This is obviously a very simple example, but is typical of how XML is being used at the present time. So, we've seen how to create a complex XML document using entities, then how to style and display it using CSS. What else are we going to cover? The rest of the chapter will deal with other topics you will hear mentioned in the context of XML. We cover them briefly to give you an idea of what is involved, but don't go into any great depth, as this is not a book on XML!

Other XML Topics

To wrap up our coverage of XML let's look briefly at some of its other aspects. They are not really related to style sheets but are necessary for a full understanding of XML's capabilities, so coverage will be just sufficient to give us insight into this.

We will look at searching XML files, linking in XML, and then look briefly at some newer XML concepts, namely namespaces, XML-data, and Resource Definition Format (RDF).

Searching and Modifying XML Files

Because this is a book on style sheets and not on programming, we won't go into very much detail here. Suffice it to say that one of the major advantages of XML is its ability to act as a data repository with its semantic markup using tags and/or attributes. This same semantic markup makes it extremely easy to search the file.

Searching can either be carried out using proprietary programs, using script or, in some instances, using style sheets. Using style sheets it is possible to hide all the contents of a file except those contents that we want to display, to suppress some contents entirely, and also to alter the order of display.

Using style sheets is fine if we want to display the majority of the document. However, if we want to pick out a small part of the document (e.g. a patients allergies or blood group from a medical record) then it is better to take the coding or scripting approach.

One of the most frequently asked questions when it comes to creating a document that is going to need to be searched is–"Do I use an element or an attribute to store the semantic information?" We'll attempt to answer this now.

Attribute or Tag?

When do I use an attribute and when do I use an element in my XML document? You will be pleased to know that this debate is at least as old as SGML and although hotly argued has never been resolved. In fact, there has never ever been a list of agreed rule of thumbs!

So essentially do what seems best to you.

Having said that, here are a few points to bear in mind.

- It is easier (and faster!) for software to search for tags than attributes.
- It is easier to modify a DTD with a tag than an attribute.
- If the content is more than a very simple choice, use a tag.

- If the content could be eliminated without changing the meaning of the document, then using an attribute is OK.
- For example: **<face eyecolor="blue"></face>** is OK in a document about body parts, but if the document was about eyes then **<face><eyecolor>Blue</eyecolor></face>** is much more appropriate.
- If in doubt use a tag.

One of the technical reviewers of this book (Benoit Marchal), however, made the great point that if you are going to search a document for tags that depend on their parentage for display then attributes are the way to go. In other words, rather than looking for all **<holdings>** elements that are contained in, or are children of **<fatcats>** elements, it is better to use an attribute and look for **<holdings type="fatcat">**.

A full review of this subject can be found at:

http://www.sil.org/sgml/elementsAndAttrs.html

After a brief overview of searching and modifying, we move on to take a look at the special ways in which we can link between documents in XML.

Linking with XML

It is necessary to say right off that a link such as:

```
<A HREF= "http://www.wrox.com"> Wrox Press </A>
```

works just fine in XML! However, like any other element **A** should be declared in the DTD as should the attribute **HREF**, even though both **HREF** and **href** are reserved keywords in XML.

However, we would be much more likely to give it a more descriptive tag such as:

```
<wroxlink href= "http://www.wrox.com"> Wrox Press </wroxlink>
```

The way to declare this link in the DTD is as follows:

```
<!ELEMENT wroxlink (#PCDATA)>
<!ATTLIST wroxlink
xml:link CDATA  #FIXED "simple"
href CDATA #REQUIRED
>
```

xml:link is a reserved XML keyword to define links. Also, just to remind you, when an attribute is given the property of **FIXED** its presence is always assumed in the tag even though it may not be typed in.

Because XML must be able to operate without a DTD, if no DTD were present the link should be written with the attribute which assigns the tag as a link tag, namely:

```
<wroxlink xml:link="simple" href= "http://www.wrox.com"> Wrox Press
</wroxlink>
```

And this will tell the processor to treat the tag as a "simple link".

You will have noticed that the attribute of **simple** has been applied, and indeed both **xml:link** and **simple** are reserved keywords of XML. (Also remember that in the last chapter we saw that **:** is reserved for XML usage.)

You might think that specifying a link as **simple** implies that there are other more complicated links possible, and you are absolutely right!

As well as

- **Simple links** (with which you are thoroughly familiar via. HTML)

XML supports:

- **Extended links**
- **Group links** (supporting role)
- **Locator links** (supporting role)
- **Document links** (supporting role)

Simple and extended links are the actual link-tags that link us to other places. The other links play a supporting role to these two. We'll take a look at each of the link types in turn, but first let's look a little at some of the terminology that is used in XML links.

Some Linking Terminology

Here are some explanations and examples of linking terminology. We have used a combination of the W3C definition and our own thoughts. When W3C definitions from **http://www.w3.org/TR/WD-xml-link** are used the wording is put in italics and enclosed by a border. Plain text is commentary on the W3C definitions.

Link

An explicit relationship between two or more data objects or portions of data objects.

In other words the highlighted text (plus the tags that contain it) that you click on and the place you end up at (usually another URL) constitute a link.

Locator

Data provided as part of a link, which identifies a resource. An URL is a locator. Any URL using **http://**, **ftp://** etc. is a locator. In HTML **#NAME** and **#ID** are locators.

Resource

Basically a resource is something we can get at using a hyperlink. Clicking on blue underlined text in a legacy browser such as Mosaic would reach a resource.

In the abstract sense, a resource is an addressable service or unit of information that participates in a link. Examples include files, images, documents, programs, and query results. To be more concrete, however, a resource is anything reachable by the use of a locator in some linking element. Note that this term and its definition are taken from the basic specifications governing the World Wide Web.

Participating Resource

This is a resource that belongs to a link. All resources are potential contributors to a link; participating resources are the actual contributors to a particular link.

Basically, if a link can take you there it is a participating resource.

Local Resource

In very simple terms, if the place you end up at is in the same document as where you started it is a local resource. If in HTML we use `<A HREF= "#top">` we are referring to a local resource.

Note that the content of the linking element could be explicitly pointed to by means of a regular locator in the same linking element, in which case the resource is considered remote, not local.

Remote Resource

A resource that is in a document other than the document that contains the link. If in HTML we use `A HREF= "http://....` we are referring to a remote resource.

Sub-Resource

In HTML we have to retrieve the whole document, even if we end up at a particular part of it by using a **fragment identifier**–`A HREF= ".......htm#index">`. In XML it is possible to retrieve just part of the document. This is referred to as a sub-resource.

A portion of a resource, pointed to as the precise destination of a link. As one example, a link might specify that an entire document be retrieved and displayed, but that some specific part(s) of it is the specific linked data, to be treated in an application-appropriate manner such as indication by highlighting, scrolling, etc.

Element Tree

An element tree is a tree like the one made by `XMLparse.exe` above. It defines the relationships of the elements one to the other.

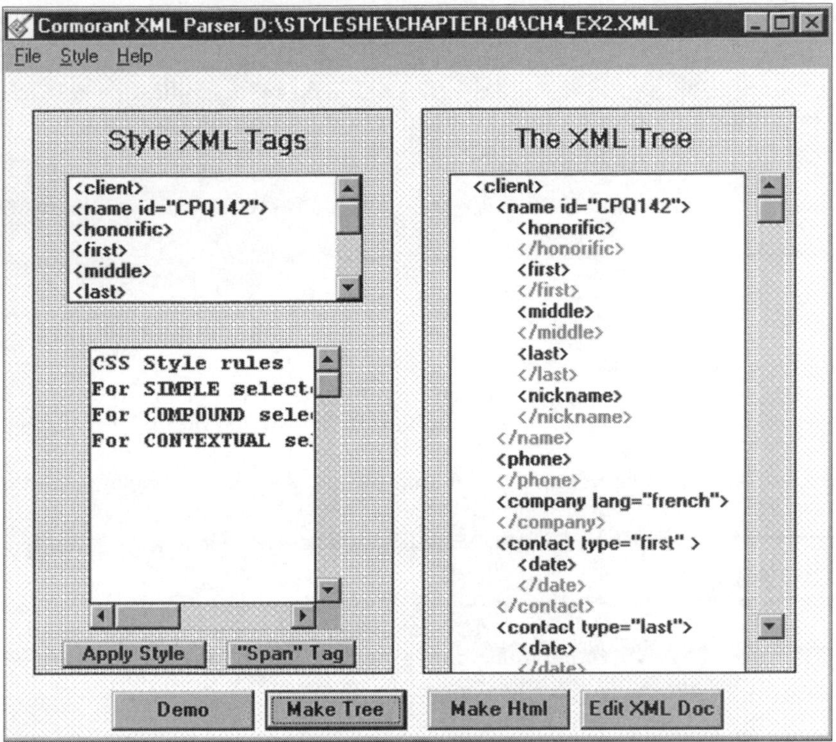

Inline Link

As defined by W3C an inline link is

> *"Abstractly, a link which serves as one of its own resources. Concretely, a link where the content of the linking element serves as a participating resource."*

This is rather a mouthful but, in practice, we all know what it means because the typical HTML **A** link is an inline link.

When we look at **extended links** we will see the difference between inline and out-of-line links.

Linking Element

Really any element that you declare in your DTD, or via an attribute to be a linking element.

Multidirectional Link

A link whose traversal can be initiated from more than one of its participating resources. Note that being able to go back after following a one-directional link does not make the link multidirectional.

Out-of-Line Link

A link whose content does not serve as one of the link's participating resources. Such links presuppose a notion like extended link groups, which indicate to application software where to look for links. Out-of-line links are generally required for supporting multidirectional traversal and for allowing read-only resources to have outgoing links.

When we look at **extended links** we will see the difference between **inline** and **out-of-line** links.

Traversal

Clicking on the Link!

The action of using a link–that is, of accessing a resource. Traversal may be initiated by a user action (for example, clicking on the displayed content of a linking element) or it can occur under program control. For example, code could automatically take you there.

That concludes our run down of linking terminology, now let's look at each of the types of link supported by XML in turn.

Simple Links

We really don't have to say anything more about simple links. Simple links are links that are essentially one way. They are inline links in that the link information is placed in the document at the place where we want the user to click.

The click will take the user to the place in the resource where we want him to go.

Extended Links

This will be a new concept to HTML folk.

Supposing that I had two paragraphs that I wanted to make inter connected, namely:

```
<P ID="para1">This idea relates to paragraph 3
</P>
<P ID="para2">This idea relates to neither paragraph 1 or 3
</P>
<P ID="para3">This idea relates to paragraph 1
</P>
```

Using simple links I would have to do the following (this is an XML document even though I have used **<P>**):

```
<P ID="para1">This idea relates to <idealink href="#para3"> paragraph 3
</idealink>
</P>
<P ID="para2">This idea relates to neither paragraph 1 or 3
</P>
<P ID="para3">This idea relates to <idealink href= "#para1">paragraph 1
</idealink>
</P>
```

And this works quite well but can get quite complicated for a large number of related ideas.

XML allows us to place the links away from the actual paragraphs by the using the reserved attribute value **extended** keyword on an element. These are now out-of-line links.

```
<relatedideas xml:link = "extended">
<idea href= "para1"/>
<idea href= "para3"/>
</relatedideas>
```

```
<P ID="para1">This idea relates to paragraph 3
</P>
<P ID="para2">This idea relates to neither paragraph 1 or 3
</P>
<P ID="para3">This idea relates to paragraph 1
</P>
```

The **<idea>** tags are locator tags–see below for an explanation.

These links can be anywhere, not even in the same document, and the main advantage from the point of view of a web site manager is that it makes link updating easier to handle.

Of course less work for the human means more work for the computer, it now has to locate where the links are. Every time it sees an element with an **xpointer** (see below) or a locator attribute (see below) it has to ask itself the question "where is the link information?" and go out and find it.

To put the above in a DTD simply use the following.

```
<!ELEMENT relatedideas  (#PCDATA)>
<!ATTLIST relatedideas
xml:link CDATA  #FIXED "extended"
href CDATA#REQUIRED
>
```

Next we look at the last three types of link, group links, locator links and document links, before moving on to cover XPointers.

Group, Locator and Document Links

These concepts will also be new to HTML folk.

In HTML we are used to linking to one place in a single document. In a group link we are essentially telling the processor here is a link, it could be contained in any of the following documents. Go find it please.

Group Links

Group links are used with extended links and simply tell an XML processor to look for links in a group of documents. In the above example

```
<relatedideas xml:link = "extended">
<idea href= "para1"/>
<idea href= "para3"/>
</relatedideas>
```

para1 may be in document **abc.xml**, and **para3** may be in document **xyz.xml** document.

```
<docgroup xml:link= "group">
<doc href= "abc.xml"/>
<doc href= "xyz.xml"/>
<docgroup>
```

The code set out above tells the processor which documents to search looking for the relevant links. The **<doc>** tag is a document link–see below.

Locator Links

We have already seen locators in action but we didn't know it because we hadn't seen the DTD! If there was no DTD we would have had to write:

```
<relatedideas xml:link = "extended">
   <idea xml:link = "locator" href= "para1"/>
   <idea xml:link = "locator" href= "para3"/>
</relatedideas>
```

Even with a DTD, putting in the attribute is not wrong, so it is probably always better to put **xml:link="locator"** in tags designed to be links.

Document Links

Again we have already seen this in action, but were not privy to the DTD.

```
<docgroup xml:link= "group">
   <doc href= "abc.xml"/>
   <doc href= "xyz.xml"/>
<docgroup>
```

can be written:

```
<docgroup xml:link= "group">
   <doc xml:link = "document" href= "abc.xml"/>
   <doc xml:link = "document" href= "xyz.xml"/>
<docgroup>
```

Again we can do no wrong by always including **xml:link="document"** in those links indicating the location of a document.

Shorthand Tags

It is likely that the XML browsers may accept the following rendition of the above example in a well-formed document, although reserving the document element may prove troublesome!

```
<extended>
   <locator href= "para1"/>
   <locator href= "para3"/>
</extended>

<group>
   <document href= "abc.xml"/>
   <document href= "xyz.xml"/>
<group>
```

Finally, in this section on linking, let's take a look at Xpointers.

XPointers

We will round off our brief overview of XML links with a word or two on XPointers.

Essentially XPointers allow us to identify fragments of a document.

We are already familiar with an XPointer from HTML. An XPointer allows us to identify a specific place in the document tree.

If in HTML we write:

```
<A HREF= "#para1"> Go to paragraph 1</A>
```

We are using an XPointer to take us to the document location marked by:

```
<A NAME= "para1" ></A>
```

or preferably as this is better practice:

```
<A ID= "para1" ></A>.
```

In XML an XPointer can take various different forms.

- **`root()`**–If this identifier is used the link goes to the root element of the document.
- **`origin`**–See the spec (3.2.2) for the definition of this term. Essentially it is the start of the document from which the link originates.
- **`id(name)`**–If the pointer is **`id(para1)`**, it would point to paragraph one in the previous sections example if the **`<A ID="para1"></A>`** form had been used.
- **`html(NAMEVALUE)`**–If the pointer is **`html(para1)`**, it would point to paragraph one in the previous sections example if the **`<A NAME= "para1"></A>`** form had been used.

It can also take the form of a relative location using the document tree's child, ancestor, descendant, and sibling information. Here is the example taken from the XPointers working draft:

http://www.w3.org/TR/1998/WD-xptr-19980303 (3.3.3)

```
<!DOCTYPE_SPEECH_[
<!ELEMENT_SPEECH_(#PCDATA|SPEAKER|DIRECTION)*>
<!ATTLIST_SPEECH
     ID    ID    #IMPLIED>
<!ELEMENT_SPEAKER_(#PCDATA)>
<!ELEMENT_DIRECTION_(#PCDATA)>
]>
<SPEECH_ID="a27"><
   SPEAKER>Polonius</SPEAKER>
   <DIRECTION>crossing_downstage</DIRECTION>
      Fare_you_well,my_lord.
   <DIRECTION>To_Ros.</DIRECTION>
      You_go_to_seek_Lord_Hamlet?_There he_is.
</SPEECH>

"The following XPointers select various sub-resources within this resource:

id(a27).child(2,DIRECTION)
Selects the second "DIRECTION" element (whose content is " To Ros.").
id(a27).child(2,#element)
Selects the second child element (that is, the first direction, whose
content is "crossing downstage").
id(a27).child(2,#text)
Selects the second text region , "Fare you well, my lord." (The line break
between the SPEAKER and DIRECTION elements is the first text region.)"
```

We are familiar with the following format

```
<A HREF= "abc.htm#para1"></A>
```

but in XML if we can use this form and we can also use the pipestem as below.

```
<LINK HREF= "abc.htm#para1"></A>
<LINK HREF= "abc.htm|para1">
```

The difference between the hashmark "**#**" and the pipestem "**|**" is in what is retrieved.

With the hashmark all of the document must be retrieved, with the pipestem how much is retrieved is left up to the processor, perhaps guided by script.

The XPointers syntax also allows us to grab and display chunks of the document, but this is beyond the scope of this simple overview.

So, we've covered searching and modifying documents and linking to and from documents and parts of documents, in the final part of this section we'll look at three XML hot topics: namespaces, XML-data and Resource Definition Format (RDF). We'll begin with namespaces.

XML Hot Topics

The only problem with writing about hot topics in a book is that by the time they are read they may well not be all that hot! However, these topics will probably stick around for a while, and are terms that are often bandied about (quite often without any comprehension as to what they mean!), so some simple explanations and definitions are given here to assist you in your further reading.

Namespaces

It is difficult to write good DTDs, as I'm sure you have discovered, thus there is tremendous benefit to be derived from being able to reference these DTDs with a unique name.

Furthermore it may be desirable to author a document which uses chunks marked up with tags from different DTDs. Rather than write a new DTD, why not have a way to associate the elements in the chunk with its own DTD?

Namespaces is a means to accomplish this. The W3C working document can be found at:

http://www.w3.org/TR/1998/WD-xml-names-19980327

For namespaces to work there must be unique identity expressed in a namespace processing instruction.

This processing instruction takes the form:

```
<?xml:namespace ns=[uri] prefix=[ "string"]?>
```

Any unique identifier can be used, often referred to as a URN (Universal Resource Number) but a URI is a good way to do this.

This is placed in the prolog after the XML declaration (if any) and before the DTD (if any).

Here is an example:

```
<!--XML declaration goes here-->
<?xml:namespace ns='http://www.wrox.com' prefix='wx'?>
<?xml:namespace ns='http://www.hypermedic.com' prefix='hm'?>

<!--DTD goes here-->
```

This would identify a DTD at Wrox and Hypermedic respectively.

Now to associate any tag with the appropriate DTD just use the correct prefix, as in this document:

```
<hm:doc>
   <hm:internetbooks> There are several books published on this subject
      <wx:book title= "Instant HTML"/>
      <wx:book title= "Instant JavaScript"/>
   </hm:internetbooks books>
</hm:doc>
```

The processor should look up the DTD for each designated tag and check the tag against the relevant DTD. This can obviously save a tremendous amount of work for the author.

This is a very simple overview of this developing subject.

Another way to share DTDs is to use a technology called **Architectural Forms**. We can't go in to this subject as even a basic description would be somewhat lengthy, but when you see the name bandied about, at least you know what the term refers to.

Architectural forms are part of the hytime standard:

http://www.hytime.com

A tutorial on architectural forms can be found at:

http://www.isogen.com/papers/archintro.html

XML-Data

XML-data is a means of describing schemas using XML syntax.

The XML-data specification can be found at:

http://www.w3.org/TR/1998/NOTE-XML-data-0105/

Schemas define the characteristics of classes of objects. The DTD is a good example of a schema in that the DTD defines the classes of the elements and the classes of attributes for each element. XML-data is a means of describing this syntax in XML.

Let's see what this means in practical terms by taking our example of a DTD. Here is a simple XML document with its DTD:

```
<?XML version="1.0"?>
<!DOCTYPE book [
<!ELEMENT book (author+, title? )>
<!ELEMENT author (#PCDATA)
<!ELEMENT title (#PCDATA)

]

<book>
   <author> Frank Boumphrey</author>
   <title> Professional style sheets</title>
</book>
```

This DTD tells us that the **<book>** element should contain one or more authors, and/or one title, i.e. the title is optional. XML-data would allow us to express this DTD in XML using certain keywords. For simplicity we will put the cart before the horse. First we will look at how it would be expressed in XML-data, and then we will explain how it was compiled.

```
<?XML version='1.0' ?>
     <?xml:namespace name="urn:uuid:BDC6E3F0-6DA3-11d1-A2A3-00AA00C14882/"
as="s"/?>
     <s:schema id='ExampleSchema'>
       <!-- schema goes here.-->

<elementType id= "book">
   <element type= "#author" occours= "ONEORMORE"/>
   <element type= "#title" occours= "OPTIONAL"/>
</elementType>

     </s:schema>

<book>
<author> Frank Boumphrey</author>
<title> Professional style sheets</title>
</book>
```

Note the following points:

The DTD for this schema is identified by a name space URN! (and if you ever want to use XML-data this is the exact URN you must use). The syntax used is a little different from what we discussed, but the meaning should be apparent to you.

- **<s:schema id='ExampleSchema'>** tags enclose our DTD substitute.
- The reserved key word **<elementType>** identifies the root document. (Note the camel back notation, XML is case sensitive.)
- The reserved key word **<element>** identifies the other tags with reserved attributes **type** and **occurs**.
- The values for **occurs** can be: **REQUIRED**, **OPTIONAL**, **ZEROORMORE**, or **ONEORMORE**.
- All these are defined in the DTD contained at the namespace URN.

I must say that personally I find the DTD easier to deal with, but XML-data concepts can be expanded to other forms of schema, and thus have the potential to be a universal language for schema. A good analogy is that HTML is to SGML what DTDs are to XML-data.

Resource Definition Format (RDF)

When the US Congress became concerned about Internet pornography, a way of being able to identify and define the content of websites called PICS–or Platform for Internet Content Selection was quickly devised.

The laws were rapidly struck down as being unconstitutional, but it was soon realized that the work done on PICS could be expanded to a generalized description and identification of DATA, and thus RDF–Resource Definition Format–came into being. And who says that politicians never accomplish anything good?

Quite simply RDF is about metadata. Metadata is data about data, and RDF would allow machines to read and understand data. This can lead to all kinds of interesting applications such as "bots" that can search web sites and correlate information for us.

The following references provide a good resource for those interested in pursuing this subject:

`http://www.w3.org/TR/NOTE-rdfarch`

This is an account of the various data formats.

Whereas:

`http://www.w3.org/TR/NOTE-rdf-simple-intro`

and

`http://www.w3.org/DesignIssues/Metadata`

are, respectively, a simple and a more lengthy account of metadata.

Summary

In this chapter we learned;

- How to create a complex XML document using entities
- How to style and display an XML document using CSS and HTML
- How to search and modify XML documents
- How to link XML documents

We then looked at some of the latest topics in XML, including how DTDs can be recycled. We also looked briefly at namespaces, XML-data, and RDF.

In this and the last chapter, we looked at XML, the powerful new language for marking up documents and describing data. In the next chapter, we will have a first look at XSL, a style sheet language created for use with XML. XSL is much more powerful than CSS in many ways, especially in the way that it can select items for styling based on the document tree, can select create and order flow objects, and can use script in presentation.

That will be the end of part 1, our basic introduction. In part 2 we will look in some detail at both CSS1 and CSS2 and how the specifications can be used to style both HTML and XML documents.

References

This is the W3C recommendation for XML dated 28 Feb 1998:

http://www.w3.org/TR/1998/REC-xml-19980210

The working document on namespaces can be found at:

http://www.w3.org/TR/1998/WD-xml-names-19980327

The following are the notes and working documents dealing with Links and Xpointers:

http://www.w3.org/TR/WD-xml-link

and

http://www.w3.org/TR/1998/WD-xptr-19980303

The Note on XML-data is at:

http://www.w3.org/TR/1998/NOTE-XML-data-0105/

References on some general reading on XML including PICs and XML are:

http://www.w3.org/TR/NOTE-rdfarch

http://www.w3.org/TR/NOTE-rdf-simple-intro

http://www.w3.org/DesignIssues/Metadata

The Dublin Core Metadata is one specific and well-advanced proposal for meta data for use in libraries and museums. The documents are very readable and can be found at:

http://purl.org/metadata/dublin_core/main.html

Exercises

1. Write a simple XML file that will need a legal disclaimer and/or a warning header.
2. Reference these headers using entities, and write the appropriate prolog.
3. Write the separate files for the disclaimer and the warning. Make both an illegal (i.e. non-nesting) and legal XML file so that you understand the difference.

5

Basic XSL Style Sheets

In this chapter we will take a first look at XSL (e**X**tensible **S**tyle **L**anguage): the new style language being designed for XML.

We will:

- Examine again the usage and needs for XSL
- Look at the learning tools available
- Examine how XSL works
- Take another look at flow objects
- Analyze a construction rule
- Look at some of the other simpler rules with examples
- Match some XML documents with XSL

CSS v. XSL v. DSSSL

We saw in the last chapter that XML can work quite well with CSS, so why the need for XSL? XSL is designed to be used with XML so that XML can take advantage of the flexibility that comes from breaking free of the HTML straight jacket. CSS is primarily a declarative language and, apart from the **`visibility`** and **`none`** properties, allows little control over content or the order of its appearance. Also it's not extensible by the user. XSL on the other hand, although primarily declarative, can be extended using ECMAScript language. ECMA is an acronym for European Computer Manufacturers Association and is an attempt to create a vendor neutral standard scripting language based on JavaScript. XSL uses XML syntax and creates its own flow objects, so it can be used for advanced formatting such as rearranging, reformatting and sorting elements. This enables the same XML document to be used to create several sub document views. XSL also adds provisions for the formatting of elements based on their context in the document, allows for the generation of text, and the definition of formatting macros.

DSSSL and its subset DSSSL-0 can also do this but there were flaws. The main one is highlighted in the following quote from the Seybold report on Internet publishing which welcomed XSL:

"DSSSL proved to be too hard; a simpler subset that applies the principles of rule-based formatting to the Web (which right now needs it more than print) makes a whole lot of sense."

Is it likely then that XSL will replace CSS and DSSSL? In the case of CSS the answer is no because CSS is simpler to use and its declarative style is ideal for multimedia and HTML. In the case of DSSSL, it will continue to be used in the print industry and elsewhere because it has advanced capabilities that XSL does not have.

A fair analogy is that CSS is to XSL what HTML is to JavaScript, and XSL is to DSSSL what JavaScript is to a full programming language.

XSL is only at the earliest stages of implementation, and it is likely that its capabilities will be expanded, but at present it has no provisions for columns and other such features. Also, although there are an increasing number of tools, there is at the time of writing no browser implementation for either XML or XSL, every thing has to be converted to HTML first.

> *A native browser implementation of XML will be able to take an XML file plus a style sheet and will be able to down load the files, and display them in the browser window. So an XML enabled browser will take* **`yourfile.xml`***, which makes reference to the style of* **`yourfile.xsl`** *or* **`yourfile.css`** *and simply display them without having to convert them to HTML or manipulate them with code. This is, of course, what the current HTML browsers do with* **`myfile.htm`** *and* **`myfile.css`**

By comparison the CSS1 specification is fairly mature and when used with HTML, much of it is implemented in the current four series browsers–even if it is implemented incorrectly in many cases. The promise is that there will be complete implementation of CSS1in the next versions of the main two browsers and in Opera version 4.0.

> *With the recent release of the Mozilla code for the Netscape 5 version, it is clear that this will have native support for XML and CSS. It is likely that the other browsers will follow suit.*

XSL Tools

It is expected that many tools will come on to the market over the next year, and that the first XML compatible browsers will give some support for XSL. At present the available tools convert XML/XSL to HTML/CSS and are really just learning tools.

There are two excellent simple tools available; Jeremie Miller's **Sparse** which operates in JavaScript and thus works on any system, and Microsoft's **msxsl.exe** which is available either as an ActiveX control or as a command line executable.

It is recommended that if possible you put both of these on your computer to work through the examples. In the process of showing you how to load these tools we will get a little ahead of ourselves. Don't worry for now about the actual meaning of the parts of the XSL file, just copy or paste them into your text editor. For those who don't like to do this just skip ahead to a later section entitled *XSL Construction Rules*, and read that first.

Sparse by Jeremie Miller

You can run this directly off the Internet by going to

`http://www.jeremie.com/Dev/XSL/`

However, we recommend that you run it off your hard drive. You can either download it from the url given above by following the instructions below, or from the Wrox web site at **`http://rapid.wrox.co.uk/books/1657`**.

1. Create a folder called "**`jmsparse`**" (or whatever you fancy really)
2. Open the above url, and save it as "**`sparse.htm`**"
3. Open **`http://www.jeremie.com/Dev/XSL/sparse.js`** and save it in the same folder as **`sparse.htm`**.
4. Open **`http://www.jeremie.com/Dev/XML/xparse.js`** and save it in the same folder as **`sparse.htm`**.
5. Open **`sparse.htm`** in your text editor and change **`<script src="/Dev/XML/xparse.js">`** at about line 37 to **`<script src="xparse.js">`**
6. Change **`<textarea name="xml" rows="10" cols="70">`** to read **`<textarea name="xml" rows="20" cols="70">`** at about row 82
7. Change **`<textarea name="xsl" rows="10" cols="70">`** to read **`<textarea name="xsl" rows="20" cols="70">`** at about row 90

The last two are not necessary, but you will find it easier to work with the larger text area.

Open **`sparse.htm`** in your browser, and you'll see two text entry windows, one headed XML: and the other headed XSL:, populated with example text and a Process button at the bottom of the page.

To run the parser you just have to type your XML in the XML text area, your XSL in the XSL text area, and hit the Process button. An alert will come up with the HTML/CSS code on it. Either press the Enter key or the OK button and a separate browser window will open with your output.

It is difficult to run large examples on this and it is essentially a teaching tool, but hopefully Jeremie will port it to Java. It has the advantage over the Microsoft tool (and mine come to mention it) in that it is cross platform. All this is true at the time of writing, but things do change, and Sparse is continually being upgraded. If you have any difficulties check Jeremie's website, or the Wrox website under the heading Tools.

Using Sparse

Sparse takes an XML file and an XSL file, and combines them to produce a styled HTML document. Let's see how this works. If you've got the **sparse.htm**, **sparse.js** and **xsparse.js** downloaded and in a directory on your hard drive, load **sparse.htm** into your browser. Delete the example code and paste this code into the XML window;

```
<?XML VERSION='1.0'?>
<xdoc>
<greeting>Hello XSL</greeting>
</xdoc>
```

and this code into the XSL window;

```
<rule>
<root/>
<HTML>
<BODY>
 <children/>
</BODY>
</HTML>
</rule>

<!--put all your rules between the italiscized headings-->

<rule>

<target-element type="greeting"/>
<DIV color="maroon" font-size="20pt">
Wow. Look you can add text!!
<BR/>
<HR/>
<children/>

</DIV>
</rule>

<!--make sure you end with this, although extraneous it is necessary to
enable the code to run properly-->

<rule><target-element/><children/></rule>
```

At the time of writing the rules must be put between the italicized headings for it to work properly. This may well not be necessary by the time you read this as the parser is being improved every day.

Click on the Process button at the bottom of the screen and first of all the HTML produced will be displayed as follows;

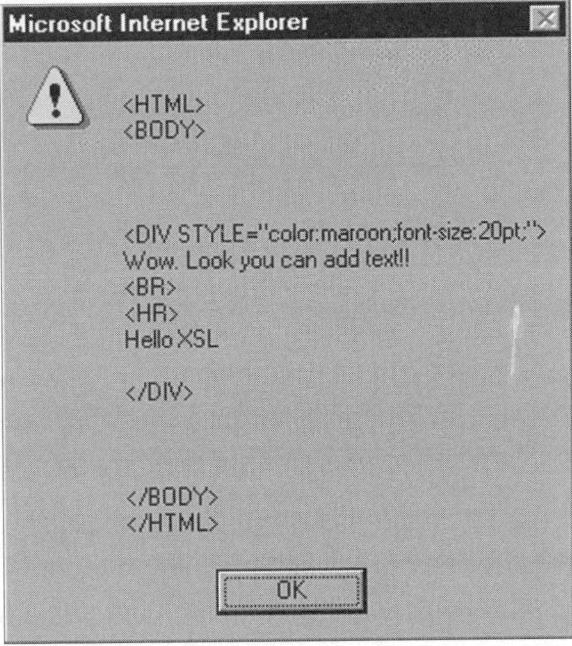

Click the OK button on the dialog illustrated above, and a new browser window will be opened up to display the HTML just created.

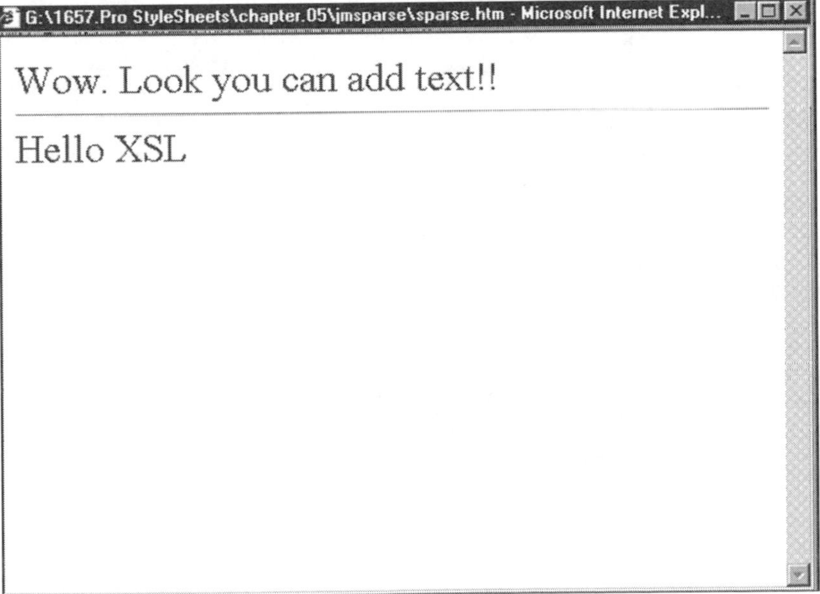

The Microsoft XSL processor does the same thing–let's take a look at how you set it up and use it.

The Microsoft XSL Processor

The Microsoft XSL processor can be downloaded from:

http://www.microsoft.com/xml

At the time of writing, you have to navigate a little from this initial address. First, hit the XSL style sheet link. Then leap to the MS XSL processor link. Then move swiftly to the Microsoft XSL command line utility. Here you will happily find a link to the Microsoft XSL Processor.

It only runs on Windows 95, Windows NT (x86 only) and on Internet Explorer 4.0 or later. It is available as one of the following two flavors:

1. As a command-line utility that, when given an XML document and a XSL style sheet, generates an HTML document using the inline **STYLE** attribute.
2. As an ActiveX control which allows display within a web page.

Download the command-line utility, and the sample files for both utilities. We'll cover downloading the ActiveX control shortly. The XSL tutorial is also well worth reading.

Using the Command-line Utility

Create a directory **xslproc** then download **msxsl.exe** (following the instructions we outlined above). It is a self unzipping file. Download the sample files and try them out later. First, try a similar example to the one we used above in the Sparse demonstration. Type the following code into a text editor and save it as **hixsl.xml**

```
<?XML VERSION='1.0'?>
<xdoc>
<greeting>Hello XSL</greeting>
</xdoc>
```

All pretty dull so far, but hang on a minute, mix it with the following style sheet and see what happens. Don't worry what it all means for now just copy it into a text editor and save it as **hixsl.xsl**. You can download these files from **http://rapid.wrox.co.uk/books/1657** if you want to save yourself some typing.

```
<xsl>
<rule>
<target-element type="greeting"/>
<DIV color="maroon">
Wow. Look you can add text!
<BR/>
<HR/>
Horizontal rules!
<HR/>
<children/>
<HR/>
```

```
<children/>
<BR/>
<children/>
<BR/>
<children/>
<BR/>
And clone as many children as you want! (move over Dolly my old chum)
</DIV>
</rule>
</xsl>
```

Now this may not seem to exciting to you, but if like me you have spent the previous few months trying to figure out what works in what version of who's browser, it' s pretty heady stuff.

From the command-line, you then need to run the following:

```
c:\xslproc\msxsl -i hixsl.xml -s hixsl.xsl -o hixsl.htm
```

For those of you too young to remember what a command-line is–in Windows 95 go to Start-Run, type the following in exactly (or substitute. whatever directory you have your files in), then hit the OK button.

As you have probably gathered **-i** is the input XML file, **-s** is the XSL style sheet and **-o** is the HTML output.

A file called **hixsl.htm** will have been created in the **xslproc** directory. Load it up in your text editor to see what it looks like.

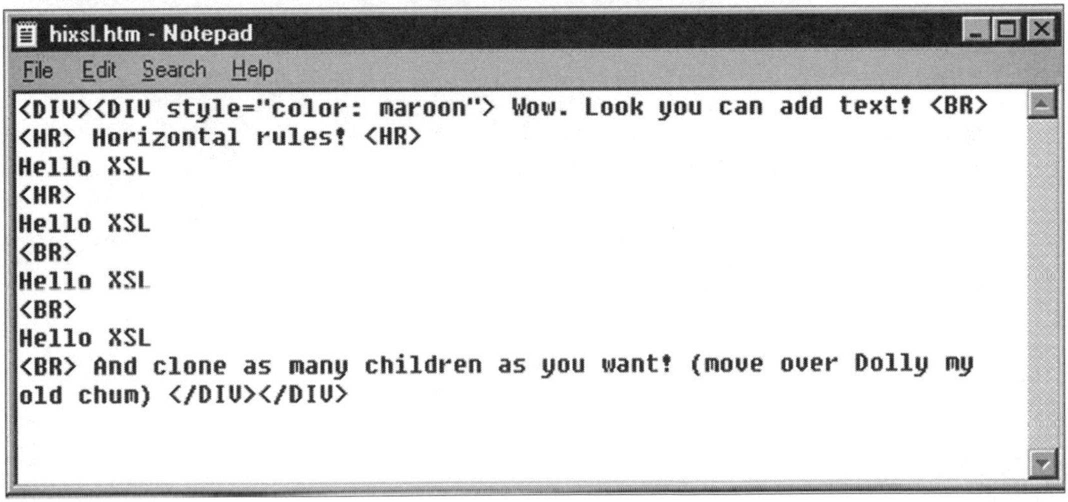

```
hixsl.htm - Notepad
File  Edit  Search  Help
<DIV><DIV style="color: maroon"> Wow. Look you can add text! <BR>
<HR> Horizontal rules! <HR>
Hello XSL
<HR>
Hello XSL
<BR>
Hello XSL
<BR>
Hello XSL
<BR> And clone as many children as you want! (move over Dolly my
old chum) </DIV></DIV>
```

Interesting huh? Note how the MS processor has converted it to HTML with inline style rules. Now run it in your browser and you will get the following screenshot.

The actual details of how the manipulation is done will be explained later.

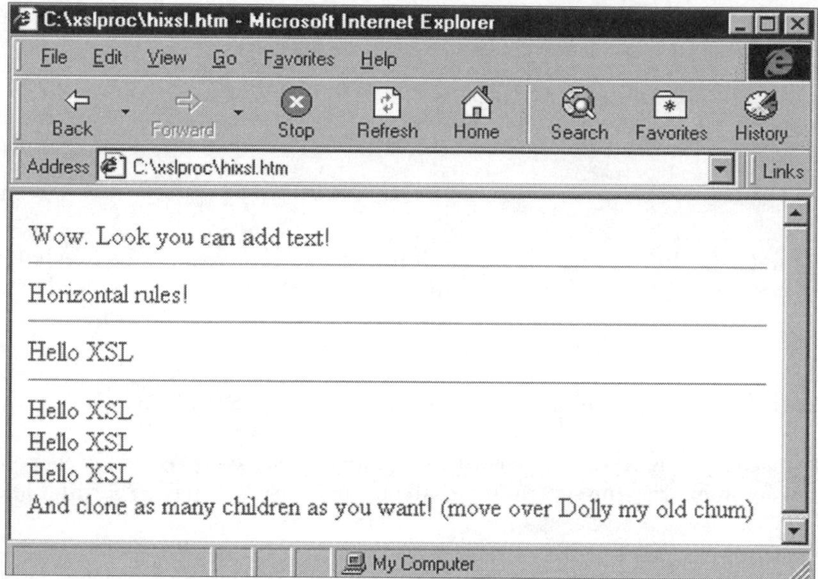

Using the ActiveX Control

To use the ActiveX control, you must place the ActiveX object in your web page. To do this you need to type or paste the following into your text editor. Save it as **actx.htm** in the same directory as **hixsl.xml** and **hixsl.xsl**.

> *This is just to remind you to use a standard text editor and not a word processor for all your examples. If you must use a word processor, make sure that you save the examples as ASCII text, but even here you may run into problems because the quotation marks may be saved incorrectly, so use Notepad or its equivalent.*

```
<HTML>
<HEAD>
<TITLE>MS ActiveX control</TITLE>

<SCRIPT FOR="window" EVENT="onload">
        var xslHTML = XSLControl.htmlText;
        document.all.item("xslTarget").innerHTML = xslHTML;
</SCRIPT>

</HEAD>

<BODY>


<OBJECT ID="XSLControl"
                CLASSID="CLSID:2BD0D2F2-52EC-11D1-8C69-0E16BC000000"
                CODEBASE="http://www.microsoft.com/xml/xsl/msxsl.cab"
```

```
                STYLE="display:none">
<PARAM NAME="documentURL" VALUE="hixsl.xml">
<PARAM NAME="styleURL" VALUE="hixsl.xsl">

</OBJECT>
<DIV id="xslTarget"></DIV>
</BODY>
</HTML>
```

Open **actx.htm** in your browser, making sure you are online at the time. The code will cause the ActiveX control to be downloaded and installed automatically. The following 3 DLLs will be registered:

- **MSXSL.DLL**
- **XSLCTRL.DLL**
- **ATL.DLL** (if you don't already have it.)

After you have downloaded the DLLs it is not necessary to be online to run the HTML files. This is what the page will look like in your browser, once the download is complete.

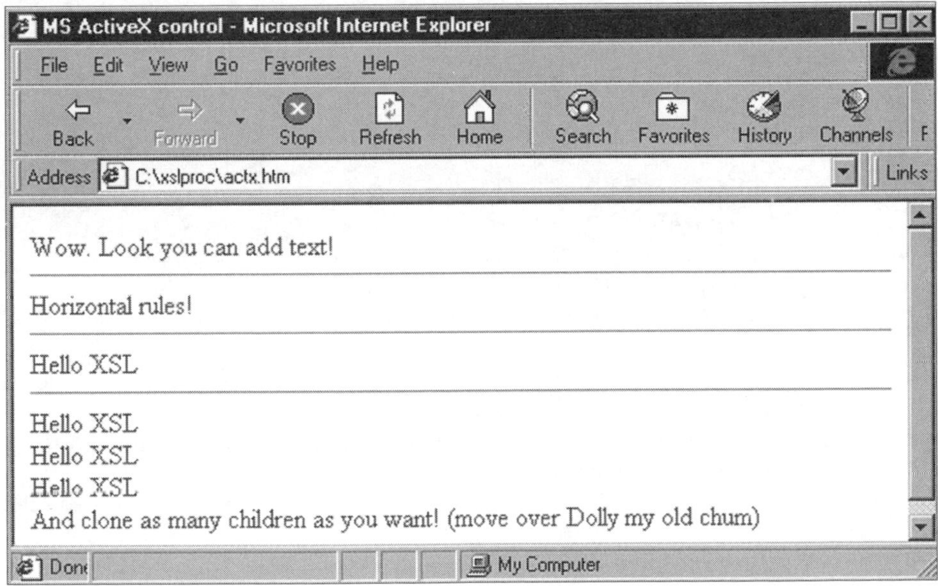

The **<PARAM>** tags point to the URLs of your files. (The files can be anywhere, but for simplicity put them all in the same directory), and **<SCRIPT>** inserts the HTML into your page at:

```
<DIV id="xslTarget"></DIV>
```

You can, in fact, use this same file to run any of the examples, just change the name of the files in the **<PARAM>** tags.

A Note on Experimentation

Experimentation is one of the best ways to learn. If you are running Windows 95 consider using the following process.

- In the Win95 command line type up your command
- Open the HTML output in your browser
- Open the XSL file in your text editor.

Now you can make changes to the XSL file, save them, rewrite your HTML file simply by clicking on the OK button of the Run command-line. You can view the results by refreshing your browser. Each of the above cycles takes no more than 3 or 4 seconds allowing you to rapidly review all your changes and giving you a feel for what you can and cannot accomplish.

In downloading and examining our tools we got a little ahead of ourselves. Let's first examine how XSL works and how it is different from CSS.

How XSL works with Flow Objects

An XML or HTML document creates flow objects. For example, the following snippet of HTML code contains three flow objects:

```
<H3>A heading</H3>
<HR>
<P>A paragraph containing text</P>
```

Actually to be pedantic, each word, or even each character could be treated as a flow object, indeed in style languages such as DSSSL they are so treated, so we should really refer to macro-flow objects. However–unless otherwise stated–by a flow object we mean a separate element.

CSS just acts on the individual flow objects. XSL, on the other hand, can create its own flow objects thus providing immense flexibility. This was shown in the example above, where a single flow object in the XML file, when combined with the XSL file, was used to create nine HTML flow objects! (we are not even counting the **
s as flow objects here). As we shall see in the next section, it does this via the **action part of a style rule.

The concept of a flow object can be a little difficult to grasp. Essentially, they are just objects that the user-agent creates for display in a window. If you have difficulty with flow objects, you may want to jump ahead to Chapter 7 and read about them in a little more detail.

The current processors convert these flow objects into HTML flow objects for display in the current generation of browsers. We covered this in some detail in the previous chapter. However, this should be looked at as an interim solution, as it is likely that in the near future, (and in this business, near is probably closer than you think), browsers will not have to go through this intermediary stage.

The following box diagrams illustrate this process. Note how in CSS no new flow objects are created or destroyed, they merely have styling applied. In XSL, however, not only is styling applied, but the flow object itself can be manipulated, added to, or even altered beyond all recognition!

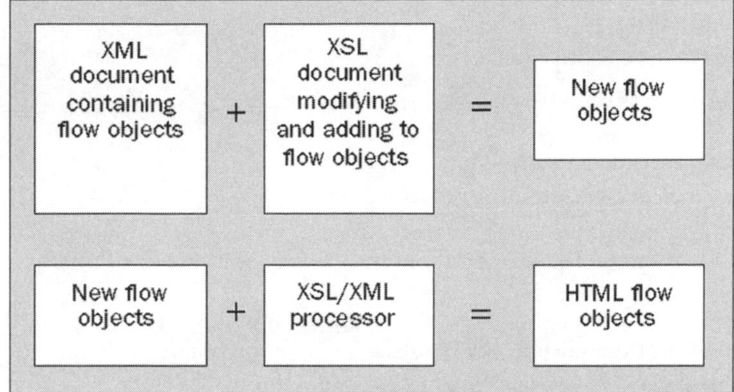

The above diagram shows how XSL can modify the flow objects in an XML document. Note that the conversion to HTML flow objects is only a temporary expedient until XML compliant browsers are developed.

The below diagram displays how CSS styles the flow objects in an XML document. No new flow objects are created. Note that the conversion to HTML flow objects is again only a temporary expedient until XML compliant Browsers are developed.

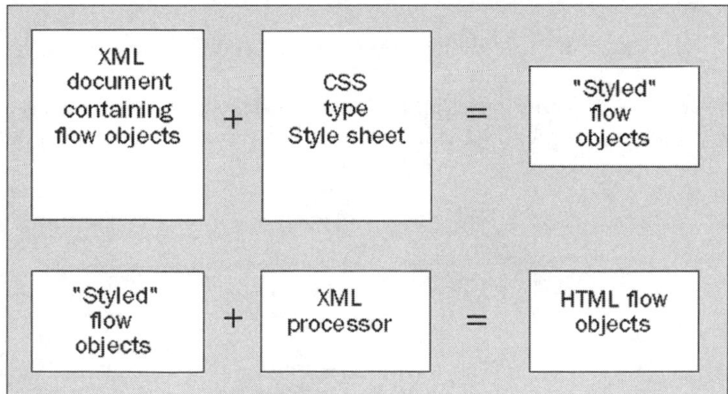

XSL Construction Rules

An XSL style sheet is an XML document, so it has to follow the XML rules for well-formedness. This basically means that there must be a unique opening and closing tag (in practice **`<xsl>....</xsl>`** suffices), and all the other tags must be nested.

The basic XSL building block is a construction rule that describes how the original XML element is to be transformed into a displayable flow object. It consists of two parts:

- A **pattern** that will identify the XML source element.
- An **action** that describes the transformation to be applied to the element.

Patterns select an XML source document element using the following criteria:

- Element ancestry
- Wildcards in the ancestry/descendant tree
- Element descendants
- The attributes on an XML source element
- Position of an element relative to its siblings
- Uniqueness of an element relative to its siblings

These will all be investigated in more depth in the *Patterns* section later in the chapter.

Once we have selected the elements we want styled, we apply the action part of the rule to tell the processor how we want them displayed. We can also take the opportunity to add text to the XML element or even to reorder the appearance of the XML source elements.

Actions, which style or otherwise modify the selected XML element, can include:

- Element children and the **`<select-elements>`** tag
- Literal text
- Generated text (via. Scripting)
- DSSSL and HTML flow objects–including images
- Rules for reordering and filtering

These will all be investigated in more depth in the *Actions* section later in the chapter.

First let's look at construction rules in action in some simple examples of XSL style sheets. We'll use our old **`hixsl.xml`** file as the XML example they'll be applied to, so let's begin by reminding ourselves of what that looks like:

```
<?XML VERSION='1.0'?>
<xdoc>
<greeting>Hello XSL</greeting>
</xdoc>
```

Here is a very simple XSL style sheet to go with **`hixsl.xml`**:

```
<xsl>

   <rule>
<!--here is the pattern part of the rule-->
      <target-element type= "greeting"/>
```

```
<!--here is the action part of the rule-->

      <DIV color= "blue">
         <children/>
      </DIV>
   </rule>
</xsl>
<!--This rule uses CSS/HTML flow objects-->
```

Let's look at this rule in some detail. First, note the opening and closing **<rule>...</rule>** tags. This is a tag that is specific for XSL and must enclose each construction rule.

Next comes the pattern part of the rule which, in this case, consists of a single empty (by XML definition) tag **<target-element/>.** Note that it has an attribute **TYPE** which takes the value of the XML tag that it is going to transform, namely **<greeting>.** Note how the empty tag takes the XML style closing slash.

```
<target-element type= "greeting"/>
```

The tag **<target-element/>** is another specific XSL tag. There is a full listing of these tags at the end of the chapter.

The action part of the tag is the bit that creates the flow object. First of all it specifies a **container** for the object, which in the current XSL specification can either be an HTML container or a DSSSL container. DSSSL flow objects will be considered in later chapters, here for simplicity we will only use the familiar HTML flow objects. This particular example uses a **<DIV>** container. Note how the HTML is put in uppercase to distinguish it from the XSL elements. Style is applied to the container by using a CSS (or a DSSSL) property as a simple attribute.

```
<DIV color="blue">
```

Also note how, in accordance with XML syntax, all attribute values must be quoted. You can use as many CSS properties as you want as long as you separate each one by a space. In the actual properties and values themselves it is best to leave no white space.

It is important that the container be closed i.e **</DIV>**. Note that we could just have easily used a **<P>** but, in accordance with the XML specification, we would have had to use a closing **</P>**.

Between the opening and closing tags of the container we put the content that we would like in the container. In this case we just include the **<children/>** of the target element, which happens to be the text "Hello XSL!". So the result–once you've converted the XML to HTML using the processor–is Hello XSL in blue, as illustrated in the screen shot below. The sample files are available at:

http://rapid.wrox.co.uk/books/1657

This is **ch5_ex1.htm**.

Note that every time we repeat children we create a new flow object. We can put any valid flow object we want in the **<DIV>** container, including images, other text, or HTML code. The code example below is the same as the one we've just seen, apart from the action part.

```
<xsl>

   <rule>
<!--here is the pattern part of the rule-->
      <target-element type= "greeting"/>
<!--here is the action part of the rule-->

      <DIV color="blue">
      <children/>
      <HR/>

<!--note the closing slashes in these empty HTML tags.-->
      <IMG SRC="smiley.gif"/>
      <BR/>
      Some plain text.
<!--here is a simple list, note the closing of the LI-->
      <UL>
      <LI/>First item
      <LI/>Second item
      </UL>
      </DIV>
   </rule>
</xsl>
```

Here in addition to the **<children/>** of the source XML document, we have added a horizontal rule, an image, a line break, some plain text and an HTML style list to the action part of the tag.

The output, when converted to HTML, looks like this:

You can run the sample yourself from our web site. It is **`ch5_ex2.htm`**.

Note how the HTML flow objects must conform to XML syntax so that it is essential to close the normal empty tags with a penultimate forward slash, and to put all attribute values in quotes.

If we had used a compact list above, we would have had to give the attribute **`COMPACT`** a value. For example:

```
<OL COMPACT> ...</OL> IS BAD

<OL COMPACT="anything"> ...</OL> IS GOOD
<OL COMPACT=""> ...</OL> IS ALSO GOOD
```

Although the **`msxsl`** processor is quite tolerant of missing closing slashes, there is no guarantee that future processors will exhibit the same tolerance, so it is always best to just put them in.

Just as a CSS style sheet is made up of style rules, an XSL style sheet is predominantly made up of construction rules, although there are other types of rules.

Let's examine the pattern part of the construction rule in a little more detail.

Containers

We made a glib reference to containers above, and it may be as well to be a little more explicit.

XSL creates flow objects, and so rather than define our own flow objects we can make use of existing flow object definitions. Two existing 'standards' create a set of flow objects for their own use, namely HTML and DSSSL. XSL makes use of these existing flow objects. The **msxsl** processor only supports the HTML set of flow objects.

So when we used **<HR>** above, we were, in fact, saying to the processor–"Please consult your internal dictionary and look up **<HR>**. You will find it is a an instruction used in HTML to draw a horizontal line on the page, so please just go right ahead and draw it."

It is possible that the mature release of XSL will provide a list of predefined flow objects. It is also likely that the HTML flow objects that are currently employed by the **msxsl** processor will be deprecated, as they allow too much room for confusion.

As we saw in the last chapter, the two basic flow objects we need are 'inline' and 'block'. Anything else is icing on the cake.

Practical XSL Examples

Consider the following XML document which details the sales and costs by country and State/Province, and let's look at some ways we can use XSL to produce several different looks to this XML file. If you want to try it out as you are reading, copy this code into a text editor and save it as **ch5_ex3.xml** in the same directory as **msxsl.exe**.

```
<document>
   <us>
      <ohio>
         <sales>
            120K
         </sales>
         <costs>
            12K
         </costs>
      </ohio>
      <arizona>
         <sales>
            50K
         </sales>
         <costs>
            3K
         </costs>
      </arizona>
   </us>
   <canada>
      <ontario>
         <sales>
            160K
         </sales>
         <costs>
            18K
         </costs>
      </ontario>
      <quebec>
```

```
            <sales>
               110K
            </sales>
            <costs>
               9K
            </costs>
         </quebec>
      </canada>
   </document>
```

For starters we will combine this with the following XSL type style sheet. Again, you can copy the code into your text editor and save as **ch5_ex3.xsl** in the same directory as **msxsl.exe**.

```
<xsl>
   <rule>
      <root/>
       <HTML>
        <TITLE>SALES BY STATE AND COUNTRY</TITLE>
        <BODY color="black" background-color="white" font-size="14pt">
      Sales in navy blue, costs in red<BR/>
         <children/>
      <BR/>
        </BODY>
       </HTML>
   </rule>

<rule>
 <target-element type="costs"/>

 <SPAN color="red">
  <children/>
 </SPAN>

</rule>

<rule>
 <target-element type="sales"/>

 <SPAN color="navy">
  <children/>
</SPAN>

</rule>

<rule>
 <target-element type="quebec"/>

 <SPAN font-size="14pt">
   <BR/>Quebec
  <children/>
 </SPAN>
</rule>

<rule>
 <target-element type="canada"/>
```

```
    <DIV color="green" font-size="18pt" background-color="#ffcccc">
      <BR/>Canadian sales
    <children/>
   </DIV>

  </rule>

  <rule>
   <target-element type="us"/>

   <DIV color="green" font-size="18pt" background-color="#ccccff">
  <BR/>US sales
    <children/>
   </DIV>

  </rule>

  <rule>
   <target-element type="ontario"/>

   <SPAN font-size="14pt">
     <BR/>Ontario
    <children/>
   </SPAN>

  </rule>

  <rule>
   <target-element type="ohio"/>

   <SPAN font-size="14pt">
     <BR/>Ohio
    <children/>
   </SPAN>

  </rule>

  <rule>
   <target-element type="arizona"/>

   <SPAN font-size="14pt">
     <BR/>Arizona
    <children/>
   </SPAN>

  </rule>


  </xsl>
```

Run the code through the command-line utility as described earlier. You should end up with a file called **ch5_ex3.htm**, which looks like the following:

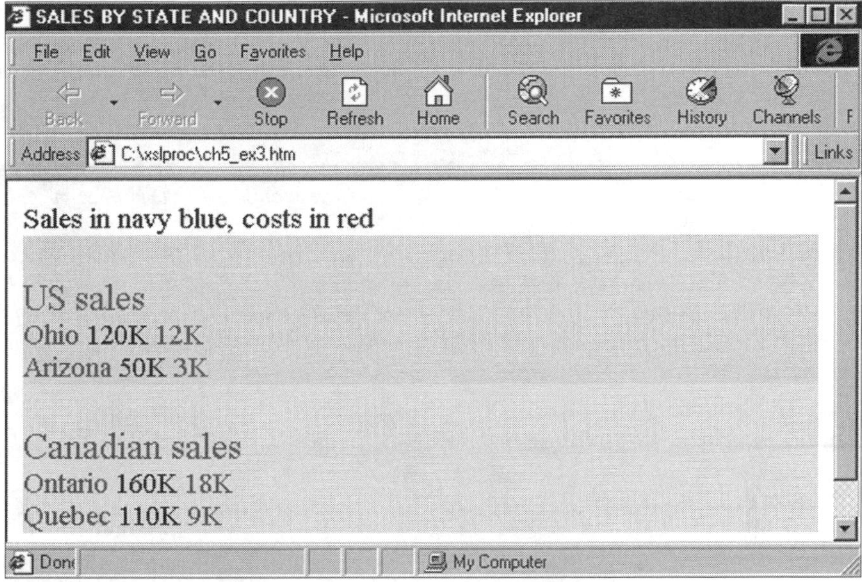

To get the full effect of the different colors, you can run the HTML output from our web site at **http://rapid.wrox.co.uk/books/1657**. The file is **ch5_ex3.htm**.

The Root Rule and Recursion

There are several things to note about this style sheet. The first thing is that we have put all the rules in a haphazard order. This is not good practice, but it is just to make a point. The XSL processor, however, follows the XML order.

The second thing to note is that we have added a special root rule namely the code below:

```
<rule>
     <root/>
     <HTML>
     <TITLE>SALES BY STATE AND COUNTRY</TITLE>
     <BODY color="black" background-color="white" font-size="14pt">
     Sales in navy blue, costs in red<BR/>
     <children/>
     <BR/>
     </BODY>
     </HTML>
</rule>
```

The XSL processor processes the XML document by a process of recursion. For each element in the XML document it will look for an applicable XSL rule. It is useful but not necessary to stipulate the root rule in the XSL document using the special XSL empty tag **<root/>**.

This enables us to put all our basic formatting in the first rule. Note that we could also have put this in a **<target-element type="document">** rule if we wanted.

The processor has to start somewhere and the **<root/>** tag is a good way to tell it where to start.

The processor finds the root rule and then looks at its children, then at its children, and then at its children etc. etc.

> *Recursion is a computing term which, basically, means that the user-agent must look back at another example before deciding how to process the present example. For example, in XSL the processor comes across the action element* **</children>** *in the root tag, so it goes off searching for children to process. What it finds is the children (the US and Canada in the above example) that have children of their own, so it must find out about these children before it starts to process its own children, and so on down the line. When the processor finds the final child, it will process the final child and then work its way back up the line, finally processing any children left over which don't have their own rules.*

Just for fun try removing **<children/>** from the above root rule and recompile the document. You will find that only the black text remains, because the recursive process stops with the root rule.

Now try commenting out or removing the whole of the root rule. The children will magically reappear (although of course the opening text and the title will have gone and the HTML document will not be strictly valid). This is because the processor will provide a default root rule, to prevent a halting of the recursion process. In the **msxsl** processor the default rule reads as follows:

```
<rule>
<root/>
 <DIV>
 <children/>
</DIV>
</rule>
```

However, different processors may provide different default rules.

If the XSL processor finds no rule to apply to an element it must apply a default one. Again, the **msxsl** processor applies the following default rule:

```
<rule>
  <target-element/>
  <children/>
</rule>
```

However, other processors may apply other rules, and you can even provide your own default rule e.g.

```
<rule>
  <target-element/>
 <DIV color="brown">
  <children/>
 </DIV.
</rule>
```

would make all the elements for which there is not an existing rule show up in brown.

Try running the above XML file with just the following style sheet and see what happens:

```
<xsl>
</xsl>
```

The following screen shot shows what we will see.

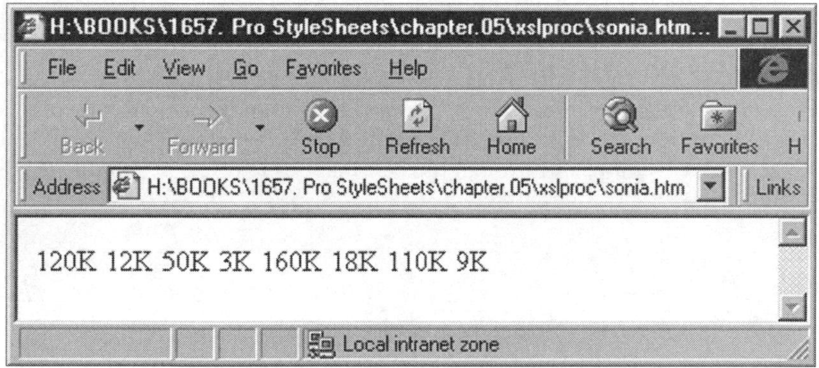

To stop halting the recursive process the processor has put in the default rule:

```
<rule>
  <target-element/>
  <children/>
</rule>
```

and produced the following rather meager HTML file.

```
<DIV> 120K  12K  50K  3K  160K  18K  110K  9K </DIV>
```

We have, of course, given the processor no styling information whatsoever.

Then try running, cutting and pasting in various rules, try removing <**children**/> from various rules, and see what happens. You will get a very good idea of how the recursive process works.

At the beginning of this section on XSL construction rules, we stated that a construction rule consisted of two parts: a pattern and an action. We are going to examine both parts in detail in the rest of this chapter, beginning with patterns.

Patterns

As we stated earlier, the **pattern** part of the construction rule identifies the XML source element. We saw this in the examples we've just been using to illustrate practical XSL.

```
<xsl>

   <rule>
<!--here is the pattern part of the rule-->
      <target-element type= "greeting"/>
```

There are several ways that a pattern can be narrowed down and we are going to examine each one in turn.

Element Selection by Ancestry

By specifying the immediate ancestry of a source document tag it is possible to sub select a descendant tag. Try adding the following code to the previous style sheet example, **ch5_ex3.xsl**, save it as **ch5_ex4.xsl** and run it through the command-line utility, changing the name of the output file to **ch5_ex4.htm**. Alternatively just run **ch5_ex4.htm** on the web site.

```
<rule>
   <element type="quebec">
      <target-element type="costs"/>
   </element>
   <SPAN color="brown">
      <children/>
   </SPAN>
</rule>
```

Now the only difference you will notice is that Quebec costs will be in brown.

What we have done is specified a **pattern by ancestry** using the XSL tag **<element>**...**</element>**. Note that we have to specify the direct ancestor. This pattern would not work because **costs** are not a direct ancestor of **canada**.

```
<rule>

   <element type="canada">
      <target-element type="costs"/>
   </element>

   <SPAN color="brown">
      <children/>
   </SPAN>
</rule>
```

The following would work, but again would make only the Quebec costs appear in brown.

```
<rule>
   <element type="canada">
   <element type="quebec">
      <target-element type="costs"/>
   </element>
   </element>
   <SPAN color="brown">
      <children/>
   </SPAN>
</rule>
```

Add the construction rule that follows to the **ch5_ex4.xsl** style sheet we created above, and save it as **ch5_ex5.xsl**.

```
<rule>
 <element type="canada">
 <target-element type="quebec"/>
 </element>
 <SPAN font-size="14pt" color="brown">
<BR/>Quebec
  <children/>
 </SPAN>
</rule>
```

Run the code through the processor, changing the name of the output file to **ch5_ex5.htm**. When you open the resultant **ch5_ex5.htm** in your browser, it should look like this:

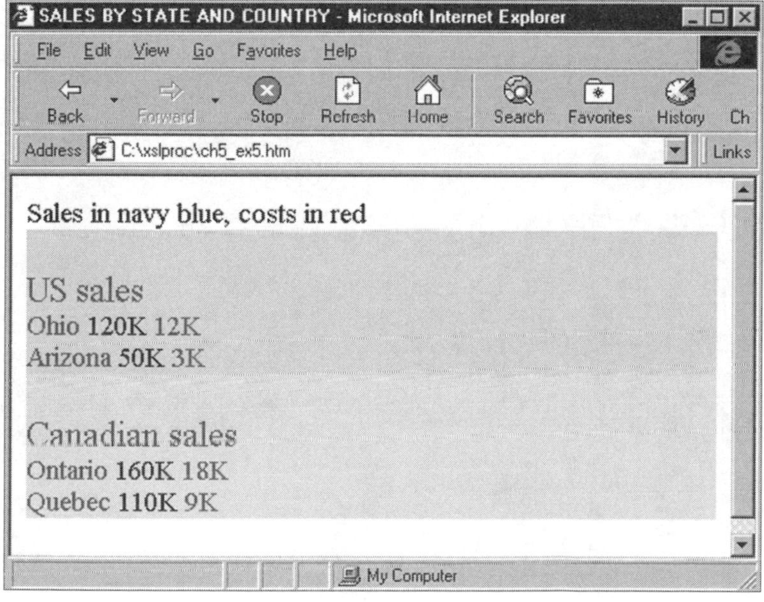

You probably can't see this in print, but both Quebec and 9K are in brown. You can run **ch5_ex5.htm** from the web site at **http://rapid.wrox.co.uk/books/1657**.

Rules not Inherited in XSL

Note that the sales figure for Quebec of 110K remains navy blue. This brings up the important point that unlike CSS, XSL rules are **not** inherited (except see style-rules, covered in Chapter 11). There is a separate construction rule for every element.

Using Wildcards to Establish a Pattern

As well as specifying a pattern, we can also use wildcards to establish a general trend. Add the following to **ch5_ex5.xsl**, comment out the two specific state rules for **<arizona>** and **<ohio>** and save it as **ch5_ex6.xsl**. We have to comment out the specific rules, otherwise they will be chosen over this wildcard rule as they are more specific (see the later section entitled *Rule Arbitration* for more details).

```
<rule>
   <element type="us">
      <target-element/>
   </element>
   <SPAN color="brown" font-size="20pt" background-color="#ccccff">
   <BR/>State
     <children/>
   </SPAN>
</rule>
```

Compile it–changing the output file name to **ch5_ex6.htm**–and run it up in your browser. Alternatively, just run **ch5_ex6.htm** from the web site and you should see this:

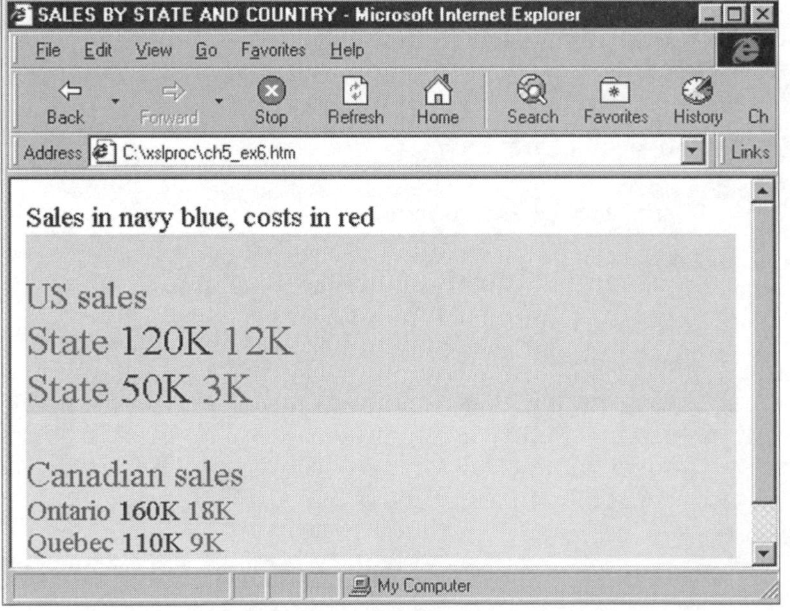

The screen shot shows the result of replacing a specific criterion with a wildcard as seen on IE4. Note how the font size is passed to all the children, but the font colors remain different because they are governed by more specific XSL construction rules.

Note that all the descendants of the element **<us>** are affected unless they are governed by a more specific rule. If we just wanted the **grandchildren** of the **<us>** tag to be affected we could do the following:

```
<rule>
<element type="us">
<element>
   <target-element/>
 </element>
</element>
 <SPAN color="brown" font-size="20pt" background-color="#ccccff">
<BR/>State
  <children/>
 </SPAN>
</rule>
```

Run this sample with **ch5_ex4.xml**. **ch5_ex4.xml** is the same as **ch5_ex3.xml** except we have added text to the **<state>** elements to show how the grandchildren, not the children are affected by this wild card pattern. You will need to comment out the existing rules for sales and costs.

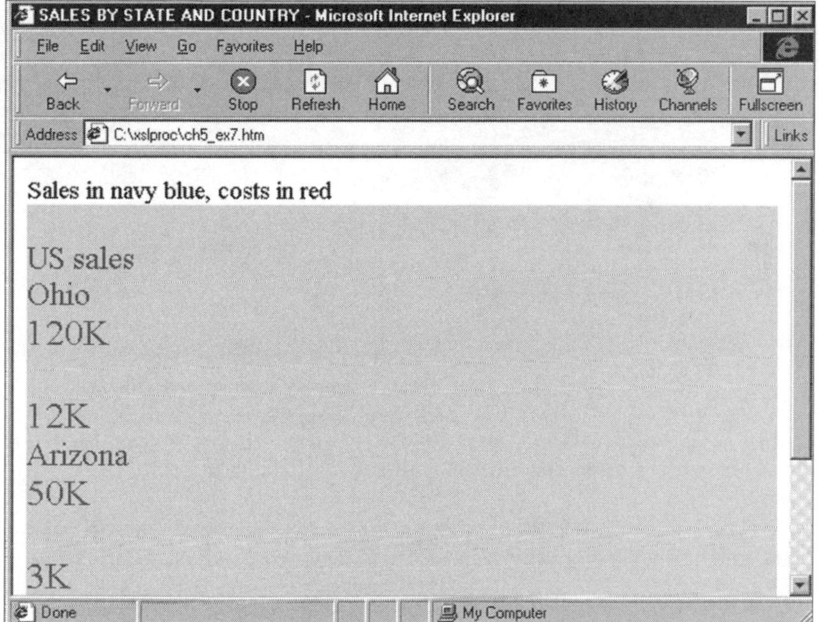

The <any> Tag

We can also use the special XSL element **<any>** to affect a wild card change. This can match a specific tag that is an ancestor of an element, no matter how deep the descent. Add the following example to **ch5_ex5.xsl** and save it as **ch5_ex8.xsl**.

```
<rule>

<element type="us">
 <any>
 <target-element type="sales"/>
 </any>
</element>

 <SPAN color="brown" font-size="20pt">
  <children/>
 </SPAN>

</rule>
```

Run it through the processor, reverting to using **ch5_ex3.xml** as the **.xml** file and calling the output file **ch5_8.htm**. This is what it will look like:

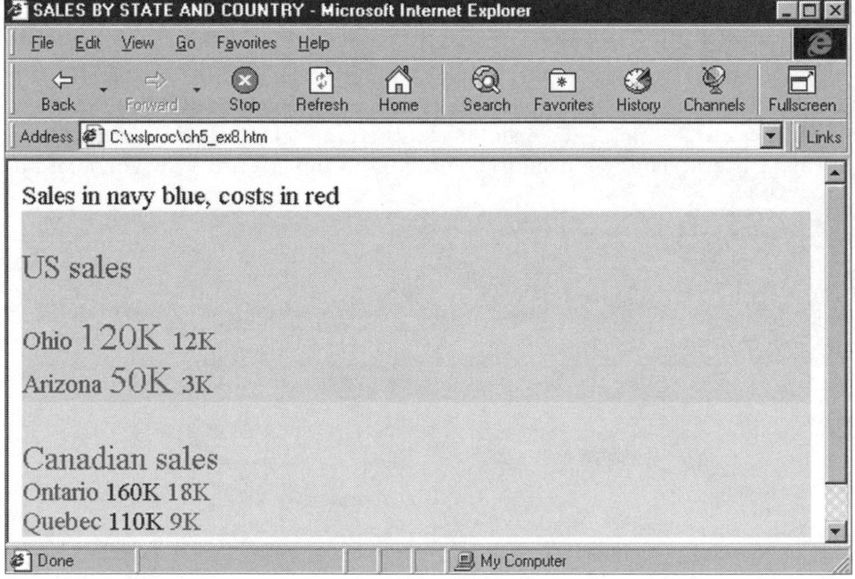

The US sales figures now appear in brown. Note that this construction rule is more specific than the original **<sales>** rule and so will be chosen by the processor in preference to the original **<sales>** rule. This is **ch5_ex8.xsl** on the web site.

It is also interesting to change **<element type="us">** to **<element type="ohio">**. Save this as **ch5_8a.xsl** and run it through the processor to create **ch5_8a.htm**, illustrated in the next screenshot.

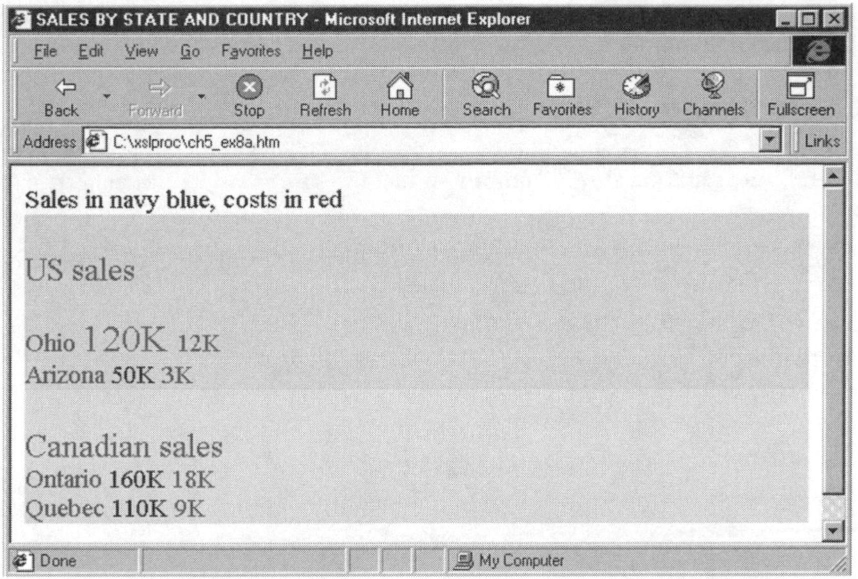

Element Selection by Descendant

Elements can also be selected by their children .The original XML file has been given extra elements for sales called **<record>** and **<best>** (**ch5_ex5.xml**). The following two rules would specify a **<sales>** element that also contained a **<record>** element, and which contained both a **<record>** and a **<best>** element.

```
<rule>
 <target-element type="sales">
<element type="record"/>

</target-element>

 <SPAN color="brown">
  <children/>
 </SPAN>

</rule>

<rule>
 <target-element type="sales">
<element type="record"/>
<element type="best"/>
</target-element>

 <SPAN color="teal">
  <children/>
 </SPAN>

</rule>
```

At the time of writing this kind of pattern is not supported by the processor, but they may be by the time you read this. Examples are on the web site in case you want to check them out.

Element Selection by Attribute

XML file tags may have attributes and the tags can be selected depending on the nature of the attribute. **ch5_ex5.xml** has been modified so that the **<sales>** tag has an attribute **progress**.

```
<document>
   <us>
      <ohio>
         <sales progress="down">
            120K
         </sales>
         <costs>
            12K
         </costs>
      </ohio>
      <arizona>
         <sales progress="up">
         <record></record>
            50K
         </sales>
         <costs>
            3K
         </costs>
       </arizona>
   </us>
   <canada>
      <ontario>
         <sales progress="steady">
            160K
         </sales>
         <costs>
            18K
         </costs>
      </ontario>
      <quebec>
         <sales>
         <record></record>
         <best/>
            110K
         </sales>
         <costs>
            9K
         </costs>
      </quebec>
   </canada>
</document>
```

As you can see, **<sales progress=**"**up**"**>** for Arizona, **<sales progress="down">** for Ohio, **<sales progress="steady">** for Ontario. Quebec has no attribute assigned to **sales**.

Comment out (using XML commenting) the specific **<ohio> <sales>** construction rule from **ch5_8a.xsl**. This rule is more specific and so would take precedence over the one we are about to add. Then add the following to create **ch5_ex10.xsl.**

```
<rule>
<target-element type="sales">
<attribute name="progress" has-value="yes"/>
</target-element>
<SPAN color="brown" font-size="24pt">
<children/>
</SPAN>
</rule>
```

As you can see we have used a special XSL element called **<attribute>** which itself can take the attributes **NAME, VALUE**, and **HAS-VALUE**. **HAS-VALUE** can take the value of yes or no.

The following screenshot shows the result. Note how any sales tag with a **progress** attribute appears in large brown type.

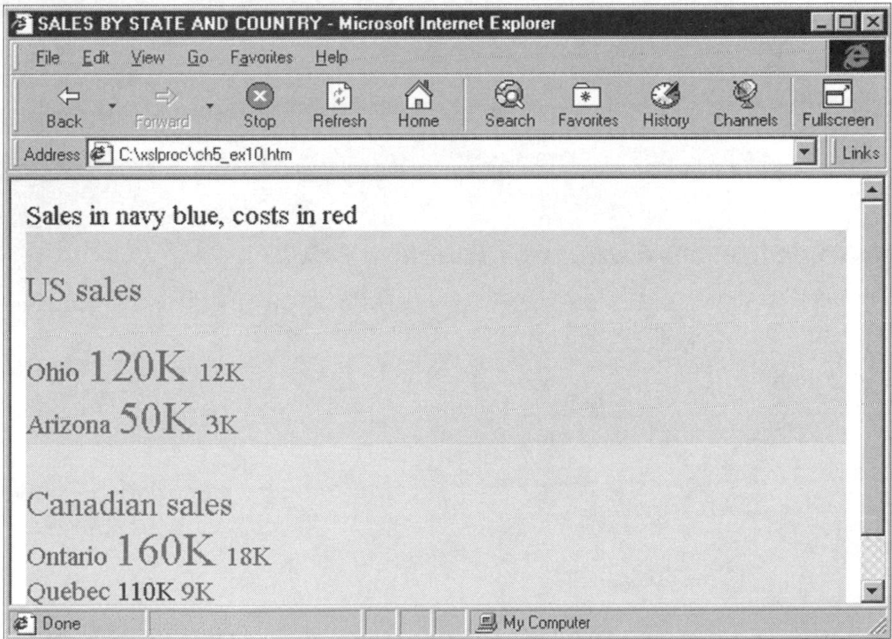

A couple of interesting alterations are the following. In both cases see if you can predict what will happen before running.

Go to the XML document and change **<sales progress="up">** to **<sales progress="">**, re-run it and see what happens.

In the XSL document change **has-value="yes"** to **has-value="no"** and re-run. The following screen shot shows the results.

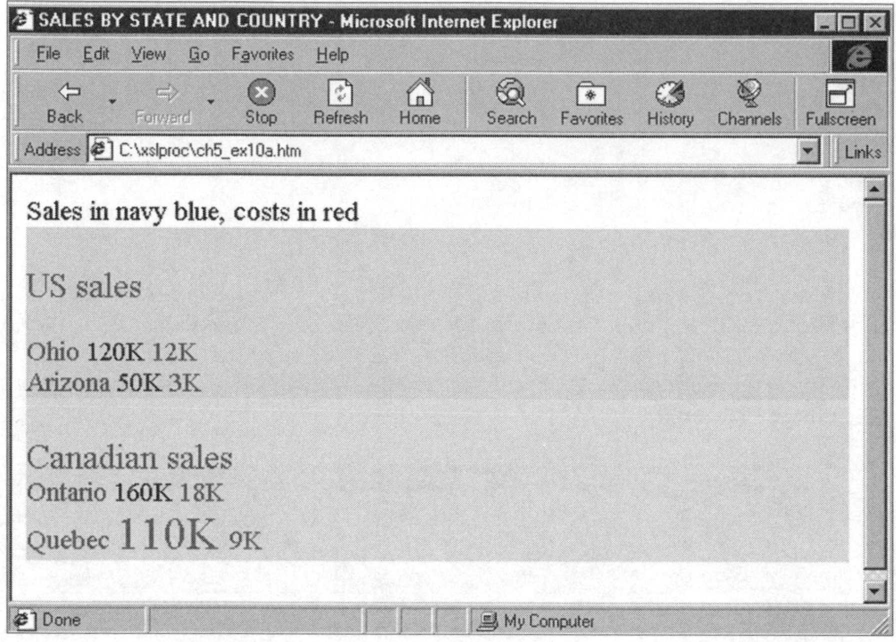

Element Selection by Attribute (Specific Value)

You can select an element by a specific value. Delete the rule you added in the example above, and replace it with the one set out below. Save it as **ch5_ex11.xsl**.

```
<rule>
<target-element type="sales">
<attribute name="progress" value="up"/>
</target-element>
<SPAN color="brown" font-size="24pt">
<children/>
</SPAN>
</rule>
```

Run it through the processor with **ch5_ex5.xml** and name the output file **ch5_ex11.htm**. This is what you should see:

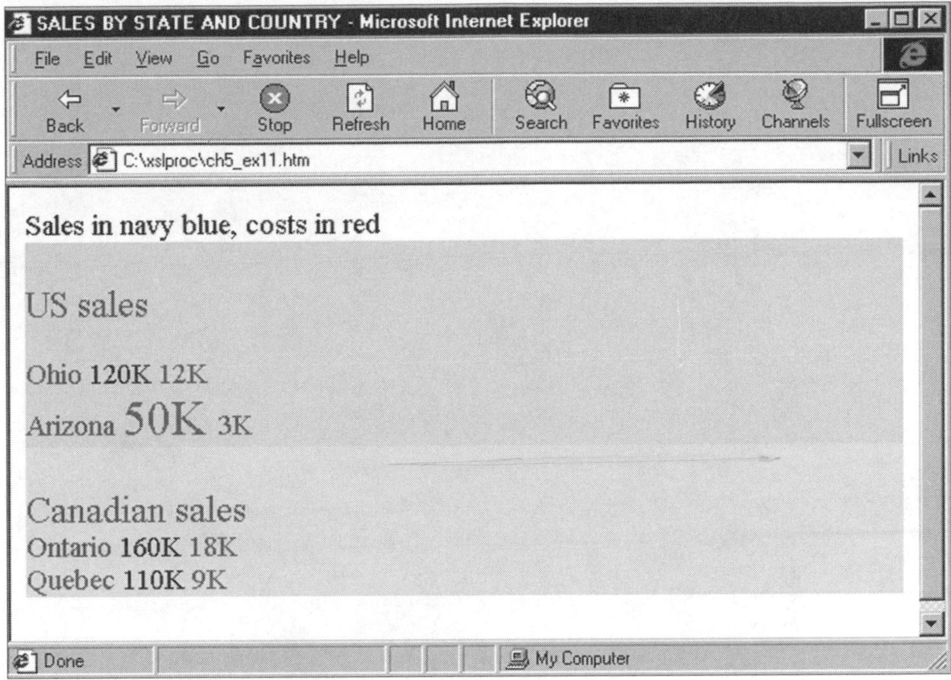

Arizona was the only state with a progress value of up, so the styling has been applied to Arizona only.

Similarly, you can select for any string value, of a named attribute.

Element Selection by Position

We will now modify the XML file to give two cost figures for the Canadian provinces, the first being in US currency the last in Canadian currency. Copy and paste this code into your text editor and save it as **ch5_ex6.xml**.

```
<document>
   <us>
      <ohio>
         <sales progress="down">
            120K
         </sales>
         <costs>
            12K
         </costs>
      </ohio>
      <arizona>
         <sales progress="up">
         <record></record>
            50K
         </sales>
         <costs>
            3K
```

```
        </costs>
      </arizona>
    </us>
    <canada>
      <ontario>
        <sales progress="steady">
          160K
        </sales>
        <costs>
          18K
        </costs>
        <costs>
          24K
        </costs>
      </ontario>
      <quebec>
        <sales>
        <record></record>
        <best/>
          110K
        </sales>
        <costs>
          9K
        </costs>
        <costs>
          12K
        </costs>
      </quebec>
    </canada>
  </document>
```

We are able to distinguish between the two by using the **POSITION** attribute of **<target-element>**. Add the following rule to the original **.xsl** file you created for this code, **ch5_ex3.xsl**, and save it as **ch5_ex12.xsl**.

```
  <rule>
    <target-element type="costs" position="last-of-type"/>
    <SPAN color="brown" font-size="24pt">
    <children/>
    </SPAN>
  </rule>
```

Run **ch5_ex6.xml** and **ch5_ex12.xsl** through the processor and save the output as **ch5_ex12.htm**. This is what you should see:

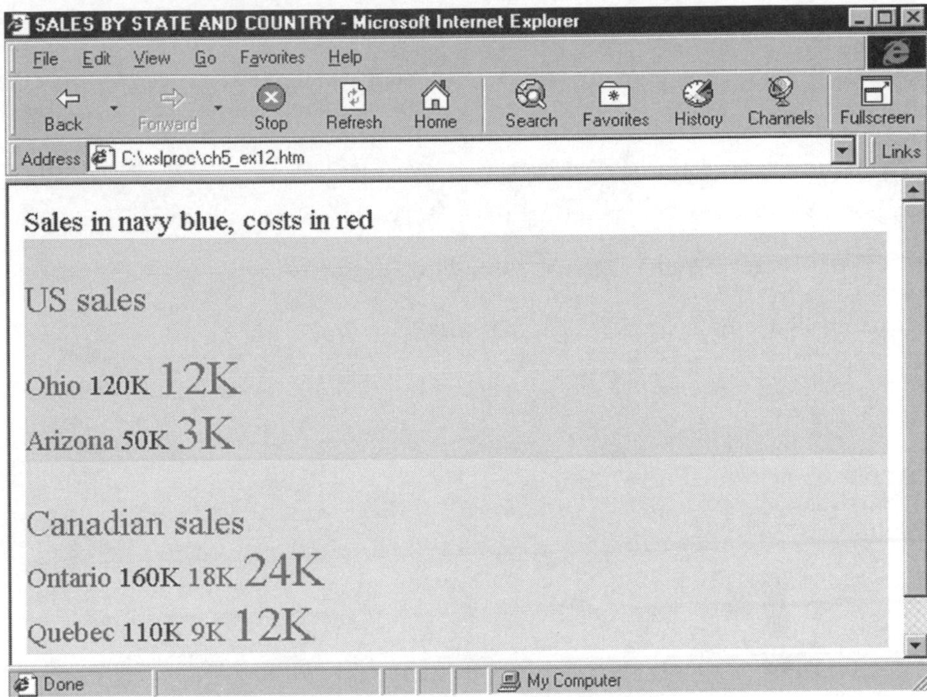

As you can see, the original costs for the US have been effected by the rule, but it's the new Canadian costs which have been effected because they occupy the last of type position in the XML file.

The position attribute can take four values:

- first-of-type
- last-of-type
- first-of-any
- last-of-any

The **-OF-ANY** attribute is used to display the first or last child of a series. To see this in action, add this rule to **ch5_ex12.xsl**, comment out the **<sales>** construction rule and save it as **ch5_ex13.xsl**.

```
<rule>
   <element type="quebec">
   <target-element position="first-of-any"/>
   </element>
   <SPAN color="brown" font-size="24pt">
   <children/>
   </SPAN>

</rule>
```

Run it through the processor to produce the output file **ch5_ex13.htm**. The output will be the same as the screenshot above, except the sales figure for Quebec will be in large brown font, because it is the first element of the **<quebec>** group. We had to comment out the sales construction rule because it was more specific and would have taken precedence over this rule.

Element Selection by Uniqueness

target-element also takes the attribute **ONLY**. This would take the form:

<target-element type="sales" only="of-type"/>

The **ONLY** attribute also takes the value "**OF-ANY**".

To modify the XSL document to display the above for Ohio, you would add a rule like this:

```
<rule>
   <element type="ohio">
   <target-element type="sales" only="first-of-type"/>
   </element>
   <SPAN color="brown" font-size="24pt">
   <children/>
   </SPAN>
</rule>
```

and comment out the more specific sales construction rule.

Element Selection: Multiple Patterns

A rule can contain multiple patterns. This can be useful when, for example, you want several tags to produce the same output. For example, in a fairy-tale all the following tags would be in bold type.

```
<rule>
   <target-element type= "shouting"/>
   <target-element type="bold"/>
   <target-element type="emphasis"/>
   <target-element type="ogre"/>
   <SPAN font-weight="bold">
   <children/>
   </SPAN>
</rule>
```

In a lot of the examples we've gone through above, you had to comment out more specific rules to get the new rule we introduced to work. This is known as rule arbitration, and we'll give you a bit more information about it next.

Rule Arbitration

The XSL note has this to say about rule arbitration.

3.2.6. Conflicts

It is possible for a source element to match patterns in several different rules. XSL has an algorithm for determining which rules should be invoked in this situation. It also allows the style sheet to override this by specifying *importance* and *priority* attributes on the *rule* and *style-rule* elements.

When an element matches more than one pattern, then the *most specific* pattern will be used. The precedence order for establishing the most specific pattern is:

1. The pattern with the highest importance; the importance of a pattern is the value of the importance attribute on the rule that contains it; this allows the CSS !important feature to be supported
2. The pattern with the greater number of id attributes
3. The pattern with the greater number of class attributes
4. The pattern with the greater number of element or target-element elements that have a type attribute
5. The pattern with fewer wildcards; a wildcard is an any element, an element element without a type attribute, or a target-element element without a type attribute
6. The pattern with the higher specified priority; the priority of a pattern is the priority of the rule that contains it; the priority of a pattern is the value of the priority attribute on the rule that contains it
7. The pattern with the greater number of only qualifiers
8. The pattern with the greater number of position qualifiers
9. The pattern with the greater number of attribute specifications

When determining which of two matching patterns is the more specific, the above criteria are applied in order until one of the criteria identifies exactly one of the patterns as most specific. For construction rules, it is an error if, for any source element, there is not a unique matching pattern that is more specific than all other matching patterns. These notes can be found at:

`http://www.w3.org/TR/NOTE-XSL.html`

This is just put here for reference. You definitely do not have to memorize this. Just remember that as a rule of thumb, the construction rule that defines the pattern most specifically is the one that applies, and experiment. If you are writing an XSL processor then you will have to memorize and incorporate these rules in your processor.

So, that concludes our detailed look at the pattern part of the construction rule. Let's look at the other part of the rule–actions.

Actions

We have been using actions all along in our examples. To recap, the action part of a construction rule is the part that styles, adds to, or otherwise modifies our XML source element after we have selected it using a pattern. Here's our original example as a reminder.

```
<xsl>
<rule>
<!--here is the pattern part of the rule-->
      <target-element type= "greeting"/>

<!--here is the action part of the rule-->

      <DIV color= "blue">
         <children/>
      </DIV>
   </rule>
</xsl>
```

So far we have looked at how the action renders out the children as flow objects, and how we can add text, an image or an HTML tag e.g.,**
, **<HR/> as a flow object. Remember that when the latter are added they are not really HTML tags any more but flow objects in their own right.

The **<children/>** tag will create flow objects of all the children of the target-element.

Element Children and the <select-elements> tag

We can also use a special XSL tag **<select-elements>** (called **<select>** in the original note, but changed to avoid confusion with the HTML tag of the same name) to select out elements for special formatting.

The **<select-elements>** tag is placed in the action part of the rule right after we specify the flow object type. It is used to select only certain elements for processing. For example, let's assume we have an XML file that lists all our investments under an element **<investments>**, and investments has the following children: **<stocks>** , **<bonds>**, **<cash>**, **<properties>**.

The following rule would display all of the children: **<stocks>** , **<bonds>**, **<cash>**, and **<properties>** in a red font.

```
<rule>
   <target-element type = "investments"/>

   <DIV color = "red">
      </children>
   </DIV>
<rule>
```

If I just wanted to display my stocks I could alter the above using the **<select-elements>** tag. In the example below only stocks would be displayed, and display of the other elements would be suppressed.

```
<rule>
   <target-element type = "investments"/>

   <DIV>
       select-elements>
       <target-element type= "stocks>/>
       </select-elements>
   </DIV>
<rule>
```

We use the same **<target-element type=>** tag as we used in the pattern part of the rule, and if you are not careful this can be confusing.

Literal Text

You can add text in the style sheet which is then displayed in the browser. For example:

```
<xsl>
<rule>
<!--here is the pattern part of the rule-->
<target-element type="greeting"/>

<!--here is the action part of the rule-->
<DIV color="maroon">
Wow. Look you can add text!
<BR/>
<HR/>
Horizontal rules!
<HR/>
<children/>
<HR/>
<children/>
<BR/>
<children/>
<BR/>
<children/>
<BR/>
And clone as many children as you want! (move over Dolly my old chum)
</DIV>
</rule>
</xsl>
```

In this example which we saw at the beginning of the chapter, "Wow look you can add text!" and "And clone as many children as you want! (move over Dolly my old chum)" are added as literal text in the action part of the style sheet, and displayed as text in the browser.

Generated Text (via Scripting)

We'll cover this in detail in Chapter 11. For now, just note that it can be very useful for generating page numbers.

DSSL and HTML Flow Objects, including Images

In the Literal Text example above, the horizontal rules and line breaks are all flow objects added by the XSL style sheet.

Reordering and Filtering

Using the **<select-elements>** element it is possible to filter and reorder the original XML flow objects. This will be discussed in more detail in Chapter 11. For now, just note that the **msxsl** processor's implementation of this feature is rather unpredictable, and run the following example:

> *The **msxml** processor is what's known in the software industry as a "technological-preview", in other words it is a pre-beta and even a pre-alpha release. **Msxsl.exe** works well for such a piece of software, but some of its actions, especially when using the **<select-elements>** tag are a little unpredictable. I had difficulty duplicating some examples using this tag. Bear this in mind if you are having problems running the examples showing the, **<select-elements>** tag.*

Here's the XML file. Copy or paste it into your text editor and save it as **ch5_ex7.xml**.

```
<document>
   <figures>
      <store>
         <location>Mentor</location>
      </store>
      <stock>
         <spades>50</spades>
         <price>25</price>
         <maker>Acme</maker>
      </stock>
      <stock>
         <spades>100</spades>
         <price>20</price>
         <maker>OKindustries</maker>
      </stock>
      <stock>
         <spades>150</spades>
         <price>10</price>
         <maker>Elcheepos</maker>
      </stock>
   </figures>
</document>
```

and here's the XSL file. Copy it into your text editor and save it as **ch5_ex15.xsl**.

```
<xsl>
  <rule>         <!--extracts <stock> elements-->
    <target-element type="figures"/>
    <TABLE>
      <TBODY>
          <select-elements>
          <target-element type="stock"/>
```

```
          </select-elements>
        </TBODY>
      </TABLE>
    </rule>

    <rule>        <!-- extracts <maker> and <price> elements -->
      <target-element type="stock"/>
      <TR>
        <TD>
          <select-elements>
            <target-element type="maker"/>
          </select-elements>
        </TD>
        <TD>
          $
          <select-elements>
            <target-element type="price"/>
          </select-elements>
        </TD>
      </TR>
    </rule>

    <rule>        <!-- formats <maker> elements -->
      <target-element type="maker"/>
      <DIV font-weight="bold"><children/></DIV>
    </rule>

  <rule>        <!-- formats <price> elements -->
      <target-element type="price"/>
      <SPAN color="blue"><children/></SPAN>
    </rule>
  </xsl>
```

Run the files through the processor and save the output file as **`ch5_ex15.htm`**. The screenshot below shows what you should see when you view the output file in your browser.

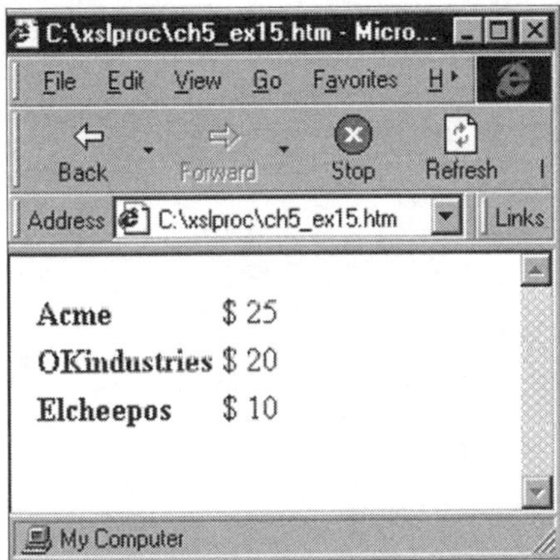

The style sheet has pulled out the maker and price elements and applied styling to them. Let's try another example.

Open **ch5_15.xsl** in your text editor and change:

```
<target-element type="figures"/>
```

to:

```
<target-element type="document"/>
```

Save the file as **ch5_ex16.xsl** and run again, changing the output file name to **ch5_ex16.htm**. (Hint–we warned you it might be unpredictable.) Here is what it does:

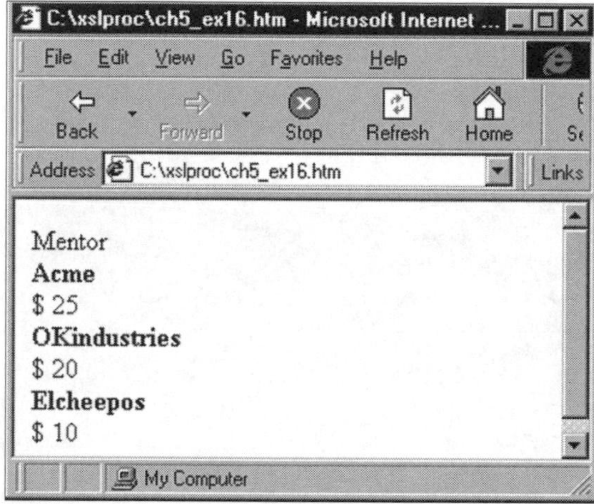

Because we've moved the selection criteria up a level, the contents of the **<store>** element are included so we see the location Mentor appear. However, we've lost the formatting of the prices.

Hiding Source Elements

To hide a source element all that is necessary is to leave the action part of the construction rule blank. However, please do note that this will hide **all** the flow objects from that element.

Another way to do this is to use the XSL element **</empty>**. Copy this into your text editor and save it as **ch5_ex17.xsl**.

```
<xsl>
  <rule>
    <target-element/>
    <DIV font-weight="bold"><children/></DIV>
  </rule>
  <rule>
    <target-element type="stock"/>
    <DIV font-weight="bold"><empty/>figures withheld</DIV>
  </rule>
</xsl>
```

Run it through the processor, output it as **`ch5_ex17.htm`**.

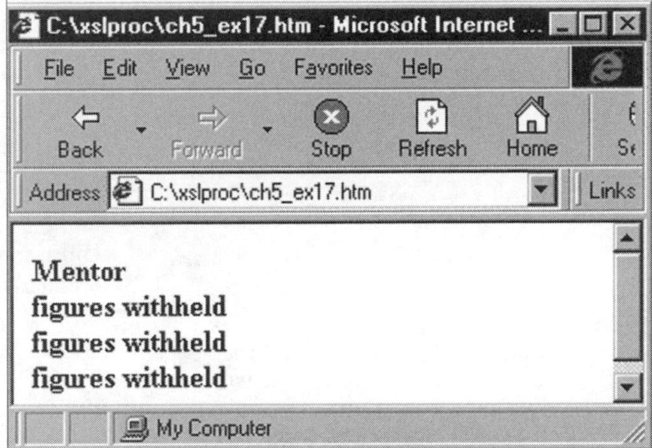

All the children of **`<stock>`**, that is **`<price>`**, **`<maker>`** and **`<spades>`**, are hidden, and replaced by the text figures withheld.

Change stock for figures and run again. Note how all the children are done away with (like at the end of *Jude the Obscure* by Thomas Hardy).

Style Rules

Style rules will be covered in a later chapter, Chapter 11. At this point, it is just important to note that they can be used to style a flow object that has already been created.

Scripting and the <eval> Tag

A whole number of transformations and created text can be achieved via scripting which we will go into later in the book. For now, just note that you can either use the = sign as in:

```
<DIV font-size= "10*3-5 + 'pt'"> <!-- a rather facile example-->
```

(this tells the processor to evaluate the expression as a JavaScript expression)

or use the XSL element **`<eval>`** as in:

```
<DIV>
<eval> formatNumber(childNumber(this),"1")</eval>
</DIV>
```

Flow Object Macros

It is also possible to create a macro for re-use, again this will be discussed later (together with a further and detailed discussion of scripting, filtering, ID's, classes and modes, and source styles in Chapter 11.)

Summary of XSL Elements

The following is a working list of XSL tags. Please note that XSL is still in its infancy and as of yet has no official DTD. This list may well change and all updates will be featured on the Wrox Press site at **`http://rapid.wrox.co.uk/books/1657`**.

Element tag	Attributes	Atrribute Values	Comments
`rule`	`MODE`	any string	**`MODE`** used to define a name to be used with children or select elements

`target-element`	`TYPE`
	`ID`
	`POSITION`
	`ONLY`
		any string
		`POSITION` takes values: **`first-of-type, first-of-any, last-of-type, last-of-any`**
		`Only` takes value **`of-type`**	

`children`	`MODE`	**`MODE`** takes value defined under rule	Displays flow objects
`root`			The primary element for recursion
`style-rule`			
`apply`			Used with style-rule to apply style properties
`element`	`TYPE`	**`name, has value`**	Yes/No
`attribute`			
`id`			
`class`			
`eval`			
`select elements`	`MODE` `FROM`	**`FROM`** takes value of **`descendants`**, or **`children`**. **`children`** is the default value	Replaces **`<SELECT>`** tag
`define-macro`	`NAME`		Used for creating a macro

Element tag	Attributes	Atrribute Values	Comments
`invoke`			
`HTML tag`	`USE`	`#source`	Applies any style attributes in the document
`"" ""`	`NAME`		
`define-script`			Similar to **<SCRIPT>** in HTML. Contains functions and constants
`define-style`	`NAME`	any string	The string is then used as an element in a style rule
`any`			Used to define a wildcard

`attribute`	`NAME`
	`VALUE`
	`HAS-VALUE`
		The source element attribute, and the source elements attribute value
		Has value takes yes or no as value	

Referencing XSL Style Sheets

Although the process of referring to an XSL style sheet from an XML document has not been finalized, it will be in the form of a processing instruction, probably as follows.

```
<?xml-stylesheet href="sales.xsl" type="text/xsl" ?>
```

An XSL style sheet can import another style sheet with the following syntax:

```
<import href="sales.xsl"/>
```

This should be placed in the prolog.

Because an XSL document is also an XML document it is also likely that the above processing instruction placed in the prolog of the XSL style sheet will also be supported.

```
<?xml-stylesheet href="sales.xsl" type="text/xsl" ?>
```

Summary

In this chapter we took an introductory look at XSL, including expanding on the following:

- The capabilities of XSL, beyond those of a mere declarative language
- The basic XSL rule, the construction rule and its constituent parts; a pattern and an action
- The pattern part of the rule, used to fine-select the source documents elements
- The action part of the rule, used to create new flow objects.
- Had a brief look at filtering and re-ordering. (More on this later, in Chapter 11)
- Had a brief look at the other potential capabilities of XSL

With this chapter we come to the end of part 1 and our basic overview of HTML, XML, and styling. Part 2 will give a full explanation of the CSS flow properties, and in part 3 we will use these to go into advanced styling and scripting and look at what may be coming down the road in the near future.

References

The XSL note:

`http://www.w3.org/TR/NOTE-XSL.html`

Sparse:

`http://www.jeremie.com/Dev/XSL/`

His home page contains good links to all of XSL and XML

The Microsoft XSL page:

`http://www.microsoft.com/XML`

This page navigates to the XSL page and contains all of the XSL links.

To be placed on the mailing list send the following command in email to–**`xsl-list-request@mulberrytech.com`**. Put "subscribe" in the body of the message

The WWW XSL page:

`http://www.w3.org/Style/XSL/`

An excellent starting point for all style sheet information is the following site:

`http://www.finetuning.com/xsl.html`

Exercises

1. Write a well-formed XML document that contains the inventory, employee records, sales records of a chain of 3 or 4 stores.
2. Write a construction rule that formats the whole document
3. Add additional flow objects to the formatting
4. Display just part of the document e.g. the inventory part (hint:–leave out the **<children/>** tag in the action part of the style rules).
5. Try using the **<select-elements>** tag to filter the document. (This will be covered in some detail in Chapter 11, *XSL Beyond the Basics*).

Part 2

In this section, comprising chapters 6 to 10, we cover styling and style sheets in-depth. We look at all the effects you can achieve and go through the properties you will use to achieve them. The section is divided up by property type.

So, in **Chapter 6** we look at font and text properties, covering font and text definitions, font control and text control and the font solutions such as bitstream technology and open type and web embedding font technology. **Chapter 7** deals with flow objects, selectors, inheritance and the cascade. What we're really doing in this chapter is starting to look at the subject of flow objects and how you select and style them. We also look in detail at inheritance and the whole cascade mechanism. **Chapter 8** covers boxes and layers. We learn about boxes and their properties, how they react as flow objects and how to display, hide and layer boxes. We also find out how to clip the contents of the box. In **Chapter 9** we move on to cover backgrounds, colors, units, links and languages. The major part of the chapter explains how to set different backgrounds for your page. The rest of it looks at the necessary minutiae such as how you set colors and what units you use for measurement. Finally in this section, in **Chapter 10**, we look at lists and tables as they can be used and styled in HTML, CSS and XML. One of the most important points for web page designers is to ensure that their pages look good in all browsers. We've made a point of specifying this in the chapters, but it's also a subject worth a section in its own right here.

What Works in which Browser?

Appendices B and C give the latest information about what works in which browser at the time of going to press. However, this continually changes as various patches are applied to the browsers. A better way to do things is to download the examples applicable to each chapter from **`http://rapid.wrox.co.uk/books/1657`**. They will let you know what is working in the browser you are using!

Testing for CSS1 properties can be found at this site:

`http://www.w3.org/Style/CSS/Test/`

Tim Boland of The National Institute of Standards and Technology (NIST) in Gaithersburg, Maryland also has a very full test site at the following URL. One can also get to the CSS2 tests through this URL:

`http://sdct-sunsrv1.ncsl.nist.gov/~boland/css.`

Web Review also keep a relatively up-to-date compatibility guide and "safe" chart, which can be found at:

`http://style.webreview.com/mastergrid.html`

6

Font and Text Properties

As I discovered, while researching for this chapter, you could spend aeons just reading the information available on fonts. As you may be aware by now, I am neither a typographer nor a graphic designer, but am rather an engineer who is more worried about what works. Before I became font aware, I thought "Who could possibly need more than, Times, Arial, Courier, and perhaps a couple of fancy fonts such as Nuptial and Brush Script BT"? I also thought that the font selection capabilities provided by the CSS1 specification were more than adequate.

I am, however, a big believer in the old adage "the customer is always right". It has, therefore, become quite obvious to me that what the customer–including presumably a large number of typographers and graphic designers–wants is a better control of the fonts in which to write their web pages than is now currently available.

The CSS2 specification, with its support of Panose numbers, Netscape's Bitstream/Truedoc technology, and Microsoft's TrueType and Font Embedding Technology are all witness to this, and provide (unfortunately non-compatible) solutions to the provision of unique fonts over the Internet. Hopefully, a merging of standards will occur and the web-author will only have to worry about one method of implementation.

In the meantime, both the major players support the CSS1 standard, and it is recommended that this is what the majority of pages are written in. However, the other technologies are certainly exciting, even to a non-typographer such as myself, and we will examine them in some detail at the end of the chapter.

This chapter will:

- Start with a review of necessary font definitions and terms.
- Look in some detail at the properties used to describe fonts provided by the CSS specs.
- Review some necessary text definitions and terms.
- Look in some detail at the properties used to describe text provided by the CSS specs.
- Survey the various font solutions provided by the W3C, Netscape and Microsoft.

These will be detailed later in this chapter. Included in this preview will be a brief look at how the API of the dominant operating system (Windows) describes fonts.

So, let's start with some definitions.

Fonts and Font Properties

In the first half of this chapter we deal with fonts and their properties, as defined in CSS. We begin with some definitions of font terminology, which will be used in our explanation of the effect the various font properties will have on your web pages. We then list the font properties available, and go through the syntax and effect of each one. Most importantly, we tell you which browser supports which property, or even which browser supports which values for each property!

So, let's start with some definitions.

Font Definitions

In this section we'll examine;

- Fonts and typefaces
- Font names and copyright issues
- Fonts on computers
- Bitmap and scalable fonts
- Font anatomy, glyphs, cells and kerning
- Font categories and availability
- Font sizes and proportions

This may not seem immediately relevant, but we will use this terminology later in our explanations of the various font properties and so it is handy to be familiar as soon as possible.

Fonts and Typefaces

We have a tendency to use the terms **Font** and **Typeface** inter changeably, but they are in fact two different things.

A typeface is a whole **family of fonts**, such as the **Times New Roman** family. A font is a single instance of that family such as **Times 12pt Bold**, which is a **font** that is a member of the **Times** family.

Having said that, expressions such as–the Arial font family–and the shorthand–Arial font–is heard much more often than the more correct–Arial typeface family. That's O.K. Just as long as we understand exactly what is meant!

A font **foundry** is a place where fonts are made. In days of yore, actually as recently as the 1970's, they actually were foundries where the **molds** for fonts were made. Nowadays foundries make digital representations of fonts.

> *To set type, the compositor or typesetter would set all the font molds in a moldboard. Molten lead was then poured on to make an impression. The resulting block was used for printing. The advantage of this two stage process was that when setting up the type, a p looked like a p rather than a q!*

Font Names and Copyright Issues

Once a font has been designed, the foundry gives it a name and, in the US, it is this name that is copyrighted. It may be imitated as long as the digital code is not copied, or the same name used. This has lead to a lot of cheap imitations of well known fonts, so that 'English Times', may well be indistinguishable from 'Times New Roman.'

In European countries the laws are more stringent and such brazen mimicry is not allowed.

The copyright issue is an important one over the Web because, although it is easy enough to transfer a font over the Internet, doing so will usually breach various copyright laws.

Fonts on Computers

The challenge for style sheet writers is to get the font that they want displayed on the users screen or printer.

I can specify whatever font name I want on my style sheet, but if it's not on your computer then I'm out of luck!

To complicate things even further, it may be on your computer, but under a different name. For example, 'Times New Roman' on a PC and 'Times' on a Mac are identical fonts.

There are a number of ways I can get round this, for example:

- Specify several names, (the CSS1 approach),
- Send a general description and let your user agent choose the nearest match, (the CSS2 approach),
- Have a user agent that is capable of building a font from data sent to it, (the Netscape approach)
- Have several fonts in the public domain and send one of those (one Microsoft approach, obtain their font set from: `http://www.microsoft.com/typography/fontpack/default.htm`),
- Send a font which has been coded so that it can only be used on the users computer in the context of the current message thus preserving copyright (another Microsoft approach).

These approaches will be discussed in more detail at the end of this chapter.

Bitmap and Scalable Fonts

Fonts on computers can be either scalable or bitmapped. In the simplest terms, a bitmapped font is made up of blocks or bits; a scalable font is made up of mathematically defined vectors. This is rather like the difference between a vector drawing, and a bitmapped photo. Large bitmapped fonts can look rather ugly. This screen capture shows a Paint screen. The two fonts are similar at smaller sizes, but note the difference when they are blown up. The blocks that the bitmapped font is composed of are very obvious.

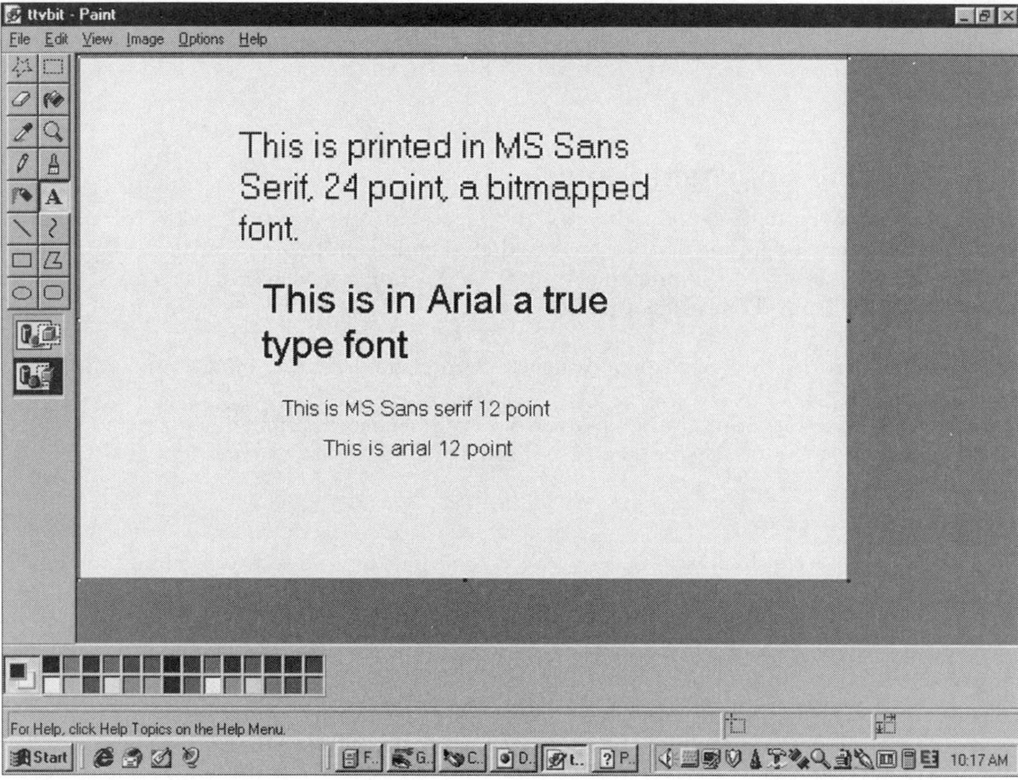

Most fonts nowadays are scalable fonts, also known as TrueType on Macs and PCs, and, unless stated otherwise, the comments in this chapter refer to them.

Font Anatomy, Glyphs, Cells and Kerning

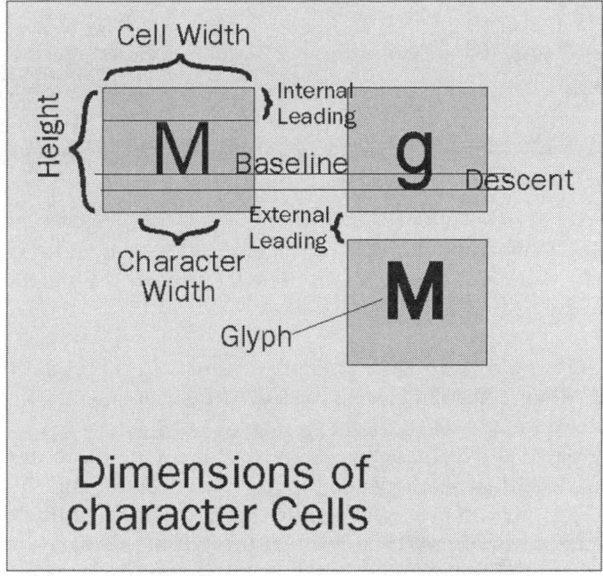

This shows the anatomy of a typical **Character** in a font. Note that the actual representation of the character is called a **Glyph**, and the whole thing is contained in a **character cell**, which has a given width.

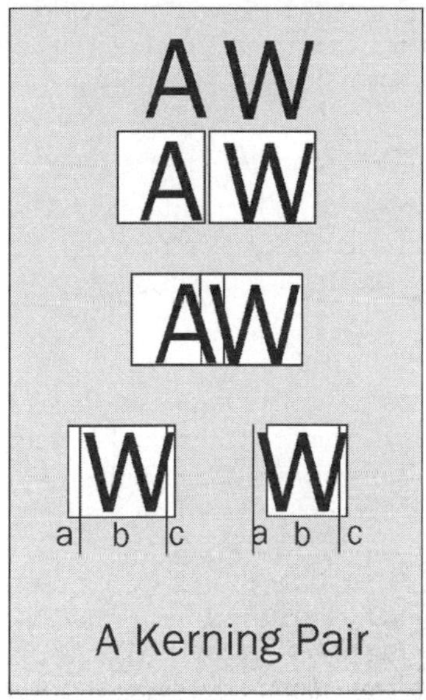

This drawing shows how two character cells are overlapped in the kerning process.

When two characters are placed side by side in a proportional font, although the width of the glyph will remain the same, the character cells will be overlapped to bring the characters closer together, for example 'AW' and 'ff' in the Times font. This relationship of overlapping cells, depending on which character it is next to, is called **Kerning**. The necessary information to enable kerning is carried in a table known as **Kerning Pairs**. In the days of physical fonts the typesetter would have different characters for "f" and "ff", because obviously the individual characters could not be physically over lapped.

> *The Windows API has 40 odd functions for manipulating text. GetKerningPairs is one of them if you ever need to retrieve kerning information.*

The drawing of a kerning pair above shows how it is done. The cell width is made up of three dimensions represented by the letters **a**, **b**, and **c**. The letter b represents the character or glyph width, and the letters a+b+c stand for the cell width.

In some situations the letters a or c are given negative values. In this situation, the Pair A-W gives a negative value to the **a** value of W. This is what causes the overlap.

Leading is the vertical space between the characters, and is divided into internal and external leading. Internal leading; the distance between the top of the Glyph and the top of the cell, is a font property. External leading; the distance between the bottom of one character cell and the top of the cell in the next line, is not a font property, it is a text formatting property, and we will discuss it in more detail in our discussion of text properties. (This discussion can be found under the later heading *Text Formatting and Formatting Properties.*)

In a **proportional font** the character cells are of varying width, compare (l) and (m). (m) is quite clearly wider than (l).

In a **mono-spaced** or **type-writer** font such as this sentence is written all the character cells are the same width, compare (l) and (m).

Font Categories and Font Availability

The CSS1 specification divides fonts up into five different categories. We'll give a brief description of each one, and then discuss their availability. A screenshot of all five types of font, as displayed by IE4 and Communicator follows these descriptions.

Serif

We talked a little about the different uses of serif and sans-serif fonts in Chapter 1. The serifs of a serif font often have a very complex structure which makes them more difficult to describe mathematically than sans-serif fonts. For example, in a study by Albrecht Durer (AD1510) the serifs in the classical Roman font were shown to be based on 9 different radii. This tends to make the digital signature of serif fonts larger.

The serifs serve to link the individual letters together so that the eye naturally reads the words rather than the letters. Most large bodies of text are written in a serif font.

Sans-Serif

These fonts are particularly useful for headings and small font sizes on the screen. The lack of serifs give a "clean" feel to these fonts. The lack of serifs makes them clearer to read at small sizes, especially in low-resolution screens.

Monospace

In the days of the typewriter we used to see mono-spaced fonts all the time, as all typewriters used them. They are really only used today for math and writing code. They are particularly appropriate for tables, where it is useful to be able to line words up in a vertical fashion.

Cursive

Cursive fonts are fonts which imitate human handwriting. Although useful and pleasing for small amounts of text, these fonts tend to be very tiring to read for an extended period of time. They tend to be used for a change of pace where it is intended for the reader to slow down.

Fantasy

This describes any font that doesn't fall into the above categories. The only ones that you can be **sure** will be on the users machine are a serif, a sans-serif, and a mono-spaced font, as this is all that default Windows and Macs have on them. In practice most users have many more loaded. As an illustration of this, let's check out the default fonts available in the two major browsers installed on your machine.

Testing your Browser's Font Defaults

To see what your browser displays for each of the five font types we've described above, copy the following code into a text editor, save it as **ch6_ex1.htm** and open it in your browser.

```
<HTML>
<HEAD>
<TITLE>
Chapter 6 Example "default fonts"
</TITLE>
<STYLE>
/*CLASSES HERE*/

BODY{
background-color:white;
font-size:16pt;
font-weight:400;
}

DIV.serif{
font-family:serif;
font-size:16pt;
font-weight:400;
}

DIV.sans{
font-family:sans-serif;
font-size:16pt;
font-weight:400;
}
```

```
DIV.mono{
font-family:monospace;
font-size:16pt;
font-weight:400;
}

DIV.cursive{
font-family:cursive;
font-size:16pt;
font-weight:400;
}

DIV.fantasy{
font-family:fantasy;
font-size:16pt;
font-weight:400;
}

</STYLE>
</HEAD>
<BODY>
This is what your browser defaults to.
<BR><BR>
<DIV CLASS="serif">This is what your browser defaults as a serifed
font</DIV>
<BR>
<DIV CLASS="sans">This is what your browser defaults as a sans serifed
font</DIV>
<BR>
<DIV CLASS="mono">This is what your browser defaults as a monospaced
font.</DIV>
<BR>
<DIV CLASS="fantasy">This is what your browser defaults as fantasy
font</DIV>
<BR>
<DIV CLASS="cursive">This is what your browser defaults as a cursive
font</DIV>
</BODY>
</HTML>
```

Here's what it looks like in my installation of IE4;

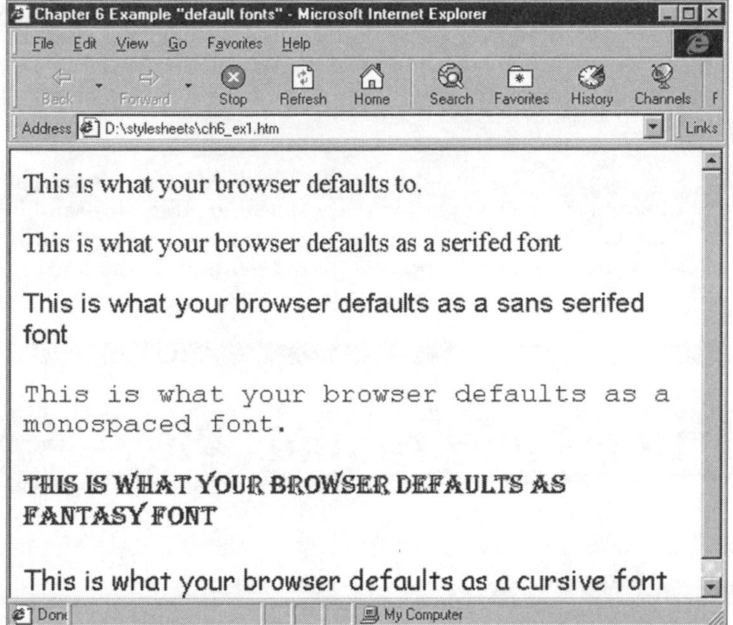

and here's the same file in Communicator.

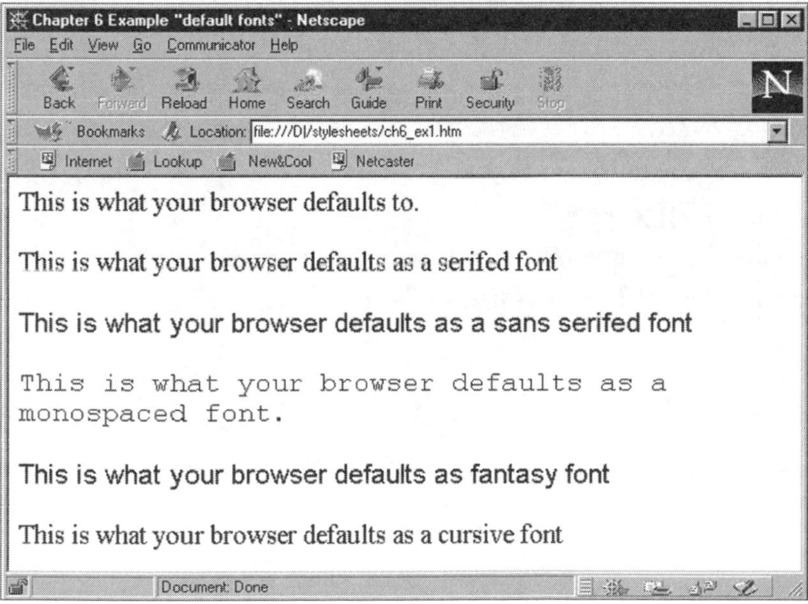

Netscape Navigator just presents Times New Roman for cursive and fantasy. IE4 is a little more adventurous!

Font Sizes and Proportions

The font size is the height of the character cell, i.e. the sum of the internal leading, the size of the body (also called the "x" or ex size), plus the ascender and descender height. It is usually measured in points there being 72 points to the inch. Note that the size the font appears on you screen may vary because of your screen size and resolution, but on your printer 72 points should produce a 1 inch high letter.

Although all fonts of the same size but of a different family will have the same cell height, their proportions may be different. Some will put the internal leading at the top, and others will split it between top and bottom. Cursive fonts will tend to have a smaller body size and larger ascenders and descenders. This screenshot shows proportions of different fonts compared to Times New Roman:

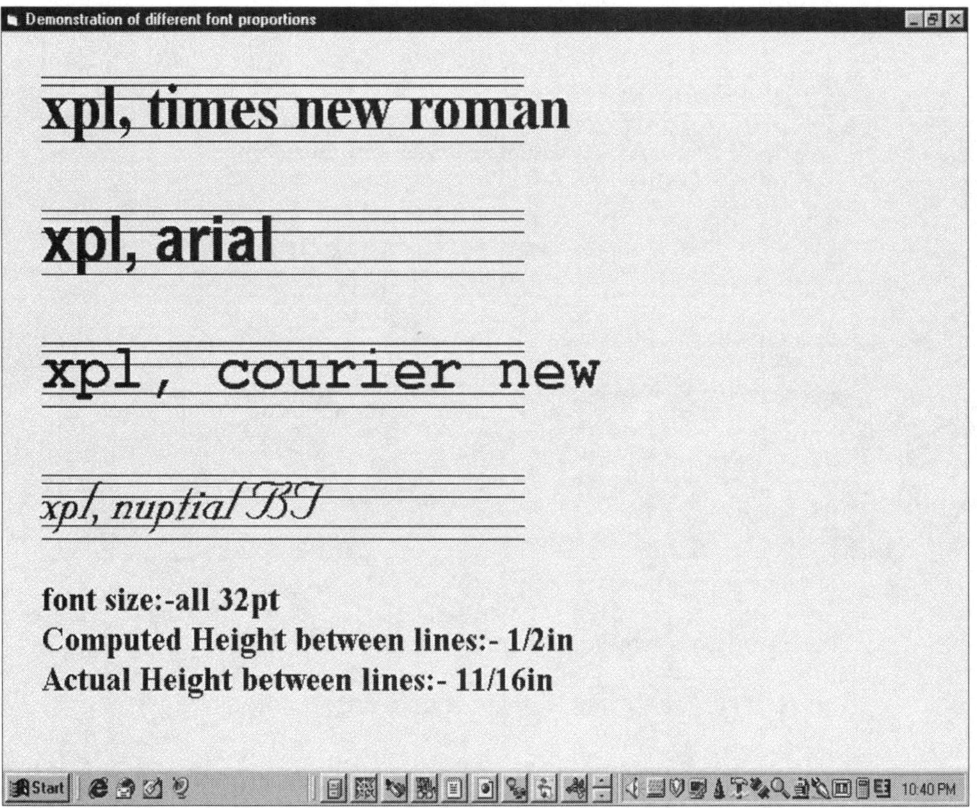

This shows a screen capture of a program used to compare font proportions. The lines were generated for Times New Roman and represent the proportions of that font. The other fonts have been over drawn on those proportions. Note that in this program, unlike a word processor, the fonts originate from the top line, so they are not all lined up on the base line.

This also demonstrates that in Times and Arial the leading is the same and all at the top, in Courier and Nuptial it is divided between the top and the bottom, and that the x size of Arial is bigger than Times, and that of Courier and Nuptial is smaller.

This has important implications, because our perception of the size of the font is tied in with the "x" or body size. The following lines all written in 12 point type illustrate this effect.

Here is Times New Roman:

The figure shows that in Times and Arial, the leading is the same and all at the top, in Courier and Nuptial it is divided between the top and the bottom, that the x size of Arial is bigger than Times, and that of Courier and Nuptial is smaller.

Here is Arial:

The figure shows that in Times and Arial, the leading is the same and all at the top, in Courier and Nuptial it is divided between the top and the bottom, that the x size of Arial is bigger than Times, and that of Courier and Nuptial is smaller.

Here is Courier New:

The figure shows that in Times and Arial, the leading is the same and all at the top, in Courier and Nuptial it is divided between the top and the bottom, that the x size of Arial is bigger than Times, and that of Courier and Nuptial is smaller.

Here is Nuptial BT:

The figure shows that in Times and Arial, the leading is the same and all at the top, in Courier and Nuptial it is divided between the top and the bottom, that the x size of Arial is bigger than Times, and that of Courier and Nuptial is smaller.

That concludes our coverage of font definitions, let's get straight into our examination of the properties used to describe font and text provided by the CSS specs.

CSS Font Properties

CSS provides various ways to describe all these font properties. Here is a table which summarizes the various properties.

Property Name	Example	Possible values	Initial value	Applies to/ inherited
`font-family`	`font-family: Arial, sans-serif;`	Any font-family name separate by a comma (,).	Determined by browser.	All/yes

Table Continued on Following Page

Property Name	Example	Possible values	Initial value	Applies to/ inherited
`font-size`	**`font-size:12pt`**	**`<absolute-size>|`** **`<relative-size>|`** **`<length>|`** **`<percentage>`** (Note relative units refer to parent elements font size)	Medium	All/yes
`font-style`	**`font-style: italic;`**	**`normal|italic|oblique`**	Normal	All/yes
`font-variant`	**`font-variant: small-caps;`**	**`normal|small-caps`**	Normal	All/yes
`font-weight`	**`font-weight: bold;`**	see text	Normal	All/yes

Now we've seen the summary, let's examine each of the properties separately. We'll explain the impact of each one in turn, and tell you which browser implements which property, fully, partially, or not at all.

Font-family

This is a list of font names separated by a comma, for example:

```
font-family: arial, helvetica, geneva, "lucida sans", sans-serif;
```

The browser will search through the fonts on the computer in the order that the fonts are listed, i.e. it will first look for Arial, then Helvetica, etc. If it doesn't find any of the named fonts it will use sans-serif, which, by definition, always exists. If your computer had just one font, say Courier, it would use this.

Note the use of double quotes to enclose a font with space in it. Although not strictly necessary, the use of single or double quotes is recommended.

We have already looked at some of the problems inherent in this system. Namely that the font may be under a different name, or there may not be a suitable font on the users system.

@font-face

CSS 2 introduces the **@font-face** rule. (Note that the browsers do not yet support this rule.) Briefly the rule works by pointing to a font description. It takes the general syntax:

@font-face {<*font-description*> **}**

where <*font-description*> has the form:

```
descriptor: value;
descriptor: value;
[...]
descriptor: value;
```

Introduce it in your style sheet as follows:

```
<STYLE TYPE="text/css" MEDIA="screen, print">
      @font-face {
        font-family: "My fantasy";
        src: url(http://mysite.com/fonts/Myfantasy)
      }
      H1 {font-family: 'My fantasy', fantasy}
</STYLE>
```

First the user agent would look on the computer to see if it had any information about "My fantasy". It could find either that it had no information, or it had some but not enough to make a match, or it had enough to attempt a match, or that it had the font itself.

If it hadn't got enough information it would then contact the web site given for further information. If for any reason it couldn't get the information at all it would fall back on the browser's default fantasy font.

Font-size

The syntax for this property is:

font-size:<absolute-size>|<relative-size>|<length>|<percentage>

where the value of **absolute-size** can take one of the following values:

xx-small|x-small|small|medium|large|x-large|xx-large

and the value of **relative-size** can be:

larger|smaller

Length can be in any unit. If a relative unit or a percentage value is used they both refer to the size of the font as a percentage or a proportion of the *parent element* unit. The following code illustrates this:

```
<HTML>
<HEAD>
<TITLE>
Chapter 6 Template
</TITLE>
<STYLE TYPE="text/css">
     /*CLASSES HERE*/

   BODY{
   background-color:white;
   font-size:16pt;
   font-weight:normal;
   }

   DIV{
   font-size:12pt;
   font-weight:normal;
   }
   H1{font-size:100%}
   SPAN{font-size:200%}

</STYLE>
</HEAD>
<BODY>
   This is 16 pt text.
   <DIV><H1>Heading of 100% </H1>Should be the same size as this text</DIV>
   Not the same size as this
   <DIV>
      <SPAN >this should be 20pt text</SPAN>
   </DIV>

   <DIV STYLE="font-size:12pt;">All this text should be the same size
      <DIV STYLE="font-size:1em;">All this text should be the same
size</DIV>
      <DIV STYLE="font-size:2ex;">All this text should be the same
size</DIV>
      <DIV STYLE="font-size:100%;">All this text should be the same
size</DIV>
      <DIV STYLE="font-size:1pc;">All this text should be the same
size</DIV>
   </DIV>
   <DIV STYLE="font-size:larger;">Fontsize should be larger</DIV>
   <DIV STYLE="font-size:smaller;">fontsize should be smaller</DIV>
   <DIV STYLE="font-size:xx-small;">Ascending size?xx-small</DIV>
   <DIV STYLE="font-size:x-small;">Ascending size?x-small</DIV>
   <DIV STYLE="font-size:small;">Ascending size?small</DIV>
   <DIV STYLE="font-size:medium;">Ascending size?medium</DIV>
   <DIV STYLE="font-size:large;">Ascending size?large</DIV>
   <DIV STYLE="font-size:x-large;">Ascending size?x-large</DIV>
   <DIV STYLE="font-size:xx-large;">Ascending size?xx-large</DIV>
```

```
<DIV STYLE="font-family:'nuptial bt',cursive;font-size:12pt;">This is 12
point nuptial bt
      <DIV STYLE="font-family: 'times new roman'; font-size:2ex;"> This
text should be 2X the height of the nuptial body type.
      </DIV>
   </DIV>

   <DIV STYLE="font-family:arial,sans-serif;font-size:12pt;">This is 12
point arial
      <DIV STYLE="font-family:'times new roman'; font-size:2ex;">This text
should be 2X the height of the arial body type.
      </DIV>
   </DIV>
</BODY>
</HTML>
```

The next two screenshots show the above code running in IE4 and Communicator. Both do a fairly good job of interpretation although they do put the heading in a bolder font. Note in particular how the em unit measures the height of the body of the parent font.

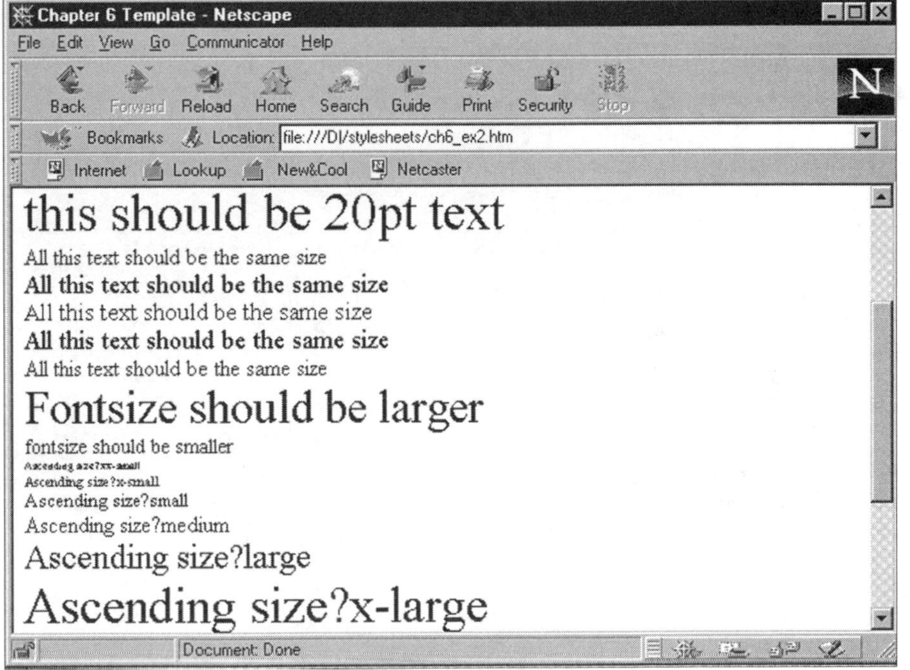

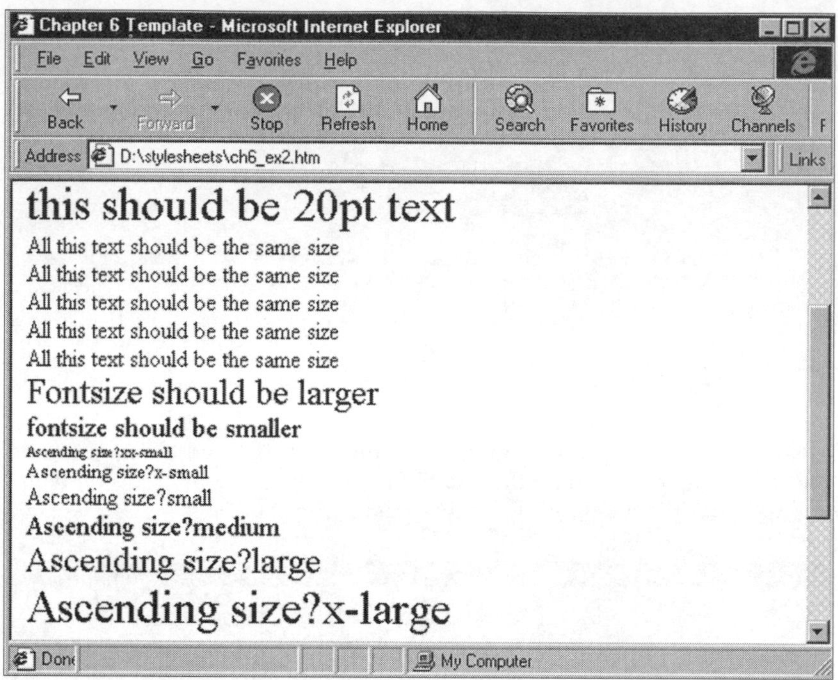

For a little variation try running this code and see what happens.

```
<DIV STYLE="font-family:nuptial bt,cursive;font-size:12pt;">This is 12
point nuptial bt
<DIV STYLE="font-family: 'times new roman'; font-size:2ex;"> This text
should be 2X the height of the nuptial body type.
</DIV>
</DIV>

<DIV STYLE="font-family:arial;,sans-serif;font-size:12pt;">This is 12 point
arial
<DIV STYLE="font-family: 'times new roman'; font-size:2ex;">This text
should be 2X the height of the arial body type.
</DIV>
</DIV>
```

It kind of works in Communicator 4.04, while IE4 treats ex like em

Font-Size-Adjust

CSS2 introduces this new property, which is designed to preserve the x height of the *first choice* font. As we mentioned above, the subjective size of the font is more dependent on its x height than on its em height.

This property takes the general syntax:

```
font-size-adjust: z|none
```

If the value z is set the user-agent sets the font size according to the following formula:

```
first_choiceFontsize =availableFontsize *  (z_available
font/z_first_choice)
```

where **z** is the ratio of the fonts em to ex i.e. em/ex. This property is not supported at present (see Appendix D for the definition of em and ex).

Color

Color could be considered a font property, but will be covered under the Background section and in Appendix E. For now note that the general syntax is:

```
color:<color>;
```

The value of color can either be expressed as a string e.g,

```
red, green, blue, black, white
```

as a six figure hex number e.g

```
#FF0000, #00FF00, #0000FF, #000000, #FFFFFF,
```

as a three figure hex number

```
#F00, #0F0, #00F, #000, #FFF
```

or as an RGB value

```
rgb(255,0,0), rgb(0,255,0), rgb(0,0,255), rgb(0,0,0), rgb(255,255,255)
```

Let's now take a look at three properties which we've grouped under the heading of font variations–**font-style**, **font-variant** and **font-weight**.

Font Variations

Most fonts come with some variations, like italic, bold and so on. Some font families have several. In the days of actual physical fonts, separate fonts represented all the various weights, italic and/or oblique styles, and small capitals. In the digital age they are more likely to be constructed 'on the fly' from the algorithm describing the base font. Note that the better fonts do not do this, i.e small caps is not just shrunk down uppercase letters, and the italic font is a separate font not a mathematically slanted regular font. As a rule 'lower quality' fonts will generate their italics, and small caps etc. by slanting or shrinking their regular font. The problem with this approach is that it messes up kerning, and can give the font a jagged appearance.

Note also that some fonts have a different name for their bold fonts, such as Arial Black. Use of this font is more likely to give a more pleasing result than just using the bold Arial. This is because the font is designed to be used as a thick font.

Here is bold Arial.

Here is Arial Black.

Instead of getting into all the problems arising from the different fonts, CSS lets you nominate the variation, and lets the browser sort out what to use, although this sometimes leads to a less than desirable result.

Let's take a look at each of the different types of variation in turn.

Font-Style

The syntax is:

```
font-style: [normal|oblique|italic]
```

If **`font-style`** is assigned a value of **`normal`**, the browser will search its database for a font labeled **`normal`**; if the value **`oblique`** is assigned it will look for an oblique font; if **`italic`** it should look for an italic font or, failing that, for an oblique one. Fonts with oblique, incline or slanted in their name will usually be called oblique, those with italic, cursive or kursive in their name will be labeled italic.

An italic font may be the normal font slanted. As we pointed out above this does not always give a good result.

Again, Navigator and IE differ in their behavior. Navigator ignores the oblique value, but whether that is a bug or whether it is following the letter of the spec in that it is not required to substitute an italic font for an oblique, I am not sure.

Both browsers will slope a font that in fact doesn't have (or need) an italic. The cursive nuptial script looks bearable this way the blocky Bedrock looks frankly awful!

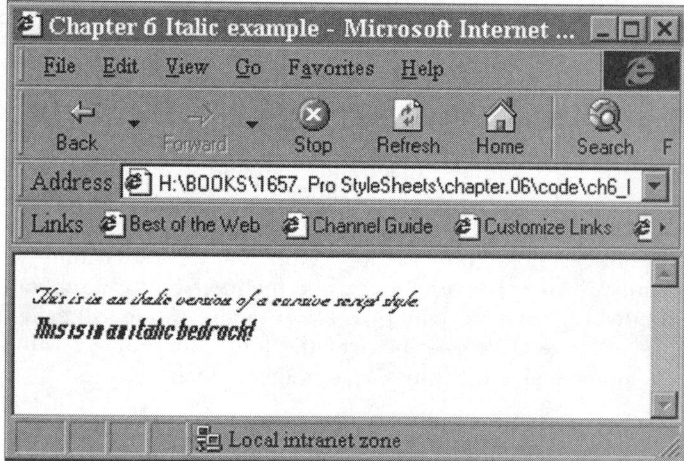

Another reason to be cautious of using italics is that the kerning values are often designed for normal text and not for italic. Note how an italic 'N' crashes into a normal 'l' making it look like a weird 'M'.

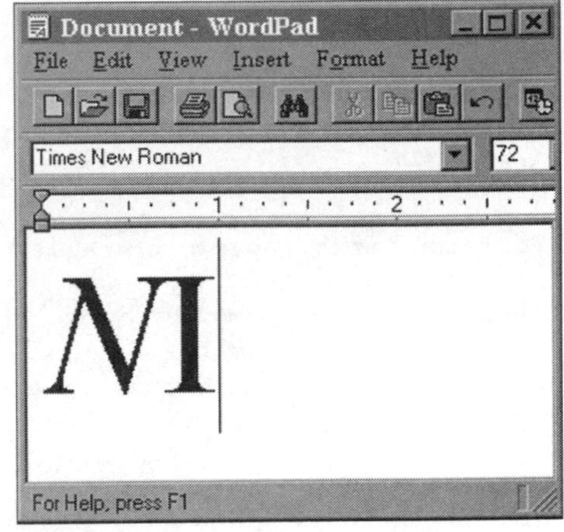

Try looking at these or check out **`fstyle.htm`** on the web-site at: **`http://rapid.wrox.co.uk/books/1657`**.

```
<DIV STYLE="font-family:'nuptial bt'font-style:normal;">This is in a normal
version of a cursive script style.</DIV>

<DIV STYLE="font-family:'nuptial bt'font-style:italic;">This is in an
italic version of a cursive script style.</DIV>

<DIV STYLE="font-family:bedrock;font-style:normal;">This is bedrock.</DIV>

<DIV STYLE="font-family:bedrock;font-style:italic;">This is in an italic
bedrock!</DIV>
```

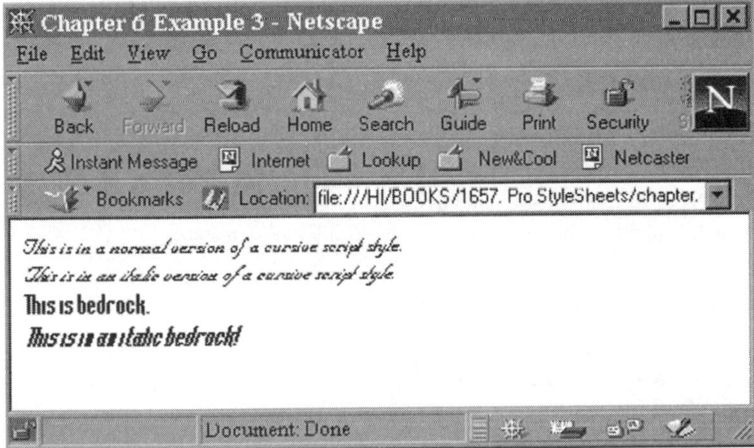

The adage is that you must check everything, because the user agent is just doing what it's been programmed to do.

Both browsers give a good implementation of this property, although Communicator ignores the oblique property.

Font-Variant

The syntax for this property is:

```
font-variant: [normal | small-caps]
```

There are two possible values for this property, normal or small-caps. A true small-caps font is **not** a scaled down version of the uppercase letterset but in practice most of the fonts do not have a 'small-caps' variation. In that case the CSS2 specification states it is acceptable (but not required) to scale down an upper case font.

The following figure shows how the following code should be rendered–namely the original uppercase letters should be larger than the characters rendered in small caps.

```
<DIV STYLE="font-variant:small-caps;">This should all be in small-caps with
THESE WORDS in slightly larger letters.</DIV>
```

THIS LINE SHOULD BE RENDERED IN SMALL CAPS WITH THESE WORDS SLIGHTLY LARGER THAN THE REST.

How small caps should be rendered.

Neither of the 4 series browsers support this property correctly. Netscape doesn't support it, and IE4 does not distinguish between regular uppercase and small-caps.

Font-Weight

Many fonts have no bold value at all. For example, the Nuptial BT font and Brushscript BT have nothing along the lines of Arial Black. These should in theory not be affected by the weight considerations, but in fact they are because the browser uses algorithms to darken or lighten the font, and just like the italics they can look pretty ugly as a result.

The syntax is:

```
font-weight: [normal| bold| bolder| lighter| 100| 200| 300| 400| 500|
600| 700| 800| 900]
```

Assignment of Weight

Numerous names can be given to the same weight of font. For example a bold font could be called all of the following:

`medium`, **`semibold`**, **`demi-bold`** **`or`** **`black`**

Normal fonts can be called:

`normal`, **`roman`**, **`Book`**, **`regular`** or even **`medium`** as well.

Because of this, CSS assigns a number to the font from 100 to 900. In assigning a number it follows these rules:

- If the font scale has a numerical scale, the font can be mapped directly.
- A name of **`regular`**, **`book`**, **`roman`**, **`normal`**, will be mapped to **`400`**, a **`bold`** to **`700`**.
- A **`medium`** will be mapped to **`500`**.
- **`Extra-bold`** will be mapped to **`800`**.
- The holes are filled in by a complex set of rules that we need not go into. If you are really interested see section 14.3.1 of the specification.

Even these few rules seem complicated, but luckily all you have to remember is to use **`normal`** and **`bold`**.

To see the weighting in action run the following sample or download it from the web-site as **`weight1.htm`**. This property is not fully supported in either Communicator or IE4 so don't expect it to work completely.

Example of font weighting

To see the effect of font weighting, copy or paste this code into your text editor, save it as a .htm file and display it in your browser. The code demonstrates the **`font-weight`** property as it is set out in the CSS specification. The screenshot that follows basically shows that it is not yet fully supported by the browsers.

```
<HTML>
<HEAD>
<TITLE>
Chapter 6 Example1
</TITLE>
<STYLE>
/*CLASSES HERE*/

BODY{
font-size:14pt;
background-color:white;
/*font-family:'times new roman',times,serif;*/
font-family:Arial,helvetica,sans-serif;
/*font-family:'courier new',courier,monospaced;*/
font-weight:normal;
}

DIV{
font-weight:400;
}

DIV.normal{
font-weight:normal;
}
```

```
DIV.lighter{
font-weight:lighter;
}

DIV.bold{
font-weight:bold;
}

DIV.bolder{
font-weight:bolder;
}

DIV.wt100{
font-weight:100;
}

DIV.wt200{
font-weight:200;
}

DIV.wt300{
font-weight:300;
}

DIV.wt400{
font-weight:400;
}

DIV.wt500{
font-weight:500;
}

DIV.wt600{
font-weight:600;
}

DIV.wt700{
font-weight:700;
}

DIV.wt800{
font-weight:800;
}

DIV.wt900{
font-weight:900;
}

SPAN.lighter{
font-weight:lighter;
}

SPAN.bolder{
font-weight:bolder;
}
</STYLE>
```

```
</HEAD>
<BODY>
This is a normal weight arial font 14 points.
<BR><BR>
<DIV CLASS="normal">
This should be normal weight, this should be <SPAN CLASS="lighter">
lighter, </SPAN>and this<SPAN CLASS="bolder"> bolder</SPAN> than the line
it is contained in.
</DIV>

<DIV CLASS="bold">
This should be bold weight, this should be <SPAN CLASS="bold"> lighter,
</SPAN>and this<SPAN CLASS="bolder"> bolder</SPAN> than the line it is
contained in.
</DIV>

<DIV CLASS="lighter">
This should be a lighter than normal weight, this should be <SPAN
CLASS="bold"> lighter, </SPAN>and this<SPAN CLASS="bolder"> bolder</SPAN>
than the line it is contained in.
</DIV>

<DIV CLASS="bolder">
This should be a bolder than normal weight, this should be <SPAN
CLASS="bold"> lighter, </SPAN>and this<SPAN CLASS="bolder"> bolder</SPAN>
than the line it is contained in.
</DIV>

<DIV CLASS="wt100">
A 100 weight font. This should be <SPAN CLASS="bold"> lighter, </SPAN>and
this<SPAN CLASS="bolder"> bolder</SPAN> than the line it is contained in.
</DIV>

<DIV CLASS="wt200">
A 200 weight font. This should be <SPAN CLASS="bold"> lighter, </SPAN>and
this<SPAN CLASS="bolder"> bolder</SPAN> than the line it is contained in.
</DIV>

<DIV CLASS="wt300">
A 300 weight font. This should be <SPAN CLASS="bold"> lighter, </SPAN>and
this<SPAN CLASS="bolder"> bolder</SPAN> than the line it is contained in.
</DIV>

<DIV CLASS="wt400">
A 400 weight font. This should be <SPAN CLASS="bold"> lighter, </SPAN>and
this<SPAN CLASS="bolder"> bolder</SPAN> than the line it is contained in.
</DIV>

<DIV CLASS="normal">Here is a normal line for comparison. CSS says that 400
should correspond to normal</DIV>

<DIV CLASS="wt500">
A 500 weight font. This should be <SPAN CLASS="bold"> lighter, </SPAN>and
this<SPAN CLASS="bolder"> bolder</SPAN> than the line it is contained in.
</DIV>
```

```
<DIV CLASS="wt600">
A 600 weight font. This should be <SPAN CLASS="bold"> lighter, </SPAN>and
this<SPAN CLASS="bolder"> bolder</SPAN> than the line it is contained in.
</DIV>

<DIV CLASS="wt700">
A 700 weight font. This should be <SPAN CLASS="bold"> lighter, </SPAN>and
this<SPAN CLASS="bolder"> bolder</SPAN> than the line it is contained in.
</DIV>
<DIV CLASS="bold">Here is a bold line for comparison. CSS says that 700
should correspond to bold.</DIV>

<DIV CLASS="wt800">
A 800 weight font. This should be <SPAN CLASS="bold"> lighter, </SPAN>and
this<SPAN CLASS="bolder"> bolder</SPAN> than the line it is contained in.
</DIV>

<DIV CLASS="wt900">
A 900 weight font. This should be <SPAN CLASS="bold"> lighter, </SPAN>and
this<SPAN CLASS="bolder"> bolder</SPAN> than the line it is contained in.
</DIV>
<DIV CLASS=""></DIV>
</BODY>
</HTML>
```

As the screenshot below illustrates, Communicator (incorrectly) interprets "**`bolder`**" as one weight number up rather than the next boldest available weight. It doesn't support "**`lighter`**" at all: (Neither does IE4)

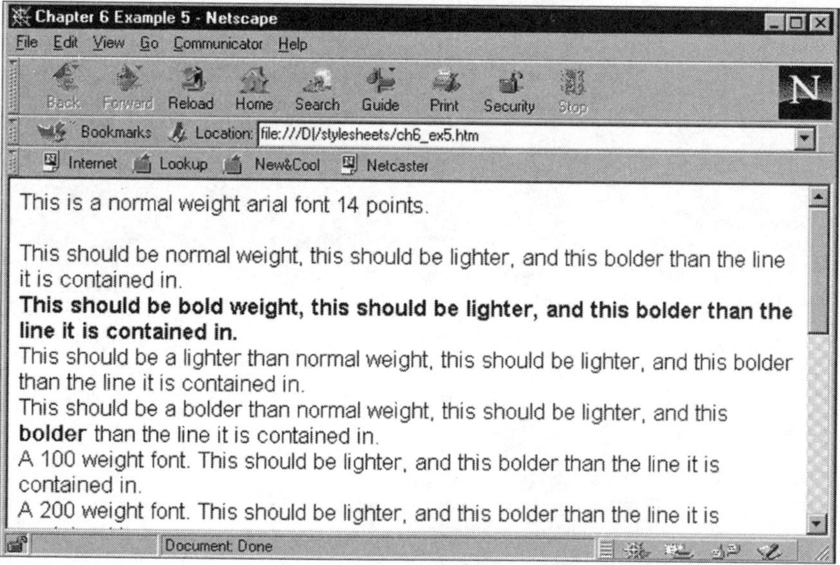

Although neither browser follows the law to the letter, if you confine yourself to **`bold`** and **`normal`** you can be confident of getting what you are expecting, otherwise check it out.

The Font Property

Instead of writing:

```
{
font-style: italic;
font-weight: bold;
font-variant: normal;
font-size: 14pt;
line-height: 18pt;
font-family: arial, helvetica, sans-serif;
}
```

CSS allows us to write:

```
{font: italic bold 14pt/18pt arial, helvetica, sans-serif;}
```

The syntax of the font property is as follows. This is covered in some detail in Appendix A in the section on *Reading the Official Specification.*

Font:[[<font-style>||<font-variant>||font-weight>]? <font-size>/[<line-height>]? <font-family>.

> *The CSS2 specification also has a provision in the font property for setting styles for the systems elements. Whether the OS makers will ever support this remains to be seen. To affect the style of the relevant part of the system, tack one of the following keywords on to the end;* **caption**, **icon**, **menu**, **messagebox**, **smallcaption**, **statusbar**.

The font property is well supported by both of the major players.

That concludes our look at the font properties outlined in CSS. Let's move on to look at text and text properties, beginning with some definitions.

Text Formatting and Formatting Properties

This section mirrors the section on fonts you have just read. First we'll take a brief look at some typesetting terms and then we'll examine the CSS text properties.

Typesetting Terms

We shall use these terms when explaining the effect the various text properties have on your web page.

Typesetters used to refer to the distance between words as the **space band** and the distance between letters they used to refer to as **tracking**. They used the terms **loose** or **very loose tracking** to refer to a lot of space between the letters and **tight, very tight**, etc. to refer to letters that had been squeezed together.

No tracking referred to the normal spacing between letters, i.e. the distance implied in the kerning. In the old days of physical type the compositors actually had **kerning pairs** as a single character. The space band was also a characteristic of the font, it is usually the width of the letter 'I'.

The vertical distance between the lines was referred to as **leading**, and was usually referred to in terms of points, e.g. 12 point type, 14 point leading

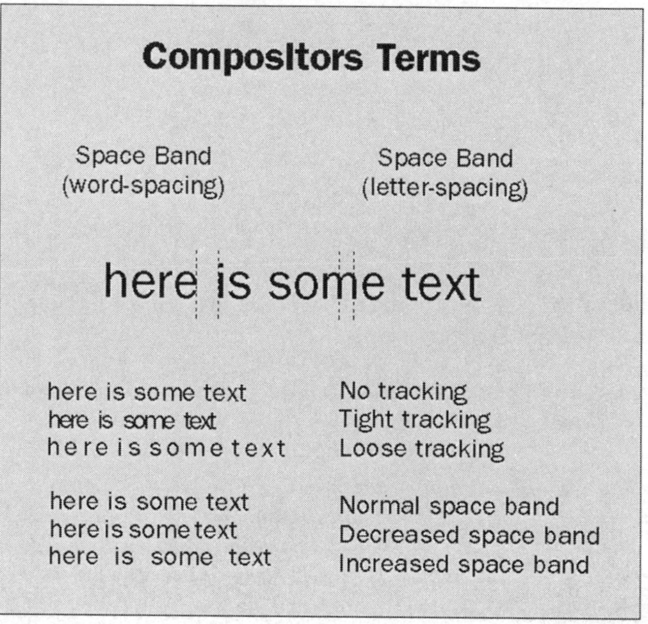

CSS leaves kerning up to the font but provides control over leading in the form of the **`line-height`** property, and control over space banding and tracking with the **`text-width`** and **`letter-width`** properties respectively.

`Line-height` is well implemented, but **`text-width`** and **`letter-width`** are very spottily implemented to say the least. Let's take a detailed look at the properties available.

CSS Text Properties

The following is a table showing the core CSS text properties.

<table>
<tr><th>Property Name</th><th>Example</th><th>Possible values</th><th>Initial value</th><th>Applies to/ inherited</th></tr>
<tr><td>word-spacing</td><td>word-spacing: 0.5em</td><td>normal | <length>
(note: Negative values permitted)</td><td>normal</td><td>All/Yes</td></tr>
<tr><td>letter-spacing</td><td>letter-spacing: 0.2em
Letter-spacing:-0.1em</td><td>normal | <length>
(Note: Negative values permitted)</td><td></td><td></td></tr>
<tr><td>text-decoration</td><td>text-decoration: underline blink</td><td>none | [underline || overline || line-through || blink]
(Note: can accept several values)</td><td>none</td><td>All/No</td></tr>
<tr><td>vertical-align</td><td>vertical-align: middle</td><td>baseline | sub | super | top | text-top | middle | bottom | text-bottom | <percentage>
(Note:% is relative to line-height property, negative values permitted)</td><td>baseline</td><td>Inline elements /No</td></tr>
<tr><td>text-transform</td><td>text-transform: uppercase</td><td>none | Capitalize | UPPERCASE | lower-case</td><td>none</td><td>All /Yes</td></tr>
<tr><td>text-align</td><td>text-align: center</td><td>left | right | center | justify</td><td>left</td><td>Block-level elements /Yes</td></tr>
</table>

Table Continued on Following Page

Property Name	Example	Possible values	Initial value	Applies to/ inherited
text-indent	**text-indent: 4em** **text-indent: 20%**	**<length> |** **<percentage>** (Note: % refers to parent elements width, negative values permitted)	**0**	Block-level elements /Yes
line-height.	**line-height: 200%** (ie. Double spaced)	**normal |** **<number> |** **<length> |** **<percentage>** (Note: Negative value not permitted)	**normal**	All/Yes
white space	**white-space: pre**	**normal | pre | nowrap**	**normal**	Block-level elements/Yes

Now let's examine each of these properties in turn.

Word-Spacing

Word spacing increases the distance between the words, what we defined at the beginning of this section as the **space band**. This property is not implemented in either browser.

The syntax is:

```
Word-spacing: [normal | <length>]
```

Negative values are permitted.

Be warned that putting this property in your style rule appears to switch off line-height (leading) properties!

Letter-Spacing

Letter spacing increases tracking. This property is not implemented at all in Navigator, and in IE it is incorrectly implemented in that it also increases the space between the words. At least this makes the text readable, because IE does not support the **word-spacing** property. (See **txtwsls.htm** for an example of the above properties.)

The syntax for this property is:

```
letter-spacing: [normal | length]
```

It increases the amount of space between the characters. It should not increase the space between the words.

The diagram below illustrates the impact of word spacing and letter spacing. We can't show you a screenshot because the properties aren't yet fully supported.

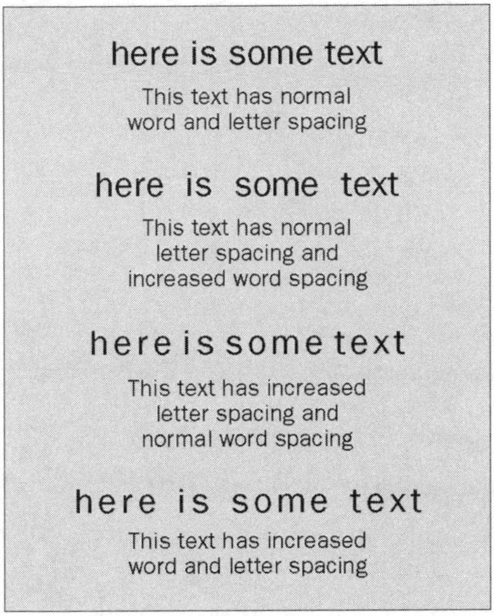

here is some text

This text has normal
word and letter spacing

here is some text

This text has normal
letter spacing and
increased word spacing

here is some text

This text has increased
letter spacing and
normal word spacing

here is some text

This text has increased
word and letter spacing

Text-Decoration

This property allows you to add underlining, overlining, strike through and a blinking on and off effect to your text. The browsers do not support all values for the property. Communicator ignores the **overline** value and IE4 ignores the **blink** value.

The syntax for this property is:

text-decoration: [none|[underline|| overline ||line-through || blink]]

Note that this property can take multiple values. For example:

```
<DIV STYLE= "Text-decoration: underline overline line-through blink;">This
should be underlined, over-lined, struck through, blinking text!
Yuck!</DIV>
```

This would produce underlined, over-lined, struck through, blinking text if browser support allowed.

Vertical-Align

This property is most useful when used with images. It is supported pretty well for dealing with images in both browsers. When dealing with text, really only the **sub** and **super** values are supported.

The syntax is:

vertical-align: baseline | sub | super | top | text-top | middle | bottom| text-bottom | <percentage>

This illustration shows how images and text should line up for each of these values, according to the CSS definition of the **vertical-align** property.

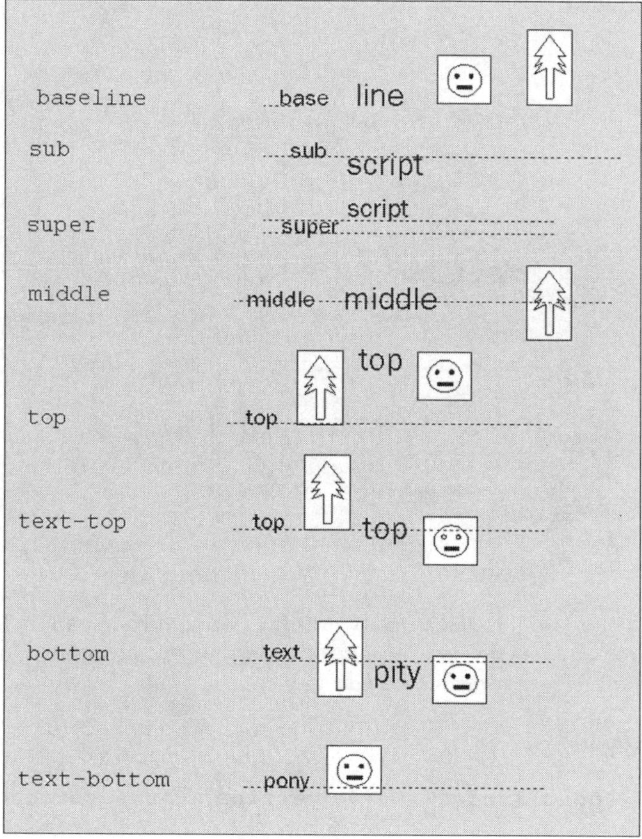

Let's examine the positioning which should be brought about by each of the values in turn.

baseline

Everything should be lined up on the baseline.

sub

The top of the image should be on the baseline. With text the top of the font body should be on the base line.

super

The bottom of the image should be on a level with the top of the font body. With text the bottom of the descender should align with the top of the font body.

top

The top of the text and the top of the image should align with the top of the tallest element on the line.

text-top

The top of the text and the top of the image should align with the top of the tallest text on the line.

middle

The middle of the text (i.e. the middle of the body) and the middle of the image should all line up with the middle of the parent text.

bottom

The bottom of the text (the descender) and the bottom of the image should align with the bottom of the lowest element on the line.

text-bottom

The bottom of the text (i.e. the descender) and the bottom of the image should align with the bottom of the lowest text on the line.

percentage

This value is given as a percentage of the elements line height value. It may be negative.

Example of use of vertical-alignment

The following code tests how the **vertical-alignment** property is implemented in your browser:

```
<HTML>
<HEAD>
<TITLE>
Chapter 6  Vertical alignment
</TITLE>
<STYLE TYPE="text/css">
/*CLASSES HERE*/

BODY{
font-size:12pt;
font-weight:normal;
background-color:white;
}

.smalltype{
font-size:12pt;
font-weight:normal;
}

.bigtype{
font-size:18pt;
font-weight:normal;
}
```

```
SPAN.{}

/*begin vertical align classes*/

.sub{vertical-align:sub;}

.super{vertical-align:super;}

.top{vertical-align:top;}

.texttop{vertical-align:text-top;}

.middle{vertical-align:middle;}

.bottom{;vertical-align:bottom;}

.textbottom{vertical-align:text-bottom;}

.percent1{vertical-align:100%;}

.percent2{vertical-align:50%;}

</STYLE>
</HEAD>
<BODY>
<BR>
<DIV CLASS="smalltype">pity
   <SPAN CLASS="bigtype">pity</SPAN>
   <IMG SRC="fir.gif">
   <IMG SRC="smiley.gif">
 All on the base line. Default rendering.
</DIV>
<BR>
<DIV CLASS="smalltype">pity
   <SPAN CLASS="bigtype">
   <SPAN CLASS="sub">pity</SPAN>
   </SPAN>
Value="sub". Sub Doesn't work on Communicator.
</DIV>
<BR>
<DIV CLASS="smalltype">pity
<SPAN CLASS="bigtype">
<SPAN CLASS="sub">pity</SPAN>
<IMG CLASS="sub" SRC="smiley.gif">
</SPAN>
Value="sub". The script gets 'subed' but not the image. Doesn't work on
Communicator.
</DIV>
<BR>
<DIV CLASS="smalltype">pity
   <SPAN CLASS="bigtype">
   <SPAN CLASS="super">pity</SPAN>
   </SPAN>
Value="super". Doesn't work on Communicator.
</DIV>
<BR>
```

```
<DIV CLASS="smalltype">pity
   <SPAN CLASS="bigtype">
   <SPAN CLASS="super">pity</SPAN>
   <IMG CLASS="super" SRC="smiley.gif"></SPAN>
Value="super". The script gets 'supered' but not the image.Doesn't work on
Communicator.
</DIV>
<BR>
<DIV CLASS="smalltype">pity
   <SPAN CLASS="bigtype">
   <SPAN CLASS="middle">pity</SPAN>
   <IMG CLASS="middle" SRC="fir.gif">
   </SPAN>
Value="middle".Middle works with the image but not with the text on both
IE4 and Communicator
</DIV>
<BR>
<DIV CLASS="smalltype">pity
   <SPAN CLASS="bigtype">
   <IMG SRC="fir.gif">
   <SPAN CLASS="top">pity</SPAN>
   <IMG CLASS="top" SRC="smiley.gif">
   </SPAN>
Value="top". Works with smiley but not large pity.
</DIV>
<BR>
<DIV CLASS="smalltype">pity
   <SPAN CLASS="bigtype">
   <IMG SRC="fir.gif">
   <SPAN CLASS="texttop">pity</SPAN>
   </SPAN>
   <IMG CLASS="texttop" SRC="smiley.gif">
Value="text-top". This is not quite correct, the specification calls for
aligning the top of the image with the top of the <I>parent</I> elements
font, ie the small text, and here it is aligned with the large text.
</DIV>
<BR>
<DIV CLASS="smalltype">pity
<IMG CLASS="middle" SRC="fir.gif">
<SPAN CLASS="bigtype">
<SPAN CLASS="bottom">pity</SPAN>
</SPAN>
<IMG CLASS="bottom" SRC="smiley.gif">
Value="bottom". IE4 gets the image right, Communicator just puts smiley on
the base line instead of aligning it with the bottom of fir.gif.
</DIV>
<BR>
<DIV CLASS="bigtype">pity
<IMG CLASS="textbottom" SRC="smiley.gif">
<IMG CLASS="middle" SRC="fir.gif">
</SPAN>
<IMG CLASS="textbottom" SRC="smiley.gif">
<SPAN CLASS="smalltype">
Value="text bottom". Navigator gets the first one right, but the second
smiley it lines up with the bottom of fir, treating it like a bottom value
rather than a text-bottom value"
</SPAN>
```

```
</DIV>
<BR>
<DIV> Pity
<SPAN STYLE="vertical-align:150%;">Pity</SPAN>
<IMG STYLE="vertical-align:150%;" SRC="smiley.gif">
</DIV>
<SPAN CLASS="">
</SPAN>
</BODY>
</HTML>
```

The code should look like this on IE4, showing reasonable implementation.

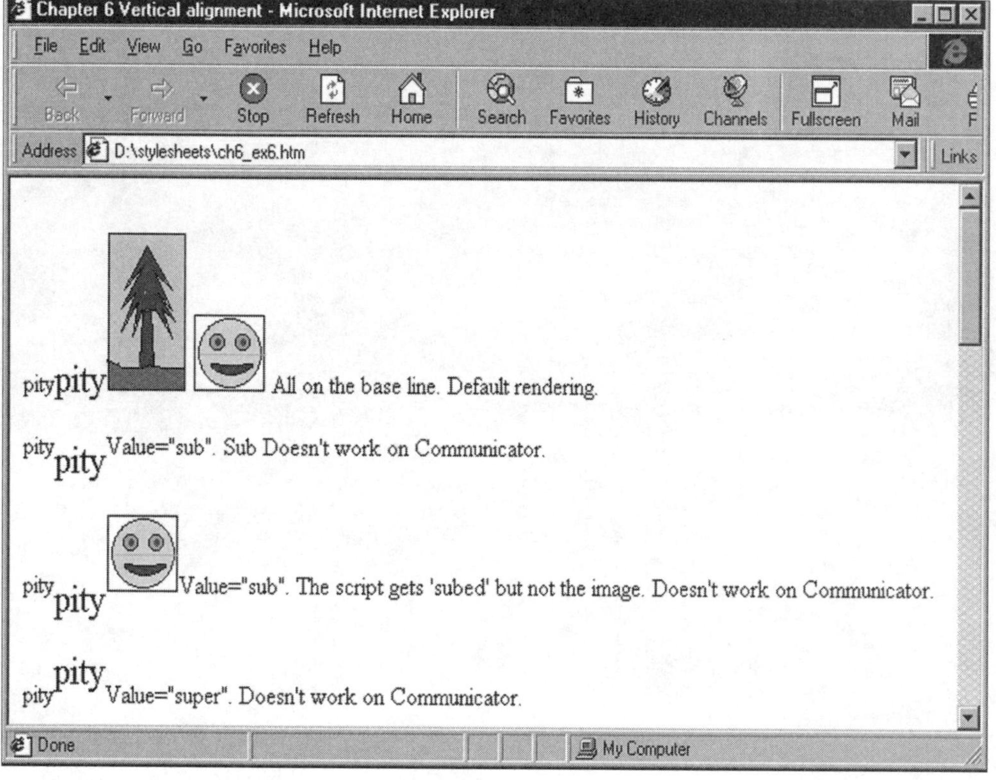

For text, only **sub** and **super** work in IE4. No values are supported for text in Communicator.

Implementation with images is much better, but still not good. As this is currently being worked on and patches are being released, any detailed information printed here would probably be out of date. (See the up to date table at the web-site, **http://rapid.wrox.co.uk/books/1657**.)

Text-Transform

The syntax for text transformation is:

`text-transform: [none | Capitalize | UPPERCASE | lowercase]`

`Capitalize`–capitalizes every first letter in the word.

This property works well in both browsers. Let's look at an example of how it works.

Example of use of text-transformation property

```
<HTML>
<HEAD>
<TITLE>
Text Transform
</TITLE>
<STYLE>
/*CLASSES HERE*/

BODY{
background-color:white;
font-size:12pt;
font-weight:400;
}

DIV.cap{
text-transform:capitalize;
font-size:12pt;
font-weight:normal;
}

DIV.upper{
text-transform:uppercase;
font-size:12pt;
font-weight:normal;
}

DIV.lower{
text-transform:lowercase;
font-size:12pt;
font-weight:normal;
}

</STYLE>
</HEAD>
<BODY>
   <DIV CLASS="">
   <SPAN></SPAN>
   </DIV>
   <DIV>Here is a normal line of text.</DIV>
   <DIV CLASS="cap">The first letters of all these words should be
capitalised.</DIV>
   <DIV CLASS="upper">ThESe shOUld aLl be in UPper cASE.</DIV>
```

```
    <DIV CLASS="lower">ThESe shOUld aLl be in lower cASE.</DIV>
</BODY>
</HTML>
```

And to prove that it works in both, here are the screenshots.

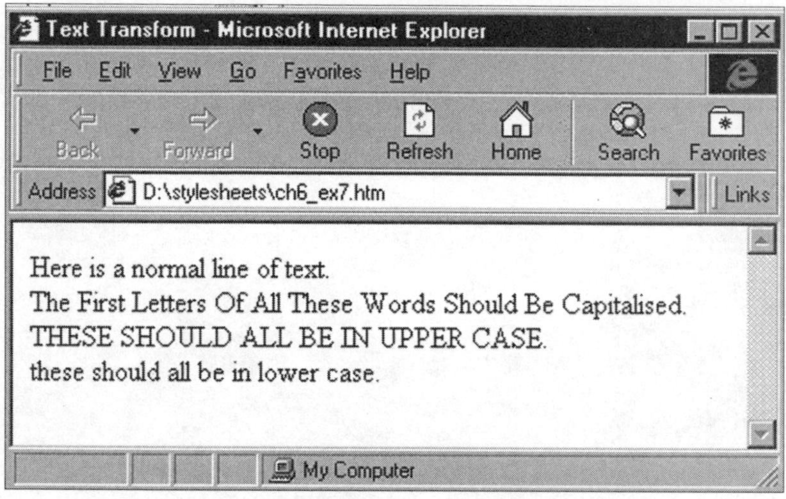

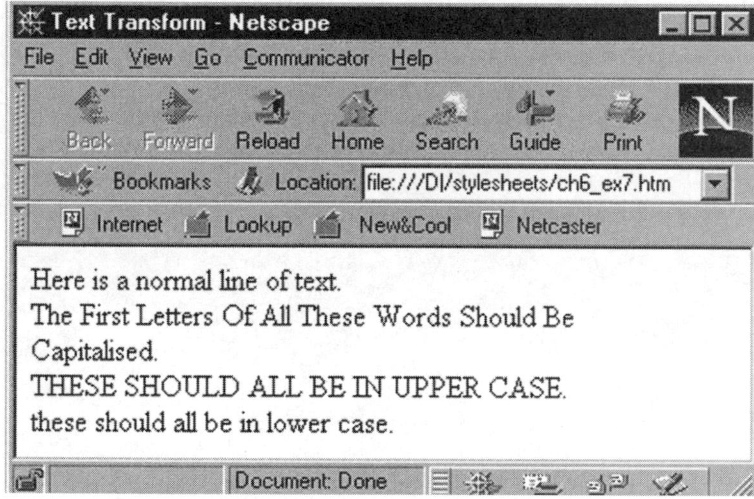

Text-Align

In a way this property is misleading, because it does not just declare how the text lines up, but rather how both the text and the line-boxes that contain them line up. Here's how the CSS specification defines it:

15.2 Alignment the 'text-align' property....
.... "This property describes how a paragraph of text is aligned. More precisely, it specifies how boxes in each line box of a block align width respect to the line box. (Note that alignment is not with respect to the viewpoint but the current containing block.)"

The syntax is:

```
text-align:[left | right | center | justify]
```

Let's look at how each of the values work in turn.

left

This is the standard way to present text, the text all lines up flush to the left. Any line-blocks or line-boxes that are contained in the parent element should also line up flush to the left.

right

Same as above, but contained units and text should be lined up flush right.

center

Same as above, but contained units and text should be centered.

justify

Here the text should be lined up flush with both margins. The CSS wording would suggest that the contained elements should as well! This seems ludicrous, and the best approach would seem to be to set it to the left as IE4 does.

Justified text should be used with caution. The extra space is put into the space band between the words, and if you have a line with a few large words in it the result can be ugly.

Further usually the font has been designed for best readability, and the space band is an important part of that readability. Many typographic gurus claim that to have to read several columns of justified text is much more tiring to the eye than reading left aligned text.

The bottom line is–use this property sparingly.

So, how do the browsers deal with **`text-align`**? IE4 does a fairly good job of rendering the text as expected. In Communicator, if the **`align`** value is set for the contents of the box, it is applied to the box itself. This can be seen in the following screenshot which shows the box aligned to the left with the text inside. The text outside the box is rendered correctly in the centre.

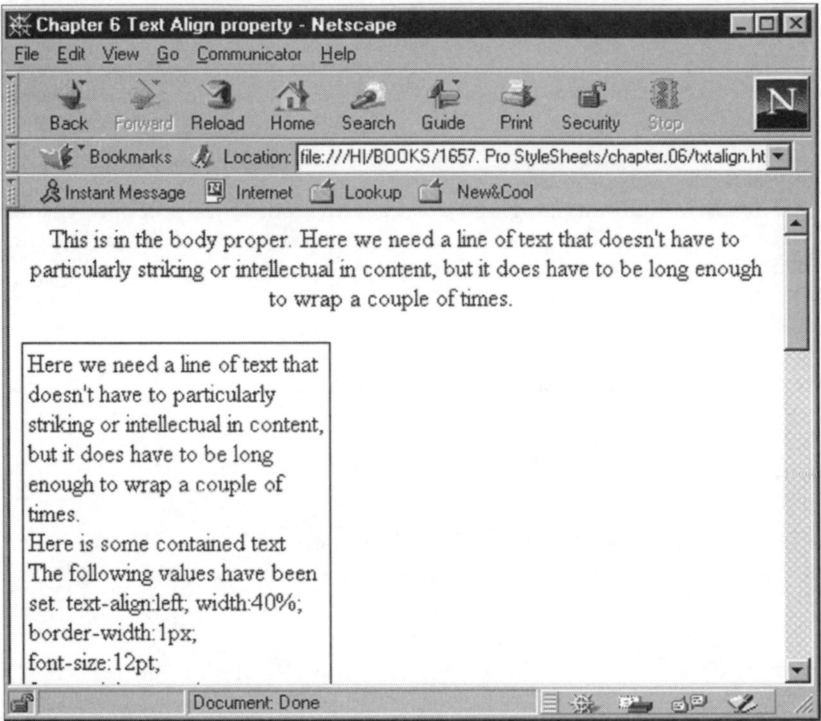

The implementation of **`justify`** is OK for the simplest pages, but it gets awfully tricky if you start trying to implement it for containers within containers! The best thing to do is to check these pages yourself if you are going to use this feature. See **`txtalgn.htm`** on the web site for examples of **`text-align`** code at: **`http://rapid.wrox.co.uk/books/1657`**

Text-Indent

This is applied to all block level elements and indents the first line of the element by the amount in the value. If **`%`** is used it refers to the width of the parent element.

The syntax is:

```
text-indent:[<length>|<percentage>]
```

IE4 doesn't support **`text-indent`** at all. Communicator does a good job. However, there is an amusing bug in the percentage value. If the percentage is less than the width of the contained box then it is interpreted as a percentage of the contained box otherwise it is interpreted (correctly) as a percentage of the containing element.

> *Try it in the example* **`txtindnt.htm`** *from the web site and change the percentage from 35 to 40.*

Line-Height

This is probably one of the most important properties in text layout, and both browsers implement it fully. Remember that, as a rule of thumb, the longer the line, the greater the amount of leading.

The syntax of this property is:

`line-height: [normal| <number> | <length> | <percentage>]`

When the value is given in the form of a number, multiply **`font-size`** by that number, the same with percentage.

For a line of text of 12 points:

```
Line-height: 200%;
line-height: 2;
line-height: 24pt;
```

The above would all give double spacing.

Check out the example at **`txtlnht.htm`** on the web site.

White-Space

White space is very important in any document layout. Not only does it add to the aesthetic appeal, but in some cases–such as the rendition of poetry–it is essential to get the meaning across. In math and code it is also vital, but perhaps here we do not worry so much about the aesthetic qualities.

The syntax of the white-space property is as follows:

`White-space:[normal | pre | nowrap]`

Let's examine the effect of each of these values in turn.

normal

Provides the normal HTML route in that it collapses multiple spaces into one.

pre

Preserves all white space just like the HTML **`<PRE>`** tag. The great thing about the CSS **`pre`** is that all the other formatting values should also apply so that you can make some thing look really good. The HTML **`<PRE>`** tags used to render everything in monospace type which looked mundane at best. OK for code and math, but for Walter de la Mere or the Bard...I don't think so.

nowrap

The text should not wrap until it meets a **`<BR>`**. this is not well supported at present.

Let's take a look at implementation of the **`white-space`** property and its values. The **`nowrap`** value is supported by neither agent at the time of writing. Communicator does a great job with the **`<PRE>`** tag while IE4 makes a mess of it. In practice to make this work put in the **`<PRE>`** tags as well as the **`pre`** value for the **`white-space`** property, because it makes no difference to Communicator and gives you what you probably intended with IE4.

Check out **wspace.htm** from the web site to see how your browser implements this property.

Text-Shadow

This is a new CSS2 property, described in section 15.3.2 of the specification, and not yet supported in browsers.

The CSS2 specification warns:

"This property is not defined in CSS1. Some shadow effects may render text invisible in UAs that only support CSS1. "

The effect is to give text a shadow. The syntax is:

text-shadow: none | [<color> || <length> <length> <length>? ,]* [<color> || <length> <length>? <length>?] | inherit

Note that the syntax allows as many shadows as you want! The first two lengths indicate the offset in X and Y direction respectively, the third length specifies a blur effect.

```
H1 { text-shadow: 0.2em 0.2em }
```

The above would specify a shadow 0.2em to the right and below,

```
H1 { text-shadow: -0.2em -0.2em 0.5em red}
```

Whereas the second example would specify a shadow to the left and above, with a blur effect of 0.5em and a shadow colored red.

```
H1 {
text-shadow: 3px 3px red,
yellow -3px 3px 2px,
3px -3px
}
```

Would specify three overlain shadows of red, yellow and black respectively. (Note the comma-separated values.)

Pseudo-Classes

There are two text pseudo-classes–**first-line** and **first-letter**.

Pseudo elements allow you to code for variable situations. Obviously the first line of a paragraph of text is going to vary depending on a number of factors not necessarily within the control of the author, for example the font size or the width of the viewing window.

first-line

The writing of a first line in a different size or weight of font is a typical typographic trick, for example:

This book should serve as an introduction
to the use of columns in the layout of text.

This book should serve
as an introduction to the
use of columns in the lay
out of text.

This trick can be very useful, and the following code should reproduce it in a conforming user agent. Unfortunately neither of the current browsers support either of these properties.

```
<STYLE TYPE="text/css">
P{color:red;
width:3in;
}
P:first-line {
font-weight: bold;
color:green; }
DIV{
color:navy;
width:3in;}
</STYLE>
```

Note how a colon is used rather than a period.

first letter

First-letter pseudo class produces a drop cap. It is not supported by either browser at the moment, but by judicious use of the position property, we can produce the effect illustrated below:

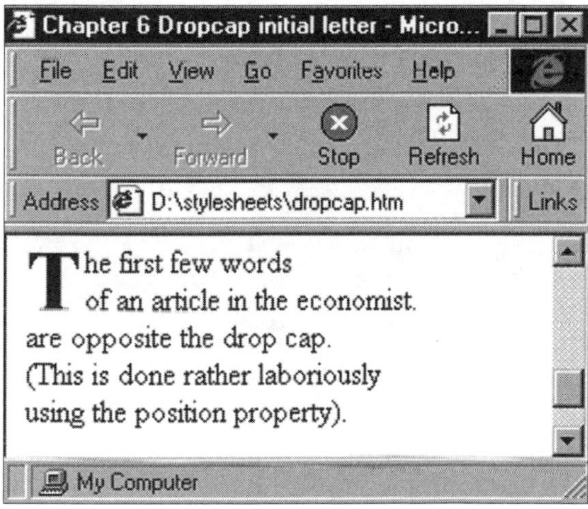

We'll cover how you can achieve this effect in the next chapter, or you can simply look at the source of **`dropcap.htm`** on the web site at: **`http://rapid.wrox.co.uk/books/1657`**.

Note how the top of the drop cap should be at the top of the main font, and the base of the drop cap should be on the same base line as the line of text it drops down to.

It would appear that even if the first-letter pseudo class was supported then just specifying a font size would not sufficiently describe this complex situation.

Font Descriptions

Before finishing off this chapter let's look at some of the ways that the font problem is being tackled. We'll cover the following topics:

- Bitstream Technology–the Netscape Solution
- Web Embedding Font Technology–the Microsoft Solution
- Panose Numbers–the Hewlett-Packard solution

Let's start with a look at what Netscape have to offer.

Bitstream Technology

Bitstream technology is being developed jointly by Bitstream and Netscape. It gives the web page author a way to reference the true-type or post-script fonts that he has on his system.

Essentially the system consists of two parts, a tool called a Character Shape Recorder (CSR), which is used to make a file called a PFR (Portable Font Resource), and a Character Shape Player.

Authors wishing to use a particular font that they have on their system use a CSR tool (contained in many web authoring tools including Netscape Communicator) to make a PFR file. When they write their HTML pages they can then reference that file either by way of the HTML **`font-face`** property or via a style sheet.

Here's an example of how it works.

```
<FONT FACE="Cataneo BT" SIZE=5>

<STYLE TYPE="text/css">
@font-face {
font-family: Chianti XBd BT;
 src: url(http://mysite/path/mypage.pfr);
  font-weight: normal
}

@font-face {
 font-family: Gothic720 BT;
 src: url(http://mysite/path/mypage.pfr);
  font-weight: normal
}
```

```
 H1 {
font-family: Chianti XBd BT, Arial, Helvetica, sans-serif;
font-weight: normal
}

BODY {
font-family: Gothic720 BT, Times New Roman, Times Roman, serif;
font-weight: normal
}
</STYLE>
```

Note how the PFR file is referenced through either a **link** or a CSS **@font-face** reference.

In order for users to download and view TrueDoc PFRs from their TrueDoc-enabled web browsers, i.e. a Netscape browser, the system administrators must set up their web servers to recognize the **PFR MIME** type.

The **MIME** type is:

```
application/font-tdpfr
```

The file extension is:

```
pfr
```

At present (of course) only Communicator supports this technology.

Readers interested in pursuing this technology are referred to the Netscape/Bitstream web page at: **http://www.bitstream.com**

Open Type and Web Embedding Font Technology

This is Microsoft's solution to providing fonts over the web. It will only work with IE4. Here's how they describe it.

"OpenType fonts may contain digital signatures, which allows operating systems and browsing applications to identify the source and integrity of font files, including embedded font files obtained in web documents, before using them."

What this means in a nutshell is that open type fonts can be designated for use only with certain user agents such as a browser, and can't be used in the end-users general applications.

Essentially a tool called a Web Embedding Fonts Tool is used to create a very compact font from an opentype font for transmission to the user as a font object.

When a user agent (at present time only IE4) encounters a page that has a font object linked to it, the font object will be downloaded and cached like any other file. The font object is decompressed and the font it contains is privately installed. Only the browser has access to this privately installed font. The privately installed font can not be accessed by other applications on the user's machine, thus getting around copyright issues.

Check out:

http://www.microsoft.com/typography/web/embedding/weft/default.htm

for more details of this technology.
Microsoft also provides a selection of core fonts that you can link to:

http://www.microsoft.com/typography/fontpack/default.htm

Panose Numbers

What do you think the chances are of Netscape and Microsoft agreeing on a technology, or even agreeing to support the others technology? As my uncle Zeke used to say, about the same as a snowflakes chance of surviving in Hell.

One of the systems W3C is considering is the Panose system, which details various metrics for describing fonts. Among the advantages is that it is a neutral technology, owned by Hewlett-Packard, and that it can be used for describing non-Latin fonts, even Kanji (which has several thousand characters).

In simple terms, it describes 10 aspects of the font and then uses a system to assign numbers to the various characteristics.

For example for a Latin text the characteristics are as follows:

- Latin Text: Family Kind (= 2 for Latin Text), Serif Style, Weight, Proportion, Contrast, Stroke Variation, Arm Style, Letterform, Midline, X-height

To use it in a style sheet use the **@font-face** selector. Here is an example, taken from the CSS2 Spec, as to how this might be used. It tells the user agent to first look for the font on the local system, then go to a URL, and, failing that, to construct a font using the Panose numbers given:

```
@font-face {
   src: local(Alabama Italic),
        url(http://www.fonts.org/A/alabama-italic) format(truetype);
   panose-1: 2 4 5 2 5 4 5 9 3 3;
   font-family: Alabama, serif;
   font-weight:   300, 400, 500;
   font-style:  italic, oblique;
 }
```

For more information on Panose numbers consult the Panose Greybook at:
http://www.fonts.com/hp/panose/greybook

and also the CSS2 specification.

Summary

This has been a long chapter. Congratulations if you have got this far!

We looked at:

- Various terminology used in describing fonts.
- The various CSS font properties.
- Terminology used in describing text layout.
- The CSS text properties.
- Various methods of specifying various fonts.

In the next chapter we will have a more detailed look at flow objects, inheritance and the meaning of cascade in cascading style sheets. We will also see how to manipulate boxes and position them to give precisely the layout we want.

Exercises

1. Download the samples for this chapter from the website at:

   `http://rapid.wrox.co.uk/books/1657`

   Make a table of how well they are supported in your browser. Make a list of the fonts available on your system and print out examples of each. (Hint, use your word processor or, if running Windows, download **`fotfin.exe`** from tools). If you have a Netscape browser, write and test a style sheet using Bitstream Technology, if IE, use Web Embedding Font Technology.

References

This reference gives a good introduction to Bitstream technology, and its various links give you all the tools that you need to implement this technology in your pages.

`http://www.bitstream.com`

This URL gives you links to all the font related technologies currently being studied by the W3C.

`http://www.w3.org/Fonts/`

The Microsoft pages, and links to all their other font related technology.

`http://www.microsoft.com/typography/fontpack/default.htm`

`http://www.microsoft.com/typography/web/embedding/weft/default.htm`

Everything that you need to know about Panose numbers. See also the current CSS2 proposal:

`http://www.fonts.com/hp/panose/greybook/`

7

Flow Objects, Selectors, Inheritance and the Cascade

In this chapter we will begin our exploration of flow objects, and how CSS applies styling to them.

- We will first redefine a flow object.
- Then we will look at the way a browser operates.
- We will take a brief look at what a document object model is.
- We will examine the Selector syntax in some detail.
- We will then have a discussion of how rules are inherited from their ancestors, and how style sheets cascade.
- Finally we will take a look at what CSS2 offers in the way of text generation, i.e. adding content to a flow object from a style sheet.

So, let's begin by giving a definition of a flow object.

What is a Flow Object?

We talked a little about flow objects in the Introduction. The concept is really quite simple. When a document is displayed on the screen or printed out, it flows from top to bottom and left to right (if it is in English). Everything that appears in the flow is a flow object. Going from the smallest up, the smallest flow object is a character, then a word, then a sentence, then a paragraph, and then the whole document. In the tradition of object oriented programming, each one can be considered as an object with its own set of properties. In XML and HTML the object size we usually deal with is an element. Remember that an image is a flow object, as well as a horizontal rule, and even a **
** tag, which is a flow object consisting of a line-feed.

The user agent will render these flow objects, and, to do so in modern browsers, it often has to have a look at the properties of objects out of their natural order. For example, if an image is aligned to the left side of a page, the preceding paragraph has to flow around it. For this reason a modern browser or user agent (usually) first makes a series of objects, figures out their relationships one to another, and then converts them into flow objects when it renders the document. If an element in the page is changed (and this is possible now with Dynamic HTML) the whole of the page has to re-flow.

Now that we've defined flow objects, it's useful to take a look at how browsers work and how they create and display flow objects.

How Browsers Work

A quick review of how browsers perform their job will help us understand some of the problems faced by the implementers, and also why some of the code is the way it is.

Legacy Browsers

The first browsers did not have to worry about different fonts and styling, and were actually pretty simple to program. All they had to do was take a document and display it, starting from the top and finishing at the bottom. I programmed a perfectly adequate viewer in VB3 which, if you excluded the .DLL, took up a miserly 56K of memory (no that is not a misprint!). Essentially, all these early browsers did was connect to the Web and download the HTML document. They then started reading the document from the beginning, and every time they came across a tag they changed the formatting and rendered the content. The following is a snippet of the VB3 code (in fact this is the bulk of the main loop) which shows how this was done.

```
Dim remtext$

    remtext = htmdoc
 Do Until InStr(remtext, "<") = 0
'loop through html document
    a% = InStr(remtext, "<")
    remtext = Mid$(remtext, a% + 1)
    x = get_next_tag(remtext)
'Get the tag

    render_tag x,remtext
'Print element content to screen.
 Loop
```

This was the main function which took the HTML text and–using two helper functions–printed it to the screen. The two helper functions which read the tags and then rendered them on the screen were a little more complex, but not much more. Things were so much easier back then!

Modern CSS Compliant Browsers

Modern CSS compliant browsers have a more complex problem. As well as providing most of the functionality of a word processor, they must read the whole of the HTML document first, make decisions about the document layout etc., and then render the document. However, the multi megabytes of the main browsers are mostly overkill and much of the code caters to special features. There are excellent browsers available that weigh in at about a megabyte. The Arena test bed browser and the Opera browser are good examples. Here are the steps–somewhat simplified–that a modern browser must go through:

- Download the HTML file.
- Build a document tree based on that file.
- Make a series of objects containing information about each element.
- Find and apply style to the objects.
- Render the objects as flow objects.

Let's examine each of those steps in more detail.

Downloading the HTML File

This, the most important step, has really changed not one bit. When a hyperlink is clicked, or a URL requested, the text string–the HTML document–is delivered to the browser over the Internet and stored in a variable. It is then passed to the browser's engine for processing.

Building a Document Tree

The first thing that the browser does is build a document tree. Here is a simple XML document.

```
<document>
<title> A Document Tree</title>
<body>
<para class= "loud"> This sentence contains some <bold> bold </bold>
text.</para>
<para  class= "quiet"> This sentence contains some <emph> italic </emph>
text</para>
</body>
</document>
```

The browser will build a tree that looks something like the tree shown here. Of course the browser doesn't actually display or construct this; it creates a digital impression of it. This visual depiction of a tree is just to make it "human readable".

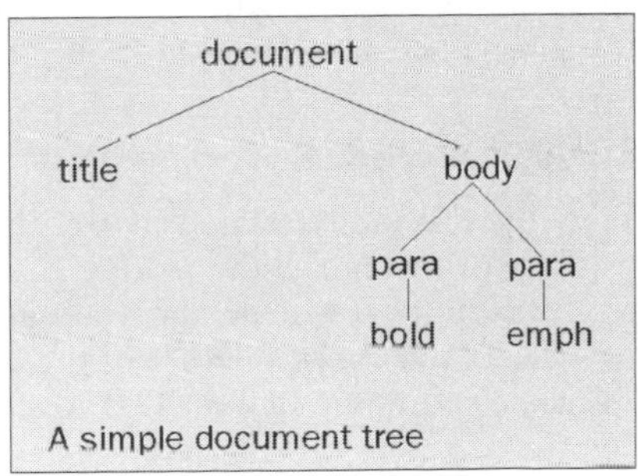

A simple document tree

The importance of this tree is that it tells the browser the relationships between the various elements. For example, **`emph`** is a child of **`para`**, which is the second child of **`body`**, which is itself the second child of **`document`**. This is the basis of the next part of the operation.

Using the notation of the W3C Document Object Model, or DOM, which we'll discuss in detail later in this chapter, each element is called a **`node`**. The **`document`** element in the above example is called the **`root element`** or, quite simply, the **`root`**.

Making Element Objects

The browser now creates an object out of each element or node. The object will contain such information as:

- The element's name.
- The element's index number (**`document`** would be 0).
- The element's parent (it will only have one parent).
- An array of the element's children.
- The element's content i.e. the text as well as pointers to the children.
- An array of its attributes.
- An array of each attribute's values.

This may seem like rather a lot of information to collect on one element and, after all, it's there in the text, but this information may be necessary for styling the object, and for using code to manipulate the object. We will discuss this a little in *Chapter 12, Scripting with Style.*

The other reason that this information is put into an array is that operations on arrays are among the fastest that a computer can do, and when a document gets quite large and complex, drawing it on the screen can consume a significant amount of time.

Applying Style to the Objects

Now that the objects have been created from the document, they must be made into flow objects by applying style. The browser may also be required to add extra text or images to them, decide in which order they are to be flowed on to the screen or on to paper, and even whether they are to be displayed at all. As we will see later we are not limited to rendering the document in the precise order in which it arrives.

The browser does this by finding style sheets (or it applies default styling) and by looking at each of the document objects in turn and applying the most appropriate style rules to them. Which rule will be applied to what element depends on the type of style sheet. In CSS it depends on the selector syntax, the inherited values, and the style cascade. These are the subjects of this chapter.

Rendering the Objects as Flow Objects

Now comes the easiest bit–just take those flow objects and plaster them all over the screen or other canvas. As anyone who has done any writing knows–the writing is the easiest bit, it is the preparation for writing that takes all the time! However, the user agent still has some work to do because it must take into account some of the characteristics of the canvas it is drawing on. Let's demonstrate this with an example. Here's a simple line of XML code:

```
<para>Here is a line of text with some <large>larger type</large> in
it</para>
```

and here's a diagram showing how the same line is displayed differently on a wide window and on a narrow window.

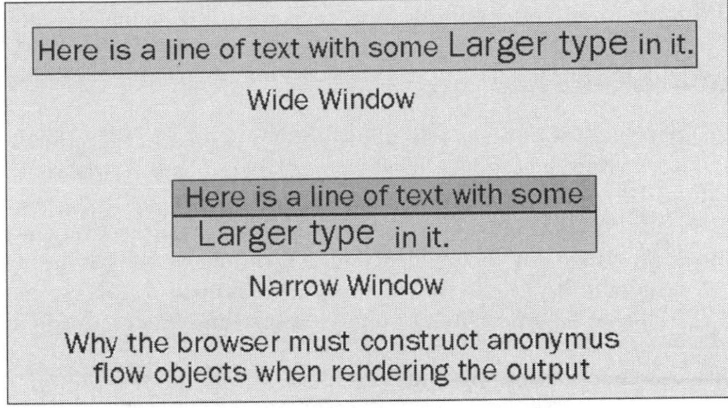

The diagram shows two flow objects, the second being an in-line flow object. The baselines of the small and the larger fonts match up, so the user agent constructs an **anonymous** flow object that contains them both to prevent the large type jutting into the line above. In fact, it must construct anonymous flow objects for each line of text, and the number of anonymous flow objects it has to construct depends on the width of the canvas.

Why anonymous? That just happens to be the name it is given in CSS. In other languages they may be called 'pseudo' flow objects, 'temporary' flow objects or 'user' flow objects.

The illustration shows what happens when the user narrows the window. A second anonymous flow object must be created.

A word processor has to go through a very similar process. If we highlight some text and then increase the font size, the whole of the page has to re-flow to keep the formatting looking good.

That concludes our look at how the browser works. Let's take a brief look at the Document Object Model, before moving on to take a detailed look at some Selector syntax.

The Document Object Model

This discussion of the Document Object Model (DOM) is put here because it follows on naturally from the discussion of flow objects. It is not, however, necessary to read this to understand inheritance or the cascade mechanism, or indeed CSS, and may be safely skipped at this stage. At least an acquaintance with the concept of a DOM is necessary, however, to understand how style can be dynamically changed through code, and how new flow objects can be created. First we'll define what a DOM actually is–then we'll give brief overviews of the Microsoft, Netscape and W3C DOMs.

Definition of the Document Object Model

Document Object Model (DOM) is one of those terms like pointers, Object Oriented Programming, prefix notation, (and EBNF!), that strikes fear into some peoples' hearts. The truth is that a Document Object Model is just a model of the document and, basically, anything that you want it to be. Like any model it can be good or bad, complete or incomplete. You can go out and write your own DOM tomorrow (getting application vendors to support it though may be a different matter!). In *Chapter 12, Scripting with Style*, we will have a look at IE4's DOM for HTML documents which is relatively complete.

A DOM then is merely a set of plans that allow you to reconstruct the document to a greater or lesser extent. By definition, a complete model is one that allows you to reconstruct the whole document down to the smallest detail. An incomplete DOM is anything less than this. It would be nice if there was a universal language to describe the DOM, then user agents could use this universal language to query the document through scripting or programming languages. At present, for example, using JavaScript you have to use different syntax–different object names and properties–depending on whether you are querying the same document in IE4 or Communicator 4.

Not surprisingly this is something that the W3C have turned their attention to and their recommendations can be found at:

`http://www.w3.org/TR/WD-DOM/level-one-core-971209`

Although not directly related to style sheets, DOMs are nevertheless important in styling, because they allow us to use code to manipulate models in various ways. The W3C version of the DOM even includes a feature called DOMfactory which will allow us to alter the document by way of code. As we will see in other chapters this can be done using XSL, DSSSL, Spice and, to a limited extent, CSS, but DOMfactory would allow you to write an almost completely new document. (Note that this feat can also be accomplished right now in IE4 using JavaScript or VBScript and Microsoft's version of the DOM.)

Before moving on to a discussion of selectors let's take a brief look at three DOMs–Microsoft's DOM for HTML, Netscape's DOM for HTML, and the W3C core DOM for XML and HTML documents.

Microsoft's DOM for HTML Documents

The diagram below shows IE4's extended document object model.

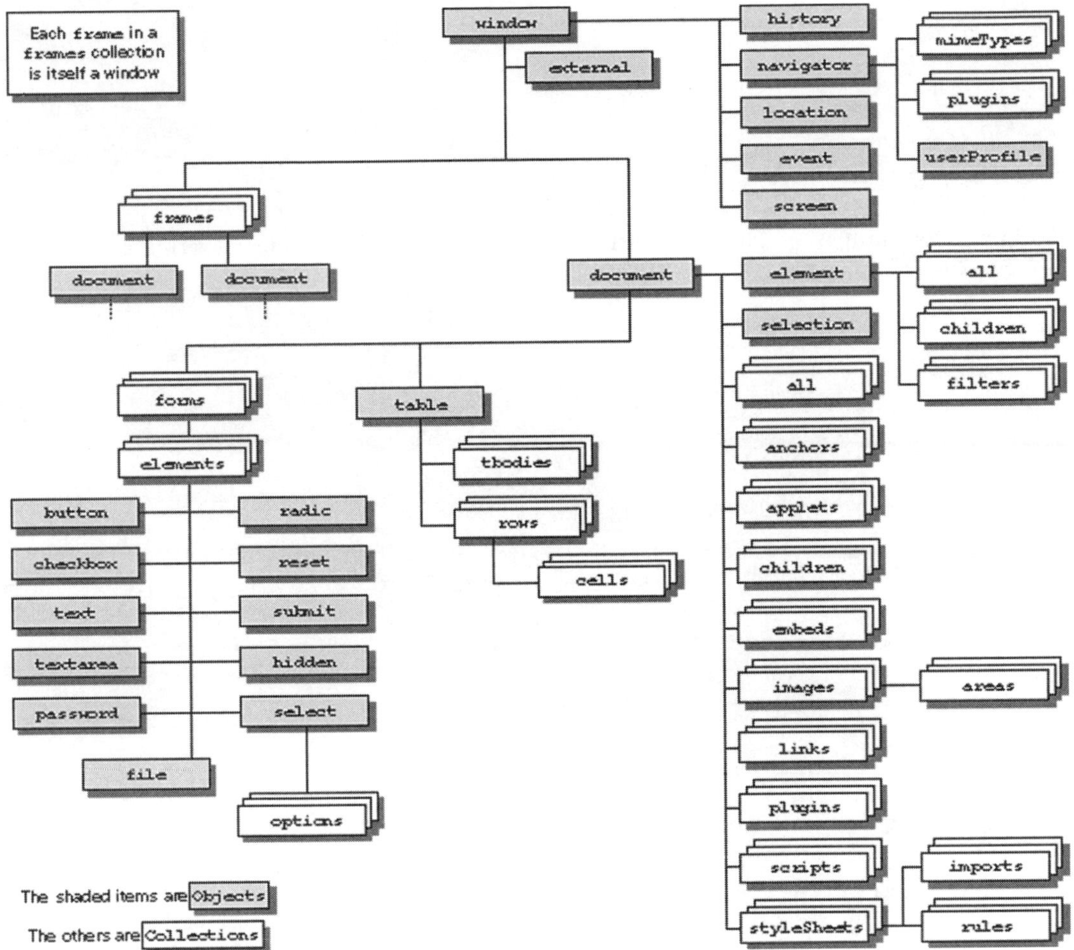

This DOM, with a little fudging, can also be used for XML. The IE4 browser indexes every tag it comes across starting from 0 to the last tag. If the tag is an HTML closing tag it does not index it. However, if it is a closing tag other than a recognized HTML tag, e.g. an XML closing tag, it will index it. Any element can be referenced using the (JavaScript) syntax:

```
document.all [indexnumber]......
```

They can also be referenced if the tag has been given an id:

```
[element id]...
```

For example:

`document.all[0].tagName` would return HTML in an HTML document.

The content of any element can be referenced using four properties:

- **`outerHTML`**
- **`innerHTML`**
- **`innerText`**
- **`outerText`**

And these four properties can also be used as methods to write new code via script. Let's look at some examples.

In the simple HTML snippet:

```
<DIV> A sentence with <I> Italic</I> text </DIV>
```

if this **`<DIV>`** had the index of **4** then:

`document.all[4].outerHTML` would return:

```
<DIV> A sentence with <I> Italic</I> text</DIV>
```

`document.all[4].innerHTML` would return:

```
A sentence with <I> Italic</I> text
```

`document.all[4].outerText` would return:

```
A sentence with Italic text
```

`document.all[4].innerText` would return:

```
A sentence with Italic text
```

The difference between **`innerText`** and **`outerText`** only becomes apparent when we use these as methods for writing content.

Other properties include the **`ancestor`** and **`children`** property. In fact, using this almost complete DOM you can do an amazing amount on the IE4 platform. This is discussed in more depth in *Chapter 12 Styling with Script.*

For a full description of the Microsoft version of the DOM see:

http://www.microsoft.com/intdev/ie4/domdoc-f.htm

and:

http://www.microsoft.com/msdn/sdk/inetsdk/help/dhtml/references/domrefs.htm.

That's our overview of the Microsoft DOM, let's see what Netscape have to offer.

Netscape's DOM for HTML Documents

Netscape's series of collections is much smaller than that of IE4, but they still allow you to dissect the document in some depth. Here you can see the collections available–the Layer collection is particularly useful:

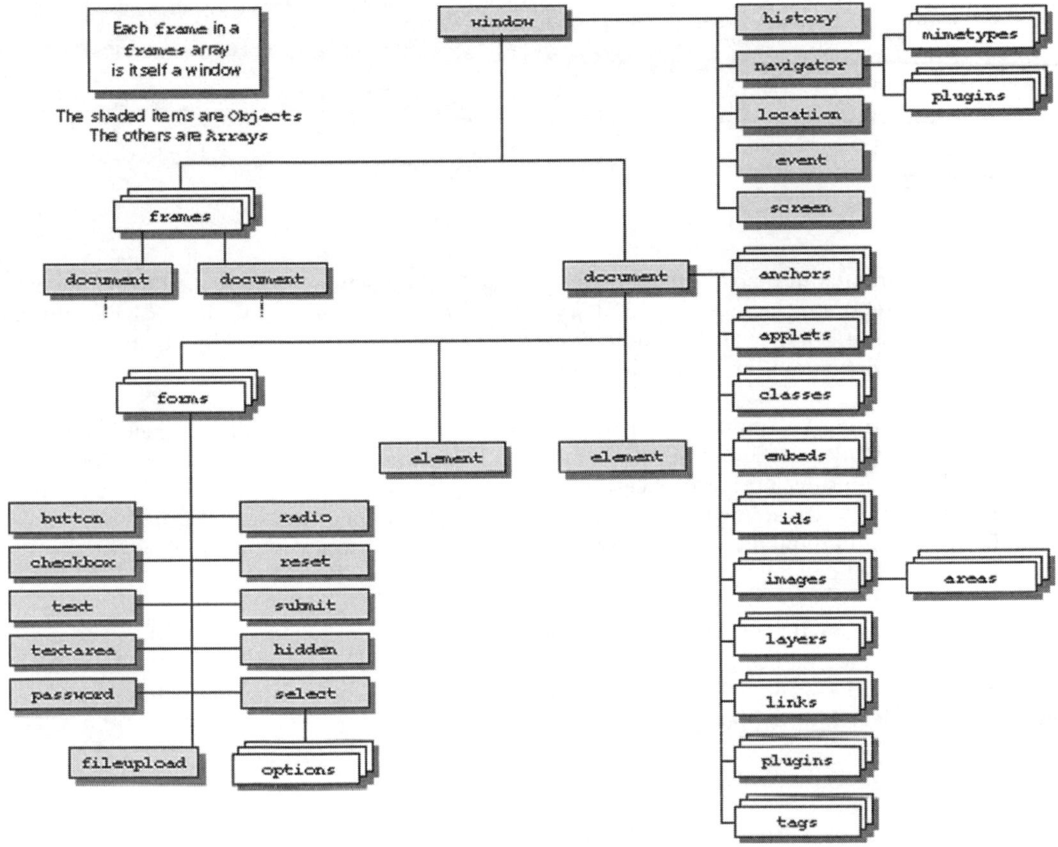

These are discussed more in Chapter 12, the scripting chapter. For a full discussion see the book *Instant Netscape Dynamic HTML Programmer's Reference ISBN 1861001193 from Wrox Press* naturally.

For a description of the Communicator version of the DOM see:

http://developer.netscape.com/library/documentation/communicator/jsguide4/index.htm.

And finally in this DOM overview, let's take a look at what the W3C have come up with.

The W3C Recommendation for the DOM

The W3C working committee has, as might be expected, taken a particularly thorough approach to creating a DOM for both XML and HTML. The model that they employ is to treat everything as a **node**, a term borrowed from DSSSL syntax, and which, in biology, corresponds to a collection of material on a plant.

The W3C DOM recognizes the following types of node:

- **Node**
- **Document**
- **Element**
- **Attribute**
- **Text**
- **Comment**
- **PI**

These are constructed into arrays that can fully describe the document. They also provide properties and methods that allow us to query any one of the **nodes** and find the **children** and **types** of the **node**. They even provide methods to completely reconstruct the document, or even construct a new document through code or script.

At the time of writing no application or user agent has been written which implements this DOM, and the DOM is still in a state of development. It is likely that the DOM will be fairly complex, and will probably be most useful for applications wishing to query an XML document that is acting as a database. It would be nice, however, and perhaps wishful thinking, to hope that the browser manufacturers could implement a common sub-set of the DOM to enable us poor web writers to write just one set of code!

There is one other small problem with the W3C DOM. The primary Document Object Model type definitions are presented using the Object Management Group's Interface Definition Language (IDL, ISO standard 14750), which is great for the inter-operation of applications, but means yet another vocabulary for the poor programmer to learn, even though its syntax is similar to C++.

More information on the W3C DOM can be found at:

http://www.w3.org/TR/WD-DOM/level-one-core-971209

That concludes our slight detour which has enabled us to gain an overview of DOMs in general and the Microsoft, Netscape and W3C DOMs in particular. Let's now move back to our main subject and look at Selectors.

Selectors

Selectors–as you will remember from *Chapter 2: Basic Cascading Style Sheets*–are the way we specify what style is to be applied to an element. We covered them briefly in Chapter 2, now we're going to look at them in detail. We'll start with a brief recap on the structure of CSS rules, then list the selector types and go through each one in turn. We'll finish the section with a table summarizing selectors and their syntax.

CSS1, CSS2 and the Browsers

Many of the selector mechanisms we will describe are new to the CSS2 Proposal, and are not well supported in the current versions of the mainstream browsers. However, new patches and updates are becoming available every day, so I have not attempted to say what is and what isn't currently supported as, by the time you read this, it will probably be out of date! I have, however, marked where a selector is a CSS2 feature, and so before using it you would do well to check it out.

CSS Rules

As we saw in Chapter 2, a CSS style rule is made up of the following parts:

`selector{[`*`property`*`:`*`value;`*`]*}`

The list of properties and their values is known as the **declaration**. The selector selects the elements that the properties and their values are to apply to. In Chapter 2 we looked at quite a number of simple selector combinations allowing multiple selectors, and element selection by ancestry. We will recap these rules here and also look at the more complex selectors.

CSS uses the document tree and pattern matching to determine what style rules apply to what elements. If the pattern matches then the style rules in the declaration will be applied. Note that if there is any bit of the property/value that the user agent does not understand, it should skip the whole of the property. For example, in the rule:

```
H1{font-size:32 ;font-weight:bold}
```

`font-size` should be excluded because no unit has been assigned to the value.

The selectors follow a set of syntactic rules that allow for matching. We'll look at selector syntax next.

Selector Syntax

The following types of selectors are recognized:

- Simple
- Universal
- Type
- Grouped
- Descendant
- Child
- Adjacent
- Attribute
- Class
- ID
- Pseudo-elements
- Pseudo-classes

We will now go through each of these selectors in turn.

Simple Selector

A simple selector is either a universal or a type selector possibly followed by attribute or id selectors. In HTML, it is case insensitive, i.e. it doesn't matter whether one writes **H1** or **h1**, but in XML case is important, in other words

```
Document{font-size:14pt; font-weight: bold}
```

and

```
document{font-size:14pt; font-weight: bold}
```

match different elements.

Universal Selector

The universal selector uses the DOS wildcard selector *.

Here is an example of a universal selector:

```
*{font-size:14pt; font-weight: bold}
```

This will match every element in the document!

Here is an example of a universal selector narrowed down by applying an attribute to it:

```
*[lang=fr]{font-size:14pt; font-weight: bold}
```

This would only match the elements that contain the attribute **[lang=fr]**.

Type Selector

The type selector matches the element type. For example:

```
subheading{font-family:sans-serif}
```

would render every subheading element in the XML document in a sans-serif font.

Grouped Selectors

If we have several elements that take the same property, we can group them together using a comma-separated list. Thus in a style sheet for an HTML document:

```
H1 {font-family:sans-serif}
H2 {font-family:sans-serif}
H3 {font-family:sans-serif}
```

could all be grouped together as follows:

```
H1, H2, H3 {font-family:sans-serif}
```

Descendant Selectors

If you understand the concept of the document tree, you will have no problem at all with the next three sections. If you don't, perhaps you might like to back up and read the section on *Building a Document Tree.*

Suppose we have the following two style rules:

```
H1{color:red}
EM{color:red}
```

Obviously in the following snippet:

```
<H1>A very <EM>important</EM> topic</H1>
```

the emphasized text is not going to stand out too well!

To get over this problem, CSS allows us to select according to ancestry. We do this by the following:

```
H1 EM{color:green}
```

This tells the user agent to render in green any **<EM>** that has an **<H1>** ancestor. It will take precedence over the previous **<EM>** rule because it is more specific (see later). Note that it doesn't matter how remote the ancestry is the match is still made:

```
<H1>This is a<SPAN> very <EM>important</EM> topic</SPAN></H1>
```

The **<EM>** would still match here even though **<H1>** is now a grandparent.

Child Selectors

The following rule matches any element that is a child of the element:

```
H1 > EM{color:green}
```

so that in our first example above:

```
<H1>A very <EM>important</EM> topic</H1>
```

important would appear in green, but in our second example:

```
<H1>This is a<SPAN> very <EM>important</EM> topic</SPAN></H1>
```

it would not.

Adjacent Selectors

This selector syntax matches an element that is adjacent to another. For example, perhaps you want the first paragraph of a section to be in bold type, in the following HTML document snippet:

```
<DIV>
   <P> The importance of being earnest is....</P>
   <P>This is quite different from Oscar Wilde's play...</P>
   <P>If he had been a little less earnest</P>
</DIV>
```

we would make the rule:

```
DIV+P{font-weight:bold}
```

This would render the first paragraph **<P> The importance of being earnest is....</P>** in bold type. The other two paragraphs, however, would be in regular type because the rule only refers to the first paragraph after the **<DIV>** tag.

Attribute Selectors

We have already seen this in use with our universal selector example, where we matched all elements with the attribute **[lang=fr]**.

We can use attribute selectors in four ways. Consider the following HTML code:

```
<DIV LANG= "fr"> Bonjour CSS </DIV>
<DIV LANG= "en-cockney"> 'allo CSS </DIV>
<DIV LANG= "en-US"> Hi, CSS </DIV>
```

The first matching syntax is **[**_attribute_**]**, which quite simply matches all elements with that attribute, regardless of the value. Thus:

```
DIV [LANG]{font-size:14pt}
```

will match all three of the elements as they all have the **LANG** attribute.

To match a specific value we use the form [_attribute=value_], so that:

```
DIV [LANG=fr]{color:red}
```

will only match the first **<DIV>** and:

```
DIV [LANG=en-cockney]{color:blue}
```

will only match the second **<DIV>**.

[_attribute_**|=**_value_] can be used to match a hyphen separated value so the rule:

```
DIV [LANG|=en]{color:green}
```

would match both the second and the third **<DIV>**.

There is one other syntax that may be of use in XML and HTML attributes that can take multiple values (such as the **REL** attribute), and that is **[**_attribute_**~=**_value_**]**. This syntax matches any occurrence of a value in a space-separated list of name values. For example:

```
A[rel~= "copyright"]
```

would match.

```
<A REL= "copyright copyleft copyeditor">
```

Default Attribute Values in XML

As we saw in Chapter 3, a default value for an attribute can be declared in the XML DTD:

```
<!ATTLIST results notation (decimal, hexadecimal) "decimal">
```

Would declare that a **results** element would take an attribute of **notation** with a value of **decimal** if nothing was specified in the document.

The trick is to set the selector to catch no attribute value for the decimal case, i.e.:

```
results{color:red}
results[notation=hexadecimal]{color:blue}
```

will style both tags **<results>** and **<results notation= "decimal">** in red, and **<results notation= "hexadecimal">** in blue.

Class Selectors

The **CLASS** attribute is treated in a special way in HTML. Of course, if you use it in XML it will mean exactly what you define it as in your DTD! (see Chapter 3)

We have already seen in Chapter 2 that the **CLASS** attribute can have several string values in HTML, so to declare it in the selector we should use the fourth of the attribute syntaxes above, namely:

```
[attribute~= value]
```

Consider the following style rules:

```
*[class~= "browns"]{color:brown;background-color:white}
```

```
*[class~= "steelers"]{color:black;background-color:yellow}
```

The first rule would match all elements with the **CLASS** value of **browns** and produce brown type on a white background, (forget about aesthetics here–we're talking American Football!). The second would match all elements with the **CLASS** value of **steelers** and produce black type on a yellow background.

HTML, as you know from Chapter 2, allows us to produce these rules in the shorthand notation of:

```
.browns{color:brown;background-color:white}
.steelers{color:black;background-color:yellow}
```

Note the prefixing period. There should not be a space between the period and the value (***.browns** would also be perfectly acceptable).

We can use the **class** notation in XML if we so desire, but we would have to use the full notation, not the shorthand:

```
*[class~= "browns"]{color:brown;background-color:white}

<nflteam class= "browns">Go pluck a Raven!</nflteam>
```

ID Selectors

In both XML and HTML the value of an **ID** attribute is unique in the whole document. Only one element can have that **ID** value, so it is a unique identifier for that element. (The IE4 DOM makes use of this uniqueness, see the scripting chapter; Chapter 12.)

In HTML, this unique attribute is always **ID**. (It is possible to use a different name for it in XML, but why make life difficult, everyone knows what **id** means?)

The style rules for an **id** are declared with a **#** immediately followed by the **id** value as shown here:

```
#xyz123{font-size:24pt}
```

Theoretically it is possible to put an element tag in front of it as shown here:

```
P#xyz123{font-size:24pt}
```

and this would match this element:

```
<P id= "xyz123"> An example </P>
```

and not match this element:

```
<DIV id= "xyz123"> An example </DIV>
```

However, as each **id** value has to be unique in the document, why bother?

Pseudo-Element and Pseudo-Class Selectors

Pseudo-classes are not well supported in browsers at the present time, so this discussion is a little hypothetical. Again hopefully, patches will introduce support. The screenshots that we have produced are cheats and indicate what the browser should show if it supported the pseudo-elements.

Definition of a Pseudo-Element

All the selectors we have seen up to now match a flow object that corresponds to an element in the document tree. As we have seen, however, when the user agent renders the flow objects on the canvas, it has to make anonymous flow objects. For example, the first line of a paragraph will vary in size depending on the width of the window. Pseudo-elements apply to these flow objects that are rendered apart from the document tree.

Definition of a Pseudo-Class

Pseudo classes are properties of elements that theoretically cannot be deduced from the document tree. For example take the HTML:

```
<A HREF=http://www.wrox.com>Wrox Press</A>
```

As you know, it usually has one color before it is clicked and another after it has been clicked. This value cannot be deduced from the document tree.

Types of Pseudo-Element

There are two types of pseudo-element:

first-line

As the name implies, this will render the first line of any element in the desired format. For example:

```
P:first-line{font-weight:bold;}
<P>In this narrow column the first line of text should be in a bold
font</P>
```

Should result in:

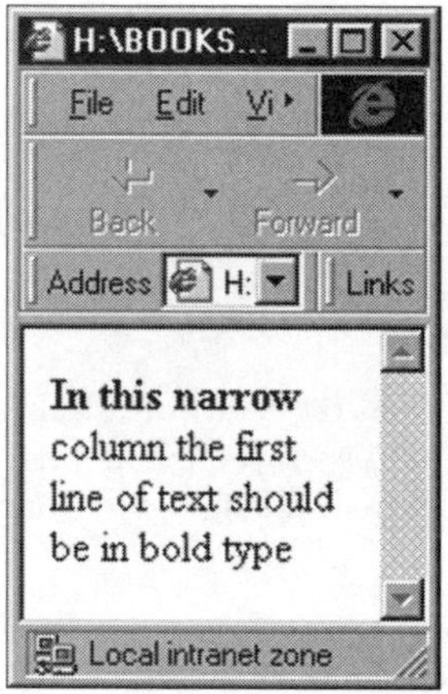

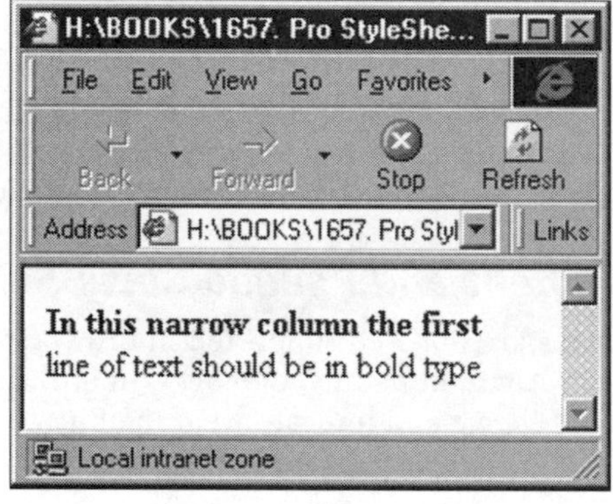

The screenshots above show what should happen. When the user narrows the window only the first line stays in bold type. (Note–because this feature is not yet supported, we have achieved this effect by other means to show you what it should do.)

first-letter

Again as the name implies, this will render the first letter of any element in the desired format. For example:

```
P:first-letter{font-size:300%;float:left}
<P> The first letter should be a drop cap spanning three lines.</P>
```

Should result in the situation shown in the following screen shot.

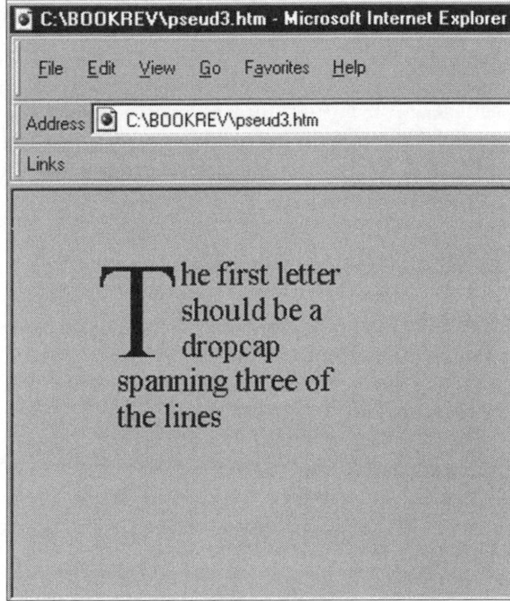

Again note that as this feature is not presently supported this is a cheat and shows what it should look like if it was supported.

Types of Pseudo-Class

There are three types of pseudo-class, and we'll look at each one in turn.

link

This class is used for setting the colors on the links, for example:

```
A:link{color:red}
A:visited{color:blue}
```

Will reverse the normal state of affairs.

dynamic

The three values that this can take are

:hover | :active | :focus

They are used for providing interactivity in the page.

The use of these pseudo agents as defined in the CSS2 specification is a little vague. They are intended to provide interactivity, so if the cursor hovered over a box one set of styling, the **hover** set, would be applied. Clicking the mouse would mean that **active** styling would be applied, and once the click was completed and the box had the focus, the **focus** styling would be applied. This is rather similar to the behavior associated with the **<A>** element in HTML, but theoretically, this could be applied to any element.

The problem is that no browser supports this type of pseudo-class, and so it is not absolutely clear how a user agent is meant to support it. If this explanation leaves you a little confused, you are not alone! Read the official spec, section 5.11.3, and see if your comprehension is better than mine is.

language

Different languages often have different formatting, for example a French document uses this form of quotes << >>. The language type of the document can be set with the **`language`** attribute, the **`META`** tag, or, in XML, with **`XML: LANG`**. To ensure that the document uses the correct form of quotes use the **`:lang`** pseudo-class as follows:

```
:lang(fr){quotes: '<<' '>>'}
```

This pseudo-class is unsupported at the time of writing, and only the **`quotes`** pseudo-class is proposed. We'll cover this later under *Generated Content.*

The official spec on selectors can be found at:

`http://www.w3.org/TR/PR-CSS2/selector.html`

Now we have covered all the various selector types. Here's a table which summarizes the various syntax types.

Table of Selectors

The following table provides a quick reference to the selector syntax types covered above.

Pattern	Example	Definition	Name
`*`	`*{font-size:12pt}`	Matches any element	Universal selector
`E`	`E {font-size:12pt}`	Matches any **`E`** element	Simple type selector
`F E`	`F E {font-size:12pt}`	Matches any **`E`** element that is a descendant of **`F`**	Descendant selector
`F>E`	`F>E{font-size:12pt}`	Matches any **`E`** element that is a child of **`F`**	Child selector
`E:first-child`	`E:first-child{font-size:12pt}`	Matches any **`E`** element that is the first child of another element	The **`:first-child`** pseudo-class

Pattern	Example	Definition	Name
`A:link` `A:visited`	`A:link{color:blue}` `A:visited{color: brown}`	Matches an unvisited link (**`A:link`**) or a visited link (**`A:visited`**)	The **`link`** pseudo-classes

`E:active`
`E:hover`
`E:focus`
	`E:hover{color:red}`	Matches **`E`** during the relevant actions	The **`dynamic`** pseudo-classes.

`E:lang(c)`	`HTML:lang(fr){ quotes: '<<' '>>'}`	Do not confuse with **`LANG`** attribute. Matches if the *document* is in (human) language c	The **`:lang`** pseudo-classes

`E:before`
`E:after`
	`BODY:after{`
	`content: "The End"`
	`}`
		Used with the **`content`** property to add text or other content	The **`:before`**, **`:after`**, pseudo-elements. (See *Generated Content* section)

`F+E`	`F+E{font-weight:bold}`	Matches any **`E`** element that immediately follows an **`F`** element.	Adjacent selector
`E[foo]`	`E[foo]{font-size:12pt}`	Matches any element **`E`** with an attribute **`"foo"`**	Attribute selector
`E[foo= "string"]`	`E[foo= "string"]{font-size:12pt}`	Matches any element **`E`** with an attribute "**`foo`**" whose value **+** string	Attribute selector
`E[foo~= "string"]`	`P[class~= "rustic"]{color: green}`	Matches any **`E`** element with a list of space separated values which has a value exactly equal to "*string*"	Attribute selector

Table Continued on Following Page

Pattern	Example	Definition	Name
`E[lang|="en"]`	**`P[lang|="en-cockney"]{font-size:12pt}`**	Matches any **`E`** element whose hyphened **`"lang"`** attribute has a pre-hyphen value equal to *val*.	Attribute selector
`.warning`	**`.warning{color:red}`**	In HTML only, the same as **`[class~=warning]`**	Class selector
`#abc123`	**`#abc123{font-size:12pt}`**	Matches the unique element with an **`id=abc123`**	ID selector

That concludes our look at selectors. We're moving on now to look at inheritance.

Inheritance

In this section we'll explain the concept of inheritance. You need to understand inheritance to be able to grasp the concepts of the cascade and rule precedence which follow, but don't worry, inheritance is phenomenally simple provided you understand the concept of the document tree. If you skipped this bit, or don't know what a document tree is go back and read the earlier section of this chapter entitled *Building a Document Tree.*

Quite simply–I inherited my dark hair from my mother, you may have inherited your dark and mysterious eyes from your father etc. etc., and an element inherits its properties from its parent and other ancestors. The element is lucky, however, all it has to do to change its properties is to make a new rule. If it doesn't have a rule applying a specific property, it will inherit the applicable rule from its parent, who may have in its turn inherited it from its parent, and so on.

The diagram below illustrates inheritance.

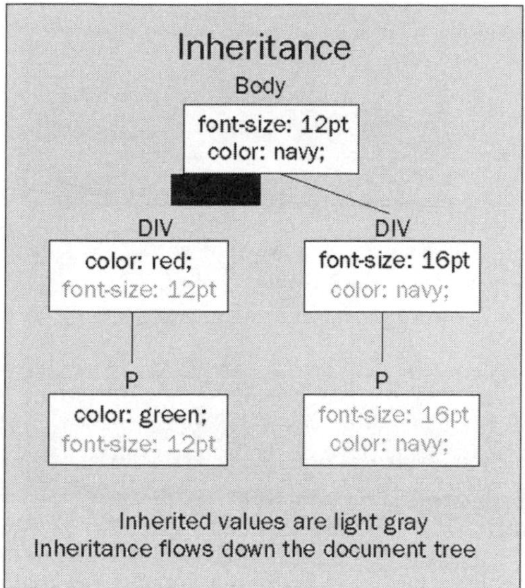

As you can see, the left hand **<DIV>** and **<P>** elements inherit their font size from the **<BODY>** element but have their own specific colors. The right hand **<DIV>** and **<P>**, by contrast, have no color rules of their own, so inherit the color navy from the **<BODY>**. However, the right hand **<DIV>** sets its own font size, and **<P>** inherits its font size from its parent, the **<DIV>** rather than its grandparent, the **<BODY>**.

Not all properties can be inherited. See Appendices B and C for a list of those that can and can't. As an example look at this simple HTML document:

```
<HTML>
<STYLE>
BODY{
color:navy;
font-size:12pt;
}
DIV{
color:red;
}
P{
color:green;
}
</STYLE>
<BODY>Here is some opening text, its color is navy.
   <DIV>This text is in the div, its color will be red
   <P>This text color will be green</P>
   </DIV>
All the text will be in 12pt font because all the elements inherited this
characteristic from the BODY element
</BODY>
</HTML>
```

This is what it looks like in IE4:

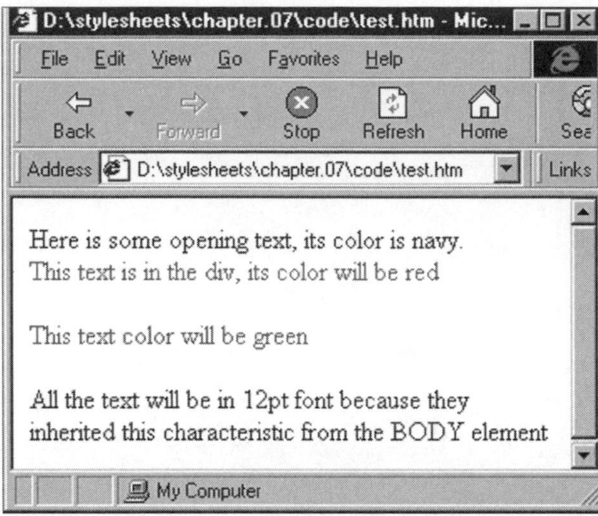

You can't see the colors in the black and white print, but you can see that the size of font remains constant. Quite simply, each of the elements had its own **`color`** property, but because they did not have their own **`font-size`** property they inherited it from the **`<BODY>`** element, which was the parent of **`<DIV>`** and the grandparent of **`<P>`**.

That's all there is to it! Make sure you understand what we've said in this section before proceeding to the next one on the cascade and rule precedence.

The Cascade and Rule Precedence

In this section, we'll define the cascade and examine the process the user agent must go through to establish rule precedence. We'll look at the **`!important`** rule and the **`@import`** rule in some detail, and then move on to see how CSS2 will allow you to generate content using your style sheets. Let's begin by defining our terms.

The cascade is the chief way that the user agent decides which style rule takes precedence. In deciding what rules to apply to an element it looks at all the rules applicable to an element from the various style sheets. If its perusal of the cascade results in a rule, it is applied. If no rule results, it looks at the ancestors of the element. If it finds a rule among the ancestors, it will apply its value to the element, provided of course that the property is one that allows inheritance. Otherwise it will apply the property's default value. Every property has a default value.

Here's a diagram to illustrate this process.

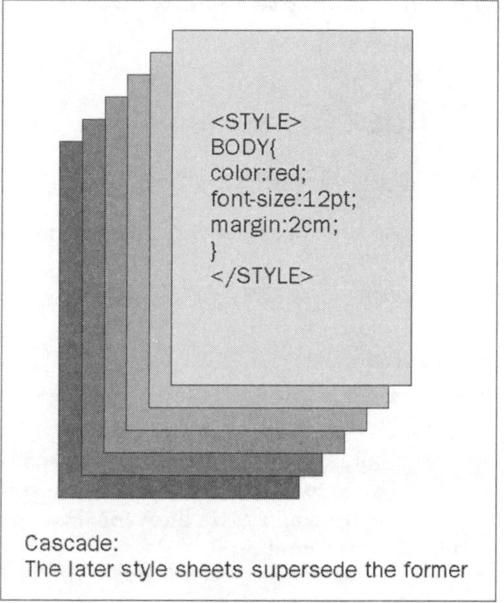

Cascade:
The later style sheets supersede the former

Before looking up rules in the applicable style sheets, the user agent must first set up a cascade, and we'll look at this next.

Setting up the Cascade

Let's look at the source of style sheets. First of all every user agent must have a style sheet built into it, or at least behave as if it did. The user agent may allow the user to generate a style sheet, or a style sheet may be imported using the **`<LINK>`** element (and this style sheet may have imported style sheets using the **`@import`** property). There may be a style sheet in the HTML document (which may also import other style sheets), and finally the element may have an inline style sheet using the **`style`** attribute. Let's list these potential sheets.

- User agent intrinsic style sheet
- User style sheet
- Imported style sheet using **`<LINK>`**–which may itself contain an imported style sheet using **`@import`**
- Style sheet in HTML–which may itself contain an imported style sheet using **`@import`**
- Inline style sheet

Thus in our hypothetical document we have a total of seven style sheets! Suppose they all have a **`DIV{font-size:`**[*value*]**`}`** rule. Which one takes precedence? The simple answer is the user agent reads the document from top to bottom, and the last one it reads is the one that takes precedence (unless the **`!important`** declaration is used, see later), because the style sheets cascade from top to bottom. Let's examine the steps the browser goes through to decide which style takes precedence.

Just to remind you the link element takes the following form:

```
<LINK REL=STYLESHEET TYPE="text/css" HREF="../style.css"
TITLE="Style">
```

Arbitrating between Values

The user agent must go through the following steps:

- For each element in the source document, and each of the elements properties, it must find all the applicable rules.
- It must sort the rules by the cascade order. The last rule is the one to be applied–unless **!important** is used.
- It must sort by specificity of selector, the most specific wins.
- In cases of equal specificity the latest rule wins.

This all may sound rather complicated but unless it's **!important** or specific, the last shall be first! (As someone famous once said.) This rule will cover 99.7% of cases that you will come across. For those who really like to beat their heads against a wall (or for those who are writing a user agent) the full set of arbitration rules can be found at:

http://www.w3.org/TR/PR-CSS2/cascade.html

Let's look at some of theses rule in more detail.

The !important Rule

The **!important** rule allows the writer to override all other selection criteria.

A style rule written as follows:

```
DIV{font-size:20pt !important}
```

overrides the whole cascade.

As a web page author you must ensure that you are not over-using the **!important** rule. There are really very few instances where **!important** should be used. In fact I can't think of a single one that stands up to any deep and probing scrutiny.

Changes to the Arbitration Process Introduced in CSS2

In CSS1 author **!important** rules took precedence over user **!important** rules, but it was soon realized that this was stupid, because the one valid reason for using **!important** was for the user with disabilities. A red/green color blind reader may want to change these colors, and a visually impaired reader may want everything at 24pt.

In CSS2 user **!important** rules take precedence over the author, which is as it should be. However, the browsers have not yet caught up, so in the meantime don't use **!important**.

Selector Specificity

Again the rules are quite complex and if you want to peruse them in detail consult the above URL. However, if you abide by the following handy quote you should be okay.

> "If it's got an **id** attribute it's specific, otherwise use your common sense."

In other words–the selector that seems to be most specific usually is.

The @import Rule

The **@import** rule allows other style sheets to be imported. They are put at the head of the style sheet before any style rules. For example:

```
<STYLE>
@import "riotous.css";
@import url(psyco.css);

BODY{color:teal;
background-color:yellow;
font-family:kidnap;
etc
}
@import "marvin.css";
</STYLE>
```

The above example shows two ways of writing the URL, either as a string, or as a parentheses enclosed URL, and it doesn't matter which form you use. Note the all-important semi-colon.

In the above example the rules in the style sheet proper take precedence over those in **psyco.css**, which take precedence over those in **riotous.css**. **Marvin.css** is simply ignored because, as usual, he is in the wrong place!

We will look at the **@media** rule in the chapter on *Other Canvases, Chapter 13*, but for now note that there is a shorthand way to attribute various style sheets to different media:

```
@import url(bigtype.css) tv, projection;
```

This tells the user agent only to download the file if it is going to project it or display it on television.

HTML Styling Tags

What about those styling tags we got to know and love in HTML 3.2, the **<FONT>** tag and all its friends?

They have not been forgotten, but in the arbitration process they are given a value of 0, in other words they are only used if there is no other rule to apply to the element!

So, we've covered flow objects, selectors, inheritance, the cascade and rule precedence–what's left? The final topic of the chapter is generated content–how CSS2 allows you to add content using a style sheet.

Generated Content

CSS2 provides the ability to generate a flow object through the use of the **content** property and the pseudo-elements **:before** and **:after**. (Of course, ordered lists have always generated content, in the form of numbers.) Although this has not yet been implemented in the browsers, when it is it will give CSS much of the utility of the other styling languages.

The subject is quite complex and space prevents more than a brief overview here, but the official spec–which is quite readable–can be found at:

http://www.w3.org/TR/PR-CSS2/generate.html

In this section we'll look at the **:before** and **:after** pseudo-elements and the **content** property, plus how to generate counters and quotation marks.

The :before and :after Pseudo-Elements

The use of these pseudo-elements is best illustrated by an example.

This style sheet:

```
P.warning:before{content: "Warning!!";
Display:block;
Font-size:24pt;
}
P.warning:after{content: "you have been warned!!";
Display:block;
Font-size:16pt;
}
```

And this HTML snippet

```
<P CLASS= "warning">Scalpels are sharp</P>
```

will produce this display

Again this property is not currently supported, and the screen shot is a cheat showing what things should look like if it were supported.

Note:

- That unless specified, the generated text inherits the properties of the element it is adding to.
- That the default display for the generated content is inline unless instructed otherwise.
- That if the element to be modified is itself an inline element, then the use of **`display:block`** in the pseudo-elements is forbidden.
- Inline elements can only take the display values of **`inline`** or **`none`**.

The Content Property

The **`content`** property can take one or more of the following values. Separate each value with whitespace.

Content Property Values	Description
<*string*>	This is a plain string text, and can be anything. They must be enclosed in quotes.
<*uri*>	(uri, universal resource indicator, is the new syntax for url, use url for now) Points to an image or even a text or HTML file for inclusion.
<*counter*>	See the section on *Counters* below
`attr(X)`	Returns the value of attribute **`X`** as a string
`open-quote`, **`close-quote`**	Returns the appropriate string from the **`quotes`** property,(see the section on *Quotation Marks* below)
`no-open-quote`, **`no-close-quote`**	Returns an empty string, but keeps incrementing any nesting counters.

Let's look at how the **`content`** property and its values are used to generate numbers and quotation marks.

Counters

CSS2 allows for automatic number writing through the use of the **`content`** property, and the **`counter()`** and **`counters()`** functions used in conjunction with the **`counter-reset`** and **`counter-increment`** properties.

The syntax for the **counter-reset** and **counter-increment** properties are as follows:

[*<identifier>* *<integer>*? **]+ | none | inherit**

Where *<identifier>* is the counter name, and *<integer>* is the amount of the increment. Default value is one.

Again the best way to show this is by way of an example:

```
H1:before {
        content: "Chapter " counter(chapter) ". ";
        counter-increment: chapter;  /* Add 1 to chapter */
        counter-reset: section;      /* Set section to 0 */
    }
    H2:before {
        content: counter(chapter) "." counter(section) " ";
        counter-increment: section;
    }.
```

This will result in output as:

Chapter 1.

1.1

1.2

1.3

etc

Chapter 2.

2.1

2.2

2.3

etc

The font size is the default **font-size** for **H1** and **H2** headings respectively.

Let's analyze this in a little more detail.

H1:before is the pseudo-element selector used to add content to the source document. It has a declaration of:

```
content: "Chapter " counter(chapter) ". ";
```

This adds the string **Chapter** , the function **counter(chapter)** which generates and returns a number, and the string **"."**. Note how these individual values are separated by whitespace.

The next line uses the property **counter-increment** to declare the identifier variable **chapter**. Because no integer has been set the default of adding 1 is used. With each call, i.e. each time **H1** appears in the parent document 1 is added to the counter total.(Cf. **chapter=chapter+1** in some languages, **chapter++** in C style.)

```
counter-increment: chapter; /* Add 1 to chapter */
```

Note that:

```
counter-increment: chapter 2;
```

Would increment the **chapter** variable/identifier by 2

The last property:

```
counter-reset: section;       /* Set section to 0 */
```

resets the value of the section identifier to 0 for each new chapter, i.e. for each new occurrence of **H1**.

The second rule:

```
    H2:before {
        content: counter(chapter) "." counter(section) " ";
counter-increment: section;
    }.
```

Simply increments the value of the identifier section for each time the element **H2** is encountered.

The following points should be noted:

- If an element is set to **display:none**, the counter will not be incremented.
- It will be incremented if it is set to **visibility:hidden**
- The **counter()** function can also take the form **counter(chapter,**<*list-style-type*>**)**, the default is **decimal**.

For those interested here is a list of the allowed list types.

disc | circle | square | decimal | leading-zero | western-decimal | lower-roman | upper-roman | lower-greek | lower-alpha | lower-latin | upper-alpha | upper-latin | hebrew | armenian | georgian |cjk-ideographic | hiragana | katakana | hiragana-iroha | katakana-iroha | none | inherit

The **counters()** function allows you to add a string to the counter output, its syntax is:

counters(<*identifier*>, <*string*>, <*list-style-type*>**)**

In our example above:

```
content: "Chapter " counter(chapter) ". ";
```

could be written as:

```
content: "Chapter " counters(chapter, ". ");
```

That's how you automate numbering using style sheets. Next we'll look at how you can ensure that you are using the appropriate form of quotation mark for the language your text will be viewed in.

Quotation Marks

The **quotes** property allows authors to use quotation marks in a context sensitive manner. The value syntax is as follows

[<*string*><*string*>]+|none|inherit

When the **quotes** property is used in conjunction with the HTML **<Q>** element and the pseudo-elements **:before** and **:after**, language specific quotes can be created. Again an example makes understanding this easier.

This style sheet first uses the quotes property to specify the quotes, it then uses the **:before** and **:after** properties with the **<Q>** element to print them:

```
Q:lang(en){quotes: ' " ' ' " ';}
Q:lang(fr){quotes: ` << ' ` >> ';}
Q:before {content :open-quote}
Q:after {content :open-quote}
```

The output for this piece of HTML:

```
<HTML lang="en">
      <BODY>
            <P><Q> A Quotation</Q></P>
      </BODY>
</HTML>
```

will be: "A Quotation".

The output for this piece of HTML:

```
<HTML lang="fr">
      <BODY>
            <P><Q> Un bon mot!!</Q></P>
      </BODY>
</HTML>
```

will be: << Un bon mot!!>>

That's it for this chapter. Let's summarize what we've learned.

Summary

We covered a lot of ground in this chapter.

- We looked at the document tree, and how it is utilized by browsers to create flow objects.
- We took a side trip to examine the Document Object Model.
- We studied the various types of selectors and took a brief look at an example that tells us how to find out what selector properties are supported by a specific browser.
- We saw the difference between Cascading and Inheritance and learnt how to import style sheets into our program.
- And finally we looked at the beginning of CSS's programming effort–the generation of content.

In the next chapter we will look at CSS's version of the flow object, the **box**, and see how we can style them, position them, layer them and otherwise manipulate them.

References

For a full description of the Microsoft version of the DOM see:

http://www.microsoft.com/intdev/ie4/domdoc-f.htm

and

http://www.microsoft.com/msdn/sdk/inetsdk/help/dhtml/references/domrefs.htm

For a description of the Netscape version of the DOM see:

http://developer.netscape.com/library/documentation/communicator/jsguide4/index.htm

The W3C working document on the DOM. Rather heavy going!

http://www.w3.org/TR/WD-DOM/level-one-core-971209

The following are the relevant URLs from the Style Sheet Recommendation. They are all quite readable.

The official spec on selectors can be found at:

http://www.w3.org/TR/PR-CSS2/selector.html

The official spec on cascading and inheritance can be found at:

http://www.w3.org/TR/PR-CSS2/cascade.html

The official spec on generating content can be found at

http://www.w3.org/TR/PR-CSS2/generate.html

Exercises

1. Write three different style sheets which give different values to the same element, and call them **cssa.css**, **cssb.css** and **cssc.css**. Write a simple HTML document and link to the style sheets using a **<LINK>** element.

```
<LINK REL=STYLESHEET TYPE="text/css" HREF="cssa.css" TITLE="Style">
<LINK REL=STYLESHEET TYPE="text/css" HREF="cssb.css" TITLE="Style">
<LINK REL=STYLESHEET TYPE="text/css" HREF="cssc.css" TITLE="Style">
```

2. Alter the order of your links and see how this affects the document display.
3. Put a style sheet in the head of your HTML document, and also include some inline styling. How does this alter the display?
4. If you are using IE4, try referencing a style sheet with the **@import** statement. Try putting this in the wrong place, and see what happens.
5. The **first-letter** pseudo-element is not supported at present. Try and figure out a way to make one using the **<SPAN>** element and the **float** property. Hint you may want to read the section on the **float** property in the next chapter before trying this.

8

Boxes and Layers

In this chapter we will look at the CSS concept of a specific flow object–the box. We will see how, by using CSS properties, we can display a box and move it around the screen. Although some of the implementation is a little buggy, and although the position properties are CSS2 rather than CSS1 properties, the major features are quite well supported by both Netscape and Microsoft.

We have concentrated on what works, and when we have provided an example of a poorly implemented property, we have shown you how the result is meant to be implemented, rather than how it is. In each screen capture we have used the browser that currently gives the closest implementation to the CSS specification. If neither of them do, then a 'pseudo-page' is usually provided. With patches coming out every day, by the time you read this, any information I give in these pages might be out of date, so the only way to be sure that an example works is to try it out!

Both W3C and the National Institute of Standards and Technology (NIST) (see the References at the end of the chapter for URLs) maintain sites where you can test the implementations of the browsers. We also refer you to an up-to-date table of what works and doesn't in various browsers on various platforms in the References section at the end of this chapter. However, we repeat the only way to be sure is to test your own pages.

In this chapter we will:

- ❑ Look at the basic flow object–the box.
- ❑ Look at the difference between block, inline, and anonymous boxes.
- ❑ Examine the box properties.
- ❑ Look at the normal flow of objects.

- See how to alter the normal flow, by floating a box, and positioning it both relatively and absolutely.
- Look at how to layer boxes, and how to alter the layering.
- Look at the options we have for displaying or hiding a box.
- Look at how to clip the contents of the box.

So, let's begin with an examination of that basic flow object–the box.

The Basic Box

The basic box has an edge, which contains the whole box. Inside this edge are content, margins and a border, and between the content and the border is padding. CSS provides properties that specify values for these areas. The following diagram shows the layout and properties of a typical block box.

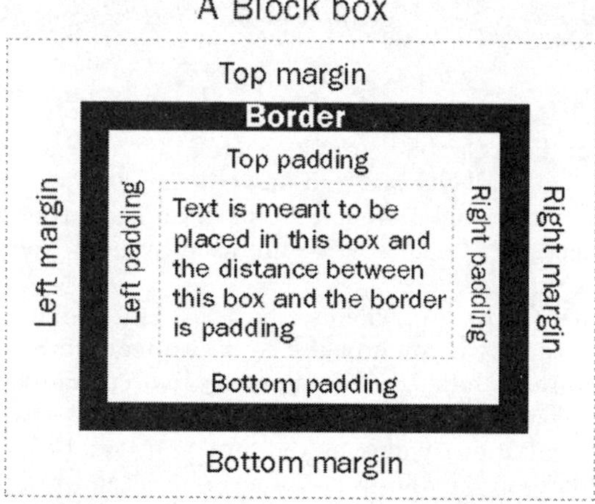

Notes
1. The thin grey lines depicting the outline of the text and margins are for illustration only.
2. The background of the parent box will shine through the margin.
3. The background of this block will shine through the padding.

*In the above diagram a reference is made to a parent box. Every element forms a box, and as every element–except the root element (**BODY** in HTML)–is contained in another element, every box–except the root box (**BODY** in HTML)–will have a parent.*

Every element will create its own box, which will enter into the normal flow. Usually the dimensions of the box will depend on its contents, however, in the following example we have specified the dimensions and background color of the box so that you can see some of the box properties.

The following code will create a box 3 inches square. We will go into the properties in detail later on.

```
<HTML>
   <HEAD>
      <TITLE>
      Chapter 8 Simple Box Example
      </TITLE>
      <STYLE TYPE="text/css">
      /*CLASSES HERE*/
      DIV{
      width:3in;
      height:3in;
      background-color:yellow;
      }
      </STYLE>
   </HEAD>
   <BODY>
      <DIV>
      Some text
      </DIV>
   </BODY>
</HTML>
```

The screenshot below shows what this looks like on IE4.

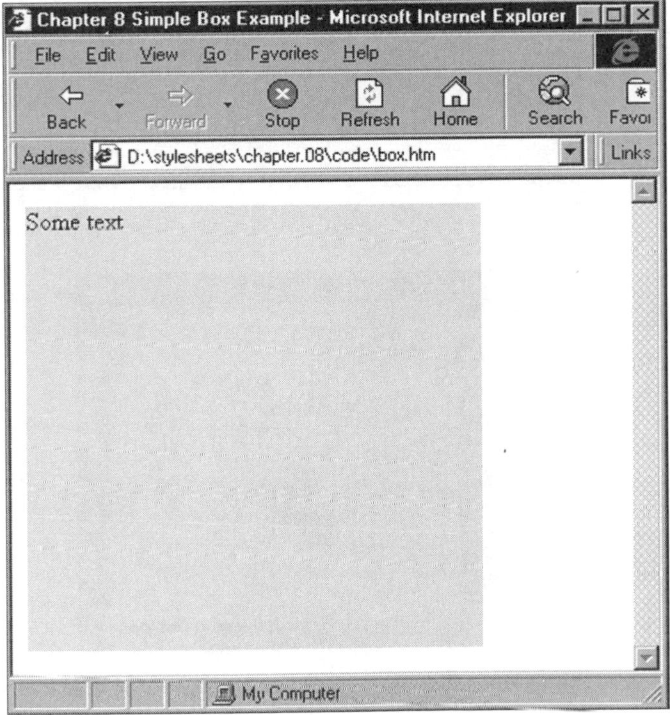

Now let's add a margin, a border and some padding to it.

```
<HTML>
   <HEAD>
      <TITLE>
      Chapter 8 Simple Box Example
      </TITLE>
      <STYLE TYPE="text/css">
      /*CLASSES HERE*/
      DIV{
      width:3in;
      height:3in;
      background-color:yellow;
      margin:.5in;
      padding:.5in;
      border-width:.25in;
      border-style:solid;
      text-align:justify;
      }
      </STYLE>
   </HEAD>
   <BODY>
      <DIV>
      Here is just enough text to wrap at least once inside of its padding. Note
how the padding is applied all around.
      </DIV>
   </BODY>
</HTML>
```

The next screenshot shows the result.

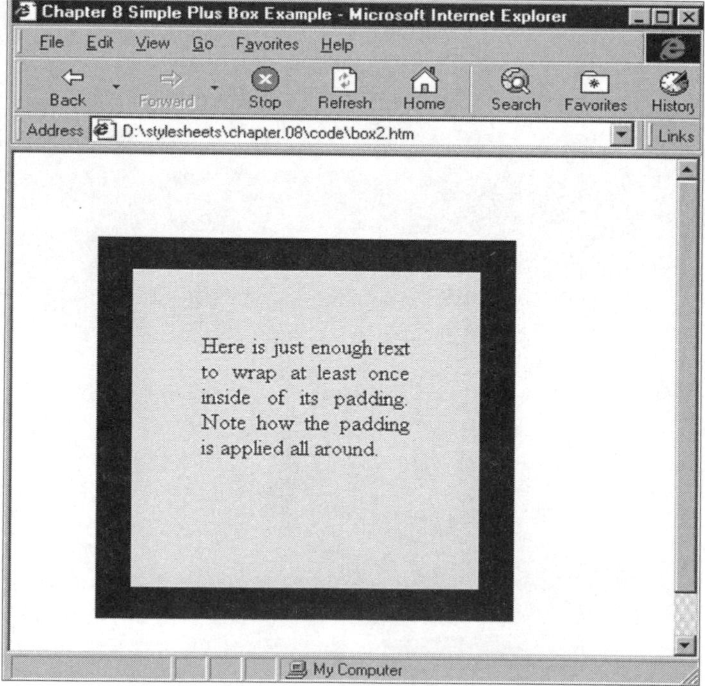

It is important to note the following:

- How adding the margin of half an inch has shifted the box down and to the right by half an inch.
- A quarter inch border has been added all around.
- There is now a half inch of padding all around between the text and the edge of the containing block.
- The background of the containing box (the **BODY** element) shines through the margin.
- The background of the contained box (the **DIV**) shines through the padding.

Actually IE4 does not quite follow the specification in this example, as the width–when stated as an absolute property–refers to the content width, so both padding and the border should have been added outside, rather than inside. We noted above that a box is created by its content. Here is a simple piece of code that illustrates this:

```
<HTML>
<STYLE>
BODY{background-color:white;}
DIV.first{background-color:red;color:white;font-size:18pt;}
DIV.second{background-color:yellow; color:black; font-size:24pt;}
DIV.third{background-color:navy;color:white;font-size:36pt;}
SPAN{background-color:green;color:yellow;}
</STYLE>
<BODY>
<DIV CLASS= "first">First line</DIV>
<DIV CLASS= "second"> Second line. In this line I have <SPAN>added enough
text so </SPAN>that the line will wrap to a second line.</DIV>
<DIV CLASS= "third">Third Line</DIV>

</BODY>
</HTML>
```

The following screenshot shows the result of this code.

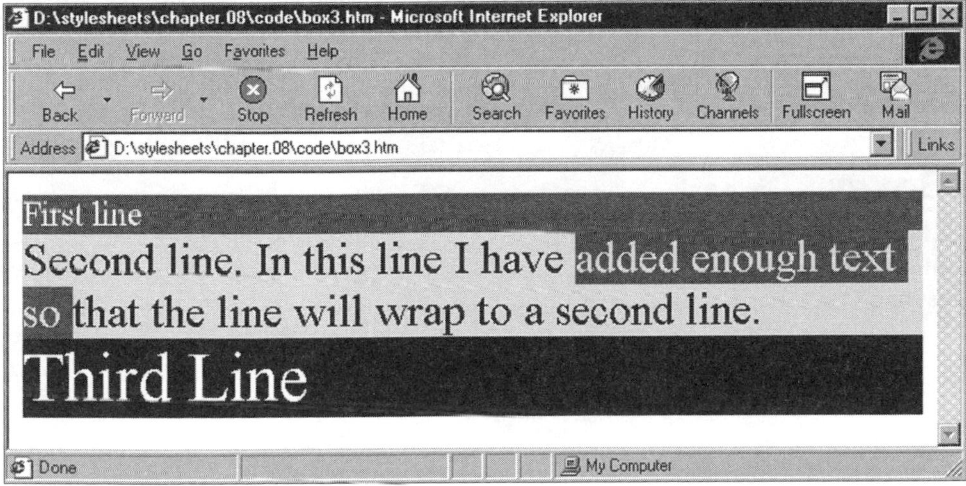

Note the following:

- In HTML the `<DIV>` element will create a block box.
- The `<SPAN>` element will create an inline box.
- How width of the block box extends across the whole page, i.e. it makes use of all the space available to it.
- The height of the block boxes are sufficient to contain the content, they have the default value of `auto`.
- The inline box that is created is just wide and high enough to contain the content.
- When a break occurs in the middle of an inline box, the user agent will create another inline box on the next line.

That concludes our look at the basic box. Before moving on to look at the properties that go with it, let's briefly examine the different types of box.

The Box Types

In our zeal to demonstrate what a box is we got a little ahead of ourselves. CSS1 recognizes three kinds of box (CSS2 recognizes several more, but they are connected with tables and lists, and will be dealt with in that chapter–Chapter 10). We will concern ourselves here with the three basic types, which are:

- The **Block** box.
- The **Inline** box.
- The **Anonymous** box.

We'll spend some time going over each box type in turn.

Block Boxes

Block boxes are the basic building block of a document display. Essentially they have a line-break before and after them. As we saw, if the width and height is not specifically set they will take up all the width available to them, and they will adjust their height so that they contain all their content. The `<DIV>` and `<P>` elements in HTML are examples of elements that form block boxes.

Inline Boxes

The inline box, as its name implies, contains content that will appear on a single line, and does not have a line break before and after it. The `<SPAN>` and `<EM>` elements are examples of HTML elements that form inline boxes.

Anonymous Boxes

Anonymous boxes are formed by the user agent to enable it to display the material correctly. In the above example we had the following text: "Second line. In this line I have", before our **<SPAN>**. In order to allow correct formatting the user agent creates an anonymous box. In fact, in this example four anonymous boxes were created, can you see where? (Answer below.) We can not set properties for anonymous boxes (except via their parents), but it is a phrase that you will see all the time, so now you know what it means!

> *Answer–The second line creates a block box that contains the whole. The* **<SPAN>** *creates an inline box. The two anonymous boxes that are created contain the text before and the text after the* **<SPAN>**. *The* **<SPAN>** *here actually creates two inline boxes, because it flows on to a second line.*

Armed with these definitions, we'll be able to gain a better understanding of what effect the following box properties can have on them.

Box Properties

As we have already noted, a box can have margins, padding, and borders. Let's have a look at the CSS properties that set the values for these various properties. We will also indicate how they vary for an inline or a block box.

Margin Properties

The margin properties are **margin-top**, **margin-right**, **margin-bottom**, **margin-left**, and the shorthand property **margin**.

They set the margins for a block and apply to all elements. The property is not inherited unless specifically stated.

The first four take the syntax:

margin-*:<*length*> | <*percentage*> | **inherit**

The shorthand property takes the syntax:

margin: <margin-width>{1,4} | inherit

- If just one value is given, it applies to all sides.
- If two are given, the first applies to the top and bottom, the second to the left and right margins.
- If three values are given, the first applies to the top, the second to left and right, the third to bottom.
- If four are given, the order is top, right, bottom, left. i.e. clockwise.

The value for margin can be a negative value. If a negative value is set for the property **`margin-left`**, the left-hand margin of the child box will be to the **left** of its parent box. If a negative value is set for the property **`margin-right`**, the right-hand margin of the child box will be to the **right** of its parent box.

In this example, just one value is given for margin.

```
<HTML>
<HEAD>
<STYLE>
BODY{background-color:white;}
DIV.first{background-color:red;color:white;font-size:18pt;}
DIV.second{background-color:yellow;color:black; font-size:24pt;border-
width:1px;border-style:solid; margin:1cm;}
DIV.third{background-color:navy;color:white;font-size:36pt;}
SPAN{background-color:green;color:yellow;}
</STYLE>
</HEAD>
<BODY>
<DIV CLASS= "first">First line</DIV>
<DIV CLASS= "second"> Second line. In this line I have <SPAN>added enough text
so </SPAN>that the line will wrap to a second line.</DIV>
<DIV CLASS= "third">Third Line</DIV>
</BODY>
</HTML>
```

The following screenshot shows how the example is rendered. Note how the background color of the **`<BODY>`** shines through the margin.

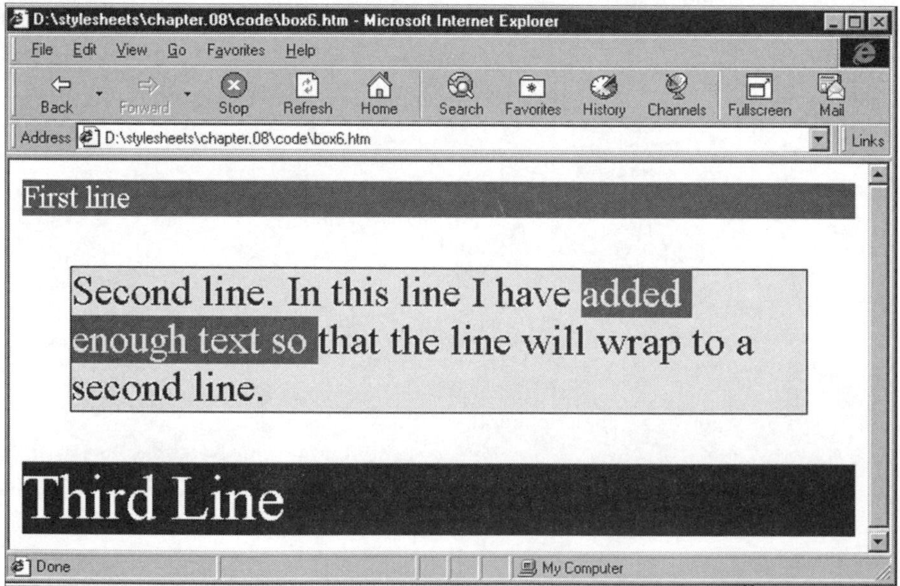

If a percentage value is used for margin, i.e. in the example above if the margin property for **DIV.second** was given the value of 10%, then the percentage refers to the width of the containing box. In other words in the example above, it would refer to the **<BODY>** width, and the margin would be 10% of the **<BODY>** width.

Adjacent Margins

In CSS, vertical margins of block boxes will collapse into each other so that the distance between the blocks is not the sum of the margins, but the greater of the two margins. This diagram illustrates the concept.

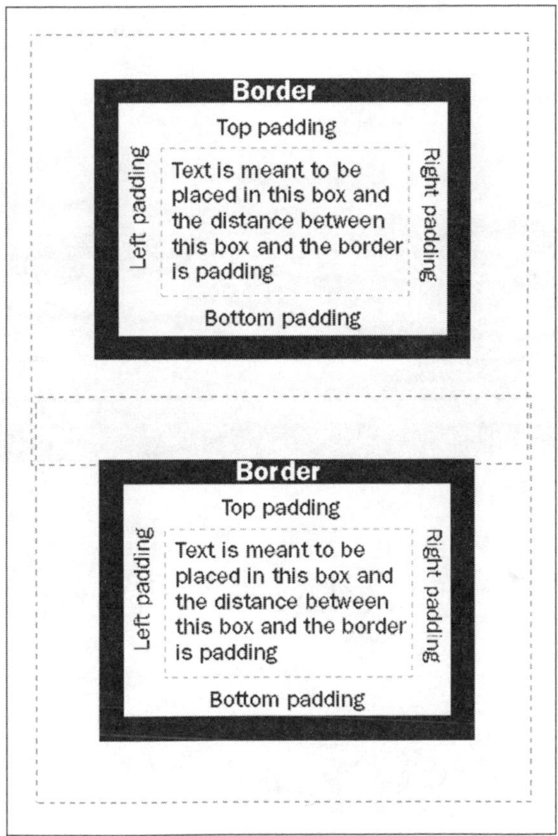

In the diagram above an outline of the margin has been included, (although of course we can't do this on the screen, margins don't have borders!). Note the overlap between the bottom margin of the top box, and the top margin of the bottom box, so that the space left between them is only equal to the greater of the two margins. This is what is known as vertical collapse. With boxes positioned side by side, the adjacent horizontal margins will not collapse in other words they are additive.

As you can see in the next section, we have altered the code to give the third **<DIV>** a margin. The result is shown in the following screenshot. Note how the margins between the second and third **<DIV>**s collapse, i.e. the distance is still only 1 cm not 2 cm.

```
<HTML>
<HEAD>
<STYLE>
BODY{background-color:white;}
DIV.first{background-color:red;color:white;font-size:18pt;}
DIV.second{background-color:yellow;color:black; font-size:24pt;border-
width:1px;border-style:solid; margin:1cm;}
DIV.third{background-color:navy;color:white;font-size:36pt;margin:1cm;}
SPAN{background-color:green;color:yellow;}
</STYLE>
</HEAD>
<BODY>
<DIV CLASS= "first">First line</DIV>
<DIV CLASS= "second"> Second line. In this line I have <SPAN>added enough text
so </SPAN>that the line will wrap to a second line.</DIV>
<DIV CLASS= "third">Third Line</DIV>
</BODY>
</HTML>
```

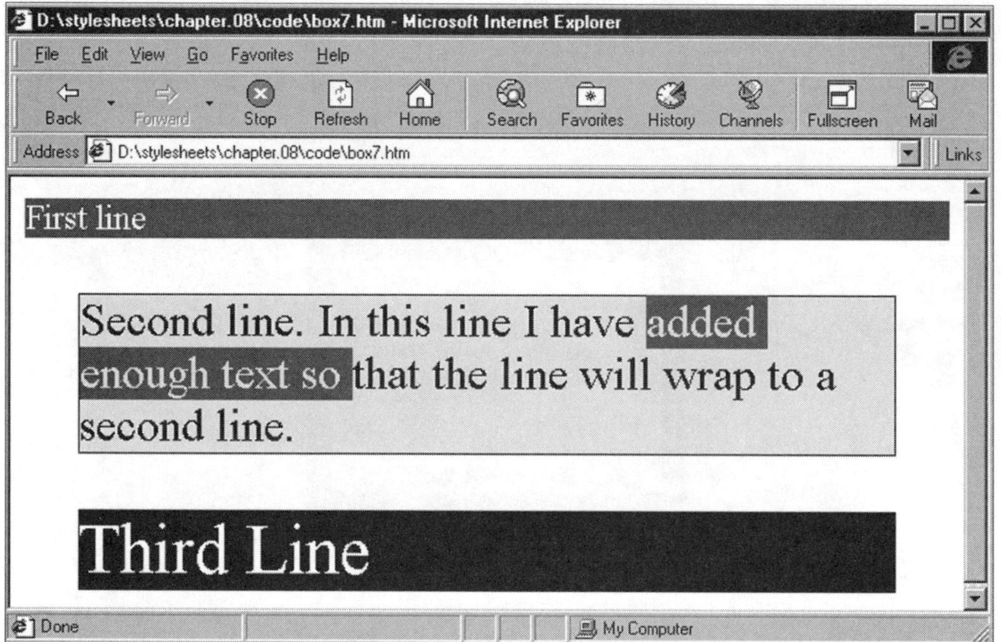

Vertical margins of block boxes collapse if they are taking part in the normal flow, but margins of floated elements and margins of absolutely positioned boxes do not collapse (see the later section on *Positioning Boxes*).

That concludes our look at margin properties, let's move on to the next set of properties in our list, the padding properties.

The Padding Properties

The padding properties are **padding-top**, **padding-right**, **padding-bottom**, **padding-left**, and the shorthand property is **padding**.

The syntax is very similar to that of margin, except that negative values are not allowed.

The first four take the syntax:

padding-*:<*length*> | <*percentage*> | **inherit**

The shorthand property takes the syntax:

padding: <padding-width>{1,4} | **inherit**

Again the percentage value is calculated in respect of the containing block. Padding properties are not inherited.

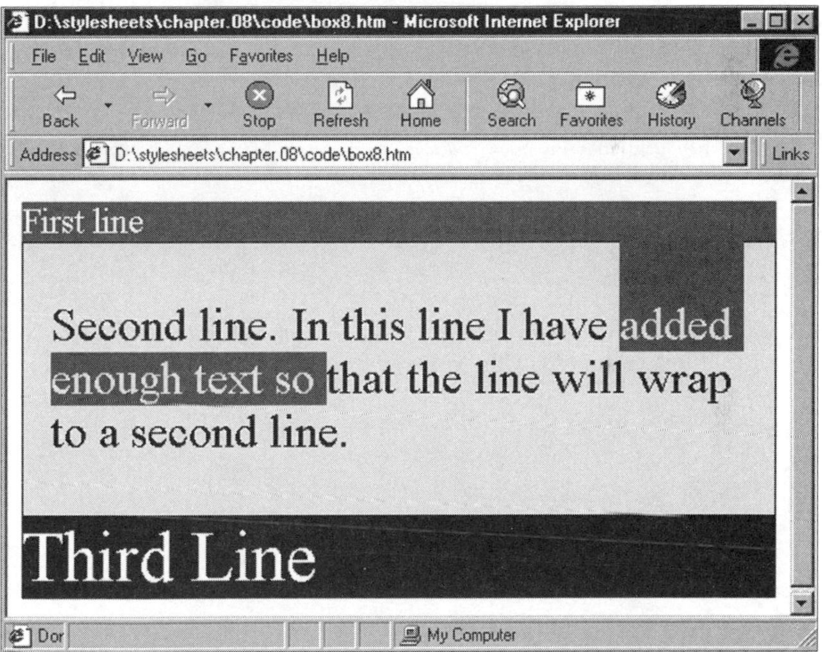

The screenshot above shows what happens when we add

```
padding:1cm .5cm;
```

to the second **<DIV>**. The full code for the example would then read as follows:

```
<HTML>
<STYLE>
BODY{background-color:white;}
DIV.first{background-color:red;color:white;font-size:18pt;}
DIV.second{background-color:yellow;color:black; font-size:24pt;border-
width:1px;border-style:solid;
padding:1cm .5cm;}
DIV.third{background-color:navy;color:white;font-size:36pt;}
SPAN{background-color:green;color:yellow;}

</STYLE>
<BODY>
<DIV CLASS= "first">First line</DIV>
<DIV CLASS= "second"> Second line. In this line I have <SPAN>added enough text
so </SPAN>that the line will wrap to a second line.</DIV>
<DIV CLASS= "third">Third Line</DIV>

</BODY>
</HTML>
```

Note what has happened to our **<SPAN>**. This is because the padding was added to the first line anonymous box. This is probably not a valid interpretation on Microsoft's part.

> *Authors would probably like any background element for their <SPAN> elements to be the same height on both lines, they do not want the padding added to their <SPAN> properties. (Padding is not meant to be inherited.) This is my reason for saying that Microsoft's interpretation is at fault, even though it doesn't actually contravene the strict letter of the CSS spec!*

The border, padding and margin properties are meant to be applicable to inline objects as well as block objects, but they are not currently well implemented in the browsers.

The following screenshot shows how padding appears when added to an inline box in Communicator:

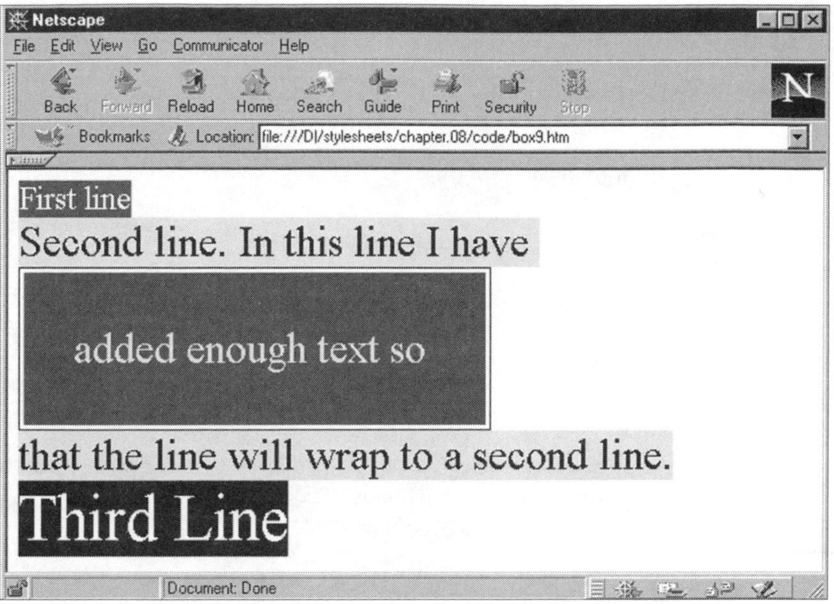

The code which produces this screenshot looks like this:

```
<HTML>
   <STYLE>
      BODY{background-color:white;}
      DIV.first{background-color:red;color:white;font-size:18pt;}
      DIV.second{background-color:yellow;color:black; font-size:24pt;}
      DIV.third{background-color:navy;color:white;font-size:36pt;}
      SPAN{background-color:green;color:yellow;padding:1cm;border-
width:1px;border-style:solid;}
   </STYLE>
   <BODY>
      <DIV CLASS= "first">First line</DIV>
      <DIV CLASS= "second"> Second line. In this line I have <SPAN>added
enough text so </SPAN>that the line will wrap to a second line.</DIV>
      <DIV CLASS= "third">Third Line</DIV>
   </BODY>
</HTML>
```

As you can see it has made a block box out of it. IE4 just ignores these properties in an inline box. If, however, we set a **width** property to an inline element we can apply these properties to them. This will be dealt with in more detail later in the chapter, in the section on *Positioning Boxes*.

Border Properties

Border properties are used to set the border width, color, and style. There are also several shorthand properties. We'll examine each of the different types of border property in turn. Border properties are not inherited.

Border Width

Border width properties are **border-top-width**, **border-right-width**, **border-bottom-width**, **border-left-width**, and the shorthand is **border-width**.

Their syntax is similar to that of **margin**. They can take a length or an absolute string value. Percentages are not permitted. The syntax is:

border-top-width: thin | medium | thick | <*length*>

If the shorthand value is used, the allotment of values to the sides is as for the **margin** and **padding** shorthand, which we explained at the start of the *Box Properties* section when we covered **margin** properties.

Border Color

Border color properties are **border-top-color**, **border-right-color**, **border-bottom-color**, **border-left-color**, and the shorthand is **border-color**.

The syntax is:

border-top-color: <*color*>

If the shorthand value is used the allotment of values to the sides is as for the **margin** and **border** shorthand, with the exception that the value **transparent** can also be used. Color values are listed in Appendix E.

Border Style

Border style properties are **border-top-style**, **border-right-style**, **border-bottom-style**, **border-left-style**, and the shorthand is **border-style**.

Style can take the following string values (and this is quoted from the spec):

> **none**–No border. This value forces the computed value of **border-width** to be **0**.
> **hidden**–Same as **none**, except in terms of border conflict resolution for table elements. (See the chapter on tables for further details.)
> **dotted**–The border is a series of dots.
> **dashed**–The border is a series of short line segments.
> **solid**–The border is a single line segment.
> **double**–The border is two solid lines. The sum of the two lines and the space between them equals the value of **border-width**.
> **groove**–The border looks as though it were carved into the canvas.
> **ridge**–The opposite of **groove**: the border looks as though it were coming out of the canvas.
> **inset**–The border makes the entire box look as though it were embedded in the canvas.
> **outset**–The opposite of **inset**: the order makes the entire box look as though it were coming out of the canvas.

The default value is **none**.

An example is as follows:

```
border-top-style:<solid>
```

For the shorthand property, the same rotation is followed as in **`margin`**.

The following screenshot shows how the various border styles are rendered in Communicator:

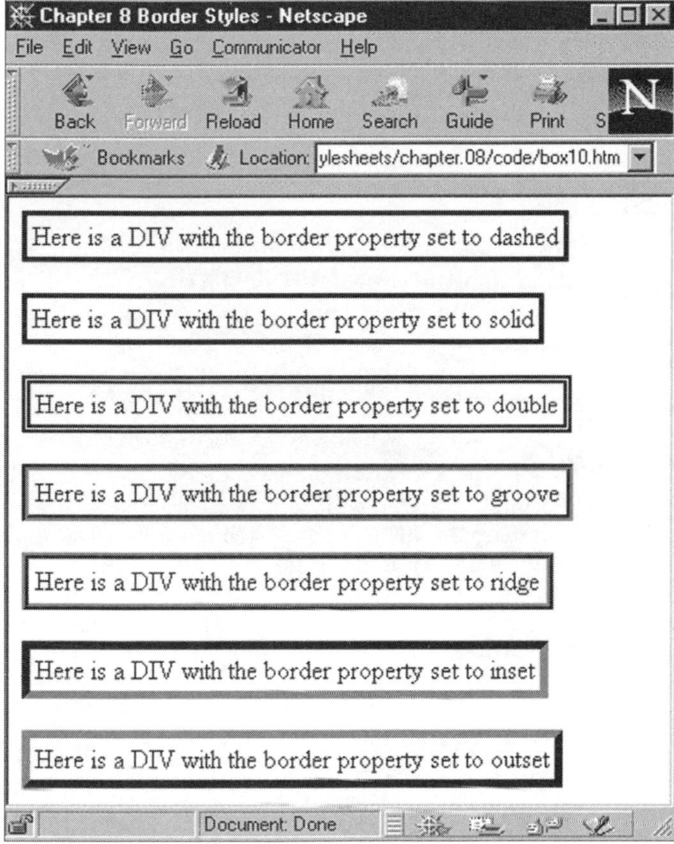

In IE4 only the **`solid`**, **`double`**, **`hidden`** and **`none`** values are supported, the rest just produce a solid border.

Other Shorthand Border Properties

The shorthand border properties are **`border-top`**, **`border-right`**, **`border-bottom`**, **`border-left`**, and **`border`**.

They will set the width, style and color of the border. The **`border`** property sets all four borders. The syntax is:

```
border: <border-width> || <border-style> || <color>
```

The following code snippet is an example:

```
H1 {border-bottom: thick solid black}
```

This will produce a thick solid black bottom border, while this code snippet:

```
H1 {border: thick solid black}
```

will produce a thick solid black border all around.

That concludes our introduction to the basic box and its properties. Now let's look at the normal flow of objects, both inline and block, and see how you can alter this using the **`float`** and **`position`** properties.

Positioning Boxes

Boxes created by XML or HTML enter into a normal flow. This flow is different for block boxes and inline boxes. It is possible to alter the normal flow of block boxes by the **`position`** and the **`float`** properties. Although **`float`** and **`position`** properties are meant to work on both block and inline boxes, in practice–at the present time–**`float`** works on inline boxes, and **`position`** on block and inline boxes. First we will look at how to take inline elements out of the normal flow, and then we will look at block elements.

Normal Inline Flow

We saw above how the various lines of text in a block box are treated as anonymous boxes within their element. We also saw that if any of this text is selected out for special treatment by way of a **`<SPAN>`**, an **`<EM>`**, or other inline element, it is treated as an inline element because it does not have a line break before or after it. We can, in fact, apply properties to this inline element to take it out of the normal flow, and because these can be a little difficult to comprehend in the abstract, we will start with an example. After working through the example, we'll go into detail on the properties we have used.

An Example using the Float Property

In this section we are going to apply the **`width`** and **`float`** properties to the **`<SPAN>`** element. This is the relevant code that we are going to start with which creates a simple **`<SPAN>`** and gives it a background color of green:

```
<HTML>
<HEAD>
<TITLE>
Chapter 8 Float Property Example
</TITLE>
<STYLE>
DIV{font-size:14pt;}
SPAN{background-color:#008800; font-size:14pt;}
</STYLE>
</HEAD>
<BODY>
<DIV CLASS="">
This is an anonymous box created in a DIV before a SPAN.
```

```
<SPAN CLASS="">We are about to take this span out of the normal flow using
the float method. First though we must give it a width.</SPAN>
 This is another anonymous box created after the SPAN.
</DIV>
<DIV CLASS=""></DIV>
</BODY>
</HTML>
```

This screenshot shows how this code appears on screen.

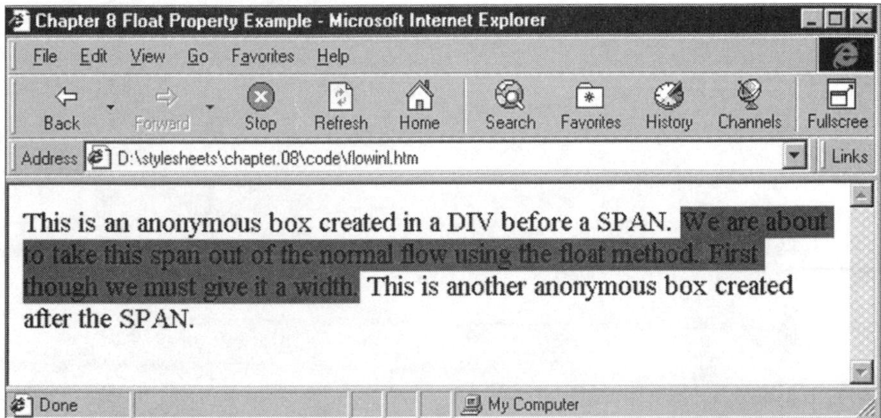

Next we set a width of 4cm for our inline **SPAN** by adding the **width** property and value to our code. We cover the **width** and **height** properties after the example. Here's how the code looks now.

```
<HTML>
<HEAD>
<TITLE>
Chapter 8 Float Property Example
</TITLE>
<STYLE>
DIV{font-size:14pt;}
SPAN{background-color:#008800;font-size:14pt;width:4cm;}
</STYLE>
</HEAD>
<BODY>
<DIV CLASS="">
This is an anonymous box created in a DIV before a SPAN.
<SPAN CLASS="">We are about to take this span out of the normal flow using the
float method. Now we have given it a width of 4 cm using the width
property.</SPAN>
 Now we have another anonymous box created after the SPAN.
</DIV>
<DIV CLASS=""></DIV>
</BODY>
</HTML>
```

This screenshot shows how this appears on the screen. Note how a box has been created, but it is still an inline box with its base resting on the font base line.

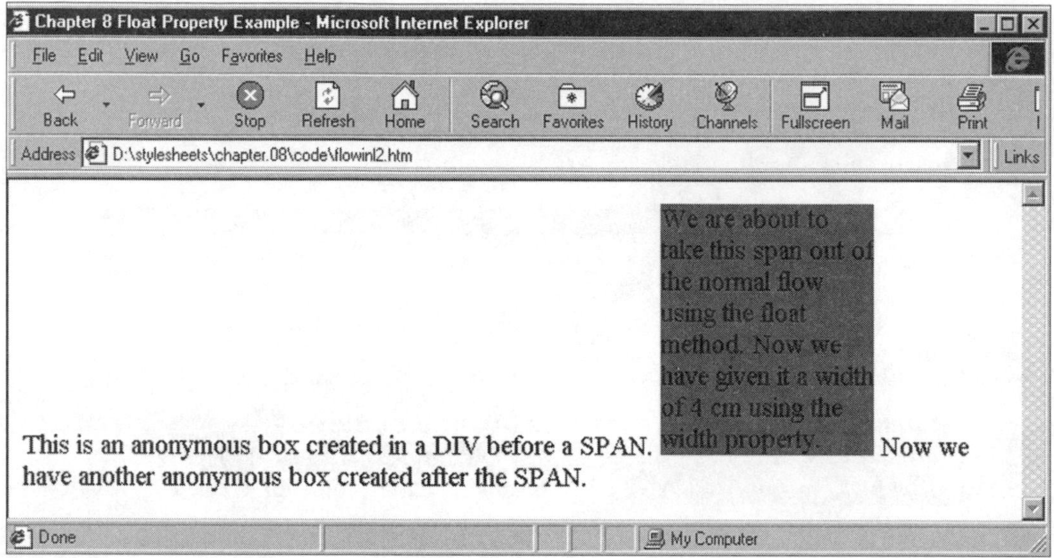

We now take this box out of the normal flow by adding the **`float`** property with a value of **`left`** to the following code. The **`float`** property is covered in its own section after the examples.

```
<HTML>
<HEAD>
<TITLE>
Chapter 8 Float Property Example
</TITLE>
<STYLE>
DIV{font-size:14pt;}
SPAN{background-color:#008800;font-size:14pt;width:4cm;float:left;}
</STYLE>
</HEAD>
<BODY>
<DIV CLASS="">
This is an anonymous box created in a DIV before a SPAN.
<SPAN CLASS="">We are about to take this span out of the normal flow using the
float method. Now we have given it a width of 4 cm using the width
property.</SPAN>
 Now we have another anonymous box created after the SPAN.
</DIV>
<DIV CLASS="">This is a second DIV and it is to demonstrate how the text flows
round the inline flow object that we have taken out of the normal flow using the
width and float properties. In a moment, using the clear property, we will make
this text start <I>after</I> the SPAN. </DIV>
</BODY>
</HTML>
```

The following screenshot shows how this appears on the screen. We have also added another **<DIV>** here, and in the next example we are going to use the **clear** property with this **<DIV>** to make it start after our floated **<SPAN>**.

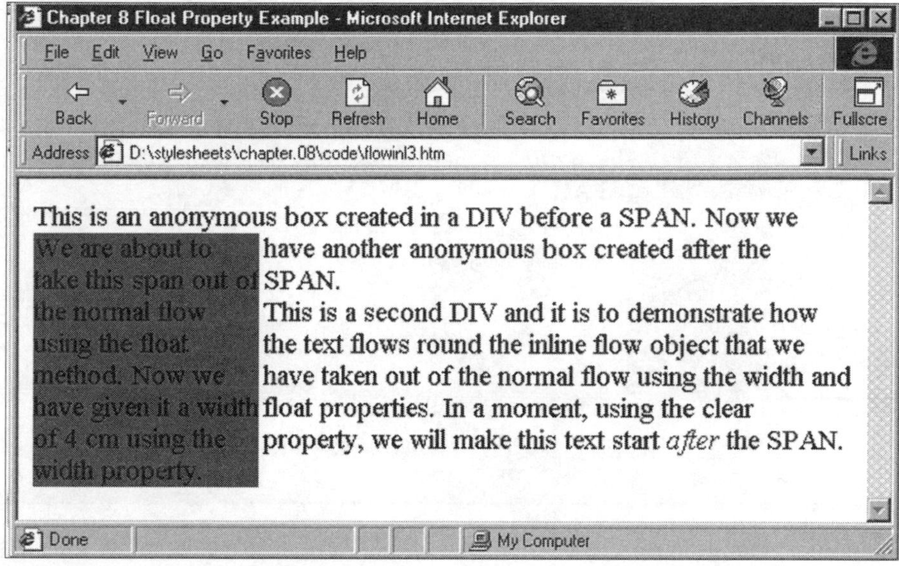

Here is the **<DIV>** with **clear:left** set on it using inline styling.

```
<HTML>
<HEAD>
<TITLE>
Chapter 8 Float Property Example
</TITLE>
<STYLE>
DIV{font-size:14pt;}
SPAN{background-color:#008800;font-size:14pt;width:4cm;float:left;}
</STYLE>
</HEAD>
<BODY>
<DIV CLASS="">
This is an anonymous box created in a DIV before a SPAN.
<SPAN CLASS="">We are about to take this span out of the normal flow using the
float method. Now we have given it a width of 4 cm using the width
property.</SPAN>
 Now we have another anonymous box created after the SPAN.
</DIV>
<DIV STYLE="clear:left;">In this final example we have now set the second
DIV's clear property "left" and we demonstrate how the text now begins
<B>after</B> the SPAN. </DIV>
</BODY>
</HTML>
```

The following screenshot shows how this appears.

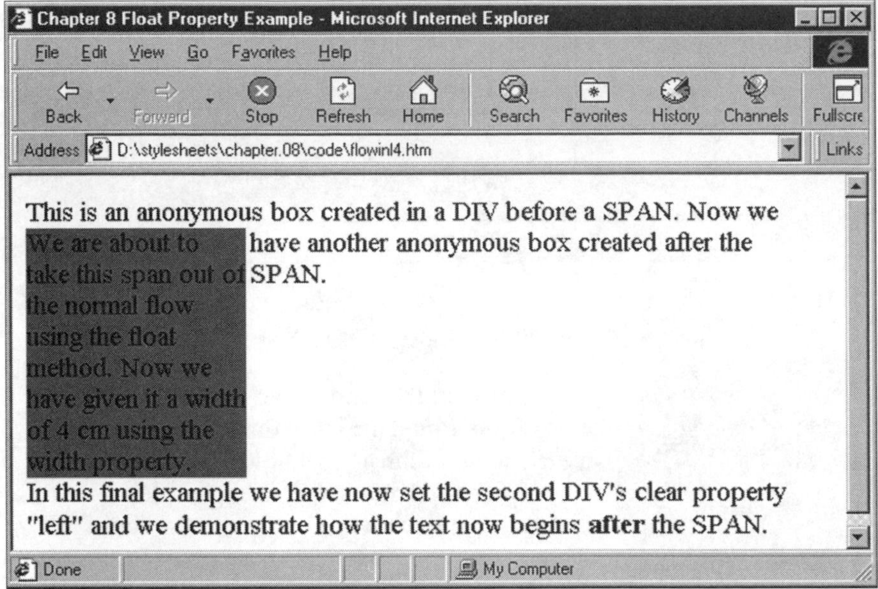

Now let us look at the properties that we have used.

Width and Height Properties

We used the **width** property in the example above to give a width to our **<SPAN>**.

The syntax for both the **width** and **height** properties is:

width | height:<*length*> | <*percentage*> | **auto**

They have an initial value of **auto**.

Note that when percentage values are used they should be calculated as a percentage of the **width** of the containing block. This applies to the **height** value as well as the **width** value.

IE4 interprets this property incorrectly at the time of writing. Here is an example:

```
<DIV STYLE="width:25%;height:25%;background-color:red"></DIV>
<DIV STYLE="width:5em;height:5em;background-color:yellow"></DIV>
<DIV STYLE="font-size:16pt;width:5em;height:5em;background-
color:red"></DIV>
```

The following screenshot shows how this is interpreted in IE4. Note the first box should be square, and the second and third boxes should be the same size.

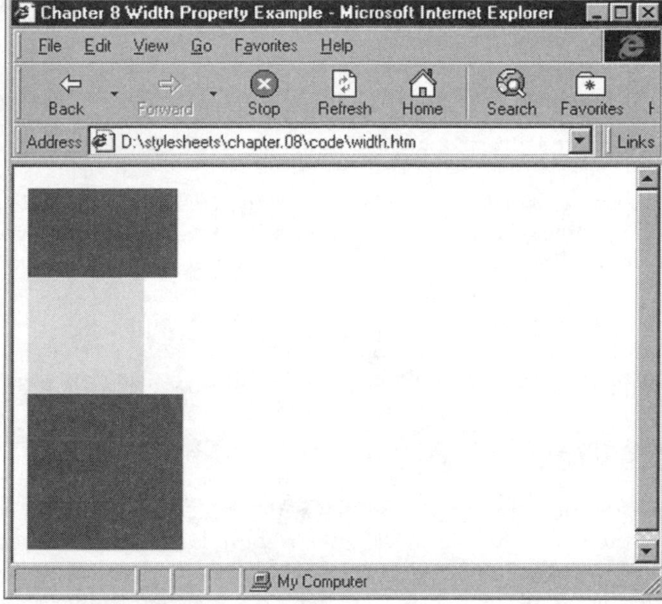

Because of the incorrect interpretations at present, it is probably best to use percentage or absolute units for widths (i.e. don't use **`ems`**) and just use absolute units for height.

Next in our example, we used the **`float`** property to remove the **`<SPAN>`** from the normal flow, so let's look at it in a bit more detail.

Float Property

This should apply to all elements that are not positioned absolutely. In practice it does not apply to block elements as they have a line-break before and after them. Use the position properties to position block elements.

A value of **`left`** takes the object out of the normal flow, and positions it to the left of the page. A value of **`right`** positions it to the right of the page.

The syntax is:

```
float: left | right | none
```

This property is used with inline flow objects that have a **`width`** value. The width can either be an intrinsic width–as in the case of an image or an object, or it can be a width generated by code–as in the case of the above examples.

Finally, in the example above, we used the **`clear`** property to make the second **`<DIV>`** start after the **`<SPAN>`**, so let's look at this property next.

Clear Property

This property is used to position blocks in respect to floated elements. It only applies to block elements, including floats. It is similar to the clear attribute used with **
** in HTML except that it can be applied to any block element.

The syntax is:

```
clear: none | left | right | both
```

If the value is set to **none**, which is the default, then the contents of the block element will flow alongside the floated element. If set to **left** or **right**, it will wait until either the left or right margins are clear before flowing. If **clear** is set to **both**, it will wait until both margins are clear before flowing.

That concludes our look at normal inline flow, and how it can be altered using the **float** property. Next we look at normal block flow, and how it can be altered using the **position** property.

Normal Block Flow

Normally block objects flow from top to bottom with a line break between each object, and the object would be to the left of the page. (Or to the right in languages that read right to left.) If the objects were stacked then the first flow object would be on the bottom of the pile, and the last flow object would be on the top of the pile. We can alter the normal position using the **position** property in conjunction with the box offset properties of **top**, **right**, **bottom**, and **left**.

If the elements were to overlay one another–and we can make this happen by using the **position** property–they would form a stack with the first in the flow order being under the next and so on. The order of the stack is called the **z-order**, and each item in the stack has an index called the **z-index**. An element with a z-index of 1 would be under an element with a z-index of 2, and so on. We can alter this normal order by assigning a z-index or changing the normal z-index with the **z-index** property.

Note that for some reason in CSS there is no easy way to center a block object on a page, as in using the HTML tag of **<CENTER>**. The officially correct way to center an object is to set both the **margin-right** and **margin-left** properties to **auto** as follows.

```
.center{margin-left:auto;margin-right:auto;}
```

But this is cumbersome and besides it is not supported! A way that does work is to set the object in a **<DIV>** with the **text-align** property set to **center**, namely:

```
<DIV STYLE= "text-align:center"><TABLE....>etc</DIV>
```

But this is really a hack! Although the **<CENTER>** tag has been deprecated, it is still probably the easiest method to use!

So, first we'll take a look at the **position** and box offset properties, and see some examples of absolute and relative positioning, then we'll examine layers and the **z-index** property.

Position Property

The **position** property–along with the list of box offset properties–is used to calculate the coordinates of a box. The syntax is as follows:

position : static | relative | absolute | fixed

The meaning of these values is as follows.

static

The box is a normal box in the normal flow. Its position is calculated by the user agent according to its established algorithms. See the following URL for details of these algorithms:

http:/www.w3.org/TR/PR-CSS2/visudet.html

relative

The position of the box is calculated with respect to its position in the normal flow. It is merely displaced from that position by an amount given using the box offset properties. We will cover this in detail below.

absolute

The box position is calculated with respect to the containing box. **0,0** would be the top left hand corner of the containing box, and these co-ordinates would place the top left hand corner of the positioned box at the top left corner of the containing box. If positive co-ordinates are used, then the box will be displaced down and to the left by the amounts specified. The box is taken out of the normal flow, which means that its position does not affect the positioning of its siblings. As you would expect, boxes that are absolutely positioned do not collapse their margins.

fixed

The position is calculated as in the absolute value, but it is calculated in relation to a reference point other than the containing block. In the case of a computer screen this is the viewing window, so its position will not change when the window is scrolled (not supported at present).

Box Offset Properties

The properties are **top**, **right**, **bottom**, or **left**.

The position of boxes which have been assigned a **relative**, **absolute**, or **fixed** value are determined by these properties.

The syntax is:

top: <*length*> | <*percentage*> | **auto**

The default is **auto**. The property specifies how far the box is offset from the border of the containing box.

Relative units, including percentages, are calculated with respect to the containing boxes' dimensions or properties. Note that **top** is calculated as a percentage of the **height** of the containing block. (Cf. The **height** property where it is (should be) a percentage of the width.)

Normal Block Flow Example

In this first example we have simply created three element blocks using **<DIV>**s which we call the first, second, and third blocks. We have given the blocks a fixed width of 6cm and a height of 3cm for illustration purposes only. This example demonstrates normal flow. Here is the relevant code:

```
<HTML>
<HEAD>
<TITLE>
Chapter 8 First Positioning Example
</TITLE>
<STYLE TYPE="text/css">
/*CLASSES HERE*/

BODY{
font-size:12pt;
font-weight:normal;
}
DIV{
font-size:24pt;
font-weight:normal;
width:6cm;
height:3cm;
}

</STYLE>
</HEAD>
<BODY>
<DIV STYLE="background-color:#FF0000">First block</DIV>
<DIV STYLE="background-color:#FFFF00">Second block</DIV>
<DIV STYLE="background-color:#00CC00">Third block</DIV>
</BODY>
</HTML>
```

The following screenshot shows what it looks like in IE4.

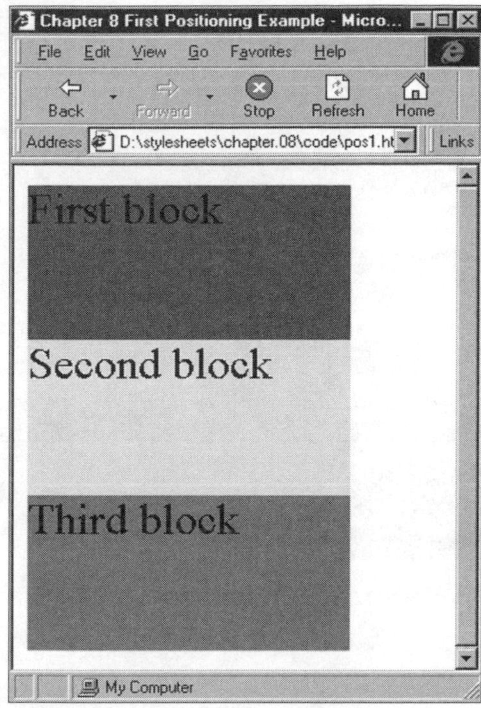

Relative Positioning Example

To demonstrate relative positioning, the code for the second **<DIV>** has been altered as follows.

```
<HTML>
<HEAD>
<TITLE>
Chapter 8 Relative Positioning Example
</TITLE>
<STYLE TYPE="text/css">
/*CLASSES HERE*/

BODY{
font-size:12pt;
font-weight:normal;
}
DIV{
font-size:24pt;
font-weight:normal;
width:6cm;
height:3cm;
}

</STYLE>
</HEAD>
<BODY>
<DIV STYLE="background-color:#FF0000">First block</DIV>
```

```
<DIV STYLE="background-color:#FFFF00;position:relative;left:1cm; top:-
1cm;">Second block</DIV>

<DIV STYLE="background-color:#00CC00">Third block</DIV>
</BODY>
</HTML>
```

So it now displays like this:

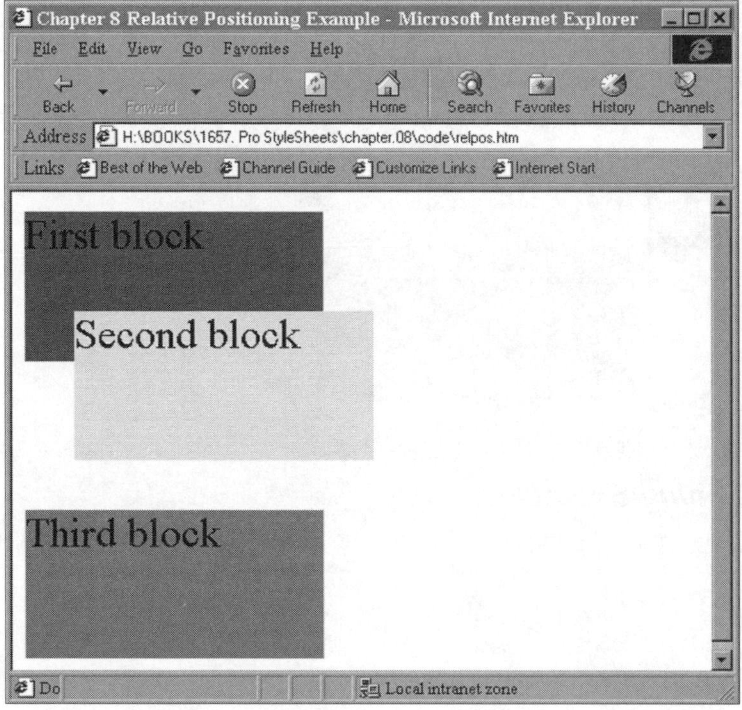

The change in the code has had the effect of pushing the box up and to the right by one centimeter (note the minus sign for the **top** value). See how the space that it originally occupied has been preserved.

Absolute Positioning Example

To demonstrate absolute positioning, we alter the code for the second **<DIV>** as follows.

```
<HTML>
<HEAD>
<TITLE>
Chapter 8 Absolute Positioning Example
</TITLE>
<STYLE TYPE="text/css">
/*CLASSES HERE*/

BODY{
font-size:12pt;
```

```
font-weight:normal;
}
DIV{
font-size:24pt;
font-weight:normal;
width:6cm;
height:3cm;
}

</STYLE>
</HEAD>
<BODY>
<DIV STYLE="background-color:#FF0000">First block</DIV>
<DIV STYLE="background-color:#FFFF00;position:absolute; left:1cm;
top:1cm;">Second block</DIV>
<DIV STYLE="background-color:#00CC00">Third block</DIV>
</BODY>
</HTML>
```

This screenshot shows the effect on the display.

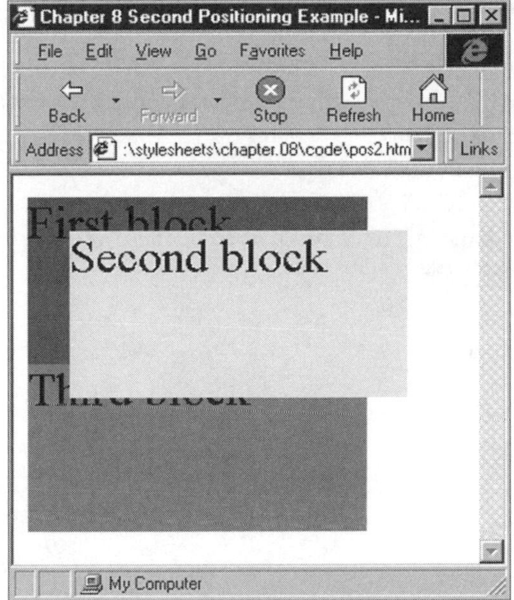

Note the following points.

- The second block is now positioned absolutely in reference to its containing box (the **<BODY>** element), one centimeter from the left edge, and one centimeter from the top edge.
- The space that it would have occupied in the normal flow is not reserved. Block Three follows hard on the heels of Block One.
- Block Two is now top of the stack. Absolute elements are always above relative ones in the z-order unless coded otherwise.

So, now we've covered relative and absolute positioning, let's move on to layers and the z-index.

Layers and the Z-index Property

If boxes are positioned so that they overlap one another, normally the last box in the flow will be on top.

This property establishes the stack level of a box within a containing box. If the z-index of three boxes are assigned a **`z-index`** of **`1`** to **`3`**, then **`1`** will be the bottom box, and **`3`** the top box with **`2`** in the middle. The **`z-index`** can also take a negative number, but the negative number **`-1`** does **not** move it back by one it puts it to z-position **`-1`**.

For example, if we had assigned the top of the three boxes a z-index of **–1** it would not go back one, it would go to the bottom of the pile because the order would now be **–1**, **1**, **2**.

See example **`pos3b.htm`** and **`pos4b.htm`** on the web site at:

`http://rapid.wrox.co.uk/books/1657`

The syntax is:

`z-index:` <*integer*> | **`auto`**

Here are some examples. We're using the same basic code that we used in our relative and absolute positioning demonstration.

Z-index

In this first example we have taken the original code and used a **`relative`** position on the second and third blocks to make them overlap. Here's the code:

```
<HTML>
<HEAD>
<TITLE>
Chapter 8 Z-Index Example
</TITLE>

<STYLE TYPE="text/css">
/*CLASSES HERE*/

BODY{
font-size:12pt;
font-weight:normal;
}
DIV{
font-size:24pt;
font-weight:normal;
width:6cm;
height:3cm;
}

</STYLE>
</HEAD>
<BODY>
<DIV STYLE="background-color:#FF0000">First block</DIV>
```

```
<DIV STYLE="background-color:#FFFF00;position:relative;left:1cm; top:-
1cm;">Second block</DIV>
<DIV STYLE="background-color:#00CC00;position:relative;left:2cm; top:-
2cm;">Third block</DIV>

</BODY>
</HTML>
```

and here's the screenshot to show you what it looks like.

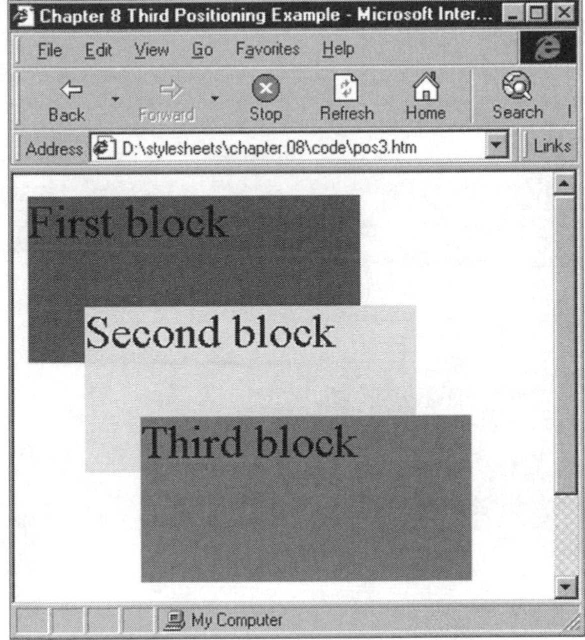

To demonstrate z-index, we've amended the code by adding a **`z-index`** property to reverse the stack or z-order.

```
<HTML>
<HEAD>
<TITLE>
Chapter 8 Z-Index Example
</TITLE>

<STYLE TYPE="text/css">
/*CLASSES HERE*/

BODY{
font-size:12pt;
font-weight:normal;
}
DIV{
font-size:24pt;
font-weight:normal;
width:6cm;
```

```
height:3cm;
}

</STYLE>
</HEAD>
<BODY>
<DIV STYLE="background-color:#FF0000">First block</DIV>
<DIV STYLE="background-color:#FFFF00;position:relative;left:1cm; top:-1cm;
z-index:-1">Second block</DIV>
<DIV STYLE="background-color:#00CC00;position:relative;left:2cm; top:-2cm;
z-index:-2">Third block</DIV>
</BODY>
</HTML>
```

This is how it looks.

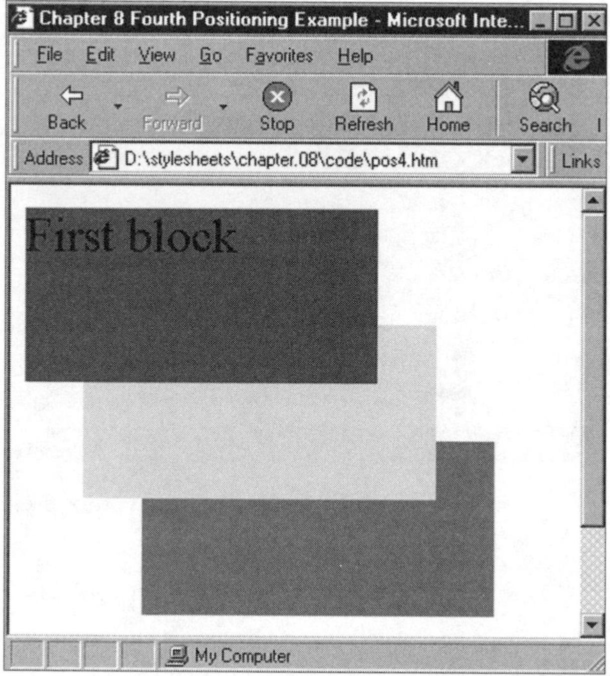

So, we've covered floating boxes, positioning them relatively and absolutely, and layering them and then altering the layer order. Next we're going to learn the options available for displaying or hiding boxes.

Displaying or Hiding a Box

The two properties that you use when displaying or hiding a box are the **`display`** and **`visibility`** properties. We'll cover both here.

The Display Property

In XML the type of box that an element becomes is set by the **display** property. In HTML, in practice, the element has an intrinsic type. In CSS1 it takes the following syntax:

display: block | inline | list-item | none

The default value is **inline**.

CSS allows the user agent to override this property for certain tags, and this happens in HTML. You can code

```
DIV{display:inline;}
```

or

```
SPAN{display:block;}
```

until you are blue in the face, and a **<DIV>** will still be a block element, and **<SPAN>** an inline one.

You can use the **{display:none;}** property/value though and this will cause the element not to appear, and indeed no space will be allotted for it in the flow. Not only that, but none of the element's children will appear either. If we just want to make the element invisible, and leave space for it in the flow then we use the **visibility** property. We'll talk about this next.

CSS2 allows the following additional values for the **display** property:

inline | block | list-item | run-in | compact | marker | table | inline-table | table-row-group | table-column-group | table-header-group | table-footer-group | table-row | table-cell | table-caption | none | inherit

Although we will be looking at most of these throughout the book, you are referred to the spec at: **http://www.w3.org/TR/PR-CSS2/visuren.html** for a full account at this stage.

The Visibility Property

The syntax for **visibility** is:

visibility: visible | hidden | collapse

If the value **hidden** is employed then the element will not appear, but the space allotted for it will still appear in the flow. To make descendants appear again the property must be set to **visible**. (This latter doesn't work too well in the current browser implementations. Even if you set a descendant's property to **visible**, it will not reappear.)

The two screenshots shown below demonstrate the difference between the **visibility** and **display** properties.

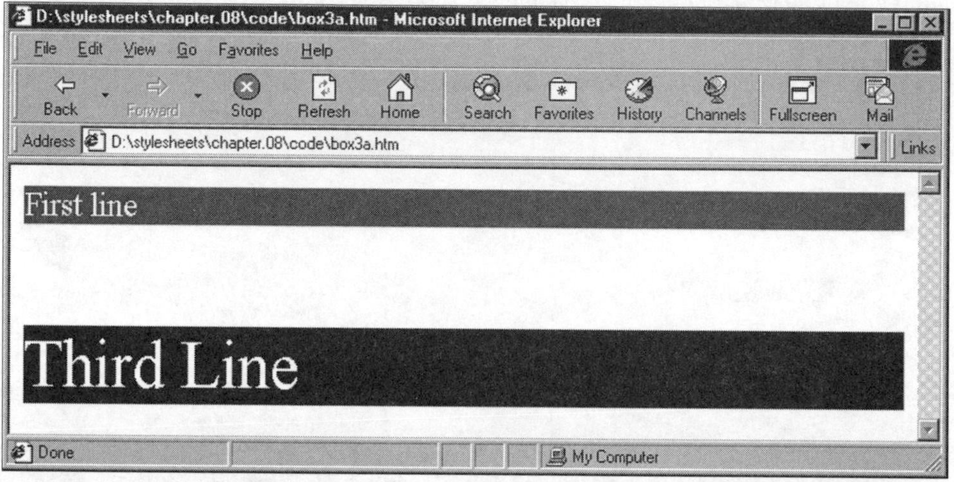

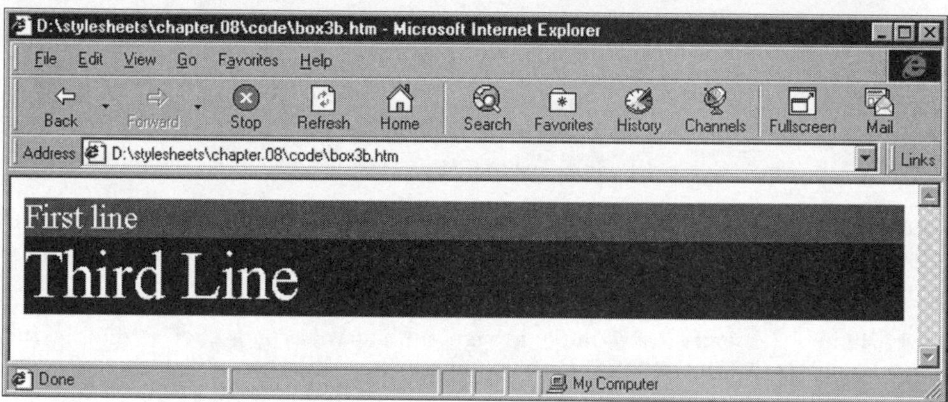

In the first, the **visibility** property for the second **DIV** was set to:

```
visibility:hidden;
```

While in the second, the property **display** was set to:

```
display:none;
```

So, now we know how to display or hide a box. The final point we said we'd cover when we started out on this chapter was how to clip the contents of a box. That's next.

Clipping the Contents of a Box

To clip the contents of a box to ensure all the content is visible, you need to know how to use the **`overflow`** and **`clip`** properties. We'll cover both these properties first, then we'll go through an example that demonstrates how to use them.

The Overflow Property

What happens if we set a container's width and height, and the content does not fit in the box? That depends on what value we have assigned to the **`overflow`** property. The default value is **`visible`** which means that the box will expand somehow to allow us to see all the content. In the case of text, it will increase the height of the containing box, in the case of an object with fixed dimensions–such as an image–it will expand the appropriate dimension.

The syntax for this property is:

`overflow: visible | hidden | scroll | auto`

visible

As mentioned above, the containing box will expand to contain the content.

hidden

Any content not contained in the box will be clipped off, and should not be visible.

scroll

The content will be hidden, but scrollbars are provided to enable the hidden content to be reviewed.

auto

This allows the user agent to handle the problem as it sees fit. Usually scrollbars will be provided.

The Clip Property

The **`clip`** property defines what portion of an elements content is visible. By default, the dimensions of the clipping region are the same as the dimensions of the box, but this region can be modified using the **`clip`** property. The **`clip`** property defines a rectangle. Suppose that we had a box with absolute dimensions and text on the right had been clipped off? If we used the **`clip`** property with these values:

```
DIV {clip: rect (1cm, -1cm, 1.5cm, 1cm);}
```

the clipping region would be extended outside of the box on the right side (note the minus sign and that the rotation is top, right, bottom, left).

This property is not supported at the present time, but the following diagram shows what it should look like if it was.

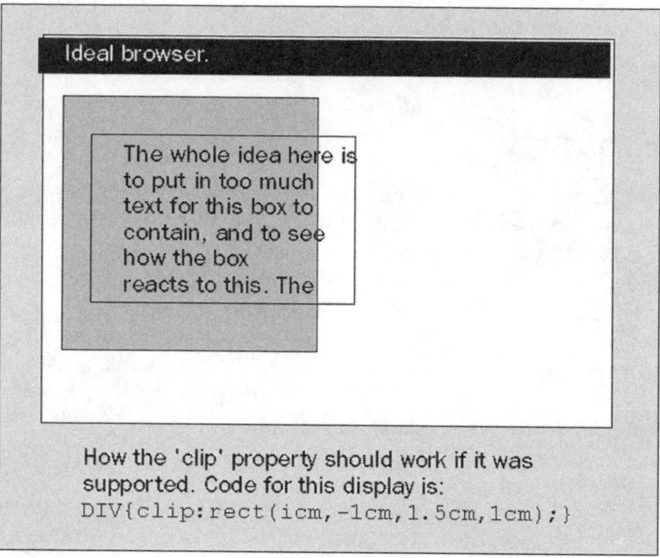

Clipping Examples

Consider the following code where a box 6cm x 6cm has been produced. The text has deliberately been made too large for the box. What happens is that, because no **`overflow`** property has been assigned, the default of **`visible`** is assigned, and the height of the box is increased to accommodate the content.

```
<HTML>
<HEAD>
<TITLE>
Clipping Properties
</TITLE>
<STYLE>
DIV{
font-size:20pt;
font-weight:normal;
background-color: yellow;
width:6cm;
height:6cm;
}
</STYLE>
</HEAD>
<BODY>
<DIV>
The whole idea here is to put in too much text for this box to contain, and
to see how the box reacts to this. The easiest way to do this is to
increase the font size!
</DIV>
</BODY>
</HTML>
```

The following screenshot shows what this looks like.

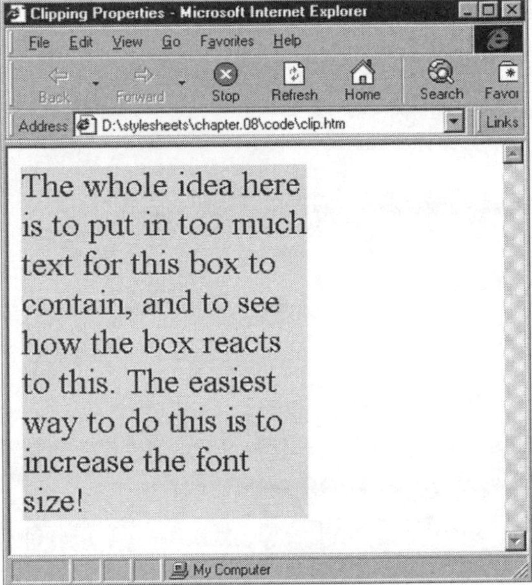

We now modify the code as follows:

```
DIV{
overflow:hidden;
```

The result looks like this.

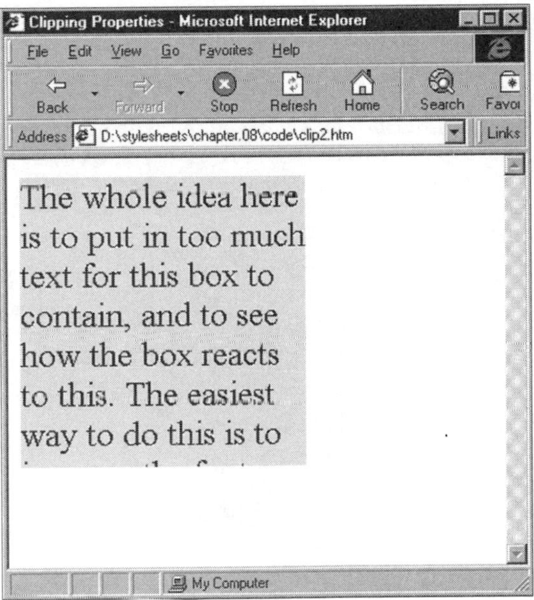

The bottom content has been cut off and we have no access to the hidden content.

We then modify the code again as follows:

```
DIV{
overflow:scroll;
```

The result now looks like this.

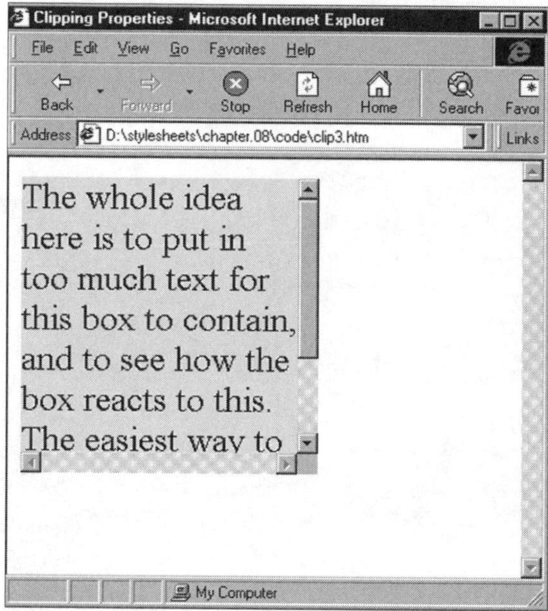

The bottom content has still been cut off but scroll bars have been added to allow us access to the hidden content.

In the following screenshot another box has been added which extends to the right, (the source code is on the web site at **`http://rapid.wrox.co.uk/books/1657`**), and here the horizontal scroll bar is active.

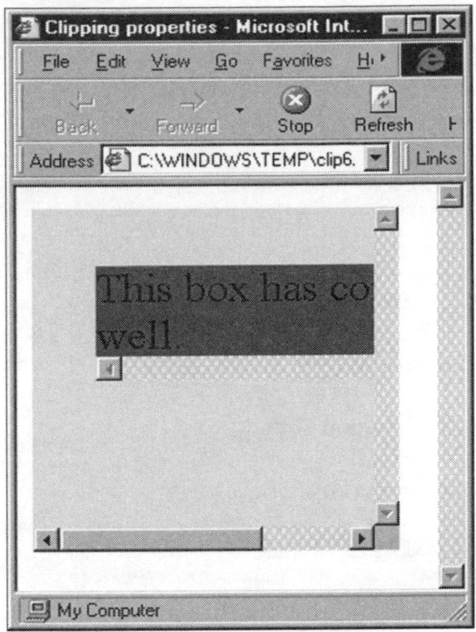

That concludes our look at boxes and layers. Let's summarize what we've covered.

Summary

In this chapter we had a look at:

- The different kinds of flow objects
- The difference between block, inline, and anonymous boxes
- The margin, padding and border properties
- The normal flow
- How to alter the normal flow using the position and float properties
- How to layer properties and manipulate layers using the **`z-index`** propery
- How to display or hide a box
- How to clip the contents of a box

In the next chapter we will finally take an official look at colors backgrounds, images and units.

References

Detailed instructions and algorithms describing the calculation of width and height under various circumstances can be found at:

http:/www.w3.org/TR/PR-CSS2/visudet.html

The W3C document on the box model:

http:/www.w3.org/TR/PR-CSS2/box.html

The W3C document on rendering and positioning:

http:/www.w3.org/TR/PR-CSS2/visuren.html

The W3C document on the clipping and overflow properties:

http:/www.w3.org/TR/PR-CSS2/visufx.html

References to check what is currently working:

http://www.w3.org/Style/CSS/Test/

NIST standards test suite for CSS:

http://sdct-sunsrv1.ncsl.nist.gov/%7Eboland/css/

(These URLs are not stable at the present time, they should become stable within the next month or so. Look out for updates on the Wrox web site.)

Exercises

1. Use the **`position:fixed`** property to write an alternative for a side Frame.

2. How could the **`z-index`** property be used to create simple animation? (You will have to use script and **`settimeinterval`** for this one.)

9

Backgrounds, Colors, Units, and Links

If this had been an academic paper this section would have come first of all. This is because the material in this chapter contains the basic building blocks for CSS style sheets.

Euclid started with his simple propositions and built up the whole structure of geometry from these foundations. An artist, however, is usually struck by the beauty of a painting or of nature, and then learns the tools of the trade, how to define perspective, how to mix colors, and how to apply them etc. By now you will appreciate what style sheets can do for you, and now we will have to look at all the bits and pieces that make the whole thing possible.

We will study the following:

- Backgrounds–how to set either a color or an image for your document.
- Colors–how they are defined and displayed.
- The various Units used in CSS.
- Linking documents to style sheets.
- The **`@charset`** rule.
- Interacting with the user interface.

The syntax used in CSS is a modified EBNF. Because its is likely that you will want to continuously reference this we have placed it in *Appendix A*.

Let's begin with a look at backgrounds.

Backgrounds

We have been using the **background-color** property in most of our examples up until now, and as you will have gathered **background-color** allows us to set the background color for any element. We can also set an image in the background of any element using the **background-image** property. We can set this image as wallpaper, as a single image or in various other ways using the **background-repeat** and the **background-position** properties. The background color is the bottom layer, so to speak, if we specify both a background color and a background image, then the image will be placed on the background.

We'll look at all the background properties one by one beginning with the most straightforward.

Background-color

The syntax for this property is:

background-color: *<color>* **| transparent**

This will set the background color for any element. The initial value is **transparent**, so that the color of the underlying element will shine through.

Background-image

This will set the background image to the image at the requested URL. The syntax is:

background-image: *<uri>* **| none**

A URI is, to all intents and purposes, the same as a URL. It is just the new identifying moniker used in CSS. URIs are only just beginning to be implemented in such standards as name spaces. Wherever you see URI it is never wrong to put an URL. For those interested here is what the CSS spec has to say about URIs.

> 4.3.4 URL + URN = URI
> URLs (Uniform Resource Locators, see [RFC1738] and [RFC1808]) provide the address of a resource on the Web. An expected new way of identifying resources is called URN (Uniform Resource Name). Together they are called URIs (Uniform Resource Identifiers, see [URI]).

Here's an example of how you use **background-image**:

```
<HTML>
<HEAD>
<TITLE>
Smiley Example
</TITLE>
<STYLE>
BODY{background-image:url(smiley.gif)
}
</HEAD>
<BODY>
</BODY>
</HTML>
```

and here's what it looks like:

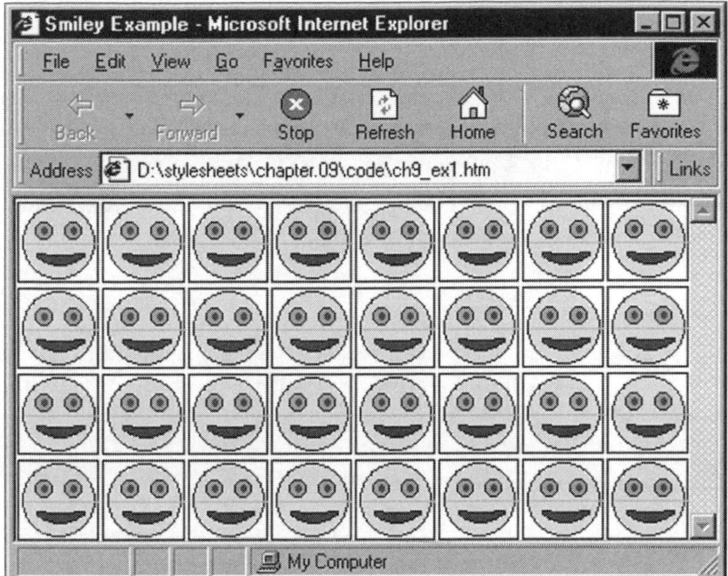

Note that–although CSS uses URI in the syntax–you actually have to put URL in the code. This is for reasons of backwards compatibility. If you wanted to use a URN to reference, the actual rendering would be as follows:

```
{background-image: Urn(123456789abcd)}
```

This, presumably, would be the Uniform Resource Number for some image. As URNs are probably still a few years away from general usage, stick to good old fashioned URLs.

As you can see, the result is a page wallpapered with **smiley.gif**–provided that **smiley.gif** is in the same directory as our style sheet, i.e. it is a Relative URL. It is wallpapered because wallpapering is the default for the **background-repeat** property. We'll look at this property next

Background-repeat

The **background-repeat** property specifies how the background image is to be displayed. The position of the image is controlled by the **background-position** property, details of which will follow this explanation. This property is well supported in IE4, but poorly supported in Communicator. We will first look at the syntax and then some samples. The syntax is:

background-repeat: repeat | repeat-x | repeat-y | no-repeat

The following table shows what each of these values does:

Value	Description
`repeat`	The image is wallpapered.
`repeat-x`	The image is repeated as a line across the x axis. The default position is the top of the page.
`repeat-y`	The image is repeated as a line across the y axis. The default position is the left hand side of the page.
`no-repeat`	A single image appears. The default position is the top left hand corner.

To demonstrate what repeat-x and repeat-y do, let's see what impact they have on our happy little example. First we'll add repeat-x to the **`<BODY>`** styling by inserting this in the styling instructions:

```
background-repeat:repeat-x
```

The effect looks like the following screen shot:

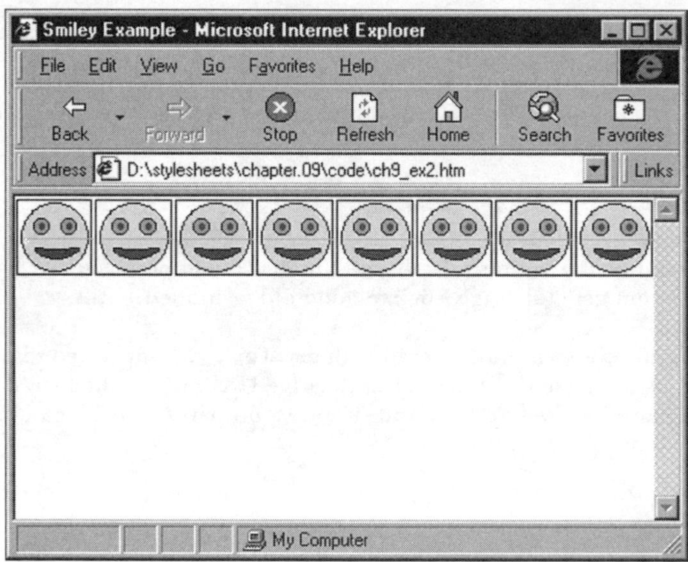

If, instead, we add this line:

```
background-repeat:repeat-y
```

we get this effect:

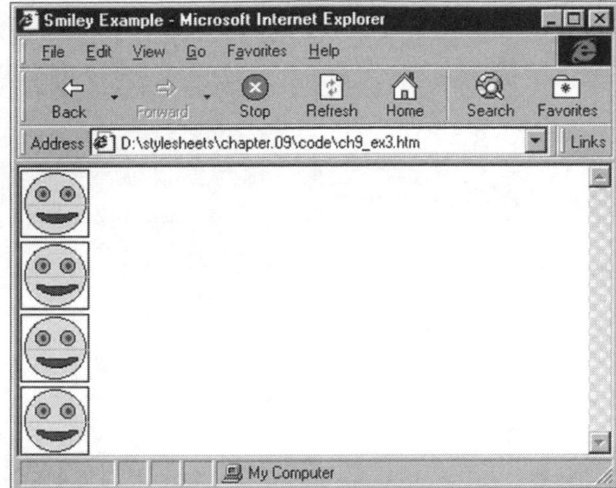

Now we will move on to our forth background property–**background-position**.

Background-position

The **background-position** property positions the image if the value for **background-repeat** is anything other than **none** or **repeat**.

It has the following syntax:

background-position:[[<*percentage*> <*length*>]{1,2}] | [[top | center | bottom] || [left | center | right]]

We'll carry our smiley example on to demonstrate this property, using the syntax:

background-position:center center

to set a single image in the center of the screen. We must remember to set our **background-repeat** property to **no-repeat**. The full code now looks like this:

```
<HTML>
<HEAD>
<TITLE>
Smiley Example
</TITLE>
<STYLE>
BODY{background-image:url(smiley.gif);
background-repeat:no-repeat;
background-position:center center;
}
</HEAD>
<BODY>
</BODY>
</HTML>
```

and the result produced looks like this:

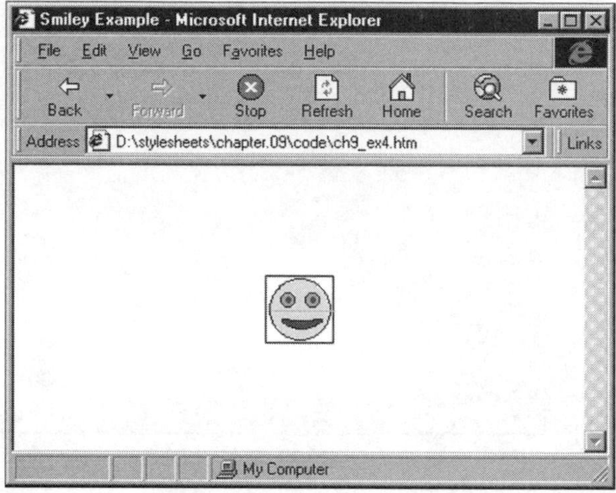

Note the following points:

- If only one value is used for percentage or length then it applies to the horizontal position only, and the vertical position is set to 50%
- You can't mix keywords and percentages/lengths. i.e. **`50% left`** is not allowed.
- You can mix percentages and lengths. i.e. **`50% 4cm`** **is** allowed.
- Keywords can be transposed i.e. **`top left`** and **`left top`** are identical.
- If using percentage values, a value of 40% 60% would take a point in the image 40% from the left, and 60% from the top edge, and position that point at 40% of the width of the containing boxes width, and 60% of the height of the containing boxes height. The diagram below illustrates this.

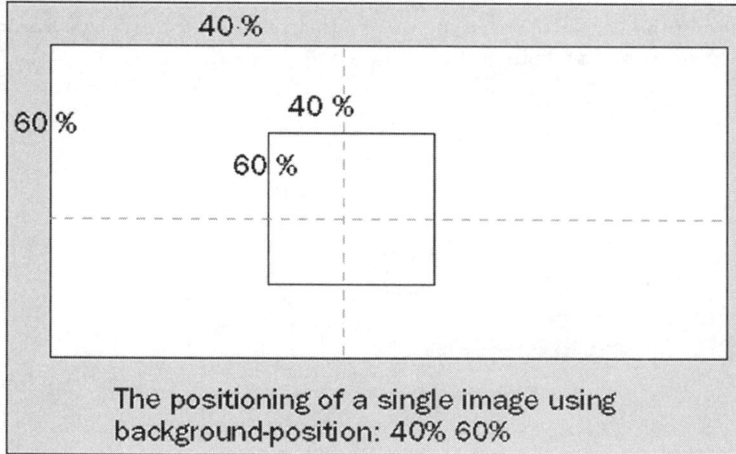

The positioning of a single image using background-position: 40% 60%

Background-attachment

This property applies to images other than wallpaper images and ordains whether the background image will scroll with the document. It can be useful in presenting a single logo that will always stay in the same place no matter where the page is scrolled. Please note, however, that the scenario just alluded to is an IE4 situation as **background-attachment** does not yet work in Communicator.

The syntax is:

background-attachment: scroll| fixed

If the value is set to **fixed** then the image will not move with scrolling. The default is **scroll**. This means that the image will move as you scroll the page.

Here's an example, where we've positioned our **smiley.gif** using **background-position.**

```
background-attachment:fixed
```

We have used the above line of code to make the text scroll right over the top of him while he stays fixed and grinning.

Here's the full code:

```
<HTML>
<HEAD>
<TITLE>
Smiley Example
</TITLE>
<STYLE>
BODY{
font-size:20pt;
background-color:white;
background-image:url(smiley.gif);
background-repeat:no-repeat;
background-position: .5cm .5cm top left;
background-attachment: fixed;
}
</STYLE>
</HEAD>
<BODY>
Here is lots of text
<BR>
so you can check whether the image moves
<BR>
when you scroll the page<BR>
</BODY>
</HTML>
```

We increased the font size of the text and inserted the **
** tags to get enough text to produce a scrollbar. The following screen shot shows what it looks like on IE4:

You'll have to copy the code into your text editor and run it, or run **ch9_ex5.htm**, from the web site at:

http://rapid.wrox.co.uk/books/1657

to really check this out. Suffice to say, the image does indeed stay fixed and the text scrolls over the top of it.

Background

This is the shorthand property for background **background-color**, **background-image**, **background-repeat**, **background-attachment** and **background-position**.

My advice would be not to use it unless you really like a life of confusion. However, just in case you do fall into that category, or are not easily confused, here is an example.

```
P{background: url(myimage.jpg) red 50% 2cm no-repeat fixed;}
```

This should place a single image on a red background in the middle of the page, and your text should scroll over the top of it.

Now that we have dealt with all the various background properties it would be handy to get these fixed in the mind by implementing them in a few examples.

Examples

The following code sets a single line of smileys starting at the left edge and going across the center of the page. (No flames please, I am well aware that this is artistically kitsch.)

```
<HTML>
<HEAD>
<TITLE>
Smiley Example
</TITLE>
<STYLE>
BODY{
font-size:12pt;
font-weight:normal;
background-color:#CCCCAA;
background-image:url(smiley.gif);
background-repeat:repeat-x;
background-position:center left;
}
</STYLE>
</HEAD>
<BODY>
</BODY>
</HTML>
```

The following screenshot shows how this appears on IE4.

The next example sets the image half way across the window and a quarter of the way down.

```
<HTML>
<HEAD>
<TITLE>
Smiley Example
</TITLE>
<STYLE>
BODY{
```

```
font-size:12pt;
font-weight:normal;
background-color:#CCCCAA;
background-image:url(smiley.gif);
background-repeat:no-repeat;
background-position:50% 25%;
}
</STYLE>
</HEAD>
<BODY>
</BODY>
</HTML>
```

This screenshot shows how it appears on IE4.

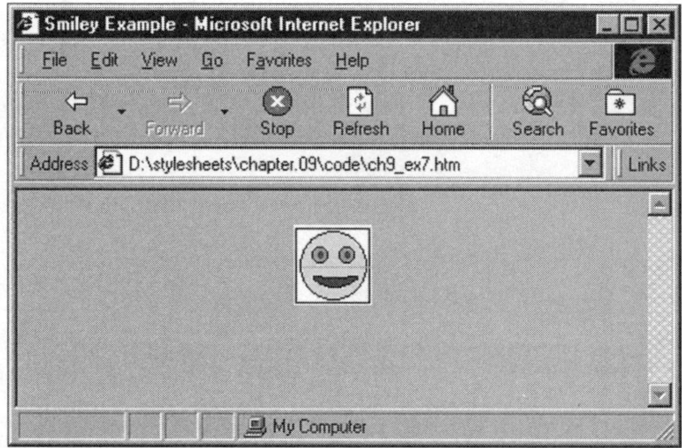

The following code attaches the image so it will not scroll. You really have to try this yourself, (either by typing the code into a text editor, saving it and viewing it in IE4, or by running the file **ch9_ex8.htm** from the web site), as this is a dynamic effect. Unfortunately, like most of the background properties, this does not work at present on Communicator, you just see the text.

```
<HTML>
<HEAD>
<TITLE>
Smiley Example
</TITLE>
<STYLE>
BODY{
font-size:12pt;
font-weight:normal;
background-color:#CCCCAA;
background-image:url(smiley.gif);
background-repeat:no-repeat;
background-position:50% 25%;
background-attachment:fixed;
}
</STYLE>
```

```
</HEAD>
<BODY>
BIG RED TEXT BIG RED TEXT BIG RED TEXT
<BR>
BIG RED TEXT BIG RED TEXT BIG RED TEXT
<BR>
BIG RED TEXT BIG RED TEXT BIG RED TEXT
<BR>
BIG RED TEXT BIG RED TEXT BIG RED TEXT
<BR>
BIG RED TEXT BIG RED TEXT BIG RED TEXT
<BR>
BIG RED TEXT BIG RED TEXT BIG RED TEXT
<BR>
BIG RED TEXT BIG RED TEXT BIG RED TEXT
<BR>
</BODY>
</HTML>
```

The screenshot shows how this appears on IE4. The text has been added so that the scrolling is blatantly apparent.

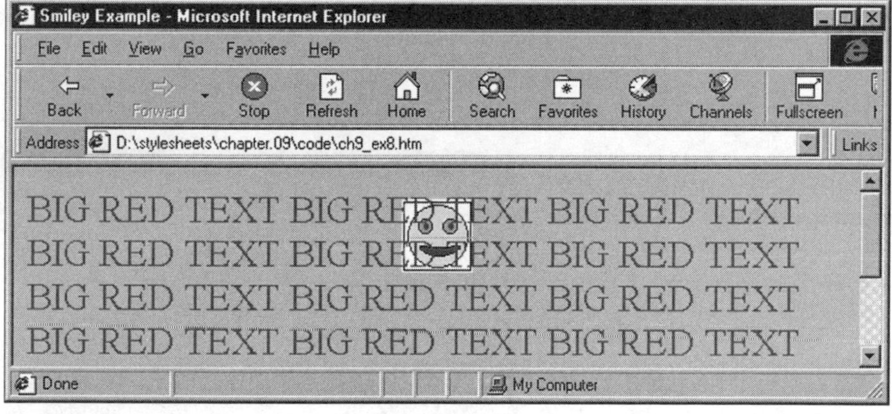

We will now move on to consider the related subject of inline boxes.

Background Images and Inline Boxes

Any block box will handle the background properties in the same way. The way inline images handle them is a bit more subtle as the following examples illustrate. Here is the relevant code from **ch9_ex9.htm**:

```
<HTML>
<HEAD>
<TITLE>
Images and inline boxes
</TITLE>
<STYLE>
BODY{
```

```
    font-size:16pt;
    font-weight:bold;
    background-color:#CCCCAA;
    background-image:url(smiley.gif);
    background-repeat:no-repeat;
    background-position:center center;
    background-attachment:fixed;
}
SPAN{background-image:url(fir.gif);
    font-size:16pt;
    font-weight:bold;
    color: red;
}
</STYLE>
</HEAD>

<BODY>
<DIV CLASS="">here is some text
   <SPAN CLASS="">This text and two line <BR>breaks are in<BR> the
span</SPAN>
Some more text
</DIV>
</BODY>
</HTML>
```

The screen shot here shows how it appears. Notice how the tiling has not appeared anew on the next line.

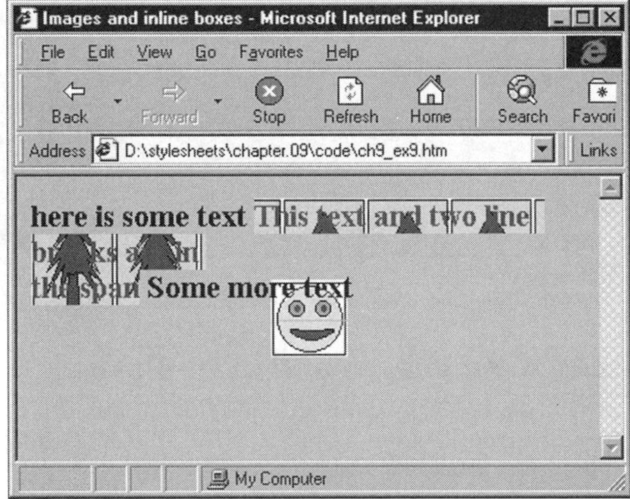

We alter the code as follows to get a single image, by setting **background-repeat** to **no-repeat** and taking the line breaks out of the **<SPAN>** element as follows:

```
<HTML>
<HEAD>
<TITLE>
```

```
Images and inline boxes
</TITLE>
<STYLE>
BODY{

 font-size:16pt;
 font-weight:bold;
 background-color:#CCCCAA;
 background-image:url(smiley.gif);
 background-repeat:no-repeat;
 background-position:center center;
 background-attachment:fixed;

}

SPAN{
    background-repeat: no-repeat;
    background-image:url(fir.gif);
    background-position:center center;
color:red;
}

</STYLE>
</HEAD>

<BODY>

<DIV CLASS="">Some text
   <SPAN CLASS="">This text is in the span</SPAN>
Some more text
</DIV>

</BODY>
</HTML>
```

This is how it appears:

However, if the text in the **<SPAN>** is prolonged so that it runs over to the next line, then the image is centered with respect to the containing block–the **<DIV>**, not the **<BODY>** This explains why it doesn't quite line up with smiley. If the text does not wrap onto the next line it lines up in respect to the **<BODY>**.

The code is the same as above, we just added additional text inside the **<SPAN>** element and this is what happens.

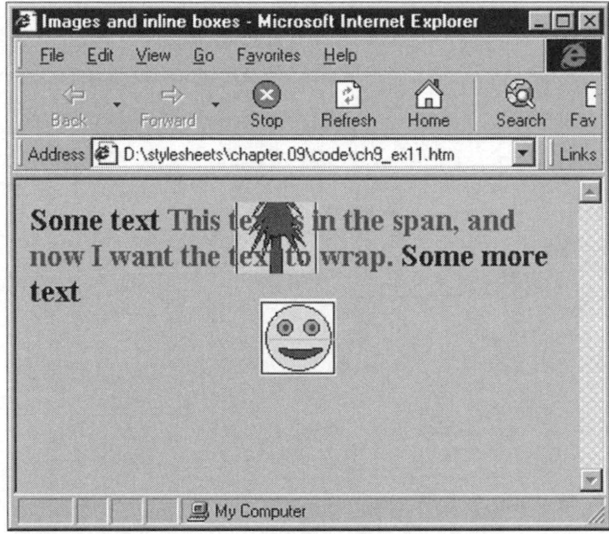

Background images give us a useful way to layer text and other images on top of an existing image. We can position a single image exactly where we want it and then either have it move with the scrolling text or not as the case may be. That concludes our look at backgrounds. Next we're going to look at another of the simple building blocks of style sheets–color.

Colors

The **background-color** and the **color** properties set colors in CSS. As you probably know, colors are presented on the screen by mixing up the pixels to produce the shade of color. How true the color representation is depends on the user's computer.

A **true-color** display stores 24 bits per pixel and is able to display 256 x 256 x 256 = 16,777,216 colors. A **high color** display stores 16 bits per pixel, and allows 255 x 255=65,536 colors. A 256 color display stores 8 bits per pixel and allows 255 x 1= 255 colors. And, of course, there are still some 16 color devices out there. The number of colors that can be displayed without dithering depends not only on the display but the amount of RAM put aside for display. A 1200 x 1600 pixel screen at 24 bit color (3bytes) will use up 1200 x 1600 x 3 =approx. 6MB of RAM!

Most designers and programmers have high-end computers, but when we are designing for the Web it must be remembered that we are designing for the average computer. There are still 16 color units around, but I don't think we need to cater for them, if someone has one of these units they don't expect great graphics. A 256 color display unit–and this probably still represents the majority of computers out there–can only show 256 colors at any one time. The user agent will create a palette of colors and those are the ones it will display. If the color is not on the palette it will dither the color. We don't, however, want dithered colors for our background colors or for our typographic lettering.

Both IE4 and Communicator 4 allow JavaScript and VBScript to access the **screen** object which is part of the browser object model. This allows the author to get information about the color depth of the user's screen.

```
<SCRIPT>
var BitsperPixel=screen.colorDepth
document.write(BitsperPixel)
</SCRIPT>
```

The code presented above returns the bits per pixel of the user's device.

The safest way to make sure that we get non-dithered colors is to use the Netscape color cube that is used by both major browsers. The color cube is a six-sided cube that produces a palette of 216 colors. Each side is 0, 51, 102, 153, 204, 255 in the decimal system, or 00, 33, 66, 99, CC, FF in the hexadecimal system. Here is the R= 00 side of the cube that will produce nothing but green/blue colors:

BLUE VALUES							
		00	33	66	99	CC	FF
GREEN VALUES	00	000000	000033	000066	000099	0000CC	0000FF
	33	003300	003333	003366	003399	0033CC	0033FF
	66	006600	006633	006666	006699	0066CC	0066FF
	99	009900	009933	009966	009999	0099CC	0099FF
	CC	00CC00	00CC33	00CC66	00CC99	00CCCC	00CCFF
	FF	00FF00	00FF33	00FF66	00FF99	00FFCC	00FFFF

Each one of these numbers refers to a RGB value in the RGB system.

There are three ways that color can be depicted. The first is by using the RGB system where a number between 0 and 255 is assigned for each of the primary colors, red, green, and blue. The second is the HSV system which stands for Hue, Saturation, and Value. Finally there is the CMYK system which specifies a percentage of cyan, magenta, yellow, and black. CSS and HTML use the RGB system.

As we have just mentioned the fact that CSS uses the RGB system it is probably helpful if this color system is explained in a little more detail before moving on to our little example.

The RGB System

The RGB system is simplicity in itself, every color is represented by a combination of red, green, or blue values, and these values are defined by an integer between 0 and 255. 0 would depict a complete absence of that color, 255 the full quota. So, black–the absence of all color–would be defined as 0,0,0 and white, the combination of all colors, is defined as 255,255,255. There are different styles for depicting the individual values. HTML uses one style. CSS uses several.

Try running this code (**color1.htm**) on an older computer to see the dithering. You will see that the safe Netscape colors are not dithered.

```
DIV{
font-size:12pt;
font-weight:normal;
height:1cm;
width:6cm;
border-style:solid;
border-width:1px;
color:white;
}

<DIV STYLE="background-color:#000">0 Netscape color</DIV>
<DIV STYLE="background-color:#100">1</DIV>
etc, etc
<DIV STYLE="background-color:#E00">E</DIV>
<DIV STYLE="background-color:#F00">F Netscape color</DIV>
```

Colors in HTML

In HTML you can depict a color as a named keyword, or as a hexadecimal. The named colors allowed are as follows, and represent the 16 colors that can be displayed on 16 color systems:

aqua	black	blue	fuchsia	gray	green	lime	maroon
navy	olive	purple	red	silver	teal	white	yellow

In addition, the browsers also support numerous other color names. Appendix D of *Instant HTML Programmer's Reference, ISBN 1861001568, from Wrox Press* gives a list of them, some 140 in all. However, you are strongly urged not to use these proprietary names for colors but rather to use the hexadecimal notation, as these names are not transferable to style sheets, whereas the hexadecimal notations, and the basic 16 colors, are transferable.

The hexadecimal notation used in HTML employs a hash mark followed by a 6 letter string, namely **#rrggbb** where a pair of digits represents the color value expressed as a hexadecimal.

#000080=navy
#FF0000=red
#FFFF00=yellow
etc, etc.

A note for Windows programmers: The Windows system depicts colors in a **`bgr`** *notation, so you will have to create a function to reverse the order if you want to interface your Windows apps with the Internet.*

Colors in CSS

In CSS you can depict a color by any of the keyword names as in HTML.

aqua	black	blue	fuchsia	gray	green	lime	maroon
navy	olive	purple	red	silver	teal	white	yellow

Or you can use one of several depictions of the RGB notation. The HTML method works perfectly well, and for inter-operability it is best to use this in everyday use. The following sub headings are the various methods that can be employed.

Long Hexadecimal Version

This is the same as the HTML version, i.e. **`#rrggbb`** where **`rr`**, **`gg`**, **`bb`**, expands to a hexadecimal between **`00`** and **`FF`**.

Short Hexadecimal Version

The format here is **`#rgb`**. Where **`r`**, **`g`**, and **`b`** expand to a hexadecimal between **`0`** and **`F`**. Note that **`A`** is shorthand for **`AA`**, not for **`A0`**, **`B`** is the shorthand for **`BB`** etc.

RGB (Integer) version

The format here is **`rgb(r, g, b)`** where **`r`**, **`g`**, and **`b`** expand to a decimal integer between **`0`** and **`255`**.

RGB (Percentage) Version

The format here is **`rgb(r%, g%, b%)`** where **`r`**, **`g`**, and **`b`** expand to a percentage value of 255.

The later methods can be useful when we are generating color variations using code. See some of the examples in *Chapter 15*, the example chapter.

Another nice thing about using the RGB numbers in CSS is that if we give an incorrect integer value, we don't just get a rude error message, and our program closing down. Instead, the value is clipped to the appropriate one, so **`-20`** would be clipped to **`0`**, and **`266`** would be clipped to **`255`**.

All of the following depict the same color–red.

```
color: #FF0000
color: #F00
color: rgb(255,0,0)
color: rgb(100%,0,0)
color: rgb(300,0,0)/*300 clipped to 255*/
color: rgb(255,-30,0)/*-30 clipped to 0*/
```

We will now move from this general discussion concerning the various color systems and how they apply to HTML and CSS to an examination of the specific color properties themselves and, therefore, how to actually use color in your style sheets.

Color Properties

The color properties are **`color`**, which sets the foreground or font colors, and **`background-color`** which depicts the background color.

The Color Property

The syntax for **`color`** is:

`color:`<*color*>

For example, **`color:blue`** or **`color:#0000FF`** or **`color:rgb(0,0,255)`** all represent the color blue.

The default color depends on the user agent.

The Background-color Property

The syntax for **`background-color`** is:

`background-color:`<*color*>

For example, **`color:green`** or **`color:#0F0`** or **`color:rgb(0,100%,0)`** all represent the color green.

Again the default color depends on the user agent.

This concludes the section devoted to one of the many CSS units–color. We will now logically move on to consider the others.

CSS Units

The units in CSS can be any of the following types.

- An integer or real number
- A length
- A percentage
- A literal
- A URI
- Counters
- A color

- An angle
- A time
- A frequency
- A string

Which type any given property can take depends on the property.
Colors have already been discussed earlier in this chapter,and counters were discussed in Chapter 7. In this section, therefore, we will have a look at all the other units.

Integers and Real Numbers

Some properties take an integer as a value e.g. the **`z-index`** and others take a real number. Both integers and real numbers must be in decimal notation both when they are used by themselves and also when they are used with a unit.

Lengths

The following units are recognized in CSS.

Relative units

Relative units and percentages are extremely useful in that they will adjust with the kind of media that a document is being shown on. The three types of relative unit are **`em`**, **`ex`** and **`px`**, and we'll examine each one in turn.

em

An **`em`** in CSS corresponds to the font size of the reference element.

Note that the reference element is not always obvious. For example, when calculating the margin of a box, **`em`** will refer to the font size of the **containing** box. However, when calculating padding it will refer to the font size being used by the box that contains the content to which the padding is being applied.

If the reference font size is 12 then an **`em`** is one sixth of an inch, no matter what type of font is used.

Note also that the size that the font appears on the screen is subject to a magnification factor. i.e. large screens will display both the font, and the related **`em`** larger than a small screen.

> *The origins of the term em (also called a mutton) is obscure. It was originally thought to relate to the width of the lower case letter m. In modern typography it is the height of the font. An en is half an em.*

ex

An **`ex`** should equal the height of the body of the lower case x glyph. In those languages that have no x, a substitute is provided.

Because various fonts of the same size have different proportions the **ex** is related to both the font size (in points) and the type of font.

For example this X is in the font 20pt Arial, and this *x* is in the font 20 point Nuptial. Obviously, an **ex** in nuptial is about half the size of an **ex** in Arial. The only problem is that the browsers do not at present respect this distinction and treat an **ex** as a scaled down **em**.

px

A pixel is the smallest unit of resolution, and will obviously depend on the resolution of the viewing agent. For example, on the screen I am using at the present time there are 96 pixels per inch in both the x and the y axis, and on my current printer there are 300 pixels per inch. Most programming languages provide a function to allow the programmer to adjust their images to the screen resolution, but in CSS this is not possible. The new **screen** object described above does not, unfortunately, provide this information. So we have the situation that if, say we set a font to a pixel size, it would look fine on the screen and impossibly small when we printed it out on a high-resolution laser printer!

When I use the following code:

```
<HTML>
<HEAD>
<TITLE>
Pixel Example
</TITLE>
<STYLE>
DIV{
font-size:72pt;
font-weight:normal;
}
SPAN{font-size:96px;}
</STYLE>
</HEAD>

<BODY>
<DIV CLASS="">72 pt,
            <SPAN CLASS="">96 px</SPAN>
</DIV>
</BODY>
</HTML>
```

It displays as follows:

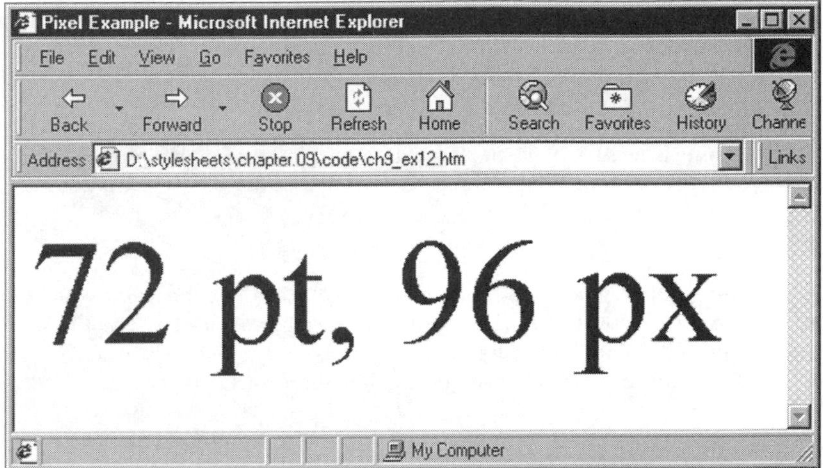

The programming language I used to calculate the number of pixels per inch does a fairly good job. (Visual Basic, using the **`TwipsperPixelx`** function). When I print it out on my printer from IE4 I also get an adjusted version, i.e. the printed sheet is just like the screen, however, when I print it in Communicator, it doesn't even print the pixel part! For this reason authors should be very careful when using **`px`**.

CSS recommends that to get round this problem user agents rescale pixel units–so that for reading at an arms length `1`**`px`** corresponds to about 0.28mm(1/90th inch). But then a pixel would not be a relative unit would it?

Absolute units

Absolute units consist of points, picas, inches centimeters and millimeters, represented by the following notation:

`pt`	A point
`in`	An inch
`cm`	A centimeter
`pc`	A Pica
`mm`	A millimeter

Inches, millimeters and centimeters really don't need much discussion, except to remind the reader that on the screen they will appear in larger or smaller sizes depending on the screen magnification. Points and Picas have a quite interesting history. First of all lets say that in the computer world, including CSS, a point is one seventy-second of an inch, and a pica is 12 points or one sixth of an inch.

This, however, has not always been the case. In fact, up until quite recently a point has been slightly more than a seventy second of an inch. A point–or pointe–was originally a French typographic measurement, and defined as 72 to the inch, but 72 to the French inch and that is slightly larger than an English inch, thus a pica was just over a sixth of an inch. Typographers took over this measure, and it existed until PostScript said enough is enough (thank you PostScript) and redefined the point as 72 to an English inch.

In typography a point is used to measure font sizes and leading, and a pica is used to measure line lengths.

Keywords

These vary with the property. For example, **`border-width`** has the values **`thin`**, **`medium`**, and **`wide`**, **`font-size`** has properties ranging from **`xx-small`** to **`xx-large`**. These units are literals and must **not** be quoted. What value they take depends on the user agent. CSS just makes the stipulation that, for example, **`small`** must be smaller than **`medium`**.

Whether or not a length can be negative depends on the individual property.

Percentages

Percentage values are always in reference to another value, for example a length. It should be noted that when a value that is set by a percentage is inherited, it is the value that is inherited, not the percentage, so in the following situation:

```
DIV{font-size:10pt;line-height:120%}/*sets line eight to 12pt*/
P{font-size:20pt}
```

If the **`<P>`** was a child of the **`<DIV>`** the **`line-height`** would only be 12 points not 24. Probably not what the author intended! Be careful to see what property and element the percentage applies to–it is not always obvious.

Literals

CSS employs numerous literals as in the naming of colors, the width of borders, the weight and size of a font, etc, etc. It is always an error to quote a literal.

So:

```
color: "red";
```

is an error.

URIs

This is the new term employed by CSS–coined on the supposition that some time in the future there will be a new way to identify resources called a Uniform Resource Number or URN. If this happens, then a URI will be a URL plus a URN.

In the meantime in CSS just use the URL as in this example.

```
background:url(http://mysite.com/bigpic.gif);
```

Do not put the URL in quotations.

Counters

See the section on *Counters* in Chapter 7.

Colors

See the large chunk in the middle of this chapter.

Angles

Angles are used in aural style sheets. See the discussion in the *CSS2 Aural Style Sheets section of Chapter 14*, the section on *The Azimuth and Elevation Properties* specifically.

The following unit identifiers are allowed in CSS:

Unit Identifier	Description
deg	degrees
grad	grads
rad	radians

Times

Times are also used in aural style sheets. See the discussion in the *CSS2 Aural Style Sheets* section of *Chapter 14*, the section on *The Pause Properties* specifically.

Allowed units are:

Unit Identifier	Description
ms	milliseconds
s	seconds

Frequencies

Frequencies are also used in aural style sheets. See the discussion in *The Voice Characteristics Properties* section of *Chapter 14*, the section on *The Pitch Property* specifically.

Allowed units are:

Unit Identifier	Description
Hz	Hertz
kHz	Kilohertz

Strings and Escapes

Strings can be written with either a single or a double quote. Double quotes cannot occur inside double quotes, so that:

```
"This string is a "nested"string"
```

is an error.

To do this one must escape the double quote with a back slash thus:

```
"This string is a \"nested\"string"
```

is alright.

The following is also correct:

```
'This string is a "nested"string'
```

as is this:

```
"This string is a 'nested' string"
```

We will now move from our basic style sheet units to another fundamental issue–that of the linking of documents.

Linking Documents to Style Sheets

In this section we will briefly cover linking to both HTML and XML documents.

Linking HTML Documents to Style Sheets

This is just a recap as this subject is covered in more detail in Chapter 2 in the section entitled *External Style Sheets.* An HTML document is linked using either the **<LINK>** element or the **@import** rule. For example:

```
<LINK REL=STYLESHEET TYPE="text/css" HREF="../style.css" TITLE="Style">
```

would link to a style sheet in the parent directory. Use the double period '**..**' to go back one directory in the path. If a relative URL is used in a style sheet it is relative to the style sheet, and not to the destination document. We can have two or more **<LINK>** tags. The later ones will take precedent over the earlier ones in setting up the cascade.

We looked at the **@import** rule in Chapter 7 under the heading *The Cascade and Rule Precedence* when we saw how it can be used to set up a cascade.

To recap **@imports** must come before all the rule sets, and can take the following two forms:

@import url(mystyle.css)

@import "ourstyle.css"

Note the second form is quoted, but the first is not.

@rules

@rules start with an **@** and an identifier such as **@media**, and include everything up to the next semi-colon, or the next block, (curly braces**{}** delimit a block), whichever come first. An **@import** rule must precede all the rule sets.

In the following example the second and third **@imports** are illegal and should be ignored by the processor, the first because it is inside an **@media** block, the second because it does not precede the rule set. Note that it would have been OK if it had been after the **@media** block but before the **<BODY>**.

```
@import "mystyle.css"
@media print{
      @import "print.css"
      BODY{font-size:12pt;}
}
BODY{font-size:14pt;}
@import "another.css"
```

That concludes our recap on linking HTML documents to style sheets, now let's look at linking XML documents.

Linking XML Documents to Style Sheets.

Although no final rule has been promulgated yet, it is most likely that XML documents will link to style sheets via a processing instruction.

```
<?XML=STYLESHEET TYPE="text/css" HREF="../style.css" TITLE="Style"?>
```

Here is an HTML link with its equivalent XML sheet.

```
<LINK href="mystyle.css" rel="stylesheet" type="text/css">
<?xml:stylesheet href="mystyle.css" type="text/css"?>
```

Note that this second version has **<?XML:stylesheet** instead of **<?XML=stylesheet**. It is probable that the colon will become universal so use it. Linking XML documents have recently been addressed in a W3 note that can be found at:

http://www.w3.org/TR/1998/NOTE-xml-stylesheet-19980405

The @charset Rule

This rule is of interest if you are going to use a character set other than the standard roman set. If we are writing a document in say Japanese, we will identify the char set to be used in the prolog in an XML document, and in the **content-type** in an HTML document.

```
<META http-equiv="Content-type" content="text/html;charset=EUC-JP">
```

see:

http://www.w3.org/TR/REC-html40/charset.html#h-5.2

for more details.

Any style sheet embedded in these documents via the **<STYLE>** tags will automatically take on the language of that document, but what about external style sheets? Use the **@charset** right at the beginning of the file and specify the character set to be employed right after it.

Interacting with the User Interface

As we saw in Chapter 6–under the heading *Font Categories and Font Availability*–CSS gives us a way to employ the users system resources in the form of fonts.

Colors and Background Colors

We can also do this with colors and backgrounds. Here are a few of the many values we can mimic. For a full list see:

http://www.w3.org/TP/PR-css2/ui.html

CSS Property	Windows Object to Mimic.
active-border	Active window border color.
active-caption	Active window caption color.
app-workspace	Background color of multiple document interface.
background	Desktop background.
button-face	Face color for three-dimensional display elements.
button-highlight	Dark shadow for three-dimensional display elements (for edges facing away from the light source).
	Shadow color for three-dimensional display elements.
button-text	Text on push buttons.
caption-text	Text in caption, size box, and scroll bar arrow box.
gray-text	Grayed (disabled) text. This color is set to #000 if the current display driver does not support a solid gray color.
window	Window background.
window-frame	Window frame.
window-text	Text in windows.

To set the background and foreground colors to the same colors as the users window we would write:

```
P{color:window-text; background-color:window;}
```

Cursor

Whereas the above is of limited utility the cursor properties are very useful, especially if we are using Dynamic HTML. They enable us to specify the type of cursor to be displayed as a pointing device.

An example is:

```
.link{Cursor:hand}
```

which would turn the cursor into a hand every time the cursor passed over a **`link`** class. Note that the CSS refers to this as **`pointer`**, which doesn't work but we have used the IE4 keyword of hand which works!

The values that cursor can take are as follows. The forms should be familiar to any windows user!

Cursor value	Description
`auto`	The shape of the cursor will change depending on the context of the area that is over .e.g. an I beam over text, a pointing hand over a link
`crosshair`	
`default:`	Usually an arrow
`pointer`	A pointing hand. However IE4 recognises the value "hand" for this value, and Communicator does not support the cursor property.
`move`	Usually a grasping hand
`*-resize`	n, nw, sw, s, w, resizing cursor
`text`	The I bar
`wait`	An hour glass
`help`	A question mark
`wait`	Usually an hour glass
`<URL>`	The source of a cursor file
`help`	Usually a question mark.

Summary

In this chapter we looked at several items that do not fit conviently into other categories.

- We looked at the color properties and how to add forecolor and background color to our elements. We included a run down of the various ways CSS uses to express color values.
- We looked at how to add images in the background, and the various CSS properties that allow us to place individual and multiple images.
- Next we looked at the various units that CSS employs for its values, both absolute and relative.
- We reviewed how to link our documents to a style sheet.
- We lastly looked at the **`@charset`** rule, and how we can interface with the user's desktop.

In the next chapter we will conclude our review of CSS with a review of Tables and Lists. After that we will start on part three, which tackles some of the more advanced and futuristic aspects of styling.

Exercises

There are no exercises for this chapter.

10

Lists and Tables

In this chapter we will look at lists and tables. Not everything we discuss is currently supported, for example, no XML parser supports lists or tables, and none of the CSS2 table properties are supported in the current browsers. However, both Netscape and Microsoft are committed to supporting standards, so we are keen to show you what will be available once they bring in support for CSS2.

Lists were in the original HTML specification and are used for organizing text into easily readable packages. They are interesting as they are the only place in HTML where content, i.e. text that does not appear in the original HTML document namely the list number or a bullet, is generated.

Tables are used for tabulating material. In HTML they have been chiefly used for formatting purposes. When the browsers fully adopt CSS (and they are getting there) they will be used for their true purpose, displaying tables!

We will study the following

- Lists in plain HTML
- Lists in HTML and CSS
- Lists in XML
- Tables in HTML
- Tables in CSS
- Tables in XML
- Table Properties
- Aural rendering of tables

Aural rendering will be discussed more fully in the section on Aural Content in Chapter 14. For now note that it will be possible to render HTML documents via a speech synthesizer (in fact special browsers for the blind can do this now), and that tables will need to be treated slightly differently in the aural format.

So, let's jump right in with our first section on lists.

Lists in HTML, CSS and XML

We'll devote a section to each of the three list types, beginning with HTML lists.

Lists in HTML

HTML offers three kinds of list:

- The ordered list **<OL></OL>**
- The unordered list**<UL></UL>**
- The definition list **<DL></DL>**

We will just take a brief look at ordered and unordered lists here. For a full description of the HTML see page 34 of *Instant HTML Programmer's Reference, ISBN 1861001568, from Wrox Press.*

In formatting terms the list element forms a block level box that contains list items **<LI>**, and each list item is another block box contained in the list box. Lists can be nested to any level.

```
<HTML>
<HEAD>
<TITLE>
Ordered and Unordered List Example
</TITLE>
</HEAD>
<BODY>

<UL>
   <LI> First unordered item
   <LI> Second unordered item
   <OL>
      <LI> First ordered item
      <LI> Second ordered item
      <UL>
         <LI> First nested unordered item
         <LI> Second nested unordered item
      </UL>
      <LI> Third ordered item
      <LI> Forth ordered item
   </OL>
   <LI> Third unordered item
   <LI> Forth unordered item
</UL>

</BODY>
</HTML>
```

The following screen shot shows how it looks in Communicator 4.

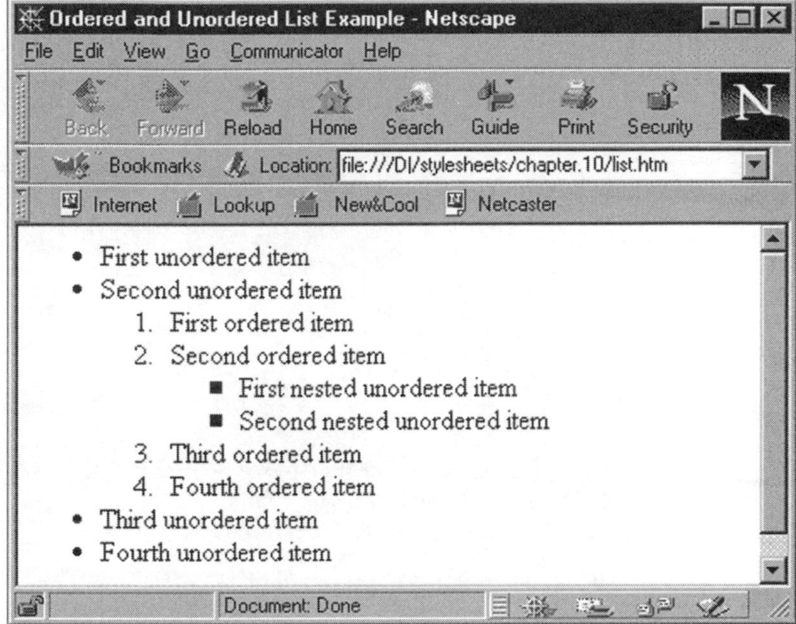

It is important here to note the following:

- How the nesting is reflected in the list. A different bullet is created, and the list further indented, for each level of nesting.
- How numbers are automatically generated for each item in the ordered list. The default numbering is Arabic numeral. Both the type of numbering and the type of bullet used can be changed as described in the next two bullets.
- The **`type`** attribute can be used to specify the type of numbering in an ordered list. The choices are:

  `type=1`–Arabic numerals (the default)
  `type=A`–Capital letters
  `type=a`–small letters
  `type=I`–Large Roman Numerals
  `type=i`–Small Roman Numerals

- The **`type`** attribute can be used to specify the type of bullet in an unordered list. The choices are: **`circle | disc | square`**.
- In ordered lists the attribute **`value=`***n* can also be used, to indicate where to start the numbering.

Lists in CSS

Any of the normal style properties can be used for the list elements. For example, we can use the **color** and the **font-size** properties to alter our text, and the **background** and **box** properties to alter the backgrounds and their surroundings. We have added the following style sheet to the above HTML to illustrate this point and also to show how each list forms a box.

```
<HTML>
<HEAD>
<TITLE>
Ordered and Unordered List Example
</TITLE>
</HEAD>
<STYLE>
     UL{
          background-color:orange;
          margin-right:1cm;
          margin-left:1cm
     }
     OL{
          background-color:blue;
          color:white;
          margin-right:1cm;
          margin-left:1cm
     }
     UL.nested{
          background-color:yellow;
          color:black;
     }
</STYLE>

<BODY STYLE="font-size:18pt;background-color:white;">

     <UL>
          <LI> First unordered item
          <LI> Second unordered item
          <OL>
               <LI> First ordered item
               <LI> Second ordered item
               <UL CLASS="nested">
                    <LI> First nested unordered item
                    <LI> Second nested unordered item
               </UL>
               <LI> Third ordered item
               <LI> Fourth ordered item
          </OL>
          <LI> Third unordered item
          <LI> Fourth unordered item
     </UL>
</BODY>
</HTML>
```

The result is shown in the following screenshot. Note, incidentally, how the generated numbers are rendered outside the box in the IE4 browser.

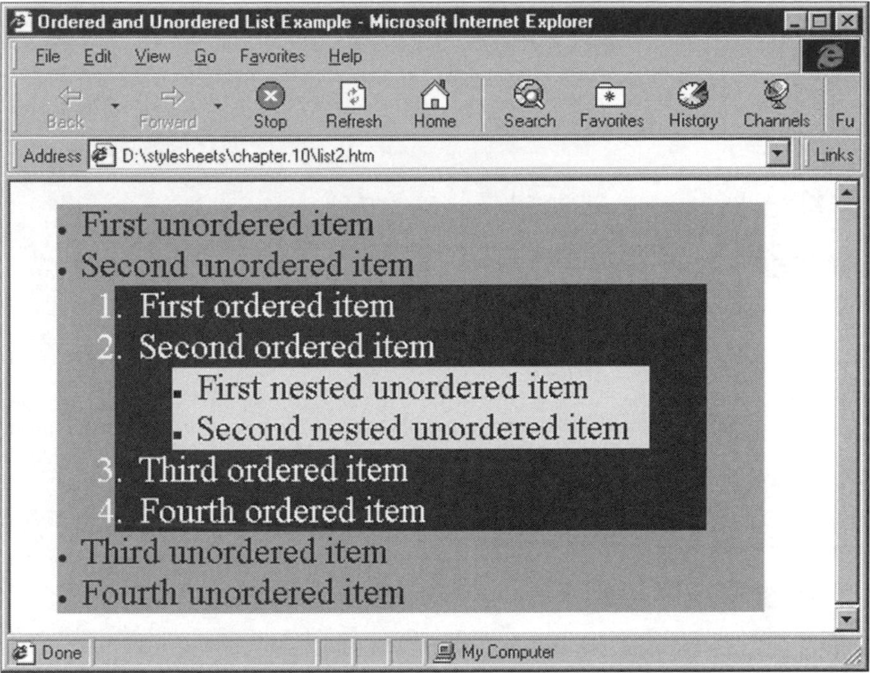

All the list attributes have been deprecated in HTML 4 in favor of CSS properties. Deprecated is a word that is used by the W3C to say "There is now a better way of doing this, and in future editions we will be phasing out this code".

CSS List Properties

These properties are **list-style-type**, **list-style-position**, **list-style-image**, and **list-style**. These properties specify what kind of marker appears before the list item, whether the marker is placed inside or outside the list item's content, and whether an image is used as a bullet. Using the additional properties of descendant selectors and child selectors (see the sections on each of these in *Chapter 7, Flow Objects, Selectors, Inheritance and the Cascade*) it is possible to specify the markers for different depths.

List-style-type

The **list-style-type** property is applied to any element with the **display** property set to **list-item** and to the **<LI>** element in HTML. The syntax is:

list-style-type : <*value*>

It can take the following values, the default being **disc**:

disc* | circle* | square* | decimal* | leading-zero | western-decimal | lower-roman* | upper-roman* | lower-greek | lower-alpha* | lower-latin | upper-alpha* | upper-latin | hebrew | armenian | georgian | cjk-ideographic | hiragana | katakana | hiragana-iroha | katakana-iroha | none* | inherit

The values marked with a * are the CSS1 values and are supported by the major browsers.

I'm afraid I have no idea what hiranga, georgian, or hebrew bullets look like, and I can't find out because the major browsers do not support the additional CSS2 values nor does the CSS2 specification describe them! I assume that they refer to the numbering systems of the languages in question, and that in right to left languages (e.g. Hebrew) they will be placed on the right of the text, and be right indented.

A **list-style** value of **none** suppresses all previous markers.

List-style-image

The syntax for this property is:

```
list-style-image: <url> | none
```

It allows an icon to be used as a bullet. It is supported in both Communicator 4 and IE4.

List-style-position

The syntax for this property is:

```
list-style-position: inside | outside
```

This is a CSS2 property and, when implemented, will allow the marker to be either inside the list-item box or outside it. The following figure shows how this property works:

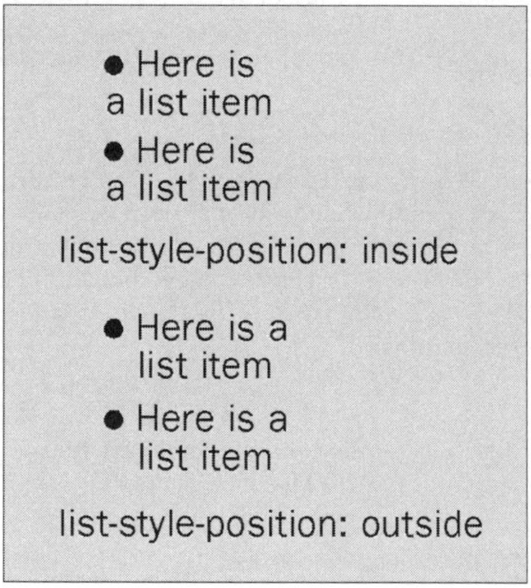

● Here is
a list item
● Here is
a list item
list-style-position: inside
● Here is a
list item
● Here is a
list item
list-style-position: outside

List-style

This is a combination property. The syntax is:

list-style: [<list-style-type> || <list-style-position> || <list-style-image>]

So, we've looked at lists in HTML and lists styled with CSS in HTML, with a quick look through the CSS properties you can use. Time to move on to our third list type, XML lists.

Lists in XML

In HTML, the browser will understand that the relevant HTML tags are participating in list formation. In XML, however, there is no such indication to the user agent that an element is participating in a list. To indicate that an element is participating in a list in XML the **display** property must be set to **list-item** e.g.

```
item{
   display: list-item;
   list-style: square;
   }
```

This tells the user agent that **<item>** should be treated the same way that **<LI>** is in HTML.

```
<flowers>
   <item>Rose</item>
   <item>Daffodil</item>
   <item>Iris</item>
   <item>Pansy</item>
</flowers>
```

The above code would result in a display as follows if you applied the styling given above to the XML document in an XML parser which supported lists, then converted it to HTML. Unfortunately, no XML parser does support lists yet. When I ran this through XMLparse, I got the flower names displayed one underneath the other, but no square bullets. I had to add **<LI>** tags to the HTML to get the display shown below.

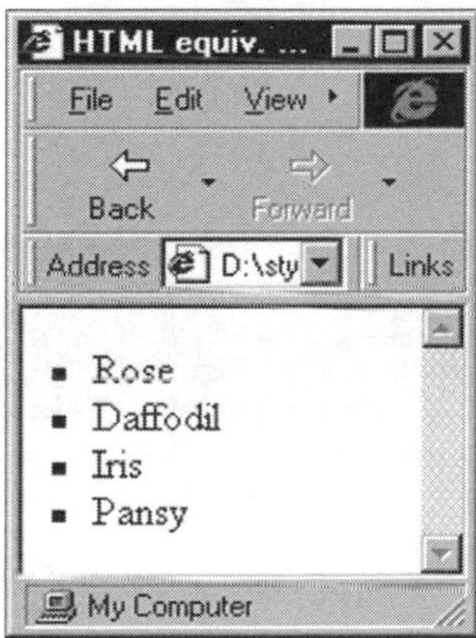

Principal and Marker Boxes

In fact when an element is given the value of **`list-item`**, two boxes are generated–the principal box which contains the list items content, and the marker box which contains the bullet or other marker. The following screen shot shows the separate boxes as demonstrated in Communicator.

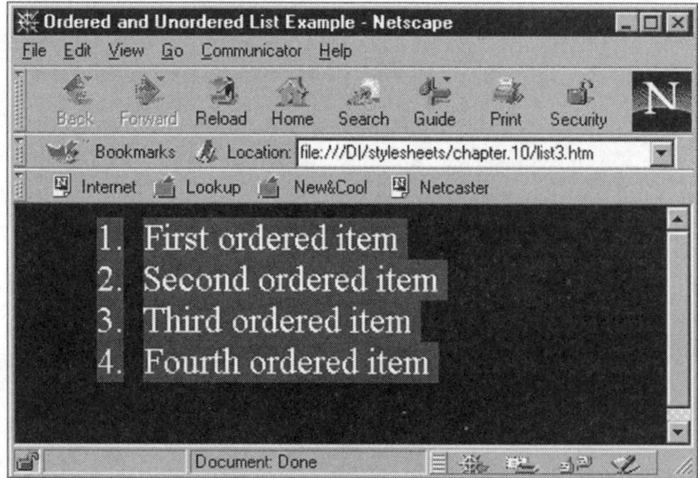

Note that this screenshot was generated using a simple HTML ordered list. Here's the code:

```
<HTML>
<HEAD>
<TITLE>
Ordered and Unordered List Example
</TITLE>
</HEAD>
<STYLE>

     OL{
           background-color:red;
           color:white;
           margin-right:1cm;
           margin-left:1cm
     }

</STYLE>

<BODY STYLE="font-size:18pt;background-color:black;">

                <OL>
                 <LI>First ordered item
                 <LI>Second ordered item
                 <LI>Third ordered item
                 <LI>Fourth ordered item
                </OL>

</BODY>
</HTML>
```

We can generate numbers for the list by using the pseudo element **before** and using the **content** and **counter-increment** properties.

If we change the style sheet as follows:

```
<STYLE>
   item{
      display: list-item;
      list-style: decimal;
   }

   item:before{
      display: marker;
      content: counter(mycounter, decimal) ".";
      counter-increment: mycounter;
   }
</STYLE>
```

the result would display as follows–when parsed and converted to HTML. However, at the moment these properties are not supported, so we've cheated to get the screenshot to show you how it should look.

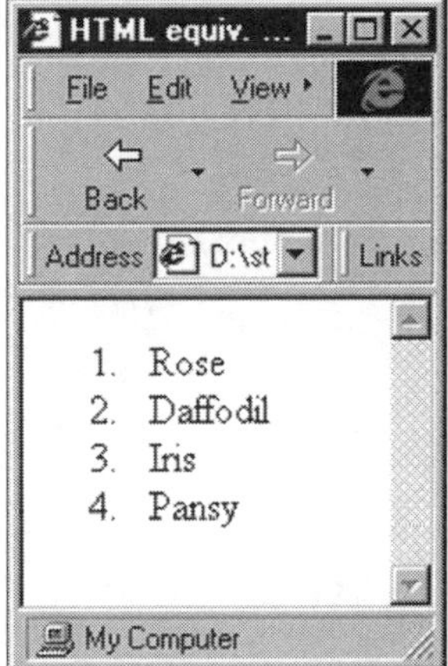

Finally, in this section on XML lists, let's take a quick look at the **marker-offset** property, which allows us to control the distance between the principal and marker boxes.

Marker-offset Property

The **marker-offset** property specifies the distance between the marker box and the principal box.

If we added to the style sheet thus:

```
item:before{
display: marker;
marker-offset: 3em;
Etc. etc.
```

Note that the following screen shot is a cheat. Because XML and CSS2 are not supported in the current browsers, we have rigged the HTML using the single pixel trick discussed in Chapter 1. This shows you how the code would display if the standards were supported.

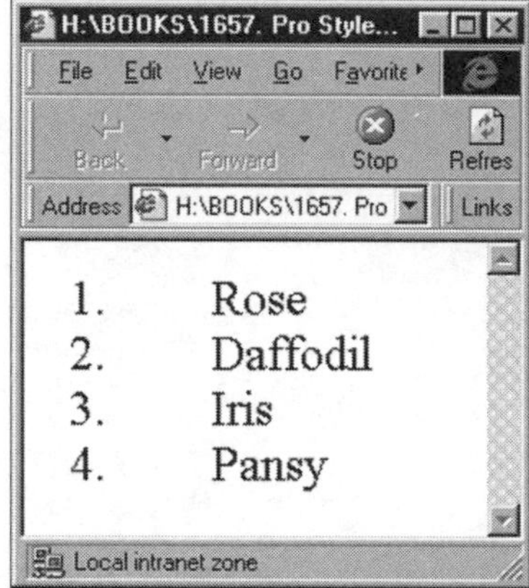

This has only been a superficial account of a fairly complex subject, but it should be enough to get you writing XML lists when the software becomes available.

For a very detailed (and quite technical account) see:

`http://www.w3/org/TR/PR/CSS2/generate.html (12.6)`

and:

`http://www.w3/org/TR/PR/CSS2/lists.html`.

So, having dealt with lists, it's time to move on to tables.

Tables in HTML, CSS and XML

This section will have the same structure as the one on lists. We'll cover HTML tables, HTML tables styled with CSS and XML tables. We'll begin with the familiar–HTML tables.

Tables in HTML

Tables in HTML have been used not only for tabulating information, but also for formatting and styling as we saw in Chapter 1. As the former they do a good job, as the latter they are rather a clumsy hack and will be supplanted by CSS.

Essentially tables consist of cells divided into rows and columns, with captions, headers and footers. Styling can be applied to the overall table as well as the individual rows, columns, and cells by using attributes. A full description of these is beyond the scope of this book, but a book such as *Instant HTML Programmer's Reference, ISBN 1861001568, published by Wrox Press* provides an excellent account of what is and is not possible using tables in HTML.

Actually most of the attributes have been deprecated in HTML 4 in favor of using Cascading Style Sheets.

> *Deprecated is a word that is used by the W3C to say "There is now a better way of doing this, and in future editions we will be phasing out this code". Although the table styling attributes work well for styling HTML tables, style sheets are to be preferred for all the reasons we mentioned in Chapter 1. Thus, the styling attributes have been deprecated in HTML 4, although, of course, they will carry on being supported for some time to come.*

Before going into the detailed CSS specification we will first show a simple example of a table with a caption, a header and a footer, with three rows and three columns. We will show how it can be displayed using no CSS and then using CSS. The following is the code for the HTML/no-CSS version.

```
<HTML>
<HEAD>
<TITLE>
chapter 10 HTML 4 no CSS example
</TITLE>
</HEAD>
<BODY>
   <TABLE BORDER=1 BGCOLOR="orange" width=100%>
      <CAPTION>
      Pure HTML 4 Tables (No CSS)
      </CAPTION>
      <COLGROUP SPAN=1 BGCOLOR="red">
      </COLGROUP>
      <COLGROUP SPAN=1 BGCOLOR="white">
      </COLGROUP>
      <THEAD>
         <TR>
         <TH>This is  cell heading COL1</TH>
         <TH>This is  cell heading COL2</TH>
         <TH>This is  cell heading COL3</TH>
        </TR>
      </THEAD>

      <TFOOT>
          <TR>
          <TD>This is  cell footer COL1</TD>
          <TD>This is  cell footer COL2</TD>
          <TD>This is  cell footer COL3</TD>
          </TR>
      </TFOOT>

      <TBODY>
         <TR BGCOLOR="yellow">
         <TD><BR>ROW 1A<BR><BR></TD>
         <TD BGCOLOR="green">ROW 1B</TD>
         <TD>ROW 1C</TD>
```

```
            </TR>
            <TR>
            <TD><BR>ROW 2A<BR><BR></TD>
            <TD>ROW 2B</TD>
            <TD>ROW 2C</TD>
            </TR>
            <TR>
            <TD><BR>ROW 3A<BR><BR></TD>
            <TD>ROW 3B</TD>
            <TD>ROW 3C</TD>
            </TR>
         </TBODY>
      </TABLE>
   </BODY>
   </HTML>
```

The following screenshot shows the table as it appears in IE4.

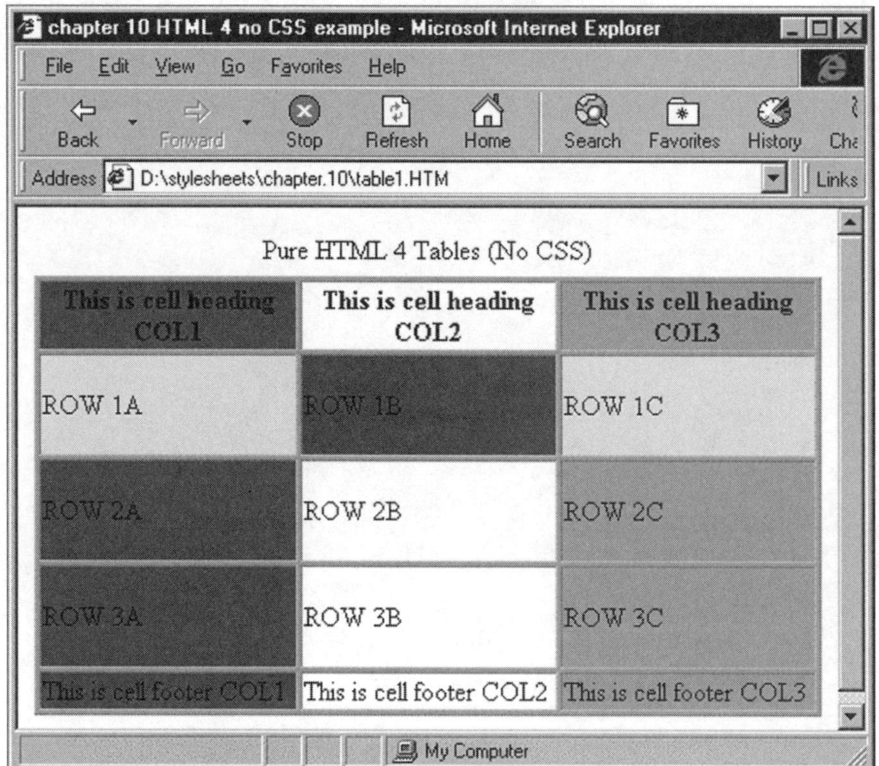

The following points should be noted:

- The basic unit is a row containing cells. The row is the **<TR></TR>** element, the cell is the **<TD></TD>** element.
- The **<COLGROUP>** element is used to add styling to a column. It is only supported by IE4 at present. In the code above you will see there are two **<COLGROUP>**s both with a **SPAN** attribute set to **1**. The first lot of code will apply to the first column, the second to the second, etc.etc. See a book on HTML for a full description of this element.
- It is not strictly necessary to add the closing elements to **<TD>**, **<TR>**, and **<TH>**, but it is better to do it as it makes your coding clearer, and some browsers get confused if you don't do it.

What colors should we see in the individual cells? This depends on whether **background-color** properties have been set to other than **transparent** (the default) on the cell, row, column, or table properties. We have used four colors here to show the layer hierarchy. The topmost is the individual cell, next down is the row, followed by the column, followed by the table body color, followed by the body color. If all four layers are transparent, then the body background color will shine through. If the cell, row and column **background-color** properties are transparent then the table background color will shine through. If only the cell is transparent, then the row background color will shine through, and finally the cell color overlies everything.

This point is illustrated below.

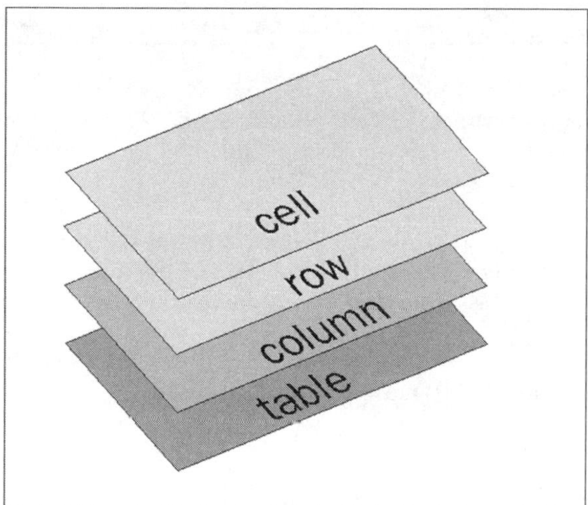

Although we have put the **<TFOOT>** section of the code above the **<TBODY>** section of the code, the table footer is still displayed at the bottom of the table. This is not so in Communicator 4, where you must place the **<TFOOT>** where you want it to appear. Here is what the code above looks like when displayed in Communicator 4.

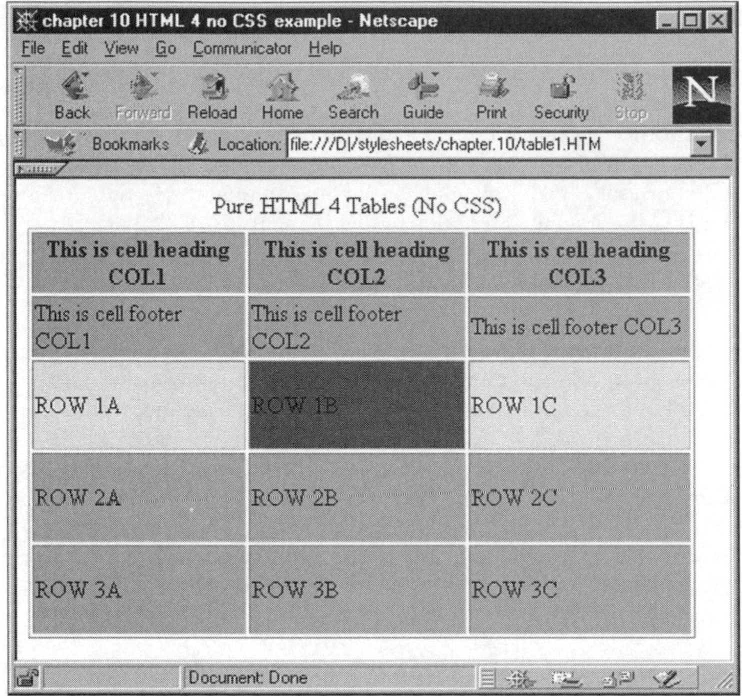

As you can see, the cell footer is displayed before the body of the table, in the location we gave it in the code. The other difference is that the cells all take the background color of orange, except Row 1 where the specific row and cell **`color`** properties take over. This is because Communicator doesn't support the **`<COLGROUP>`** element.

The overall width of the table is controlled by the **`width`** property, found in the **`<TABLE>`** element, either in pixels or as a percentage. The width and height of the individual cells is controlled by the content. To make sure the width is what you want it to be you have to use the single pixel trick, which we demonstrated in Chapter 1.

That concludes our look at an HTML table with no CSS styling. Next we'll look at the same example styled using CSS.

Tables in CSS

In the next example, we have converted the above example to a table using style sheets. In other words we have moved all the style information out of the HTML code and put it in a style sheet. The only difference we have made is that we have specified the height of the cell to show you this is indeed possible. (Leave out the **`height`** properties and the two would be identical.)

Just one word of caution, some of the properties are not well supported by Communicator 4, so be sure to test in both browsers.

When the HTML elements are used, properties can be applied to the elements just like any other box. **<TABLE>**, **<CAPTION>**, **<THEAD>**, **<TFOOT>**, **<TBODY>** and **<TR>** are block level boxes–**<TD>** and **<TH>** are in-line elements. **<COL>** and **<COLGROUP>** do not, of course, create boxes, but serve as handy racks on which to hang properties. These elements can take all the CSS properties, plus the special properties for tables.

The table elements of HTML have display properties built into them. For example, when a user agent that understands HTML comes across **<TABLE>** it knows how to format its contents. Because XML elements used for tables have no such instant recognition, they must declare themselves to be table elements using the **display** properties. This is not necessary in HTML (although we have put a few in the following example). In fact, CSS specifically exempts HTML from following the **display** property for its elements, although **<SPAN>** and **<DIV>** should recognize them (they don't at present). The **display** property for a table can be changed to in-line in HTML/CSS by using the **display:inline-table** declaration but this is not implemented in the browsers.

```
<HTML>
<HEAD>
<TITLE>
Chapter 10 CSS example
</TITLE>
<STYLE TYPE="text/css">

   TABLE{
      display:table;
      border-width:1px;
      border-style:solid;
      width:100%;
      background-color:orange;
   }

   COLGROUP#col1{
      display:table-column-group;
      background-color:red;
      column-span:2;
   }

   COLGROUP#col2{
      display:table-column-group;
      background-color:white;
      column-span:1;
   }

   #row1{background-color:yellow;}
      .greenbg{
      background-color:teal;
      vertical-align:top;
      text-align:center;
   }

   TD{border:solid 1px white;}
   TR{height:2cm;}
   TR.head{height:1cm;}
   TR.foot{height:1cm;}
```

```
</STYLE>
</HEAD>
<BODY>

The following is an example of a block level table.

<TABLE>
   <CAPTION>
   Pure HTML 4 Tables (Using CSS)
   </CAPTION>
   <COLGROUP id="col1">
   </COLGROUP>
   <COLGROUP id="col2">
   </COLGROUP>

   <THEAD>
      <TR CLASS="head">
      <TH>This is cell heading COL1</TH>
      <TH>This is cell heading COL2</TH>
      <TH>This is cell heading COL3</TH>
      </TR>
   </THEAD>

   <TFOOT>
      <TR CLASS="foot">
      <TD>This is cell footer COL1</TD>
      <TD>This is  cell footer COL2</TD>
      <TD>This is cell footer COL3</TD></TR>
   </TFOOT>

   <TBODY>
      <TR id="row1">
      <TD>ROW 1A</TD>
      <TD class="greenbg">ROW 1B</TD>
      <TD>ROW 1C</TD>
      </TR>
      <TR>
      <TD>ROW 2A</TD>
      <TD>ROW 2B</TD>
      <TD>ROW 2C</TD>
      </TR>
      <TR>
      <TD>ROW 3A</TD>
      <TD>ROW 3B</TD>
      <TD>ROW 3C</TD>
      </TR>
    </TBODY>
</TABLE>
</BODY>
</HTML>
```

Here is what it looks like in IE4:

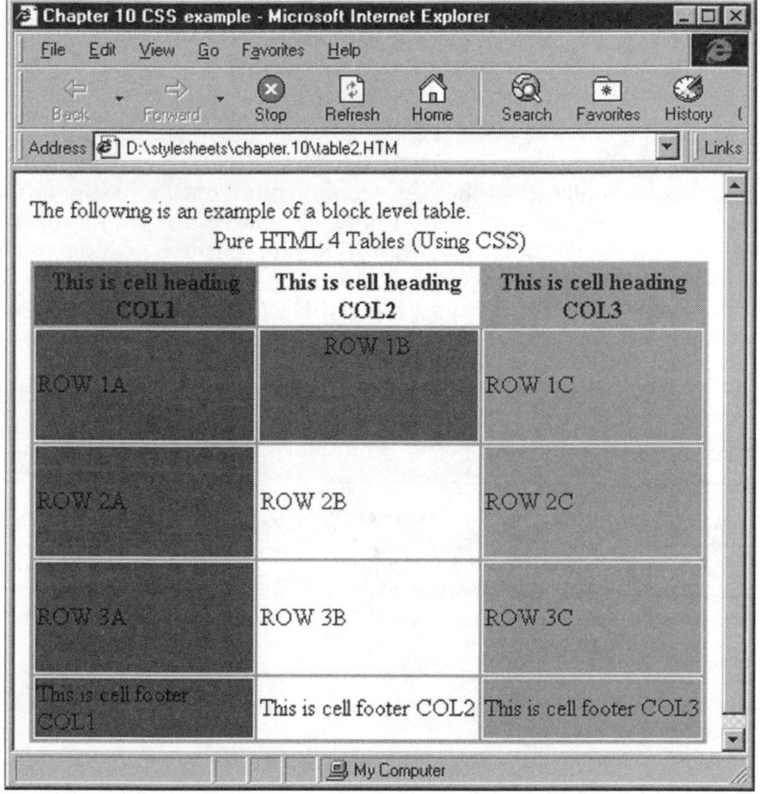

Important points to note are:

- We have used the **display** property to define the elements. This is not necessary in HTML, (in fact you can't change a **<TABLE>** to a **<COL-GROUP>**), and has just been included by way of illustration.
- We have made use of the **id** element to define the two columns. This gives us an easy peg on which to hang our CSS code.
- We have used the **column-span** property to define how many columns the properties should be applied to. In fact, this doesn't work in the current implementations–we still have to use the HTML **SPAN** attributes.
- In HTML **border** attributes set on the **<TABLE>** tag are, by default, applied to all the individual cells. In CSS the **border** property simply surrounds the table, and we must put individual border attributes on the cells.
- Using CSS the width and heights of individual cells can be defined.
- The **vertical-align** and **text-align** properties are used to align text in the cells. The default is **vertical-align:middle**, and **text-align:left**.

So, we've done tables in plain HTML and tables styled using CSS, let's see how we handle them in XML.

Tables in XML

As mentioned above, XML elements have no intrinsic formatting capabilities, so elements that are used for tables in XML have to declare their nature by using the **display** property. Several display properties exist solely for use in XML. Let's have a look at what properties are available.

We have a similar situation here to the XML lists. User agents which recognize HTML know that when they come across a tag that says **<TABLE>** they must format them in a certain fashion. In XML we make our own elements, and the XML compliant user agent has no intrinsic knowledge of the meaning of the tag. Even if we decided to call an element **<table>**, for all the XML compliant user agent knows we may be referring to a piece of furniture made by Chippendale. If we want one of our elements to act like a table element, we have to tell the user agent and use a property and a value. The property we use is the **display** property which informs the user agent what kind of flow object to make.

XML Display Properties

The following table is a list of these properties with their HTML equivalents.

XML Display Properties	HTML Equivalents
table	**TABLE**
in-line-table	No HTML equiv.
table-row	**TR**
table-row-group	**TBODY**
table-header-group	**THEAD**
table-footer-group	**TFOOT**
table-column	**COL**
table-column-group	**COLGROUP**
table-cell	**TD**, **TH**
table-caption	**CAPTION**

Let's examine each of these properties in turn.

Table, Inline-table

To see the difference between a table and an inline table, we need to look first at an HTML table, then move on to examine an example of a table in XML. A table, in many ways, is an anomaly in HTML. It acts as a block element when its float value is **none**, (which is the default), but acts as an inline element when its CSS float property is set to **left** or **right**, or if the **align** attribute is set to **right** or **left**. The next example illustrates this point. In the first rendering the HTML attribute **align=left** is used, in the second the CSS property **float: left** is used. Here is the code.

```
<HTML>
<HEAD>
<STYLE>
Body{font-size:14pt;
}
</STYLE>
</HEAD>
<BODY>
Here is a line of text written before the table,
<TABLE BORDER=1 ALIGN=left>
<TR>
<TD>A table with a <BR>solitary cell</TD>
</TR>
</TABLE>
and here is some text written after the table to demonstrate how text will
align itself around a table whose align property has been set to left.
<HR>
Here is a line of text written before the table,
<TABLE BORDER=1 STYLE="float:left">
<TR>
<TD>A table with a <BR>solitary cell</TD>
</TR>
</TABLE>
and here is some text written after the table to demonstrate how text will
align itself around a table whose float property has been set to left.
</BODY>
</HTML>
```

The rendering is identical, as you can see from this screenshot:

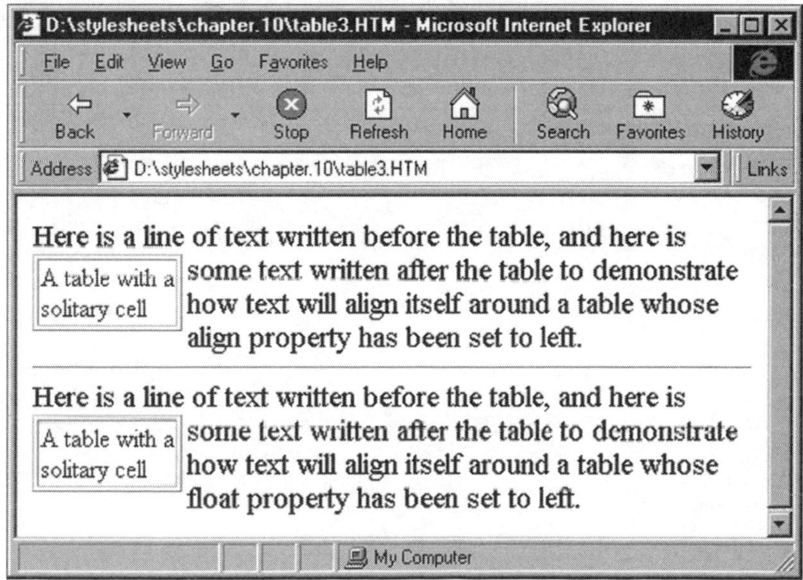

Note also how the table does not inherit the **`font-size`** properties.

In XML to get the same effect, namely to make your table an inline flow object rather than a block object, you must set the **display** property to **in-line-table**. If the **display** property is set to **table** then we will have a block flow object.

In the following XML code, we want to create an element called **<yearlysales>** to act as a table, with a separate row for each **<salesperson>**, and a separate cell called **<quarterlysales>** to act as a place to put each salesperson's sales by quarter. We will also add a caption to our table.

Here is what the code may look like.

```
<yearlysales year= "1997">
<salescaption> Sales for 1997 by salesperson and by quarter.
</salescaption>
     <salesperson name= "brown">
          <quarterlysales>Dan Brown</quarterlysales>
          <quarterlysales period= "first">40,000</quarterlysales>
          <quarterlysales period= "second">127,000</quarterlysales>
          <quarterlysales period= "third">38,000</quarterlysales>
          <quarterlysales period= "fourth">62,000</quarterlysales>
     </salesperson>
     <salesperson name= "smith">
          <quarterlysales>John Smith</quarterlysales>
          <quarterlysales period= "first">104,000</quarterlysales>
          <quarterlysales period= "second">91,000</quarterlysales>
          <quarterlysales period= "third">23,000</quarterlysales>
          <quarterlysales period= "fourth">76,000</quarterlysales>
     </salesperson>
     <salesperson name= "white">
          <quarterlysales>Pat White</quarterlysales>
          <quarterlysales period= "first">85,000</quarterlysales>
          <quarterlysales period= "second">72,000</quarterlysales>
          <quarterlysales period= "third">69,000</quarterlysales>
          <quarterlysales period= "fourth">93,000</quarterlysales>
     </salesperson>
</yearlysales >
```

To display this information in the form of a table we need to associate this XML document with the following CSS style sheet.

```
salescaption{
display: table-caption
}
yearlysales{
display: table
}
salesperson{
display: table-row
}
quarterlysales{
display: table-cell
}
```

When this is processed by an XML/CSS compliant user agent (please note that **XMLparse** does not support tables or lists,) it will produce output like the following.

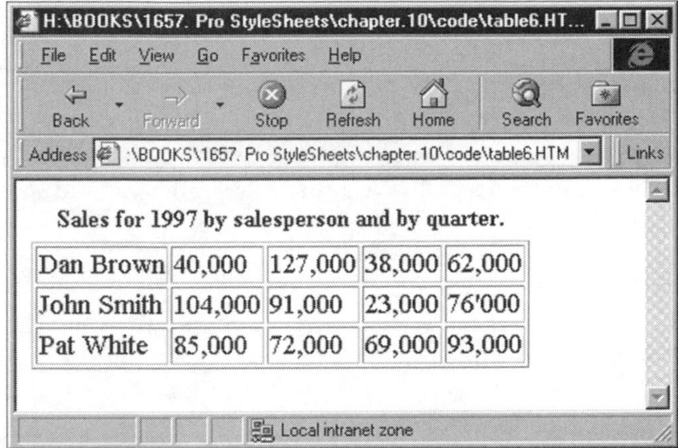

(Note that the above screen shot is a cheat. Because XML an CSS2 are not supported in the current browsers, we have rigged HTML to show you how the code would display if the standards were supported.) It is an easy matter to highlight various parts of the table. To highlight a row the best way would be to use the **id** property. To highlight **smith** we add an **id** attribute thus

```
<salesperson name= "smith" id="xyz">
```

and then add this to our CSS code

```
#xyz{
background-color:orange;
}
```

which will produce this:

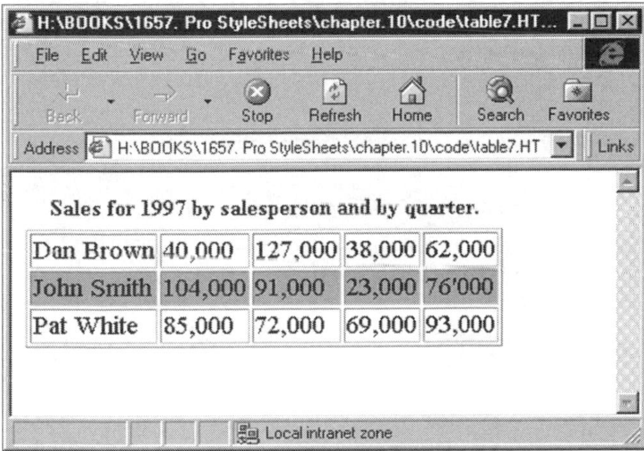

Table-row, Table-row-group

CSS is row orientated, as is HTML. The individual table cells are set up in rows rather than in columns. A **`table-row-group`** creates a block flow object. This will contain **`table-rows`** as block flow objects.

Table-header-group, Table-footer-group

Also contains **`table-rows`**. In HTML, this is limited to a single row, but in XML more than one row could be used. The header group is always displayed after a top caption, but before any **`table-row-group`**. The footer group is always displayed before a bottom caption, and after any **`table-row-group`**.

Table-column, Table-column-group

These do not create flow object boxes but refer to parts of the row flow objects. They are useful abstractions for applying a group of properties to a column of cells, and allow us to hang properties on them.

Table-cell

This is the basic unit of the table, and is an inline flow object. It corresponds to **`<TD>`** in HTML.

Table-caption

Displays the caption for the table. The **`caption-side`** property–which we cover in detail in the section on *Table Properties* below–allows positioning of the caption in relation to the table. As such it is an integral part of the table. If either an inline-table and a caption, or a table and a caption are created, CSS creates an anonymous box which includes both. By moving one you must move the other. The next two figures show how the captions should be displayed in relation to the table itself.

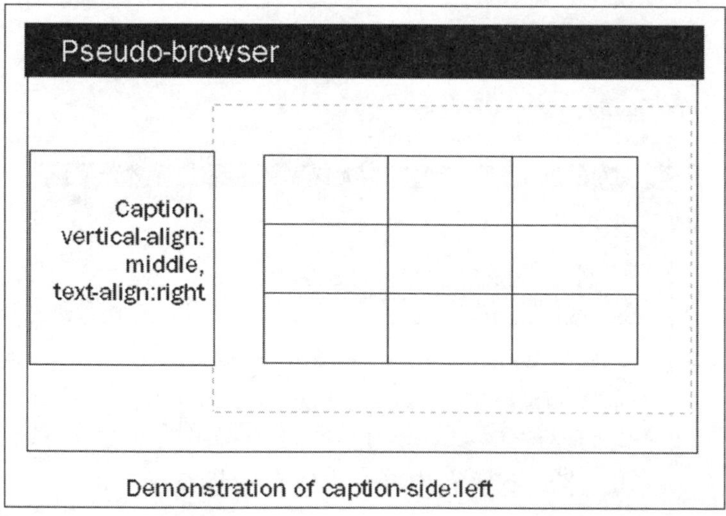

Demonstration of caption-side:left

The CSS code needed to create a caption to the left of the table would look something like the following:

```
BODY{
   margin-left:10em;
}

CAPTION{
   caption-side:left;
   margin-left:-10em;
   width:10em;
   text-align:right;
   vertical-align:middle;
}
```

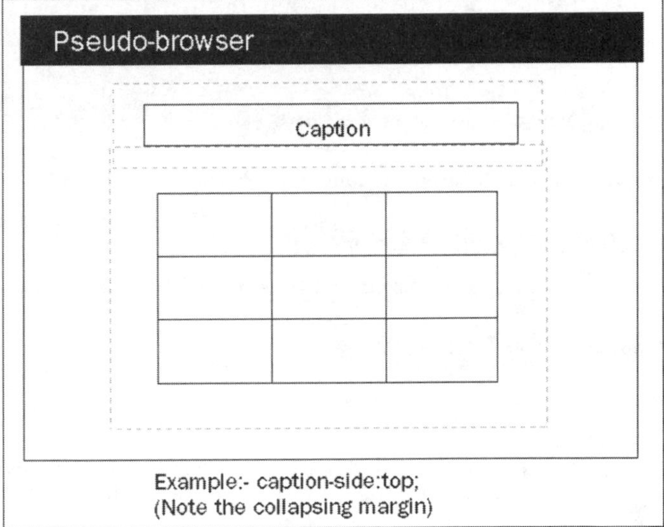

Example:- caption-side:top;
(Note the collapsing margin)

To create CSS code to put the caption at the top we really have to do nothing, as **caption-side:top** is the default. However, if we wanted to include the code (and this is often a good idea for clarity's sake) it would look as follows.

```
CAPTION{
   caption-side:top;
   text-align:center;
   }
```

No user agent supports these properties at present, and because it is almost impossible to write HTML to support the property **caption-side:left**, we have just shown what a **caption-side: left** would look like in an imaginary browser.

So, we've covered tables in HTML, CSS and XML. To conclude our look at tables, we'll look at some of the new properties which CSS2 has introduced for tables, although at present there is no support for them.

CSS2 Table Properties

CSS2 provides several properties specifically for tables, which will eventually replace the styling attributes for tables, deprecated in HTML 4.0. They will hopefully be implemented by the next generation of CSS/XML aware browsers. Neither of the current browsers support these table properties.

Caption-side Property

This is not quite equivalent to the HTML **CAPTION ALIGN=** "**[***value***]**" attribute.

In the HTML attribute, the values **top** and **bottom** will put the caption either at the top or bottom of the table. However, the value **left** will put it at the left side of the top, and the value **right** will put it at the right side of the top. This CSS property, when implemented, will place the caption either to the right or left side of the table as shown in the first diagram in the section above.

The syntax is:

caption-side: top | bottom | left | right

It only applies to **<table-caption>** elements and the default is **top**.

Column-span and Row-span Properties

These are the same as the HTML **COLSPAN** and **ROWSPAN** attributes for cells.

The syntax for **row-span** is as follows:

row-span:<*integer*>

This can be applied to individual cells. HTML **<TD>** elements and XML elements with the **display: table-cell** value will act the same way. *integer* is the number of rows that the cell will span. Here's some example code:

```
<HTML>
<BODY STYLE="font-size:18pt;background-color:white">

   <TABLE BORDER=1 STYLE="font-size:18pt">

   <TR>
   <TD>A table with three rows and columns. A1</TD>
   <TD STYLE="row-span:3;">A table with three rows and columns.B1,2,&
3</TD>
   <TD>A table with three rows and columns. C1</TD>
   </TR>
   <TR>
   <TD>A table with three rows and columns. A2</TD>
   <TD>A table with three rows and columns C2</TD>
   </TR>
   <TR>
   <TD>A table with three rows and columns. A3</TD>
   <TD>A table with three rows and columns C3</TD>
```

```
    </TR>

</TABLE>

</BODY>
</HTML>
```

and here's a screenshot showing what it would look like if **row-span** were supported.

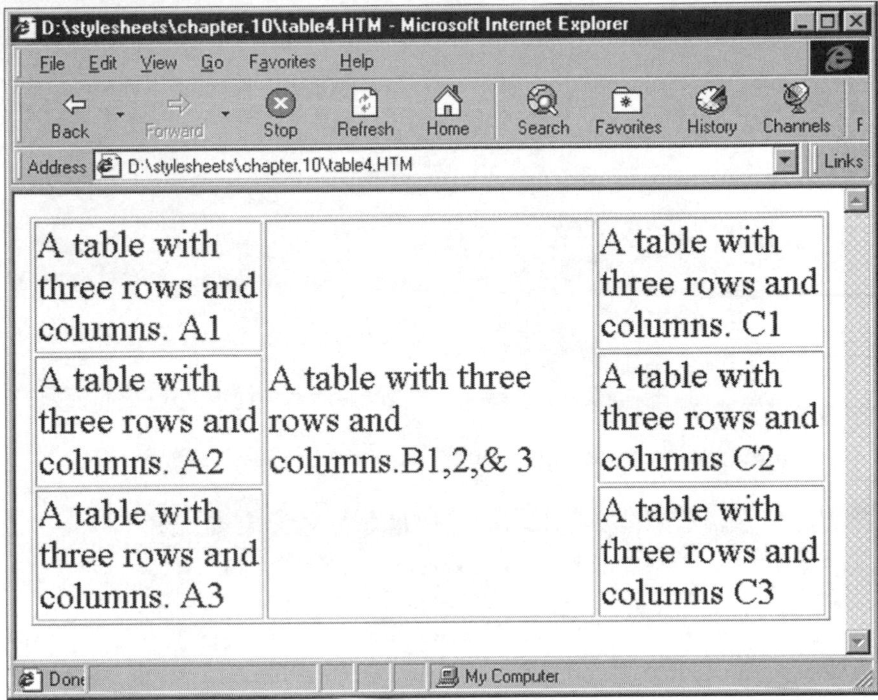

The screen shot is a cheat because neither of the browsers support this property. In fact,

```
<TD ROWSPAN=3>
```

was used instead of,

```
<TD STYLE="row-span:3;">
```

column-span can be applied to elements with the **display** property of **table-cell**, **table-column**, and **table-column-group**. It is similar to the HTML **COLSPAN** attribute that can be applied to **<TD>** and **<TH>**.

The syntax for **column-span** is as follows:

column-span:<*integer*>

Here's some code to demonstrate how it should be used:

```
<HTML>
<BODY STYLE="font-size:18pt;background-color:white">

<TABLE BORDER=1 STYLE="font-size:18pt">

<TR>
<TD STYLE="column-span:2;">A table with three rows and columns. A & B1</TD>
<TD>A table with three rows and columns. C1</TD>
</TR>
<TR>
<TD>A table with three rows and columns. A2</TD>
<TD>A table with three rows and columns. B2</TD>
<TD>A table with three rows and columns. C2</TD>
</TR>
<TR>
<TD>A table with three rows and columns. A3</TD>
<TD>A table with three rows and columns. B3</TD>
<TD>A table with three rows and columns. C3</TD>
</TR>

</TABLE>
</BODY>
</HTML>
```

and here's what it would like, if it was supported by a current browser version;

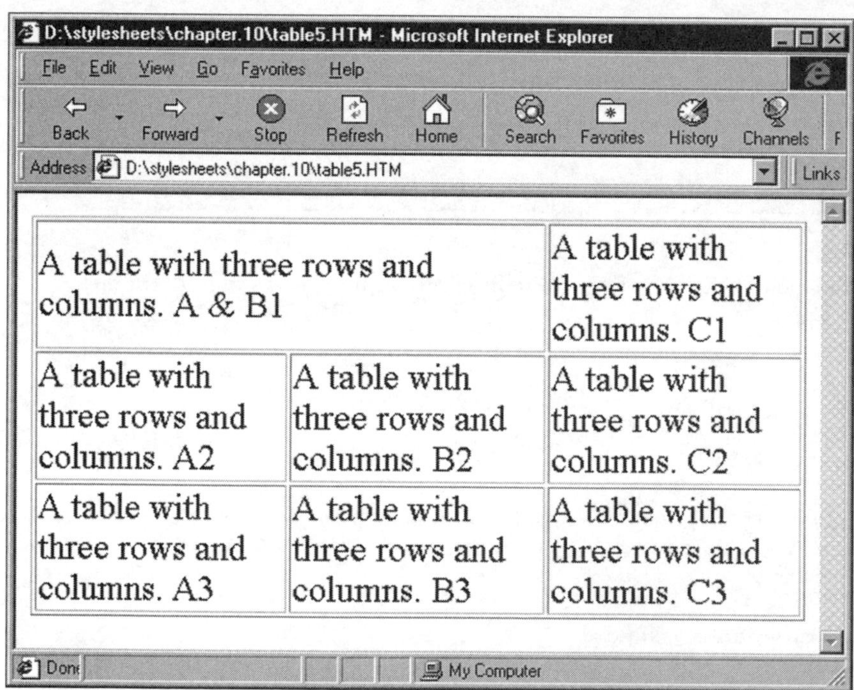

However, to achieve this screenshot we've had to cheat again, and have used:

```
<TD COLSPAN=2>
```

in place of

```
<TD STYLE="column-span:2;">
```

Table-layout Property

The syntax of this property is

```
table-layout:fixed|auto
```

The default being **auto**.

If the property is set to **auto**, CSS makes no effort to tell the user agent how to lay out the table. The user agent will have to go through a complex (and time consuming) process and the author will not have control over the final formatting.

In order to layout the content of a table with no fixed dimensions, the user agent has to make several passes at the code. The following shows some of the processes that it must go through.

- Make an array of the content of each cell.
- Determine the maximum and minimum width of all the cells necessary to display the content.
- Find out which cells have the **colspan** properties.
- Calculate the widths of the columns, based on the width of the cells in that column and the cell spacing, border width etc.
- If a table width (W) is given and the width of all the columns (w1+w2..+w*n*) is less than this width, (w1+w2..+wn)<W , then divide the remainder between the columns somehow.
- If the table width is less than the necessary width, (w1+w2..+wn)>W, the user agent must decide how to display the content. The obvious options are increase W, add a scrollbar, or clip the contents.
- If no table width is given (**width:auto** , the default), use some algorithm to decide how to layout the columns.

Using **table-layout: auto** the author can be sure that his material will be displayed somehow. If he sets the declaration to **table-layout: fixed** the author is responsible for the display, and CSS requires that conforming user agents use a certain algorithm (which, incidentally, only requires one pass, and displays much faster than any auto algorithm).

The full details of the algorithm can be found at:

http://www.w3.org/TR/PR-CSS2/tables.html (18.5.3)

The following is a summary:

- The table's width is either set with the **width** property or is as wide as the space available to it.
- If a column width is set, this value is used.
- If a cell in the first row has a **width** property set, this value is used.
- In this way the first row is set out immediately and all the other rows follow with the same widths. Heights may be adjusted if no height properties have been set.
- If there is overflow this is dealt with according to the **clip** property.

Table (and Image) Alignment

As we saw above, tables can be aligned to the left or right of a page using the **float** property, but how do we align the table in the center of the page?

The correct CSS approved method is to set the **margin-left** and **right** properties to **auto**. For example,

```
TABLE.center {margin-left: auto; margin-right: auto;}
```

This should center the table, but unfortunately it is not implemented. If a table or an image is set in a **<DIV>**, however, then this will work.

```
<DIV STYLE="text-align:center"><IMG SRC="smiley.gif"></DIV>
```

On the other hand, just use the deprecated HTML **<CENTER>** tag if you are using HTML.

A full discussion of this can be found at:

http://home.att.net/~sjacct/centre.html

This is courtesy of Sue Jordan of the CSS pointers group.

Cell Box Alignment

The text in the cells are aligned using the standard **text-align** and **vertical-align** properties. The cells may also be aligned in a row or a column using the **vertical-align** and the **text-align** properties. Although the cells may be positioned and floated using the relevant properties this is not recommended as it will break up the formatting of the table.

Vertical Alignment

A cell is constrained by the row it is in. If the height of the cell box is smaller than the height of the row, then the cell is aligned according to its **vertical-align** property. The default value for this property is **baseline**. The properties that can apply to rows and cells are:

baseline, **top**, **bottom**, **middle**.

The other values do not apply to table cells.

The baseline of a row is computed from the content of the cells that have a **baseline** value, and is equal to the largest cell baseline.

The baseline of a cell is calculated based on the first line of text. If there is no text, the baseline is the bottom of the object contained in the cell. For example, an image or an applet, or if the cell contains no content then the baseline is the bottom of the cell.

The following two figures show how this is done.

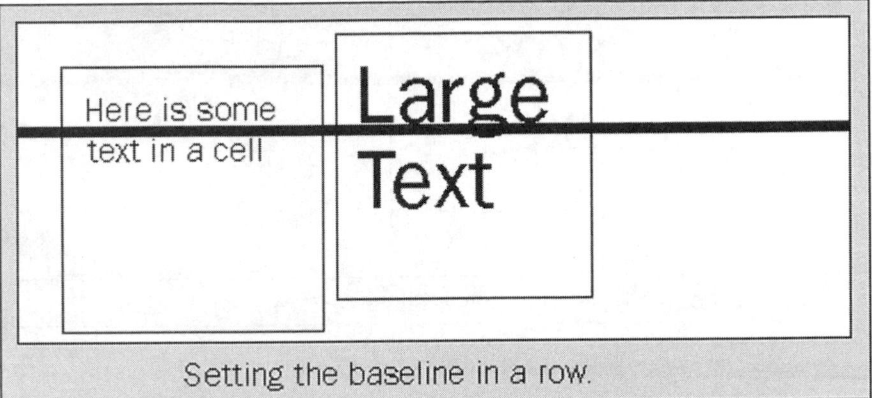

Setting the baseline in a row.

In the above figure the baseline of the "Large Text" establishes the base line because it has the greatest distance between its baseline and the top of the table.

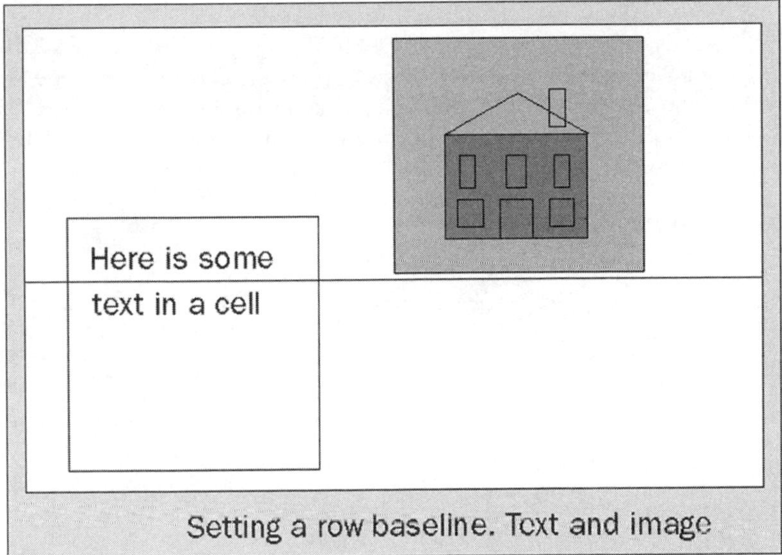

Setting a row baseline. Text and image

In the above figure the baseline of the house image, i.e. the bottom of the image, establishes the baseline because it has the greatest distance between its baseline and the top of the table. Once a baseline is established the cells with a **`vertical-align`** value other than **`baseline`** can be positioned. The height of the row may have to increase to accommodate the other cells (provided its height is set to **`auto`**).

The following figure shows how this is done. The **vertical-align** property of each cell is shown.

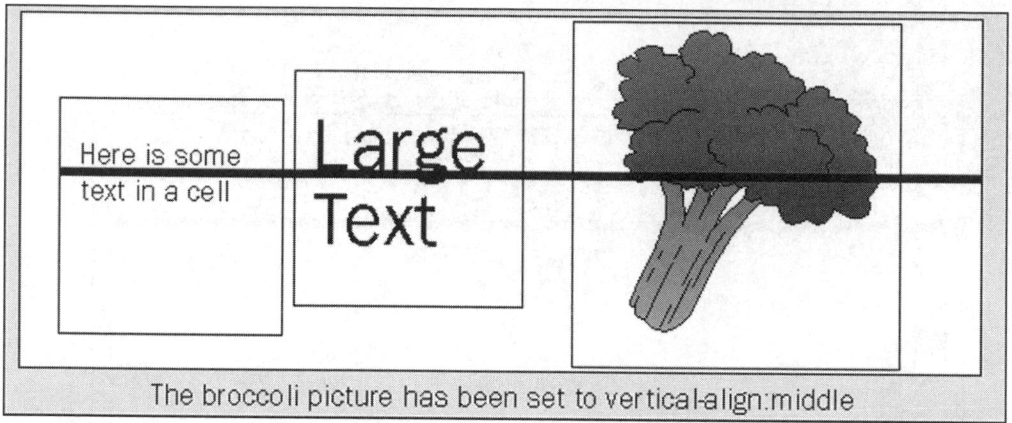

The broccoli picture has been set to vertical-align:middle

In the drawing above the **vertical-align** value for the broccoli has been set to **middle**, i.e.

```
vertical-align:middle
```

Note how the top of the table row is increased to accommodate the whole picture.

Horizontal Alignment

This is done using the **text-align** property. Note that this property can take a value of <*string*> when used in conjunction with a table. The following is an example of using the *string* value. The figures will line up on the first instance of the beginning of the string in the cell. The **text-align** property is set for the period, and so the table contents will line up on the period.

```
TD{ text-align: "."; width: 5em;}
TD:before {content:"$"}

<TABLE>
   <TR>
   <TH> Jan Gas</TH>
   <TH> Feb Gas</TH>
   </TR>
   <TR>
   <TD>12.40</TD>
   <TD>6.05</TD>
   </TR>
   <TR>
   <TD>8.60</TD>
   <TD>7.63</TD>
   </TR>
   <TR>
   <TD>11.85</TD>
   <TD>14.40</TD>
   </TR>
   <TR>
   <TD>6.42</TD>
```

```
    <TD>9.50</TD>
    </TR>
    <TR>
    <TD>10.00</TD>
    <TD>13.20</TD>
    </TR>
</TABLE>
```

This would produce the following result if supported by a browser.

- Jan Gas Feb Gas
- $12.40 $6.05
- $8.60 $7.63
- $11.85 $14.40
- $6.42 $9.50
- $10.00 $13.20

Visibility Property

The **visibility** property takes the values of **visible**, **hidden** or **collapse**. This latter value is for use only with tables. If used with other elements it should be interpreted as **hidden**. It can be used with a row, a row-group, a column, or a column-group.

The main use of this property is to create dynamic effects. What the property does is hide the content of the element without re-flowing the table. The space that the element occupied then becomes available to be used by another element.

Borders

Table elements can take any of the border styles listed in Appendices B and C. They are set on the elements according to two distinct models which are declared using the **border-collapse** property. The default value for this is **collapse**. However, some of the values for **border-style** have different meanings when used on table elements:

- **hidden** has the same value as **none**, but will also inhibit the display of borders on adjacent cells.
- **inset** makes the whole cell appear as if it were embedded in the canvas.
- **outset** makes the whole cell appear in relief.

Border-collapse Property

The syntax for this is:

```
border-collapse: collapse | separate
```

The default is **collapse**. These are two distinct models with their own properties, which we'll cover next.

The Collapse Model

The horizontal borders will be collapsed and the vertical borders will abut. There are complex rules of conflict resolution when various styles and size of border collapse on one another and these can be found at:

http://www.w3.org/TR/PR-CSS2/tables.html (18.6.2)

As a rule of thumb the most eye-catching border is chosen over the more drab border.

The Separated Borders Model

In the separated borders model two additional properties control the border presentation.

Border-spacing Property

The syntax for this property is:

border-spacing: <*length*><*length*>?

This declaration specifies the distance that separates adjacent border cells. If just one value is given it specifies both vertical and horizontal borders, if two are given, the first refers to the horizontal spacing, the second to the vertical spacing.

The space is filled with the background of the table element.

Empty-cells Property

This property simply declares whether a border should be drawn round an empty cell.

The syntax is:

empty-cells: borders | no-borders

The default is **borders**.

That's the end of the CSS2 table properties coverage. All that's left in the tables section is a quick look at aural rendering, which follows.

Aural Rendering

Aural rendering will be discussed more fully in the section on *Aural Content* in Chapter 14. The properties specifically for tables are best discussed here.

When tables are used in aural presentation, a speech generator will declare the header at the top of the column. The speak-header property specifies whether this is just declared once at the head of the property or whether it is spoken before each cell in the column.

The syntax is:

speak-header: once | always

That concludes our coverage of tables. Let's review what we've learned in this chapter.

Summary

In this chapter we have looked at the special circumstances surrounding lists and tables when they are used with Style Sheets and when they are used with XML. We saw that:

- In HTML the tags carry special meaning that enables the user agent to correctly format them.
- In XML role of the elements partaking in lists and tables must be indicated using the **`display`** property.
- We looked at the current situation in HTML, and noted that in HTML 4 the attributes associated with table and list tags have been deprecated.
- We looked at the CSS properties that will replace the deprecated attributes.
- We briefly re-visited counters and content generation, and how they can be used to provide list numbering.

With this chapter, we wrap up our review of the CSS properties. In the remaining chapters we will be looking in more detail at XSL, and we will also look at how scripting can be used in styling and some of the newer types of style sheets waiting in the wings.

References

The following have been nicknamed the CSS Pointers Group and they provide many useful CSS tips, including the one given above on centering tables.

`http://www.enhanced-designs.com/`	Toby Brown
`http://home2.swipnet.se/%7Ew-20547/`	Jan Roland Eriksson
`http://home.att.net/%7Esjacct/`	Sue Jordan
`http://www.macvirus.com/`	Susan Lesch

The following site contains an in depth article on the above group, and references to other CSS sites.

`http://microsoft.com/sitebuilder/columnists/site042098.asp`

The following URL's contain the official specification for the material contained in this chapter.

`http://www.w3.org/TR/PR-CSS2/tables.html`
`http://www.w3/org/TR/PR/CSS2/generate.html` (12.6)
`http://www.w3/org/TR/PR/CSS2//lists.html`

Exercises

Because much of tables and lists are not supported at the present it is difficult to make a meaningful exercise. However, try the following.

1. Make a list using XML, and then write a style sheet that numbers the list from 20 to 30.
2. Make a table in XML, and make the vertical cell-padding twice as large as the horizontal cell-padding.

Part 3

This is the alternative section! We've covered the basics of CSS and XML styling in Part1, then looked in-depth at what you can achieve today with CSS in Part 2. Part 3 addresses the future of styling.

In **Chapter 11** we look at advanced XSL– much of which is still unsupported in browsers or tools– including formatting and filtering, defining styles and using modes and macros. We cover the use of script for styling in **Chapter 12**, including using script to differentiate between browsers, calling external script files and dynamic styling in both IE4 and Communicator 4. In **Chapter 13** we look to the future of styling for XML and two potential alternatives to XSL, namely XS and Spice. **Chapter 14** deals with one of the major issues of CSS2, styling for canvases other than the computer screen. We cover styling for paged media, aural content and tactile content, including a discussion on braille styling and formatting. Finally, as a treat, in **Chapter 15** we run through lots of example code showing how you can achieve some stunning effects on your web pages.

Happy styling!

11

XSL: Beyond the Basics

This chapter looks at some of the more advanced possibilities of formatting using XSL. The features we examine are:

- Formatting and filtering using XSL.
- Using style rules.
- Defining styles .
- Inline styling.
- **`Class`** and **`ID`**.
- Modes.
- Macros.
- Built in XML and XSL functions.
- Scripting with XSL.
- Dynamic scripting.
- Flow objects from DSSSL and HTML supported in XSL.
- XSL output other than HTML.
- Possible changes to the spec.

It must be remembered that XSL is still at the Note stage, i.e. at the earliest level of W3C discussion, and there is a strong possibility that much will be changed in the review process that the note is undergoing. Indeed it is possible (but unlikely) that XSL will not be adopted at all! All the examples we'll see in this chapter will use the MSXSL processor, which you used in Chapter 5. We'll begin with a quick overview of what this processor doesn't support, before going on to use it to demonstrate some features that it does support!

The MSXSL Processor

Somewhat predictably the MSXSL processor does not support any of Netscape's specialized HTML tags, so examples of Dynamic HTML have been kept to a minimum, and of course the compiled IE4 DHTML file will not work on Communicator 4!

Many of the more advanced features are not incorporated in the MSXSL processor at the present time, but we have given examples just the same as it is possible that these features may be incorporated at the time you are reading this! As of March 20th the following were not included.

(Taken from **http://www.microsoft.com/workshop/author/xml/xmldata-f.htm**. Check out this site for the latest information.)

The Microsoft XSL Processor implements XSL as described in the Proposal for XSL with these changes and omissions:

- The current drafts of the XML language specify that XML is case sensitive. For MSXSL, all tag and attribute names must be lower case, except for HTML flow object names and attributes, which may be in upper case, lower case, or mixed case. MSXSL retains this case in the HTML output.
- CSS properties applied as attributes must be in lower case for them to be recognized as styles and output within a **STYLE** attribute. Because some of the CSS properties (like **border**) may conflict with HTML attributes, we recommend the convention of using upper or mixed case for all HTML attributes.
- (The following sections refer to the sections used in the XSL note itself.)
- Section 2.2: **<?xml-stylesheet?>** processing instructions within the XML document are ignored.
- Section 2.3: Importing of style sheets is not implemented (**<import>**).
- Section 3.2.1: Only ancestor patterns are supported, children patterns should not be used.
- Section 3.2.4: **ID** and **CLASS** attribute categories are not implemented (**<id>** and **<class>**) .
- Section 3.3.3: **<select>** has been renamed to **<select-elements>** to avoid conflicts with the HTML **<SELECT>** element.
- Section 3.3.4: Flow object macros are not implemented.
- Section 4.1: Named styles are not implemented.
- Section 5: Modes are not implemented.
- Section 6.1: DSSSL Core Flow Objects are not implemented.
- Section 6.2: HTML/CSS Core Flow Objects are not limited to those listed in this section. Any HTML element may be used.
- Section 7.2: Side effects within ECMAScript are not detected or prevented.
- Section 7.3: Units within ECMAScript are not implemented.
- Section 7.4: The built-in functions are a subset of those provided in DSSSL. See the XSL Tutorial for details. The XML object model is that of the Microsoft XML Parser.
- Section 7.4: Script is not allowed in the **from** attribute of **<select-elements>**.

So, now we know what we can't do with the processor, let's take a look at what we can do with it. We'll begin with formatting and filtering with XSL.

Formatting and Filtering

Consider the following longish XML document, and just suppose that we want to display one item from it, the inventory of regular hoes at the Chagrin store. How would we go about it?

Example of Filtering and Formatting

To reproduce this example yourself, you can download the files **ch11_ex1.xml** and **ch11_ex1.xsl** from the web site at **http://rapid.wrox.co.uk/books/1657** or copy the code below into a text editor and save it as **ch11_ex1.xml**.

```
<xdoc>
   <inventory>
   This text is in the inventory
      <store location="mentor">
         <hoes>
           21
         </hoes>
         <spades>
           25
         </spades>
         <rakes>
            29
         </rakes>
      </store>

      <store location="chagrin">
         <hoes>
           h31
         <tobaccohoes>11</tobaccohoes>
         <reghoes>20</reghoes>
         </hoes>
         <spades>
           s35
         </spades>
         <rakes>
           39
         </rakes>
      </store>

      <store location="burton">
         <hoes>
           h41
         <reghoes>30</reghoes>
         </hoes>
         <spades>
           s45
         </spades>
         <rakes>
           49
         </rakes>
         </store>
   </inventory>
   <employees>
```

```
        Put all the information about employees here.
        <store location="mentor">
           <payroll>
              mthly:-$12,500
           </payroll>
        </store>
     </employees>
  </xdoc>
```

One way to pull the figure for regular hoes at the Chagrin store out of this document is to use the **<select-elements>** tag. Let's look at the XSL style sheet that allows us to do this.

The <select-elements> Tag

The first thing to do is to get rid of the employees flow objects. We do this by targeting the ancestor **employees**, and not putting in any action part of the rule. Voila! Ancestor and children all gone. (Don't you wish that you could get rid of Uncle Ed that easily!)

```
<rule>
<target-element type="employees"/>
<!--Note the lack of any action-->
</rule>
```

Next we use the **<select-elements>** tag, and progressively select our way down the tree until we get to the Chagrin regular hoes. Note how we use the **<attribute>** element to select the Chagrin store from its siblings. To try the example yourself, copy the code below into your text editor and save it as **ch11_ex1.xsl**.

```
<xsl>
  <rule>
      <target-element/>
      <DIV color="blue" title="='&lt;' + tagName + '&gt;'">
      <children/>
      </DIV>
  </rule>

<rule>
      <target-element type="inventory"/>
            <select-elements>
            <target-element type="store">
            <attribute name="location" value="chagrin"/>
            </target-element>
            </select-elements>
</rule>

<rule>
      <target-element type="store"/>
            <select-elements>
            <target-element type="hoes"/>
            </select-elements>
</rule>

<rule>
      <target-element type="hoes"/>
```

```
            <select-elements>
            <target-element type="reghoes"/>
            </select-elements>
</rule>

<rule>
      <target-element type="reghoes"/>
      <SPAN color="teal" title="='&lt;' + tagName + '&gt;'"><BR/>
      <children/>
      </SPAN>
</rule>

<rule>
<target-element type="employees"/>
</rule>

</xsl>
```

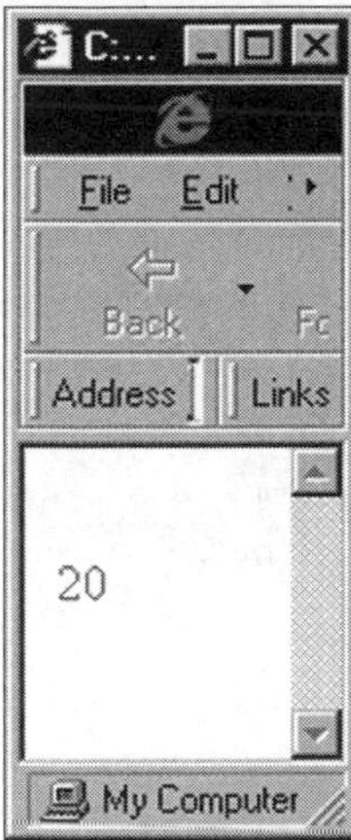

If you run these two files through the MSXSL processor, as we described in Chapter 5, and save the output as **`ch11_ex1.htm`**, the final out put will be 20 in a teal color.

We could have made the XSL code slightly shorter by using the **`from`** "**`descendants`**" attribute/value pair thus:

```
<rule>
      <target-element type="store"/>
         <select-elements from "descendants">
            <target-element type="reghoes"/>
         </select-elements>
</rule>
```

to replace the two rules;

```
<rule>
      <target-element type="store"/>
            <select-elements>
            <target-element type="hoes"/>
            </select-elements>
</rule>
<rule>
      <target-element type="hoes"/>
            <select-elements>
            <target-element type="reghoes"/>
            </select-elements>
</rule>
```

Note how the element is selected before the styling is applied and the flow object created.

This may strike you as rather a lot of work, and it is. It is very rarely that we would want to do this to a document, but it does illustrate the power of XSL for selection, and filtering of a document. That concludes our look at formatting and filtering. The next topic we'll examine is the use of style rules in XSL.

Using Style Rules

CSS allows us to cascade style sheets and merge properties from different sheets. A construction rule cannot do this because it produces a flow object. If one construction rule specified an inline object, another a block object and yet another a list, then there is room for all kinds of trouble. XSL gets round this predicament by the use of style rules.

Consider the following two CSS rules applied to an XML tag **<title>**:

```
title {color: red; font-size: 20pt;}
```

and later:

```
title {color: blue; font-style: italic;}
```

These would cascade or merge into a single rule:

```
title {color: blue, font-size: 20pt; font-style: italic;}
```

The color blue would be chosen in preference to the color red, because it was part of the later rule. We can do the same thing in XSL using the **<style-rule>** element.

Book Example

All the following examples use the same XML document, which looks like this;

```
<?xml version="1.0"?>

<xdoc>
      <book>
             Professional Style Sheets
             <chapter title="introduction">Introduction</chapter>
             <chapter title="chapter1">Style Sheets in General</chapter>
             <chapter title="chapter2">Basic CSS</chapter>
             <chapter title="chapter3">Basic XML</chapter>
             <chapter title="chapter4">More XML</chapter>
      </book>
</xdoc>
```

You can download it as **ch11_ex2.xml** from our web site at **http://rapid.wrox.co.uk/books/1657**, or copy it into your text editor and save it as an XML file.

We'll demonstrate the use of **<style-rule>** and show how the rules merge or cascade by using the following XSL rules:

```
<xsl>
<style-rule>
<target-element type= "chapter"/>
<apply color= "red" font-size= "20pt"/>
</style-rule>

<style-rule>
<target-element type= "chapter"/>
<apply color= "blue" font-style= "italic"/>
</style-rule>
```

Note that the style rules do not create a flow object, the processor must still search around for a construction rule to create the flow object. It finds one here.

```
<rule>
<target-element type="chapter"/>
<DIV color="green" background-color="white">
<children/>
</DIV>
</rule>
</xsl>
```

Copy the code above into your text editor and save as **ch11_ex2.xsl** or download this file from the web site. Run it through the MSXSL processor and save the output as **ch11_ex2.htm**. This is what you should see:

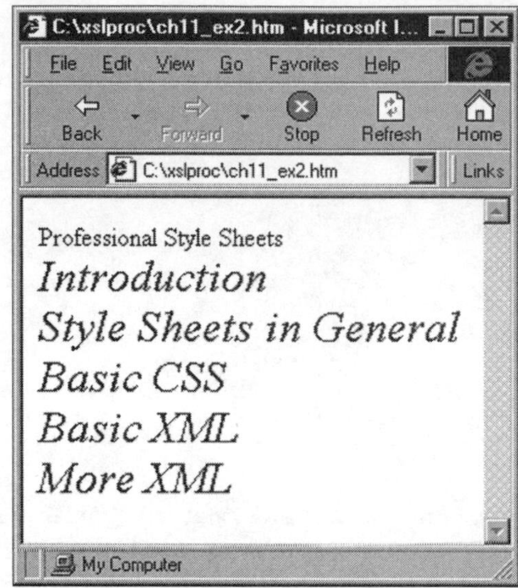

You can see from the screenshot that the selected text has taken the font size specified by the first style rule, and the font style specified by the second rule. What you can't tell from the black and white of the printed page is that the text color is blue. The style rules obey the same rules of precedence that the CSS rules follow, i.e. the rough and ready rule is that the most specific and the latest rules take precedence. This explains why the blue of the second style rule was applied rather than the red of the first style rule. However, why wasn't the green specified by the construction rule applied, as that was the final rule given? Although not mentioned in the specification, it appears that in the MS implementation, style rules take precedence over construction rules.

So, we've seen how you use style rules in XSL, let's take a look at how you define styles themselves.

Defining Styles

The XSL style object creates a list of styles to go with an element. It is possible to produce a named style using the syntax:

<define-style name= "stylename">

For example, we could create a style called "**subheading**" style.

```
<define-style name= "subheading"
              font-size= "12pt"
              font-style= "bold"
              font-family= "arial ,sans-serif"
              margin-left= "-2em"/>
```

Then every time we wanted to use it we would just have to refer to it by name.

In a style rule the form would be:

```
<style-rule>
<target-element= "subtitle"/>
<subheading color= "navy">
</style-rule>
```

In a construction rule the form would be:

```
<rule>
  <target-element= "subtitle"/>
   <DIV use= "subheading" color= "navy">
    <children/>
   </DIV>
</rule>
```

An alternate syntax is given for style rules that must comply with a strict DTD:

```
<style-rule>
<target-element= "subtitle"/>
<apply use= "subheading" color= "navy">
</style-rule>
```

As you can see this creates **"subheading"** to be a value of the attribute **use**.

Named styles are not implemented in the technological preview of the MSXSL processor, so we can't show you what this example looks like yet. Another unimplemented feature is inline styling, which we'll look at next.

Inline Styling

The specification provides a method for employing styles declared in the source document. It is by no means certain that this will make it into the proposal. However, for completeness here it is:

In the original document declare the intent to transmit a style as follows:

```
<subtitle xsl :: font-weight="bold">
```

In the style sheet refer to it as follows:

```
<rulc>
   <target-element type= "subtitle">
   <DIV use= "#source"
   <children/>
   </DIV>
</rule>
```

Enough of unimplemented features, let's get back to things we can demonstrate–classes and ids in XSL.

Class and ID

Consider the following lines of code:

```
<title id= "xyz123">

<title class= "heading">
```

As we saw in the section on *ID Selectors* in Chapter 7, the first line gives a unique identifier to a tag, the second declares the tag to be a member of the class "**heading**". XSL can specify these using the XSL **<attribute>** element, namely:

```
<target-element type= "title">
<attribute name= "id" value= "xyz123"/>
</target-element>

<target-element type= "title">
<attribute name= "class" value= "heading"/>
</target-element>
```

XSL allows us to specify a source document attribute that should behave like an **id** or a **class** by using:

```
<id attribute= "name"/>
```

or:

```
<class attribute= "name"/>
```

This latter piece of arcana is not supported in the MSXSL processor, and it is difficult to see where it may be of use. It could possibly be of value where a DTD is not supplied with the XML document, and it is necessary to validate it.

Modes

It is not unusual for elements from a source document to be displayed in several different places with a different kind of formatting. For example, in the book example XML file we saw above we may want to use the chapter headings in a table of contents, at the head of the chapters themselves, and as a heading in a footnotes section. Each appearance would require different formatting. Let's see how we could achieve that.

First let's remind ourselves what the XML code looks like.

```
<?xml version="1.0"?>

<xdoc>
      <book>
              Professional Style Sheets
              <chapter title="introduction">Introduction</chapter>
              <chapter title="chapter1">Style Sheets in General</chapter>
              <chapter title="chapter2">Basic CSS</chapter>
              <chapter title="chapter3">Basic XML</chapter>
              <chapter title="chapter4">More XML</chapter>
      </book>
</xdoc>
```

To apply different types of formatting to the same element at different points in the document we could use the XSL **mode** attribute to the **rule** and then declare it in the action. The following code:

```
<rule mode = "footnotes">
 <target-element type= "chapter"/>
<DIV font-size= "12pt" font-style= "italic">
<children/>
</DIV>
```

would create a mode called **"footnotes"**, and assign the specified style values to it. Now whenever we wanted to invoke these values in a flow object we would just assign it the mode value of **"footnotes"** e.g.

```
<DIV>
<children mode= "footnotes"/>
</DIV>
```

would style the children in 12pt italic.

This feature is not supported in the MSXSL processor.

Macros

Just as we can associate a set of style rules with a name, we can combine various flow objects into a macro using the XSL **<define-macro>** element.

The following would define a macro called **"disclaimer"**.

```
<define-macro name= "disclaimer">
  <HR/>
     Warning!! <BR/>

          The above opinions are the opinions of the writer and do not
          necessarily reflect the views of Wrox Press. Wrox Press can in no
          way be held liable for anyone idiotic enough to actually believe
          such ramblings.

  <HR/>
</define-macro>
```

You have now created an element called **"disclaimer"** defining a flow object. To use it, just declare it as follows:

```
<rule>
 <target-element type= "polemic"/>
  <DIV>
            <children/>
            <disclaimer color= "red" font-size= "16pt">
            <children/>
            </disclaimer>
  </DIV>
</rule>
```

The MSXSL processor does not support macros.

Built-in XML Functions

A Document Object Model (DOM) provides a mechanism for software developers and web script authors to access and manipulate parsed HTML and XML content. All markup, text, comments, as well as any document type declarations are made available. W3C is working on a document model for both HTML and XML, which is at present incomplete.

See **http://www.w3.org/TR/WD-DOM/level-one-core-971209** for further details.

Microsoft have written their own XML Document Object Model, and not surprisingly the MSXSL processor makes use of this. The MSXSL processor supports manipulations on the XML DOM. While the MS XML DOM provides a means by which we can navigate and alter an XML tree, the MSXSL processor allows access to the read-only functions of the XML DOM. The full model has built-in functions with which actual tree elements can be added, removed or otherwise manipulated. Obviously if a style sheet could do this it would become more than a style sheet.

The read-only element functions are:

Functions	Description
tagName	Returns the element type of the requested element. See below.
text	Returns the text of the requested element. The tags and other markup are stripped off.
parent	Returns the immediate ancestor of the requested element.
getAttribute()	Returns the attribute value as a string. See below.
children	Returns an enumeration of the children elements of the requested elements.
item()	Rather involved, see example below for details.
length	Returns the number of elements as a string. Takes the form **this.children.length**

For an exploration of the full Microsoft implementation of the XML DOM see:

http://www.microsoft.com/xml/articles/xmlmodel.htm

We will just look at a few relatively simple examples and one more complicated one to give an idea of how the model works, and to see how the XML DOM can be used in formatting the document.

The tagName Function

Let's look at an example using our old favorite, **ch11_ex2.xml**.

```
<?xml version="1.0"?>

<xdoc>
      <book>
              Professional Style Sheets
              <chapter title="introduction">Introduction</chapter>
              <chapter title="chapter1">Style Sheets in General</chapter>
              <chapter title="chapter2">Basic CSS</chapter>
              <chapter title="chapter3">Basic XML</chapter>
              <chapter title="chapter4">More XML</chapter>
      </book>
</xdoc>
```

Match it with this style sheet, **ch11_ex3.xsl** and process, saving the output as **ch11_ex3.htm**. **tagName** is a method that returns the element name tag as a string. Note that the keyword **this** could quite easily have been omitted in the following example:

```
<!--mark each element with its tag name.
tagName returns the element type of the requested element-->
<xsl>
  <rule>
```

```
        <target-element/>
        <DIV>
        <SPAN color="teal">
        [<eval>this.tagName</eval>]:-
        </SPAN>
        <children/>
        </DIV>
    </rule>
</xsl>
```

The tag is matched with the element content to produce an output which looks something like this:

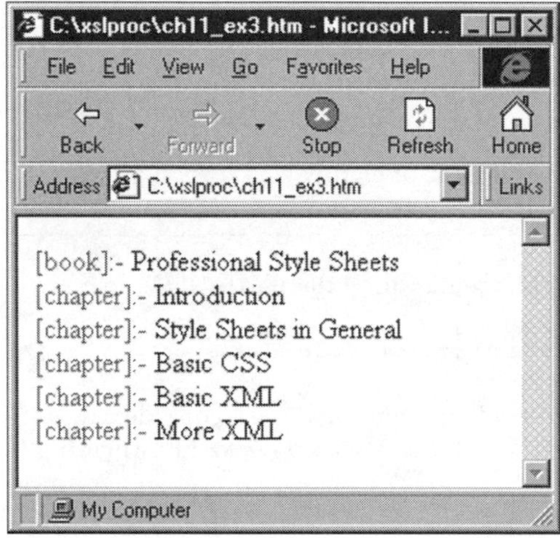

The <eval> Tag

The **eval** tag was used in the above example and is a way to include script in your XSL document. It is an XSL tag that has been borrowed from ECMAScript. Every time the processor sees it, it knows to treat the contents as code.

The getAttribute Function

The **getAttribute** function returns the value of the specified attribute of the requested element as a string. It takes the general form:

getAttribute(*attributeName***)**

The following example uses this function to match the element content with the attribute name:

```
<!--getAttribute returns a string with the value of the attribute.
This attribute is written as a flow object.-->

<xsl>
   <rule>
       <target-element type="chapter"/>
```

```
            <DIV color="teal">
            <SPAN color="blue">
            <eval>this.getAttribute("title")</eval>
            </SPAN>
            <BR/>
            <children/>
            <HR/>
            </DIV>
        </rule>
    </xsl>
```

The output will be similar to this:

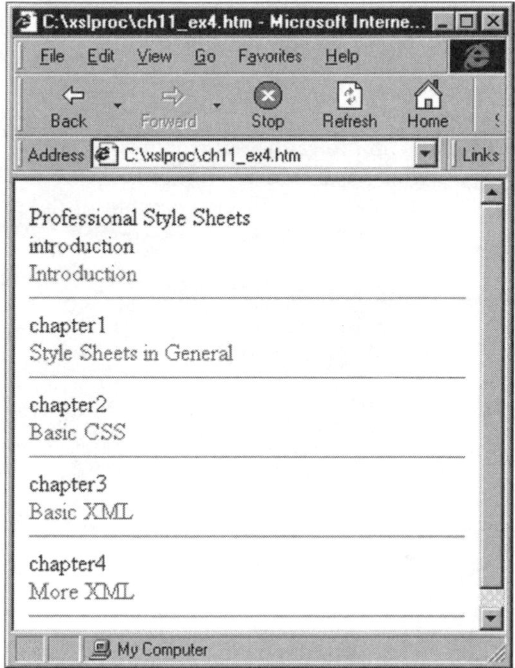

The item() Function

This is a fairly complicated function which is best explained by an example. Essentially, it returns information about elements from a collection. This can be skipped if you want but it is included to show how it is possible to get information about a document using the XML DOM.

We have modified our XML file as follows and saved it as **ch11_ex3.xml**.

```
<?xml version="1.0"?>
<xdoc>
      <!--here is a comment-->
      <book>
            Professional Style Sheets
            <chapter><emphasis>Chapter1</emphasis></chapter>
            <!--comment-->
            <aside/>
            More text
             <chapter>Chapter2</chapter>
             <chapter>Chapter3</chapter>
             <chapter>Chapter4</chapter>
             <chapter>Chapter5</chapter>
        </book>
</xdoc>
```

We will now use the **item()** function to return information about the children of the **book** element. All the immediate flow objects are ordered into an array, and we can query the array to find the tag name, the type of flow object, or the text content of the flow object. Here's the style sheet, **ch11_ex5.xsl**.

```
<!--the item() returns the item from a collection, either taking an index
as an argument, or an element name-->
<xsl>
   <rule>
<target-element type="book"/>
      <DIV>
      <SPAN color="teal">
      <eval>children.item(0)</eval><BR/>
      <eval>children.item(1).parent</eval><BR/>
      <eval>children.item(1).children</eval><BR/>
      <eval>children.item(8).children</eval><BR/>
      <eval>children.item(1).tagName</eval><BR/>
      <eval>children.item(1).type</eval><BR/>
      <eval>children.item(1).text</eval><BR/>
      <eval>children.item(2).type</eval><BR/>
      <eval>children.item(3).type</eval><BR/>
      <eval>children.item(3).tagName</eval><BR/>
      <eval>children.item(4).type</eval><BR/>
      <eval>children.item(4).text</eval><BR/>
      </SPAN>
      </DIV>
   </rule>

</xsl>
```

The output, **ch11_ex5.htm**, looks like this;

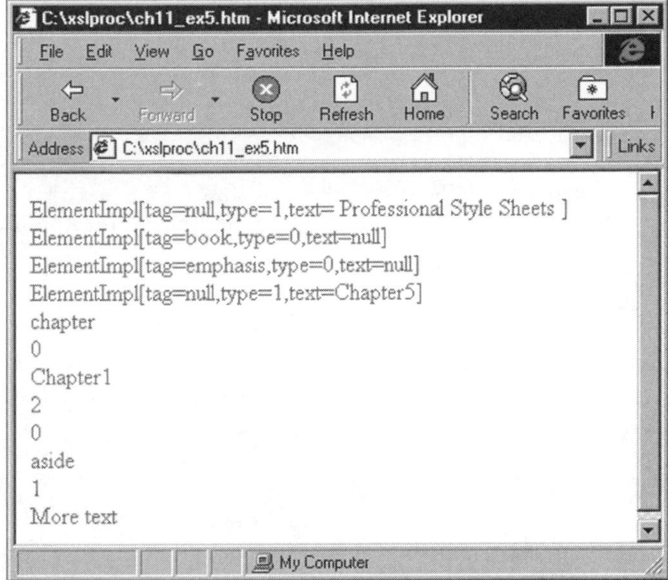

Not exactly intuitive is it? Let's go through it line by line and explain what we're looking at. Remember up front that the array starts from 0 and note that type 0 = element, 1 = text and 2 = comment. Note also that we are asking for a list of items of the book element. Here to make this simpler I have listed the flow objects.

0. Professional Style Sheets
1. **<chapter>** (note that **<emphasis>** is a child of **<chapter>** and is included in that flow object, so doesn't take part in the flow object count for book).
2. **<aside/>**
3. The comment
4. More text
5. **<chapter>**
6. **<chapter>**
7. **<chapter>**
8. **<chapter>**

So the first line we see on screen is:

ElementImpl[tag=null,type=1,text= Professional Style Sheets]

which is produced by the code:

```
<eval>children.item(0)</eval><BR/>
```

which was a general query for the first flow object. The first flow object in the target element **<book>** is a piece of text, so the screen tells us that it is type 1, and then produces the text which is Professional Style Sheets.

Next we see the line:

ElementImpl[tag=book,type=0,text=null]

produced by the code:

```
<eval>children.item(1).parent</eval><BR/>
```

Now the parent of flow object 1 is the element **<book>**, and we can see that it does contain text, however the processor just ignores it. This is probably a bug, sorry, unsupported feature, of the processor.

The next line of output reads:

ElementImpl[tag=emphasis,type=0,text=null]

and is produced by the code:

```
<eval>children.item(1).children</eval><BR/>
```

which asks for information about the child of item 1. The child of the first **<chapter>** element is the **<emphasis>** element, so the output line tells us that the tag is emphasis, that its an element (type=0) and it contains no text. (This again is probably a bug, because of course **<emphasis>** does contain text!)

The final query of this type produces this output:

ElementImpl[tag=null,type=1,text=Chapter5]

from the code:

```
<eval>children.item(8).children</eval><BR/>
```

which is requesting information about the child of Item 8. Item 8 in the array is the final **<chapter>** element, and its child is the text which it encloses. The output therefore tells us that this child is not a tag, it's a piece of text (type=1) and the text is Chapter 5.

The next three lines of code are querying the properties of item 1, the first **<chapter>** element:

```
<eval>children.item(1).tagName</eval><BR/>
<eval>children.item(1).type</eval><BR/>
<eval>children.item(1).text</eval><BR/>
```

In simple terms this is saying, what is the tag name of **<chapter>**, what is its type and what text does it contain? The output produced in response is:

chapter
0
Chapter1

which accurately reports that the tag name is chapter, the type is element (type=0) and the text it contains is Chapter1.

The next lines of code both ask for a report on the type of an item, in this case for the type of item 2, the comment and item 3, the **</aside>** element:

```
<eval>children.item(2).type</eval><BR/>
<eval>children.item(3).type</eval><BR/>
```

The output of:

2
0

accurately identifies the types as comment (type 2) and element (type 0) respectively.

The last three queries are as follows and are querying the tag name of item 3, the **</aside>** element, and the type and text of item 4, "More text".

```
<eval>children.item(3).tagName</eval><BR/>
<eval>children.item(4).type</eval><BR/>
<eval>children.item(4).text</eval><BR/>
```

The output produced is:

aside
1
More text

which correctly gives the tag name of item 3 as aside, and identifies item 4 as a line of text (type=1) and gives the text as More text.

As you can see using these XML DOM properties it is possible to deconstruct and construct the whole document.

Built-in XSL Functions

XSL also has a number of built-in functions. These are a subset of those included in the DSSSL standard, but because hyphens are not allowed in JavaScript, the hyphenated notation has been converted to camelBack notation.

XSL Functions	Syntax	Description
ancestor	**ancestor(***elementType, element***)**	Returns the nearest ancestor to the element
childNumber		See below
ancestorChildNumber	**ancestorChildNumber** **(***elementType, element***)**	Returns the number of the nearest ancestor of an element to the requested element type
path	**path(***element***)**	Returns the path of the element
heirarchialNumber Recursive	**heirarchialNumberRecursive** **(***elementType, element***)**	Returns the child numbers of the requested element type
formatNumber		See below
formatNumberList	**formatNumberList (list, format,seperator)**	Returns a formatted representation of **list** where **list** is an array of integers

We will just look at one example.

The childNumber and formatNumber Functions

The function **childNumber** returns the elements number (as a string) in relation to its siblings. Its general form is:

childNumber(*element***)**
Element is usually represented by **this**.

The function **formatNumber()** takes two arguments, a number and the type of format it is to take. The general form is:

formatNumber(*number, format***)**

Format can be as follows:

"1" means use 0,1,2,3.....
"01" means use 01,02,03.......
"a" means use 0, a, b, c..... aa, bb, cc....
"A" means use 0, A, B, C...
"i" means use 0, i, ii, iii...(not implemented)
"I" means use 0, I, II, III...(not implemented)

To demonstrate, we'll take our original book XML file, **ch11_ex2.xml**, which looks like this:

```
<?xml version="1.0"?>

<xdoc>
      <book>
              Professional Style Sheets
              <chapter title="introduction">Introduction</chapter>
              <chapter title="chapter1">Style Sheets in General</chapter>
              <chapter title="chapter2">Basic CSS</chapter>
              <chapter title="chapter3">Basic XML</chapter>
              <chapter title="chapter4">More XML</chapter>
      </book>
</xdoc>
```

and marry it up with this style sheet, which we've saved as **ch11_ex6.xsl**.

```
<xsl>
   <rule>
      <target-element type="chapter"/>
      <DIV color="teal">
    <!--Note how +is used to concatenate-->
      <eval>"Chapter" + " " + formatNumber(childNumber(this),"1")</eval>
      <SPAN color="navy">
      <children/>
      </SPAN>
      </DIV>
   </rule>
</xsl>
```

Then process using the MSXSL processor, saving the output as **ch11_ex6.htm**. This is what you should see:

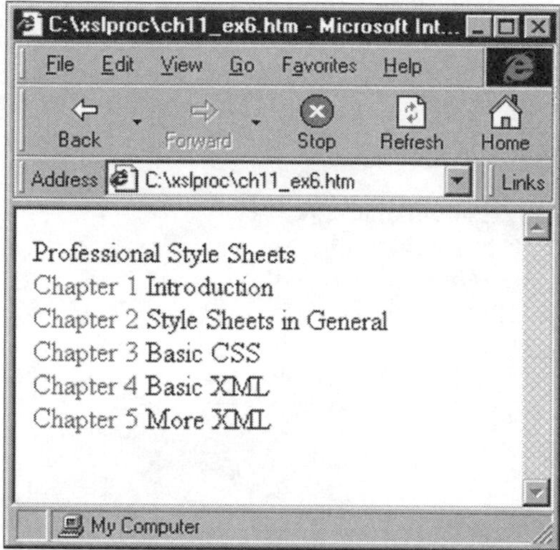

As you can see, it's inserted the word Chapter and a sequential number in the format specified in front of the contents of each **<chapter>** element.

Script and XSL

As well as the built-in functions, XSL allows us to use script in two ways:

- In processing our source document, it allows us to add power to the formatting abilities of XSL and to generate text .
- It allows us to pass script through to the HTML to make the document active.

Throughout this discussion of XSL we have been producing HTML, but that is really because that is what the tools we have enable us to do. XSL can be used to produce other types of documents such as RTF and PDF, as well as producing direct output both on the screen or as print or other media. It is just that the tools to do this do not exist as of yet.

The define-script Tag

This is similar to the **<SCRIPT>** element in HTML, and contains functions and constants. Note that, although global variables can, in fact, be placed in the element, their use in this way is strongly discouraged, as they can cause peculiar side effects. Indeed their use is prohibited in the XSL Spec. Usually there is just one **<define-script>**, and this is put at the beginning of the XSL style sheet.

The **<define-script>** tag is used when you want the JavaScript to work while the document is loading. Our example shows how the **getAttribute** value is passed to a function, and text is generated depending on the chapter number.

It is likely that the **<define-script>** tag will take the attribute **language** just as the **<SCRIPT>** tag does. At present, only JavaScript is supported in the MSXSL processor.

Here is an example of it in action, using our old friend **ch11_ex2.xml** again:

```
<?xml version="1.0"?>

<xdoc>
      <book>
              Professional Style Sheets
              <chapter title="introduction">Introduction</chapter>
              <chapter title="chapter1">Style Sheets in General</chapter>
              <chapter title="chapter2">Basic CSS</chapter>
              <chapter title="chapter3">Basic XML</chapter>
              <chapter title="chapter4">More XML</chapter>
      </book>
</xdoc>
```

And here is a somewhat more complex XSL style sheet, which we'll save as **ch11_ex7.xsl**. These files are available on the Wrox web site at **http://rapid.wrox.co.uk/books/1657** if you can't face the prospect of typing all this out.

```
<!--a function writeString takes getAttribute as an argument and uses it to
return an appropriate string
.-->

<xsl>
    <define-script>
    <![CDATA[
    var myColor="#888800";
    function writeString(e)
         {
         var myString="No comment for this chapter";
         if (e=="introduction")
               {myString="A gentle introduction";}
         if (e=="chapter1")
               {myString="Explores the idea of style sheets in general";}
         if (e=="chapter2")
               {myString="Teaches you how to write your first style
sheet.";}
        return myString}
      ]]>
      </define-script>

   <rule>
      <target-element type="book"/>
      <DIV background-color="#CC0000" color="DDDD00" text-align="center"
font-size="32pt">
      <children/>
      </DIV>
      <HR/>
   </rule>

   <rule>
      <target-element type="chapter"/>
```

```
        <HR/>
        <DIV background-color="#FFFFFF" color="=myColor" font-size="18pt"
   text-align="left"
        padding-left="2em">
        <children/>
        <BR/>
        <SPAN color="teal" font-size="14pt">
        <eval>" " + writeString(this.getAttribute("title"))</eval>
        </SPAN>
        </DIV>
     </rule>
   </xsl>
```

Run both files through the MSXSL processor and save the result as **`ch11_ex7.htm`**. This is what it should look like:

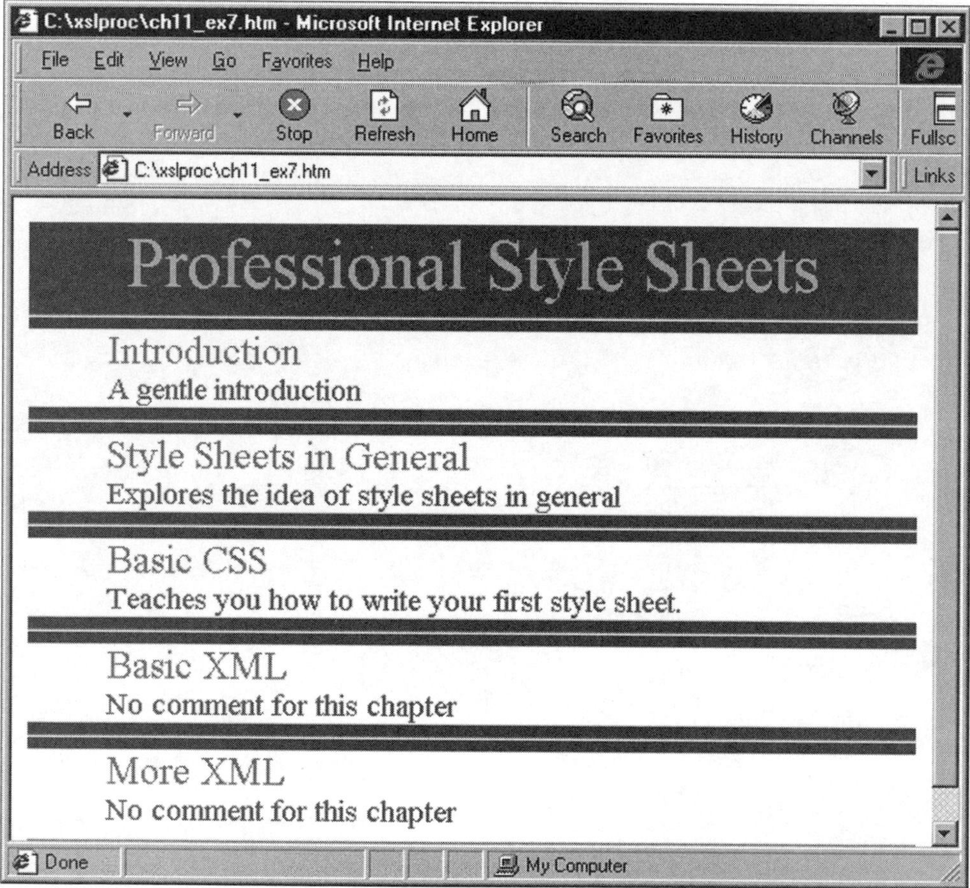

This screenshot shows what the above document looks like on IE4. Apart from the styling, we have used a simple JavaScript function to generate the text.

Let's look at this in a little more detail. The **<define-script>** element is used to define script that is executed while the XSL file is being linked with the XML file, using the syntax;

```
<xsl>
     <define-script>
```

To pass JavaScript through to the final document just use the **<SCRIPT>** tag in the **<root/>** element. (See the section on *Scripting* below)

The whole of the script is marked as character data (see Chapter 3 under *XML Comments*), to ensure that it will be passed through to the output document:

```
<![CDATA[
```

We could easily have just declared this:

```
var myColor="#888800";
```

in the body of the style sheet, but we included it in this format as a demonstration of how constants should be passed to the action part of the style sheet.

We have created a JavaScript function **writeString()** which accepts an argument **e** which represents a string of the **title** attribute of the **<chapter>** element. It is tested for in the conditional statement.

```
        function writeString(e)
             {
             var myString="No comment for this chapter";
             if (e=="chapter1")
                  {myString="A gentle introduction";}
             if (e=="chapter2")
                  {myString="Explores the idea of style sheets in general";}
             if (e=="chapter3")
                  {myString="Teach's how to write your first style sheet.";}
      return myString}
      ]]>
      </define-script>
```

What would happen if we used the **else** statement to place the text "No comment for this chapter"? (Try it and see what happens.)

Here is the part of the code that passes the argument to **writeString**. It is put inside a special **<eval>** tag that tells the processor to treat the content as script.

```
<SPAN color="teal" font-size="14pt">
<eval>writeString(this.getAttribute("title"))</eval>
</SPAN>
```

As we saw briefly in Chapter 5, the section on *Scripting and the* **<eval>***Tag*, another way to tell the processor to treat content as script is to use the equals sign. For example:

```
<SPAN color="blue" title="='&lt;' + tagName + '&gt;'">
```

This can be useful when we use script for simple concatenation, as you'll see in the example in the *Inline JavaScript* section later in the chapter.

Each instance of the element **"chapter"** is scanned and its **title** attribute is isolated using the XML method **getAttribute**. The attribute is then passed to **writeString** as an argument, and a string is returned which is used to create a flow object.

Dynamic Scripting

XSL can add dynamic behavior to our documents by passing through the **<SCRIPT>** tag to the generated HTML output. Note that the use of **<SCRIPT>** is different from **<define-script>**. The latter defines script that is executed during the processing of the document, the former executes in the processed document. The following only works in IE4 as this it is their version of Dynamic HTML.

Here's the style sheet:

```
<xsl>

   <rule>
      <root/>
         <HTML>
         <SCRIPT LANGUAGE="JAVASCRIPT">
            <![CDATA[
            function changecolor(e){
             if (e.style.backgroundColor!='red')
             (e.style.backgroundColor='red')
             else
             (e.style.backgroundColor='green')
            }
            ]]>
         </SCRIPT>
         <BODY>
            <children/>
         </BODY>
         </HTML>
   </rule>

   <rule>
      <target-element type="chapter"/>
      <DIV id='=tagName + formatNumber(childNumber(this),"1")' background-
      color="red" onClick='="changecolor("+tagName +
      formatNumber(childNumber(this),"1")+")"' color="blue"
      font-size="12pt">
         <children/>
      </DIV>
   </rule>

</xsl>
```

and it looks like this:

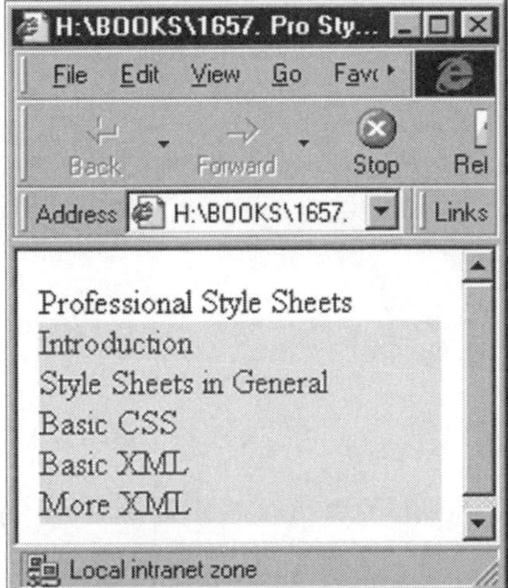

In this screenshot the text is blue and the background color is red. The really clever bit is that when you click on one of the chapter titles, the background color changes to green, like this:

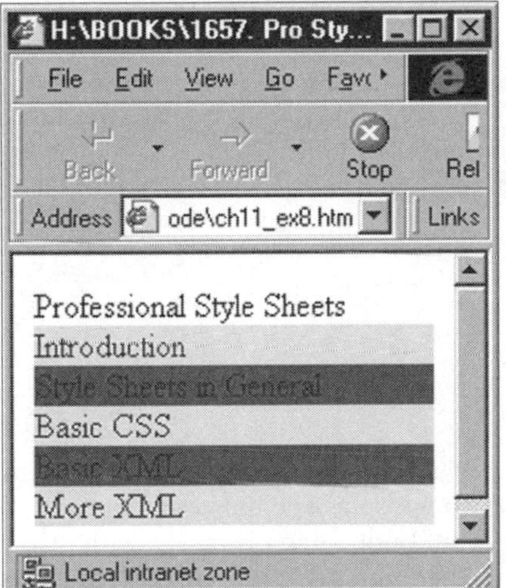

The only bit that needs a little explanation is the following.

For the first child:

```
        <DIV id='=tagName + formatNumber(childNumber(this),"1")'
                background-color="red"
                onClick='="changecolor("+tagName +
   formatNumber(childNumber(this),"1")+")"'
                color="blue" font-size="12pt">
                <children/>
```

produces:

```
<DIV id="chapter1" onClick="changecolor(chapter1)" style="background-color:
red; color: blue; font-size: 12pt">
```

Specifically

```
'=tagName + formatNumber(childNumber(this),"1")'
```

generates

```
"chapter1"
```

so that when you click on the tag with the **id** of **chapter1** the background color changes.

Predictably we are not able to use the MSXSL processor to pass through any of Netscape's DHTML tags such as **<LAYER>**.

Inline JavaScript

We can add JavaScript to our style sheets either by using the **<eval>** tag or simply using the **=** sign which tells the XSL processor that the attribute value should be calculated as a JavaScript expression. Here's a neat piece of code lifted from the Microsoft tutorial, which can be found at:

http://www.microsoft.com/xml/xsl/tutorial/tutorial.htm.

It relies on the fact that, in IE4, when the mouse pointer rests over text from an HTML element with the **title** attribute, the value of **title** will appear in a little yellow tool box.

Here is the simple XML file, which we'll save as **ch11_ex4.xml**.

```
<xdoc>
<publisher>Wrox Press</publisher>
</xdoc>
```

Here is the XSL file, which we save as **ch11_ex9.xsl**. Note how the equals sign inside the quotes is used to concatenate the **tagName** with the opening and closing angled brackets. (You must use **>**. Using the generic **>** would not work.) If mixed with other style rules this would be a wildcard applying to any element that had not had a specific rule written for it. In a large XML file this can be a useful tool in the authoring process.

```
<xsl>
<rule>
      <target-element/>

      <SPAN color="blue" title="='&lt;' + tagName + '&gt;'">
      <children/>
      </SPAN>
</rule>
</xsl>
```

This generates this HTML, in a file called **ch11_ex9.htm**, after it has been through the processor.

```
<DIV>
<SPAN title="<publisher>" style="color: blue">
Wrox Press
</SPAN>
</DIV>
```

which looks like this:

This does not work in Communicator 4 (what else is new!). Here, however, is a similar piece of code that works in both.(Now that's a change!) Clicking on the text will bring up an alert box with the tag's name in it.

```
<xsl>
<rule>
      <target-element/>
      <A HREF="='#top&quot; '+ 'onClick=&quot;alert('+'\''+tagName+'\');'">
      <children/>
      </A>
</rule>
</xsl>

<!--(It is necessary to put in the #top otherwise after the alert the
parent directory will appear)-->
```

The only part of the code you need to be careful with are the apostrophes. See how we use the escape character `'\'` to put in the single quote. This is necessary because, surprisingly, HTML does not provide an entity for it, and `'` (the ASCII value) will not work in this situation. It looks like this in IE4:

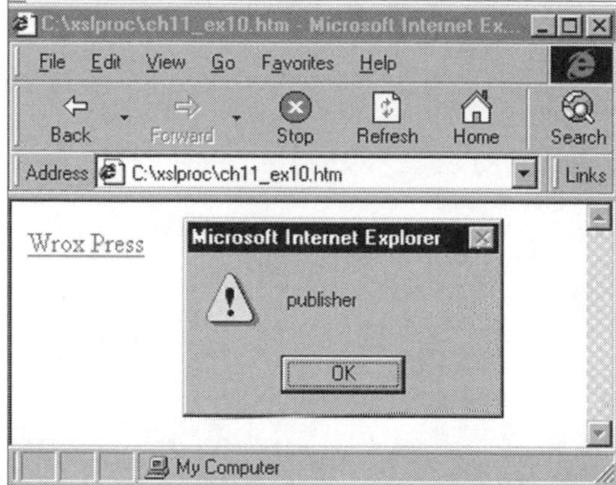

and like this in Communicator 4:

The ability to pass through code to work on our source document adds tremendous power to XSL. It means that virtually everything that can be done with JavaScript can be accomplished through the style sheet, and allows numerous presentations and manipulations of the same document.

For further examples of Dynamic HTML see *Instant HTML Programmer's Reference, ISBN 1861001568* and *Instant JavaScript, ISBN 1861001274.*

XSL Output other than HTML

Throughout our review of XSL we have been producing HTML documents as an output. This does not mean that we cannot use XSL to produce other forms of output, it is just that we do not have the tools to do this yet, as the MSXSL processor just outputs HTML.

All that XSL does is perform various manipulations on the original source document, and there is no reason for an XSL compliant browser to go through the intermediary stages. DSSSL was used to print documents, and it is probable that user agents will be developed to both print and convert the XML/XSL document to other media such as Braille or sound.

Flow Objects from DSSSL and HTML supported in XSL

The HTML flow objects will be familiar to the readers of this book, the trick is to think of them as flow objects rather than switches. DSSSL flow objects are internationalized so that languages with different writing directions can be supported. The following flow objects are the subset that it is proposed to support in XSL (taken from the spec).

Flow Object	Description
scroll	Used for online display
paragraph, **paragraph-break**	Used for paragraphs
character	Used for text
line-field	Used for lists
external-graphic	Used for including graphic images
horizontal-rule, **vertical-rule**	Used for horizontal rules (note that the DSSSL "rule" flow object will be split into these two rules to eliminate the name conflict) (like **HR** in HTML) and vertical rules
score	Used for underlining and scoring
embedded-text	Used for bi-directional text
box	Used for borders

Table Continued on Following Page

Flow Object	Description
`table`	Flow objects for tables
`table-part`	
`table-column`	
`table-row`	
`table-cell`	
`table-border`	
`sequence`	Used for specifying inherited characteristics
`display-group`	Used for controlling the positioning of groups of displayed flow objects
`simple-page-sequence`	Used for simple page layout
`link`	Used for hypertext links

Possible Changes to the Spec

XSL is a rapidly evolving language, and discussion about its future takes place on an XSL discussion list. To subscribe to this list send an email with the word "subscribe" in the body of the text, as follows:

```
To:- xsl-list-request@mulberrytech.com
Subject:- [blank]
Body:- subscribe
```

Recent discussion may suggest that XSL may be modulised into a tree to tree transformation language for conversion into HTML and a separate formatting grammar, based on DSSSL flow objects. Only time will tell, but it is likely that the basics will remain the same.

Here is a quote from one of the W3C working group to the XSL list.

> *"This formatting grammar will be based initially on DSSSL flow objects, with some unification of concepts from CSS and HTML. But by splitting XSL, we can independently use the two parts–HTML can be generated with only the transformation language, the formatting grammar can be used with alternate creation methods, including hand-authoring and Active Server Pages. More details to the list when the WG gets further along on this."*

Summary

In this chapter we had a more detailed look at the possibilities of XSL.

- We looked at how to use the **`<select-elements>`** element to filter and reorder our sheet.
- We looked at the use of style rules, modes, and macros and looked at how to cascade rules.
- Examined the basic document object model and how it can be used with XSL.
- Saw how scripting can be used to extend XSL.
- Looked a little at the future direction of XSL.

That completes our look at XSL. We will have a look at some of the possible alternatives to XSL in the next chapter.

References

The XSL Discussion List

All the technical discussion on XSL. Also available in a digest form. To subscribe:

```
<xsl-list-request@mulberrytech.com>:  subscribe
```

Document Object Models

The still incomplete draft of the W3 DOM for XML and HTML:

```
http://www.w3.org/TR/WD-DOM/level-one-core-971209
```

Microsoft's implementation of the XML DOM for IE4. Used in this chapter.

```
http://www.microsoft.com/xml/articles/xmlmodel.htm
```

Tutorials

Microsoft's tutorial to use with their processor. An excellent adjunct to this book.

```
http://www.microsoft.com/xml/xsl/tutorial/tutorial.htm
```

Paul Prescott's tutorial on DSSSL. An outstanding tutorial from a true educator. It even makes DSSSL seem easy!

```
http://itrc.uwaterloo.ca:80/~papresco/dsssl/tutorial.html
```

Specs

The original note:

```
http://www.w3.org/TR/NOTE-XSL.html
```

General

Links to every where!

```
http://www.finetuning.com/xsl.html#xsl
```

Exercises

1. Write a simple piece of JavaScript using the CSS visibility property, and pass it through to your output using XSL, so that when you click on an item it disappears and reappears again.

12

Scripting with Style (or Styling with Script)

This chapter reviews some of the ways that scripting can be used to help in styling documents. If you don't know any JavaScript, or are a little rusty in it, you may want to review a text such as *Instant JavaScript, ISBN 1861001274 from Wrox Press. Instant HTML Programmer's Reference, ISBN 1861001568, from Wrox Press* also has an excellent section on JavaScript. This book contains a JavaScript tutorial at Appendix G that you might find helpful. This is in no way meant to be exhaustive, and gurus of DHTML may want to skip this chapter. This chapter is really here to demonstrate some of the possibilities that script has for styling.

We will review what is commonly known as Dynamic HTML and look at Communicator 4 and IE4's versions of it. Here are some of the topics we will cover

- Differentiating between browsers using script.
- Creating different style sheets for different browsers.
- Calling external script files.
- Dynamic styling in IE4, including rewriting pages, animation, movement, and drag and drop.
- Dynamic styling in Communicator including using the **<LAYER>** tag to create special effects in Communicator.

Let's begin by taking a look at how you differentiate between browsers using script.

Differentiating between Browsers

As we have seen time and again throughout this book the Browser Wars continue to wreak havoc on the front line soldiers (us!). In their zeal to create a loyal customer base the major players keep adding new features that don't operate in the others browsers. Their interpretation of the W3C CSS standard is also different.

I try to think of a non-Machiavellian interpretation for the different interpretation of the W3C standard, but I can't. If in doubt as to what something means, all you have to do is *ask* the author of the standard, Bert Bos, how something should be interpreted and he will tell you. I know, I did it several times in researching to write this book. As both major players are members of the W3C you would think that this would be easier for them than it is for me. (Unless of course it's the same kind of psychology as not asking for directions when lost!) To see a list of the members go to **`http://www.w3.org/ Consortium/Member/List.html`**.

Perhaps it's just that it is too hard to alter the browser? Well, writing code for most of the implementations is not difficult, particularly if using the Windows API, I have done it several times. Plugging it into the current edition of the browser could prove a little more troublesome. However, if the browsers are written in an object-oriented fashion, it shouldn't be too difficult to change, particularly with the wealth of programming talent that they have at their disposal. Perhaps the following comment from the CSS style list sums it all up!

> *"We all know that both major market browsers have sacrificed standards compliance in favour of backwards compatibility. Netscape was always worried that web pages that displayed under an old version would be broken under a new version, and hence carried implementation bugs (oh, I'm sorry, implementation ISSUES) up to the fourth generation. And IE was initially so caught up in mimicking Netscape in implementation so people would not prefer it over IE, that it copied most of the bugs. And now we're in a feature race, especially when it comes to DOM/scripting, and the two browsers look as much alike as, well, two things that aren't very much alike :-)"*
>
> *Stephanos Piperoglo*

Whatever the reason the fact is that us poor souls have to live with it. We can do one of several things.

- We can write code to the lowest common denominator. (Best viewed in Mosaic 1.0)
- We can ignore one of the major players and hope that it doesn't look too ugly in the other. This will cater for about 45% of our viewers. (However, this is a great option if writing for an Intranet where you know what version of browser is going to be used.)
- We can try and write code that works in all browsers and is backwards compatible in all other versions. (I've tried this. This solution is fine if you don't mind poor sleep patterns, ulcers, and no love life!)
- We can write just for the latest versions i.e. 4 and above, use style sheets and make sure that our documents degrade gracefully to simple HTML.

This latter method strikes me as the way to go, as it has several advantages.

- It will reach 90% of the browser users with great looking pages.
- The content just has to be written once.
- We just have to write different style sheets, and different scripts for the places where the browsers differ.

Luckily it is not too difficult to distinguish between the different types of browsers using JavaScript and the browser object model:

Method	Description
navigator.userAgent	Returns a string containing the browser version, brand, and platform.
navigator.appName	Returns a string with the Name of the maker.
navigator.appVersion	Returns a string with several items, the first letter(number) of which happens to be the version number

You can also differentiate between browsers using the Navigator Object, which we'll cover next. The Navigator object is part of browser object model and is supported by both Microsoft Internet Explorer and Netscape Communicator. It contains four properties, which allow us to get information about user agent. These properties are listed below.

Property	Contents
appCodeName	The code name of the browser
appName	The product name of the browser
appVersion	The version of the browser
userAgent	The user-agent (browser name) header sent in the HTTP protocol from the client to the server

The example below shows how to get the values of these properties.

```
<HTML>
<HEAD>
 <TITLE>Navigator Object Properties</TITLE>
</HEAD>
<BODY onLoad=broType();>
<script language="JavaScript">
 function broType()
 {
  document.forms[0].elements[0].value = navigator.appName;
  document.forms[0].elements[1].value = navigator.appVersion;
  document.forms[0].elements[2].value = navigator.appCodeName;
  document.forms[0].elements[3].value = navigator.userAgent;
 }
```

```
</script>
<P align="center"><font size=5 color="blue">
 <b>Navigator Object Properties</b>
</P>
<center>
 <form>
  <table border=2>
   <tr>
    <td>appName</td><td><input type=text size=60></td>
   </tr>
   <tr>
    <td>appVersion</td><td><input type=text size=60></td>
   </tr>
   <tr>
    <td>appCodeName</td><td><input type=text size=60></td>
   </tr>
   <tr>
    <td>userAgent</td><td><input type=text size=60></td>
   </tr>
  </table>
 </form>
</BODY>
</HTML>
```

and the results you get from running it on Communicator and IE4 are as follows;

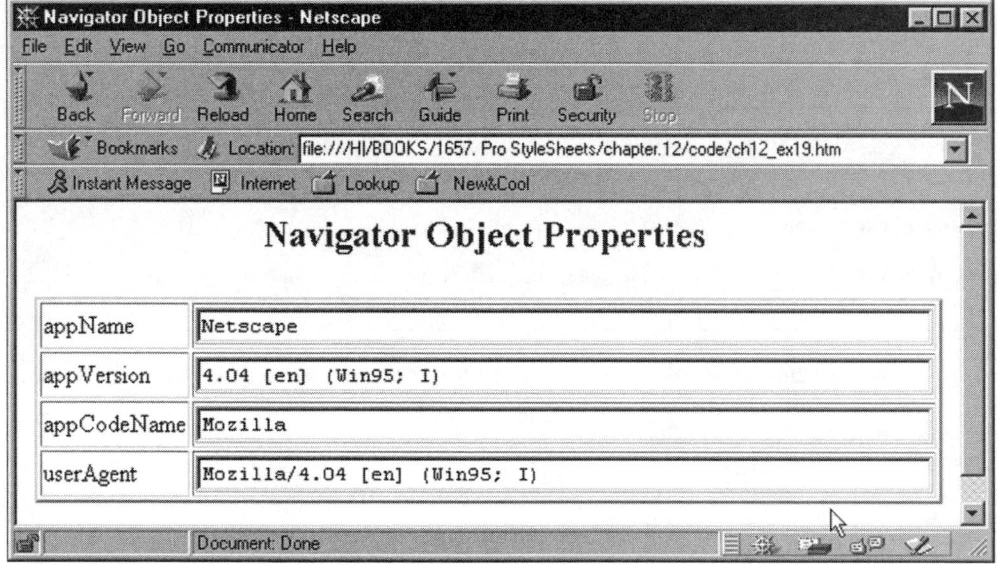

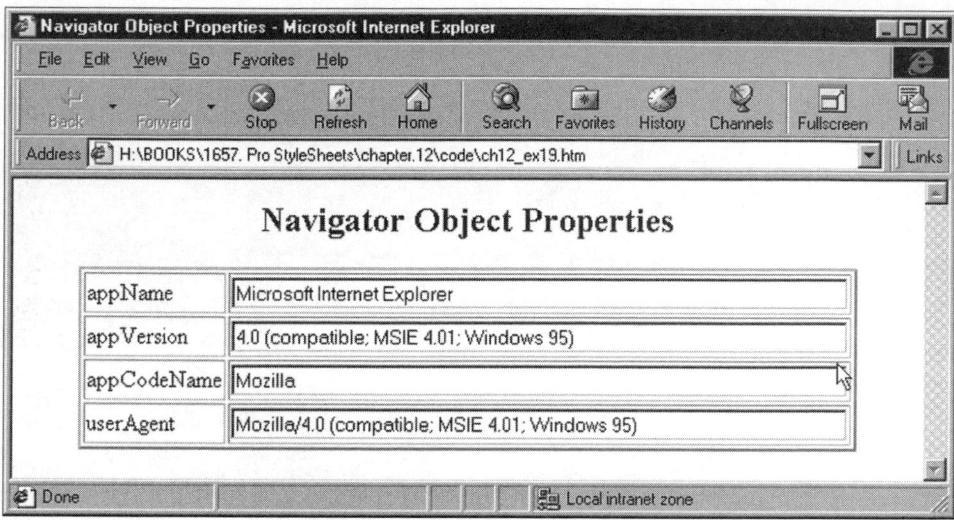

As you can see from the screenshots above, using Navigator object methods we can determine the name of the browser, its version and the platform the client is running. This can help us to make programming decisions about the features supported by particular client. So, once you've identified what browser the client is running, how do you adjust your styling to fit? The next section gives you some ideas.

Writing Differential Style Sheets

The following code shows one approach to this problem. It writes different style sheets for different browsers, and offers an alternate site for those viewers with neither of the major browsers.

This code could be easily modified to link to outside style sheets, outside JavaScript files etc.

```
<HTML>
<HEAD>

<TITLE> Differentiating Browsers</TITLE>
<SCRIPT>

      //This script loads different style sheets for different browser
//versions.
      //Author Frank Boumphrey
      //Written 11/5/97
      //Last revised 3:59 PM 3/13/98

function vertype(){

      ////////////////////////////////////////////////////////////////
      //this function returns the version type of the browser      //
      //ie4 if IE4 or greater                                       //
      //nav if Navigator4 or greater                                //
      //other if none of the above                                  //
      ////////////////////////////////////////////////////////////////
```

```
//declare function variables

var browType=""
var vnum=""
var isie4
//load function variables

      browType=navigator.appName;

//returns first character of appVersion(which is the version number)

      vnum=navigator.appVersion.charAt(0);


      if(browType=="Microsoft Internet Explorer" && vnum > 3)
            {
            isie4="ie4";
            }
      else if(browType=="Netscape" && vnum > 3)
            {
            isie4="nav";
            }
      else
            {
            isie4="other";

      //Use a confirm to reroute others or tell them to get lost!!

      if(confirm("This browser probably does not support Dynamic
HTML.\nClick OK to go to our non-DHTML website \nClick Cancel to continue
here.")==true)
      {location.href="altern.htm";}
            }
      return isie4
            }

function writestyle(e){


//////////////////////////////////////////////////////////////////////////////
//                                                                          //
//this function writes different stylesheets for the different browser     //
//                                                                          //
//      versions                                                            //
//                                                                          //
//////////////////////////////////////////////////////////////////////////////

      if(e=="ie4")
            {
            //write the style sheet for IE4
            document.write("<STYLE>.ie4{color:navy; font-size:40pt; font-
style:italic;}</STYLE>");
            }
      if(e=="nav")
```

```
            {
            //write the style sheet for Communicator 4.
            //Also demonstrates how to split between lines.
             document.write(
             "<STYLE>.nav{color:teal;"
            +" font-size:36pt;"
            +"font-style:bold;}"
            +"</STYLE>");
             }
            if(e=="other")
            {
      //note this alert still appears even if you select OK in alert above
in vertype().
            alert("No styling is being applied to this document");
            }
            return ;
            }

      //the following code calls the functions

      var browtype=vertype();

      var e=writestyle(browtype);

</SCRIPT>
</HEAD>
<BODY>

<DIV CLASS="ie4">This text will be in Navy 40 point italic script if being
run on IE4 or higher.</DIV>
<DIV CLASS="nav">This text will be in Teal 36 point bold script if being
run on Communicator 4 or higher.</DIV>

</BODY>
</HTML>
```

Note that there are several places where the lines of code wrap. This of course should not happen in your code. If you want to use this code it is best to download it as file **ch12_ex1.htm** from the web site at **http://rapid.wrox.co.uk/books/1657**.

Here are a couple of screenshots which illustrate the effect, and then we'll go through the code which produces it in some detail.

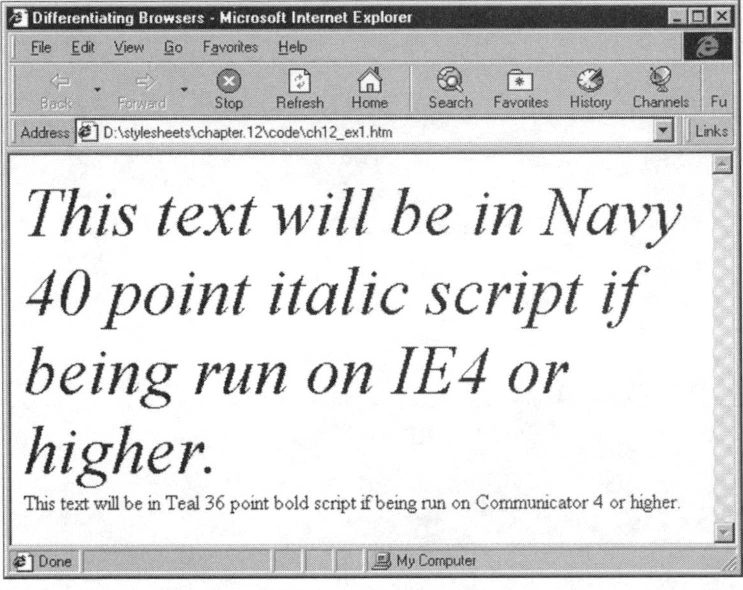

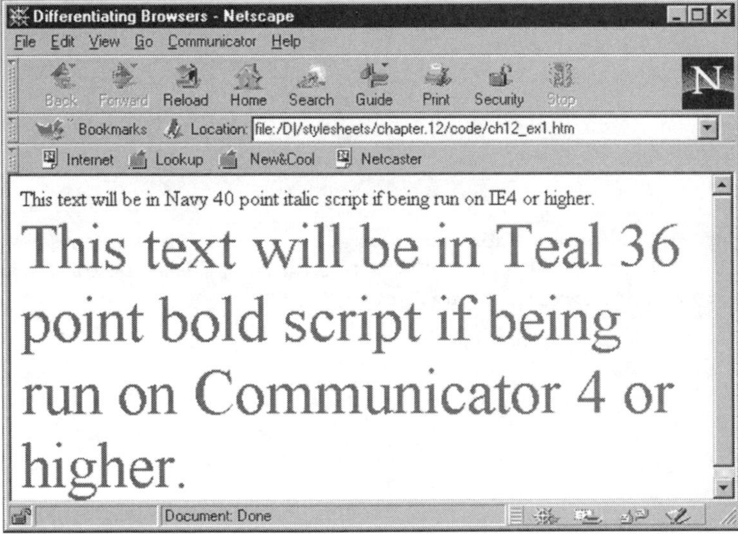

Comment on the Code

Let's take a look at the code we used to achieve this effect.

```
function vertype()
```

This function is the main function, which returns a string depending on the type of browser it is operating on. The string is returned in the variable **isie4**.

```
browType=navigator.appName;
```

This loads the maker's name into the variable **browType**.

```
vnum=navigator.appVersion.charAt(0);
```

This uses the string objects method **charAt(index)** to return the first character (i.e. the zeroth character) of the **appVersion** string, which conveniently happens to be the version number!

```
if(browType=="Microsoft Internet Explorer" && vnum > 3)
```

A simple flow choice **if** (notice the double ampersand and double equals). The joy (and the curse!) of JavaScript is that it is so loosely typed, so our string **3** is automatically converted into a numerical 3.

```
return isie4
```

Now whenever we call our function, a string containing **ie4**, **nav**, or **other** will be returned.

We use this in the rest of the code to write our style sheets. Remember that JavaScript functions return a string.

```
document.write(
      "<STYLE>.nav{color:teal;"
            +" font-size:36pt;"
            +"font-style:bold;}"
      +"</STYLE>");
```

We have to concatenate if we want to spread the code over several lines.

You may have noticed a lack of terseness in the JavaScript that I have written. In many places I have put in redundant expressions, and I have put in a lot of comments. There are several reasons for this

- I am not a "code-head". I like my code to be reasonably understandable!
- I like to comment all my code. My memory isn't what it was! (See Chapter 2, section on *Commenting*)
- The extra time to download a few additional lines of code is negligible compared to downloading a small image.
- If I do want to compact the code, I keep a non-compacted version in a separate file for reference.

Having said that, most of the following files have had their comments removed for the sake of space in the book!

Referring to an External JavaScript File

We can of course put the code in an external file (remember to leave off the **<SCRIPT>** tags), and just call that file. In the following example **browver.js** contains the function **vertype()** and looks like this;

```
function vertype(){
var browType=""
var vnum=""
var isie4
//load function variables

      browType=navigator.appName;

//returns first character of appVersion(which is the version number)

      vnum=navigator.appVersion.charAt(0);


      if(browType=="Microsoft Internet Explorer" && vnum > 3)
            {
            isie4="ie4";
            }
      else if(browType=="Netscape" && vnum > 3)
            {
            isie4="nav";
            }
      else
            {
            isie4="other";

      //Use a confirm to reroute others or tell them to get lost!!

      if(confirm("This browser probably does not support Dynamic
HTML.\nClick OK to go to our non-DHTML website \nClick Cancel to continue
here.")==true)
      {location.href="altern.htm";}
            }
      return isie4
            }
```

Note that you must put the next call in another pair of tags (somebody told me the reason why once, and it made sense at the time, but the explanation would take up a few pages, and really life's too short...).

The next call simply calls our function name directly. It is as if we have pasted in the contents of **browver.js** between the first set of **<SCRIPT>** brackets.

```
<HTML>
<HEAD>
<SCRIPT SRC="browver.js">
</SCRIPT>
<SCRIPT>
```

```
if(vertype()=="ie4")
      document.write("<STYLE>P{color:red}</STYLE>")
if(vertype()=="nav")
      document.write("<STYLE>P{color:blue}</STYLE>")

//remember to use the double equals and quote the returned string

</SCRIPT>
</HEAD>
<BODY>
<P>If this text is in red, you are running IE4 or higher, if its blue you
are running Communicator 4 or higher.</P>

</BODY>
</HTML>
```

Screenshots of the result of this example won't help you much, as you have to be able to see which color text is displayed in the browser to check that it works. However, the files **browver.js** and **ch12_ex2.htm** are available on the web site at **http://rapid.wrox.co.uk/books/1657**.

Calling Differential Pages

Sometimes it's just easier to generate different pages for different browsers. One good way to do this is to have a "Please wait" page. To prevent it from flashing on and off, which can be annoying, in the following example we have used the JavaScript **setTimeout()** function to call the function **vertype()** after 3 seconds.

To try this code out for yourself, you'll need to create a couple of simple **.htm** files called **nav1.htm** and **ie41.htm**, so that you can check that the right brower is calling the right file after the 3 second interval. These are available on the web site, along with the code set out below, **ch12_ex3.htm**.

```
<HTML>
<HEAD>
<SCRIPT>

function vertype(){

//declare function variables

      var browType=""
      var vnum=""
      var isie4

//load function variables

      browType=navigator.appName;

//returns first character of appVersion(which is the version number)

      vnum=navigator.appVersion.charAt(0);

      if(browType=="Microsoft Internet Explorer" && vnum > 3)
            {
```

```
            isie4="ie4";
            {location.href="ie41.htm";}
            }
      else if(browType=="Netscape" && vnum > 3)
            {
            isie4="nav";
            {location.href="nav1.htm";}
            }
      else
            {
            isie4="other";
            {location.href="other.htm";}
            }

      return isie4
}

</SCRIPT>
<STYLE>
...styling goes here
</STYLE>
</HEAD>
<BODY STYLE="background-color:white;">
<DIV id=xyz1>Wrox Press</DIV>
<BR>
<DIV id=xyz2>We are preparing the page that your particular browser
requires.</DIV>
<BR>
<DIV id=xyz3>Please wait</DIV>

<!--the following script will call the appropriate HTML page 3 seconds
after the index page is launched-->
<SCRIPT>
setTimeout('vertype()',3000)
</SCRIPT>
<!--This is for browsers with no scripting abilities-->
<NOSCRIPT>If you do not run script go to our <A HREF=
"noscr.htm">noscript</A> page</NOSCRIPT>
</BODY>
</HTML>
```

We have not, in either of the previous examples, hidden the script or the style sheets from non-compliant browsers. It goes without saying that in fact we should have used comment tags.

```
<SCRIPT>
<!--
//Hide from non-compliant browsers
code here.....
//End hiding-->
</SCRIPT>
```

This is just plain good practice!

Active or Dynamic Styling

Having shown you various ways to differentiate between the two major players, we can now get on with the next topic of dynamic styling. Unfortunately (and predictably) both Microsoft and Netscape use very different methods, so if you want to use dynamic styling you are going to have to write two sets of pages.

We will look at Microsoft's version first, and particularly at their use of the HTML Document Object Model.

Document Object Model

We had a look at what a Document Object Model (DOM) was in the last chapter and we took a quick look at the Microsoft, Netscape and W3C Document Object Models in the *Document Object Model* section of Chapter 7. We will go into a little more detail in this chapter, because it is such an important concept. Why?

Well a full document object model gives a complete description of the whole document. By way of analogy, if I made a model plane, there are two ways that I could find out about the model, I could look at the model itself, or I could look at a description of the model.

If I have a document I can do the same thing, I can look at the document itself or I can look at a description of the document. A DOM is a detailed description of that document. A full DOM allows you to completely reconstruct the document from the DOM. Why is this so important in styling and in JavaScript?

Well basically any JavaScript method consists of:

`[object].[method]`

e.g. **`document.write`**(*this and that*)

and the DOM now gives us access to the whole document as a set of objects to restyle it, rewrite it or otherwise manipulate it. We are now only limited by the methods and the user agent's implementation of the methods.

Consider the following simple HTML document, which is on the web site as **`ch12_ex4.htm`**.

```
<HTML>
<HEAD>

<TITLE> DOM Demonstration</TITLE>
<SCRIPT>
//here's a comment
</SCRIPT>
<STYLE>
P{font-size:16pt}
BODY{background-color:white}
</STYLE>
</HEAD>
<BODY>
```

```
<H2>A heading</H2>
<P ID="XYZ"> A paragraph with <EM>emphasised</EM> text</P>
<DIV> A div containing a <SPAN STYLE="font-weight:bold"> span </SPAN> in
it</DIV>
<P> the last text before the script</P>
</BODY>
</HTML>
```

This could either be listed as a collection of tags, or as a tree shown here:

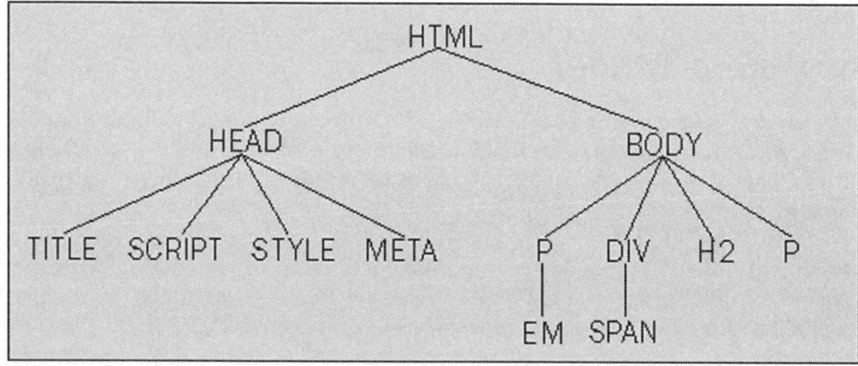

In a now familiar fashion, we can say that every element has a parent (except **<HTML>**) and children (except the end elements). For example, the **<DIV>** has **<BODY>** as a parent and **<SPAN>** as a child.

If we wanted to refer to **<DIV>** we could use the following:

```
HTML.BODY.DIV
```

but this could refer to more than one **DIV** if they were present. So the DOM also makes an array or collection of all the tags, and labels them from 0 (remember in computing nearly all arrays start from 0) to as many as the document has (also referred to as the document's **length** in the DOM). In the example shown above, **<HTML>** would be item number 0 and the last **<P>** would be item number 13.

To refer to a tag in JavaScript we can use the syntax:

document.all [*indexnumber*]

To show how this works out in practice add the following code to your HTML document above: (note that the line breaks in the book where it shouldn't, if in doubt check out the code on the website at **http://rapid.wrox.co.uk/books/1657**).

```
HTML>
<HEAD>

<TITLE>DOM Demonstration</TITLE>
<SCRIPT>
```

```
//heres a comment
</SCRIPT>
<STYLE>
P{font-size:16pt}
BODY{background-color:white}
</STYLE>
<META>
</HEAD>
<BODY>

<H2>A heading</H2>
<P id="XYZ"> A paragraph with <EM>emphasised</EM> text</P>
<DIV> A div containing a <SPAN style="font-weight:bold"> span </SPAN> in
it</DIV>
<P> the last text before the script</P>

<SCRIPT>

      var tagnums=document.all.length

      document.write("Number of tags before we start generating breaks :-
"+document.all.length +"<BR>")
      for(var num=0;num <=tagnums-1;num++)
      {
      document.write("Tag Number" + num + ":-"+";  Name:-
"+document.all[num].tagName+"<BR>");
      }
      document.write("Number of tags after we stop generating breaks :-
"+document.all.length);
</SCRIPT>
</SCRIPT>
<P> the last text</P>
</BODY>
</HTML>
```

Now run the script on IE4.

The document object model is only supported in IE4, but for once this is probably not deliberate. IE4 came out after the standard was postulated, in fact they delayed its release to support the standard, Navigator came out before. This is such a powerful concept that Netscape will almost certainly bring it out in their next release. It is currently partially supported through their Tags collection.

The result is shown in the screenshot:

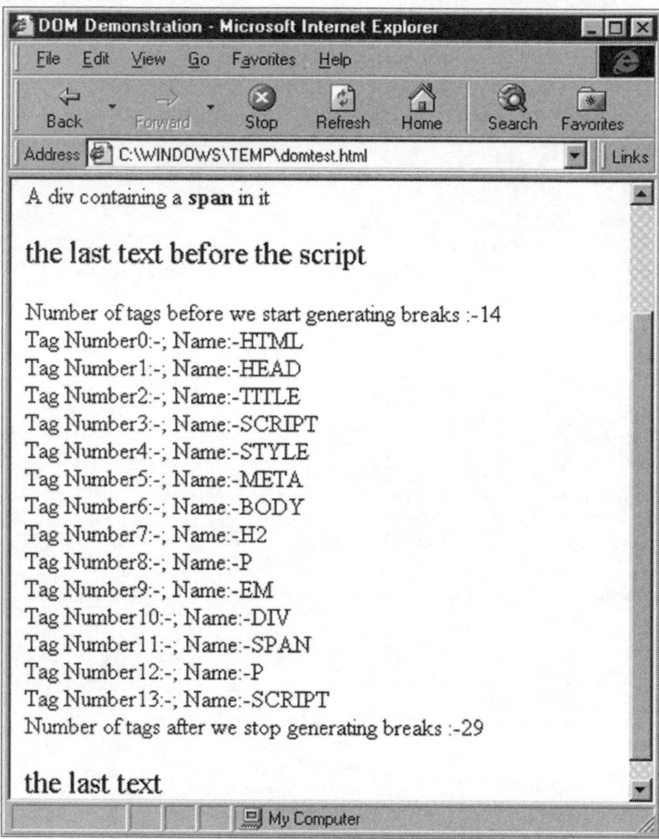

Notes on the Code

`document.all.length` makes use of the DOM property **`length`** and returns the number of tags which we load into the variable **`tagnums`**.

```
document.write("Number of tags before we start generating breaks :-
"+document.all.length +"<BR>")
```

(Should all be on one line.) This writes out the number of tags before we start the loop.

```
for(var num=0; num <=tagnums-1;num++)
```

will be familiar to most readers. For those who it is not, it is a way of repeating a number of actions called a loop. The first expression **`num=0`** tells the loop where to begin, **`num <=tagnums-1;`** tells the loop when to run. i.e. while **`num`** is less than or equal to **`tagnums-1`** it will run, when **`num`** becomes greater than **`tagnums-1`** the loop will stop. The third expression **`num++`** increases the value of **`num`** by one each time we run through the loop. Note how we declare **`num`** as a variable in the loop i.e. **`var num`**. Note that **`num`** only runs to **`tagnums-1`**. This is because the length starts from 0 not 1.

```
document.write("Tag Number" + num + ":-"+";  Name:-
"+document.all[num].tagName+"<BR>");
```

(This should all be on one line) actually writes out the tag number and tag name using the DOM **tagName** property. This also generates a new **
** tag each time , so that after the loop the number of tags will increase.

```
document.write("Number of tags after we stop generating breaks :-
"+document.all.length);
```

(Should be all on one line.) Writes out the new total of tags.

Referring to Document Objects

We saw one way above to refer to a document object, namely:

document.all[*indexnumber***]**

There are several other ways, namely

document.all["ID"]

or just plain

ID

or by its position relative to another item in the array;

document.all[*indexnumber***].all[***indexnumber***]** (see example below under *Getting Element Content*)

If we are writing inline script we can just use **this** to refer to the tag the code is embedded in e.g.

```
<H1 Onmouseover= "this.style.color= 'blue'">this heading feels blue!!<H1>
```

Getting Element Content

IE4 offers four interesting properties to let us get at our elements

OuterHTML - returns all the text and its tags including the enclosing tags
OuterText - just returns the text (see further explanation below)
InnerHTML - returns all the text and the enclosed tags but excludes the enclosing tags of the element itself
innerText - just returns the text (see further explanation below)

The difference between inner and outer text emerges when we use these properties to remove text. Then **innerText** will remove just the text enclosed between the tags, **outerText** will remove the tags as well. Add the highlighted script to our simple HTML document, **ch12_ex4.htm** above, save it as **ch12_ex5.htm** and run it. Here's what the code looks like:

```
<HTML>
<HEAD>

<TITLE> DOM Demonstration</TITLE>
<SCRIPT>
//here's a comment
</SCRIPT>
<STYLE>
P{font-size:16pt}
BODY{background-color:white}
</STYLE>
<META>
</HEAD>
<BODY>
<H2>A heading</H2>
<P ID="XYZ"> A paragraph with <EM>emphasised</EM> text</P>
<DIV> A div containing a <SPAN STYLE="font-weight:bold"> span </SPAN> in
it</DIV>
<P> the last text before the script</P>
<SCRIPT>
      //document.write(XYZ.outerHTML+"<BR>")
      document.write(XYZ.innerHTML+"<BR>")
      document.write(XYZ.outerText+"<BR>")
      document.write(XYZ.innerText+"<BR>")
      alert(document.all[8].outerHTML+"<BR>")
      document.write(document.all[8].innerHTML+"<BR>")
      document.write(document.all["XYZ"].tagName+"<BR>")
      document.write(document.all["XYZ"].innerHTML+"<BR>")
      //all[6] is the body, P is the second child of the body
      document.write(document.all[6].all[1].innerHTML+"<BR>")

</SCRIPT>
</BODY>
</HTML>
```

Firstly, you will see that we are illustrating the different ways of referring to the tag, **<P ID="XYZ">**, as follows:

By its ID **document.write(XYZ.innerHTML+"<BR>")**
By its index number **alert(document.all[8].outerHTML+"<BR>")**
By its ID using different syntax
document.write(document.all["XYZ"].tagName+"<BR>")
By its position relative to another item in the array
document.write(document.all[6].all[1].innerHTML+"<BR>")

Secondly, you will note that I have commented out the **document.write** that would have written out the complete tag. If I had not done this, I would have written a **P** with an identical ID to the first, and I would have broken the rule that all the IDs in a document must be unique. The script compiler would have got confused and returned an **undefined** for the rest of my objects.

Try it and see!

Thirdly you will see that we are also demonstrating the different effects which **innerText** and **outerText** and **innerHTML** and **outerHTML** have on the object we have selected. To fully understand this, we need to see what the code produces on screen. We show two screenshots, the first up to and including the alert line of code, the second showing what the screen looks like once the code has run its course.

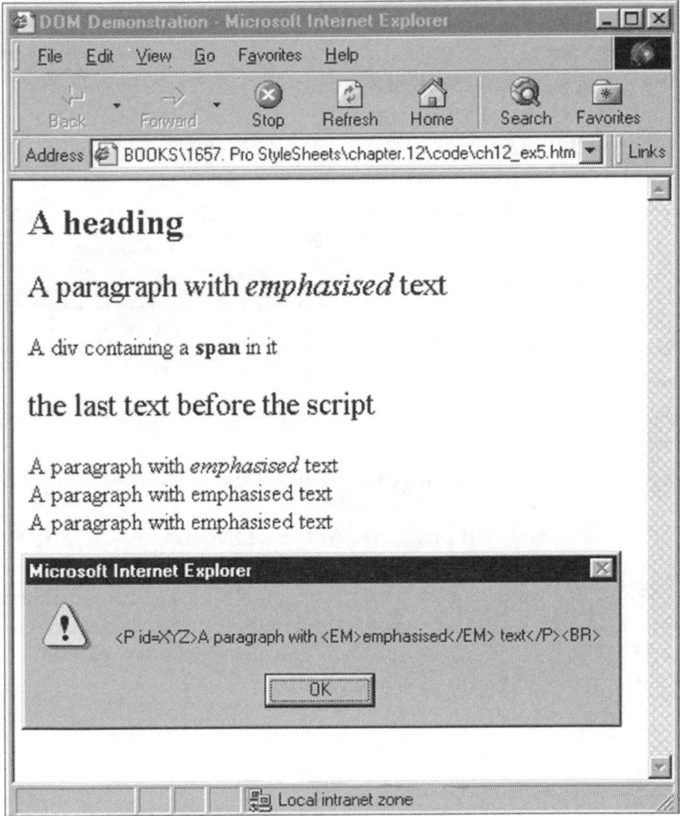

Note how the alert dialog box doesn't give a literal rendering of our HTML, but rather what the browser stores it as. This is the browser's interpretation of what we have written. The property **text** will render a literal interpretation, however this property only works with a **<SCRIPT>** tag!

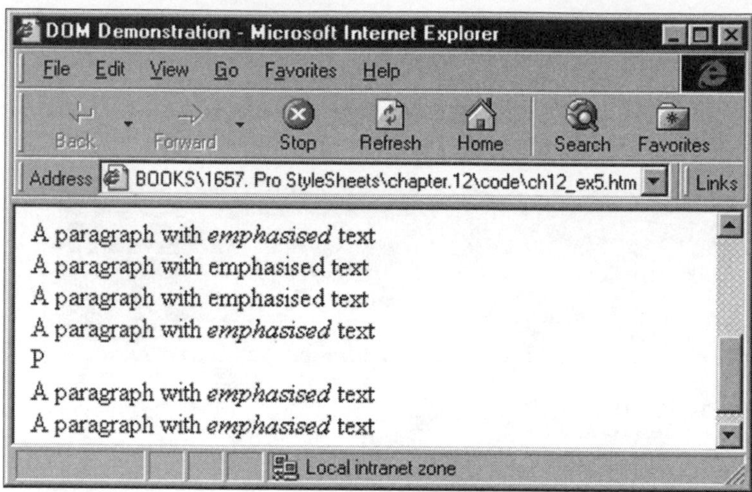

To summarize, let's go over the output illustrated above and see how the tag:

```
<P ID="XYZ"> A paragraph with <EM>emphasised</EM> text</P>
```

has been shown in the browser according to the different properties assigned to it.

The first line used the **innerHTML** property, so the **<EM>** tags are included and we see their effect. The second and third lines use **outerText** and **innerText** respectively, so we see just the text enclosed by the **<P>** with no emphasis. The alert box above used the **outerHTML** property, so we saw the entire tag. The fourth line on screen used **innerHTML** again, so the emphasis returned. The fifth line asked for the tag name, and so we see the P. The last two lines both use **innerHTML** so we see the effect of the **<EM>** tags at work again.

Event Model

With the advent of the DOM, Microsoft also introduced some great new events. Every element is capable of expressing these events.

Keyboard Events	Description
onkeypress	Will trigger an event when a key is pressed AND released.
onkeydown	The even will be triggered when the key is pressed.
onkeyup	The even will be triggered when the key is released.

Mouse Events	Description
`onmouseover`	The event will be triggered when the mouse passes over the object.
`onmouseout`	The event will be triggered when the mouse leaves the object.
`onmousedown`	The event will be triggered when the mouse button over the object is depressed.
`onmouseup`	The event will be triggered when the mouse button over the object is released.
`onmousemove`	The event will be triggered every time the mouse moves and is over the object.
`onclick`	The event will be triggered when the mouse button over the object is clicked.
`ondblclick`	The event will be triggered when the mouse button over the object is double clicked.

Dynamic Styling in IE4

Now that we've had a good look at the DOM and how it accesses objects, let's have a look at some of the ways we can use it to create some dynamic styling in IE4. Although the examples are very simple (they have been kept so purposely), we can develop and adorn them to create some quite complex and dramatic effects.

Just a word of warning before we start. Remember Brady's three laws. (Brady is Murphy's dumb brother in law.)

- When the only tool you have is a hammer, everything looks like a nail!
- Just because you can do something doesn't mean you have to do it!
- The enemy of good is perfect!
- Keep it simple stupid!

I know that's four, but Brady never was too good at counting. Remember the **`<BLINK>`** tag? Enough said! However, we can produce some really neat effects.

CSS Properties and JavaScript

CSS properties contain a hyphen in the middle. This, of course, is a no-no in JavaScript as the hyphen is too easily confused with the minus operater. To overcome this problem, convert all hyphenated properties to camelBack notation. E.g. **`font-size`** becomes **`fontSize`**

Remember that JavaScript is case-sensitive, so remember to Capitalize that second word! I'd swap all my royalties in exchange for a penny for each time the readers of this book are going to forget this!

Highlighting Text

One of the simplest (and easiest) effects that we can achieve is to highlight text as the mouse pointer passes over it.

At its simplest this is almost trivial.

```
<SPAN ONMOUSEOVER="this.style.color='red'" ONMOUSEOUT
="this.style.color='navy'">Heading </SPAN>
```

`this` is a keyword that refers to the tag it is embedded in. Notice the use of the single quotes around the values **`red`** and **`navy`** inside the double quotes. This simple line of code will make the word Heading appear in red when the mouse pointer is over it, and navy when the mouse pointer leaves it.

If we want to get a few more effects, such as combining a change of font, or altering a background color then we have to use a function. Here, **`this`** is passed to the function as a parameter, and both the background and the foreground colors are changed.

It is possible to make quite fancy drop-down menus using this technique.

```
<SCRIPT LANGUAGE=JAVASCRIPT>

      function changecolor(e){
            e.style.color="red";
            e.style.backgroundColor="yellow"
      }

      function changecolor2(e){
            e.style.color="navy";
            e.style.backgroundColor="#FFFF88"
      }

</SCRIPT>

<BODY>
<DIV>
<SPAN id=xyz1 ONMOUSEOVER="changecolor(this)"
ONMOUSEOUT="changecolor2(this)">First</SPAN>
<SPAN ONMOUSEOVER="this.style.color='red'"
ONMOUSEOUT="this.style.color='navy'">Second</SPAN>
<SPAN ONMOUSEOVER="changecolor(this)"
ONMOUSEOUT="changecolor2(this)">Third</SPAN>
<SPAN ONMOUSEOVER="this.style.color='red'"
ONMOUSEOUT="this.style.color='navy'">Fourth</SPAN>
<SPAN ONMOUSEOVER="changecolor(this)"
ONMOUSEOUT="changecolor2(this)">Fifth</SPAN>
</DIV>
```

*For those not too familiar with JavaScript, a **function** is a collection of code that does something every time it is called by an event. It can be fed data at one end (called **passing a parameter**) and it either uses that data to perform an action (as in this case), or it manipulates the data and returns the manipulated data.*

In this case the function **changecolor** is called by the event **onmouseover** and it is passed the name of the tag that the event is embedded in. However, instead of using **SPAN** as the name of the tag, **this** is used as an identifier object referring to the tag's name.

In this case the function **changecolor** is called by the event **onmouseover**. When the mouse moves over the **<SPAN>** element the identity of the particular **<SPAN>** element it is moving over is passed to the function by using the **this** keyword, and the code in the function is executed with respect to that particular **<SPAN>**.

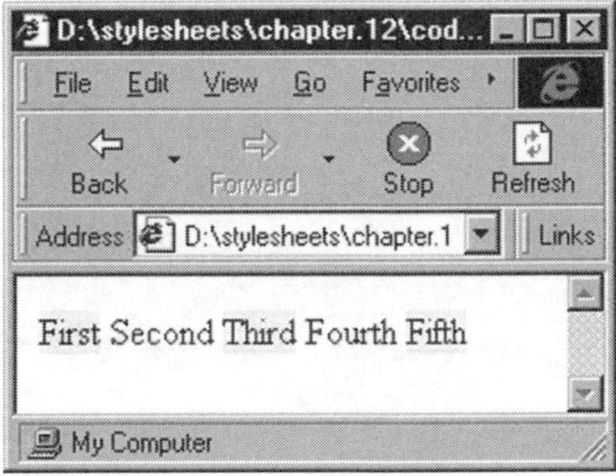

It then carries out various manipulations on the tag, in this example it changes the background colors of the words First Third and Fifth when the mouse pointer is moved over them.

Replacing or Toggling Text

We can use the **innerText** property to not only to read text but also to write it! This simple demonstration demonstrates this.

Rewrite the H2 tag as follows, save it as **ch12_ex8.htm**.

```
<HTML>
<HEAD>
</HEAD>
<BODY>
<H2 id="xyz1" STYLE="cursor:hand" onclick="changetext();">A heading</H2>
</BODY>
</HTML>
```

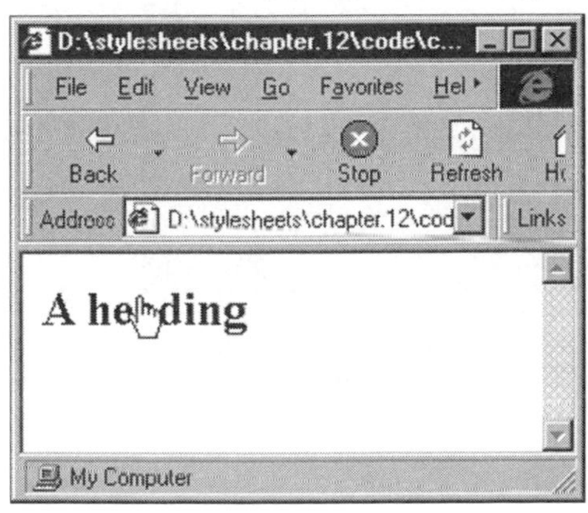

Note the **STYLE** property of **cursor**, which turns the pointer into a hand when it passes over the text, like this.

We use the event **onclick** to call the function **changetext()**
Add the highlighted script to **ch12_ex8.htm** and save it as **ch12_ex9.htm** as shown below.

```
<HTML>
<HEAD>
<SCRIPT LANGUAGE=JAVASCRIPT>

      function changetext(){
            if(xyz1.innerText=="A brand new heading")
            {
            xyz1.innerText="A heading";
            xyz1.style.fontSize="16pt";
            }
      else
            {
            xyz1.innerText="A brand new heading";
            xyz1.style.fontSize="22pt";
            }
            }

</SCRIPT>
</HEAD>
<BODY>
<H2 id="xyz1" STYLE="cursor:hand" onclick="changetext();">A heading</H2>
</BODY>
</HTML>
```

The function uses a simple **if..else** statement to rewrite the heading when we click on it. Note how we use **innerText** in two capacities. The first time we use it, it reads the inner text, and the second time we use it as a method to write the heading. In this example, we just use the **id** of the tag (**xyz1**) to refer to it in the function. The screenshot below shows what happens when you click on A heading.

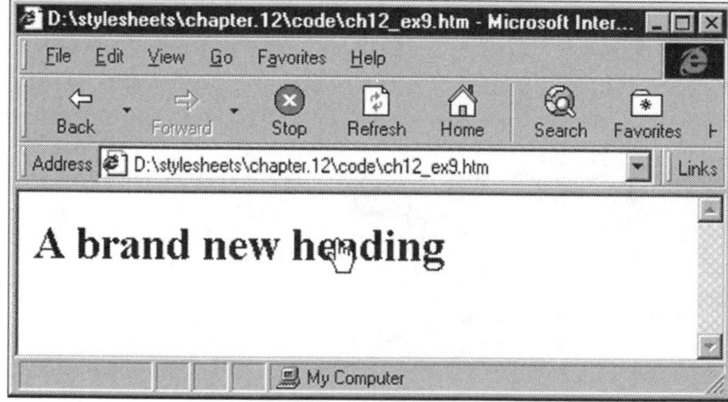

Another important point that this simple demonstration shows, is that when we substitute the larger font the whole of the HTML page re-flows to accommodate it just like a word processor would.

Extra credit: replace **innerText** with **outerText** and see what happens. (Hint it won't work because the tags with the **id#** disappear along with the text!)

Hiding an Element

By using either the CSS **visibility** or **display** property we can create some quite useful effects. If we make an element invisible by using **visibility:hidden** then we hide the element but leave untouched the space it occupied. If we use **display:none** then we not only hide the element we get rid of the space it occupied, causing the whole document to re-flow.

This can be useful in creating menus, dictionaries, etc. Let's see an example.

Change **<H2>** to read as follows, and add a **<DIV>** with the following **ID**:

```
<H2 id="xyz1" STYLE="cursor:hand" onclick="changetext2();">Hide the
text</H2>
<DIV id="xyz2">
      (Put what ever text you want to put here.)
</DIV>
```

Now add the following function.

```
<SCRIPT LANGUAGE=JAVASCRIPT>

      function changetext2(){
      if(xyz2.style.display==""||xyz2.style.display=="block")
            {
            xyz1.innerText="Display the text";
            xyz1.style.fontSize="16pt";
            xyz2.style.display="none";
            }
      else
            {
            xyz1.innerText="Hide the text";
            xyz1.style.fontSize="22pt";
            xyz2.style.display="block";
            }
      }

</SCRIPT>
```

So the full code looks like this;

```
<HTML>
<HEAD>
<SCRIPT LANGUAGE=JAVASCRIPT>

      function changetext2(){
      if(xyz2.style.display==""||xyz2.style.display=="block")
            {
            xyz1.innerText="Display the text";
            xyz1.style.fontSize="16pt";
            xyz2.style.display="none";
            }
      else
            {
            xyz1.innerText="Hide the text";
```

```
                xyz1.style.fontSize="16pt";
                xyz2.style.display="block";
                }
        }

</SCRIPT>
</HEAD>

<BODY>
<H2 id="xyz1" STYLE="cursor:hand" onclick="changetext2();">Hide the
text</H2>
<DIV id="xyz2">
        Now you see me, now you don't
</DIV>
<DIV>Does this line stay in the same position?</DIV>
</BODY>
</HTML>
```

Save it as **ch12_ex10.htm** and load it into your browser. The first thing you'll see is this;

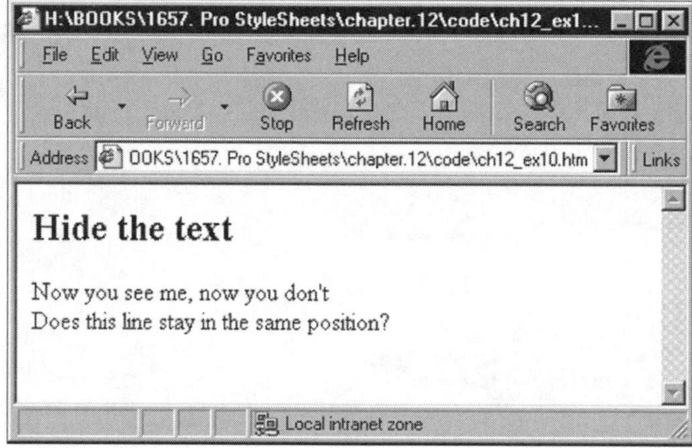

but when you click the heading Hide the text, it changes to this;

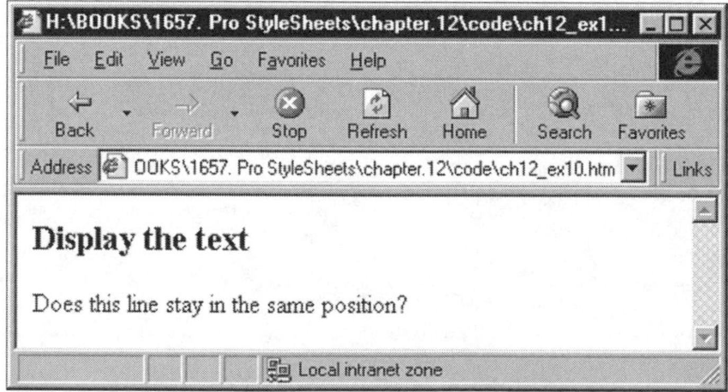

Note that by turning the **display** property to **none**, not only is the element not displayed, but neither are any of the children.

The default value for **display** is null or **""**, i.e. the **display** property takes the value assigned by the user agent for that particular tag which is **""**. For this reason we have to use the **or** operator (**||**) to cater for the situation where **display** is either **""** or **"block"**.

```
if(xyz2.style.display==""||xyz2.style.display=="block")
```

Note how we just use the id (**xyz2**) to identify the object.

The following function uses the **visibility** property instead of the **display** property. Amend **ch12_ex10.htm** using the code below and save it as **ch12_ex10a.htm**. Run them both and notice the difference.

```
function changetext2(){
        if(xyz2.style.visibility==""||xyz2.style.visibility=="visible")
                {
                xyz1.innerText="Display the text";
                xyz1.style.fontSize="16pt";
                xyz2.style.visibility="hidden";
                }
        else
                {
                xyz1.innerText="Hide the text";
                xyz1.style.fontSize="16pt";
                xyz2.style.visibility="visible";
                }
        }
```

The screenshots show the difference. If you look carefully you will see that when **display=none** is used (the screenshot on the right), the space occupied by the line disappears, whereas when **visibility=hidden** is used the space is preserved (the screenshot on the left).

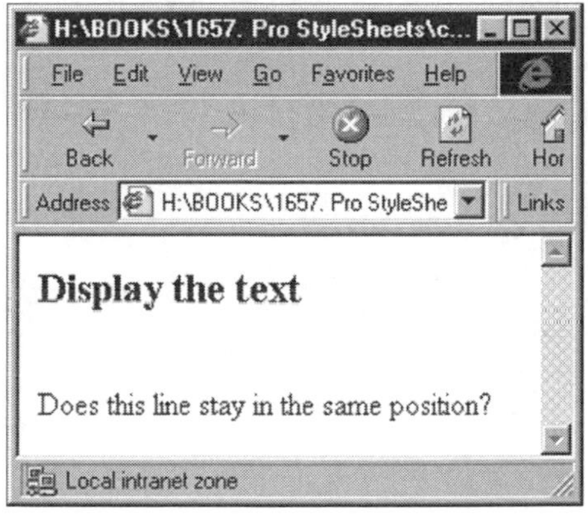

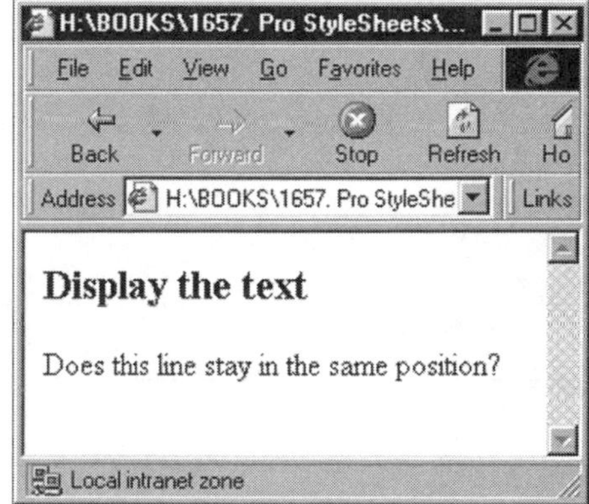

Using setInterval()

You thought that the **<BLINK>** element was bad? Wait and see what is possible with the **setInterval()** method! The **setInterval()** function causes events to fire at a regular interval. It has a similar use to the timers which are found in languages such as Visual Basic.

It takes the general syntax

setInterval('[function]',[interval in milliseconds])

Again, watch that upper case **I**.

As an example change the last example to read this:

```
<H2 id="xyz1" STYLE="cursor:hand"
onclick="setInterval('changetext2()',2000);">Hide the text</H2>
```

Now when you run the sample and click on the heading the whole page will change every two seconds. Now you can really drive your readers crazy!

Seriously though this is very useful for animated effects.

Animation

Simple or even quite complex animation is possible through the **setInterval()** function. Here we create our animation by positioning three images one above the other, using **setInterval** to change the z-index of the pictures.

```
<HTML>
<HEAD>
<TITLE>Winking Smiley I</TITLE>

<STYLE>
      .center{position:absolute;
            top:50%;
            left:50%;
            }
</STYLE>
<META>
</HEAD>
<BODY>

      <IMG ID="xyz2" CLASS="center" SRC="smiley2.gif">
      <IMG ID="xyz3" CLASS="center" SRC="smiley3.gif">
      <IMG ID="xyz1" CLASS="center" SRC="smiley.gif" STYLE="cursor:hand"
onclick="setInterval('timer()',500);">


<SCRIPT LANGUAGE=JAVASCRIPT>

      var counter=0;
            var runanimation=true;   //a boolean
```

```
        function timer(){

                counter++;

                if(counter==1 && runanimation==true)
                {
                        xyz1.style.zIndex="0";
                        xyz2.style.zIndex="-1";
                        xyz3.style.zIndex="-2";
                }

                if(counter==2  && runanimation==true)
                {
                        xyz2.style.zIndex="0";
                        xyz1.style.zIndex="-1";
                        xyz3.style.zIndex="-2";
                }

                if(counter==3  && runanimation==true)
                {
                        xyz3.style.zIndex="0";
                        xyz2.style.zIndex="-1";
                        xyz1.style.zIndex="-2";
                        counter=0;
                }

        }

/*This function toggles the animation. Note how counter needs to be reset
to 0*/

        function toggle(){

                if(runanimation==true)
                {
                        //alert(runanimation);
                        runanimation=false;
                        xyz4.innerText=runanimation;
                }

                else{
                        runanimation=true;
                        xyz4.innerText=runanimation;
                        counter=0
                }
        }
</SCRIPT>
<DIV onclick="toggle();">Click on the face to start animation click here to
toggle.Run animation=<SPAN id="xyz4">true</SPAN></DIV>
</BODY>
</HTML>
```

And here's what it looks like;

The code is very straight forward, essentially consisting of two functions, the second one being purely to switch on and off the animation.

Notice how we declare **`counter`** as a global function, and increment it by one each time **`timer()`** is called. We included the **`toggle`** function to show how to call a boolean variable, and also to illustrate the importance of re-setting variables when we interrupt a function.

A boolean type is a type that either returns true or false.

Movement

Movement is particularly easy using the CSS properties of **`top`** and/or **`left`**.

The following code causes the smiley to climb up the page. The amount of movement you can generate is limited only by the extent of your desire to annoy the viewer. The timer interval has been set for 50. You can set it for a lower interval than this, but 50 milliseconds is the smallest time interval you will be able to obtain on the Windows platform.

```
<HTML>
<HEAD>

<TITLE>Moving Smiley</TITLE>

<STYLE>
      .center{position:absolute;
            top:100%;
            left:50%;
            }
</STYLE>
<META>
</HEAD>
<BODY>
```

```
<IMG ID="xyz1" CLASS="center" SRC="smiley.gif" STYLE="cursor:hand"
onclick="setInterval('timer2()',50);">

<SCRIPT LANGUAGE=JAVASCRIPT>
      var counter=0;


      function timer2(){
            //this function move the image.
            counter++;
            var pos
            pos=100-counter + "%"
                  xyz1.style.top=pos//pos as an integer
                  xyz4.innerText=pos//pos as a string value
            if (counter==100)
                  counter=0;
            }

</SCRIPT>
<DIV onclick="toggle();">Click on the face to start its climb.Percentage of
climb remaining=<SPAN id="xyz4">true</SPAN></DIV>
</BODY>
</HTML>
```

The above example illustrates very neatly how JavaScript handles variable assignment. In strongly typed languages we would have to manually reassign the variable **pos** to make it into a string. However JavaScript does this for us. Because it knows that **innerText** has to take a string value it automatically reassigns the variable type. Although convenient for the most part, in larger programs this can be a source of incredibly hard to find bugs!

Let's see what it looks like part way through the climb!

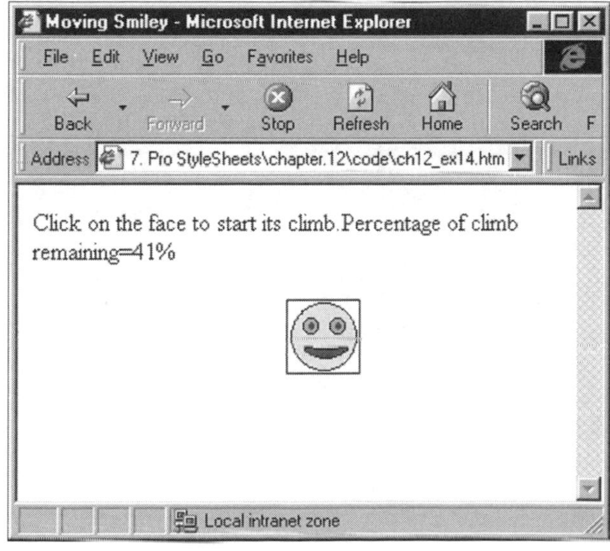

Drag and Drop

There are several different ways to carry out drag and drop operations, the one shown here is one of the simplest and probably the easiest to conceptualize. For other methods see books such as *Instant JavaScript, ISBN 1861001274* and *Instant IE4 Dynamic HTML Programmers Reference, ISBN 1861000685.*

```
<HTML>
<HEAD>

<TITLE>Drag Smiley I</TITLE>

<STYLE>
      #xyz1 {position:absolute;
             top:100;
             left:100;
      }
</STYLE>

</HEAD>

<SCRIPT LANGUAGE=JAVASCRIPT>

      var moveit=false;

      function drag_it(e,f){

             if (moveit==true)
                    {
                    xyz1.style.left=e-5 +"px";
                    xyz1.style.top=f-5 +"px";
                    }
      }

      function dragmode(){

             if(moveit==false)
                    {
                    moveit=true;
                    xyz2.innerText="movemode=true";
                    }
             else
                    {
                    moveit=false;
                    xyz2.innerText="movemode=false";
                    //Put any "drop" code here.
                    }
      }
</SCRIPT>

<BODY onmousemove="drag_it(window.event.x,window.event.y)">

      <IMG ID="xyz1" SRC="smiley.gif"  onclick="dragmode()">

<DIV>Click on image to start drag, and click again to end it.</DIV>
<DIV id="xyz2">movemode=false<DIV>
```

```
</BODY>
</HTML>
```

It's difficult to illustrate, but here's what it looks like!

The operation depends on a single global boolean variable and two functions.

First of all look at the **<BODY>** tag. It uses the event **onmousemove** to capture the x and y position of the cursor in the window, namely **window.event.x** and **window.event.y** which returns a value in pixels.

> *If you have difficulty understanding* **window.event.x** *try putting this code in the* **BODY** *of any HTML document.*
>
> ***<BODY onclick="alert(window.event.x)">***
>
> *and try clicking all over the screen. Repeat with* **window.event.y**.

We pass these values as parameters to our function **drag_it**, which checks the value of **dragmode**, and if it is true uses the CSS **top** and **left** properties to position our image. See how we subtract 5 pixels to ensure that the pointer stays over the image.

To start the drag operation we click on the image, which calls **dragmode()**, and if our boolean variable **moveit** is **false** it turns to **true**. To stop the drag operation we simply click again.

We could also carry out a drop operation by putting the necessary code in **dragmode()**

We have only just scratched the surface of what is possible using Dynamic HTML and CSS in IE4, but we will use these few simple effects to produce some neat pages later on. For a much more comprehensive view see the Reference Section at the end of the chapter.

Dynamic Styling in Communicator 4

Almost all the effects that can be produced in IE4 can also be produced in Netscape with their version of Dynamic HTML.

We are not going to say so much about Communicator, not out of any sense of favoritism, or because I think it is an inferior product, but because Communicator uses a proprietary tag, **<LAYER>**, to achieve most of its dynamic content, and this tag will NOT be adopted by W3C. Indeed Communicator is moving towards adoption of the W3C standard, and already supports the positioning properties, which probably means that the **<LAYER>** tag will be deprecated. However, it is likely to be with us in the next 2-3 years, so we had better learn a little about it.

Documentation on this and several other topics can be found at:

http://developer.netscape.com/library/documentation/index.html

well worth a visit.

For a great summary of JavaScript see:

http://developer.netscape.com/library/documentation/communicator/jsguide4/index.htm

The Wrox Press books, *Instant JavaScript, ISBN 1861001274,* and *Instant HTML Programmer's Reference, ISBN 1861001568,* contain excellent summaries, and *Instant Netscape Dynamic HTML Programmer's Reference, ISBN 1861001193,* contains all you need to know (and more) on this subject.

The Document Object Model in Netscape

The DOM for Netscape browsers provides an incomplete, but large and useful set of collections.

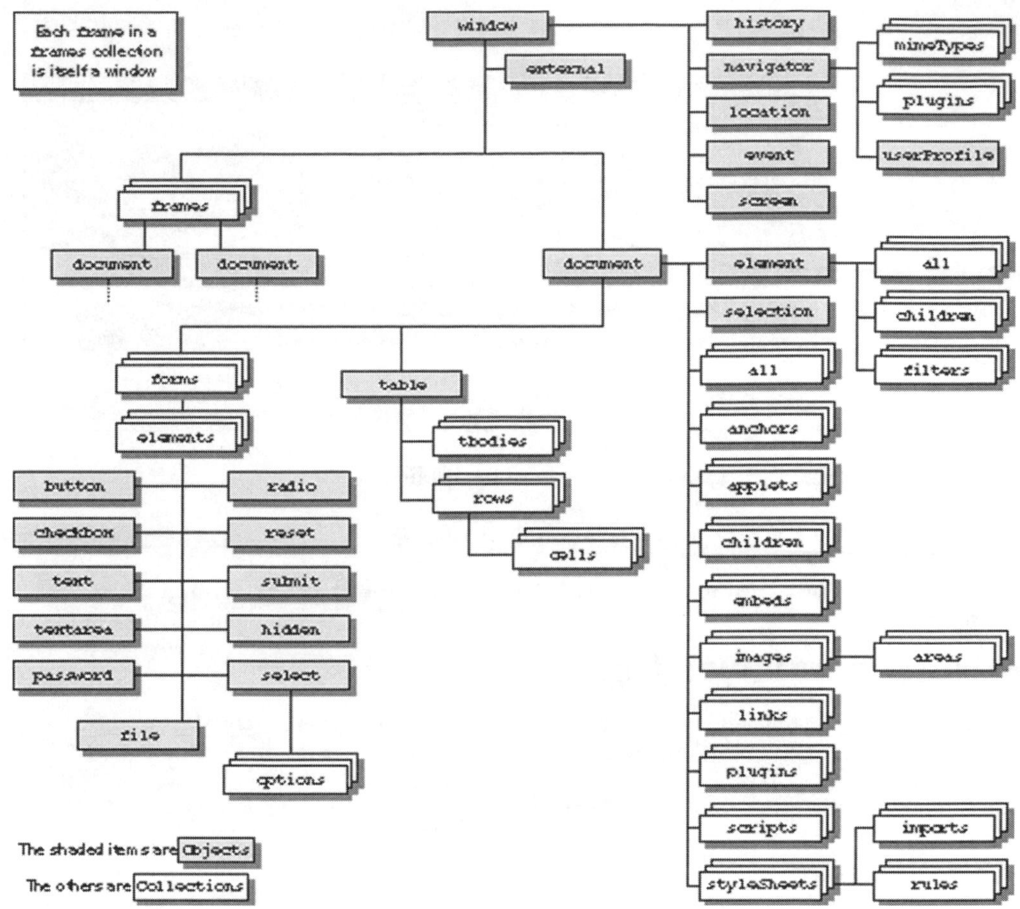

Most of the dynamic styling capabilities of Communicator are centered around the **<LAYER>** element.

JavaScript Style Sheets

Communicator also adds a new kind of style sheet called a JavaScript style sheet which has much of the functionality of CSS style sheets. It's difficult to see why you would want to use this type of style sheet instead of CSS style sheets, but for completeness here is an example.

```
<HTML>
<STYLE TYPE="text/javascript">
tags.DIV.color= "red";
tags.DIV.backgroundColor= "navy";
tags.DIV.fontSize= "20pt"
//note the camelback notation.
</STYLE>
<DIV>Hello and Goodbye JavaScript Style Sheets!</DIV>
</HTML>
```

Save it as **ch12_ex16.htm** and open the file in Communicator and this is what you'll see.

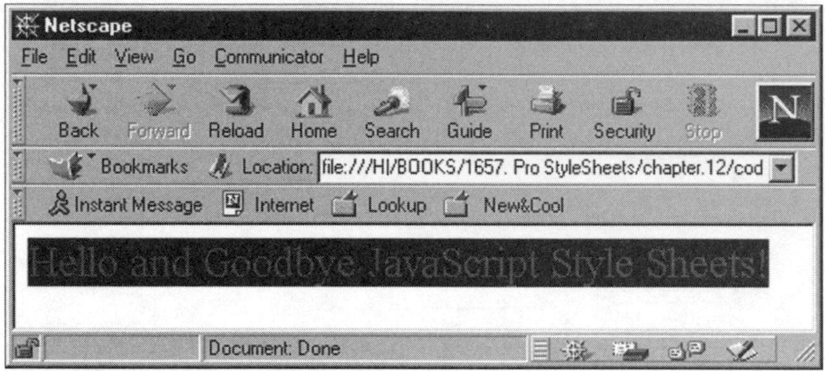

If you open the same file in IE4, no styling will be applied at all.

For further reference see the Netscape developers site.

http://developer.netscape.com/library/documentation/index.html

The Netscape Layer Tag

In a way, it is a pity that this is not going to be the future of Dynamic HTML, because this tag offers wonderful functionality, with numerous attributes, properties and methods attached to it.

The following table gives some of the main attributes

Layer Attributes.

Attribute	Description
above	Above in the z-order
background	URL of the image for the layer
below	Below in the z-order
bgcolor	Background color, use **#000000** notation or string
class	The style class
clip	Clipping co-ordinates
height	Pixels
id	Same as name
left	x position in reference to the containing box

Table Continued on Following Page

Attribute	Description
`name`	Same as id
`pagex`	x in relation to window
`pagey`	y in relation to window
`src`	URL
`top`	y position in reference to the containing box
`visibility`	Hidden or visible
`width`	Pixels
`z-index`	The z-order

Many of the properties mimic the attributes above.

Layer Properties

Properties	Description
Position and clipping properties	
`left`	As above
`top`	As above
`pageX`	As above
`pageY`	As above
`above`	As above
`below`	As above
`zindex`	As above
`parentLayer`	The layer that contains the current layer
`siblingAbove`	The previous sibling
`siblingBelow`	The next sibling
`clip.bottom`	The y2 co-ordinate of the clipping rectangle
`clip.top`	The y1 co-ordinate of the clipping rectangle
`clip.left`	The x1 co-ordinate of the clipping rectangle

Table Continued on Following Page

Properties	Description
`clip.right`	The x2 co-ordinate of the clipping rectangle
`clip.height`	The height of the clipping rectangle
`clip.width`	The width of the clipping rectangle
Content Properties	
`background`	As above
`bgcolor`	As above
`name`	As above
`src`	As above
`visibility`	As above

The **<LAYER>** tag also has several methods associated with it.

Layer Methods

Method	Description
`moveAbove`	In the z-order
`moveBelow`	In the z-order
`moveBy`	Move by x ,y
`moveTo`	Move to an x, y co-ordinate in relation to the container
`moveToAbsolute`	As above in relation to the page
`resizeTo`	x, y
`resizeBy`	Adds or subtracts x , y
`load`	Loads an HTML page into the layer
`captureEvents`	Instructs the layer what kind of events to capture
`handleEvent`	Invokes the handling code
`releaseEvents`	Stops capturing the events
`routeEvent`	Passes the event through the event hierarchy

We will use some of these methods in the examples below. For further examples *see Instant Netscape Dynamic HTML Programmer's Reference, ISBN 1861001193 from Wrox Press.*

Highlighting Text

Here's how you do this in Communicator using the **<LAYER>** tag.

```
<HTML>
<HEAD>

<TITLE>Dynamic Page</TITLE>
<SCRIPT LANGUAGE=JavaScript1.2>
      function changecolor(color,display){
            //alert(color)
            document.altercolor.bgColor=color;
      }

</SCRIPT>

<STYLE>
      DIV{
      color:navy;
      font-size:80pt;
      font-family:arial,sans-serif;
      font-weight:bold;
      text-align:center;
      }

      .yel{
      color:yellow;
      font-size:65pt;
      }

</STYLE>
</HEAD>
<BODY>


<LAYER NAME=altercolor BGCOLOR="white"  onmouseover="changecolor('red')"
onmouseout="changecolor('white')">
      <DIV>
      Professional <br> Stylesheets
      </DIV>


<DIV CLASS="yel">Wrox Press</DIV>
</LAYER>
</BODY>
</HTML>
```

You refer to the **<LAYER>** tag by name (or ID they are the same for a **<LAYER>**). Otherwise there is really nothing new here. By and large to accomplish anything dynamically you have to put it inside a **<LAYER>** tag. Here's what it looks like when you move the cursor over the text. When you move the cursor off the text, the red background disappears.

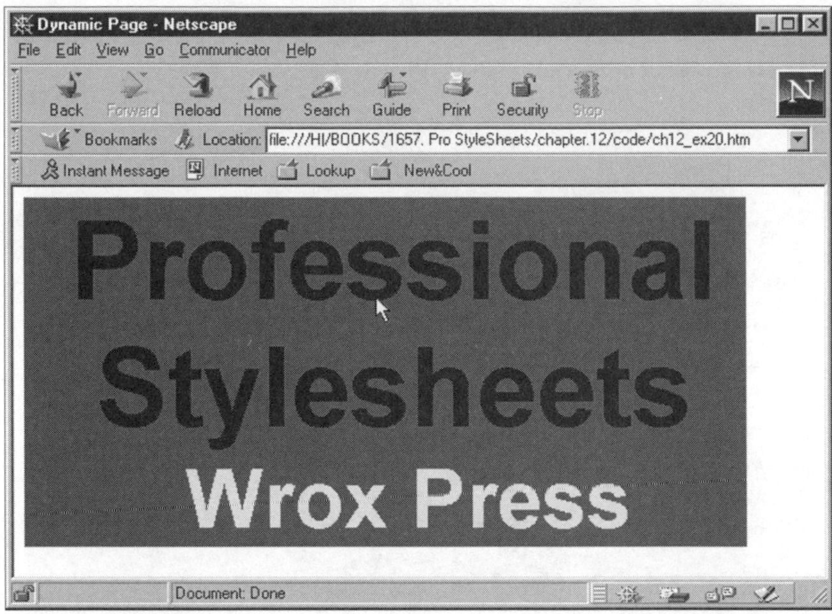

Actually you don't have to create a function to accomplish the above. This will do the trick just as well!

```
<LAYER NAME=altercolor BGCOLOR="white" onmouseover="this.bgColor='red'"
onmouseout="this.bgColor='white'">
```

Animation

Here is the slimmed down Communicator version of the Winking Smiley. We have taken out the **id** from the images themselves and put them as names on the enclosing **<LAYER>**. We have also substituted the **visibility** property for the **z-index** property. We could have used the CSS property for visibility just as easily for the IE4 version.

The **<LAYER>** does not support (surprisingly) the **onClick** event, so we initiate movement with the **onmouseover** event. Notice again that the style object is not supported, so we just refer to the object as:

document.[*layer-name or layer-id*]**.**[*layer-property*]**=***value*

```
<HEAD>

<TITLE>Winking Smiley II</TITLE>

<STYLE>

</STYLE>
</HEAD>
<BODY>
      <LAYER NAME="xyz1" >
```

```
        <IMG  CLASS="center" SRC="smiley2.gif">
        </LAYER>
        <LAYER NAME="xyz2" >
        <IMG CLASS="center" SRC="smiley3.gif">
        </LAYER>
        <LAYER NAME="xyz3">
        <IMG  CLASS="center" SRC="smiley.gif" >
        </LAYER>
<LAYER  TOP=100 LEFT=50 onmouseover="setInterval('timer()',200)">
        <DIV>Run your mouse over this line to start the animation.</DIV>
        </LAYER>

<SCRIPT LANGUAGE=JAVASCRIPT>
        var counter=0;

        function timer(){

               counter++;

               if(counter==1 )
               {
                      document.xyz1.visibility="visible";
                      document.xyz2.visibility="hidden";
                      document.xyz3.visibility="hidden";
               }

               if(counter==2  )
               {
                      document.xyz2.visibility="visible";
                      document.xyz1.visibility="hidden";
                      document.xyz3.visibility="hidden";
               }


               if(counter==3 )
               {
                      document.xyz3.visibility="visible";
                      document.xyz2.visibility="hidden";
                      document.xyz1.visibility="hidden";
                      counter=0;
               }

        }
</SCRIPT>

</BODY>
</HTML>
```

And it looks like this:

Disappearing Text and other Tricks

While we cannot rewrite text to a **<LAYER>**, we can reload the whole of the **<LAYER>** from an external source using the **src** property. We can also give the appearance of writing new text etc. by using several **<LAYER>**s in conjunction with the **source** and **clip** properties.

Movement is possible using **setInterval** and the positioning properties.

Other Useful Styling Tricks with Script

We don't have room to cover all that we can accomplish with script, with the full implementation of the DOM what you will be able to achieve is limited only by your imagination. However, here are a couple of very useful tricks that you can use right now.

Repetitive Text

One of the other things that script is good for is writing repetitive text. All we have to do to back drop the whole page with text, (we would have to use the **position:absolute** property to add the other elements), is to write two lines of code.

```
For(var num=0; num<=100;num++)
{document.write("Wrox Press Birmingham U.K.")}
```

The following code produces a pyramid of text:

```
<SCRIPT>
      function pyramid(e)
            {
            document.write("<DIV align=center>")
            for(var num=0;num<=e;num++)
                  {document.write("cairo");}
            document.write("</DIV>")
            }
      for(var num=0;num<=10;num++)
            {
            pyramid(num);
            }
</SCRIPT>
```

which looks like this:

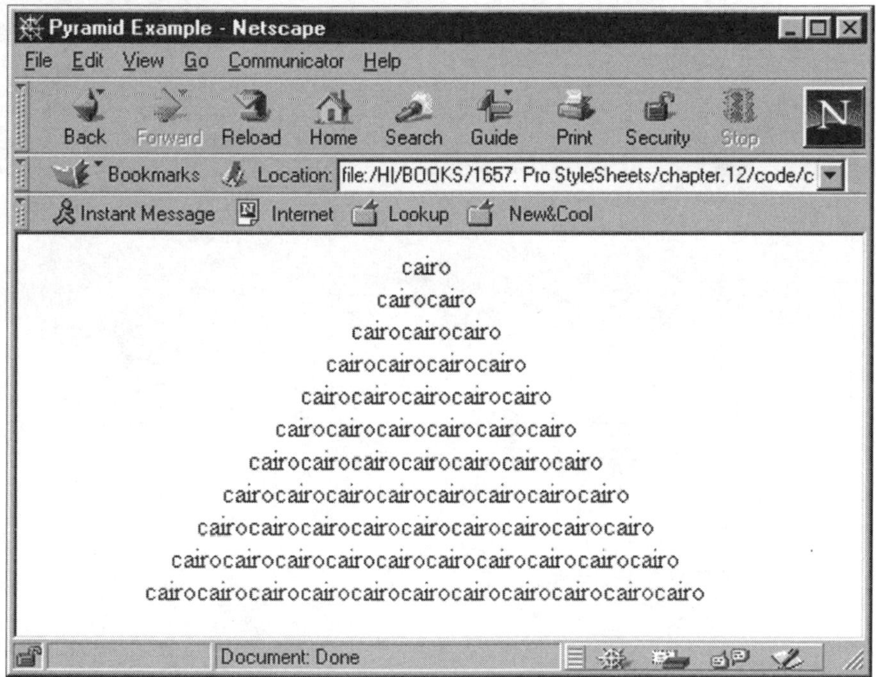

Numerous other text shapes are possible with a little ingenuity. The examples in Chapter 15 use this trick quite extensively.

Creating Macros

Another potentially very useful way to use script in styling is to create macros. A style macro in this concept is code that will create a given type of styling image or effect. This is usually done by putting your code in a separate **.js** file, and then the macro is called simply by declaring it.

Unfortunately if you want to use the **position:absolute** property to position your macro it does not work well in Communicator. You can get them to semi-function, but it takes a lot of tweaking.(See below.) Macros usually need to be positioned, so because Communicator does not support absolute positioning, the usefulness of macros is limited.

The following code places a Wrox logo at the positions x and y (expressed as a percentage) on a page. All it does is write an appropriate **<DIV>** tag with inline styling.

First of all, however, some code for IE4 that positions a macro. This should all, of course, be on one line. Type it into a text editor and save it as **wroxlogo.js**.

```
//creates macro OF WROX LOGO
function wroxlogo(x,y){
   document.write("<DIV STYLE= 'background-color:red; padding:.3em;
border:solid .5em gray; width:35pt; font:bold 30pt/50% arial,sans-serif;
position:absolute; top:"+y+"%; left:"+x+"%'>WROX<BR></DIV>");
      }
```

The function is called in the target document quite simply as follows:

```
<HTML>
<HEAD>

<TITLE>Call Macro</TITLE>
<SCRIPT SRC="wroxlogo.js">
</SCRIPT>
<SCRIPT>
     var dummy=wroxlogo(40,90)
</SCRIPT>
<STYLE>
</STYLE>
</HEAD>
<BODY>
<H2 STYLE="text-align:center; font-size:36pt; color:red">Wrox Press</H2>
</BODY>
</HTML>
```

And it looks like this:

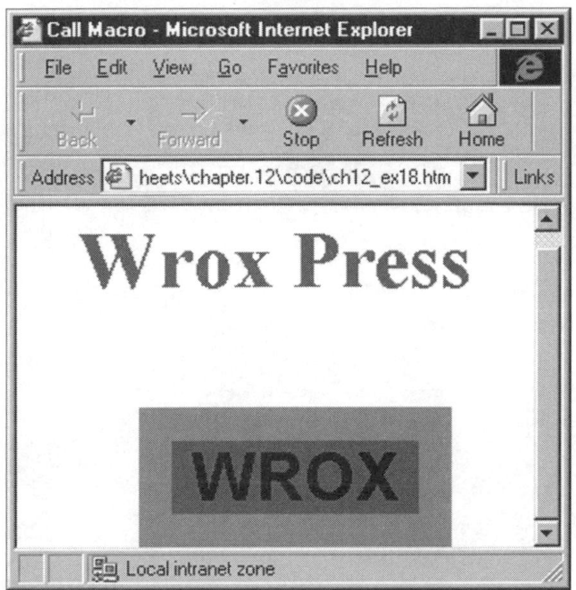

For those who want to see how it works in Communicator see the **`junknav`** *samples. The problem is twofold, first one has to write a style sheet (***`junknav1.js`***), and then write the text (***`junknav2.js`***). We now must import two files. The problem with Communicator is that the absolute position only displays in the inheritance. So you have to write two styles, one with the position and one with the display version. Of course both will appear in IE4, so that means we have to differentiate between the two systems. I mean you might as well make a graphic! Don't even try and run the samples on IE4. (To find all this out must have taken almost a day of tweaking.)*

On the other hand if you just want your macro to appear in the normal flow, and don't want to position it on the page, macros work fine on both browsers. The following code creates a warning macro. Note that to make it work on Communicator we have to call our style sheet first and then our flow object. Copy and save this code as **`warning1.js`**.

```
//style sheet for warning2.macro .Needs to be called before warning 2
      function writewarning1(){

      document.write("<STYLE>.logo{color:red; font-size:40pt;font-
family:bedrock,sans-serif; font-weight:bold;text-
align:center;}.sub{color:purple;font-size:16pt;font-style:normal;text-
align:center;}.text{color:red;font-size:14pt;font-style:normal;}</STYLE>");

      }
```

Here is the macro that creates the flow object. Copy and save this as **warning2.js**.

```
function writewarning2(e){

      document.write("<HR width=50% align=center>")
      document.write("<DIV CLASS=logo>WARNING!!</DIV>")
      document.write("<DIV CLASS=sub>Read this carefully</DIV>")
      document.write("<HR>")
      document.write("<SPAN CLASS=text>"+e+"</SPAN>")
      document.write("<HR>")
}
```

Here is an example of a document that uses these macros demonstrating how they are called. Copy and save it as **ch12_ex20.htm**.

```
<HTML>
<HEAD>
<SCRIPT SRC="warning1.js">
</SCRIPT>

<SCRIPT SRC="warning2.js">
</SCRIPT>

<SCRIPT>
      //
    var dummy=writewarning1()//dummy variable calls js functions
    var dummy=writewarning2("READ ALL WARNINGS IN THIS DOCUMENT CAREFULLY.
THEY ARE PUT THERE FOR A PURPOSE!!")
</SCRIPT>


</HEAD>
<BODY>
Here is some text


      <SCRIPT>
            var dummy=writewarning1()
            var dummy=writewarning2("This bomb will explode if not handled
carefully")
      </SCRIPT>
Some more text
</BODY>
</HTML>
```

And this is what it looks like displayed in Communicator:

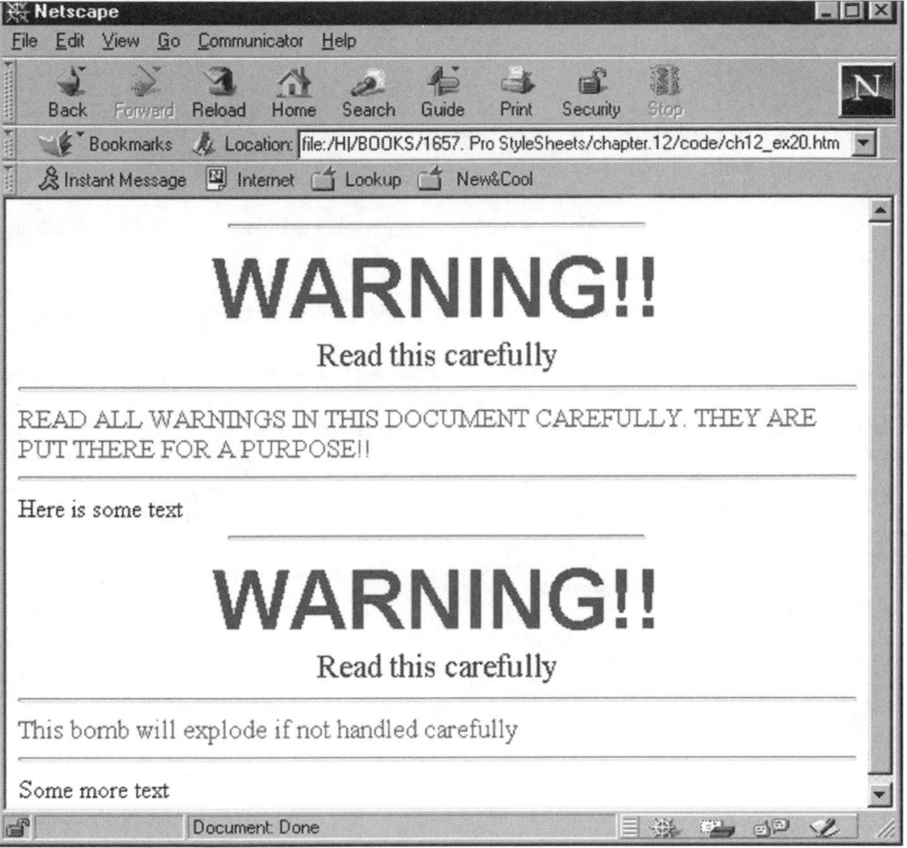

Summary

In this chapter we saw how JavaScript acts as a natural adjunct to style sheets. Unfortunately some of the more complicated combinations of JavaScript and CSS properties do not work well on the Communicator browser, so some of scripts potential usefulness is limited. Some of the uses we investigated were:

- Client side browser detection
- The DOM and Dynamic HTML according to Microsoft
- The DOM and Dynamic HTML according to Netscape
- Using script to write repetitive and patterned text
- Creating style macros using script

This brings us to our discussion of style sheets as applied to the screen. In the next chapter we will look at other kinds of style sheets, then we will have a look at canvases other than the computer screen.

References

The following books from Wrox Press are all well worth reading.

Instant JavaScript, ISBN 1861001274.
Instant HTML Programmer's Reference, ISBN 1861001568.
Instant IE4 Dynamic HTML Programmer's Reference, ISBN 1861000685.
Instant Netscape Dynamic HTML Programmer's Reference, ISBN 1861001193

The following URL gives access to all of Netscape's articles and digital books. Although there is much dross there is also much of value.

http://developer.netscape.com/library/documentation/index.html

There is also an excellent beginner's tutorial here, as well as a more comprehensive one at:

http://developer.netscape.com/library/documentation/communicator/jsguide4/index.htm

This is where to find the W3C documentation on the Document Object Model:

http://www.w3.org/TR/WD-DOM/requirements-971009.html

Exercises

1. Write a simple HTML program which makes two or three bordered boxes.
2. Use the CSS **`position`** property and differential style sheets to make them display the same on Communicator and IE4 (Not a trivial exercise)
3. Design an overhead menu bar. Create drop down boxes for each item. (Save this in a **`.js`** file you may want to use it again and again.)

13

Other Style Languages: SPICE, XS, DSSSL flow objects

In this chapter we are going to have a look at other types of style sheets that can be used with XML and HTML. One is extremely new–Spice, whereas the other–XS–has been around for quite some time (at least its parent DSSSL has). We will finish up with a brief look at DSSSL flow objects and some of their properties, as these will be utilized in XSL.

The two languages we've concentrated on so far in this book are CSS and XSL. These languages are intended for styling print on the screen, although as we have seen CSS is branching into other media.

Essentially CSS takes an XML or an HTML document and applies styling to it. This document is then presented on the screen or in other media.

XSL takes a document marked up in XML and creates styled flow objects. In its present form it can create either an HTML type flow object, or a DSSSL type flow object, although the only parsers available just use HTML type flow objects. We will look at the DSSSL flow objects that XSL can use at the end of this chapter. Although the MSXSL parser outputs HTML, there is no reason why future tools for use with XSL should not output RTF, printed documents or screen documents.

> *Note there is a clear distinction between the potential of a language, and the tools available to employ that language. XSL is potentially a very powerful language, but at the present we have very crude tools to work with it, namely the MSXSL parser that has only one form of output, in line HTML. It is rather like taking a tree. The potential to make a lovely piece of furniture is there, but we are unlikely to do this with a hand axe!*

The other languages we will look at in this chapter are XS (do not confuse with XSL!) or DSSSL-o, and Spice. DSSSL-o is a subset of DSSSL, which has been around for a long time, and is extremely powerful. It has been used mainly for styling in the print industry, and will continue to be used there for the foreseeable future. It can work on any SGML document including XML and HTML. As we have mentioned before it can be very complicated, and XS (DSSSL-o), is a simplified subset designed to be used on the Web. Activity on the development of XS has almost come to a halt and has been supplanted by XSL. (The same group of people are working on both at W3C.)

We have included a section on XS here both as an introduction to DSSSL, and because it is quite possible that new life may be breathed into the XS language.

Spice, on the other hand, is a language with great potential. Essentially it can create any kind of flow object, from any kind of marked up document, and display it in any kind of media, using any kind of script or style language! The only drawback is that there are no tools currently available. One of its creators is Dave Raggett the chair of the W3C HTML committee. We have included Spice in this chapter because, if it fulfills its promise, it may well become *the* styling language on the Web!

A word of warning–if I went to school to learn about carpentry, I would attend both lectures and practical classes. The first would be interesting, but the teaching and my understanding would not be complete until I had been let loose with chisels, hammers, nails and a lump of wood. The problem with this chapter is that we don't have the practical classes, mainly because we don't have the chisels or the hammers to work with. Admittedly, in the section on XS, I do tell you where to find the tools to work with SGML and DSSSL. You are also encouraged to get them and hack away. However, to tell you how to start using them would require more space than is available in this book, so I have just given examples, and you will have to take it from me that they are correct!

Spice

Spice is a new styling language written by Dave Raggett and Robert Stevahn of Hewlett Packard. It leverages user's knowledge of CSS and JavaScript, which can be used to style both XML and HTML documents. Like XSL and DSSSL–but unlike CSS–it allows manipulation of the flow objects, and even allows the user to write his own kind of flow object in the form of a macro. Although there are no tools available at the time of writing, a browser will probably be available in the fall of '98, as well as plug-ins to enable the mainstream browsers to read Spice style sheets.

This language is only in its formative stage, so the following may well change.

Spice in Concept

For such a powerful language, the concepts are remarkably simple. The basic construct is a style rule, which has been written utilizing CSS type properties. Here is an example of such a rule:

```
Style H1
{
       fontFamily: "Arial";
       fontSize: 12pt;
       display: block;
}
```

There are some important points to note here:

- The hyphens have been removed from **`font-family`** and **`font-size`** and have been replaced with a camelBack notation, (capitalizing the second word in a hump like fashion) in order to avoiding confusion with the JavaScript subtraction operator.
- The type of flow object, **`block`**, has been declared. Block is derived from a library of flow objects maintained by the Spice engine or referenced from a URL (see later).
- The flow object definitions have to be specifically imported (see next section).

Here is a simple HTML document showing one way that Spice rules can be included in it.

```
<HTML>
<STYLE TYPE= "text/spice">

import document, block, inline;
      import wroxheader from "http://www.wrox.com/Spice/std.lib"
      /*the above is hypothetical!*/
      import "Mystyle.css"
      import "Hisstyle.spi"
      Style HTML
            {
                  fontFamily: "Times New Roman";
                  fontSize: 12pt;
                  display: block;
            }
      style H1
            {
                  fontFamily: "Arial";
                  fontSize: 1.5em;
                  display: wroxheader;
            }
      Style H2
            {
                  fontFamily: "Arial";
                  fontSize: 1.5em;
                  textAlign: center;
                  display: block;
            }
      Style P
            {
                  textAlign: left;
                  display: block;
            }
      Style EM
            {
                  FontStyle: italic;
                  display: inline;
            }
</STYLE>
      <H1> 15 Spice and XS</H1>
      <H2> Spice</H2>
      <P> Hello Spice!</P>
      <P> This is a<EM> really cool</EM> language.</P>
</HTML>
```

Spice Points to Note

We have included the rules in **<STYLE>** tags here, but it is probable that they will also be able to be included in **<SCRIPT>** tags. This will have several advantages as **<SCRIPT>** allows an **SRC** attribute which we can use to include any modifying code that we might write (see later under the heading–*Spice Flow Objects*).

Just like CSS, Spice style sheets cascade. This example has imported both a CSS and a Spice type style sheet. (In a CSS type style sheet we would use **@import**, here we just use **import**.) We will discuss this in more detail in a moment.

Just like CSS (and unlike XSL) Spice style sheets inherit, so in addition to the stated styles of **align:left** our **<P>** will also be rendered with the **document** styles–**fontFamily: "Times New Roman"; fontSize:12pt;** (this is contained in the **document** block).

Note at the head of the document the **import** statement. This is completely analogous to the Java language **import** or the C language **include**, and imports a library of functions. In this case they are functions that tell the rendering engine how to display the flow objects. We will discuss this in more detail in a moment.

This simple example will create 5 flow objects, an **HTML**, an **H1**, two **P**s and an **EM**. They will be displayed according to the definitions given in the imported libraries.

So far Spice may just seem to be a slightly more complex way of writing CSS type style sheets, but the real power of Spice can be seen both in the way that it manipulates flow objects, and also how it allows for creation of new flow objects. First, however, it would be helpful to understand a little about the way that the Spice engine renders documents.

Document Rendering

When the user agent receives a Spice style sheet it iterates through the parent document and examines each element in turn. It then looks for a rule that it can apply to it and then creates a flow object based on that rule. If it finds no rule it will apply a **default** rule (c.f. XSL).

Spice Flow Objects

In XSL we laid out the creation of the flow object in the action part of the XSL rule. This is shown in the following code (this is just the action part of the rule):

```
<DIV>
      <children/>
      <HR/>
</DIV>
```

where we make a flow object of all the children, and place a horizontal rule after each child.

In Spice there is no need to do this, the flow objects are included in a library. This library may be hard-wired into the user agent itself, it may be cached, or it may be referenced in an outside URL.

In our sample above the **<H1>** tag is to be rendered as a **wroxheader** flow object. The user agent needs to find the code describing how this kind of flow object is to be rendered. First it will look in its hard-wired library, then in its cache to see whether it has been recently downloaded, then it will look at the URL and import the necessary code. If all this fails–the user may be off-line–it will use a default rendering.

Note that in XSL all you have to do to avoid displaying an item is to omit the action part of the rule. Because properties are inherited, this will not work in Spice. The rule will inherit the root rule for **display**, in this case **block**. To avoid displaying an item we must use the property **display:none;**.

Modifying a Flow Object

Spice allows us to create our own flow objects. This is either from scratch, or by modifying an existing flow object. To do this we can use Java, JavaScript, Spice itself or even create an ActiveX object.

Here is how we would go about modifying the block object to create a **wroxheader** flow object using Spice.

```
//note similarity to java 'extends' keyword

        Prototype wroxheader extends block
                {
                        function layout(element)
                        {
                                this.style.borderStyle=solid;
                                this.style.backgroundColor=black;
                                this.style.color=white;
                                this.style.position=absolute;
                                this.style.top=0;
                                this.style.left=0;
                                this.append(new Text("Chapter "));
                                ProcessChildren(element,this);

                        }
                }
```

Note the use of the keyword **prototype** that tells the Spice engine that we are creating a new prototype and calling it **wroxheader**. Note also the use of the keyword **extends** which tells the Spice engine what object we are modifying to create our prototype **wroxheader**. This is very similar to its use in Java.

Now whenever we use the **display:wroxheader;** property/value pair we will produce white text on a black background at the top left hand corner of the page, and the text will be pre fixed with "Chapter ". So in our earlier example:

```
<H1> 13 Spice and XS</H1>
```

would appear in Arial 1.5*12=18pts (our base font size is 12) from the style sheet instructions. From the **display** instructions it would be at the top left corner of the page, with white text on a black background.

As a reminder here is the relevant part of the style sheet.

```
style H1
            {
                    fontFamily: "Arial";
                    fontSize: 1.5em;
                    display: wroxheader;
            }
```

We would put this code in our file **std.lib** which, as we saw, was referenced from the head of the style sheet.

There are a few Spice keywords here. The **layout** function is passed the name of the element that the layout is to be applied to (i.e. **H1**). The **append** keyword is used to append a new child to the sequence, in this case a **Text** type child **"Chapter"**, and **processChildren** is a built-in method that iterates through the flow tree processing the children of the element. (In our example there are no children.) As well as appending text, Spice allows us to append graphics from a standard library (see the section on *Graphics* below).

Next let's look at how Spice will let us manipulate the order and sequence of our document.

Modes and Out of Sequence Rendering

Just as in XSL, Spice allows us to do modes and out of sequence renderings. Consider the following simple XML document:

```
<document>

      <contents></contents>
      <chapter> Introduction</chapter>
      <chapter_text> In this chapter....</chapter_text>
      <chapter> CSS</chapter>
      <chapter_text> Cascading Style....</chapter_text>
      <chapter> Spice </chapter>
      <chapter_text> Spice is a new...</chapter_text>

</document>
```

I would like to pull out all the chapter headings and print them in my **contents** tag, using a different style to the one I use at the top of each chapter. How do I go about this?

In CSS one would have to rewrite the parent document and use separate style rules to accomplish this. For example:

```
<document>

<contents>
      <chapter class="toc"> Introduction</chapter>
      <chapter class="toc"> CSS</chapter>
      etc, etc
```

```
</contents>
       <chapter class= "heading"> Introduction</chapter>
       <chapter_text> In this chapter     </chapter_text>
       etc, etc
```

Here I've had to include all the chapter headings within the **<contents>** element, and give them a class of **toc** when used in this element and a style of **heading** when I use them at the beginning of each chapter. So, I have to reference a CSS style sheet that would contain the following rules:

```
.toc{font-size:10pt}
.heading{font-size:18pt}
```

In Spice there is a better way to do it using the mode rule. The first step is to create a style rule for the **<chapter>** element as a whole:

```
style chapter
       {
       fontSize:18pt;
       }
```

The next thing is to create a special mode to display the chapters as a table of contents.

```
mode toc
       {style*
       {
              Display:none;
       }

       style chapter
       {
              FontSize:10pt;
       }
}
```

Note what we have done. The asterix ***** tells the processor to apply this rule to every element, so none will be displayed except the **<chapter>** element, which will be displayed using a font size of 10 points. Now to display this in our **<contents>** we just give our tag a unique **id** as an attribute. For example:

<contents id= "toc"></contents>

When the processor sees this it will create a flow object, which contains the content of every **<chapter>** element, rendered in a 10 point font.

Note that if we hadn't included

```
        style*
        {
                Display:none;
        }
```

in our mode rule, the whole content of the book would have been displayed in contents!

Another way to do this would be to write a prototype for a flow object called say **body**.

```
    Prototype body extends block
    {
            //lay out the table of contents

            With mode toc       //just displays chapter elements.
                    {
            ProcessChildren(element,this)
                    }

                    // Now layout the document proper

                    ProcessChildren(element,this)
    }
```

Now using the style rule in our above example:

```
        Style document
                {
                Display:body;
                }
```

our document will now be laid out with a table of contents at the top. Note how we don't even have to use the **<contents>** tag. Spice gives us a shorthand way to do this, which will accomplish exactly the same effect.

```
    Style document
            {
            Display: block with mode toc, block with mode regular
            }
```

For further information on this you are directed to the notes and tutorials contained in the References section at the end of this chapter.

Media Dependant Style Sheets

Spice also allows us to specify separate media to use, for example in a "show and tell" you may want some of the presentation in sound and some in vision. To accomplish this we use the **media** rule

```
media aural
{
        style body
        {
                volume: medium;
                voiceFamily: male;
        }

        style abbr
        {
                volume: medium;
                voiceFamily: female;
        }
```

So, anything in the presentation with a style of **body** applied to it will be rendered aurally in a male voice, anything with a style of **abbr** will be rendered in a female voice. We can now use this statement in our prototypes with **media aural** as follows:

```
with media aural
{
        ProcessChildren(element,this);
}
```

to create auditory flow objects.

Graphics

When we looked at our first attempt at creating a prototype

```
Prototype wroxheader extends block
```

we used

```
this.append (new Text("Chapter "));
```

to add text to our flow object. We could also have made reference to a graphic, either by means of a URL or by referring to a standard library. For example:

```
this.append (new Graphic("Wroxlogo "));
```

or

```
this.append (new Graphic("http:/www.wrox.com/graphics/logo.gif"));
```

Spice Style Sheets

In our original example we saw how we could import a style sheet into another style sheet to take part in the cascade. Here is how you would associate a spice style sheet with your XML or HTML document.

To specify a style sheet use the standard processing instruction in XML. For example:

```
<?xml-stylesheet href= "docstyle.spi" type= "text/spice"?>
```

In HTML use the **LINK** tag:

```
<LINK REL= "stylesheet" href= "docstyle.spi" type= "text/spice">
```

Summary of Spice

At present Spice is just at the Note stage (submitted 3 Feb 1998) and as far as I know there is no W3C activity as of yet. As I have said before, anyone who predicts in this game is a fool. I will, however, stick my neck out and say that if the tools become available; Spice will be the style language of choice for XML. This is mainly on account of its versatility, and also because it fits in with the XML philosophy of encouraging creativity.

DSSSL-O and XS

DSSSL is a style language designed to be used with SGML, and is used predominantly for book and print layout. When XML was invented as an on line version of SGML suitable for the Web, it was natural that a slimmed down version of DSSSL, named DSSSL-online should be developed. This soon got nicknamed XS. This is what we will be talking about in this section.

We have said several times in this book that DSSSL is incredibly complicated and, in fact, the more advanced aspects of it are. The basics, however, are relatively simple. It is only when we get on to the more advanced parts of the language that things become more difficult. The main reason for the perceived difficulty of DSSSL is that it is based on the programming language SCHEME which uses an exotic style of syntax that programmers accustomed to mainline languages find very confusing!

XSL is based on DSSSL but uses an XML style syntax, however XSL has also inherited DSSSL flow objects, so if, after reading this section, we decide that we never want to see DSSSL again at least we will know the ancestry of XSL flow objects!

In this section we will look at enough of the basics to allow us to write a simple style sheet that can be applied to an XML document. Then we will just give a few examples of the more powerful, and complex, parts of the language with a enough references to allow you to delve further into the subject if you wish.

DSSSL Rules

DSSSL is for the most part made up of rules and definitions, and we will have a look at both. To start off with here is a simple DSSSL rule:

```
(element para
      ( make paragraph
      font-size:12pt line-spacing:13.2pt))
```

What this rule does is tell the user agent how to create a flow object. The user agent will search through the parent document looking for **para** elements, and it will render them as a paragraph flow object with a font of 12pt and line spacing of 13.2pt. This concept should be quite familiar to you by this stage.

Let's analyze the parts of the rule. First note that there are two sets of parentheses, one contained within the other. The selector **element para** selects the elements in the parent document of the type **<para></para>**. The instruction **make paragraph** uses the DSSSL keyword **make** to tell the user agent to make a flow object of the **paragraph** type. (There are numerous built-in types of flow objects in DSSSL, and there is a section called *DSSL Flow Objects* at the end of this chapter which shows the ones recognized by XS and XSL.)

Included within the parentheses containing the **make** statement, and following the flow object type, in this case, **paragraph**, are as many property/value pairs as we want. These are separated by white space (in DSSSL anything following a semi-colon (**;**) is a comment.). These property/value pairs consist of a DSSSL property, a colon (**:**) and its value. All rather similar to CSS, except that the property names can be confusingly different. **Line-spacing**, for example, is the equivalent of the CSS property **line-height**. Also note that there is no use of a semi-colon because, as I mentioned earlier, anything following a semi-colon is considered a comment in DSSSL.

So the general syntax for a DSSSL rule is:

(element [*element name from source doc***] (make [***flow object type***] [***dsssl-property***:** *value***]**
[[*whitespace***] [***dsssl property***:** *value***]]*))**

(I think it's just easier to remember the example, don't you?)

A More Detailed Example

Here is a simple XML document with an XS type style sheet to go with it.

First the XML document:

```
<document>
      <heading> XS or DSSSL-O</heading>
      <para> Perhaps DSSSL isn't as <emph>difficult</emph> as they
say?</para>
      <para> Maybe, but let's <bold>wait<bold> for a while!</para>
</document>
```

Here is the XS type style sheet to go with it, utilizing construction rules.

```
(element document
      ( make simple-page-sequence))
      ; this is a comment,anything after a semi-colon is a comment

(element heading
      ( make paragraph
            font-family-name: "Arial"
            font-weight: 'bold
            font-size: 22pt
            line-spacing: 24pt
            space-before: 15pt
            start-indent: 6pt
            quadding: 'center ))

(element paragraph
      ( make paragraph
            font-family-name: "Times New Roman"
            font-size: 12pt
            line-spacing: 14pt
            space-before: 6pt
            start-indent: 6pt
quadding: 'start ))

(element emph
      ( make sequence
            font-posture: 'italic))

(element bold
      ( make sequence
            font-weight: 'bold))
```

You should at this stage have no difficulty understanding this. There are, however, a few traps and a few points to be made.

Like Spice and XSL these are construction rules, in other words the user agent runs through the source document and then merges it with the style construction rule to produce a flow object. This is not surprising as XSL and Spice are based to a large extent on DSSSL.

`make simple-page-sequence` makes the whole document a flow object of pages for printing, the flow-object **`scroll`** would be used to make a document for screen display. **`paragraph`** is the equivalent of a block flow object. **`sequence`** is the equivalent of an inline flow object.

You should be able to work out what most of the property names mean! Here are a few of the more esoteric:

> **`space-before`**–The space to leave above the **`paragraph`** flow object, almost the equivalent of CSS **`margin-top`**.
> **`start-indent`**–The space to leave between the page edge and the beginning of the **`paragraph`** flow-object (in left to right writing the left edge, in right to left the right edge), almost the equivalent of the CSS **`margin-left`**.

quadding–almost the equivalent of the CSS **text-align** property. It takes the values of **'start**, **'end**, **'center**, and **'justify** (note the single apostrophe).

You are referred to the on line spec at:

http://sunsite.unc.edu/pub/sun-info/standards/dsssl/dssslo/do960816.htm

for a full list of the properties.

At Appendix H there is a table of the subset of DSSSL flow objects and properties that are designated by the XSL note for use with XSL.

Note how **"Arial"** and **"Times New Roman"** are put in quotes, this tells the processor that it is dealing with a variable.

On the other hand the **quadding**, **font-posture**, and **font-weight** values are preceded by a single apostrophe (**'**). This tells the processor that it is dealing with a literal, and that it must look up its value.

So far everything has been quite simple. Let's now complicate things slightly by looking at a DSSSL definition.

DSSSL Definitions

The DSSSL style language allows us to make our value definitions. Here is an example:

```
(Define heading-font "Arial")
```

Now you can use this in your style rules, so instead of having:

```
(element heading
      ( make paragraph
            font-family-name: "Arial"
            Etc
```

We can put:

```
(element heading
      ( make paragraph
            font-family-name: heading-font
                  Etc., etc.
```

This may not seem like too much of a big deal until we realize that, as in HTML, we may have 6 different types of heading, and then if we wanted to revise the font–to "Verdana" say–all we would have to do is change our definition.

DSSSL Expressions

This is where DSSSL becomes a little sticky for most people. The problem is that it uses the dialect of a rather unusual programming language called Lisp. That dialect is called Scheme.

Most of the mainstream programming languages such as C, Java, and VB use expressions in the same way we learned in high school algebra. For example, 7=(3+4). The plus is called an operand and it is said to be in-fixed–it comes between the two values it is operating on.

Here is another more complex example, x=(5y+3z)(yz/2)

The problem with DSSSL is that it does not use in-fixed operands, it uses pre-fixed operands. Instead of 7=(3+4) we have 7=(+ 3 4).

And the second expression looks even more unfamiliar:

x=(*(+ (* 5 y)(* 3 z)) (/(*y z) 2)))

I personally love a statement on this subject made by Paul Prescod:

"Once you get used to it, DSSSL's syntax may actually be more comfortable to you than the traditional math notation".

This is an interesting opinion, but not one that I believe holds any water.

> *Actually I am quite wrong to pick on Paul like this because he has written an outstanding simple and easy to understand tutorial which can be found at:*
>
> **`http://itrc.uwaterloo.ca/~papresco/dsssl/tutorial.html`**

This tutorial enabled even me to think that DSSSL may not be quite as difficult as I thought it was. It is a model of clarity and lucid thought and an example of what all educators should strive for. This does not, however, detract from the fact that it is a tricky old subject. However, that's the way it is and if you want to use the full power of DSSSL (and it is incredibly powerful) you'll just have to get used to it. If you are going to do much programming with DSSSL then get a word processor that matches parentheses. To get back to our subject–we could use an expression in the following manner:

```
(Define heading-font-size 12pt)
```

and then for our 6 different types of heading we would use

```
(element heading1
      ( make paragraph
            font-size: (* 2 heading-font-size)
            Etc
(element heading2
      ( make paragraph
            font-size: (* 1.5 heading-font-size)
            Etc
```

```
(element heading3
      ( make paragraph
            font-size: (* 1.2 heading-font-size)
            Etc
```

You can really put parentheses anywhere, and the user agent will evaluate the expression.

SOSOFO

This acronym stands for **S**pecification **O**f a **S**equence **O**f **F**low **O**bjects.

What it means is that we do not, in fact, make a flow object with a rule such as

```
( make paragraph font-size: 12pt line-spacing: 13.2pt)
```

we just specify how to make one. This is, in fact, a SOSOFO, and it is the SOSOFO that is passed to the user agent, which uses it to construct a flow object. If you get into DSSSL it is something you will see all the time.

Selecting Elements for Processing

What is missing from the above expression is the method **`process-children`**. Do you remember how in XSL we had to put in **`</children>`** in the action part of the rule, or else a flow object was not created? Well here we have to put in **`process-children`**, but the difference is that if we leave it out (and we do most of the time, why do extra work) the processor puts it in for us. In other words, the processor automatically converts the above into:

```
( make paragraph font-size: 12pt line-spacing: 13.2pt
                        ( process-children))
```

If for any reason we didn't want the children to be processed we would use the property **`empty-sosofo`** as follows:

```
( make paragraph font-size: 12pt line-spacing: 13.2pt
                        (empty-sosofo))
```

There are several other methods we can use–here are just a few of them:

`process-matching-children ' [`*element name***`] [`***element name***`] *`**

Will process just the children with the ancestry in the depicted element order.

`process-first-descendant ' [`*element name***`]`**

Will process the first children of the depicted element.

`process-element-with-id (attribute-string "idref")`

Will process the element with that unique id.

See the on line references for other processing properties, all 200 of them!

Introducing Text

As in XSL we can introduce added material in the style sheet. For example to add an automatic warning to a **<danger>** element in the following XML snippet:

```
<danger> Scalpels are sharp. They can cut you!</danger>
```

we would make the following rule:

```
(element danger
      ( make paragraph
            font-family-name: "Arial"
            font-size: 12pt
                  (make sequence
                        font-weight: 'bold
                        font-size: 18pt
                        (literal "Warning:!"))
                  (Process-children)))
            ;careful with those parentheses!
```

This will produce in our output:

Warning:!Scalpels are sharp. They can cut you!

The key word **literal** has introduced some text in our flow object before processing the children.

Selectors

Just as in CSS we can refine our selectors. The CSS rule

```
H2 EM {font-size:10pt}
```

would just mach those emphasized words in an **<H2>** heading.

In DSSSL this will give the same effect:

```
(Element (H2 EM) ( make ...
```

Programming

DSSSL allows us to program using the full power of a programming language. We will only look at one simple example here, you are directed to the References for further examples. This example employs a conditional statement. The syntax in most languages is

In Basic

```
If [statement to test]=true then
[action]
```

For example

```
if raining=true then
      take_umbrella
```

In C

```
If(raining==true)
      {take_umbrella();}
```

In Scheme it is

```
(if test consequent alternate)
(If (raining?) (take_umbrella)( leave_umbrella))
```

Here is a concrete example

```
(element para
      (if (first-sibling?)
            (make paragraph first-line-start-indent: 0pt)
            (make paragraph first-line-start-indent: 6pt)))
```

And in our document this would indent every paragraph that is NOT the first paragraph of a section.

Summary of DSSSL-O and XS

Perhaps DSSSL is not quite as fearsome as its reputation. Like most true programming languages however it takes time to learn and the syntax is different from the mainstream languages. If you are going to be doing a lot of print output it may be worth your while to go into more than the basics of DSSSL. However, if your interest is mainly in producing material for the Web, then it is probably wiser to invest your time elsewhere.

If you want to look into this subject a little further, start with Paul Prescod's tutorial, and then move on to Dan Germán's. URLs for both are given under References at the end of the chapter. Download the specification written by Jon Bosak. It is in fact quite readable. Numerous other contacts are given at James Clark's site. He is also the author of Jade, a processor for SGML/DSSSL, which is the tool that you should download if you want to practice DSSSL.

Summary

In this chapter we had a look at an up and coming language Spice, which shows great promise, and an old-timer DSSSL. Don't count DSSSL out yet. As well as being an international standard, DSSSL's strength is that all the other languages try to be just like it. With some simple tools and better documentation it may well make a comeback.

References

Spice

A brief overview of the subject, read this before reading the note.

http://www.w3.org/People/Raggett/spice

The original note on Spice presented to W3C:

http://www.w3.org/TR/1998/NOTE-spice-19980123.html

A comparison of XSL and Spice:

http://www.sil.org/sgml/spice-XSL980224.html

DSSSL-Online or XS

Paul Prescod's tutorial on DSSSL. Well worth a read even if you don't want to learn about the subject:

http://itrc.uwaterloo.ca/~papresco/dsssl/tutorial.html

Daniel M. Germán tutorial, goes into slightly more detail than Paul Prescod. Another excellent tutorial:

http://www.sil.org/sgml/dssslGerman.html

James Clark's home page with numerous DSSSL references:

http://www.jclark.com/dsssl

The DSSSL-Online spec can be found at:

http://sunsite.unc.edu/pub/sun-info/standards/dsssl/dssslo/do960816.htm

All the references on Scheme that you could possibly want are at:

http://www-swiss.ai.mit.edu/scheme-home.html

Exercises

None for this chapter.

14

Other Canvases

Up until this point we have predominantly been dealing with computer screen based presentation. However, style sheets can be, and are even now, used for painting on other canvases. The CSS2 specification recognizes nine different canvases; aural, braille, embossed pages (i.e. braille printers), hand held devices, print, projection, screen, teletypes (or devices with a fixed width character grid) and television. We'll cover most of these canvases in this chapter–showing how you can adapt your styling depending on whether your content is primarily aural, visual or tactile.

We will cover Braille in the most detail because it is a canvas which technology is clearly addressing. Braille should be paid more attention than it currently receives to fulfill the democratic aspirations of the Web. Plus, there would not be this development if there were not a need. Added to this is the fact that the information that follows is not all that easily available elsewhere. I am indebted to Joe Sullivan of Duxbury software and Jim Bliss of VpinfoNET for their help in writing the sections on braille.

Warning! Hardly any of this has been implemented in the main-line browsers yet. I have, however, included a few examples on the web site that you can play around with to test for implementation. Check out the samples for this chapter at **http://rapid.wrox.co.uk/books/1657**.

Styling for Different Types of Content

There are basically three kinds of content and two types of presentation.

Content can be, visual, aural or tactile. Presentation can be either continuous or paged.

A continuous presentation is like the typical computer screen presentation, with scrollbars if the content runs over the edge of the screen. Obviously aural presentation can only be continuous, although poor speakers reading from notes often act as if aural paged presentation is possible.

Visual web material becomes paged presentation whenever we print out a page. The demands for printed material are quite different from continuous material, and CSS2 has introduced a number of new properties to assist us. Visual material also becomes a paged presentation when we put on a slide show, and here we often have mixed material. We may want to intersperse our visual slides with aural material, sound bites etc.

Tactile material again can be continuous or paged. When braille is sent to a braille printer, paged material is produced.

We're going to examine the styling options for each of the three types of content, beginning with visual content.

Visual Content

We have been dealing with continuous presentation of visual content on the computer screen for most of this book so now let's have a look at the special requirements of paged material. It is helpful to first acquaint ourselves with some definitions that are used in the page world.

Definitions of Paged Material Terms

Here are definitions of some terms we'll use frequently later in this section.

Widows

A widow is a small piece of text from the end of a paragraph that runs over to the next page. For example, a piece of text left all by itself at the top of a page

Orphans

An orphan is a small piece of text from the beginning of a paragraph which is left on one page when the bulk of the text is on another page. For example, a piece of text left all by itself at the bottom of a page.

Page Break

A page break is the place in the text where a break is made in order to start a new page.

Single-sided Printing

Printing on just one side of the sheet.

Double-sided Printing

Printing on both sides of the sheet.

N-up Printing

Transferring a lot of small page boxes to one sheet of paper, rather like a lot of thumb nails on a screen.

Tiling

Transferring one image or page box to several sheets of paper. (Note that this is the opposite of what we think of when we tile a screen with an image, where several copies of one image are repeated).

Signatures

A series of page boxes printed on one sheet, which, when folded in the correct manner, produces a book or a card etc. This is a typographic term.

General Considerations.

When transferring a flow object designed for the screen to a page we must bear several points in mind. Here are some of the more obvious ones.

- When printing to a page, because the resolution of the printed media is much higher than a screen, we can get away with a smaller font, and serif fonts also tend to look better on a page.
- There are several circumstances where we may want to force a page break, either before or after a flow object, and there are other circumstances where we may want to prevent a page break, such as in the middle of a table.
- We will certainly want to prevent excessive widows and orphans. We will want to be able to define what is an acceptable widow or orphan for any given flow object.
- We may have a flow object, such as an image, which is too big for a screen, and thus probably too big for a page. We will want to have some say as to whether this flow object should be scaled, allowed to flow across several pages, clipped, or not shown at all.
- We may want some of our flow objects to appear only on a left or a right page.
- We will want to be able to vary the width of the margins and the position of the folio (a folio in typography is the page number) of the page depending on whether it is a right or a left hand page.
- We may want some of our flow objects to appear in a landscape rather than a portrait orientation.
- If we have positioned something absolutely in relation to our screen it may be in an inconvenient location on the page. We must be able to either relocate it or discard it.
- Finally we would like some control over the size of the page and the margin size.

Let's see how CSS2 addresses these requirements.

CSS2 Properties and Syntax for Paged Media

Let's look at some of the tools that CSS2 gives us for redesigning our flow objects for the paged media.

The Page Box

The page box is a box that contains the material to be printed out. It can have a **`margins`** and a **`size`** property which are set with the **`@page`** rule. The margin is the distance between the content material and the edge of the page box. At present CSS2 does not support a border or a padding property for paged material.

Note that the **`@page`** rule does not have any idea what is going to be placed inside the box, so units based on font sizes, **`em`** and **`ex,`** cannot be used. As you know-when it comes to setting widths and margins these units are derived from the containing box rather than the container, and of course a page box has no container.

When printing double sided documents the left and the right pages need to be different, so the **@page** rule has two pseudo classes-**:left** and **:right**. Crop marks can also be set with the **marks** property.

The following figure depicts the page box on a sheet of paper.

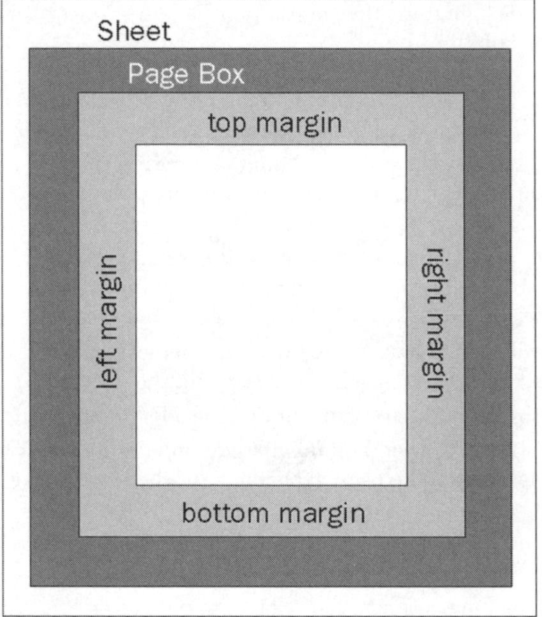

The @page Rule

The **@page** rule sets the **margin**, **size**, and **marks** property.

For example:

```
@page {
margin:2cm
Size:landscape
}
```

This will create a page box with a landscape orientation, and there will be a 2cm margin between the content and the page box. By using the landscape value for **size** we allow the user agent to make the best fit it can to the page. In other words, landscape creates a relative size.

The Margin Property

The normal **margin** properties apply as for continuous media, except, as already noted, **em** and **ex** cannot be used as units.

The Size Property

The syntax is:

size: <*length*>{1,2} | **auto** | **portrait** | **landscape**.

Here's an example of its use:

```
@page {
size:7.25in 9.25in; /* width height */
}
```

This will create a page the size of this book. This is the way to make an absolute or fixed sized page. Using **auto**, **portrait** or **landscape** makes a relative size page and allows the user agent to fit the page as best it can.

The Marks Property

The syntax is:

marks: [crop||cross] | none

This will place crop marks, crosses or both just outside the page box when an absolute size has been specified. They will of course be invisible when a relative size is used.

Left, Right, and First pseudo classes.

These allow us to specify different properties for left, right and first pages.

```
@page :left{
margin-left:2cm;
margin-right:3cm;
}

@page :right{
margin-left:3cm;
margin-right:2cm;
}
@page :first{
margin-left:3cm;
margin-right:2cm;
margin-top:4cm;
}
```

Whether the first page is left or right depends on the reading direction. It will be a right page in English, a left page in Hebrew.

Handling Content outside of the Page Box

It is up to the author to make sure that material is not outside the page margins, as if the material is outside the page margins, CSS lets the user agent handle this problem in any way it sees fit.

Handling Page Breaks

Normally the user agent will start a new page when it comes to the end of a page! If we don't want that to happen, we can use the **page-break** properties, with an element, to control where page breaks should take place, (within the confines of the page size - if fixed). We can also use the **widows** and **orphans** properties to control the allowable size of these. Note that these properties are declared with the **document** element properties, not with the **@page** rule.

The Page-break Properties.

The **page-break** properties are

- **page-break-before**
- **page-break-after**
- **page-break-inside**

page-break-before and **page-break-after** take the following values:

auto | always | avoid | left | right | inherit

The default is **auto**.

page-break-inside takes the values of:

avoid | auto

The following code would make sure that a paragraph with the class of **floater** was always printed on a single page, as it would force a break before and after the element.

```
P.floater{
page-break-before: always;
page-break-after: always;
}
```

Whereas the following would force one or more page breaks to ensure that a paragraph with the class of **left** was always printed on a left side page.

```
P.left{
page-break-before: left;
}
```

Finally, the code snippet below would ensure that a page break never took place inside the paragraph, unless of course that paragraph was longer than the page.

```
P.intact{
 page-break-inside: avoid;
}
```

Paragraph breaks, however, can never take place inside an absolutely positioned box. If the box is absolutely positioned the paragraph will be clipped. Thus if we wish to absolutely position a flow object on a page, it is up to us to make sure that it fits!

The Page Property

It is possible to declare a class of pages using the **@page** rule. For example, the following slice of code would create three classes of page-**rotated**, **narrow**, and **wide**.

```
@page rotated {size: landscape}
@page narrow {size: 4in 8in}
@page wide {size: 6in 9in}
```

To refer to them just use the **page** property.

```
TABLE {page: rotated:left}
```

The above would put all tables on a left landscape type page.

One doesn't have to specify whether it is left or right of course, we just put this in here to show how to add it if you wanted to specify the page.

The following would print a paragraph with a narrow page box.

```
P{page:narrow}
```

Here is a diagram of a left and right page using the following code:

```
@page narrow {size: 4in 8in}
@page wide {size: 6in 9in}
DIV.lpagenarrow {page: narrow:left}
DIV.lpagewide {page: wide:left}
DIV.rpagenarrow {page: narrow:right}
DIV.rpagewide {page: wide:right}
```

```
<DIV CLASS= "lpagenarrow">Ipse lorem sequiter etc.</DIV>
<DIV CLASS= "rpagewide"> Ipse lorem sequiter etc </DIV>
```

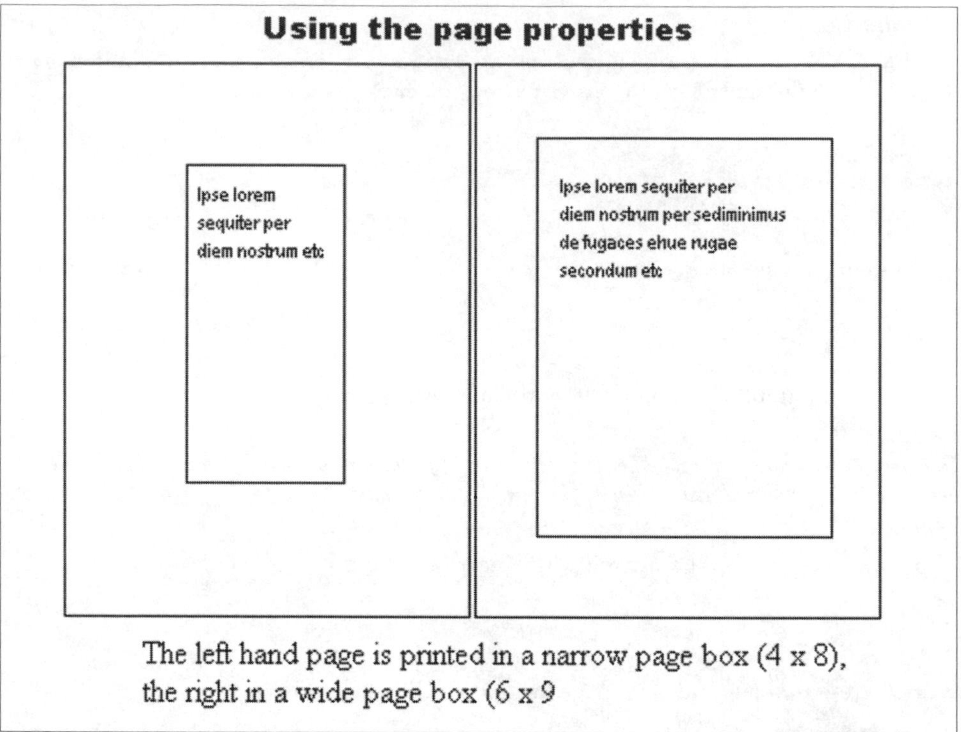

Using the page properties
Ipse lorem
sequiter per
diem nostrum etc
Ipse lorem sequiter per
diem nostrum per sediminimus
de fugaces ehue rugae
secondum etc
The left hand page is printed in a narrow page box (4 x 8),
the right in a wide page box (6 x 9

Widows and Orphans

The syntax of the value for widows and orphans is: <*integer*>

Where integer stands for the minimum number of lines that must be left at the bottom of a page for orphans, or the top of a page for widows.

```
P{
widows:3;
orphans:3;
}
```

The above would specify that if the paragraph starts near the end of the page and if less than three lines can be got in-it must break. Similarly if the paragraph is going to run over on to another page, then there must be at least three lines on the other page, or the page break must occur sooner.

Obviously, if the **`page-break-inside`** property is set to **`avoid`** then **`widows`** and **`orphans`** properties are not used unless the page is forced to break due to length.

That concludes our look at your options for displaying paged visual content, next we'll look at the styling challenges and solutions available for aural content.

Aural Content

Aural browsers are not just for the sight impaired, they are useful in cars, for the dyslexic, for slide shows, and for multi-media, and numerous other situations.

There are three broad aspects of aural media that must be considered:

- The navigation aspect of browsing
- The text-to-language conversion aspect
- The styling of the speech aspect

Only the last one really falls within the realm of this book, but we need to consider the first two at least briefly as they do impact on styling. Let's look at each one in turn.

Navigation

The normal way to navigate the Web is with a mouse and a click on a link. The link is usually in some different color for identification purposes and the mouse pointer changes when it is over the link. This type of identification and interactivity is not available to the aural browser. The following are possible solutions.

- The links are spoken in a different tone of voice, perhaps with a pause afterwards, during which the user could say "follow" to connect.
- The user could request links by specifically requesting "links". The user agent could then give a numbered list that the user could select from by saying the number.
- The user agent could give a list of links at the end of the page.
- The user agent may give a list of headings at the top of the page. This would be the equivalent of the normal reader scanning the page, which 85% of us do. (See Chapter15 *Examples–example2* for more information on visual scanning.)

In any case, there will need to be a mechanism for error correction, abortion of a link-the equivalent of pressing *Escape*-and for recapping.

In most cases the user will be able to use a keyboard to input. However, there are cases where this won't be possible. For example, when driving or when there are physical disabilities that prevent keyboard use. In such cases the browser will have to have voice recognition.

Aural browsers will also need to consider the case of forms. Sophisticated browsers will, in the future, have voice recognition facilities (already, numerous stand-alone voice recognition software packages exist) less sophisticated browsers will have the equivalent of a drop down list-"Choose from the following options...". Authors must take all this into account when designing pages for the aural media.

Text-to-Language Conversion

Aural browsers take the written word and synthesize spoken language. Speech synthesis from the written word is well advanced, but there are still many problems. Here are three of the most obvious ones:

- Pronunciation-is read pronounced "red", as in I read the book, or is it pronounced "reed" as in I will read that.
- Context-different contexts require different pronunciations. "I love that" will have at least three different renderings depending on whether it is said in an ironic, an exclamatory, or an intimate setting.
- Inflection-in English (and certain other languages) sentences, phrases and words can acquire different meaning depending on the inflection imparted to them.

There is, at the present time, no way to represent this in a style language, and authors writing for aural media may want to word sentences differently. Aural browsers may need to be amenable to such spoken commands as "stop", "back up three", "go forward one", and "spell".

It is likely that aural browsers will, on coming across an image, spell out the **<ALT>**. When the author knows that the target audience may use an aural browser, he may want to provide a fuller description. Indeed, there is a place for the use of a different tag, or else, the author could use the **cue-before** style property, which we'll cover shortly in the *CSS2 Aural Style Sheets* section.

Styling Speech

Here are some of the styling considerations which authors need to take account of when creating an aural style sheet. After a brief look at these we will see how CSS2 begins to handle them.

General Aural Styling Considerations

Volume

Volume is not quite as simple as measuring the loudness in decibels. In speech there is certainly a large variation in absolute volume in a single sentence. Therefore, when we speak of volume in this context, we are referring to average volume. Users typically should have control over the average volume, and authors should have control over volume range and relative volume. See the section on *The Volume Property* below.

Voice Characteristics

There are many characteristics here apart from the obvious ones of male or female, speech rate, and dialect (James Bond with a Texan accent, or John Wayne with an Oxford accent). Such characteristics are stress, inflection and richness. A rich voice comes from the belly and carries. Naval officers and opera singers have rich voices. The wave form looks very rich (very wavy) and so is difficult to describe in words. See the section on *The Voice Characteristics Properties* below.

Spatial Effects

A stereo effect. Where are the sounds coming from? See the section on *The Azimuth and Elevation Properties* below.

Pauses

Listen to any radio show. The pauses will signal a change of scene or mood. See the section on *The Pause Properties* below. We need to be able to designate pauses.

Cues

"This is the BBC world service, here is the news" is a cue to the upcoming news. See the section on *The Cue Properties* below. We need to be able to provide cues.

Background Noise and Mixing

Should background sound be present, should it be continuous, loud, soft, should it continue from one element to the next, should an element's background be mixed with sound from the previous element? Next time you go to a film, try and pay attention to the background sound to realize how complex a subject this is. See the section on *The Play-during Properties* below.

CSS2 Properties and Syntax for Aural Style Sheets

Let's look at some of the ways that CSS2 allows us to implement these characteristics. At the present time there are no aural browsers that implement style sheets-although some of those designed for the sight impaired are contemplating it.

The Volume Property

The volume refers to the median value of the wave form, so that a flat voice would be around the set value, but a highly inflected voice may have values much higher or lower than the set value. The syntax is:

volume:<*number*> | <*percentage*> | **silent** | **x-soft** | **soft** | **medium** | **loud** | **x-loud**

<*number*> refers to a number between 0 and 100, where 0 is the minimum audible level, and 100 is the maximum comfortable level. Note that the overall values are likely to be adjustable, by use of physical volume controls. <*percentage*> is a percentage of the inherited value, which is clipped if it exceeds the comfortable range. For example, if the base sound of the containing element is 80, and a value is set at 200% for a contained element, the value of the volume would not be 160, it would be 100. **silent** is not the same as 0-it means no sound at all. The absolute values increment by 25. For example, **x-soft=0**, **soft=25**.......**x-loud=100**.

The Voice Characteristics Properties

These properties have to do with how the voice is rendered by a speech synthesizer. It should be emphasized that, at present, there are no voice synthesizers available that can make use of all the properties CSS has enumerated. They are put there to encourage developers to make higher-end products.

The Speech-rate Property

The rate of speech is measured in words per minute. The syntax for this property is:

speech-rate:<*number*> | **x-slow** | **slow** | **medium** | **fast** | **x-fast** | **faster** | **slower**

x-slow is 80 wpm, **slow** 120 wpm, **medium** 180-200 wpm, **fast** 300 wpm, **x-fast** 500 wpm, and **faster**/**slower** adds or subtracts 40 wpm from the value.

The Voice-family Property

This is really the equivalent of the **`font-family`** property in visual media, and has a similar syntax. It is expected that each user agent will support 3 generic voices, male, female, and child, but it is not clear how specific voice 'fonts' will be stored on the client's computer. For example:

```
rancher {voice-family: 'John Wayne', western, male;}
```

could be possible values for voice-family in the future. However, as they have not been developed yet, we will we have to wait and see whether we get voice "fonts".

The Pitch Property

The pitch of a voice is measured in hertz **`[Hz]`** or kilohertz **`[kHz]`**. The **`pitch`** property allows you to set pitches of individual voices. A typical male voice averages about 120 Hz, and a female voice about 200 Hz.

The user agent will have to arbitrate between this value and **`voice-family`** if both properties are used.

The Pitch-range Property

The range of the voice on a scale of 0 to 100. 0 would be a completely flat robotic voice, and anything above 50 highly inflected.

The Stress Property

A value that is put in to allow for higher quality auditory production. It would specify the height of the local peaks in any dialect, and would be used in conjunction with the **`pitch-range`** property.

The Richness Property.

Another property put in to encourage the design of high-end synthesizers. It is a numerical value that defines the richness or brightness of a voice.

The Azimuth and Elevation Properties

These properties are for use with stereo speakers and define where the voice is coming from. **`azimuth`** defines the bearing in a plane parallel to the floor, and **`elevation`** defines the bearing on a plane at right angles to the floor.

The syntax for **`azimuth`** is:

`azimuth:<angle>| [[left-side | far-left | left | center-left | center | right | far-right | right-side] ||behind] | leftwards | rightwards`

The syntax for **`elevation`** is:

`elevation:` <*angle*> **`| above | level | below | higher | lower`**

Angles can be described in degrees **`[deg]`**, grads, **`[grad]`**, or radians **`[rad]`**. **`higher`** or **`lower`** adds or subtracts 10 degrees. **`leftwards`** or **`rightwards`** adds or subtracts 20 degrees.

The figures below show the positions of the absolute values.

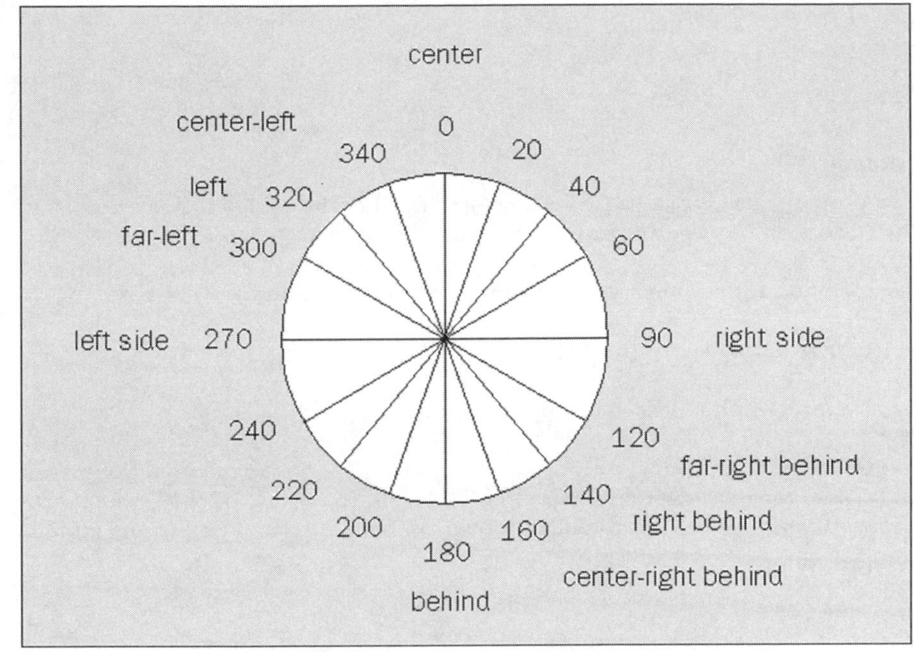

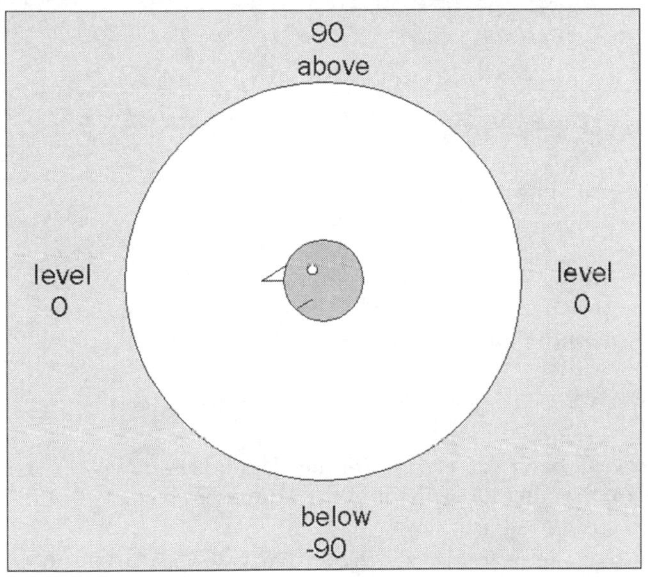

The following code would have the speaker voice appearing to come from over ones left shoulder.

```
speaker{
azimuth:far-left behind;
elevation:45deg;
}
```

The Pause Properties

The **pause** property specifies a pause both before and after the element. It is a combined form of **pause-before**, and **pause-after** and they all take the same values.

The syntax for **pause**, the short hand of **pause-before** and **pause-after** is:

pause: [[<*time*> | <*percentage*>] {1,2}]

where *time* is expressed in milliseconds (ms) or seconds (s).

The *percentage* value is a percentage related to the speech rate. For example, if the speech rate is 180 words per second, then each word takes 333 milliseconds, so a pause of 300% would create a one second pause. If only one value is provided it refers to both the pause before and after.

For example:

```
.dramatic{
pause-before: 1000ms;
pause-after: 750ms;
}
```

and

```
.dramatic {pause: 1000ms 750ms;}
```

would both have the same effect.

The Cue Properties

These properties can provide an auditory icon before and after the element. It takes a URL where the URL is the location of the sound file. For example:

```
.correct{ cue-before: url(c:\windows\media\tada.wav)}
```

Would play a **tada** wave before an element of the class **correct**. Whereas the following would make an appropriate noise after an element of the **incorrect** class:

```
.incorrect{ cue-after: url(c:\windows\media\utopia~17.wav)}
```

Again **cue** is a shorthand property, and again if only one value is given it applies to both before and after. If two URLs are given, just separate them with white space.

The Play-during Property

This property controls the background sound of the spoken element. The syntax is as follows:

play-during:<*url*> **mix? repeat?** | **auto**| **none** | **inherit**

> *To re-cap the meaning of the syntax, the pipe-stem | means alternation occurs, a space between values means that all three may be present, the* **?** *mark means it may be present 0 or 1 times (****** *means 0 or several,* **+** *means one or several)*

This is best explained by examples.

```
dramatic{play-during:url(c:\windows\media\beethoven.rmi)}
```

The playing time for this piece is about 6 minutes and 20 seconds.

Take this XML document snippet.

```
<dramatic>
Gustav was on his way to the war together with his companions....
<battle>
Suddenly, shells exploded frightening the horses...
</battle>
</dramatic>
```

Suppose that the **battle** element occurred about 3 minutes into the narrative, let us have look at how specifying **play-during** properties for the **battle** element would affect the original background music.

First of all, if no **play-during** was specified then the default property **auto** would apply and the piece would carry on playing until it was finished and it would not restart. However, if the property had been set to **inherit** as in:

```
battle{play-during:inherit}
```

then the music **would** restart. This time we set the **play-during** property to a URL.

```
battle{play-during:url(batsnds.wav)}
```

Now the Beethoven piece would stop, and the battle sounds piece would start playing. If that piece were too short for the whole of the **battle** element it would stop. To get it to repeat over and over we must put in the **repeat** property.

```
battle{play-during:url(batsnds.wav)repeat}
```

To get the Beethoven piece to carry on playing and be mixed with the battle piece, we would have to put:

```
battle{play-during:url(batsnds.wav)mix}
```

To have a silent background we would, of course, have to put:

```
battle{play-during: none}
```

The Speak Property

The speak property is somewhat analogous to the **display** property in visual media. It takes the values **normal**, **none**, or **spell-out**, for example:

```
.suppressed {speak: none}
```

This would suppress all elements of the class **suppressed**, and furthermore would allot no time space for them. To keep the time space intact use the **volume: silent** property/value combination. **Display: none**, and **volume: silent** in aural media are exactly analogous to display: none, and visibility: hidden in visual media.

The code below tells the browser to spell out all the elements of the class **acronym**, so NATO would become "en", "ay", "tee", "oh".

```
.acronym {speak: spell-out}
```

The Speech Properties

Now, let`s examine the speak property in more detail by presenting its related properties.

The Speak-punctuation Property

This property is for use when reading code or other text where the punctuation is of vital importance. It takes the values of **code** or **none**.

The Speak-numeral Property

Takes the values of **digits** or **continuous**. For example:

```
artsgrad{speak-numeral:continuous;}
```

will say 237 as "two hundred and thirty seven". While:

```
scigrad{speak-numeral:digits;}
```

will say "two three seven"

The Speak-header Property

Used when rendering tables aurally. It takes the value of **once** or **always**. If it is set to **once** the header is spoken just at the beginning of a group of cells, if it is set to **always**, it is spoken before every cell.

So, we've covered styling of visual and aural content, what's left? That's right, tactile content, which we'll cover now.

Tactile Content

This section covers the styling options available for tactile content. The main audience for tactile content are those with some form of visual impairment, so let's begin with a look at the various types of visual disabilities.

Types of Visual Disability

There is a whole range of visual disability, which authors need to take into account when developing web pages.

Color Blindness

Visual disabilities other than blindness are common. Some 10% of the population suffer from some form of color blindness. This visual impairment makes it difficult to distinguish between various colors. Red/green color blindness is the most common, but some 5% of the male population is totally colorblind. Authors may want to take this into account when designing pages. The simplest way to check that your pages are readable to a colorblind person is to print them out on a black and white printer

Presbyopia

This is the most common disability, indeed it is so common that it is hardly considered one. All people, as they grow older, lose the ability to focus on things close at hand, hence the need for reading glasses. This is due to the fact that the lens of the eye gets thicker and thus more difficult to squeeze into the round shape necessary for reading closely. By the age of 55 most people will need a 2x magnifying lens for reading.

Authors may want to take this into account, particularly if the target audience is an older population, and use larger font sizes. Most older people have difficulty reading serif font sizes smaller than 12 on the screen, although they can usually handle sans-serif fonts of 10.

Blindness—Partial to Total

There are numerous causes and degrees of blindness. Some are blind from birth and others become blind through accident or disease. Some people are able to read very large or bright type others are totally sightless.

However sophisticated aural presentation becomes, it will never be the complete answer to communicating with the blind. Because aural and written materials are processed in different parts of the brain, there is a need for both. (Witness that the demand for books has been increased and not lessened by television.) For this reason sites-particularly public sites-should always present a version suitable for Braille translators. Luckily for authors, the format that HTML is written in-a tagged language-is ideal for Braille translators. Indeed the disability acts of various States in the US (passed before the advent of the WWW!) require the publication of documents in SGML so that they can be readily transcribed to Braille. The other reason that aural translators will not be the total answer is that a significant proportion of the people who are blind are also deaf.

As you can see, there will always be a need for tactile content for sight impaired readers. No matter how sophisticated aural browsers become, the written word will not be replaced for deep psychological and neuro-physiological reasons. The spoken word and the written word go through different neurological processes, and, for the sightless, Braille is the written word.

Braille is a remarkable achievement. It is a 19th century technology that appears to be more established than ever as we enter the 21st century. In many ways it anticipated computer technology in the methods that it employs.

A Short History of Braille

As with many technologies, it was war that gave the impetus to implementation. A French army captain, Charles Barbier de la Serre invented a system of raised dots for reading and writing to allow military orders to be read at night. It was a complex system based on phonetics and word representation rather than the alphabet and never caught on– even in the military. He presented it to the Royal Institute for the Blind Youth in Paris hoping it might be of help.

Louis Braille, born in France in 1809, lost his sight at the age of three when his eye was pierced by a sharp awl in his father's saddle-making workshop. Infection set in and spread to the other eye and that was that. He was, however, a remarkably gifted child, and at age ten he was sent to the Paris blind school, where he learned about the system of dots, realized its problems, analyzed and corrected them. By the age of 15, he had refined and produced the system still in use today. By the age of 16, he was chief organist at a Paris church, and by the age of 17 was elected professor of the Institute.

The system he invented used a series of six dots to represent the alphabet, what we would call a six bit system. It used these 64 combinations to allow formatting, what XML gurus would call an entity system for common words, a music and a mathematical vocabulary. He also made allowance for representation in other languages. A mark of his genius is that the system he invented is virtually unchanged to this day. Using this system a blind reader can read at speeds comparable to a sighted reader.

The Braille Alphabet

The Braille alphabet is shown in the following figure:

A	B	C	D	E	F	G	H	I	J
K	L	M	N	O	P	Q	R	S	T
U	V	X	Y	Z	and	for	of	the	with
ch	gh	sh	th	wh	ed	er	ou	ow	W

The positions of the 6 dots are universally numbered from 1 to 3 from top to bottom on the left and from 4 to 6 from top to bottom on the right. Each character is called a cell in Braille. In print they are conveniently represented by the format [()()]. To represent numbers the first ten symbols are used, prefixed by a number indicator [(3)(456)], so to represent 35 we would put [(3)(456)][(1)(4)][(1)(5)](ie "c"=3, and "e"=5). Luckily we don't have to remember any of this because Braille translators do all the work for us. To see a Braille translator in action visit:

`http://www.access2020.com/new.html`

The use of contractions such as "the" is common in Braille. Braille without contractions is called Grade I Braille, and with contractions is called Grade II.

Braille Styling and Formatting

When a page is laid out for a sighted reader, the object is to make the site look pleasing to the eye. Certain colors have certain connotations, as do certain fonts. In Braille the idea of formatting is to reduce bulk as much as possible (Braille books are very bulky, see below) while maintaining readability.

There is no equivalent in Braille to fonts, weight, or style.

To emphasize a letter in Braille the italics symbol 4-6 is placed before it. To emphasize a whole passage, a double italics symbol is placed before it and another is placed before the last word.

Indent and Runover

Braille uses the term indent and runover. The placement of the first cell in the paragraph is called an indent, that of the subsequent lines of text is called the runover. Instructions such as "indent to cell three, runover to cell one", produce the typical paragraph indent, "indent to cell one, runover to cell three" would produce the equivalent of a hanging indent.

Headings

There are three kinds of headings in Braille: major, minor, and paragraph. What do these terms mean?

- A major heading is centered with a blank line before and after.
- A minor heading is blocked to cell 5, and any runover is also blocked to cell 5. (Blocking is the equivalent of indenting, a cell is the equivalent of a letter space). Usually a blank line is left after it.
- A paragraph heading is just emphasized using the 4-6 symbol, and text will usually follow on, on the same line.

Braille rules require at least one line of text on a page following a heading.

Braille Paged Media

Braille is bulky. Each line of Braille contains only about 34-40 characters so a typical page only contains about 1000 characters compared with about 3500 for print. Secondly because the pages are embossed, they cannot lie flat. Thus, a standard desktop dictionary will take up an entire bookshelf.

Because Braille books are copied for the most part from inkprint books, Braille printed documents have a double page number, that of the actual Braille page, and a number corresponding to the inkprint version. This allows for easy reference. Books laid out with this double number system are said to be laid out in **textbook format**, those where exact correspondence to an inkprint book is not necessary can be laid out in **literary format**.

Braille Browsers

As you can see HTML and XML are well suited to Braille, and really very little styling is necessary, just three forms of heading, a text indent property, and a print layout property. Current Braille browsers just strip off all the formatting except for the basic tags, and give a good interpretation. For this reason authors who may have Braille readers in their audience should probably go easy on the use of **`<DIV STYLE= "">`** tags to convey headings, as the Braille browser will just interpret them as another heading.

Current Braille browsers often have a speech engine attached as well as having a Braille screen and the user has the option which to use. The Braille screen is a series of pins that can be raised or lowered to correspond to the cell dots. One advantage Braille readers have over their sighted peers is that it is often easier to read from a Braille screen than from a book, because the "resolution" is sharper.

So, we've seen the styling options available for visual, aural and tactile content, let's see how we can specify the type of media we are styling using CSS2.

CSS2 Media Dependant Style Sheets

The type of media required can be specified in several ways. Perhaps the easiest in HTML is to specify the target media using our old friend the **`<LINK>`** element. This can be done as follows:

```
<LINK REL= "stylesheet" TYPE= "text/css" MEDIA= "print" HREF=
"printme.css">
```

We also saw how the type of media can be specified when setting up our cascade using the **`@import`** rule in *The **`@import`** Rule* section of Chapter 7.

```
@import url(cowboy.css) aural;
```

We can also use the **`@media`** rule, which we'll cover next.

The @media Rule

To specify a style sheet for a special kind of media just do the following:

```
<STYLE TYPE="text/css">
@media screen{
BODY{font-family:serif;font-size:14pt;}
}
@media print{
BODY{font-family:serif;font-size:10pt;}
}
</STYLE>
```

Note how the style sheets are included inside the curly brackets. The **@media** rule is not yet implemented by browsers, but when it is, the values available will be:

all, **aural**, **braille**, **embossed**, **handheld**, **print**, **projection**, **screen**, **tty**, and **TV**.

You can try out the example given above if you want, but I'm afraid all you will get is the default browser values. However, for what it's worth it is called **atmed.css**. At the present moment, the only way you can specify a media type is through the **<LINK>** element. If you try adding the **@media** type to your **@import** none of it works.

You can, however, use the **<LINK>** tag to specify a special style sheet for printing, but be warned that if you put another style sheet after your LINK, it will overrule your **MEDIA= "print"** style sheet. For this reason it is, at present, best not to use the **@media** property, and perhaps just provide a separate page for printing.

With hand held devices, teletypes, and TV, it is up to the user agent to identify what kind of device it is being run on. Obviously different style sheets will be needed for these different display types. These style sheets can be specified with the **@media** rule.

Summary

This chapter has been a little nebulous because we have been dealing with subjects for which there is at present no implementation. These are really signposts to the future.

- We looked at the different requirements for printed (paged) and continuous media, and what properties CSS2 provides to let us handle these different requirements.
- We then examined the requirements of aural browsers, and what will be needed to write style sheets for them
- We had a brief look at sight disabilities, the history of Braille and at the special requirements and formatting for embossed media.
- Finally, we looked at how we specify separate style sheets for the different types of media using the **`@media`** rule.

References

Paged Media

The CSS2 spec on media types:

http://www.w3.org/TR/PR-CSS2/media.html

The CSS2 spec on paged media:

http://www.w3.org/TR/PR-CSS2/page.html

Aural Media

The CSS2 spec on aural style sheets:

http://www.w3.org/TR/PR-CSS2/aural.html

The W3C note on voice browsers:

http://www.w3.org/TR/1998/NOTE-voice-0128

Tactile Media

A paper on the background of Braille:

http://www.rdcbraille.com/backbrl.html

History of Braille

http://world.std.com/~duxbury/braille.html

SGML and Braille

http://world.std.com/~duxbury/hksb96.html

Biography of Louis Braille

http://www.duxburysystems.com/braille.html

Access to Material needed for Developers Writing for Braille

http://www.access2020.com/develop.html

The Braille Alphabet

http://www.access2020.com/alpha.html

15

CSS Examples

This has been the most fun part of this book to write, and I hope that it will be the most fun part for you to read, because it is here that we can apply everything that we have learned. Most of the examples up to now have been to illustrate a point, or demonstrate a principle, and I don't think even my mother would see any artistic merit in them! I make a disclaimer at this point, I claim no artistic merit myself, I leave that to my daughter, she tells me what is cool and I render it into code as best I can.

Although all these examples were designed for the IE4 browser, with suitable adjustments they could be run on Communicator as well. A word of warning, however, some of these pages will freeze up the Communicator browser (at least they do mine) so if you want to run them on Communicator be prepared to reboot! The Communicator browser does not render the position property well, so use **<LAYERS>** to write the equivalent Netscape code. Perhaps by the time you read this some patches will have been introduced. I know that Netscape is working on improving their CSS compliance both for further releases of their 4 series and for their upcoming release of version 5.

If you want to put any complicated page on the Web, especially one that uses a lot of script containing a lot of loops, be sure to test it on both platforms and if necessary write a fallback version which will look good on older browsers. For some reason viewers don't take kindly to a page that crashes their computer.

We will describe each example using the following routine:

- Describe the rationale behind the graphics (if any).
- Iterate what parts of the CSS2 specification they use, if any (they all use the CSS1 specification).
- If JavaScript code is used, look at the main code routines and how they are written.

Notes on Writing Pages with CSS

All your pages should degrade gracefully to standard HTML. If they don't or can't then you should run a differentiation routine.

The easiest way to do this is:

- Write your page in strict HTML 4.0. Now your pages will look fine on HTML 2.0 browsers and will look great on HTML 4.0 browsers.
- Add style sheets. There should be no change in backward compatibility with pure style sheets. However, if you are using a lot of positioning code, make sure that it looks OK in both browsers.
- Add deprecated style tags and attributes to improve rendering in HTML 3.2 browsers (no problem with HTML 2.0 here).
- Publish the pages.

Example 1 A Simple Technical Discussion

With the advent of style sheets there is no possible reason for your technical documents to be boring and difficult to read. A few lines of code in an external file should convert your dull documents into something like the following medical web page, with the added advantage that they should be able to degrade gracefully in non-CSS compliant browsers.

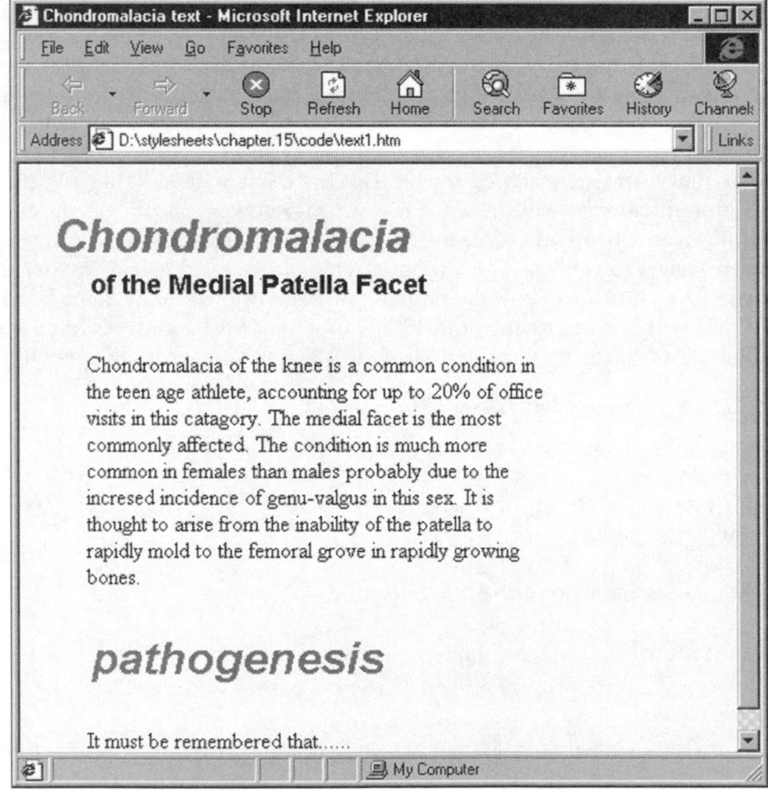

The body of the text is in 12pt Times New Roman, an excellent if dull choice for reading long lines of text. The serifs help to combine the letters into words and make for faster reading. (If you ever want the reader to slow down consider using a sans-serif font.)

For reading large blocks of text the optimum number of words per line should be between 10 and 16. Those wall to wall texts so common on the web are all right for occasional reading, but, if you are like me, you are soon heading for the Print menu if you have to study it. Most well laid out books have a number nearer the upper limit, for the screen it should be nearer the lower limit. Setting the width of the text area to 22-26 ems, which is a measurement relative to the font, guarantees that the correct number of words per line even if the viewer overrides your choice of font size.

The default background color on most browsers is either light gray or white, the former being perceived as being the best back drop for images, the latter for text. Text on a gray background looks rather stodgy, and white can appear rather glaring if viewed for a long period. The best compromise for an extended reading experience is a light pastel color, and here we have selected light lemon. For a full discussion of backgrounds, see Siegel's "Web Wonk" at:

http://www.dsiegel.com/tips/wonk7/vertical.html

The headings in this example are very different from the headings that demand attention. The idea is to demarcate the text without being overly distracting. They are not designed to say "Read me", they are deliberately understated. They do this in two ways, firstly they are complementary to the background color, namely a darker shade with a touch of brown thrown in, and secondly they are offset to the side. Note the secondary heading is almost the same size, but shows its secondary position by not being offset, and employing a lower case letter to start with. The primary heading uses the tertiary heading to create an underlining effect, emphasizing the primary heading without distracting from it.

Technical Points

There is nothing fancy or tricky here, just some simple style rules. Here's the code, it is simple CSS1 and employs no JavaScript:

```
<HTML>
<HEAD>
<TITLE>Chondromalacia text</TITLE>
<SCRIPT>

</SCRIPT>
<STYLE>
     BODY{
     color:#000000;
     background-color:#FFFFDD;
     }
    .heading1{
     margin-top:1em;
     margin-left:3%;
     margin-bottom:1em;
     color:#888800;
     font-size:25pt;
     font-family:arial,sans-serif;
     font-style:italic;
```

```
        }
      .runheading2{
        margin-top:-1.5em;
        margin-left:8%;
        margin-bottom:2em;
        color:#000000;
        font-size:14pt;
        font-family:arial,sans-serif;
        font-style:normal;
        }

      .heading2{
        margin-top:1em;
        margin-left:8%;
        margin-bottom:1em;
        color:#888800;
        font-size:24pt;
        font-family:arial,sans-serif;
        font-style:italic;
        }

      .textbody{
        font-size:12pt;
        font-family:'times new roman',sans-serif;
        width:21em;
        margin-left:8%;
        }

    </STYLE>
    </HEAD>

    <BODY>
    <H2 class=heading1>Chondromalacia</H2>
    <H4 class=runheading2>of the Medial Patella Facet</H4>
    <DIV class=textbody>Chondromalacia of the knee is a common condition in the
    teen age athlete, accounting for up to 20% of office visits in this
    catagory. The medial facet is the most commonly affected. The condition is
    much more common in females than males probably due to the incresed
    incidence of genu-valgus in this sex. It is thought to arise from the
    inability of the patella to rapidly mold to the femoral grove in rapidly
    growing bones. </DIV>
    <H3 class=heading2>pathogenesis</H3>
    <DIV class=textbody>It must be remembered that......</DIV>
    </BODY>
    </HTML>
```

The next screenshot shows how it appears on a Navigator 3 browser, i.e. it degrades quite gracefully and is perfectly readable.

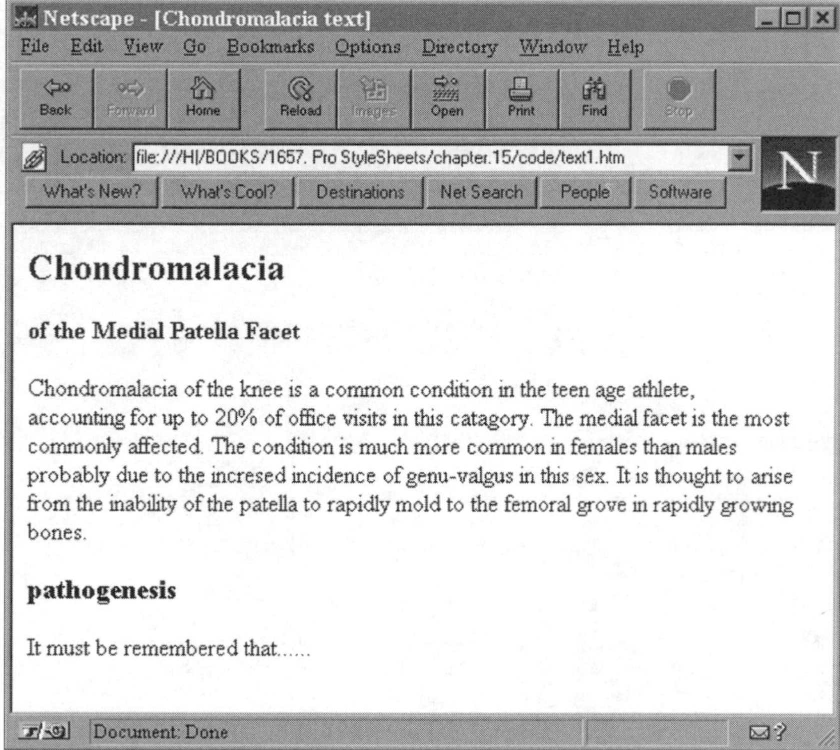

The code for the example is on the web site at **`http://rapid.wrox.co.uk/books/1657`** and can be run from there as **`text1.htm`**.

Example 2 A News Item

Here's a screenshot of our next example. There is certainly nothing fancy about this page. It was thrown together to illustrate the difference between a technical page and a news page. The code is available on the Web site, see **`text2.htm`**.

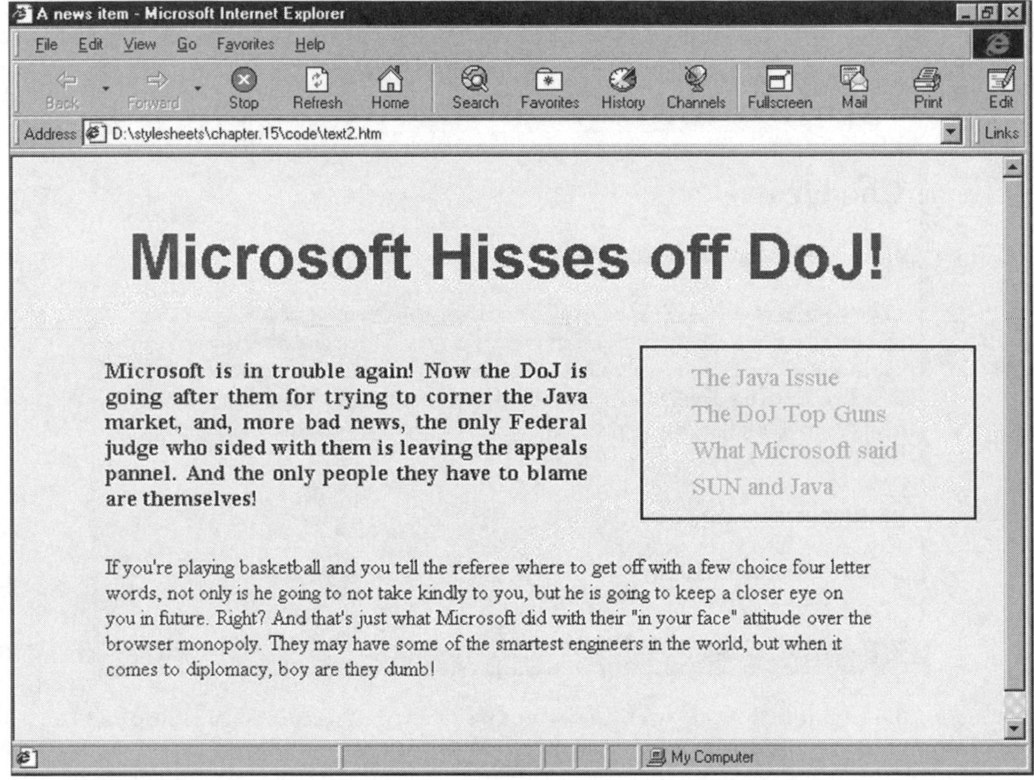

One of the great brains on the Web is Dr. Jakob Nielsen, and he has done actual research into a wide range of web related issues, so when he talks he is not just spouting an opinion, he is expressing as close as we can get to scientific fact on the Web. For example, he shows that people don't like to read from the screen (because of the lower resolution), and that they read 25% slower than the printed page. In fact, most people (80%) don't read the page at all, they just scan picking out highlights. For this reason a page that is designed for news should have a lot of highlights. Only 70% of web readers ever scroll a page, so get the stuff on the first page, with links if necessary.

Pages written for the Web should be written in what Nielsen calls the "inverted pyramid" style, i.e. put your conclusions first and then say how you reached them. This of course is the exact opposite of the way we learnt to do things at school and college. The following example of a news page reflects some of his thoughts. Unlike the first technical page, the headings are here designed to catch the eye. The color of this heading is in direct contrast to its light mauve background. Note the bolder type at the top working down to the smaller type, and note the handy references that are themselves eye catchers. We could probably have made the individual words Java and Judge stand out in the opening paragraph.

To really see how inverted pyramid reporting is done, read the cheap tabloids next time you are checking out at the supermarket. How can you resist a heading that says "Titanic survivor found on iceberg!" even though you know it's impossible.

For a real education on the Web check out some of Nielsen's pages. Here are three of the most relevant:

- Jakob Nielsen's *How Users Read on the Web:* **`http://www.useit.com/alertbox/9710a.html`**
- Jakob Nielsen's *Inverted Pyramids in Cyberspace:* **`http://www.useit.com/alertbox/9606.html`**
- *Be Succinct! (Writing for the Web):* **`http://www.useit.com/alertbox/9703b.html`**

Technical Points

Try resizing this page, particularly so that the heading flows on to two lines. Note that although the right hand box is not in an optimum position, it is not too bad.

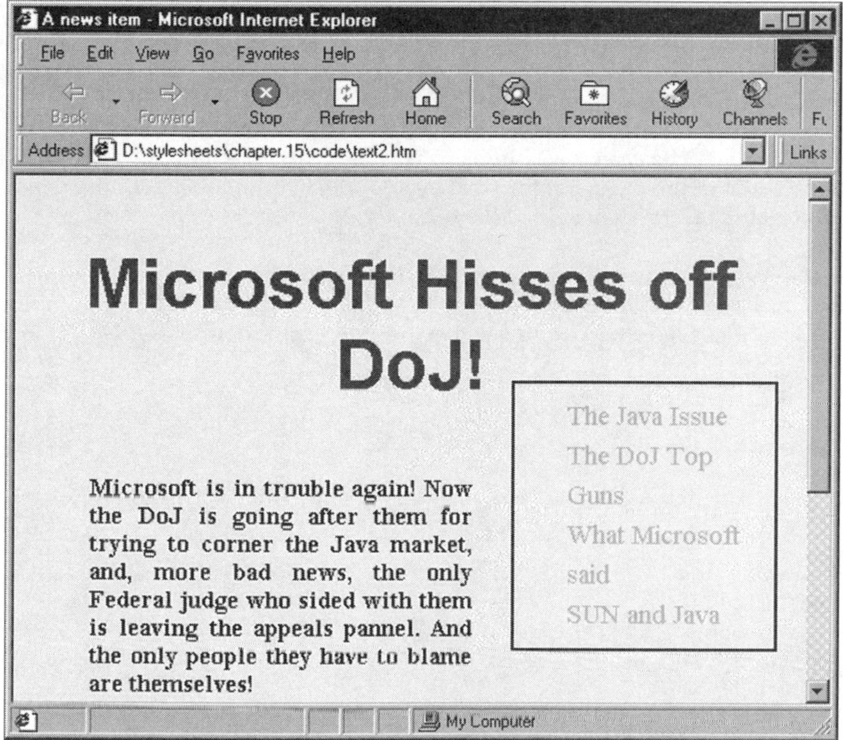

The **top** of the box remains the same, and we put it at 3 times the font size of our heading.

```
.heading1{
 margin-top:1em;
 margin-bottom:1em;
 color:#CC0000;
 font-size:35pt;
 font-family:arial,sans-serif;
 font-style:bold;
 text-align:center;
 }

.box{
 font-size:14pt;
 position:absolute;
 top:105pt;
 left:65%;
 width:35%;
 border:2px solid navy;
 padding:.5em .5em .5em 2em;
 line-height:140%;
 }
```

The **left** property is expressed as a percentage, as are the widths, ensuring that everything remains proportional. The easiest way to manage things from the point of view of coding is to put stuff on the left side of the page, but for right eye dominant people (95% of the population) things are more noticeable on the right side of the page.

Here's the code which we used for the page. We have just used simple CSS1 properties with the CSS2 **absolute** position property. Note that if we had wanted to put the box on the left side of the page we would not have needed to use the absolute position property. No JavaScript is used.

```
HTML>
<HEAD>
<TITLE>A news item</TITLE>
<SCRIPT>

</SCRIPT>
<STYLE>
     BODY{
     color:#000000;
     background-color:#EEEEFF;
     }

    .heading1{
     margin-top:1em;
     margin-bottom:1em;
     color:#CC0000;
     font-size:35pt;
     font-family:arial,sans-serif;
     font-style:bold;
     text-align:center;
```

```
      }

     .box{
      font-size:14pt;
      position:absolute;
      top:105pt;
      left:65%;
      width:35%;
      border:2px solid navy;
      padding:.5em .5em .5em 2em;
      line-height:140%;
      }

     .textbodybold{
      font-size:13pt;
      font-family:'times new roman',sans-serif;
      text-align:justify;
      font-weight:bold;
      width:50%;
      margin-left:8%;
      margin-bottom:2em;
      }

     .textbody{
      font-size:12pt;
      font-family:'times new roman',sans-serif;
      text-align:left;
      font-weight:normal;
      width:80%;
      margin-left:8%;
      margin-bottom:2em;
      }

      A:link{color:#880000;text-decoration:none;}
      A:visited{color:#dddd44;text-decoration:none;}
</STYLE>

</HEAD>
<BODY>
<A NAME="top"></A>
<H2 class=heading1>Microsoft Hisses off DoJ!</H2>

<DIV class=textbodybold>Microsoft is in trouble again! Now the DoJ is going
after them for trying to corner the Java market, and, more bad news, the
only Federal judge who sided with them is leaving the appeals pannel. And
the only people they have to blame are themselves! </DIV>
```

```
<DIV class=textbody>If you're playing basketball and you tell the referee
where to get off with a few choice four letter words, not only is he going
to not take kindly to you, but he is going to keep a closer eye on you in
future. Right? And that's just what Microsoft did with their "in your face"
attitude over the browser monopoly. They may have some of the smartest
engineers in the world, but when it comes to diplomacy, boy are they dumb!
</DIV>
<DIV class=box>
     <A HREF="#top">The Java Issue</A><BR>
     <A HREF="#top">The DoJ Top Guns</A><BR>
     <A HREF="#top">What Microsoft said</A><BR>
     <A HREF="#top">SUN and Java</A> </DIV><BR>
</BODY>
</HTML>
```

One other point, the **absolute** position property works terribly in Communicator, so avoid it in your web pages. Try viewing this page in Communicator, as is shown below, you can see the problem.

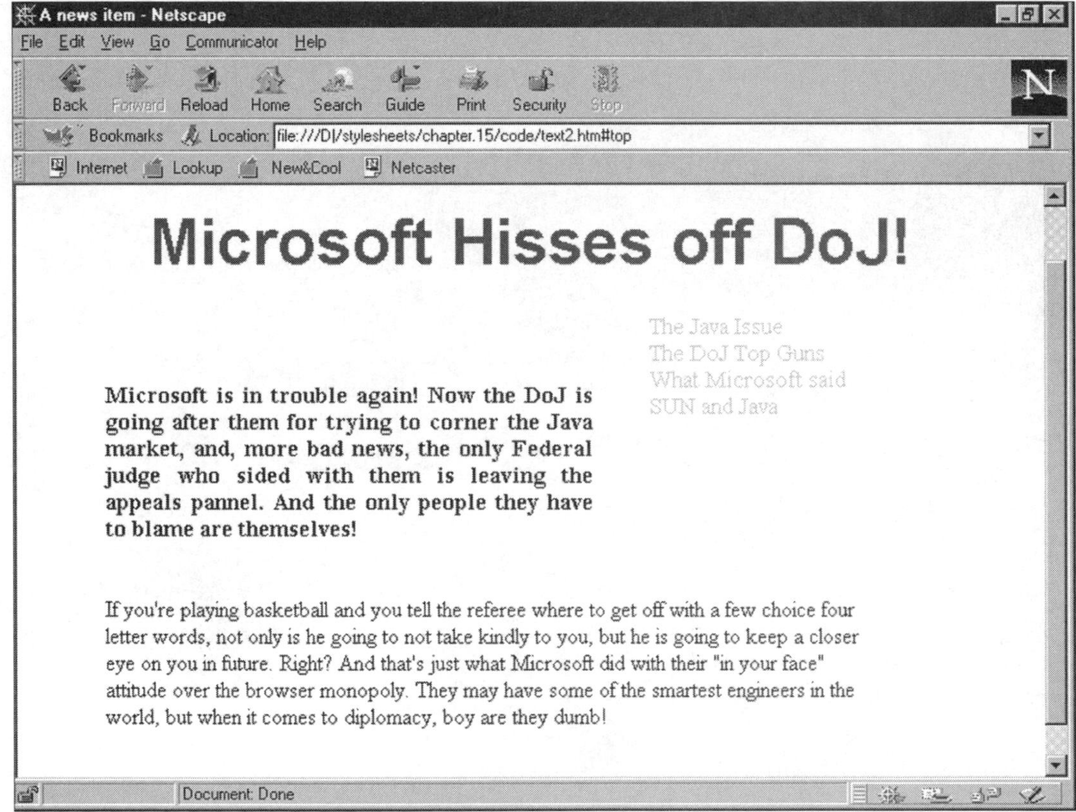

You will, I am afraid, have to use the **<LAYER>** tag and write differential code!

Example 3 Choosing Subjects

Here's our next example:

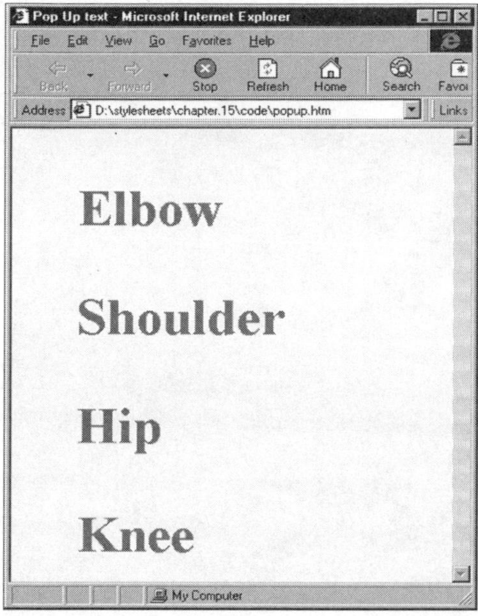

The example is taken from a web page advertising an up-coming medical meeting on sports injuries. By clicking on any of the headings on the left a short description of the lecture is bought up, as shown in the following screen shot.

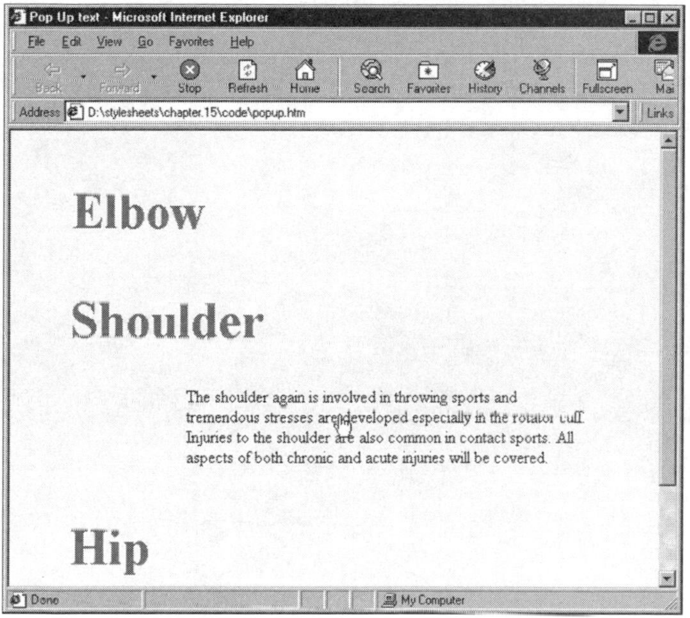

To get rid of the description, simply click on it again. By using the **`cursor`** property we are able to turn our arrow into a hand every time it is over a click-able area.

Technical Points

Here's the full code for the example, available on the web site as **`popup.htm`**:

```
<HTML>
<HEAD>
<TITLE>Pop Up text</TITLE>
<SCRIPT>

     function showbox(e){

            document.all(e).style.display="block";}
</SCRIPT>
<STYLE>
     BODY{
     color:#000000;
     background-color:#ffFFdd;
     }

   .left{
     background-color:#ffFFdd;
     color:#888800;
     font-size:36pt;
     margin-top:1em;
     margin-left:1em;
     cursor:hand;
     }

    .box{
     color:#000000;
     background-color:#ffFFdd;
     width:24em;
     font-size:12pt;
     margin-top:1em;
     margin-left:10em;
     display:none;
     cursor:hand;
     }
</STYLE>


</HEAD>
<BODY>
<BR>
<H2 CLASS=left onclick="showbox('xyz1');">Elbow</H2>
<DIV CLASS=box id=xyz1 onclick="this.style.display='none'">The elbow is
most often involved in chronic injuries in throwing sports. The elbow
itself acts as a flail that passes the acceleration to the hand resulting
in a high speed throw. However this flail action puts an enormous stress on
the medial aspect of the elbow.Prevention and treatment of injuries will be
treated in some depth.</DIV>
<H2 CLASS=left onclick="showbox('xyz2');">Shoulder</H2>
```

```
<DIV CLASS=box id=xyz2 onclick="this.style.display='none'">The shoulder
again is involved in throwing sports and tremendous stresses are developed
especially in the rotator cuff. Injuries to the shoulder are also common in
contact sports. All aspects of both chronic and acute injuries will be
covered.</DIV>
<H2 CLASS=left>Hip</H2>
<H2 CLASS=left>Knee</H2>

</BODY>
</HTML>
```

Now let's examine it in more detail. Clicking on the caption calls the very simple function **`showbox`**.

```
<SCRIPT>

     function showbox(e){

           document.all(e).style.display="block";}
</SCRIPT>
```

The box had been styled as follows and its **`display`** property set to **`none`** thus ensuring that no space was allocated to the box in the initial flow.

```
.box{
color:#000000;
background-color:#ffFFdd;
width:24em;
font-size:12pt;
margin-top:1em;
margin-left:10em;
display:none;
cursor:hand;
}
```

The function is called by the following inline code:

```
<H2 CLASS=left onclick="showbox('xyz1');">Elbow</H2>
<DIV CLASS=box id=xyz1 onclick= "this.style.display='none'"> The elbow is
most often involved.........
```

And inline code sets the **`display`** property back to **`none`** again after user has finished with it. The interesting part of CSS2 that this code uses is the **`cursor`** property, but note that IE4 supports a value of **`hand`** rather than a value of **`pointer`**.

Example 4 A Banner Ad

This page was made to demonstrate relative positioning, and the principles enunciated in the articles by Dan Brown and Jeanne Taylor on the use of banner ads. It is written for an online clothes supplier "Clothes make the Man".

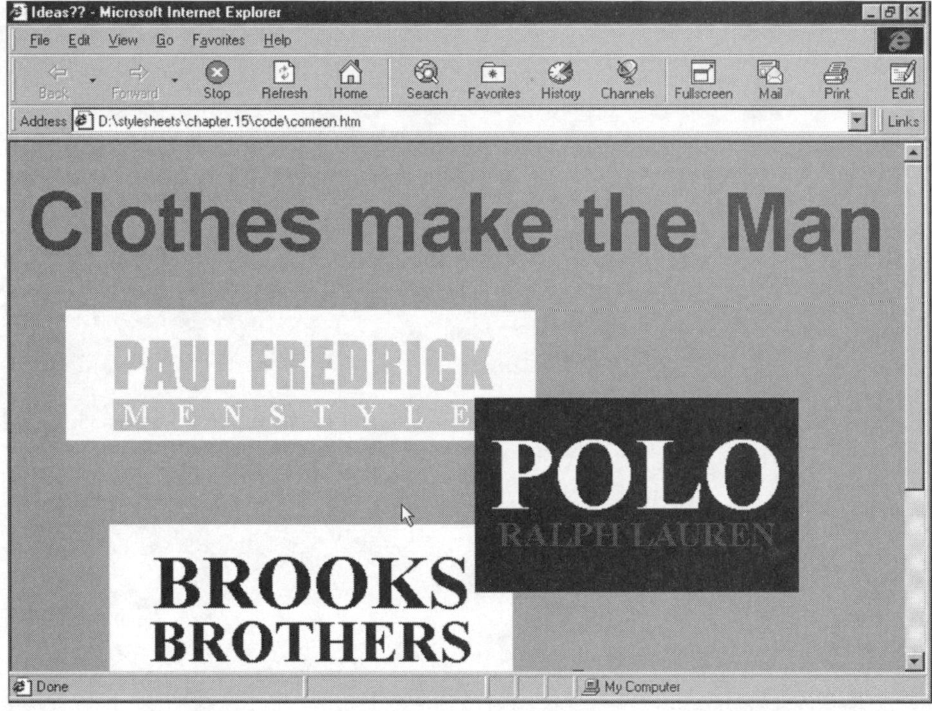

The main difference between web-based advertising and television is that in TV you have the viewer for a full thirty seconds, and all you want to do is leave an idea in the viewer's mind. You want to do that with web ads as well, but you also want them to click, and people love clicking on things that they recognize, hence the prominent logos for menswear. Clicking on these will take them to a catalog or another part of your web page. As well as hooking the reader you also have to land him, so always, always, always provide a way for them to purchase. He should not and will not look around your web site for a way to buy your products.

Why use style sheets instead of graphics? Well, the whole of this file weighs in at 2.7K, and loads in a split second. As a graphic with color reduced to the max, it still weighs in at a hefty 35K. If you do want to use graphics, you can always position them over your text when they load.

The Dan Brown and Jeanne Taylor articles (there are four of them) can be found at:

`http://www.zdnet.com/icom/webcoach/effect.ads/2.html`

Also search the root **webcoach** for numerous other interesting articles on web authoring.

Technical Points

Here's the full code for the example, available on the web site as **comeon.htm**.

```
<HTML>
<HEAD>
<TITLE>Come on ad.</TITLE>
<SCRIPT>

</SCRIPT>
<STYLE>
    BODY{
     background-color:#FFAA00;
     /*background-color:black;*/
     }

    .top{
     color:#FFFF00;
     /*background-color:black;*/
     color:#CC0000;
     font-size:50pt;
     font-weight:bold;
     font-family:arial;
     margin-top:.4em;
     margin-bottom:.4em;
     text-align:center;
     }

    .polo{
     color:white;
     background-color:#000022;
     width:200pt;
     height:120pt;

     font-weight:bold;
     font-family:"Times New Roman";
     margin-top:0.3em;
     position:relative;
     top:-10%;
     left:52%;
     }

    .polo2{
     font-size:64pt;
     font-weight:bold;
     font-family:"Times New Roman";
     text-align:center;
     margin-top:10pt;
     }

    .polo3{
     color:#DD0000;
     font-size:22pt;
     font-weight:bold;
     margin-top:-10pt;
     font-family:"Times New Roman";
```

```
         text-align:center;
         }

        .brooks{
         color:black;
         background-color:white;
         width:250pt;
         height:100pt;

         font-weight:bold;
         font-family:"Times New Roman";
         margin-top:0.3em;
         position:relative;
         top:-25%;
         left:10%;
         z-index:-1;
         }

        .brooks2{
         color:black;
         font-size:46pt;
         font-weight:bold;
         font-family:"Times New Roman";
         text-align:center;
         margin-top:10pt;
         text-decoration:none;
         }

        .brooks3{
         color:black;
         font-size:36pt;
         font-weight:bold;
         margin-top:-10pt;
         font-family:"Times New Roman";
         text-align:center;
         text-decoration:none;
         }

        .paul{
         color:#FFFF00;
         background-color:white;
         width:280pt;
         height:80pt;

         font-weight:bold;
         font-family:"Times New Roman";
         margin-top:0.3em;
         position:relative;
         left:5%;
         }

        .paul2{
         color:#FFCC00;
         font-size:38pt;
         font-weight:bold;
         font-family:'impact';
         padding-left:15pt;
```

```
      text-align:center;
      margin-top:10pt;
      }

     .paul3{
      color:white;
      background-color:#FFCC00;
      font-size:18pt;
      font-weight:bold;
      margin-top:-2pt;
      margin-left:30pt;
      margin-right:24pt;
      padding-left:5pt;
      letter-spacing:1.45em;
      font-family:"Times New Roman";
      text-align:left;
      }

     .caption{
      color:#880000;
      font-weight:bold;
      font-family:arial;
      font-size:36pt;
      margin-top:0.6em;
      text-align:center;
      }

</STYLE>
</HEAD>
<BODY>
<DIV class=top align=center>
Clothes make the Man
</DIV>

<DIV class=paul align=center>
<DIV class=paul2> PAUL FREDRICK</DIV>
<DIV class=paul3>MENSTYLE</DIV>
</DIV>

<DIV class=polo >
<DIV class=polo2>POLO</DIV>
<DIV class=polo3>RALPH LAUREN</DIV>
</DIV>

<A HREF=""><DIV class=brooks >
<DIV class=brooks2>BROOKS</DIV>
<DIV class=brooks3>BROTHERS</DIV>

</DIV></A>
<A HREF="">
<DIV class=caption STYLE="text-align:left;position:relative;top:-
35%;left:60%;">
Shop on line
</DIV>
</A>
</BODY>
</HTML>
```

There are really no special tricks here, each logo is a series of two `<DIV>` tags nested in a third `<DIV>`. The style needs to be tweaked to get it to look just right, and we need to use absolute units.

Although we have used relative units to move the logos from their place in the natural flow order, this can lead to problems if the screen is too small, but the trade off is that small screens do not have to scroll. Only experimentation will show what unit–relative or absolute–is right for your design.

One other small point, the logos have been put within a pair of `<A>` tags, and this will normally underline all text, so **`text-decoration`** has been set to **`none`**.

Example 5 A Borrowing from Print

Advertising executives like to keep a consistency to their ads, and want to reproduce on the Web the ads from the print media, not really realizing that the demands of the two media are quite different. The poor web designer is handed an ad and told to "put this on the Web".

Style sheets can really help here by allowing the designer to use a lot of small graphics interspersed by text, and position them absolutely using the position property, or layers.

Here is an example of an advert that Sun Microsystems have been running in their on-going battle over Java.

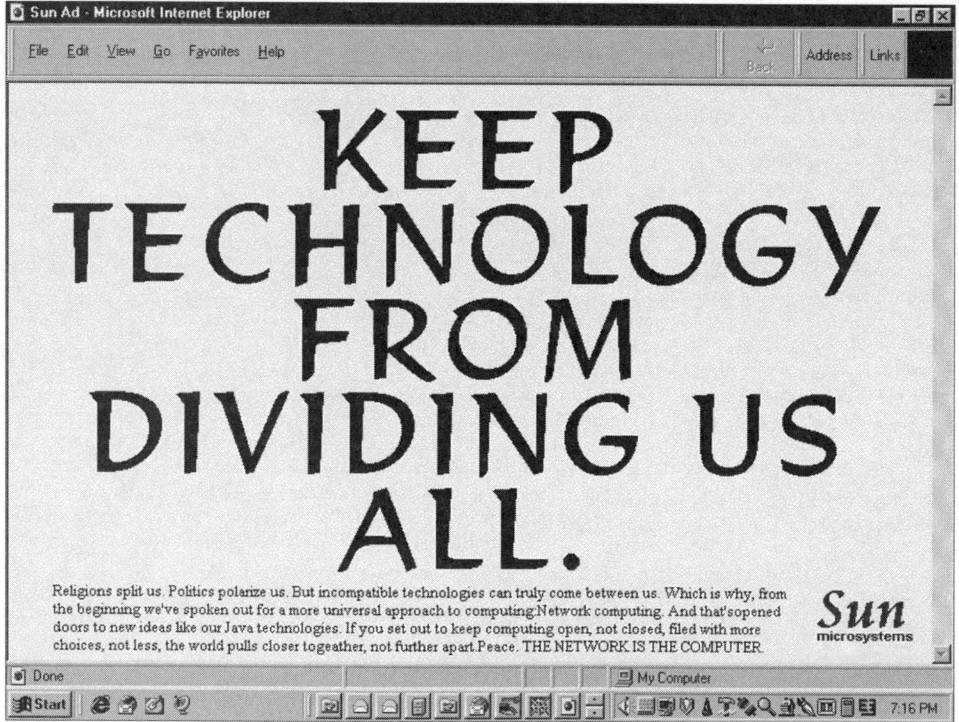

The logo in the bottom right corner would probably be better done using a small graphic, but we couldn't resist using a script macro, as described in Chapter 12, to do the job instead.

In the original ad, the text at the bottom of the page was smaller and confined to two lines. This, however, would be unreadable on a monitor because of its much lower resolution.

Another issue, the font used is **`formal436 bt`**, which, although not unusual, may well be missing on several machines. This is not the font used in the print ad, but is the closest match in common computer fonts. Times and Arial, or their equivalents are always available, so make sure that your page degrades gracefully if these fonts are used.

Technical Points

Here is the full code. Only the basic CSS1 values are used for the main caption, but the CSS2 position values are used to position the sub heading and the macro, although a point could be made for just letting the sub heading follow directly on from the main text.

```
<HTML>
<HEAD>
<TITLE>Sun Ad</TITLE>
<SCRIPT SRC="sunlogo.js">
</SCRIPT>
<SCRIPT>

     /*function sunlogo(x,y){
           document.write("<DIV STYLE='width:35pt;font:bold 14pt
    cateneo bt,sans-serif;font-style:italic;position:absolute;
    top:"+y+"%;left:"+x+"%'>Sun<BR></DIV>");
     }*/
     var dummy=sunlogo(90,90)
</SCRIPT>
<STYLE>
    BODY{
     background-color:white;
     }

    .caps{
     font-size:70pt;
     font-family:formal436 bt,Times new roman;
     line-height:85%;
     letter-spacing:0.5em;
     text-align:center;
     }

    .subtext{
     font-size:10pt;
     font-family:arial bt;
     width:82%;
     position:absolute;
     left:5%;
     top:92%;
     text-align:left;
     }
</STYLE>
</HEAD>
```

```
<BODY>
<DIV CLASS=caps align=center>
                    KEEP<BR>
                     TECHNOLOGY<BR>
                    FROM<BR>
                     DIVIDING US<BR>
                    ALL.<BR>

</DIV>
<DIV CLASS=SUBTEXT align=left>
Religions split us. Politics polarize us. But incompatible technologies can
truly come between us. Which is why, from the beginning we've spoken out
for a more universal approach to computing:Network computing. And
that'sopened doors to new ideas like our Java technologies. If you set out
to keep computing open, not closed, filed with more choices, not less, the
world pulls closer togeather, not further apart.Peace. THE NETWORK IS THE
COMPUTER.
</DIV>

</BODY>
</HTML>
```

Macros were discussed in the scripting chapter, Chapter 12, the section on *Creating Macros.* The macro creating the Sun logo is most conveniently kept in a separate file in this case, **`sunlogo.js`**, and called from within another pair of **`<SCRIPT>`** tags.

```
<SCRIPT>
     /*function sunlogo(x,y){
            document.write("<DIV STYLE='width:35pt;font:bold 14pt cateneo
bt,sans-serif;font-
style:italic;position:absolute;top:"+y+"%;left:"+x+"%'>Sun<BR></DIV>");
     }*/
     var dummy=sunlogo(90,90)
</SCRIPT>
```

This is a convenient way of calling the function. Note how the function is passed; the proposed x and y position of the logo as a percentage.

There is nothing unusual about the macro, we are just using JavaScript to write to the screen.

```
function sunlogo(x,y){

document.write("<DIV STYLE='color:#660066;width:35pt;font:bold 36pt cataneo
bt,sans-serif;font-
style:normal;position:absolute;top:"+y+"%;left:"+x+"%'>Sun<BR></DIV>");

document.write("<DIV STYLE='color:#660066;width:35pt;font:bold 8pt
arial,sans-serif;font-
style:normal;position:absolute;top:"+[y+10]+"%;left:"+x+"%'>microsystems<BR
></DIV>");
}
```

The sub-text is put here as a relative position, we would probably be better off calculating the height of our main text, and placing it as an absolute position. (Try resizing the window to see what the problem is.)

Example 6 Using Text as a Shape I

Interesting shapes can be made out of text, and you don't have to use fancy scripting to achieve this, although scripting certainly takes a lot of the sweat out of creating some shapes.

This example–copied from an old 1930's poster– creates a light bulb. Here the choices of color are important, and if you are "design illiterate" like myself, get some help in this department. (I use my wife and daughter, to whom I owe many thanks.)

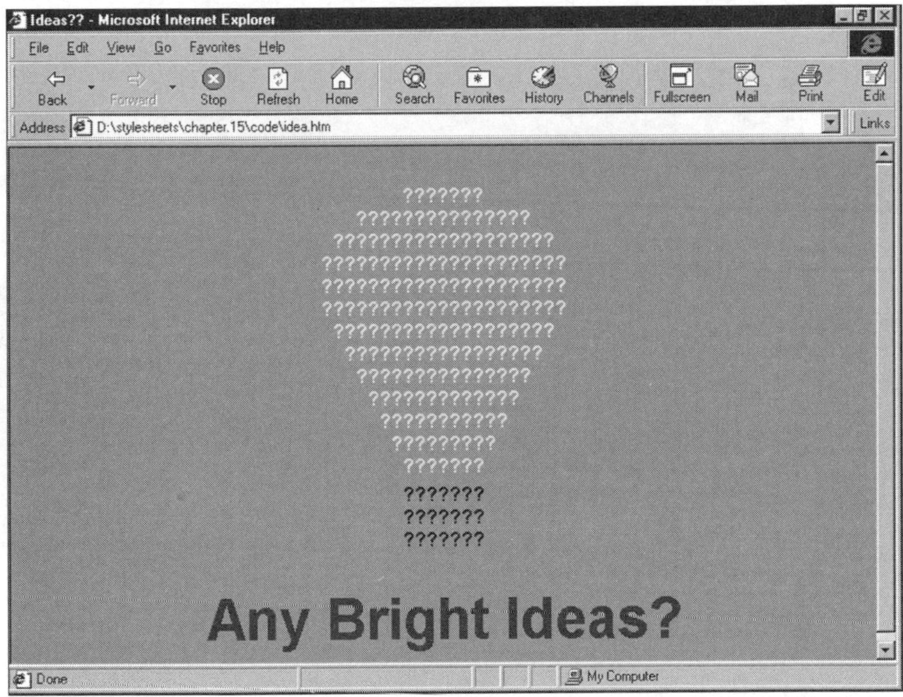

Technical Points

Here is the source code. I think you will be surprised at how simple this was. It can be downloaded as **idea.htm** from **http://rapid.wrox.co.uk/books/1657**

```
<HTML>
<HEAD>
<TITLE>Ideas??</TITLE>
<SCRIPT>

</SCRIPT>
<STYLE>
    BODY{
     background-color:#CC8800;
     }
```

```
    .top{
     color:#FFFF00;
     font-weight:bold;
     font-family:arial;
     margin-top:2em;
     text-align:center;
     }

    .bottom{
     color:#000000;
     font-weight:bold;
     font-family:arial;
     margin-top:0.3em;
     text-align:center;
     }

    .caption{
     color:#880000;
     font-weight:bold;
     font-family:arial;
     font-size:36pt;
     margin-top:0.6em;
     text-align:center;
     }
</STYLE>
</HEAD>
<BODY>
<DIV class=top align=center>
                      ???????<BR>
                    ???????????????<BR>
                  ???????????????????<BR>
                 ?????????????????????<BR>
                 ?????????????????????<BR>
                 ?????????????????????<BR>
                  ???????????????????<BR>
                   ?????????????????<BR>
                    ???????????????<BR>
                     ?????????????<BR>
                      ???????????<BR>
                       ?????????<BR>
                           ???????<BR>
</DIV>
<DIV class=bottom align=center>
                           ???????<BR>
                           ???????<BR>
                          ???????<BR>



</DIV>
<DIV class=caption align=center>
Any Bright Ideas?
</DIV>
</BODY>
</HTML>
```

All we are really doing in this example is centering lines of text (`?????`) and giving them color! We don't need an iota of code or CSS to do this, although we have used CSS for convenience.

Example 7 Using Text as a Shape II

Here's another example of using text as a shape.

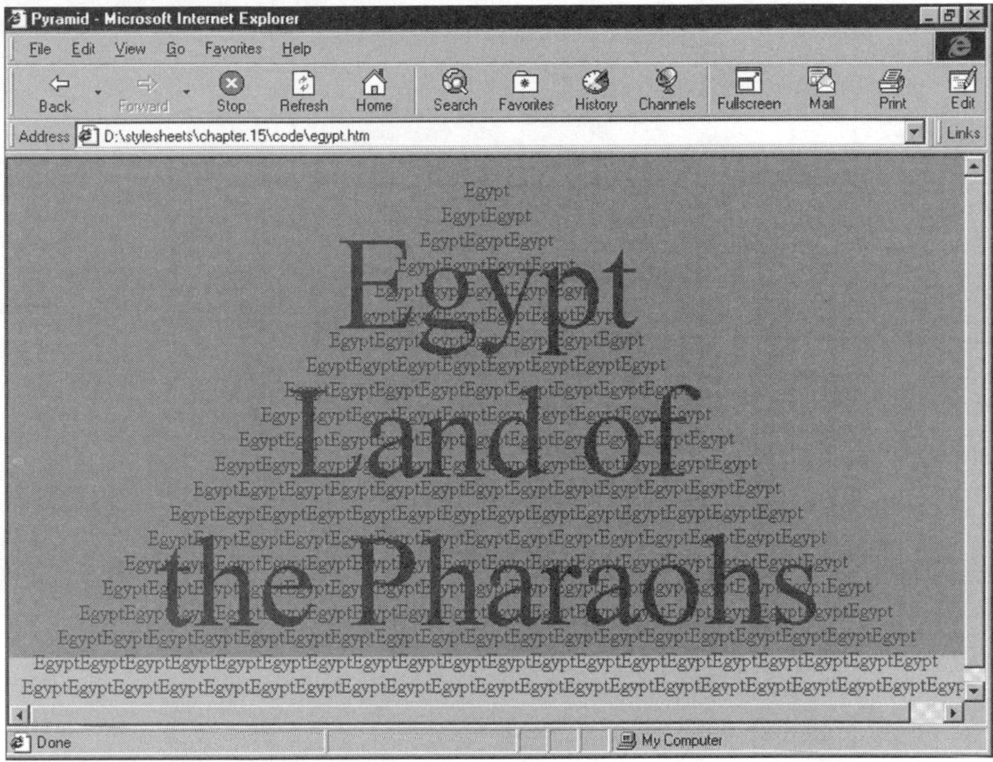

This is a somewhat more complicated example, certainly from the point of coding. The colors were copied from a wonderful color photo of the pyramids taken at sunset, but of course you'll only be able to see them if you run this code, **`egypt.htm`**, from the web site.

As I have mentioned several times, I am quite design illiterate, but I can recognize good work, so, if you are like me, always be on the look out for material that you may be able to use or alter to suit your needs at a future date.

I would like to put in a plug here for a book by Marion March called *Creative Typography* from North Light Books. (This book is currently available through **`http://www.Amazon.com`**) It will take you through all the steps of using print to create displays and, more importantly, give you several ideas about how to get ideas.

Technical Points

Here is the full code:

```
<HTML>
<HEAD>
<TITLE>Pyramid</TITLE>
<SCRIPT>
     function write_e(number){
     for(var num=0;num<=number;num++)
          {document.write("Egypt");}
     }
     for(var num=0;num<=20;num++)
          {
          write_e(num);
          document.write("<BR>")
          }
//document.write("<DIV class=xyz1>Egypt<BR> Land of <BR>the
Pharaohs</DIV>")
</SCRIPT>
<STYLE>
     BODY{
     text-align:center;
     color:#CC0000;
     background-color:#FFCC00;
     }

     .xyz1{
     padding-top:40px;
     margin-left:-25px;
     margin-bottom:20px;
     z-index:-1;
     position:absolute;
     top:0;
     left:0;
     height:85%;
     width:110%;
     background-color:#cc8800;
     color:#bb0000;
     font-size:75pt;
     }
</STYLE>


</HEAD>
<BODY>
<DIV class=xyz1>Egypt<BR> Land of <BR>the Pharaohs</DIV>

</BODY>
</HTML>
```

The center of this document is a script that will build a pyramid. Just remember that if a shape can be defined by a mathematical formula, it can be converted into a text shape with a little ingenuity.

```
<SCRIPT>
function write_e(number){
for(var num=0;num<=number;num++)
{document.write("Egypt");}
}
for(var num=0;num<=20;num++)
{
write_e(num);
document.write("<BR>")
}

</SCRIPT>
```

This code is simplicity itself, it employs a loop within a loop to write out the word Egypt a specified number of times. This is pure JavaScript. CSS2 position properties are used to place the large text over the pyramid in the position we want.

Example 8 Text as Art I

This striking example uses the cover of the West Geauga High School year book as a model, and shows what can be achieved with simple fonts. Times is used throughout. The effects are achieved by manipulating size and color, and positioning them appropriately.

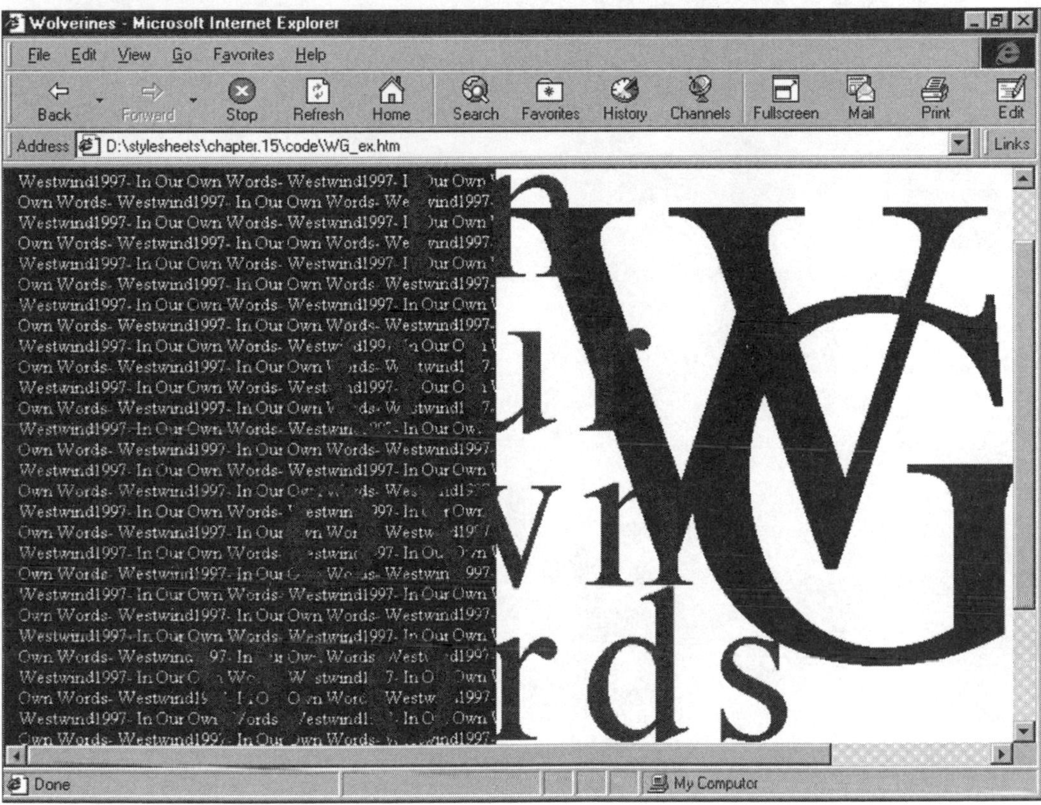

Technical Points

Here's the full code, it's available on the Web site as **WG_ex.htm**:

```
<HTML>
<HEAD>
<TITLE>Wolverines</TITLE>
<SCRIPT>
     for(var num=0;num<=130;num++)
            {document.write("In Our Own Words- Westwind1997- ")}


</SCRIPT>
<STYLE>
     BODY{background-color:#000030;color:white;font-size:10pt;}
     .xyz1
     {
     position:absolute;
     top:0;
     left:50%;
     width:55%;
     height:140%;
     background-color:#FFFFEE;
     color:#000050;
     font-size:290pt;
     letter-spacing:-0.4em;
     }

     .xyz2{
     position:absolute;
     left:0;
     top:30px;
     z-index:+2;
     text-align:center;
     color:#B00000;
     font-size:120pt;
     line-height:70%;
     letter-spacing:0.1em;
     }

     .xyz3
     {
     position:absolute;
     top:18%;
     left:68%;
     width:55%;
     height:120%;

     color:#000050;
     font-size:290pt;
     letter-spacing:-0.4em;
     }
</STYLE>


</HEAD>
```

```
<BODY>
<DIV class=xyz1>W</DIV>
<DIV class=xyz2>In<BR> our<BR> own<BR>  words</DIV>
<DIV class=xyz3>G</DIV>

</BODY>
</HTML>
```

The blocks of text are contained in 3 **<DIV>** elements positioned absolutely, and the repetitive text was generated by a **for** loop.

```
for(var num=0;num<=130;num++)
{document.write("In Our Own Words- Westwind1997- ")}
```

Again CSS2 position properties were used to place the text in their own containers.

Example 9 Text as Art II

This interesting piece makes use of contrasting colors, and a little code to achieve its effects. You can run it from the web site as **contrast.htm**.

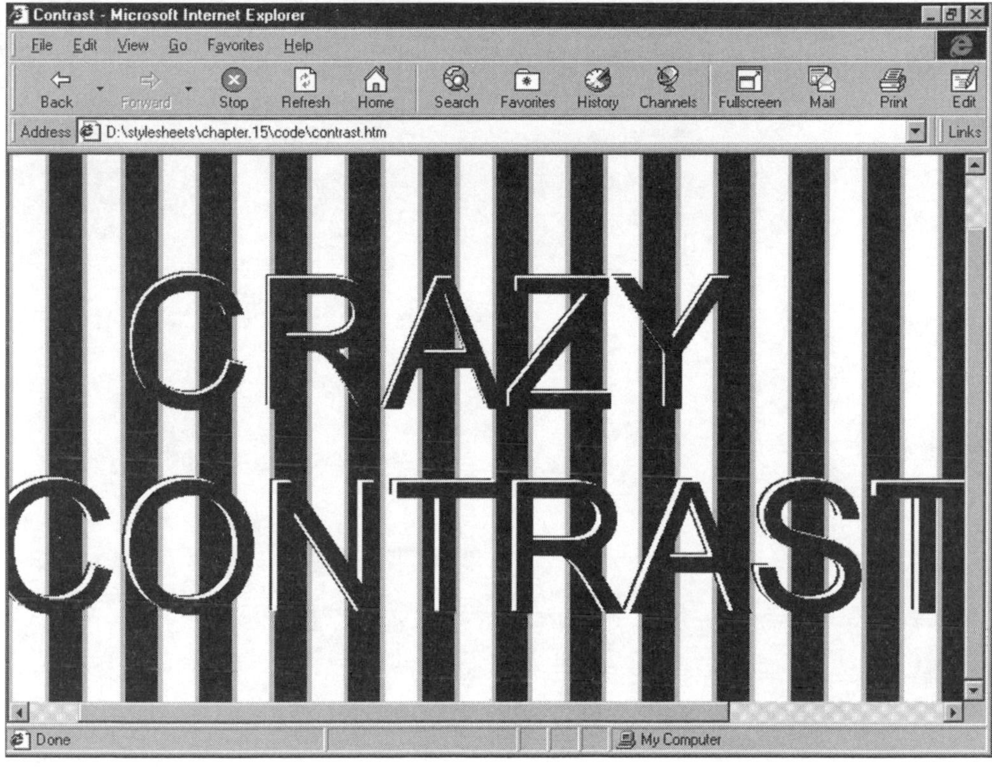

To make text stand out on a severely contrasting background, it is necessary to sandwich it as is done here, otherwise the outline of the letters will be lost.

Technical Points

Here's the full code:

```
<HTML>
<HEAD>
<TITLE>Contrast</TITLE>
<SCRIPT>

      for(var num=0;num<=35;num++)
             {
             if(num%2==1)
                    {
                    document.write("<DIV
style='position:absolute;left:"+[num*4]+"%;top:0;width:3.5%;height:120%;bac
kground-color:black'></DIV>");
                    }
             else
                    {
                    document.write("<DIV
style='position:absolute;left:"+[num*4]+"%;top:0;width:3.5%;height:120%;bac
kground-color:white'></DIV>");
                    }
             }
</SCRIPT>
<STYLE>
      BODY{
      text-align:center;
      color:#CC0000;
      background-color:#FFCC00;
      }

      .white{
      position:absolute;
      top:30%;
      left:5%;
      font-family:bedrock,sans-serif;
      color:#FFFFFF;
      font-size:105pt;
      }

      .black{
      position:absolute;
      top:30.5%;
      left:5.5%;
      font-family:bedrock,sans-serif;
      color:#000000;
      font-size:105pt;
      }

      .sand{
      position:absolute;
      top:29.7%;
      left:4.7%;
      font-family:bedrock,sans-serif;
      color:#000000;
```

```
        font-size:105pt;
        }
</STYLE>
</HEAD>

<BODY>
<DIV CLASS=sand>CRAZY CONTRAST</DIV>
<DIV CLASS=white>CRAZY CONTRAST</DIV>
<DIV CLASS=black>CRAZY CONTRAST</DIV>
</BODY>
</HTML>
```

First of all the background color is set and then the bars are drawn using a simple loop.

```
for(var num=0;num<=35;num++)
{
if(num%2==1)
{
document.write("<DIV
style='position:absolute;left:"+[num*4]+"%;top:0;width:3.5%;height:120%;bac
kground-color:black'></DIV>");
}
else
{
document.write("<DIV
style='position:absolute;left:"+[num*4]+"%;top:0;width:3.5%;height:120%;bac
kground-color:white'></DIV>");
}
}
```

Although we can get the width of the screen using JavaScript code and the screen width property, we have in fact set the width of the bar to 3.5%, so this guarantees the whole window is covered (**35*3.5=122.5**).

The sandwiched text is created by absolutely positioning three lots of text, and slightly offsetting them each time.

```
<DIV CLASS=sand>CRAZY CONTRAST</DIV>
<DIV CLASS=white>CRAZY CONTRAST</DIV>
<DIV CLASS=black>CRAZY CONTRAST</DIV>

<!--use style sheets and the position:absolute property to offset this
type-->
```

Note that this easy trick can also be used to create shadow text until the time that this property is supported by the browsers.

Example 10 Text as Art III.

The word spamming (misspelt purposely-the correctly spelt version looked wrong) marches out of a black background gaining in size and whiteness until it hits the bright red fence of Xs.

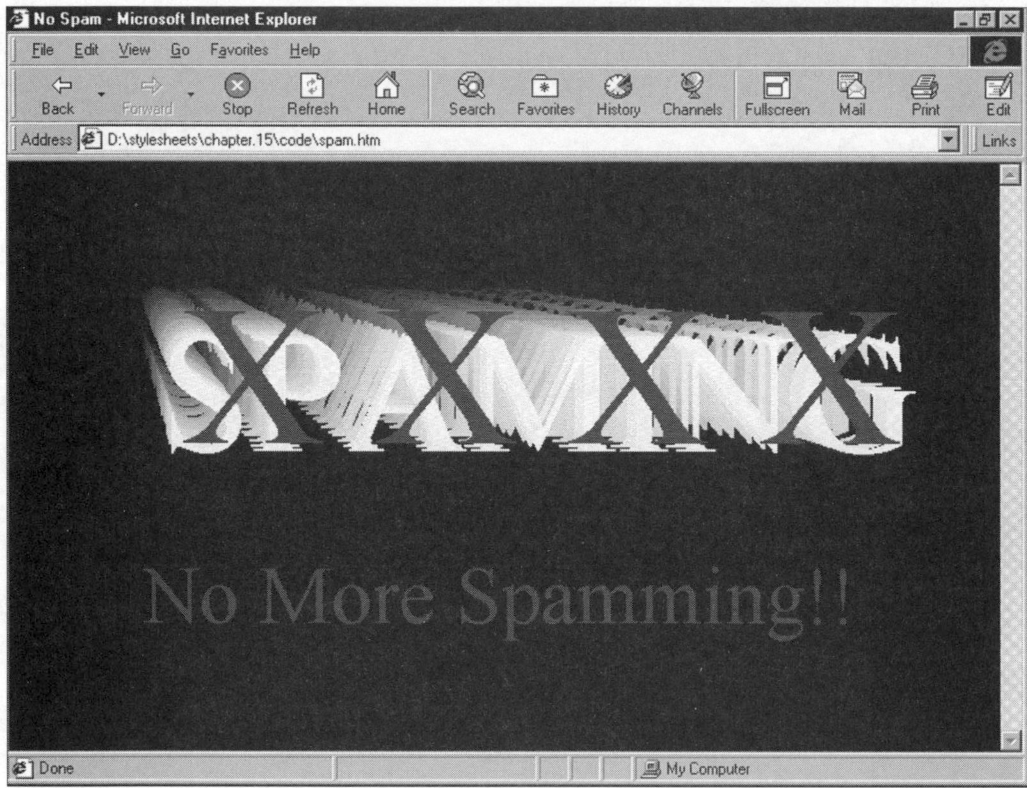

A highly effective use of text, and very easy to achieve with a little code and the position absolute property.

Technical Points

Here is the complete code that generates this effect (note that many of the lines are broken to fit them on the page). You can view it on the Web site as **`spam.htm`**

```
<HTML>
<HEAD>
<TITLE>No Spam</TITLE>

<STYLE>

</STYLE>


</HEAD>
<BODY STYLE="background-color:#000000;">
```

```
<SCRIPT>

for(var num=0;num<=25;num++)
{
document.write("<DIV
style='position:absolute;top:"+(75+num)+";left:"+(95+num*3/4)+";font-size:"
+(44+num*2)+"pt;color:rgb("+(num*10)+","+(num*10)+","+(num*10)+")'>SPAMING<
/DIV>")
}
document.write("<DIV
style='position:absolute;top:75;left:130;font-size:110pt;color:#CC0000;font
-family:geoslab703 md bt,serif'>X X X X</DIV>")
document.write("<DIV
style='position:absolute;top:285px;left:100px;font-size:45pt;color:#CC0000;
font-family:geoslab703 md bt,serif'> No More Spamming!! </DIV>")
</SCRIPT>
</BODY>
</HTML>
```

The loop not only moves each writing of "spaming" down and to the right, but it also changes the color through the use of the RGB method, and increases the size of the text. We have also used the script to also write the subscript text. Again the only CSS2 properties we use are the position properties. You can run the code from the web site as **spam.htm**.

Example 11 Text as Art IV

This really needs to be seen in color to be appreciated. You can find it on our Web site under **outbnd.htm**

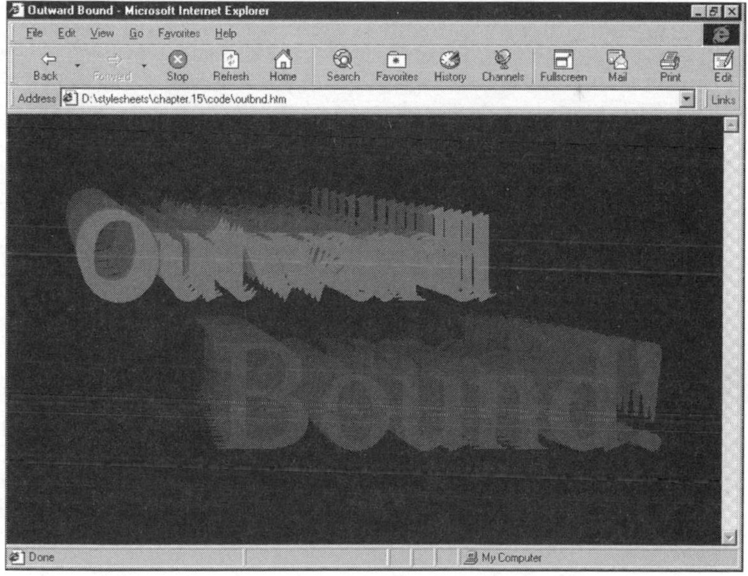

This is a title page designed for the well known adventure course. It really uses the same techniques as the last example.

Technical Points

Again, nothing new here, just a simple loop. Again the only CSS2 property we use is the position property.

```
<HTML>
<HEAD>
<TITLE>Outward Bound</TITLE>

<STYLE>

</STYLE>
</HEAD>

<BODY style="background-color:#000042">

<SCRIPT>
for(var num=0;num<=25;num++)
{
document.write("<DIV
style='position:absolute;top:"+(50+num)+";left:"+(50+num*3/4)+";font-
size:"+(44+num*2)+"pt;color:rgb("+(num*7)+","+(num*4)+",0)'>Outward</DIV>")
document.write("<DIV
style='position:absolute;top:"+(170+num)+";left:"+(180+num*4/3)+";font-
size:"+(70+num*2)+"pt;color:rgb("+(40+num*6)+",0,0)'>Bound!</DIV>")
}
</SCRIPT>
</BODY>
</HTML>
```

Summary

In this chapter we just looked at a few examples of what can be achieved using CSS and in some cases a little script.

Why use CSS instead of graphics?

Probably the most compelling reason is that your page will load much faster, but there are several additional ones which include dynamic re-flowing which can make you pages totally interactive, ease of maintenance and easy searching.

The support of Netscape for the positioning properties is currently limited, but this should change shortly, hopefully before you read this.

References

Dave Siegal is one of the acknowledged experts on web page design and font design. Begin accessing his web pages from this URL. He is an expert at laying out long passages of text.

www.dsiegel.com/tips/wonk7/vertical.html

Dan Brown is one of the gurus of the Web. In the following article he teams up with Jeanne Taylor to explain how to make a site for selling goods. Notes on banner headlines can be found at:

http://www.zdnet.com/icom/webcoach/effect.ads/2.html

Jakob Nielsen has been accused of being the smartest man on the Web. He has done scientific research on many topics, so when he speaks it is not just an ego-blown opinion. Here are the locations of three of his articles. From here you can link to many more.

How Users Read on the Web: **http://www.useit.com/alertbox/9710a.html**

Inverted Pyramids in Cyberspace: **http://www.useit.com/alertbox/9606.html**

Be Succinct! (Writing for the Web): **http://www.useit.com/alertbox/9703b.html**

Marion March is not a web denizen, but has been long acknowledged as one of the most creative typographers around. Her 1988 book *Creative Typography* from North Light Books is still in print, which should tell you how good (and timeless) it is. It takes you through all the steps of the creative process, and is one that even "right-brainers" like myself will want to read time and again.

Epilogue

There is one thing that you can be certain of, by the time you read this book much of it will be out of date! This is of course true of any technical book, but it is particularly true of any book that is written on the subject of the Internet. As one humorists put it: "There are two types of time in this world, regular time and Internet time, and I always know when I am on Internet time because I'm always behind!"

To give a specific example–during the writing of this book (a three month time span Feb-Apr 1998) the CSS2 recommendation went from a working document to proposal to a recommendation, with changes that accompanied each stage. The papers on Xlinks were revised 3 times, and new papers came out on a whole variety of subjects connected with XML–although the original XML spec has stayed rock-solid!

The speed of change is also true as regards implementation and tools. In the same period of time the CSS1 recommendation has gone from being poorly supported to quite well supported in the major browsers. At the beginning of the time period there were virtually no good tools for XML, now there are a number of them–but most are in the beta stage and not "user friendly" at present. Incidentally most of these tools are written in Java, which is rapidly becoming the default language for the Internet. One reason for this is that Java has two byte characters, and so can support the whole range of Unicode characters–not just the ASCII set.

To ensure that this book is useful for some time to come, I have tried to emphasize the basics which will not change. I have also tried to give references to the source documents so that you can check out the material for yourself. If you find a broken link then please let us know. We will endeavor to keep an updated list on the web site at:

`http://rapid.wrox.co.uk/books/1657`.

Standards

Now I am going to put on my Seer's hat and try and make a few comments on where the standards are going.

CSS1

We will start off with an easy one! This recommendation is rock solid, and is well supported in the major browsers. If you stick to CSS1 you can be fairly sure that your pages will be implemented.

A test suite is maintained by W3C at:

```
http://www.w3.org/Style/CSS/Test
```

You can test your current browser model against this suite.

CSS2

This is a massive recommendation, and it is going to take some time for the browser manufacturers to catch up, but both major players have promised full support for the recommendation. At present the positioning properties are supported well in IE4, but poorly in Communicator–although this is likely to change (see Mozilla below).

XML

There is no browser that supports XML although Netscape will give limited support in the next version of their browser. It is anybody's guess what Microsoft will do! Here's a quote from some recent correspondence of mine.

"The conference was...weird. Most people appear to be shying away from the idea of pure XML, and instead are talking about standardizing tagged subsets (a la HTML) or transforming XML documents into other formats. It's frustrating. Although Netscape is planning limited XML support (a la RDF), Microsoft's reps made it clear that they are going for tag-based interpretation, rather than interpretation of the DTD."

I predict that browsers will support XML, because that is what the public wants. Plus now that Mozilla code has been made public, there will be (is!) a group working out there making sure that at least this will happen in the next releases of the Netscape browsers.

In the meantime documents will continue to be marked up in XML, and more tools will become available to translate the XML into HTML for distribution on the Net.

For your amusement download:

`http://sunsite.unc.edu/pub/sun-info/xml/eg/shakespeare.1.10.xml.zip`

and:

`http://sunsite.unc.edu/pub/sun-info/xml/eg/religion.1.10.xml.zip`

which marks up all of Shakespeare's plays and the Bible and Koran.

You can in fact use the MSXSL parser to style these plays into HTML and display them!

XSL

The XSL working group have just (May 1998) released their blue print for XSL. It can be found at:

`http://www.w3.org/TR/WD-XSLReq`

If all the requirements ever get formulated and implemented it will be a massively powerful language! All the syntax that has been discussed in this book is likely to remain the same, except that instead of using HTML flow objects (and this can be confusing) XSL will probably define its own set of flow objects.

It is likely that CSS2 will be used for the majority of XML document styling, and that XSL will be used where more complex formatting and collating is required.

Keep an eye on:

`http://www.w3.org/style`

for updates on the XSL front.

Mozilla

"Netscape Communications made two important announcements on January 23rd, 1998: First, that the Netscape Communicator product would be available free of charge; Second, that the source code for Communicator would also be free. On March 31st, the first developer release of the source code to Communicator was made available."

Thus starts the Mozilla Mission statement.

If you think of it this is a move unprecedented in the Western world. A major corporation actually gave away the source of its wealth! Admittedly there was some smart thinking behind this move, but it is still a gesture that 99% of us would not have been able to make.

Now that Netscape has made their core code public, we really do have a "peoples browser", and we can be sure that at least one of the major players will be following the public interest.

If you want to get involved in the process you can. Sign up at:

http://www.mozilla.org/

A quick look at the code shows that XML will be supported in the next release. See:

http://www.mozilla.org/rdf/doc/xml.html

Core Styles

Wouldn't it be great if rather than writing our own style sheets, we could just link in with professionally designed and tested style sheets, knowing that they will work in any browser?

Well the future is here! Just link your document to one of the sheets maintained at:

http://www.w3.org/StyleSheets/Core/

This is the code we would use to link to the "modernist" style sheet:

```
<HTML>
<HEAD>
<TITLE>Document title</TITLE>
<LINK REL=stylesheet HREF="http://www.w3.org/StyleSheets/Core/Modernist"
TYPE="text/css">
</HEAD>
```

Internationalization

One of the big advantages of XML is that it supports (human) languages and alphabets other than the Roman alphabet through the use of Unicode.

The ASCII set can only support 255 characters (hexadecimal FF) or one byte.

The Unicode range is two bytes and so supports 65025 characters (hexadecimal FFFF).

Information on Unicode can be obtained from:

http://www.unicode.org/

Key References

Numerous references have been included throughout this book. A list of all the key ones can be obtained at the Wrox web site at:

`http://www.wrox.com`

The W3C home page is at:

`http://www.w3.org`

Other useful references that can lead you a variety of handy places are:

`http://www.hypermedic.com/style/index.htm`

`http://www.sil.org/sgml/xml.html`

`http://www.sil.org/sgml/xsl.html`

From these you can go anywhere on the Web–well kind of anyway.

Examples

All the examples in this book are available on the Wrox web site at:

`http://rapid.wrox.co.uk/books/1657`

As well as the individual examples there is a zip file of all the chapters examples.

Languages and notations

The following appendix explains the syntax used in the various specs. Although you should have a general understanding of the syntax, a detailed understanding (or reference to a guide such as this) is only necessary for detailed perusal of the Spec. Most of the syntaxes are based on a form of EBNF.

Extended Backus-Naur Form (EBNF) notation

The formal grammar of XML is given using a simple Extended Backus-Naur Form (EBNF) notation. EBNF is designed primarily to be read by machines but is also designed to be human readable. (I suppose that depends on your definition of human readable!)

EBNF or a modified form of it is used in several other W3C specs as well as having widespread use throughout the computing world. A modified form is used in DTDs. We highlight the terms and their definitions in boxes, then give detailed examples of their use.

#xN

#xN This represents a hexadecimal integer **N** as defined in ISO/IEC 10646.

For example in the XML document white space is defined as follows:

```
White Space
_ S ::=  (#x20 |_#x9 |_#xD |_#xA)+
```

Which means that white space is one or more (that's what the **+** means) combination in any order (that's what the pipestem (**|**) means) of the ISO/IEC 10646 characters.

Hexadecimal number 20 (=ASCII decimal32, a space)
Hexadecimal number 9 (=ASCII decimal9, a tab)
Hexadecimal number D (=ASCII decimal 13, a new line)
Hexadecimal number A (=ASCII decimal 10, a line feed)

[a-zA-Z], [#xN-#xN]

`[a-zA-Z], [#xN-#xN]` Matches any character with a value in the range(s) indicated (inclusive).

For example in the XML spec a permitted character (**`char`**) is defined as follows:

```
Char ::=  #x9 |_#xA |_#xD |_[#x20-#xD7FF] |_[#xE000-#xFFFD] |_[#x10000-
#x10FFFF]
```

`[#x20-#xD7FF]` means that any character in the range **`#x20`** to **`#xD7FF`** can be used as a legal character. (This includes all the ASCII characters.) **`#x9`**, **`#xA`**, **`#xD`** means that white space can be included.

Again note the pipestem which indicates alternatives.

[^abc], [^#xN#xN#xN]

`[^abc], [^#xN#xN#xN]` The ^ symbol means 'excluding'

```
AttValue ::=  '"' ([^<&"] |_Reference)* '"'   |_ "'" ([^<&'] |_Reference)*
"'"
```

In the above reference for **`AttValue`** the **`[^<&]`** means that Reference (defined else where in the spec) can be any value as long as it does not include the characters **&** or **<**.

[^a-z] [^#xN-#xN]

`[^a-z] [^#xN-#xN]` This refers to a range of values.

I couldn't find a reference in the XML spec but here's an example:

```
FirstHalfAlphabet::=([n-z] | alphabet)
```

This means that **`FirstHalfAlphabet`** can be any letter in alphabet (presumably defined else where as the characters a-z) except in those in the range n-z.

"string" 'string'

"string" 'string'	Both refer to a literal string.

In the XML spec we have the following:

```
DefaultDecl ::=  '#REQUIRED' |_'#IMPLIED'
```

Which means that the default declaration can take one of two string values '**#REQUIRED'** or '**#DEFAULT'**.

(expression)

(expression)	Expression is treated as a unit and may be combined as described in this list. This form of notation is very common in all the W3 specs.

A?

A?	Matches **A** or nothing; optional **A**.

This means that the inclusion of **A** is optional. In the XML spec we have this definition of a general entity declaration, where **S** stands for white space.

```
GEDecl ::=  '<!ENTITY' S Name S EntityDef S? '>'
```

The first two white spaces are compulsory, but the last one is optional.

A B

A B	Matches **A** followed by **B**.

For example in the following definition of a public ID:

```
PublicID ::=  'PUBLIC' S PubidLiteral
```

We are told that a **PublicID** must take the form of the string '**PUBLIC'**, followed by white space, followed by **PubidLiteral** (which is defined else where in the spec).

A | B

A | B	Matches **A** or **B** but not both.

We have already seen examples of this above, but to recap, in the following definition of **PEDef**, its value can be **EntityValue** or **_ExternalID** but not both.

```
PEDef ::=  EntityValue |_ExternalID
```

A - B

A - B Matches any string that matches **A** but does not match **B**.

For example in the XML declaration the following example is given:

```
PITarget ::=  Name - (('X' |_'x') ('M' |_'m') ('L' |_'l'))
```

This means that a **PITarget** can have any name value (which is defined elsewhere) as long as the sequence XML or any combination in upper or lower case is excluded)

A+

A+ Matches one or more occurrences of **A**.

```
CharRef ::=  '&#' [0-9]+ ';'  |_'&#x' [0-9a-fA-F]+ ';'
```

The above means that a character reference must consist of the beginning string **'&#'** plus one or more numeric characters (1 through 9) or one or more numeric characters or the letters **A** through **F**, terminated by a semi-colon.

A*

A* Matches zero or more occurrences of **A**.

```
EncName ::=  [A-Za-z] ([A-Za-z0-9._] |_'-')*
```

Which means that an encoding character must have one character in the range **a-z** (upper or lower case) plus an optional additional number of characters which can be in the range **a-z**, **0-9** numeric, a period or an underscore, or can be a hyphen.

The XML spec.

The XML spec uses EBNF as defined above.

The XML recommendation can be found at:
http://www.w3.org/TR/1998/REC-xml-19980210

The CSS1 spec.

The CSS1 spec uses a modified (and more human readable!) EBNS syntax. It can be found at:

http://www.w3.org/TR/REC-CSS1

Example Syntax	Explanation
`<Fish>`	All values are enclosed in angle brackets.
`Fish`	This represents a keyword that must appear literally (case immaterial). Commas and slashes should also appear literally.
`A B C`	**A** must occur, then **B**, then **C**, in that order.
`A | B`	Expresses alternatives. **A** or **B** must occur.
`A || B`	Note this syntax is not really EBNF. **A** or **B** or both must occur, but in any order.
`[Fish]`	Brackets are used to group items together.
`Fish*`	**Fish** is repeated zero or more times. (Pure EBNF)
`Fish+`	**Fish** is repeated one or more times. (Pure EBNF)
`Fish?`	**Fish** is optional. (Pure EBNF)
`Fish{A,B}`	Note this syntax is not really EBNF. **Fish** must occur at least **A** times and at most **B** times.

The CSS2 spec.

The CSS2 spec uses a modified EBNS syntax. The spec can be found at:

http://www.w3.org/TR/PR-CSS2/

The Grammar can be found at:

http://www.w3.org/TR/PR-CSS2/grammar.html

If you understand EBNF you should have no difficulty reading the spec or understanding the Grammar. Just as a final aid to understanding, we've taken a couple of definitions from the spec, and will walk through them with you below.

Reading the Official Specification

The following two properties are analyzed in some detail. With this under your belt you should have no difficulty analyzing the rest of the spec.

Next we show the specification for the **fontsize** property pasted from the W3C web site. First we will paste the whole spec and then we will analyze it in detail.

14.2.4 Font size: the 'fontsize' property

'fontsize'
Property name: **'fontsize'**_
Value: <absolutesize> | <relativesize> | <length> | <percentage>
Initial: *medium*
Applies to: *all elements*
Inherited: *yes*
Percentage values: relative to parent element's font size

<absolutesize> _
An <absolutesize> keyword is an index to a table of font sizes computed and kept by the UA. Possible values are:
[xxsmall | xsmall | small | medium | large | xlarge | xxlarge]

On a computer screen a scaling factor of 1.5 is suggested between adjacent indexes; if the 'medium' font is 10pt, the 'large' font could be 15pt. Different media may need different scaling factors. Also, the UA should take the quality and availability of fonts into account when computing the table. The table may be different from one font family to another.

<relativesize>_
A **<relativesize>** keyword is interpreted relative to the table of font sizes and the font size of the parent element. Possible values are**: [larger | smaller]**

For example, if the parent element has a font size of 'medium', a value of 'larger' will make the font size of the current element be 'large'. If the parent element's size is not close to a table entry, the UA is free to interpolate between table entries or round off to the closest one. The UA may have to extrapolate table values if the numerical value goes beyond the keywords.

Length and percentage values should not take the font size table into account when calculating the font size of the element.

Negative values are not allowed.

An application may reinterpret an explicit size, depending on the context, for example, inside a VR scene a font may get a different size because of perspective distortion.

Examples:
```
  P { fontsize: 12pt; }
  BLOCKQUOTE { fontsize: larger }
  EM { fontsize: 150% }
  EM { fontsize: 1.5em }
```

Now let's look at some of this in detail:

Property name: **'fontsize'**

The property-name "font-size" is quite straightforward and we are told that it can take the following possible types of value.

Value: **<absolutesize>** | **<relativesize>** | **<length>** | **<percentage>**

The four types of value that it can take are separated by a single vertical slash. The single slash means that only one of these must be chosen. i.e. **<absolute-size>** or **<relative-size>** or **<length>** or **<percentage>**.

Initial: *medium*

This applies to the initial value that the user-agent should give the property if it is not stated in the style sheet.

Applies to: *all elements*

This is self-explanatory.

If we choose to give the property an absolute value, here are our choices:

<absolutesize> _

An **<absolutesize>** keyword is an index to a table of font sizes computed and kept by the UA. Possible values are:

[xxsmall | xsmall | small | medium | large | xlarge | xxlarge]

This is the list of the absolute values. Again note the vertical slash that means we must choose one, and one only.

<relativesize>

If we choose to give the property a relative value here are our choices. Possible values are:

[larger | smaller]

You are required to choose one or the other. It is all pretty straightforward.

Length means a specified size in any of the recognized units (see chapter on units and colors). Pts are the usual measurement for fonts. There are 72 pts to an inch . In passing, please note that the singular **pt** is always used, and there is no white space between the number and the unit type. For example,

```
Font-size:72pt;
```

is correct, whilst all of the following are incorrect.

```
Font-size:72;
Font-size:72pts;
Font-size:72 pt;
```

Experience teaches that this is the most usual place for beginners and old hands alike to mess up their style sheet.

The first section of the following extract tells us what is assumed if a specific font-size is not quoted.

Initial: *medium* i.e. if no value is specified, **font-size:medium**; is assumed.
Applies to: *all elements*
Inherited: *yes*
Percentage values: relative to parent element's font size

Only the last really needs expansion. If the parent element had a font size of 12 points then **"Font-size:200%;"** would produce a font of 24 points. The following is the specification for the **font** property pasted from the W3C web site. It is one of the more complex descriptors. For space reasons we have not pasted the whole property.

14.2.5 Shorthand font property: the 'font' property

'font'
Property name: **'font'**
Value: [[<'font-style'> || <'font-variant'> || <'font-weight'>]? <'font-size'> [/ <'line-height'>]? <'font-family'>]

The value breaks down into three parts separated by a space i.e. A B C where:

A = **[<'font-style'> || <'font-variant'> || <'font-weight'>]?**
B = **<'font-size'> [/ <'line-height'>]?**
C = **<'font-family'>**

When you have values separated by a space, it means they **must** appear in the given order. For example, A followed by B followed by C.

Looking at A we have three values followed by a double vertical slash. When this occurs it means that one or all of the values can appear in any order. There is also a **?** after it. This means that whether it occurs at all is optional. A* would mean the value A could be repeated 0 or more times, i.e. it doesn't have to be there at all. A+ means it is to be repeated one or more times, i.e. there must be at least one value. This is really a modified EBNF notation that is covered in Appendix?.

Looking at B **= <'font-size'> [/ <'line-height'>]?** we have two values. **font-size** must be there, but **line-height** is optional (denoted by the **?**). The forward slash must also be there if you put in **line-height**.

C **= <'font-family'> font-family** must be there. It is not optional.

So a minimal declaration for the font property is **{font:12pt Arial;}**

Initial: see individual properties
Applies to: all elements
Inherited: yes
Percentage values: allowed on **'font-size'** and **'line-height'**

The rest of the above is quite straightforward.

CSS 1 Properties

We have deliberately separated CSS1 and CSS2 properties, because CSS1 properties are almost completely implemented by the two main browsers, whereas CSS2 properties, (with the exception of some of the position properties), are not. If you find a property in this appendix you can be reasonably sure that it will cause an appropriate display in the two mainstream browsers.

We have noted where the properties are not well applied in Communicator 4 or IE4, but as implementation of CSS is being upgraded all the time, this may be moot information.

The following is a list of properties from the CSS1 Recommendation. We follow the section division of the Recommendation, so you will find the properties divided into the following types:

- Font Properties
- Color and Background Properties
- Text Properties
- Box Properties
- Classification Properties

The proposal can be found at:

http://www.w3.org/TR/REC-CSS1

We will point to the appropriate part of the specification for each set of properties as we go through them. You will find more details on each property in the specification.

Font Properties

These are covered in Section 5.2 of the CSS1 specification.

<table>
<tr><th>Property Name</th><th>Property Syntax</th><th>Possible Values</th><th>Initial Value</th><th>Applies to</th><th>Inherited</th></tr>
<tr><td><code>font-family</code></td><td><code>font-family:[[<family-name> | <generic-name>],]*[<family-name> | <generic-name>]</code></td><td>Use any font family name.

<generic-family> values are:

serif

sans-serif

cursive

fantasy

<code>monospace</code></td><td>Browser determines initial value</td><td>All</td><td>Yes</td></tr>
<tr><td><code>font-style</code></td><td><code>font-style:</code> <<i>value</i>></td><td><b>normal | italic | oblique</b></td><td><b>normal</b></td><td>All</td><td>Yes</td></tr>
<tr><td><code>font-variant</code></td><td><code>font-variant:</code> <<i>value</i>></td><td><b>normal| SMALLCAPS</b></td><td><b>normal</b></td><td>All</td><td>Yes</td></tr>
<tr><td><code>font-weight</code></td><td><code>font-weight:</code> <<i>value</i>></td><td><b>normal |bold | bolder | lighter | 100 | 200 | 300 | 400 | 500 | 600 | 700 | 800 | 900</b></td><td><b>normal</b></td><td>All</td><td>Yes</td></tr>
<tr><td><code>font-size'</code></td><td><code>font-size:</code> <<i>value</i>>

<i>value</i>=

<code><absolute-size> | <relative-size> | <length> | <percentage></code></td><td><b><absolute-size></b>

<b>xx-small | x-small | small | medium | large | x-large | xx-large</b>

<b><relative-size></b>:-

<b>larger | smaller</b>

<<i>length</i>> |

<<i>percentage</i>>:-

In relation to parent element</td><td><b>medium</b></td><td>All</td><td>Yes</td></tr>
</table>

Property Name	Property Syntax	Possible Values	Initial Value	Applies to	Inher-ited
font	**font:** <*value*>	**[<font-style> || <font-variant> || <font-weight>]? <font-size> [/<line-height>] <font-family>**	Undefined	All	Yes

Color and Background Properties

These are covered in section 5.3 of the CSS1 specification.

Property Name	Property Syntax	Possible Values	Initial Value	Applies to	Inher-ited
color	**color:** <*value*>	**keyword | numerical RGB specification**			
background-color	**background-color:** <*value*>	<*color*> | **transparent**	**transp-arent**	All	No
background-image	**background-image:** <*value*>	**<url> | none**	**none**	All	No
background-repeat (Buggy in Communicator 4)	**background-repeat:** <*value*>	**repeat | repeat-x | repeat-y | no-repeat**	**repeat**	All	No
Background-attachment (not supported in Communicator 4)	**background-attachment:** <*value*>	**scroll | fixed**	**scroll**	All	No
background-position (Buggy in Communicator 4)	**background-position:** <*value*>	**[**<*length*> | <*percentage*>**]{1, 2} | [top | center | bottom] || [left | center | right]**	**0%,0%**	Block and replaced elements	No

Table Continued on Following Page

Property Name	Property Syntax	Possible Values	Initial Value	Applies to	Inherited
`background`	`background:` *<value>*	`<background-color> || <background-image> || <background-repeat> || <background-attachment> || <background-position>`	Undefined	All	No

Text Properties

These are covered in section 5.4 of the CSS1 specification.

Property Name	Property Syntax	Possible Values	Initial Value	Applies to	Inherited
`Letter-spacing` (not supported in Communicator 4)	`letter-spacing:` *<value>*	`normal |` *<length>*	`normal`	All	Yes
`text-decoration`	`text-decoration:`*<value>*	`none | [underline || overline || line-through || blink]`	`none`	All	No
`vertical-align` (Implementation partial and buggy)	`vertical-align:` *<value>*	`baseline |sub | super | top | text-top | middle | bottom | text-bottom |` *<percentage>* *<percentage>* is relative to elements line-height property	`baseline`	Inline Elements	No
`text-transform`	`text-transform:` *<value>*	`none | Capitalize | UPPERCASE | lowercase`	`none`	All	Yes

Property Name	Property Syntax	Possible Values	Initial Value	Applies to	Inherited
`text-align`	**`text-align:`** *<value>*	**`left	right	center	justify`**  (**`justify`** not supported in Communicator 4)	**`left`**	Block elements	Yes
`text-indent`	**`text-indent:`** *<value>*	*<length>* | *<percentage>*	**`0`**	Block elements	Yes
`line-height`	**`line-height:`** *<value>*	**`normal`** | *<number>* | *<length>* | *<percentage>* *<number>*:- **`line-height=font-size`** x num. *<percentage>*:- relative to font-size.	**`normal`**	All	Yes

Box Properties

These are covered in section 5.5 of the CSS1 specification.

Property Name	Property Syntax	Possible Values	Initial Value	Applies to	Inherited
`margin-top`	**`margin-top:`** *<value>*	*<length>* | *<percentage>* | **`auto`** *<percentage>*:- refers to the **parent** elements **width**. Negative values are permitted	**`0`**	All	No

Table Continued on Following Page

Property Name	Property Syntax	Possible Values	Initial Value	Applies to	Inherited
margin-right	**margin-right:** <*value*>	-:ditto:-	0	All	No
margin-bottom	**margin-bottom:** <*value*>	-:ditto:-	0	All	No
margin-left	**margin-left:** <*value*>	-:ditto:-	0	All	No
margin	**margin:** <*value*>	**[**<*length*> | <*percentage*> | **auto]{1,4}** If 4 values are given they apply to top, right, bottom, left, in that order. 1 value applies to all 4 If 2, or 3 values are given, the missing value is taken from the opposite side. <*percentage*>**:-** refers to the **parent** elements **width**. Negative values are permitted	Undefined	All	No
padding-top	**padding-top:**<*value*>	<*length*> | <*percentage*> **<percentage> :-** refers to the **parent** elements **width**. Negative values are **NOT** permitted	0	All	No

Property Name	Property Syntax	Possible Values	Initial Value	Applies to	Inherited
padding-right	**padding-right:** *<value>*	-:ditto:-	**0**	All	No
padding-bottom	**padding-bottom:** *<value>*	-:ditto:-	**0**	All	No
padding-left	**padding-left:***<value>*	-:ditto:-	**0**	All	No
padding	**padding:** *<value>*	**[***<length>* | *<percentage>* | **auto]{1,4}** If 4 values are given they apply to top, right, bottom, left, in that order. 1 value applies to all 4 If 2, or 3 values are given, the missing value is taken from the opposite side. *<percentage>***:-** refers to the **parent** elements **width**. Negative values are **NOT** permitted	**0**	All	No
border-top-width	**border-top-width:** *<value>*	**thin** | **medium** | **thick** | *<length>*	**medium**	All	No
border-right-width	**border-right-width:** *<value>*	**thin** | **medium** | **thick** | *<length>*	**medium**	All	No
border-bottom-width	**border-bottom-width:** *<value>*	**thin** | **medium** | **thick** | *<length>*	**medium**	All	No

Table Continued on Following Page

Property Name	Property Syntax	Possible Values	Initial Value	Applies to	Inherited
border-left-width	**border-left-width:** <*value*>	**thin | medium | thick |** <*length*>	**medium**	All	No
border-width	**border-width:** <*value*>	**[thin | medium | thick |** <*length*>]**{1,4}** If 4 values are given they apply to top, right, bottom, left, in that order. 1 value applies to all 4 If 2, or 3 values are given, the missing value is taken from the opposite side.	Undefined	All	No
border-color	**border-color:** <*value*>	<*color*>**{1,4}** (see Appendix E) If 4 values are given they apply to top, right, bottom, left, in that order. 1 value applies to all 4 If 2, or 3 values are given, the missing value is taken from the opposite side.	The element color property	All	No
border-style	**border-style:** <*value*>	**[none | dotted | dashed | solid | double | groove | ridge | inset | outset]{1,4}**	**none**	All	No
border-top	**border-top:**<*value*>	**<border-top-width> || <border-style> ||** <*color*>	Undefined	All	No
border-right	**border-right:** <*value*>	**<border-right-width> || <border-style> ||** <*color*>	Undefined	All	No

Property Name	Property Syntax	Possible Values	Initial Value	Applies to	Inherited
border-bottom	**border-bottom:** <*value*>	**<border-bottom-width>** || **<border-style>** || < *color* >	Undefined	All	No
border-left	**border-left:**<*value*>	**<border-left-width>** || **<border-style>** || < *color* >	Undefined	All	No
border	**border:** <*value*>	**<border-width>** || **<border-style>** || < *color* >	Undefined	All	No
width	**width:** <*value*>	<*length*> | <*percentage*> | **auto** % refers to parent elements width. A replaced element is an element such as **IMG** or **OBJECT** in HTML.	**auto**	Block and replaced elements	No
height	**height:** <*value*>	<*length*> | **auto**	**auto**	Block and replaced elements	No
float	**float:**<*value*>	**left** | **right** | **none** **note:-float** removes inline elements from the line.	**none**	All	No
clear	**clear:**<*value*>	**block** | **inline** | **list-item** | **none**	**none**	All	No

Classification properties

These are covered in section 5.6 of the CSS1 specification.

Property Name	Property Syntax	Possible Values	Initial Value	Applies to	Inherited
`display`	`display:` *<value>*	`block | inline | list-item | none`	Dependant on browser. If tag is unknown as in the case of XML, default is usually inline, although CSS1 default specifies block	All	No
`white-space`	`white-space:` *<value>*	`normal | pre | nowrap`	`normal`	Block Elements	No
`list-style-type`	`list-style-type:` *<value>*	`disc | circle | square | decimal | lower-roman | upper-roman | lower-alpha | upper-alpha | none`	`disc`	List-items	Yes
`list-style-image`	`list-style-image:` *<value>*	`<url> | none`	`none`	List-items	Yes
`list-style-position`	`list-style-position:` *<value>*	`inside | outside`	`outside`	List-items	Yes
`list-style`	`list-style:` *<value>*	`<list-style-type> || list-style-position ||` *<url>*	Undefined	List-items	Yes

CSS2 Properties

CSS2 includes all of the CSS1 properties, although in many cases new values have been added. Most of the new CSS2 properties are not implemented in the current browsers, with the exception of most of the position properties. The absolute position properties are, however, not implemented in Communicator 4.

We cover the properties under the same headings as the specification:

- Box Model
- Visual Rendering Model
- Visual Rendering Model Details
- Visual Effects
- Generated Content and Automatic Numbering
- Paged Media
- Colors and Backgrounds
- Font Properties
- Text Properties
- Lists Tables
- User Interface
- Aural Style Sheets

Where there have been no changes since CSS1, we state this and refer you to Appendix B.

We refer you to the section of the specification which gives you more detail on each section of properties. The specification can be found at:

`http://www.w3.org/TR/PR-CSS2/`

As ever, to see if a property works, just try it.

The only way CSS2 alters CSS1 is in cascade order. In CSS1, an **!important** in an author's style sheet took precedence over an **!important** in a user's style sheet. This has been (correctly) reversed in CSS2.

Box Model

The box properties are essentially unmodified from CSS1, see Appendix B for details of the property names and values.

Visual Rendering Model

This is a new category of property in CSS2, made up as follows:

Two existing CSS1 properties, **float** and **clear**, which are unchanged from CSS1 and are fully detailed in Appendix B.

The CSS1 **display** property adds the following values in CSS2. Otherwise it is unchanged.

| run-in | compact | marker | table | inline-table | table-row-group | table-column-group | table-header-group | table-footer-group | table-row | table-cell | table-caption

Two new properties, **position** and **z-index**, are detailed below. There is variable support for them in IE4 and Communicator 4. (Netscape does not support the **absolute** value for the **position** property. Use their **<LAYER>** tag instead.) Both the makers promise that their version 5 releases will give full support.

These are covered in section 9 of the CSS2 specification and Chapter 8 of this book in the *Normal Block Flow* section.

Property Name	Property Syntax	Possible Values	Initial Value	Applies to	Inherited
position	position: *<value>*	static | relative | absolute | fixed	static	All	No

Property Name	Property Syntax	Possible Values	Initial Value	Applies to	Inherited
box offsets	**box offsets: [top | left | bottom | right]**	*<length>* | *<percentage>* | **auto** *<length>*:-The offset is a fixed distance from the reference edge. *<percentage>*: -The offset is a percentage of the containing block's width (for **left** or **right**) or height (for **top** and **bottom**). **auto**:-The value depends on which of the other properties are **auto** as well.	**auto**	All	No
z-index	**auto** | *<integer>*		**auto**	Elements that produce absolutely and relatively positioned boxes	No

Visual Rendering Model Details

This is another new section in CSS2. It is made up of the CSS1 **width**, **height**, **line-height** and **vertical-align** properties, which remain unchanged and are detailed in Appendix B, plus four new properties, **min-height**, **max-height**, **min-width** and **max-width**, details of which are set out below.

These are covered in section 10 of the CSS2 specification.

Property Name	Property Syntax	Possible Values	Initial Value	Applies to	Inherited
min-width	**min-width:***<value>*	*<length>* | *<percentage>*	**0**	All	No
max-width	**max-width:***<value>*	*<length>* | *<percentage>*	**100%**	All	No

Table Continued on Following Page

Property Name	Property Syntax	Possible Values	Initial Value	Applies to	Inher-ited
min-height	**min-height:**<*value*>	<*length*> | <*percentage*>	**0**	All	No
max-height	**max-height:**<*value*>	<*length*> | <*percentage*>	**100%**	All	No

Visual Effects

This is a new category of property in CSS2. It is covered in section 11 of the specification and Chapter 8 of this book, the *Clipping and Overflow* section of the chapter and the *Visibility Property* section.

Property Name	Property Syntax	Possible Values	Initial Value	Applies to	Inher-ited
overflow	see spec	**visible** | **hidden** | **scroll** | **auto**	**visible**	Block level and replaced elements	No
clip	see spec	<*shape*> | **auto**	**auto**	Block level and replaced elements	No
Visibil-ity	**visibility:** <*value*>	**visible** | **hidden** | **collapse** | **inherit**	**inherit**	All	No

Generated Content and Automatic Numbering

Again, this is a new category of property in CSS2 covered in section 12 of the specification. In CSS2 it is possible to generate content in several ways:

- Using the **content** property in conjunction with the **:before** and **:after** psuedo elements.
- In conjunction with the **cue-before** and **cue-after** aural properties.
- Elements with a value of **list-item** for the **display** property.

The style and location of generated content is specified with the **:before** and **:after** psuedo elements. These are used in conjunction with the **content** property, which specifies what is inserted. Unsurprisingly, **:before** and **:after** psuedo elements specify content before and after an element's document tree content. See the specification (section 12) for further details, or read the *Generated Content* section in Chapter 7 of this book.

<table>
<tr><th>Property Name</th><th>Property Syntax</th><th>Possible Values</th><th>Initial Value</th><th>Applies to</th><th>Inherited</th></tr>
<tr><td><b>content</b></td><td>see spec</td><td>[<<i>string</i>> | <<i>uri</i>> | <<i>counter</i>> | <b>attr(X)</b> | <b>open-quote</b> | <b>close-quote</b> | <b>no-open-quote</b> | <b>no-close-quote</b>]+</td><td><b>empty string</b></td><td><b>:before</b> and <b>:after</b> pseudo elements</td><td>No</td></tr>
<tr><td><b>quotes</b></td><td>see spec for specifying the <b>quotes</b> property and inserting quotes with the <b>content</b> property</td><td>[<<i>string</i>>.,<<i>string</i>>.] + | <b>none</b> | <b>inherit</b></td><td>Depends on user agent</td><td>All</td><td>Yes</td></tr>
</table>

Paged Media

All the following paged media properties are new to CSS2 and are covered in section 13 of the specification and Chapter 14 of this book, the section on *Visual Content.*

<table>
<tr><th>Property Name</th><th>Property Syntax</th><th>Possible Values</th><th>Initial Value</th><th>Applies to</th><th>Inherited</th></tr>
<tr><td><b>size</b></td><td><b>size:</b><<i>value</i>></td><td><<i>length</i>><b>{1,2}</b> | <b>auto</b> | <b>portrait</b> | <b>landscape</b></td><td><b>auto</b></td><td>Page context</td><td>N/A</td></tr>
<tr><td><b>marks</b> (crop marks)</td><td><b>marks:</b><<i>value</i>></td><td>[<b>crop</b> || <b>cross</b>] | <b>none</b></td><td><b>none</b></td><td>Page context</td><td>N/A</td></tr>
<tr><td><b>page</b> (for using named pages)</td><td><b>page:</b> <<i>identifier</i>> <<i>value</i>></td><td>[<b>left</b> | <b>right</b>]? | <b>auto</b></td><td><b>auto</b></td><td>Block level elements</td><td>Yes</td></tr>
<tr><td><b>page-break-before</b></td><td><b>page-break-before:</b> <<i>value</i>></td><td><b>auto</b> | <b>always</b> | <b>avoid</b> | <b>left</b> | <b>right</b> | <b>inherit</b></td><td><b>auto</b></td><td>Block-level elements</td><td>No</td></tr>
<tr><td><b>page-break-after</b></td><td><b>page-break-after:</b> <<i>value</i>></td><td><b>auto</b> | <b>always</b> | <b>avoid</b> | <b>left</b> | <b>right</b> | <b>inherit</b></td><td><b>auto</b></td><td>Block-level elements</td><td>No</td></tr>
<tr><td><b>page-break-inside</b></td><td><b>page-break-inside:</b> <<i>value</i>></td><td><b>avoid</b> | <b>auto</b></td><td><b>auto</b></td><td>Block-level elements</td><td>Yes</td></tr>
</table>

Table Continued on Following Page

Property Name	Property Syntax	Possible Values	Initial Value	Applies to	Inher-ited
orphans	**orphans:** *<integer>*		**2**	Block-level elements	Yes
widows	**widows:** *<integer>*		**2**	Block-level elements	Yes

Colors and Backgrounds

These properties are unchanged from CSS1, to read about them in the CSS2 specification check out Section 14, to see the property listing and values in this book, turn to Appendix B.

Font Properties

The CSS1 properties are unchanged in CSS2, and are listed in Appendix B. There are two new CSS2 font properties, Font Properties are covered in section 15 of the CSS2 specification and Chapter 6 of this book, the section on *CSS Font Properties.*

Property Name	Property Syntax	Possible Values	Initial Value	Applies to	Inherit ed
font-stretch unsupported	**font-stretch:** *<value>*	**normal | wider | narrower | ultra-condensed | extra-condensed | condensed | semi-condensed | semi-expanded | expanded | extra-expanded | ultra-expanded**	**normal**	All	Yes
font-size-adjust	**font-size-adjust:** *<value>*	*<number>* | **none**	**none**	All	Yes

Text Properties

The CSS1 properties are unchanged in CSS2, and are listed in Appendix B. There is one new CSS2 text property. The text properties are covered in section 16 of the CSS2 specification and Chapter 6 of this book, the section on *CSS Text Properties.*

Property Name	Property Syntax	Possible Values	Initial Value	Applies to	Inherited
text-shadow	**text-shadow:** <*value*>	**none** | **[**<*color*> || <*length*> <*length*> <*length*>**? ,]*** **[**<*color*> || <*length*> <*length*> <*length*>**?]** | **inherit**	**none**	All	No

Lists

The list properties remain unchanged from CSS1, apart from **list-style-type** which has the following new values. They are all covered in section 17 of the specification.

Property Name	Property Syntax	Possible Values	Initial Value	Applies to	Inherited
list-style-type	**list-style-type:** <*value*>	**leading-zero** | **western-decimal** | **lower-latin** | **upper-latin** | **hebrew** | **armenian** | **georgian** | **cjk-ideographic** | **hiragana** | **katakana** | **hiragana-iroha** | **katakana-iroha**	**disc**	Elements with the **display** property set to **list-item**	Yes

Tables

All the **table** properties are new to CSS2 and can be found in section 18 of the specification and Chapter 10, the section on *Table Properties.*

Property Name	Property Syntax	Possible Values	Initial Value	Applies to	Inherited
column-span	**column-span:** < *integer*>		**1**	**table-cell**, **table-column** and **table-column-group** elements	No

Table Continued on Following Page

Property Name	Property Syntax	Possible Values	Initial Value	Applies to	Inherited
`row-span`	`row-span:` *<integer>*		`1`	`table-cell` elements	No
`table-layout`	`table-layout:` *<value>*	`fixed` | `auto`	`auto`	`table` and `in-line-table` elements	No
`empty-cells`	`empty-cells:` *<value>*	`borders` | `no-borders`	`borders`	`table-cell` elements	Yes
`speak-header`	`speak-header:` *<value>*	`once` | `always`	`once`	Elements that have header information	Yes

User Interface

The user interface properties are new to CSS2 and can be found in section 19 of the specification, and Chapter 9 of this book, the section on *Interacting with the User Interface.*

Property Name	Property Syntax	Possible Values	Initial Value	Applies to	Inherited
`cursor`	`cursor:` *<uri><value>*	`[ [`*<uri>*`,]* [ auto` | `crosshair` | `default` | `pointer` | `move` | `e-resize` | `ne-resize` | `nw-resize` | `n-resize` | `se-resize` | `sw-resize` | `s-resize` | `w-resize`| `text` | `wait` | `help ] ]`	`auto`	All	Yes
`outline`	`outline: [<outline-color> || <outline-style> || <outline-width>]`	`<outline-color> || <outline-style> || <outline-width>`	See individual properties	All	No
`outline-width`	`outline-width:` *<value>*	`border-width`	`medium`	All	N/A

Property Name	Property Syntax	Possible Values	Initial Value	Applies to	Inherited
outline-style	**outline-style:** *<value>*	**border-style**	**none**	All	N/A
outline-color	**outline-color:** *<value>*	**border-color** | **invert**	**invert**	All	N/A

Aural Style Sheets

These are a new addition in CSS2 and can be seen in further detail in section 20 of the specification and Chapter 14 of this book, in the section on *Aural Content.*

Property Name	Property Syntax	Possible Values	Initial Value	Applies to	Inherited
volume	**volume:** *<value>*	*<number>* | *<percentage>* | **silent** | **x-soft** | **soft** | **medium** | **loud** | **x-loud**	**medium**	All	Yes
speak	**speak:** *<value>*	**normal** | **none** | **spell-out**	**normal**	All	Yes
pause-before	**pause-before:** *<value>*	*<time>* | *<percentage>*	Depends on user agent	All	No
pause-after	**pause-after:** *<value>*	*<time>* | *<percentage>*	Depends on user agent	All	No
pause (shorthand)	**pause:** *<value>*	**[[***<time>* | *<percentage>***] {1,2}]**	Depends on user agent	All	No
cue-before	**cue-before:** *<value>*	*<uri>* | **none**	**none**	All	No
cue-after	**cue-after:** *<value>*	*<uri>* | **none**	**none**	All	No
cue (shorthand)	**cue:***<value>*	**[<cue-before> || <cue-after>]**	Not defined for shorthand properties	All	No

Table Continued on Following Page

Property Name	Property Syntax	Possible Values	Initial Value	Applies to	Inherited
`play-during`	`play-during:` <*uri*><*value*>	<*uri*> `mix? repeat?` | `auto` | `none` | `inherit`	`auto`	All	No
`azimuth`	`azimuth:` <*value*>	<*angle*> | `[[ left-side` | `far-left` | `left` | `center-left` | `center` | `center-right` | `right` | `far-right` | `right-side ]` || `behind ]` | `leftwards` | `rightwards`	`center`	All	Yes
`elevation`	`elevation:` <*value*>	<*angle*> | `below` | `level` | `above` | `higher` | `lower`	`level`	All	Yes
`speech-rate`	`speech-rate:`<*value*>	<*number*> | `x-slow` | `slow` | `medium` | `fast` | `x-fast` | `faster` | `slower`	`medium`	All	Yes
`voice-family`	`voice-family:` <*value*><*value*>	`[[<specific-voice>` | `<generic-voice> ],]* [<specific-voice>` | `<generic-voice> ]`	Depends on user agent	All	Yes
`pitch`	`pitch:` <*value*>	`<frequency>` | `x-low` | `low` | `medium` | `high` | `x-high`	`medium`	All	Yes

Property Name	Property Syntax	Possible Values	Initial Value	Applies to	Inherited
`pitch-range`	`pitch-range:` *<value>*	*<number>*	`50`	All	Yes
`stress`	`stress:` *<value>*	*<number>*	`50`	All	Yes
`richness`	`richness:` *<value>*	*<number>*	`50`	All	Yes
`speak-punctuation`	`speak-punctuation:` *<value>*	`code` | `none`	`none`	All	Yes
`speak-numeral`	`speak-numeral:` *<value>*	`digits` | `continuous`	`continuous`	All	Yes

Units and values in CSS.

CSS properties have values that can be expressed in a numeric or percentage units, as a length, as a keyword value, as an URI, or as a string value.

String Values

An example of a string value is the following font-family property value.

```
font-family: "Times New Roman"
```

String values may be quoted although there is no requirement that they should be.

Keyword Values

These occur with several properties. For example:

```
color:red
font-weight:bold
border-style:solid
text-align:center
```

These keywords **MUST NOT** be quoted!

URI

A **URI=URL+URN**.

URNs (Uniform Resource Name) are an expected new way of identifying resources. For practical purposes at the present time, a URI is the same as an URL

Here is an example of the use of an URL

```
BODY { background: url(http://www.abc.com/paper.gif) }
```

The URL may be left unquoted, or quoted with single or double quotes, but the quotes must match i.e.:

```
url(http://www.abc.com/paper.gif)
url("http://www.abc.com/paper.gif")
url('http://www.abc.com/paper.gif')
```

are all correct, but:

```
url("http://www.abc.com/paper.gif')
```

is an error.

A full description of URLs can be obtained from:

ftp://ds.internic.net/rfc/rfc1738.txt(url)

A full description of URN's can be obtained from

http://www.ics.uci.edu/pub/ietf/uri/draft-fielding-uri-syntax-01.txt(urn)

Integers

Some times a pure integer may be employed. e.g.:

```
font-weight:400
```

The integer must never be quoted.

Lengths

Lengths refer to horizontal and/or vertical measurements. All lengths (except 0) must take a unit or a percentage value after it. e.g.:

```
font-size: 12pt
```

```
margin-top: 80%
```

There must be no **`white-space`** between the number and the unit.

Some properties (e.g. **`margin-*`**) support negative values.

Units

Units are either absolute or relative. Which are used depends on a number of factors, but as a rule of thumb always use relative units unless the actual spatial distances are critical.

Relative units

Relative units are:

em

This is the actual font size. So if relative to a 36pt font, the value for 1 em would be 0.5 of an inch.

ex

This is the **`x-height`** of the font, which approximates to the height of the **`x`** character if the font possesses one. If not (i.e. the font is non-roman) it will still be defined. Different fonts of the same size may have different x-heights.

px

The pixel is related to the viewing device, and is the smallest unit of resolution of that device. Whereas this unit works well with computer screens where there is not an enormous difference in resolutions, it can cause problems when transferred to another medium.

For example if we set a **`font-size`** to 40 pixels, this would appear as a font 0.5 inches height on a screen with a resolution of 80dpi.

However, on a Laser printer of 400dpi, the font would appear 0.1 inches high!

For this reason the CSS2 specification recommends that where there is a large disparity in resolution:

> *"It is recommended that the reference pixel be the visual angle of one pixel on a device with a pixel density of 90dpi and a distance from the reader of an arm's length. For a nominal arm's length of 28 inches, the visual angle is therefore about 0.0227 degrees."*

Authors should probably use this unit sparingly. One good place to use it is when it is desirable to depict the thinnest possible line, e.g.:

```
border-width:1px
```

Absolute Units

The absolute units used in CSS are as follows:

`in` **inches**. 1 inch is equal to 2.54 centimeters.
`cm` **centimeters**
`mm` **millimeters**
`pt` **points**. The points used by CSS2 are equal to 1/72th of an inch.
`pc` **picas**. 1 pica is equal to 12 points.

Percentages

Percentage values are always relative to another value, and the property determines what they are relative to.

Percentage values may be negative where the property allows this.

Colors

Color values are covered in Appendix E.

Colors in CSS

Named Colors

There are only 16 named colors in CSS. Although both Communicator 4 and IE4 recognize almost 125 other named colors for reasons of forward compatibility you are advised to stick to either these 16 and to use the numeric equivalent for any other colors.

Color Name	Hexadecimal equivalent.
aqua	00FFFF
black	000000
blue	0000FF
fuchsia	FF00FF
gray	808080
green	008000
lime	00FF00
maroon	800000

Color Name	Hexadecimal equivalent.
navy	000080
olive	808080
purple	800080
red	FF0000
silver	C0C0C0
teal	008080
white	FFFFFF
yellow	FFFF00

Numeric colors

CSS allows several ways of declaring the **RGB** (**R**ed, **G**reen, **B**lue) components of color, using Hexadecimal's integers or percentages.

Hexadecimal Long Method

The color value takes the form:

```
#rrggbb
```

where **rr**, **gg**, **bb** stand for the primary color component in hexadecimal numbers.

Hexadecimal Short Method

The color value takes the form:

```
#rgb
```

To find the full hexadecimal component just double up the r, g, b, component. For example,

```
#C8A
```

is short for:

```
#CC88AA
```

Decimal Integer Method

This method takes the form:

```
rgb(x,x,x)
```

Where **x** is any integer from 0-255. If x is outside this range it will be clipped to the nearest legal value, For example, -50 will be clipped to 0, and 300 to 255.

```
rgb(255,255,0)
```

is yellow.

Percentage Method

This method takes the form:

```
rgb(x%,x%,x%)
```

Again user agents will clip percentages outside the range 0-100% to the nearest legal value.

```
rgb(100%,100%,0%)
```

is yellow.

Note that you can't mix integers and percentages i.e. **rgb(255,100%,0)** is **not** allowed.

Examples

The following examples all represent the same color:

```
#00CC00
#0C0
rgb(0,204,0)
rgb(0%,80%,0%)
```

Case Specificity.

In the hexadecimal notation there is **no** case specificity. i.e. **#00cc00**, **#00cC00**, **#00Cc00**, and **#00CC00** are identical colors.

Demo using JavaScript and the IE4 DOM to Show Styled XML in a Browser

Here is one way that you can display XML in an Explorer type browser. To understand what is going on a knowledge of JavaScript is necessary. If you are a little rusty on this please read the brief JavaScript tutorial at Appendix G. This code makes use of the IE4 DOM, so it will not work in Navigator. Even without knowledge of JavaScript you can still use this code by cutting and pasting.

The Demo

Download **js1.htm** and **js2.js** from the Wrox web site at:

http://rapid.wrox.co.uk/books/1657

or from

http://www.hypermedic.com/style/tips

(or manually copy from this appendix). Make sure you put these files in the same directory or folder.

In **js1.htm** you will see a wrapper **<XMLDOC>** and **<XSTYLE>**. Put your well-formed XML file in **<XMLDOC>** right after **</XSTYLE>**, and paste the style sheet between **<XSTYLE></XSTYLE>**.

Make sure that your XML file has no HTML tags in it. If it has (**`<TITLE>`** is one of the commonest) then alter the tag name. Run **`js1.htm`** in your browser and this is what you should see.

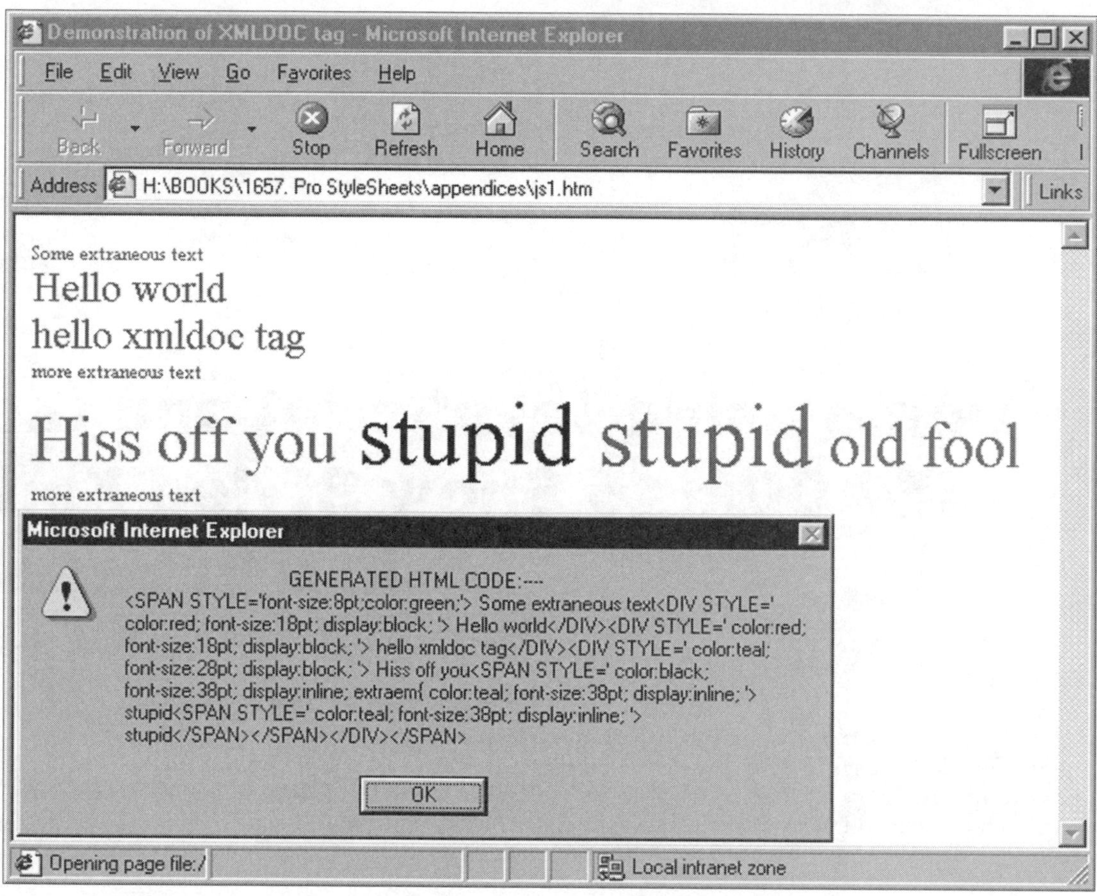

The script generates HTML from the XML. This HTML is shown in an alert. (Hit *Alt.+ F4* to close the alert if you can't see the button). If you don't want the alert to appear go to **`js2.js`** and find the first function:

```
funtion.printarray(e,f)
```

The last line of code of this function is:

```
alert(htmstring)
```

Comment it out thus:

```
//alert(htmstring)
```

The following is an annotated description of the code. There is a lot of commented out code that has been deliberately left in, in case you want to make alterations.

js1.htm

Any XML document is put in a wrapper **<XMLDOC>**, which is put in a **<DIV>** with the **id** of XML. The style sheet is put between the **<XSTYLE>** tags.

Using the **id** of the **<DIV>**, an array of all the tag names contained in the **<XMLDOC>** wrapper is made and passed to the function **printarray** together with a complete copy of the string contained in the **<XMLDOC>** wrapper namely: **xml.innerHTML**.

```
printarray(tagnames, xml.innerHTML);
```

is the code that accomplishes this.

Note that the array **tagnames[]** is filled by the following loop:

```
for (i=0;i<=xml.all.length-1;i++)
{
tagnames[i]=xml.all[i].tagName;

}
```

If an HTML tag name is used **xml.all[i].tagName** will ignore the closing tag name, causing an error when the XML file is parsed.

Here is the file **js1.htm**, with a well formed XML document inserted in it. Run it in your browser and see what happens–remember you have to have **js2.js** in the same directory as this file for it to work.

```
<!--File js1.htm-->

<HTML>
<HEAD>

<TITLE>Demonstration of XMLDOC tag</TITLE>

<STYLE>
</STYLE>

</HEAD>
<BODY>
   <DIV id=xml style="display:none;">
   <XMLDOC>
   <XSTYLE>
      document{font-size:8pt;color:green;}
      greeting{
      color:red;
      font-size:18pt;
      display:block;
```

```
}
    insult{
        color:teal;
        font-size:28pt;
        display:block;
}
    emphasis{
        color:black;
        font-size:38pt;
        display:inline;
        extraem{
        color:teal;
        font-size:38pt;
        display:inline;
}
    </XSTYLE>
    <document>Some extraneous text
    <greeting voice="nice">Hello world</greeting>
    <greeting>hello xmldoc tag</greeting>more extraneous text
    <insult>Hiss off you <emphasis>stupid<extraem>
    stupid</extraem></emphasis> old fool </insult>
more extraneous text
<!--a comment-->
    </document>
    </XMLDOC>
    </DIV>
    <SCRIPT SRC="js2.js">
    </SCRIPT>
    <SCRIPT>
//this script must be placed after the XML document.
var tagnames=new Array();

for (i=0;i<=xml.all.length-1;i++)
{
tagnames[i]=xml.all[i].tagName;

}
printarray(tagnames,xml.innerHTML);

    </SCRIPT>

</BODY>
</HTML>
```

Parsing the XML File using js2.js

The whole contents of the XML file and style sheet are passed to **`printarray`** in **`js2.js`**.

`printarray` calls various helper functions to create an HTML document out of the XML document and XML style sheet. Here is the full **`js2.js`** file. I have included comments and commented out alternative ways of doing things in the file.

```
//This script makes use of the IE4 document object model, it will not work
on Navigator.
//You cant use HTML tags
//you cant use empty tags of the type <empty/>
//all tags in stylesheet in lowercase

////////////////////////////////FRANK
BOUMPHREY//////////////////////////////////////////////////
//Written by Frank Boumphrey bckman@ix.netcom.com. March 21 1998. Comments
welcome.    //
//This code is placed in the public domain and may be freely copied and
distributed,    //
//but I would be grateful if you left this header in place.
//
////////////////////////////////FRANK
BOUMPHREY//////////////////////////////////////////////////


var htmstring="\t\tGENERATED HTML CODE:----\n"


function printarray(e,f)

// begin function
// e should be an array of all the XML tag names from <DIV id=xml>
// f should be all the XML text taken from innerHTML

{

var remtext=f
var el_text=""
var tagstack=0
var stylesheet=getXstyle(f)

//alert(stylesheet)
//document.write("<DIV STYLE='color:red'>")
//loop through the tags, exclude</XMLDOC>

for(var i=0;i<=e.length-2;i++)
{
//   alert(e[i])
el_text=(trimText(getText(e[i],e[i+1],remtext)));//the text between the
tags

remtext=remtext.substring(remtext.indexOf(e[i+1]));//advance the text

if (gettagtype(e[i])==0 && e[i].charAt(0)!="X")    //ignore or wrapper
{tagstack++}                             //add to stack if opening tag
else if(gettagtype(e[i])==1 && e[i].substring(0,2)!="/X")
{tagstack--}                             //take off stack if closing tag

if(e[i].charAt(0)!="X")
{

if(gettagtype(e[i])==0)
{
makeFlowobject(e[i],el_text,stylesheet);
```

```
}

else if(tagstack==0 && gettagtype(e[i])==1 && e[i].substring(0,2)!="/X")
     //exclude special tags
{
makeFlowobject(e[i],el_text,stylesheet);
}
else if(tagstack >0 && gettagtype(e[i])==1 && e[i].substring(0,2)!="/X")
     //print the text
{
//var this
makeFlowobject(e[i],el_text,stylesheet);
document.write(el_text);
}
}
}
alert(htmstring)
}

////////////////////////////
//end function printarray//
///////////////////////////

function gettagtype(e)

//cannot at present identify empty tag as in text / is not returned.
//Will need another routine to do this, probably identify from innerHTML
//opening tag=0,closing tag=1,emptytag=2,comment=3
{

var tagtype=0
if (e.charAt(0)=="/")
{tagtype=1}
else if (e.charAt(0)=="!")
{tagtype=3}
return tagtype
}

////////////////////////////
//end function gettagtype//
///////////////////////////


//the following code is commented out but is left in place to //demonstrate
an alternative method
/*------------------------------------------BEGIN REMOVED

function areTagsSameType(e,f)

//e is present tag,f is next tag

{
var sametype=true
if(f.substring(1)==e)
{sametype=true}
else sametype=false
//return true or false
```

```
return sametype
}
/////////////////////////////////
//end function areTagsSameType//
/////////////////////////////////
-------------------END REMOVED*/

function getText(e,f,g)

//e is present tag,f is next tag,g is the remnant text
//returns the text between two tags

{
var Uppertext=g.toUpperCase();

var endindex=Uppertext.indexOf(f,e.length);
var el_text=g.substring(e.length+1,endindex-1);
return el_text;
}

////////////////////////
//end function getText//
////////////////////////

function trimText(e)

//e is text to trim
//removes all text to the left of > and returns the edited string

{
var textstr=e;
var startnum=e.indexOf(">",0);
textstr=e.substring(startnum+1);
return textstr;
}

/////////////////////////
//end function trimText//
/////////////////////////

//-------------------------------------------------BEGIN REMOVED
/*
function getStylingtag(e,f)

// e is opening tag,f is closing tag.
//adds the appropiate style to the text and prints it.

//check to see what type the closing tag is, if it is the same type then
return the opening tag
//if it is another opening tag then just apply the style.
//if it is a different tag and a closing tag, apply the style of the
closing tag
{
if(areTagsSameType(e,f)==true)
{return e;}
else if(gettagtype(f)==0)
{return e;}
```

```
else {return f.substring(1);}
}
///////////////////////////////
//end function getStylingtag//
//////////////////////////////
//-----------------------------------------------END REMOVED*/


function makeFlowobject(e,f,g)

//Get type of tag if opening style it ,if closing close it with appropiate
DIV or SPAN
//Will need to link with style sheet of <XSTYLE> TYPE
//e is the tag, f the text to style, g the style sheet to pass through to
styling


{

//htmstring=htmstring+"A"
//alert(htmstring)

e=e.toLowerCase();          //IE4 DOM represents all tags in upper case.
if(gettagtype(e)==0)
{
if (g.indexOf(e,0)!=-1)
{

var ss=getStyleString(e,g);
//alert(ss)
if(ss.indexOf("display:block",0)!=-1)
{
document.write("<DIV STYLE='"+ss+"'>"+f);
htmstring=htmstring+"<DIV STYLE='"+ss+"'>"+f;
}
else
{
document.write("<SPAN STYLE='"+ss+"'>"+f);
htmstring=htmstring+"<SPAN STYLE='"+ss+"'>"+f;
}
}

//demonstrates possibility of hard wiring style(Commented out)
//-----------------------------------------------
/*else if(e=="greeting")
{
document.write("<DIV STYLE='color:red'>"+f);
//alert("<DIV STYLE='color:red'>"+f);
}
else if(e=="insult")
{
document.write("<DIV STYLE='color:blue'>"+f);
//alert("<DIV STYLE='color:blue'>"+f);
}
else if   (e=="emphasis")
{
document.write("<SPAN STYLE='color:green'>"+f);
```

```
//alert("<SPAN STYLE='color:red'>"+f);
}*/
//----------------------------------------------------
else {
document.write("<SPAN>"+f);
htmstring=htmstring+"<SPAN>"+f;
//alert("<SPAN STYLE='color:red'>"+"S"+f);
}
}
else if(gettagtype(e)==1)

{
e=e.substring(1)
//alert(e)
if (g.indexOf(e,0)!=-1)
{
var ss=getStyleString(e,g);

if(ss.indexOf("display:block",0)!=-1)
{
document.write("</DIV>");
htmstring=htmstring+"</DIV>";
}
else
{
document.write("</SPAN>");
htmstring=htmstring+"</SPAN>"
}
}

//demonstrates possibility of hard wiring style
//-------------------------------------------------
/*else if(e=="greeting")
{
document.write("</DIV>");
//alert(e+"</DIV>");
}
else if(e=="insult")
{
document.write("</DIV>");
//alert(e+"<DIV>");
}

else if(e=="emphasis")
{
document.write("</SPAN>");
//alert(e+"<DIV>");
}*/
//-------------------------------------------------
else {
document.write("</SPAN>");
htmstring=htmstring+"</SPAN>";
//alert(e+"</DIV>");
}
}

//
```

```
}
////////////////////////////////
//end function makeFlowobject//
////////////////////////////////


function getXstyle(e)

//gets the style sheet in innerHTMLand returns it as a string
//e should =innerHTML
{
var beginnum=e.indexOf("XSTYLE",0);
//alert(beginnum)
var endnum=e.indexOf("/XSTYLE",0);
//alert(endnum)
var stylesheet= e.substring(beginnum+7,endnum-1);
//alert(stylesheet)
return stylesheet;

}


///////////////////////////
//end function getXstyle//
///////////////////////////


function getStyleString(e,f)

//e is the tag in lowercase, f the style string
//returns the style string of the requested tag

{
var beginnum=f.indexOf(e,0)+e.length;
var remstring=f.substring(beginnum);
var endnum=remstring.indexOf("}",0);
var stylestring=remstring.substring(1,endnum);
//alert (stylestring);
return stylestring;
}

////////////////////////////////
//end function getStyleString//
////////////////////////////////



//-----------------------------------------------------
/*

//--------------------------------------------------------------------------
//Note cannot use empty tags with this very primitive first coding.
//Document must be well formed
//Need to add code to check for well formedness before running.
//(Quick and dirty check,tagstack should =0 at end)

//sample XML document
```

```
//<DIV id=xml style="display:none;">
//   <XMLDOC>
//<XSTYLE>
//   document{font-size:8pt;color:green;}
//   greeting{
//         color:red;
//         font-size:18pt;
//         display:block;
//   }
//   insult{
//         color:teal;
//         font-size:28pt;
//         display:block;
//   }
//   emphasis{
//         color:black;
//         font-size:38pt;
//         display:inline;
//   }
//   </XSTYLE>
//
//
//         <greeting voice="nice">Hello world</greeting>
//         <greeting>Hello XMLDOC tag</greeting>
//         <insult>Hiss off you emphasis>stupid<extraem>stupid
//        </extraem></emphasis> old fool!! </insult>
//
//         <!--a comment-->
//   </XMLDOC>
//</DIV>
//<SCRIPT SRC="js2.js">
//</SCRIPT>
//<SCRIPT>
//
//   var tagnames=new Array();
//
//   for (i=0;i<=xml.all.length-1;i++)
//         {
//         tagnames[i]=xml.all[i].tagName;
//
//         }
//   printarray(tagnames,xml.innerHTML);
//
//</SCRIPT>*/
```

G

JavaScript tutorial

This tutorial is not meant to be exhaustive, nor is it meant to prepare the reader to write code. It is designed as a 'quick and cheerful' tutorial to teach the reader enough JavaScript to be able to follow the JavaScript examples in the book intelligently.

You should be able to work through this tutorial in a couple of hours. The examples have been kept very simple. None of the more esoteric parts of the language are covered, nor is any attempt made to differentiate between the different versions of JavaScript.

To learn more about this surprisingly powerful language see *Instant JavaScript* ISBN 1861001274. *Instant HTML Programmer's Reference* ISBN 1861001568 is also handy as it contains a very good appendix to use as a reference and an excellent chapter on JavaScript. Both books are published by Wrox Press.

Working through this brief tutorial should give you enough of a nodding acquaintance with JavaScript to get you started, and to at least let you intelligently paste code into your documents.

NOTE: in the book code will wrap on to the next line, however, all statements should be on a single line.

Embedding JavaScript

JavaScript is included in an HTML document by enclosing it in a pair of **`<SCRIPT>`** tags. There is no limit to the number of pairs of tags you may employ.

The tags may be placed anywhere, but are usually included in the head of the document.

The script takes a **LANGUAGE** attribute, which in the case of JavaScript is **JavaScript**, which happens to be the default if JavaScript is omitted.

It is usual to wrap the JavaScript code in HTML comments to prevent older browsers trying to read the code.

Example js1.htm

```
<HTML>
<HEAD>
<SCRIPT>
      <!--hide code from older browsers
            alert("Hello JavaScript");
      -->
</SCRIPT>
</HEAD>
<BODY>
      <P>That was a simple JavaScript alert.</P>
</BODY>
</HTML>
```

Note that for the rest of the examples we will omit all the HTML tags except the **<SCRIPT>** *tags. To write a valid HTML document though they should still be employed!*

SCRIPT content

The script consists of code or comment.

Comments

Comments in JavaScript are similar to C++ comments

```
//This is a single line comment
```

```
/*this is a multiline comment,
do not try to nest these comments.*/
```

Multiline comments should not, of course, be nested.

Code

Code consists of a series of statements, separated by semi-colons (**;**).

There is no need to put in the semi-colon if a statement rests on its own line, but it is always good practice to put them in.

Example js2.htm

```
<SCRIPT>
      <!--hide code from older browsers
            document.write("First Statement"+"<BR>");
            document.write('Second Statement');
      -->
</SCRIPT>
```

We will cover the above code **`document.write()`** in more detail later on. For now just note how it enables us to write text on the screen. Note the following three points:

- How the text must be quoted with either a double or a single quote, it doesn't matter which, but they must match.
- How the **`<BR>`** tag is passed on to the browser, and creates a new line. (Try adding **`<HR>`** to the above) For example:

```
document.write('Second Statement'+ '<HR>');
```

- How the plus sign is used to concatenate strings together. (See later)

Outputting JavaScript

We can output JavaScript on the screen in a number of ways. For this simple tutorial we will just look at two ways, both of which we have already employed.

alert

An alert allows you to put a message box on the screen, as seen above.

```
<SCRIPT>
      alert ("Hello JavaScript")
</SCRIPT>
```

Note that literal text has to be quoted.

document.write

The write method allows you to write on the screen as below.

```
<SCRIPT>
      document.write ("Hello JavaScript")
</SCRIPT>
```

Note that literal text has to be quoted.

To be technically correct note that **`document`** in fact refers to the document object (see below), and **`write`** is a method that can be used with the document object.

Writing HTML Code using JavaScript

Note that what we put in the **document.write** is literally passed on to the browser, so in fact if we pass on HTML tags these will not be displayed, but will be interpreted. So:

```
<SCRIPT>
      document.write ("<B>Hello JavaScript<\/B>")
</SCRIPT>
```

will appear in bold type on the screen, i.e.:

This is because the rules of HTML will allow treating the string **</** as a closing tag for script, we must escape the forward slashes with backward slashes.

escaping characters

As mentioned just above we can escape characters in JavaScript by using backslashes. However, if we wanted the tags to appear on the screen in the example above we would have to use HTML type escapes (**&*;**) as follows:

Example js1d.htm

```
<SCRIPT>
      document.write ("&lt;B&gt;Hello JavaScript&lt;/B&gt;")
</SCRIPT>
```

The above would cause:

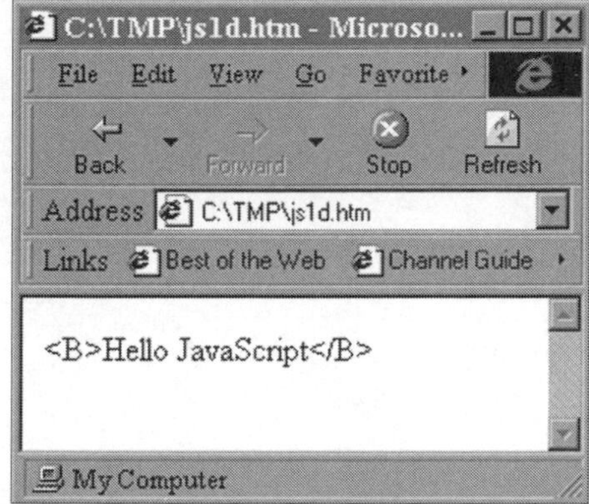

Values and Variables

There are three data types in JavaScript:

- Strings e.g. any thing in double or single quotes **"Hello Javascript"**, **'Hello JScript'**
- Numbers e.g. 1, 5, 3.14, 65000
- Boolean i.e true or false

Data is contained in Variables. These must be declared before being used by using the **var** keyword.

Data is assigned to a variable using the assignment operator =.

For example, to create a variable called quote:

var quote

and to assign a value to it:

quote= "to be or not to be"

This can be done in one step i.e.:

```
var quote="to be or not to be"
```

Points to note:

JavaScript is case sensitive–**QUOTE**, **Quote** and **quote** are all different variables.

Variables must start with either a letter or an underscore, and then can contain any combination of letters, numerals and underscores.

JavaScript is loosely typed. This means that variables don't have to contain one data type. Conversion between data types is done automatically. However for clarity it is always better to assign a type to a variable when it is declared, thus:

```
var lastName = ""
var age = 0
var alive = true
```

In assigning values the variable is always on the left side, the value being assigned is on the right side.

Variables may be reassigned at any time.

Example js3.htm

```
<SCRIPT>
      var name="John";
      var age = 40;
            document.write("My name is " + name +"<BR>");
            document.write("I am aged " + age +"<BR>");
//reassign the variables.
      name="Jane";
      age = 30;
            document.write("My wifes name is " + name +"<BR>");
            document.write("She is aged " + age +"<BR>");
</SCRIPT>
```

This should produce a screen that looks something like this:

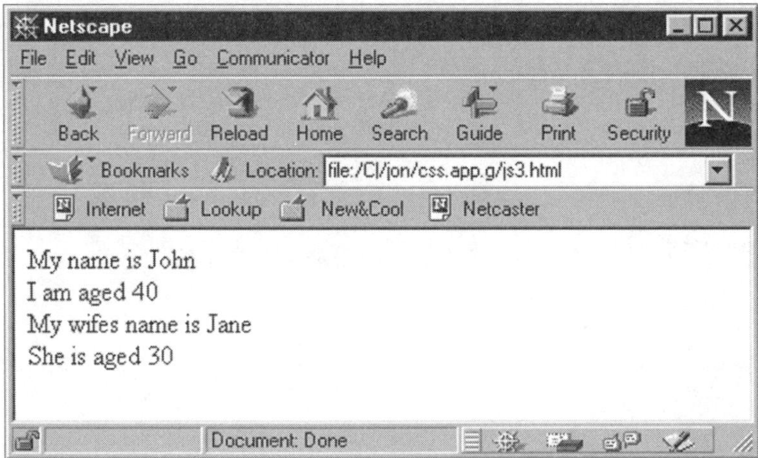

Note in passing how an HTML tag can be passed on to the HTML document using the **`write`** method.

String Operators

Although there are other string operators the only one we will concern ourselves with is the concatenation operator that we have already seen in action. This is the same as the plus sign **+** or the addition operator.

The concatenation operator joins strings or string variables together. We saw it in the example above.

`string1 + string2 + string3`

Example js4.htm

```
<SCRIPT>
//first concatenation example
      var rhyme="Mary ";
      rhyme=rhyme + "had a ";
      rhyme=rhyme + "little lamb ";
            document.write(rhyme);
            document.write("<BR>");

//second concatenation example

            document.write("Tom, "+"Tom, "+"the "+"Pipers "+"Son,");

</SCRIPT>
```

Numeric operators

Numeric operators do operations on numbers and should be familiar to you from your high school (actually primary school!) Math.

+ addition
- subtraction
***** multiplication
/ division

The following operators may not be so familiar:

% modulus–Finds the remainder of a division. For example:

7 % 3=1
8 % 3=2
9 % 3=0

++ increment–Increases a numeric variable by 1 so

y=x++

Is the same as

y=x+1

-- decrement–Decreases a numeric variable by 1 so

y=x--

Is the same as

y=x-1

Example js5.htm

```
<SCRIPT>
//various numeric  examples

      var stringnum="";

      var number1= 3+4;
      document.write("testing addition:-<BR> 3+4 = " + number1 +"<BR>");
      var number2= 5-3;
      document.write("testing subtraction:- <BR> 5-3 = " + number2
      +"<BR>");

      var number3= 3*4;
      document.write("testing multiplication:- <BR> 3*4 = " + number3
      +"<BR>");

      var number4= 3/4
      document.write("testing division:-<BR> 3/4 = " + number4 +"<BR>");

      number1= 3%4
      document.write("testing modulus:-<BR> 3%4 = " + number1 +"<BR>");

      var x=3;
      document.write("testing increment:-<BR>starting with x=3  ++x = "+
      ++x +"<BR>");
         x=3;
      document.write("testing decrement:- <BR> starting with x=3  --x = "+
      --x +"<BR>");

</SCRIPT>
```

The result should look as follows:

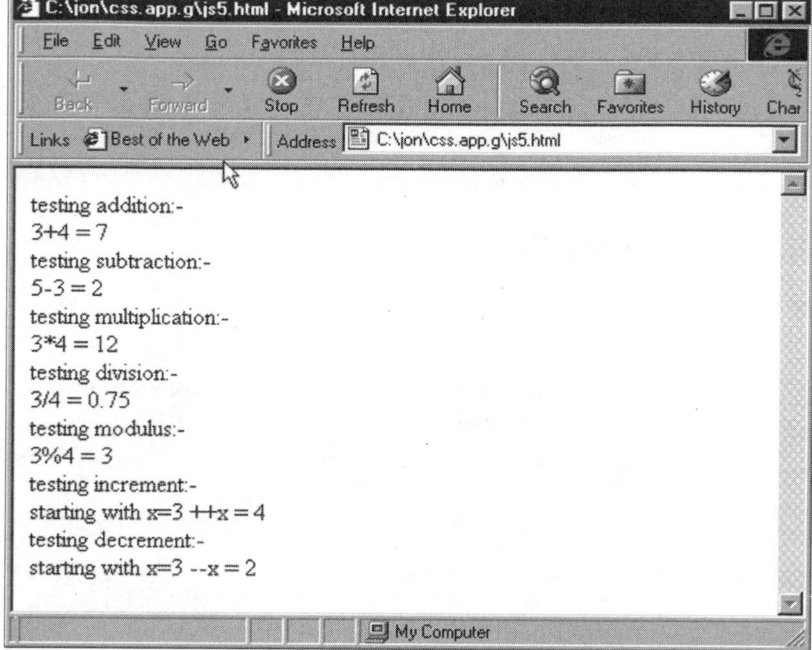

Note in the last two examples we put **++x**, and **--x** respectively. This incremented (or decremented) the x variable before we printed it.

If we had put **x++** it would have been incremented after we had displayed it. Try it and see, change the code line to read

```
var x=3
        document.write("testing increment:-<BR>starting with x=3 x++ =
        "+ x++ +"<BR>" + x +"<BR>")
```

Equality operators.

Equality operators are usually used in conditional statements (see later) to test if a variable meets certain conditions.

== is equal to (this is a double = sign)

!= is NOT equal to

> is greater than

>= is greater or equal to

< is less than

<= is less than or equal to

Other Operators

There are several other operators. Those we will cover are:

`&&` logical AND

`||` logical OR

`!` Not

Controlling Program Flow

For programs to do something useful they have to do more than flow in a linear direction. Printing 'Hello World' is all well and good, but even our own mothers would fail to get excited after a time!

Allowing programs to react to external input, or to produce variable results depending on the initial input requires that we **control program flow**.

We have two main ways to do this in JavaScript (and most other programming languages), the **conditional** statement and the **loop**.

Conditional Statements

Conditional statements and loops are how we make our code 'do things'. A conditional statement is of the form:

'**`If`** such and such is true then do this, **`else if`** such and such is true do the other, **`else`** do that'

JavaScript just has one conditional statement. The general syntax is:

```
if([test the condition here])
       {
              (This block of code will be executed if the condition is met)
}

else
       {
              (This block of code will be executed if the condition is NOT
               met)
       }
```

Example js6.htm

```
<SCRIPT>
       var color="blue"

              if(color=="red")
              {
              document.write("the color is red");
              document.write("<HR>");
              }
```

```
        else if(color=="blue")
              {
              document.write("the color is blue");
              }

        else
              {
              document.write("the color is neither red or blue");
              }
</SCRIPT>
```

Note:

Use of the equality operator **==** the double equal sign, as opposed to the assignment operator **=**, the single equal sign.

> *If you ever mess up here, don't worry there is not a single C, Java, or Script programmer who hasn't made this mistake...AND continues to make it from time to time!*

The use of curly brackets to group all the statements together (as in the first condition) that apply to a single condition.

The use of **else if**–repeat this as many times as you want.

Conditional statements can be nested.

Use **&&** to test if two variables meet the condition. i.e.

```
If (color== "red" && num < 4)
```

The condition is only true if **both** conditions are met.

Use | | to test if **either** of two variables meet the condition. i.e.

```
If (color== "red" || num < 4)
```

The condition is true if **either** condition is met i.e. if color is "**red**" OR **num** is less than **4**.

Use **!=** to test for a negative result

```
If (color!= "red")
```

The condition is true if color **does not** equal **"red"**.

Loops

Loops are the second main way that we can control flow in programming.

There are two basic kinds of loops in JavaScript

- The **`for`** loop will repeat a block of code a certain number of times.
- The **`while`** loop will execute a block while a certain condition remains true.

The For Loop

The for loop executes a block of code a certain number of times. It takes the general syntax:

```
for(var i=0;1=10;i++)
        {
        [block of code to be executed];
        }
```

`i` (or any other variable) is the start condition.
The variable has been declared here using the keyword **`var`**
The first statement in the brackets is the starting condition i.e. **`i=0`**.
The second statement is the finishing condition i.e. **`1=10`**
The third statement is how **`i`** is changed each time a loop occurs, in this case **`i`** is increased by 1 each time through the loop.

> **Warning:-If you don't alter the condition of `i` so that the finishing condition is met you will get a loop that will run forever!**

The code between the curly brackets will be executed each time the **`for`** statement loops.

The following example will write out a list of 0 to 1000 in steps of a hundred on the screen.

Example js7.htm

```
<SCRIPT>
        var i
        for(i=0;i<=1000;i=i+100)
                {
                document.write(i + "<BR>")
                }
</SCRIPT>
```

The While Loop

The **while** loop will execute while a certain condition is true. Its general syntax is:

```
while (condition)
      {
      [block of code to be executed];
      }
```

The output of the following **while** loop will be exactly the same as the **for** example above.

Example js8.htm

```
<SCRIPT>
      var i=0
      while(i<=1000)
            {
            document.write(i + "<BR>");
            i=i+100;
            }
</SCRIPT>
```

These **while** loop are particularly useful in XML for reading through XML files in conjunction with string functions, and extracting elements. A couple of examples are given at the end of this appendix.

Input/Output

There are three kinds of pop-up messages we can use in JavaScript. We have already seen one of them–the Alert–in our first example.

Alert

The alert displays a simple message. It is closed by clicking on the OK button.

```
<SCRIPT>
      alert ("Hello JavaScript")
</SCRIPT>
```

Confirm

A **confirm** gives the user a choice of OK, or cancel. If the user selects OK then the boolean value **true** (see values and variables below) is returned to the program, if he chooses cancel a value of **false** is returned.

We have used confirm with a conditional statement and an equality operator to test the value returned. For fun we have written some in line styling into our **document.write()**.

Don't worry if you don't understand this just read on for now.

Note that some of the code goes on to another line in the book. This mustn't happen in our real script.

Example js1b.htm

This example does not work too well in Navigator 4.

```
<SCRIPT>
      <!--hide code from older browsers

      if(confirm("Do you want print some big red text?")==true)
            {
            document.write("<DIV STYLE='color:red;font-size:36pt;'>
            Big Red Text <\/DIV>");
            }
      else
            {
            document.write("Small black text");
            }
      //-->
</SCRIPT>
```

Prompt

Notice how the prompt has a space for two strings. The first string is the instruction on the prompt, and the second one is the default text (which is often set to **""**). Whatever is typed in the box is returned to the program if the OK button is pressed, otherwise a value of null is returned.

Note how we declare the variable **"yourname"** and assign the value returned by the prompt all in one line of code.

Example js1c.htm

```
<SCRIPT>
      <!--hide code from older browsers

      var yourname=prompt("Please write in your name","(overwrite this text
      with your name)")

      document.write("Your name is:- " + yourname)
      //-->
</SCRIPT>
```

Arrays

Arrays are very useful in any computer language because they allow the creation, sorting and manipulation of lists using loops.

An array is simply a numbered list of variables usually of the same type. Here is a numbered list of all the cats our family has had in the last ten years:

- **[0]Merry**
- **[1]Pippin**
- **[2]Hergie**
- **[3]Adam**
- **[4]Pierre**
- **[5]Ben**
- **[5]Pickle**
- **[6]Calloway**

In JavaScript in fact the variables can be of any type, i.e. we can mix up numbers with strings, but this is bad practice for reasons we can't go into here.

Note:

The numbering starts from 0 not 1

To refer to a cat just use the number e.g. **cat[5]** is **"Ben"**

To create an array in JavaScript simply declare it using the following syntax:

```
arrayname= new Array()
```

This creates an 'empty' array, in other words the number of items has not been decided.

```
arrayname= new Array(10)
```

This will create an array which can hold ten items.

To fill your array simply assign values to the numbers. In our cat example:

```
cats=new Array(8)      //declaring the array

cats[0]=Merry
cats[1]=Pippin
cats[2]=Hergie
cats[3]=Adam
cats[4]=Pierre
cats[5]=Ben
cats[5]=Pickle
cats[6]=Calloway
```

or another way to do this in JavaScript is to simply put a comma delimited list right after the declaration.

```
cats=new Array("Merry", "Pippin", "Hergie", "Adam", "Pierre", "Ben",
"Pickle", "Calloway")
```

Length property

The length property allows us to find the length of an array using the syntax:

```
arrayname.length
```

Example js9.htm

The following example creates a cat array and populates it. It then uses a loop to print out the cats names. It then alters the sixth cats name (remember we count from 0) from Ben to Periwinkle and we prove this by asking it to write the list again.

```
<SCRIPT>

      cats=new Array("Merry", "Pippin", "Hergie", "Adam", "Pierre", "Ben",
      "Pickle", "Calloway")

            document.write("The cats array has " +cats.length+"
            members<BR>")
            var i=0
            while(i<=cats.length-1)
                  {
                  document.write(cats[i]+"<BR>");
                  i=i+1;
                  }

      cats[5]="Periwinkle"

document.write("The cats array has " +cats.length+" members<BR>")
            var i=0
            while(i<=cats.length-1)
                  {
                  document.write(cats[i]+"<BR>");
                  i=i+1;
                  }

</SCRIPT>
```

The next screen shot shows how this page should look in a browser:

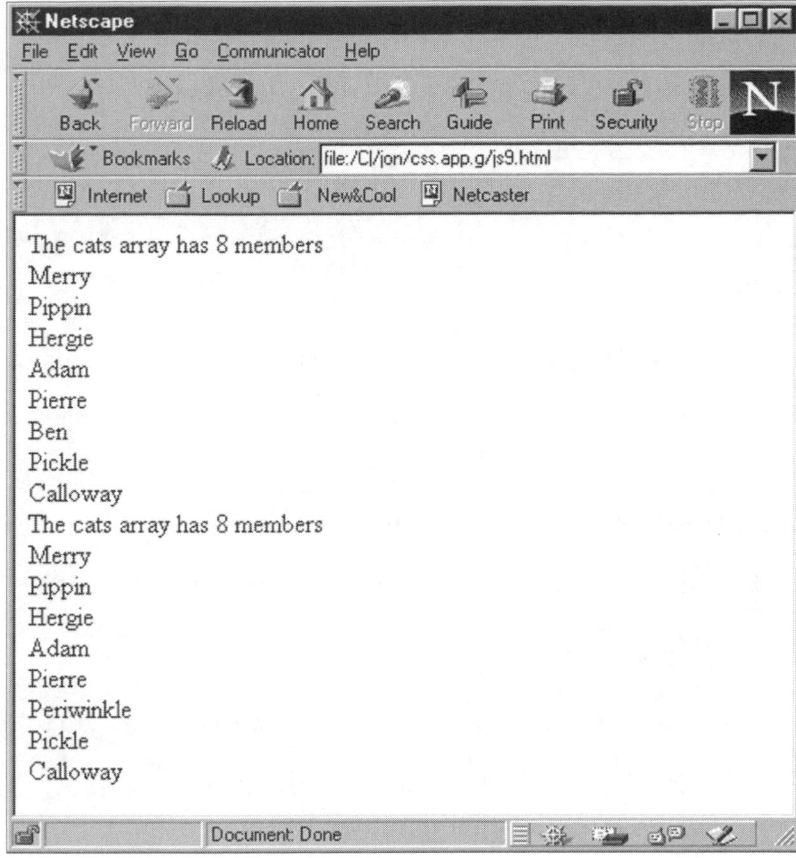

Note:

How the array is populated at the time it is declared.

How the length of the array is obtained using the array property **`length`** and the syntax **`cats.length`**

How we run to **`while (i<=cats.length-1)`** in the loop, because the array numbering starts from **`0`**.

To alter a member of an array, simply assign a new value.

> *The Array keyword is new in version 1.2. Before arrays had to be created using JavaScript's object mechanism. See Instant JavaScript for details. As you are writing for the 4 series browsers you can forget about this!*

Extending an array

Adding to an array is simplicity itself. Simply add a new member with an index greater than the existing length, and JavaScript will increase the length of the array to cover it.

Add the following to the above example:

```
cats[9]="Fluffy";

        document.write(cats[8]+"<BR>");
        document.write(cats[9]+"<BR>");
```

And you will see that **`cats[8]`** is undefined (naturally, because we haven't put any thing there yet), and **`cats[9]`** is fluffy.

Functions

Functions are encapsulated blocks of code that perform some useful function.

The basic idea is that the program will **call** a function that then executes the code contained in the function.

Functions come in two basic flavors.

- Functions that do some thing, e.g. Print out a warning. (Called a sub-routine in some programming languages)
- Functions that take in data at one end, manipulate data, and return a value.

Declaring a function

The easiest way to declare a function in JavaScript is simply to use it.

```
function functionName()
        {
                [code goes here];
        }
```

Note that JavaScript is case sensitive, and the function keyword starts with a lowercase **`f`**

Calling a function

To execute the code contained in the function the function must be **called**.

The easiest way to do this is to assign the function to a variable.

```
Var x=functionName()
```

Example js10.htm

The following function prints out a warning. It is an example of a function that executes an action. Note how the function is called.

Warning–this example may freeze some versions of Communicator4.

```
<SCRIPT>

      function warning()
            {
            document.write("<DIV STYLE ='color:red; text-align:center;
            font-size:32pt'>  Warning!! </DIV>");

            document.write("<BR> <DIV STYLE= 'color:green; text-
            align:center; font-size:24pt'> You have been warned!!.
            </DIV>");

             }

             var x=warning();
</SCRIPT>
```

Passing Arguments and Returning a Result

We've just had a look at one kind of function, what about functions that take data, manipulate it and return a result. Putting data into a function is called **passing an argument**.

The data to be manipulated is simply passed to the function by putting it in the parentheses following the function name.

The data is manipulated in the function and returned to the calling function using the **`return`** keyword.

Example js11.htm

The following simple function accepts two numbers as arguments, multiplies them together and returns the result of the multiplication.

```
<SCRIPT>
      function multiply(e,f)

            {
            var product=0;
            product=e*f;
            return product;
            }

            var x=multiply(3,4);
            document.write(x)
</SCRIPT>
```

Note:

How the numbers are passed to the function: **`var x=multiply(3,4);`**

How the function declaration accepts these numbers into variables (in this case **`e`** and **`f`** but we can give them any legal name we want).

The variable **`product`** is declared inside the function. The value of this variable **cannot** be accessed outside the function. However variables declared outside the function can be accessed inside it.

Objects

A JavaScript object allows us to gather a whole lot of variables and properties together in one place.

They are particularly important in that the Browsers have their own objects (such as the document object, which we've been using all along to print out our examples), and we can access the properties with code.

To create an object use the following syntax:

```
var objectName = new Object
```

Lets create a **`hat`** object and assign some properties to it.

```
<SCRIPT>

var hat = new Object

hat.color = "blue"
hat.size=8
hat.type="Stetson"

document.write(hat.color + "<BR>")
document.write(hat.size + "<BR>")
document.write(hat.type + "<BR>")

</SCRIPT>
```

Built-in Methods, Functions and Objects

JavaScript has a number of built-in objects and functions for manipulating dates, numbers, strings and arrays. We will just have a look at a few of the ones which are more useful for manipulating XML files.

Methods

A method is a piece of code that works on an object, the syntax is:

```
ObjectName.method()
```

We will use some methods below with built in objects.

Date Object

The date object gets the current date. There are numerous methods that can be used with the date object, here we use the **`toGMTString()`** to convert the current date to GMT time.

Example js13.htm

This example may give Universal time in IE4.

```
<SCRIPT>

      var myDate = new Date();

            document.write(myDate + "<BR>");
            var x=myDate.toGMTString();
            document.write(x + "<BR>");

</SCRIPT>
```

Note:

How we create the **`myDate`** variable and fill it with the current date by leaving the parentheses empty.

We could have put our own date inside the parentheses, and then the methods would work on that date.

The way we get the method to operate on the variable **`myDate`**.

String Objects and Methods

The string object is of particular interest to us because we will want to be manipulating strings in XML. Here is a demonstration of some of the more useful methods. Be very careful about the case of the methods e.g. **`charat`** or **`Charat`** will **not** work!

Example js14.htm

```
<SCRIPT>

var myString = "To be or not to be that is the question";

      //demo of charAt method
            document.write(myString.charAt(0) + "<BR>");

      //demo of big method
            document.write(myString.big()+ "<BR>")

            document.write(myString.indexOf("be",0)+ "<BR>")

            document.write(myString.lastIndexOf("be")+ "<BR>")

            document.write(myString.substring(3,5)+ "<BR>")

            document.write(myString.substring(3)+ "<BR>")

            document.write(myString.toUpperCase()+ "<BR>")

</SCRIPT>
```

On screen, the result should look like this:

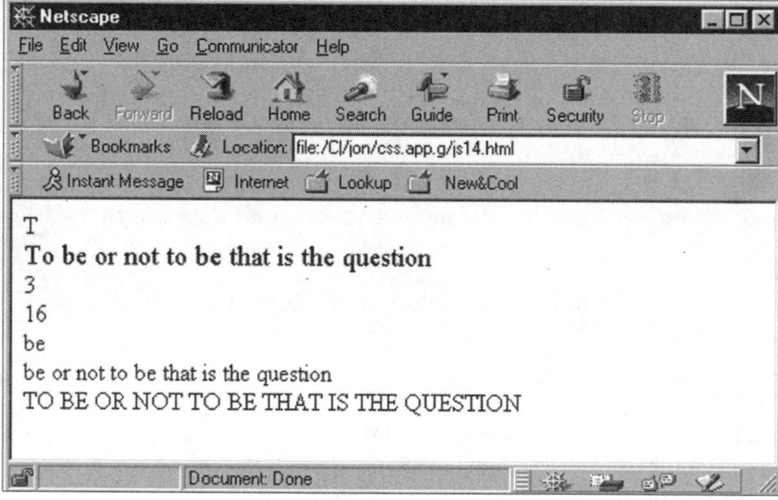

The **`charAt`** method returns the character at the given index number starting from **`0`**. Here **`charAt(0)`** returns **`T`**

There are numerous methods that will surround the string in HTML tags. Here we use the big method to enclose our string in **`<BIG></BIG>`** tags.

Other similar methods include **bold()**, **fixed()** (encloses in **<TT>**), **italics()**, **sub()**, and **strike()**.

The **indexOf** (**searchvalue, fromindex**) method searches the string starting at the **fromindex** value, and returns the index of the occurrence of the string **searchvalue**. In this example we start our search from **0** and look for **be**. The first occurrence of this is at character number 3.

The **lastIndexOf** (**searchvalue, fromindex**) looks for the last occurrence of the string before the **fromindex** value. Because in this example we did not specify a value for **fromindex**, the search will go to the end of the string. The last occurrence of the string **be** is 16 characters from the beginning of the string.

The **substring** (**index a, index b**) chops out the string between the two indexes. In the first example here it takes the chunk between character 3 and character 5, namely **be**. In the second example, **index b** is left out, so it starts at character 3 and returns the whole string.

Using this method with a while loop we can go through a long document and return all the elements of a certain type.

toUpperCase is self explanatory. There is also a **toLowerCase** method.

The Document object

The document object has various properties and methods. We have, of course, been using the **document.write()** method all along!

Some of the properties double up as methods, for example the **bgColor** method/property.

Example js15.htm

This example works in version 3 of Netscape, but not in version 4.

```
<SCRIPT>

      var bgcol=document.bgColor
      document.write(bgcol + "<BR>")
      document.bgColor="#FF0000"
      document.write(document.bgColor)

</SCRIPT>
```

Notes:

We discover the existing background color of the document by reading **document.bgColor** into a variable.

We then change the background color by using **bgColor** as a method

We then read the new **bgColor**. Note that we have skipped the variable stage in this demo.

The Navigator object

The navigator object returns information about the browser that is being used to access the HTML document. The following example demonstrates some of the more important properties.

Example js16.htm

```
<SCRIPT>
      document.write(navigator.appCodeName + "<BR>")
      document.write(navigator.appName + "<BR>")
      document.write(navigator.appVersion + "<BR>")
      document.write(navigator.language + "<BR>")
</SCRIPT>
```

This information can be useful when we need to know the type of browser the user is employing.

The Screen object

The screen object contains properties describing the display screen and colors.

Example js17.htm

```
<SCRIPT>
      document.write("Color Depth " + screen.colorDepth + "<BR>")
      document.write("screen height in pixels:-" + screen.height + "<BR>")
      document.write("screen width in pixels:-" + screen.width + "<BR>")

</SCRIPT>
```

Here is the result for my screen:

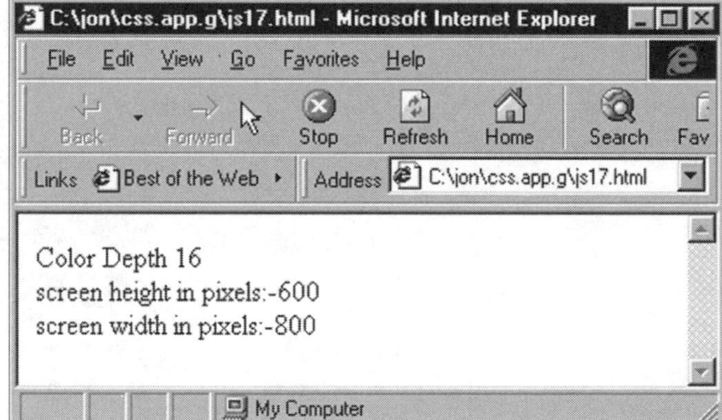

The Window object

The window object actually describes the browser window.

Whenever we put the code:

```
document.write
```

this is in fact short for:

```
window.document.write
```

We can make a new window by creating a new window variable, opening it, writing to it, and then closing it.

Example js18.htm

```
<SCRIPT>
      myNewWindow=window.open();
      myNewWindow.document.open();

      //three ways to write to the original window

      this.document.write("the original window  <BR>")
      window.document.write("the original window <BR>")
      document.write("the original window <BR>")

      myNewWindow.document.write("Here is a new window");
       myNewWindow.document.close();

</SCRIPT>
```

Note the three ways we can write to the original window.

JavaScript Events

Events are what trigger JavaScript actions. In all the above examples we have been using the **`onload`** event to display our code i.e. the code runs when we load our document.

Other events supported by both browsers include the **`onclick`** event but unfortunately even this doesn't work with all the tags in Navigator. For the other events–which are often supported by only one of the browsers–see one of the standard JavaScript references such as can be found in *Instant HTML Programmer's Reference.*

Example js19.htm

```
<HTML>
<HEAD>
<SCRIPT>
      function clickFunction()
            {
            alert("You clicked me!!");
            }

</SCRIPT>

</HEAD>
<BODY>
<H2 onclick ="clickFunction()">Click Me</H2>

</BODY>
</HTML>
```

Note how we have called the function inline.

Unfortunately the **`onclick`** doesn't work with regular tags in Navigator so we have to put them in **`A`** tags, and to make the **`A`** tag look like a regular tag we have to restyle it!

```
<A NAME="here"></A>
<A HREF="#here" onclick ="clickFunction()"STYLE="color:black;text-
decoration:none;"><H2>Click Me</H2></A>
```

We also have to link back to ourselves otherwise the directory containing our file will be opened!

Summary

This very brief tutorial should have acquainted you with most of JavaScripts possibilities.

To learn more about this and scripting in general it would be useful to get hold of some good reference books and just start experimenting. *Instant JavaScript* by Nigel McFarlane (Wrox 1998) comes highly recommended.

DSSSL Flow Objects

This appendix details a few of the DSSSL flow objects adopted by XSL. We have met some of them before. Each flow object can take numerous properties, but it is not clear yet how many of the properties will be supported by the XSL standard. I have just included a few of the more obvious ones. They probably represent 5% of those available–there are actually 193 properties. You are directed to the standard below for a full listing:

`http://sunsite.unc.edu/pub/sun-info/standards/dsssl/dssslo/do960816.htm`

DSSL Flow Object	Description	Properties	Possible Values
`scroll`	Used for online display	**`filling-direction`**	**`top-to-bottom`**, **`left-to-right`**, **`right-to-left`**, **`top-to-bottom`**
		`writing-mode`	**`left-to-right`**, **`right-to-left`**, **`top-to-bottom`**
		`background-color`	color
		`background-layer`	integer
		`background-tile`	#f, external graphic
		`start-margin`	length-spec
		`end-margin`	length-spec

DSSL Flow Object	Description	Properties	Possible Values
paragraph	The standard paragraph, almost analogous to the HTML **<P>**.	**line-spacing, glyph-alignment-mode, font-family-name, font-weight, font-posture, font-name font-size**	
		quadding	**start** | **end** | **center** | **justify**
		language	
		start-indent Similar to margin-left	
		end-indent Similar to margin-right	
		space-before Similar to margin-top	
		space-after Similar to margin-bottom	
paragraph-break	Used with paragraph. Really analogous to a ** ** in HTML		
character	Used for text . Writes single characters as flow objects. Takes most of the properties of paragraph		
line-field	Used for lists	**field-align**	**start | end | center**
		writing-mode	default is **left-to-right**
		field-width	the width of the list, will grow to accommodate

DSSL Flow Object	Description	Properties	Possible Values
`external-graphic`	Used for including graphic images.	**`display`**	**`(#t|#f)`** which is Scheme lingo for true or false
		`scale`	Takes one or two numbers, max or max-uniform
		`max-width`	Number in points
		`max-height`	Number in points
		`layer`	The z order
		`display-alignment`	**`start`** | **`center`** | **`end`**
`horizontal-rule`, **`vertical-rule`**	Used for horizontal rules (note that the DSSSL "rule" flow object will be split into these two rules to eliminate the name conflict) (like HR in HTML) and vertical rules	**`Score`**	used for underlining and scoring
		`type`	**`before`**, **`through`**, **`after`**, **`length-spec`**, **`character`**
		`color`	The z-order, default is 0
		`layer`	
`embedded-text`	Used for bi-directional text		
`box`	Used for borders	**`display`**	**`#t |#f`**
		`box-type`	**`border`**, **`background`**, **`both`**
		`background-color`	
		`box-corner-rounded`	
`table`, **`table-part`** **`table-column`** **`table-row`** **`table-cell`** **`table-border`**			

Table Continued on Following Page

DSSL Flow Object	Description	Properties	Possible Values
`sequence`	Almost equivalent to in-line in CSS Takes many of paragraphs properties.		
`display-group`	Used for controlling the positioning of groups of displayed flow objects		
`simple-page-sequence`	Used for simple page layout for printing		
`link`	Used for hypertext links		

Support and Errata

One of the most irritating things about any programming book can be when you find that bit of code you've just spent an hour typing simply doesn't work. You check it a hundred times to see if you've set it up correctly and then you notice the spelling mistake in the variable name on the book page. Grrr! Of course, you can blame the authors for not taking enough care and testing the code, the editors for not doing their job properly, or the proofreaders for not being eagle-eyed enough, but this doesn't get around the fact that mistakes do happen.

We try hard to ensure no mistakes sneak out into the real world, but we can't promise that this book is 100% error free. What we can do is offer the next best thing by providing you with immediate support and feedback from experts who have worked on the book and try to ensure that future editions eliminate these gremlins. The following section will take you step by step through the process of posting errata to our web site to get that help. The sections that follow, therefore, are:

- Wrox Developers Membership
- Finding a list of existing errata on the web site
- Adding your own errata to the existing list
- What happens to your errata once you've posted it (why doesn't it appear immediately?)

There is also a section covering how to e-mail a question for technical support. This comprises:

- What your e-mail should include
- What happens to your e-mail once it has been received by us

So that you only need view information relevant to yourself, we ask that you register as a Wrox Developer Member. This is a quick and easy process, that will save you time in the long-run. If you are already a member, just update membership to include this book.

Wrox Developer's Membership

To get your FREE Wrox Developer's Membership click on Membership in the navigation bar of our home site

www.wrox.com.

This is shown in the following screen shot:

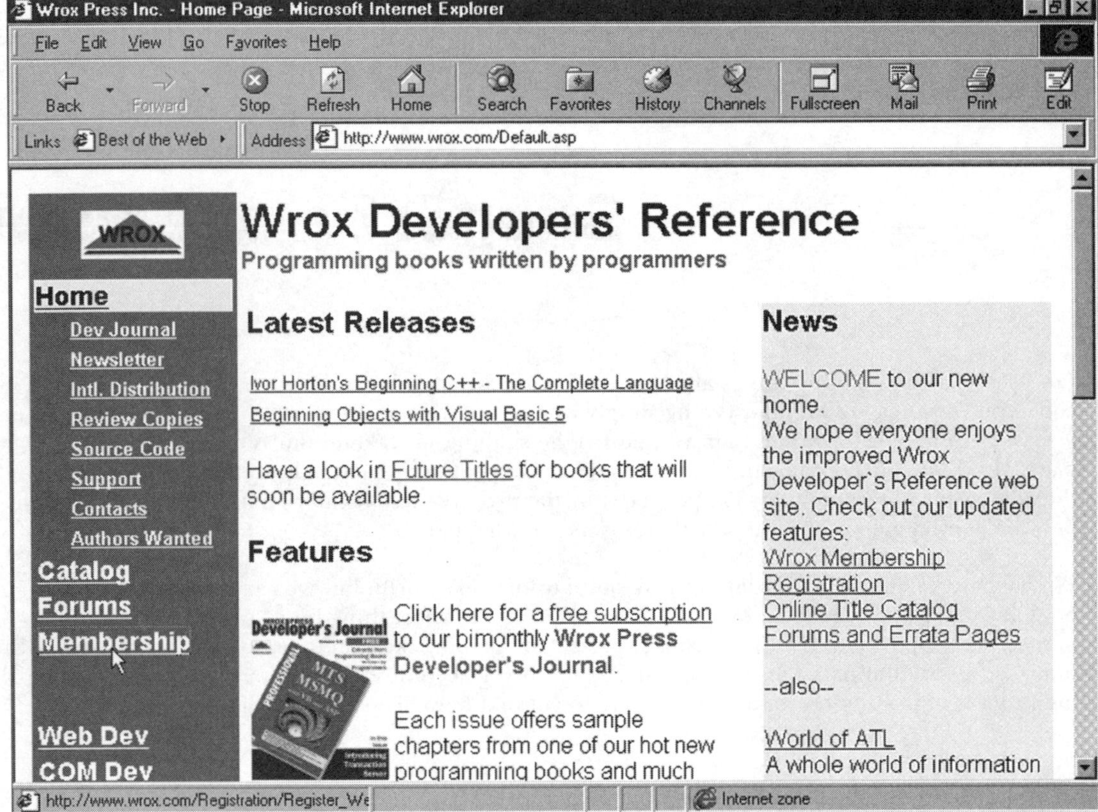

Then, on the next screen (not shown), click on New User. This will display a form. Fill in the details on the form and submit the details using the submit button at the bottom. Before you can say 'The best read books come in Wrox Red' you will get the following screen:

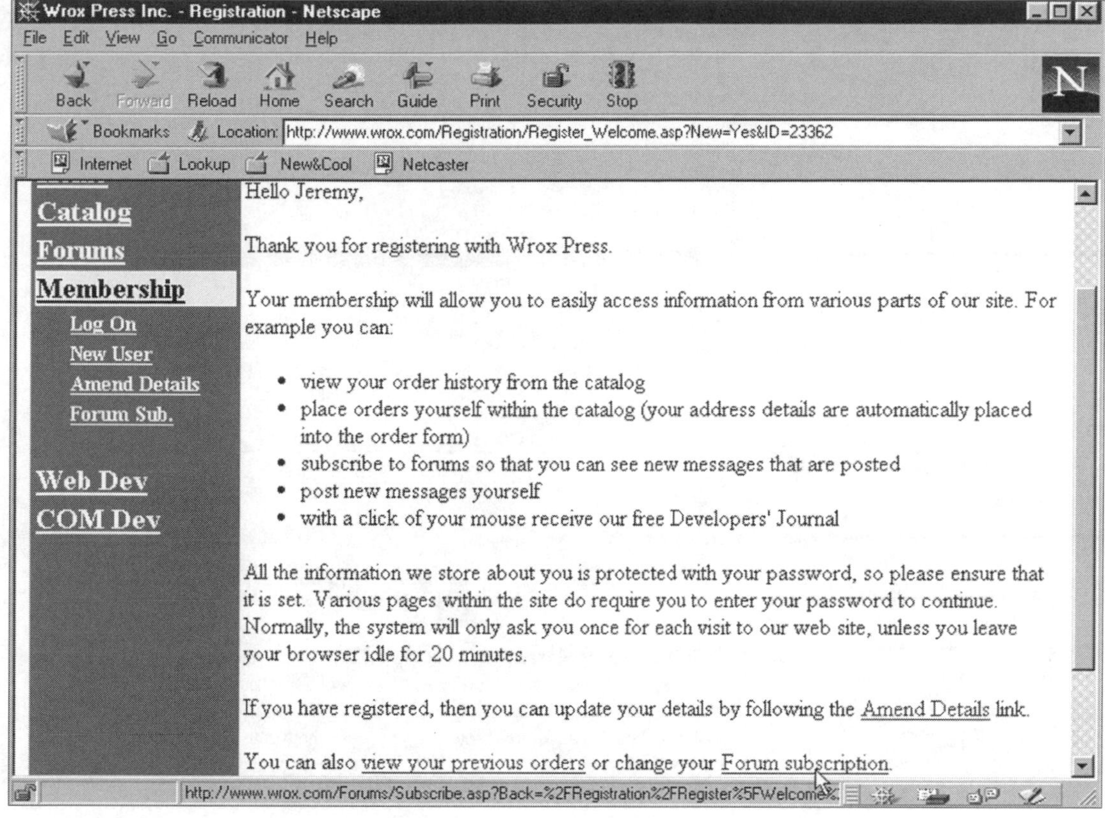

Finding an Errata on the Web Site.

Before you send in a query, you might be able to save time by finding the answer to your problem on our web site: **`http:\\www.wrox.com`**.

Each book we publish has its own page and its own errata sheet. You can get to any book's page by clicking on support from the left hand side navigation bar.

From this page you can locate any books errata page on our site. Select your book from the pop-up menu and click on it.

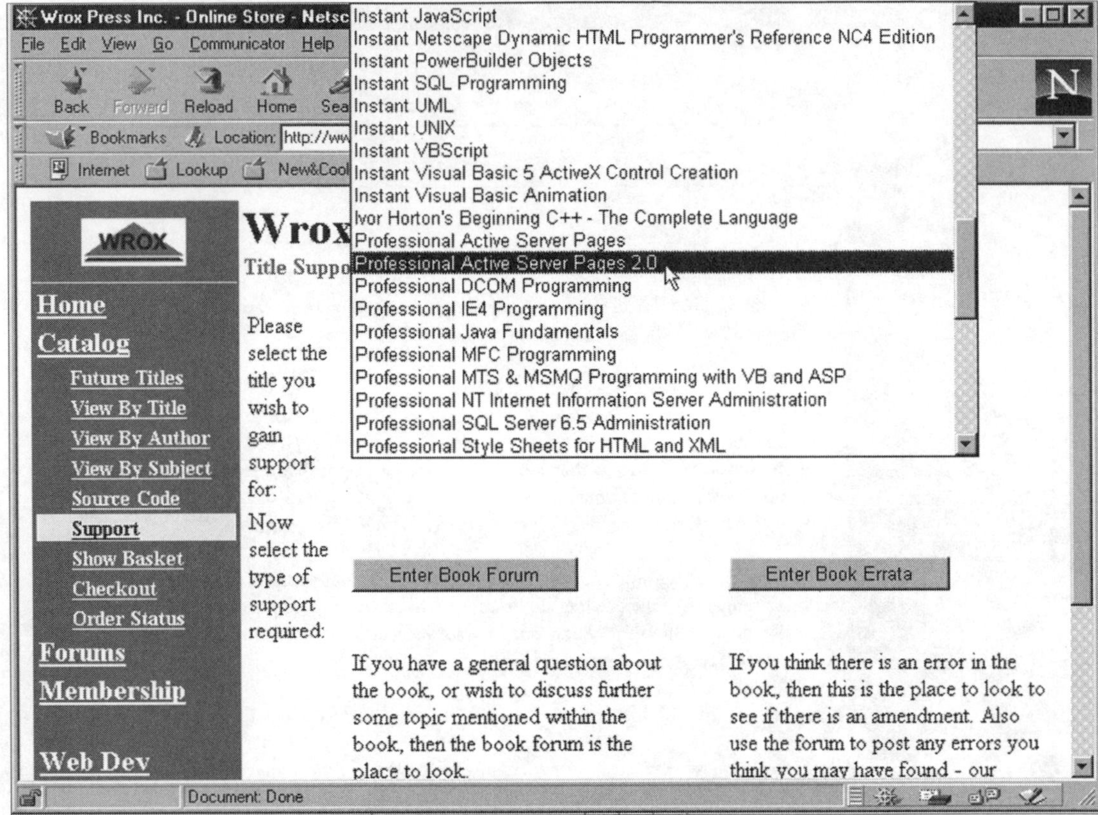

Then click on Enter Book Errata. This will take you to the errata page for the book. Select the criteria by which you want to view the errata, and click the apply criteria button. This will provide you with links to specific errata. For an initial search, you are advised to view the errata by page numbers. If you have looked for an error previously, then you may wish to limit your search using dates. We update these pages daily to ensure that you have the latest information on bugs and errors.

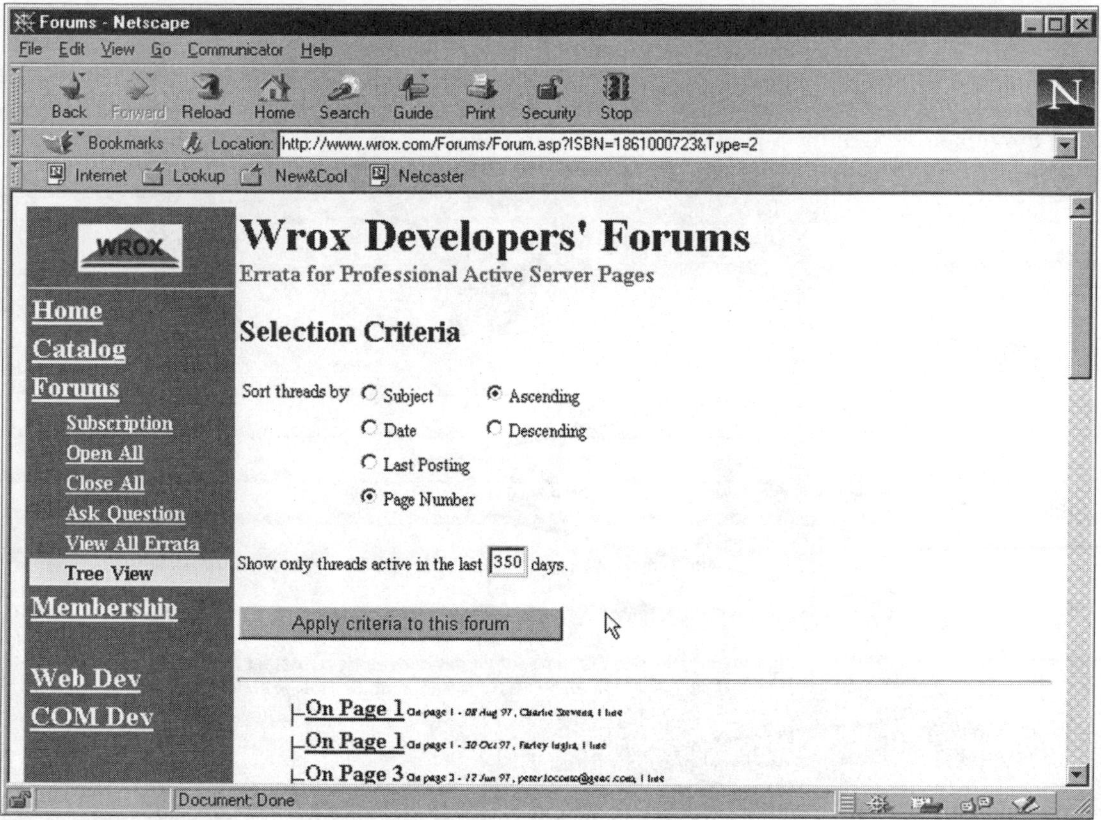

Adding an Errata to the Sheet Yourself.

It's always possible that you may find your error is not listed, in which case you can enter details of the fault yourself. It might be anything from a spelling mistake to a faulty piece of code in the book. Sometimes you'll find useful hints that aren't really errors on the listing. By entering errata you may save another reader hours of frustration, and of course, you will be helping us provide even higher quality information. We're very grateful for this sort of advice and feedback. You can enter errata using the 'ask a question' of our editors link at the bottom of the errata page. Click on this link and you will get a form on which to post your message.

Fill in the subject box, and then type your message in the space provided on the form. Once you have done this, click on the Post Now button at the bottom of the page. The message will be forwarded to our editors. They'll then test your submission and check that the error exists, and that the suggestions you make are valid. Then your submission, together with a solution, is posted on the site for public consumption. Obviously this stage of the process can take a day or two, but we will endeavor to get a fix up sooner than that.

E-mail Support

If you wish to directly query a problem in the book with an expert who knows the book in detail then e-mail **support@wrox.com**, with the title of the book and the last four numbers of the ISBN in the subject field of the e-mail. A typical e-mail should include the following things:

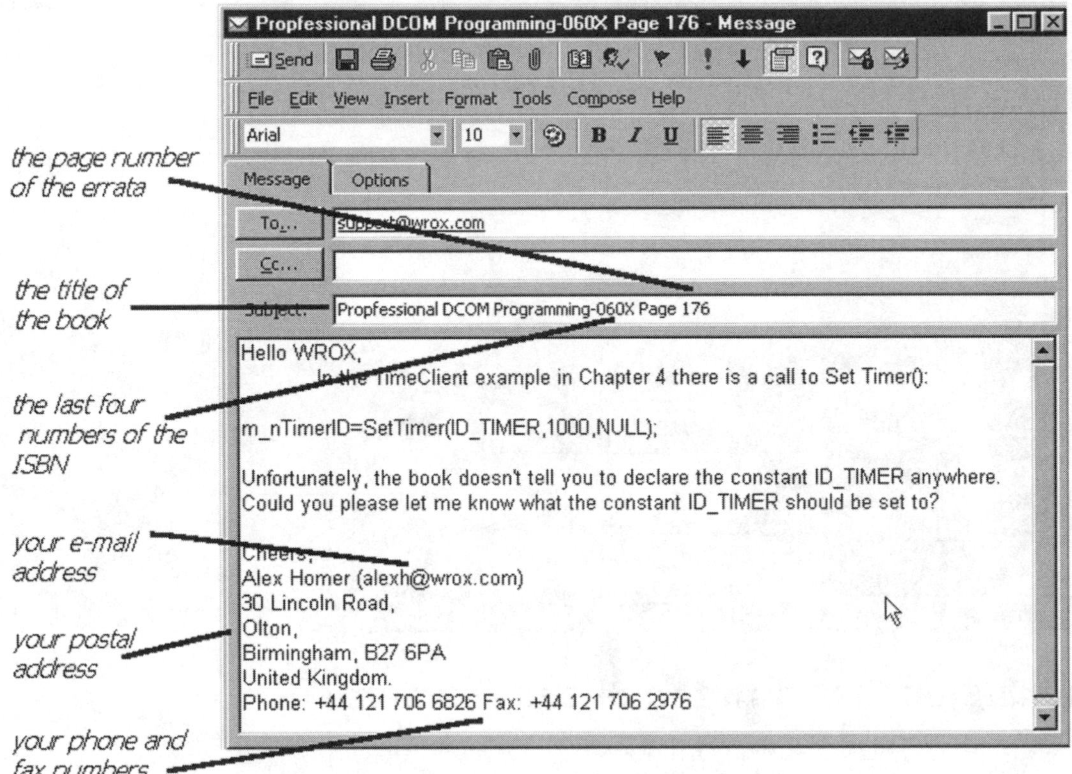

We won't send you junk mail. We need the details to save your time and ours. If we need to replace a disk or CD we'll be able to get it to you straight away. When you send an e-mail it will go through the following chain of support:

Customer Support

Your message is delivered to one of our customer support staff who are the first people to read it. They have files on most frequently asked questions and will answer anything general immediately. They answer general questions about the book and the web site.

Editorial

Deeper queries are forwarded to the technical editor responsible for that book. They have experience with the programming language or particular product and are able to answer detailed technical questions on the subject. Once an issue has been resolved, the editor can post the errata to the web site.

The Authors

Finally, in the unlikely event that the editor can't answer your problem, s/he will forward the request to the author. We try to protect the author from any distractions from writing. However, we are quite happy to forward specific requests to them. All Wrox authors help with the support on their books. They'll mail the customer and the editor with their response, and again all readers should benefit.

What we can't answer

Obviously with an ever growing range of books and an ever-changing technology base, there is an increasing volume of data requiring support. While we endeavor to answer all questions about the book, we can't answer bugs in your own programs that you've adapted from our code. So, while you might have loved the help desk systems in our Active Server Pages book, don't expect too much sympathy if you cripple your company with a live adaptation you customized from Chapter 12. But do tell us if you're especially pleased with the routine you developed with our help.

How to tell us exactly what you think.

We understand that errors can destroy the enjoyment of a book and can cause many wasted and frustrated hours, so we seek to minimize the distress that they can cause.

You might just wish to tell us how much you liked or loathed the book in question. Or you might have ideas about how this whole process could be improved. In which case you should e-mail `feedback@wrox.com`. You'll always find a sympathetic ear, no matter what the problem is. Above all you should remember that we do care about what you have to say and we will do our utmost to act upon it.

Index

Symbols

A

C

D

F

G

H

Q

R

S

U

V

W

Instant HTML Programmer's Reference

Authors: Various

ISBN: 1861001568

Price: $19.95 C$27.95 £18.49

This book is a bargain! We've packed it with information, beginning from the basics of creating an HTML document, going right through to looking at the implementations of Dynamic HTML by Microsoft and Netscape. Along the way we take in formatting, styling, forms and tables, objects and applets, and even a chapter on scripting. However, the real added value comes in the reference section, particularly the appendix that lists every HTML tag and its attributes and tells you which versions of HTML, Microsoft's browser's and Netscape's browser's support those tag/attribute combinations. There's even an on-line version up on the Wrox Web Developers site. If you want a fast paced tutorial or an in-depth reference book, this is the one to get.

Instant JavaScript

Authors: Nigel McFarlane

ISBN: 1861001339

Price: $24.95 C$34.95 £22.99

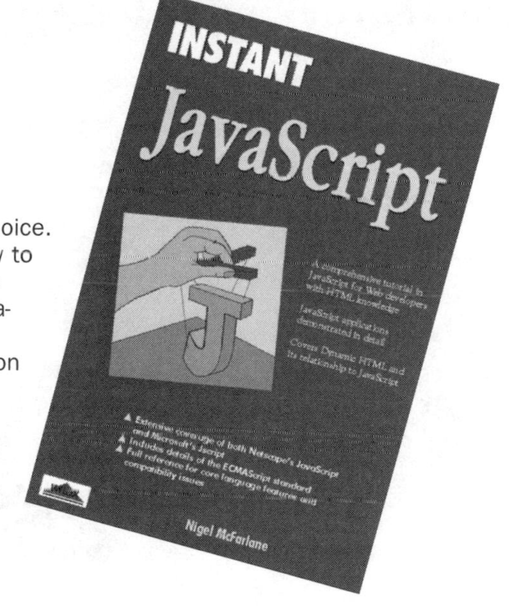

JavaScript is the web developer's programming language of choice. This tutorial and reference covers everything you need to know to use this flexible programming tool. It covers the core language details, including both the Netscape and Microsoft implementations, plus the ECMAScript standard. It explains how you can incorporate JavaScript in your web pages, including a chapter on JavaScript and Dynamic HTML. In addition we look at using forms and CGI, security and tips for avoiding compatibility problems. The reference section contains appendices on the ECMAScript core language and browser specific implementations of JavaScript. If you want a fast paced tutorial on JavaScript, which is up to speed with the new standard, this is the one to get.

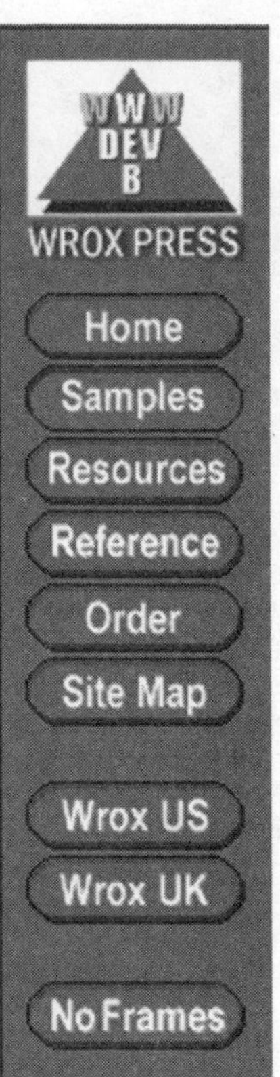

To Be Continued.......

This may be the end of *Professional Style Sheets for HTML and XML* as far as a physical page count goes but it is not even nearly the end as far as Wrox Press are concerned. This book is, in fact, a door into an online Web Development community which goes far beyond the constraints of the printed page...

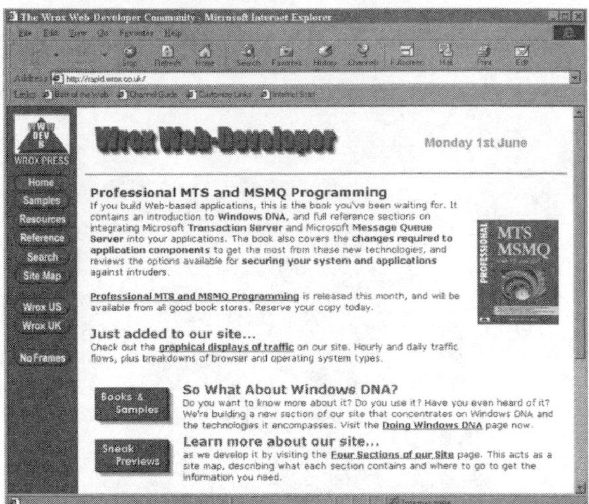

Wrox Web-Developer

http://rapid.wrox.co.uk

Reference Tools

Resources and Links

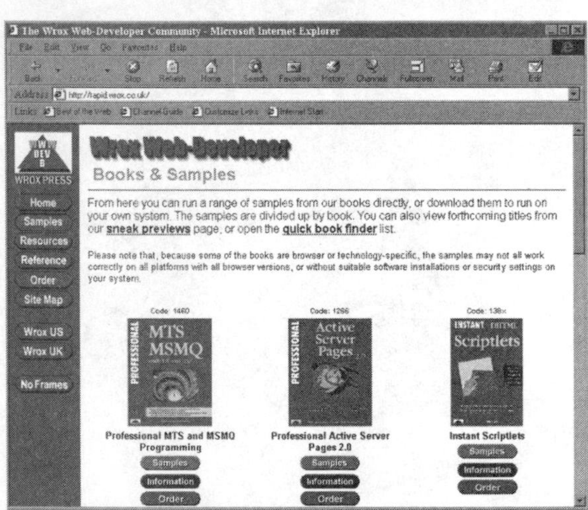

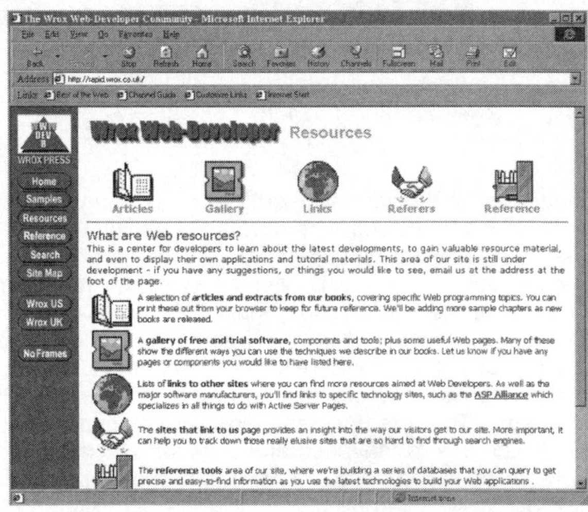

Sample Files And Much More....

Previews of Coming Attractions